THE MEDITERRANEAN DIET COOKBOOK FOR BEGINNERS

1200 RECIPES FOR EASY & DELICIOUS HOMEMADE MEALS. WITH 30-DAY MEAL PLAN TO HELP YOU BURN FAT AND BUILD HEALTHY HABITS

Ashley Hayes

TABLE OF CONTENTS

Chapter 4: Beans, Rice and Grains Recipes 85

INTRODUCTION

The Mediterranean diet has various health benefits that people who eat a lot of red meat don't have. For example, the diet has been linked to a decreased risk of cancer, heart attacks, strokes, and a reduced incidence of Alzheimer's fatalities. There's also a list of other benefits, such as a lower risk of high blood pressure, depression, and other chronic diseases and a better quality of life. So if you ever wanted a taste of the good life, here are some of the top benefits of the Mediterranean diet.

Lower Risk of Heart Disease

Unlike most people associated with the term "diet" with losing weight, this diet, as stated earlier, will help you live longer. In the United States, heart disease is one of the significant causes of death. This diet simply enables you to reduce some of the factors that lead to a heart attack. In the study done on British men, those who opted for the Mediterranean diet had a 41% lower risk of dying from a heart attack when compared to those who followed the more traditional high-fat diet such as the Atkins diet.

Lower Risk of Stroke

It is not just the heart that benefits from the diet, but your brain too. People who consumed the Mediterranean diet regularly had a 22% lower risk of suffering an ischemic stroke than following a high-fat diet. The study also found out that strokes caused by other factors such as bleeding tended to be less severe in people who ate vegetables and fish as the diet recommended. People who suffer strokes commonly have a hard time recovering from it, and the factors that lead to it need to be avoided.

Boost Immunity

You wouldn't know it, but your body's immune system is a vital part of your vulnerability to some diseases that plague you. This diet regulates the immune system and keeps the body strong and protected in the fight against infections.

Lower Risk of Cancers

Eating the proper meals can ward off different types of cancer without resorting to painful treatments or harsh pharmaceuticals. In the United States alone, death by cancer is the second leading cause of death. This diet is known for its cancer-fighting properties. In general, the Mediterranean diet has been linked to a decreased incidence of cancer. Not only does it help in killing various existing cancers, but it also prevents cancer cells from forming in the first place—the Phytochemicals in fruits and vegetables found in this diet cover all of the cancer-fighting departments. The diet also has Omega 3 fatty acids that help fight inflammation and even help prevent cancerous cells.

Lower Risk of Diabetes

The Med-diet or Mediterranean diet is the magic diet to lower the risk of diabetes in both men and women. People who eat this type of diet reduce their risk of getting diabetes to begin with, but they also boost protection. This diet keeps blood sugar levels under control and helps people avoid the need to get medication for the condition. This diet has also been demonstrated to reduce the risk of heart disease and stroke, both of which can contribute to diabetes.

Protection from Diabetes

People who have a rich diet of fruits and vegetables will have an easier time keeping diabetes at bay. The diabetic diet resembles the Mediterranean diet. The diet helps people control their weight by eating healthy foods. These foods are rich in complex carbohydrates. The elimination of red meat and sugar from one's diet will also boost metabolism.

It is never too late to start a healthier diet. You can begin at any time and change yourself into a healthier person. Start with small changes and make a beeline towards the Mediterranean diet. You will be surprised at how your body will change for the better. There is no need to suffer from diseases, complications, and even death because you decided to overeat regularly. You can protect yourself by eating healthy. There's no need to be brutal to your body to make up for the damage you caused previously.

1. Almond and Maple Quick Grits

Ingredients for 4 servings

- 1 ½ cups of water
- ½ cup of unsweetened almond milk
- Pinch sea salt
- ½ cup of quick-cooking grits
- ½ teaspoon of ground cinnamon
- ¼ cup of pure maple syrup
- ¼ cup of slivered almonds

Directions and Total Time: approx. 11 minutes

Heat the water, almond milk, and sea salt until it boils. Stir with a wooden spoon, slowly add the grits. Continue stirring to prevent lumps and bring the mixture to a slow boil. Reduce the heat to medium-low—stew for 5 to 6 minutes, frequently stirring, until the water is completely absorbed. Stir in the cinnamon, syrup, and almonds. Cook for 1 minute more, stirring.

Per Serving: Calories 151, Fat 12g, Carbs 10g, Protein 15.4g

2. Almond Banana Pancakes

Ingredients for 3 servings

- ¼ cup of almond flour
- ½ teaspoon of ground cinnamon
- 3 eggs
- 1 banana, mashed
- 1 tablespoon of almond butter
- 1 teaspoon of vanilla extract
- 1 teaspoon of olive oil
- Sliced banana to serve

Directions and Total Time: approx. 10 minutes

Beat your eggs in a mixing bowl until they become fluffy. In another bowl, mash the banana using a fork and add to the egg mixture. Add the vanilla, almond butter, cinnamon, and almond flour. Mix into a smooth batter. Heat the olive oil in a skillet. Add one spoonful of the batter and fry them on both sides. Keep doing these steps until you are done with all the batter. Add some sliced banana on top before serving.

Per Serving: Calories 306, Fat 26g, Carbs 3.6g, Protein 14.4g

3. Almond Grits with Honey

Ingredients for 4 servings

- ¼ cup of slivered almonds
- ½ cup of milk
- ½ teaspoon of almond extract
- ½ cup of quick-cooking grits
- ½ teaspoon of ground cinnamon
- ¼ cup of honey
- ¼ teaspoon of sea salt

Directions and Total Time: approx. 15 minutes

Bring to a boil the milk, salt, and 1 ½ cups of water in a pot over medium heat. Gradually add in grits, stirring constantly. Lower the heat and simmer for approximately about 6 minutes until all the liquid is absorbed. Mix in almond extract and cinnamon and cook for another minute. Ladle into individual bowls, top with almonds and honey, and serve. Enjoy!

Per Serving: Calories 131, Fat 3.8g, Carbs 23g, Protein 2.6g

4. Artichoke and Spinach Frittata

Ingredients for 4 servings

- 4 ounces of canned artichokes, chopped
- 2 teaspoons of olive oil
- ½ cup of whole milk
- 8 eggs
- 1 cup of spinach, chopped
- 1 garlic clove, minced
- ½ cup of Parmesan, crumbled
- 1 teaspoon of oregano, dried
- 1 Jalapeño pepper, minced
- Salt to taste

Directions and Total Time: approx. 55 minutes

Preheat oven to 360 F. Warm the olive oil in a skillet over medium heat and sauté garlic and spinach for 3 minutes. Beat the eggs in a bowl. Stir in artichokes, milk, Parmesan cheese, oregano, jalapeño pepper, and salt. Add in spinach mixture and toss to combine. Transfer to a greased baking dish and bake for 20 minutes until golden and bubbling. Slice into wedges and serve.

Per Serving: Calories 190, Fat 14g, Carbs 5g, Protein 10g

5. Artichoke Frittata

Ingredients for 3 servings

- 8 large eggs
- ¼ cup of Asiago cheese, grated
- 1 tablespoon of fresh basil, chopped
- 1 teaspoon of fresh oregano, chopped
- Pinch of salt
- 1 teaspoon of extra virgin olive oil
- 1 teaspoon of garlic, minced
- 1 cup of canned artichokes, drained
- 1 tomato, chopped

Directions and Total Time: approx. 15 minutes

Pre-heat your oven to broil. Take a medium bowl and whisk eggs, Asiago cheese, oregano, basil, sea salt, and pepper. Blend in a bowl. In a large ovenproof skillet, heat the olive oil. Sauté for 1 minute after adding the garlic. Take the skillet from the heat and add the egg mixture. Return skillet to heat and sprinkle artichoke hearts and tomato over eggs. Cook frittata without stirring for 8 minutes. Broil skillet for 1 minute until lightly browned. Cut frittata into 4 pieces and serve. Enjoy!

Per Serving: Calories 199, Fat 13g, Carbs 5g, Protein 16g

6. Avocado Bruschetta with Tomatoes

Ingredients for 4 servings

- 1 tablespoon of olive oil
- 1 baguette, sliced
- 2 sun-dried tomatoes, chopped
- 1 avocado, chopped
- 2 tablespoons of lemon juice
- 8 cherry tomatoes, chopped
- ¼ cup of red onion, chopped
- 1 teaspoon of dried oregano
- 2 tablespoons of parsley, chopped
- 4 Kalamata olives, chopped
- Salt and black pepper to taste

Directions and Total Time: approx. 5 minutes

Preheat oven to 360 F. Arrange the bread slices on a greased baking tray and drizzle with olive oil. Bake until golden, about 6-8 minutes. Mash the avocado in a large-sized bowl with lemon juice, salt, and pepper. Stir in sun-dried tomatoes, onion, oregano, parsley, and olives. Spread the avocado mixture on toasted bread slices and top with cherry tomatoes to serve.

Per Serving: Calories 120, Fat 11g, Carbs 7g, Protein 2g

7. Avocado Egg Scramble

Ingredients for 2 servings

- 4 eggs, beaten
- 1 white onion, diced
- 1 tablespoon of avocado oil
- 1 avocado, finely chopped
- ½ teaspoon of chili flakes
- 1 ounces of Cheddar cheese, shredded
- ½ teaspoon of salt
- 1 tablespoon of fresh parsley

Directions and Total Time: approx. 23 minutes

In a hot pan, heat the avocado oil. Toss in the chopped onion and roast until golden brown. Meanwhile, combine chili flakes, beaten eggs, and salt in a mixing bowl. Pour the prepared egg mixture over the onions and boil for 1 minute. Finally, using a fork or spatula, scramble the eggs well. Cook the beaten eggs until they are firm but not overcooked. Add the diced avocado and shredded cheese after that. Stir the scramble well and transfer in the serving plates. Sprinkle the meal with fresh parsley.

Per Serving: Calories 236, Fat 20g, Carbs 34g, Protein 8.6g

8. Avocado Milkshake

Ingredients for 3 servings

- 1 avocado, peeled and pitted
- 2 tablespoons of liquid honey
- ½ teaspoon of vanilla extract
- ½ cup of heavy cream
- 1 cup of milk
- ⅓ cup of ice cubes

Directions and Total Time: approx. 5 minutes

Chop the avocado and put it in a food processor. Add the liquid honey, vanilla extract, heavy cream, milk, and ice cubes. Blend the mixture until smooth. Pour the milkshake into tall serving glasses. Serve with pancakes or waffles. Use almond or maybe coconut milk for a vegan milkshake.

Per Serving: Calories 291, Fat 22.1g, Carbs 22g, Protein 4.4g

9. Avocado Muffins

Ingredients for 12 servings

- 6 bacon slices; chopped.
- 1 yellow onion; chopped.
- 1/2 teaspoon of baking soda
- 1/2 cup of coconut flour
- 1 cup of coconut milk
- 2 cups of avocado; pitted, peeled and chopped
- 4 eggs
- Salt and black pepper to the taste

Directions and Total Time: approx. 30 minutes

Heat up a pan, add onion and bacon; stir and brown for a few minutes. In a bowl, mash avocado pieces with a fork and whisk well with the eggs. Add milk, salt, pepper, baking soda and coconut flour and stir everything. Add bacon mix and stir again. Add coconut oil to muffin tray, divide eggs and avocado mix into the tray, heat oven at 350 degrees F and then you bake for 20 minutes. Divide muffins between plates and serve.

Per Serving: Calories 200, Fat 7g, Carbs 7g, Protein 5g

10. Avocado Toast

Ingredients for 2 servings

- 1 tablespoon of goat's cheese, crumbled
- 1 avocado, peeled, pitted, and mashed
- A pinch of salt and black pepper
- 2 whole-wheat bread slices, toasted
- ½ teaspoon of lime juice
- 1 persimmon, thinly sliced
- 1 fennel bulb, thinly sliced
- 2 teaspoons of honey
- 2 tablespoons of pomegranate seeds

Directions and Total Time: approx. 10 minutes

Combine the avocado flesh with salt, pepper, lime juice, and the cheese and whisk in a bowl. Spread this mixture onto toasted bread slices, top each slice with the remaining ingredients and serve for breakfast. Serve with scrambled eggs.

Per Serving: Calories 348, Fat 20.8g, Carbs 38.7g, Protein 7.1g

11. Bacon and Brie Omelet Wedges

Ingredients for 6 servings

- 2 tablespoons of olive oil
- 7 ounces of smoked bacon
- 6 beaten eggs
- Small bunch of chives, snipped
- 3 ½ ounces of brie, sliced
- 1 teaspoon of red wine vinegar
- 1 teaspoon of Dijon mustard
- 1 cucumber, halved, deseeded, and sliced diagonally
- 7 ounces of radish, quartered

Directions and Total Time: approx. 20 minutes

Dissolve In a large saucepan over medium heat, melt 2 tablespoons of butter. Mix in the thyme and halibut and cook. Uncover and put it back into the oven for another 20 minutes until it's bubbling. Let it rest for 15 minutes. You can sprinkle it with some parsley before serving.

Per Serving: Calories 343, Fat 15.4g, Carbs 39.4g, Protein 13.8g

12. Baked Chicken Thighs

Ingredients for 4 servings

- 1 and ½ pounds of chicken thighs, boneless and skinless
- 2 tablespoons of harissa paste
- ½ cup of Greek yogurt
- Salt and black pepper to taste
- 1 tablespoon of lemon juice
- 1 tablespoon of mint, finely chopped

Directions and Total Time: approx. 30 minutes

Put chicken thighs in a lined baking dish, add salt and pepper to taste and leave aside for now. Meanwhile, in a bowl, mix lemon juice with yogurt, salt and pepper and stir. Add harissa, stir again and spread over chicken pieces. Place chicken thighs in the oven at 165 degrees F and bake for 20 minutes. Transfer dish to your preheated broiler and broil for 5 minutes. Divide chicken on plates, sprinkle mint on top and serve.

Per Serving: Calories 250, Fat 12g, Carbs 2g, Protein 31g

13. Baking Powder Biscuits

Ingredients for 2 servings

- 1 egg white
- 1 cup of white whole-wheat flour
- 4 tablespoons of Non-hydrogenated vegetable shortening
- 1 tablespoon of sugar
- 2/3 cup of low-fat free milk
- 1 cup of unbleached all-purpose flour
- 4 teaspoons of Sodium-free baking powder

Directions and Total Time: approx. 11 minutes

Preheat oven to 450°F. Merge flour, sugar, and baking powder and whip well. Attach the egg white and milk and whip to combine. Set rounds on the baking sheet and bake for 10 minutes. Take out the baking sheet and set biscuits on a wire rack to cool.

Per Serving: Calories 118, Fat 12g, Carbs 8g, Protein 19g

14. Banana and Chocolate Porridge

Ingredients for 4 servings

- 2 bananas
- 4 dried apricots, chopped
- 1 cup of barley, soaked
- 2 tablespoons of flax seeds
- 1 tablespoon of cocoa powder
- 1 cup of coconut milk
- ¼ teaspoon of mint leaves
- 2 ounces of dark chocolate bars, grated
- 2 tablespoons of coconut flakes

Directions and Total Time: approx. 20 minutes

Place the barley in a saucepan along with the flaxseeds and two cups of water. Bring to a boil, then you can actually lower the heat and simmer for 12 minutes, stirring often. Meanwhile, in a food processor, blend bananas, cocoa powder, coconut milk, apricots, and mint leaves until smooth. Once the barley is ready, stir in chocolate. Add in banana mixture. Garnish with coconut flakes. Serve.

Per Serving: Calories 476, Fat 22g, Carbs 65g, Protein 10g

15. Barley Porridge

Ingredients for 4 servings

- 1 cup of pearl barley
- 3 cups of milk
- ¼ cup of agave nectar
- ¼ cup of dried dates, pitted and chopped
- 2 small bananas, peeled and sliced
- 4 tablespoons of walnuts, chopped

Directions and Total Time: approx. 30 minutes

In an instant pot, place all ingredients except for walnuts and stir to combine. Close the lid and adjust the vent in a sealed position. Select "Manual" and cook at "High Pressure" for 20 minutes. After cooking time is completed, press "Cancel" and do a "Natural" release. Open the lid and with a spoon, stir the barley mixture well. Transfer the porridge into serving bowls and serve immediately with the topping of banana slices and walnuts.

Per Serving: Calories 452, Fat 9.1g, Carbs 84.5g, Protein 13.7g

16. Basil with Strawberry Ricotta Toast

Ingredients for 2 servings

- ½ cup of crumbled ricotta cheese
- 1 tablespoon of honey, plus additional as needed
- Pinch of sea salt, plus additional as needed
- 4 slices of whole-grain bread, toasted
- 1 cup of sliced fresh strawberries
- 4 basil leaves, sliced into thin shreds

Directions and Total Time: approx. 10 minutes

Mix together the cheese, honey, and salt in a small bowl until well incorporated. Taste and add additional salt and honey as needed. Spoon the 2 tablespoons of the cheese mixture onto each slice of bread and spread it all over. Sprinkle the sliced strawberry and basil leaves on top before serving.

Per Serving: Calories 273, Fat 7.8g, Carbs 39.7g, Protein 15g

17. Black Olive Toast with Herbed Hummus

Ingredients for 2 servings

- ¼ cup store-bought plain hummus
- 2 tablespoons of finely chopped fresh flat-leaf parsley
- 1 tablespoon of finely chopped fresh dill
- 1 tablespoon of finely chopped fresh mint
- 1 teaspoon of finely grated lemon peel
- 2 slices (½" thick) black olive bread
- 1 clove of garlic, halved
- 1 tablespoon of extra-virgin olive oil

Directions and Total Time: approx. 10 minutes

In a small bowl, combine the hummus, herbs, and lemon peel. Toast the bread. Immediately rub the warm bread with the garlic. Spread half the hummus over each slice of bread and drizzle with the oil.

Per Serving: Calories 178, Fat 10g, Carbs 17g, Protein 5g

18 Blue Cheese Egg Scramble

Ingredients for 4 servings

- 2 tablespoons of olive oil
- 1 cup of white mushrooms, sliced
- 2 cloves of garlic, minced
- 16 ounces of blue cheese
- ½ cup of spinach, sliced
- 6 fresh eggs

Directions and Total Time: approx. 16 minutes

Heat the oil in a small-sized skillet over medium-heat and sauté the mushrooms and garlic for 5 minutes. Crumble the blue cheese into the skillet and cook for 6 minutes. Add the spinach and sauté for five more minutes. Crack the eggs into a small-sized bowl, whisk until well combined and creamy in color, and pour all over the spinach. Use a spatula to immediately stir the eggs while cooking until they're scrambled and no longer runny. Serve and enjoy.

Per Serving: Calories 562, Fat 46.2g, Carbs 4.4g, Protein 33.3g

19. Breakfast Chives Frittata

Ingredients for 6 servings

- 8 whisked eggs
- 1 teaspoon of red pepper flakes
- 2 garlic cloves, minced
- ½ cups of goat's cheese, crumbled
- 2 tablespoons of chives, chopped
- 2 tablespoons of dill, chopped
- 4 tomatoes, diced
- 1 tablespoon of olive oil
- Salt and pepper, to taste

Directions and Total Time: approx. 45 minutes

Grease a medium-sized baking pan and preheat the oven to 325°F. Mix all the ingredients thoroughly in a large bowl and pour into the prepared pan. Place in the prepared preheated oven and bake until the middle is cooked through, around 30–35 minutes. Remove from the oven and serve. Garnish with fresh chopped cilantro.

Per Serving: Calories 149, Fat 10.28g, Carbs 9.93g, Protein 13.26g

20. Breakfast Farro with Dried Fruit and Nuts

Ingredients for 8 servings

- 16 ounces of farro, rinsed and drained
- 4 ½ cups of water
- ¼ cup of maple syrup
- ¼ teaspoon of salt
- 1 cup of dried mixed fruit
- ½ cup of chopped toasted mixed nuts
- 2 cups of almond milk

Directions and Total Time: approx. 30 minutes

Place farro, water, maple syrup, and salt in the Instant Pot® and stir to combine. Close lid, set steam release to Sealing, press the Multigrain button, and set time to 20 minutes. When the timer beeps, let pressure release naturally, about 30 minutes. Press the Cancel button, open lid, and add dried fruit. Close lid and let stand on the Keep Warm setting for 20 minutes. Serve warm with nuts and almond milk.

Per Serving: Calories 347, Fat 7g, Carbs 65g, Protein 9g

21. Breakfast Quinoa

Ingredients for 4 servings

- 1 cup of quinoa, rinsed
- ½ teaspoon of nutmeg
- 1 teaspoon of cinnamon
- ⅓ cup of flax seeds
- ½ cup of slivered almonds
- ½ cup of dried apricots, chopped
- 2 cups of water

Directions and Total Time: approx. 26 minutes

Add quinoa and water in a large-sized saucepan and bring to boil over medium heat. Turn heat to low and simmer for 8-12 minutes or until liquid is absorbed. Stir in nutmeg, cinnamon, flax seeds, almonds and apricots and cook for 2-3 minutes. Drizzle with little milk and serve. If sweetness is desired, add splash of honey.

Per Serving: Calories 287, Fat 11.7g, Carbs 35.2g, Protein 10.5g

22. Brown Rice Salad with Cheese

Ingredients for 4 servings

- 2 tablespoons of olive oil
- ½ cup of brown rice
- 1 pound of watercress
- 1 Roma tomato, sliced
- 4 ounces of feta cheese, crumbled
- 2 tablespoons of fresh basil, chopped
- Salt and black pepper to taste
- 2 tablespoons of lemon juice
- ¼ teaspoon of lemon zest

Directions and Total Time: approx. 10 minutes

Bring to a boil salted water in a pot over medium heat. Add in the rice and cook for 15-18 minutes. Drain and let cool completely. Whisk the tablespoons of olive oil, lemon zest, lemon juice, salt, and pepper in a salad bowl. Add in the watercress, cooled rice, and basil and toss to coat. Top with feta cheese and tomato. Serve immediately.

Per Serving: Calories 480, Fat 24g, Carbs 55g, Protein 14g

23. Buckwheat Apple-Raisin Muffin

Ingredients for 12 servings

- 1 cup of all-purpose flour
- 3/4 cup of buckwheat flour
- 2 tablespoons of brown sugar
- 1 1/2 teaspoons of baking powder
- 1/4 teaspoon of baking soda
- 3/4 cup of reduced-fat buttermilk
- 2 tablespoons of olive oil
- 1 large egg
- 1 cup peeled and cored, fresh diced apples
- 1/4 cup of golden raisins

Directions and Total Time: approx. 44 minutes

Prepare the oven at 375 degrees F. Line a 12-cup muffin tin with a non-stick cooking spray or paper cups. Set aside. Incorporate all the dry ingredients in a mixing bowl. Set aside. Beat together the liquid ingredients until smooth. Transfer the liquid mixture over the flour mixture and mix until moistened. Fold in the diced apples and raisins. Fill each of the muffin cup with about 2/3 full of the mixture. Bake until it turns golden brown. Use the toothpick test. Serve.

Per Serving: Calories 117, Fat 1g, Carbs 19g, Protein 3g

24. Buckwheat Buttermilk Pancakes

Ingredients for 9 servings

- 1/2 cup of buckwheat flour
- 1/2 cup of all-purpose flour
- 2 teaspoons of baking powder
- 1 teaspoon of brown sugar
- 2 tablespoons of olive oil
- 2 large eggs
- 1 cup of reduced-fat buttermilk

Directions and Total Time: approx. 20 minutes

Incorporate the first four ingredients in a bowl. Add the oil, buttermilk, and eggs and mix until thoroughly blended. Put griddle over medium heat and spray with non-stick cooking spray. Pour ¼ cup of the batter over the skillet and cook for 1-2 minutes on each side or until they turn golden brown. Serve immediately.

Per Serving: Calories 108, Fat 3g, Carbs 14g, Protein 4g

25. Buckwheat Pancakes

Ingredients for 4 servings

- ¼ teaspoon of vanilla extract
- 1 cup of buckwheat flour
- 1 ¼ teaspoons of baking powder
- ½ teaspoon of sugar
- ¼ teaspoon of salt
- 1 ¼ cups of buttermilk
- 1 egg
- 1 tablespoon of olive oil

Directions and Total Time: approx. 20 minutes

Whisk the wet ingredients in one bowl and the dry ingredients in another. Mix the content of both bowls together. Heat the olive oil in a small-sized skillet over medium heat. Pour in the batter in batches and cook on both sides, about five minutes. Top with some honey and fresh berries.

Per Serving: Calories 196.4, Fat 5.8g, Carbs 25.7g, Protein 9.1g

26. Butternut Squash Spinach Toast

Ingredients for 4 servings

- 1 large butternut squash
- 1 tablespoon of oil
- 2 garlic cloves, chopped
- 1 bunch of spinach, chopped
- ¼ teaspoon of salt
- ¼ teaspoon of black pepper
- 4 pieces of bread
- ⅓ cups of Gruyere cheese
- 4 eggs

Directions and Total Time: approx. 18 minutes

Peel and cut the butternut squash into half-inch pieces. Sauté these pieces with oil in a skillet for 8 minutes. Stir in the garlic, then sauté until squash turns golden. Toss in the black pepper, salt and spinach. Toast the bread slices in a skillet until golden brown. Grease this skillet and fry the eggs one after another over medium heat. Top each slice with Gruyere, squash and fried eggs. Serve warm.

Per Serving: Calories 250, Fat 11.9g, Carbs 24.9g, Protein 13.4g

27. Cayenne Tomato Oatmeal

Ingredients for 4 servings

- 1 tablespoon of olive oil
- 1 cup of milk
- 3 cups of water
- 1 cup of steel-cut oats
- 10 cherry tomatoes, halved
- 1 teaspoon of cayenne pepper

Directions and Total Time: approx. 35 minutes

Combine milk and 3 cups of water in a saucepan over medium heat and bring to a boil. Warm the olive oil in a large-sized skillet over medium heat and sauté oats for 2 minutes. Remove into the milk saucepan. Mix in oats and cherry tomatoes and simmer for 23 minutes over medium heat. Serve in bowls sprinkled with cayenne pepper and serve.

Per Serving: Calories 180, Fat 20g, Carbs 4g, Protein 2g

28. Cheese Egg Quiche

Ingredients for 6 servings

- 1 tablespoon of melted butter
- 1 ¼ cups of crumbled feta
- ½ cup of ricotta, crumbled
- 2 tablespoons of chopped fresh mint
- 1 tablespoon of chopped fresh dill
- ½ teaspoon of lemon zest
- Black pepper to taste
- 2 large eggs, beaten

Directions and Total Time: approx. 45 minutes

Preheat the oven to 350 F. In a large-sized bowl, combine the feta and ricotta cheeses and blend them well with a fork. Stir in the mint, dill, lemon zest, and black pepper. Slowly add the beaten eggs to the cheese mixture and blend well. Pour the batter into a greased baking dish and drizzle with melted butter. Bake until lightly browned, 35-40 minutes. Serve.

Per Serving: Calories 182, Fat 17g, Carbs 2g, Protein 7g

29. Cheesy Kale and Egg Cupcakes

Ingredients for 2 servings

- ¼ cup of kale, chopped
- 3 eggs
- 1 leek, sliced
- 4 tablespoons of Parmesan, grated
- 2 tablespoons of almond milk
- 1 red bell pepper, chopped
- Salt and black pepper to taste1
- 1 tomato, chopped
- 2 tablespoons of mozzarella, grated

Directions and Total Time: approx. 30 minutes

Preheat the oven to a heat of 360 F. Grease a muffin tin with cooking spray. Whisk the eggs in a bowl. Add in milk, kale, leek, Parmesan cheese, bell pepper, salt, black pepper, tomato, and mozzarella cheese and stir to combine. Divide the prepared mixture between the cases and bake for approximately 20-25 minutes. Let cool completely on a wire rack before serving.

Per Serving: Calories 320, Fat 20g, Carbs 9g, Protein 26g

30. Cherry Oats Bow

Ingredients for 1 serving

- ½ cup of organic rolled oats
- ½ cup of unsweetened almond milk
- 1 tablespoon of chia seeds
- 1 teaspoon of hemp seeds
- 2 teaspoons of almonds, sliced
- 1 tablespoon of almond butter
- 1 teaspoon of vanilla extract
- ½ cup of fresh berries
- 1 cup of frozen cherries
- 1 cup of plain Greek yogurt

Directions and Total Time: approx. 10 minutes

Soak the oats in the unsweetened almond milk. Prepare a smooth blend of the soaked oats, frozen cherries, yogurt, chia seeds, almond butter, and vanilla extract. Pour the mixture into two bowls. Add equal amounts of hemp seeds, sliced almonds, and fresh cherries to each bowl.

Per Serving: Calories 889, Fat 35.3g, Carbs 112g, Protein 33.6g

31. Cherry Tomato and Mushroom Frittata

Ingredients for 4 servings

- 1 cup of Italian brown mushrooms, sliced
- 2 tablespoons of olive oil
- 2 spring onions, chopped
- 8 cherry tomatoes, halved
- 6 eggs
- ½ cup of milk
- Salt and black pepper to taste
- ¼ cup of grated Parmesan
- ½ tablespoon of Italian seasoning mix

Directions and Total Time: approx. 30 minutes

Preheat oven to 370 F. Mix eggs, milk, Italian seasoning, salt, and pepper in a bowl. Warm olive oil in a large-sized skillet over medium heat until sizzling. Add in mushrooms, spring onions, and tomatoes and sauté for 5 minutes. Pour in the prepared egg mixture and cook for 5 minutes until the eggs are set. Scatter Parmesan cheese and bake in the oven for 6-7 minutes until the cheese melts. Slice before serving.

Per Serving: Calories 227, Fat 15g, Carbs 13g, Protein 13g

32. Chickpea Pancakes

Ingredients for 4 servings

- 1 cup of water
- 1 cup of chickpea flour
- ½ teaspoon of salt
- ½ teaspoon of pepper
- 1 teaspoon of turmeric
- 1 tablespoon of olive oil
- 3 spring onions, diced
- 1 red bell pepper, diced, optional
- ½ teaspoon of chili flakes, optional

Directions and Total Time: approx. 15 minutes

Add the water, flour, salt, pepper, chili flakes (optional), and turmeric to a blender. Blend and then set aside. Heat the oil in a non-stick pan. Add the spring onions to the flour mixture. Add a tablespoon of the mixture to the hot pan and cook for 3 minutes. Flip each pancake with a spatula and cook for approximately another 2 minutes. Serve warm.

Per Serving: Calories 253, Fat 11g, Carbs 34g, Protein 10g

33. Chili and Cheese Frittata

Ingredients for 6 servings

- 2 tablespoons of olive oil
- 12 fresh eggs
- ¼ cup of half-and-half
- Salt and black pepper to taste
- ½ chili pepper, minced
- 2 ½ cups of shredded mozzarella

Directions and Total Time: approx. 35 minutes

Preheat oven to a heat of 350 F. Whisk the eggs in a bowl. Add the half-and-half, salt, and black and stir to combine. Warm the olive oil in a large-sized skillet over medium heat. Sauté the chili pepper for 2-3 minutes. Sprinkle evenly with mozzarella cheese. Pour eggs over cheese in the skillet. Place the large-sized skillet in the oven and bake for 20–25 minutes until just firm. Let cool the frittata for a few minutes and cut into wedges. Serve hot.

Per Serving: Calories 381, Fat 31g, Carbs 2g, Protein 25g

34. Chorizo and Cheese Omelet

Ingredients for 2 servings

- 4 eggs, beaten
- 4 ounces of mozzarella, grated
- 1 tablespoon of butter
- 8 chorizo slices, thin
- 1 tomato, sliced
- Salt and black pepper to taste

Directions and Total Time: approx. 20 minutes

Whisk the eggs with salt and pepper. In a cast-iron skillet, add the butter and cook the eggs for 30 seconds. Create a layer with the chorizo slices. Arrange the sliced tomato and mozzarella over the chorizo and cook for about 3 minutes. Cover the skillet and continue cooking for 3 more minutes, or until the omelet is completely set. With a spatula, run around the edges of the omelet and flip it onto a plate folded-side down. Serve.

Per Serving: Calories 451, Fat 36.5g, Carbs 25g, Protein 30g

35. Cinnamon and Pecan Porridge

Ingredients for 2 servings

- ½ teaspoon of cinnamon
- ¼ cup of pecans, chopped
- ¼ cup of unsweetened coconut, toasted
- ¼ cup of coconut milk
- ¼ cup of almond butter
- ¾ cup of unsweetened almond milk
- 1 tablespoon of extra virgin coconut oil
- 2 tablespoons of hemp seeds
- 2 tablespoons of whole chia seeds

Directions and Total Time: approx. 15 minutes

Place a small saucepan over medium heat. Combine the coconut milk, coconut oil, almond butter, and almond milk. Bring to simmer and remove from heat. Add the toasted coconut (leave some for toppings), cinnamon, pecans, hemp seeds, and chia seeds. Mix the ingredients well and allow to rest for 5–10 minutes. Divide between two bowls and serve.

Per Serving: Calories 580, Fat 14g, Carbs 3g, Protein 8g

36. Cinnamon Roll Oats

Ingredients for 4 servings

- ½ cup of rolled oats
- 1 cup of milk
- 1 teaspoon of vanilla extract
- 1 teaspoon of ground cinnamon
- 2 teaspoons of honey
- 2 tablespoons of Plain yogurt
- 1 teaspoon of butter

Directions and Total Time: approx. 17 minutes

Pour milk into the saucepan and bring it to a boil. Add rolled oats and stir well. Close the lid and simmer the oats for 5 minutes over medium heat. The cooked oats will absorb all milk. Then add butter and stir the oats well. In the separated bowl, whisk together Plain yogurt with honey, cinnamon, and vanilla extract. Transfer the cooked oats to the serving bowls. Top the oats with the yogurt mixture in the shape of the wheel.

Per Serving: Calories 243, Fat 20.2g, Carbs 2.8g, Protein 13.3g

37. Citrus French Toasts

Ingredients for 4 servings

- Ingredients for 4 servings
- 1 tablespoon of butter
- 1 orange, juiced and zested
- 4 bread slices
- 1 ½ cups of milk
- 2 eggs, beaten
- 1 teaspoon of vanilla extract
- 1 teaspoon of ground cinnamon
- 1 tablespoon of powdered sugar

Directions and Total Time: approx. 30 minutes

Beat milk, eggs, vanilla, orange zest, and orange juice in a bowl. Lay the bread in a rectangular baking dish in an even layer. Cover with the egg mixture and let it stand for 10 minutes, flipping once, to absorb well. Melt the butter in a large-sized skillet over medium heat and fry the bread in batches until golden brown on each of the both sides, about 6-8 minutes. Dust with powdered sugar and cinnamon. Serve.

Per Serving: Calories 160, Fat 7.3g, Carbs 17g, Protein 6.9g

38. Coriander with Honey Glazed Carrots

Ingredients for 2 servings

- ½ pound of rainbow carrots, peeled
- 2 tablespoons of fresh orange juice
- 1 tablespoon of honey
- ½ teaspoon of coriander
- Pinch of salt

Directions and Total Time: approx. 30 minutes

Preheat the oven to a heat of 400°F (205°C). Cut the carrots lengthwise into slices of even thickness and place in a large bowl. Stir together the orange juice, honey, coriander, and salt in a small bowl. Pour the orange juice mixture over the carrots and toss until well coated. Spread the carrots in a baking dish in a single layer. Roast for 15 to 20 minutes until fork-tender. Let cool for 5 minutes before serving.

Per Serving: Calories 84, Fat 1g, Carbs 20g, Protein 0.9g

39. Dilly Salmon Frittata

Ingredients for 4 servings

- 2 tablespoons of olive oil
- 1 cup of cream cheese
- 1 cup of smoked salmon, chopped
- 8 eggs, whisked
- 1 teaspoon of dill, chopped
- 2 tablespoons of milk
- Salt and black pepper to taste

Directions and Total Time: approx. 35 minutes

Preheat oven to a heat of 360 F. In a bowl, place all the ingredients and stir to combine. Warm olive oil in a large-sized pan over medium heat and pour in the mixture. Cook until the base is set, about 3-4 minutes. Place the large-sized pan in the oven and bake until the top is golden, about 5 minutes. Serve sliced into wedges.

Serving: Calories 418, Fat 37g, Carbs 3g, Protein 19.6g

40. Egg Breakfast Bowl

Ingredients for 1 serving

- 2 eggs
- 1 teaspoon of olive oil
- ½ bell pepper, chopped
- ½ scallion, chopped
- ¼ cup of Feta cheese, crumbled
- ¼ cup of olives, pitted
- Salt and pepper

Directions and Total Time: approx. 15 minutes

In a large-sized bowl, whisk eggs with pepper and salt. Add olives, scallion, bell pepper and cheese and stir well. Heat oil in a large-sized pan over medium-high heat. Add egg mixture to the pan and let it cook for 2 minutes, then start scrambling the egg mixture. Stir for 3 minutes more. Garnish with parsley and serve.

Per Serving: Calories 325, Fat 25.2g, Carbs 9.4g, Protein 17.4g

41. Eggs and Salsa

Ingredients for 2 servings

- 3 cups tomatoes
- 1 green onion (bunch)
- 1 bunch of cilantros, chopped
- 1 cup of red onion, chopped
- Juice from 1 lime
- 2 small habanero chilies, chopped
- 2 garlic cloves, minced
- 8 eggs, whisked.
- A drizzle of olive oil
- Sea salt

Directions and Total Time: approx. 10 minutes

Mix tomatoes, green onions, red onion, habaneros, garlic, cilantro, and lime juice and toss well. Add just a pinch of salt, toss again and keep this in the fridge until you serve it. Heat up a medium-sized pan with a drizzle of oil, add eggs, and scramble them for 4–5 minutes. Divide scrambled eggs on plates, add salsa on top and serve.

Per Serving: Calories 383, Fat 14g, Carbs 3g, Protein 8g

42. Eggs Florentine

Ingredients for 3 servings

- 2 tablespoons of olive oil
- 2 cloves of garlic
- 3 tablespoons of cream cheese
- ½ cup of mushroom
- ½ cup of spinach
- Salt and black pepper, to taste
- 6 eggs

Directions and Total Time: approx. 20 minutes

Put the oil in a medium-sized non-stick skillet and heat. Mix in the mushrooms and garlic until the garlic is fragrant for about 1 minute. Add the spinach to the mushroom paste and cook until the spinach softens for 2–3 minutes. Combine the mushroom-spinach mixture, then add salt and pepper. Add the eggs and cook, mixing, until the eggs are stiff; turn. Pour the cream cheese over the egg mixture and cook until the cheese starts melting, about 5 minutes.

Per Serving: Calories 278.9, Fat 22.9g, Carbs 4.1g, Protein 15.7g

43. Eggs on Greens

Ingredients for 4 servings

- 2 tablespoons of olive oil
- 2 large bunches of chard, leaves shredded
- 4 garlic cloves, sliced
- ½ cup of grape tomatoes halved
- 4 large eggs

Directions and Total Time: approx. 29 minutes

Sauté the greens with 1 tablespoon of oil in a skillet over medium heat for 10 minutes. Stir in the tomatoes and garlic, then sauté for 5 minutes, then divide this mixture into four plates. Add the remaining oil to the used same skillet. Crack the eggs in this skillet and add 1 tablespoon of water. Cover and cook for 4 minutes, then remove from the heat. Add one egg on top of each plate with greens. Serve.

Per Serving: Calories 158, Fat 12.1g, Carbs 5.9g, Protein 8.3g

44. Eggs Scramble with Veggies

Ingredients for 1 serving

- 2 eggs, beaten
- 3 asparagus, chopped
- 1 carrot, shredded
- 1 tablespoon of fava beans
- 1 tablespoon of Parmesan cheese
- 2 teaspoons of EVO
- 1 garlic clove, chopped
- Pinch of fresh rosemary
- 1 tablespoon of butter, softened
- Salt and Pepper

Directions and Total Time: approx. 20 minutes

Take a skillet, heat EVO on medium heat and add garlic, rosemary plus the veggies. Stir them to cook until soft (about 4 minutes). Take a bowl add the beaten eggs, whisk in butter, salt and pepper. Pour the eggs mixture onto the veggies, cook for about 2 minutes then add parmesan cheese or Cheddar cheese, cook until cheese is melted. Serve.

Per Serving: Calories 338, Fat 23g, Carbs 6.9g, Protein 18.5g

45. Eggs with Zucchini Noodles

Ingredients for 2 servings

- 2 tablespoons of extra-virgin olive oil
- 3 zucchinis, cut with a spiralizer
- 4 eggs
- Salt and black pepper to the taste
- A pinch of red pepper flakes
- Cooking spray
- 1 tablespoon of basil, chopped

Directions and Total Time: approx. 21 minutes

In a bowl, combine the zucchini noodles with olive oil, salt, and pepper and mix well. Grease a tray with cooking spray and divide the zucchini noodles into four nests. Crack an egg onto each nest, sprinkle with pepper, salt, and red pepper flakes and bake at 350 degrees F for 11 minutes. Divide between plates, sprinkle the fresh basil on top and serve.

Per Serving: Calories 296, Fat 23.6g, Carbs 10.6g, Protein 14.7g

46. Flatbread with Caramelized Onions

Ingredients for 8 servings

- 3 tablespoons of olive oil, divided
- 1 large onion, sliced
- 1 pound of pizza dough
- 1 teaspoon of rosemary, chopped
- 1 ¼ teaspoon of kosher salt

Directions and Total Time: approx. 55 minutes

Preheat the oven to 425°F. 15 minutes over moderate flame, sauté onion in 1 tablespoon heated oil until golden color. Squeeze batter into a 15 x 12" jelly-roll pan to a thickness of approximately 1/4 inch. Indent 1-inch intervals in the dough with the wooden spoon handle; drizzle with remainder 2 Tbsp. oil and sprinkle with rosemary, salt, and caramelized onions. Bake for 20 minutes at 425°F on the lowest oven rack or until lightly browned.

Per Serving: Calories 137, Fat 7g, Carbs 16g, Protein 2.4g

47. Frittata with Sweet Potatoes and Kale

Ingredients for 4 servings

- 6 eggs, beaten
- 1/2 teaspoon of ground pepper
- 1 teaspoon of salt
- 2 tablespoons of EVO
- 2 sweet potatoes, cut into chunks
- 1/2 red onion
- 2 cups of kale
- 4 tablespoons of goat cheese
- 2 cloves of garlic

Directions and Total Time: approx. 30 minutes

Heat oven at 350 F. Whisk egg with pepper and salt. Saute the sweet potatoes in pan for around 6 minutes and then remove from the pan and set aside. Saute kale and the other ingredients in the same pan with oil. Add egg mixture in the vegetables and cook for around 3 minutes. Top with goat cheese. Bake for around 14 minutes and serve.

Per Serving: Calories 325, Fat 11.3g, Carbs 8.9g, Protein 6.8g

48. Garlic Bell Pepper Omelet

Ingredients for 2 servings

- 2 tablespoons of olive oil
- 2 red bell peppers, chopped
- ¼ teaspoon of nutmeg
- 4 eggs, beaten
- 2 garlic cloves, crushed
- 1 teaspoon of Italian seasoning

Directions and Total Time: approx. 10 minutes

Heat the oil in a small-sized skillet over medium heat. Stir-fry the peppers for 3 minutes or until lightly charred; reserve. Add the garlic to the skillet and sauté for 1 minute. Pour the eggs over the garlic, sprinkle with Italian seasoning and nutmeg, and cook for 2-3 minutes or until set. Using a spatula, loosen the edges and gently slide onto a plate. Add charred peppers and fold over. Serve hot.

Per Serving: Calories 272, Fat 22g, Carbs 6.4g, Protein 12g

49. Goat Cheese with Avocado Toast

Ingredients for 2 servings

- 2 slices of whole-wheat thin-sliced bread
- ½ avocado
- 2 tablespoons of crumbled goat cheese
- Salt, to taste

Directions and Total Time: approx. 10 minutes

Toast the bread slices in a toaster for 2 to 3 minutes on each side until browned. Scoop out the avocado flesh into a medium-sized mixing bowl and mash it with a fork until it reaches the appropriate consistency. Each slice of bread should have a thin layer of mashed potatoes on it. Season with salt and pepper to taste after scattering the crumbled goat cheese on top. Serve as soon as possible.

Per Serving: Calories 135, Fat 5.8g, Carbs 17.4g, Protein 4.9g

50. Grain Bowl with Sauteed Spinach

Ingredients for 4 servings

- 2 cups of cooked farro grains, warmed
- 1 tablespoon of olive oil
- 1 garlic clove, chopped
- 1 bunch of spinach leaves, chopped
- ¼ teaspoon of kosher salt
- ¼ teaspoon of black pepper
- 1 medium tomato, cut into 1-inch pieces
- ½ avocado, diced
- 2 large eggs

Directions and Total Time: approx. 16 minutes

Sauté the garlic with oil in a skillet for 1 minute. Stir in the spinach, black pepper, and salt then cook for 2 minutes. Divide the grains into 2 serving bowls and top them with spinach mixture, tomato and avocado. Fry each egg in a skillet for 3 minutes then place on top of each bowl. Serve.

Per Serving: Calories 458, Fat 21g, Carbs 29g, Protein 14g

51. Greek Beans Tortillas

Ingredients for 4 servings

- 1 red onion, chopped
- 2 garlic cloves, minced
- 1 tablespoon of olive oil
- 1 green bell pepper, sliced
- 3 cups of canned pinto beans, drained and rinsed
- 2 red chili peppers, chopped
- 4 tablespoons of parsley, chopped
- 1 teaspoon of cumin, ground
- A pinch of salt and black pepper
- 4 whole-wheat Greek tortillas
- 1 cup of cheddar cheese, shredded

Directions and Total Time: approx. 25 minutes

Heat up a large-sized pan with the oil over medium heat, add the onion and sauté for 5 minutes. Add the rest of the remaining ingredients except the tortillas and the cheese, stir and cook for 15 minutes. Divide the beans mix on each Greek tortilla, also divide the cheese, roll the tortillas and serve for breakfast.

Per Serving: Calories 673, Fat 14.9g, Carbs 75.4g, Protein 39g

52. Grilled Chicken and Vinaigrette

Ingredients for 4 servings

- 2 tablespoons of vegetable oil
- 4 chicken breast halves, skinless and boneless
- Salt and black pepper to taste
- 1 tablespoon of shallot, chopped
- 1 tablespoon of vinegar
- ½ teaspoon of sugar
- ½ teaspoon of mustard
- 6 tablespoons of olive oil
- 2 tablespoons of parsley chopped
- 2 tablespoons of kalamata olives, chopped

Directions and Total Time: approx. 20 minutes

Place each chicken piece between 2 parchment paper pieces, brush meat with the vegetable oil, season with salt and pepper, and you can actually place on preheated grill pan, cook for 10 minutes turning once. Transfer to a cutting board and leave aside for a few minutes. In a bowl, mix shallot with vinegar, mustard, sugar, salt, pepper, olive oil, parsley and olives and whisk well. Cut chicken in thin slices, arrange on a platter and serve with the vinaigrette on top.

Per Serving: Calories 400, Fat 32g, Carbs 2g, Protein 24g

53. Ham, Bean and Sweet Potato Frittata

Ingredients for 4 servings

- 2 sweet potatoes, boiled and chopped
- 2 tablespoons of olive oil
- 4 eggs, whisked
- 1 red onion, chopped
- ¾ cup of ham, chopped
- ½ cup of white beans, cooked
- 2 tablespoons of Greek yogurt
- Salt and black pepper to taste
- 10 cherry tomatoes, halved
- ¾ cup cheddar cheese, grated

Directions and Total Time: approx. 25 minutes

Warm the olive oil in a large-sized skillet over medium heat and sauté onion for 2 minutes. Stir in sweet potatoes, ham, beans, yogurt, salt, pepper, and tomatoes and cook for another 3 minutes. Pour in eggs and cheese, lock the lid and cook for an additional 10 minutes. Cut before serving.

Per Serving: Calories 280, Fat 18g, Carbs 9g, Protein 12g

54. Ham Muffins

Ingredients for 6 servings

- 9 ham slices
- 5 eggs, whisked
- 1/3 cup of spinach, chopped
- ¼ cup of feta cheese, crumbled
- ½ cup of roasted red peppers, chopped
- A pinch of salt and black pepper
- 1 and ½ tablespoons of basil pesto
- Cooking spray

Directions and Total Time: approx. 15 minutes

Coat a large-sized muffin pan with cooking spray and place 1-12 ham slices in each mold. Divide the peppers and the rest of the ingredients except the eggs, pesto, salt, and pepper into the ham cups. Whisk together the eggs, pesto, salt, and pepper in a mixing dish, then pour over the pepper mixture. Bake the muffins for just approximately 15 minutes at 400°F.

Per Serving: Calories 343, Fat 15.4g, Carbs 39.4g, Protein 13.8g

55. Hummus Deviled Egg

Ingredients for 6 servings

- 1/4 cup of finely diced cucumber
- 1/4 cup of finely diced tomato
- 2 teaspoons of fresh lemon juice
- 1/8 teaspoon salt
- 6 hard-cooked peeled eggs, sliced half lengthwise
- 1/3 cup of roasted garlic hummus or any hummus flavor
- Chopped fresh parsley (optional)

Directions and Total Time: approx. 10 minutes

Combine the tomato, lemon juice, cucumber, and salt together, and then gently mix. Scrape out the yolks from the halved eggs and store them for later use. Scoop a heaping teaspoon of hummus in each half egg. Top with parsley and half-teaspoon tomato-cucumber mixture. Serve immediately.

Per Serving: Calories 40, Fat 1g, Carbs 9g, Protein 4g

56. Jalapeno Cheddar Waffles

Ingredients for 2 servings

- 3 ounces of Cream Cheese
- 3 large Eggs
- 1 tablespoon of Coconut Flour
- 1 teaspoon of Psyllium Husk Powder
- 1 teaspoon of Baking Powder
- 1 ounces of Cheddar Cheese
- 1 small Jalapeno
- Salt and Pepper to Taste

Directions and Total Time: approx. 15 minutes

Mix all ingredients except for the cheese and jalapeno using an immersion blender. Once the ingredients are mixed well and smooth, add cheese and jalapeno. Use an immersion blender again to make sure that all of the ingredients are mixed well. Heat your waffle iron, and then pour on the waffle mix. It took about 5-6 minutes in total to cook for me. Top with your favorite toppings, and serve!

Per Serving: Calories 338, Fat 28g, Carbs 3g, Protein 16g

57. Kale Egg Cupcakes

Ingredients for 2 servings

- 1 whole-grain bread slice
- 4 large eggs, beaten
- 3 tablespoons of milk
- Salt and black pepper to taste
- ½ teaspoon of onion powder
- ¼ teaspoon of garlic powder
- ¾ cup of chopped kale

Directions and Total Time: approx. 40 minutes

Heat the oven to a heat of 350 F. Break the bread into pieces and divide between 2 greased ramekins. Mix the eggs, milk, salt, onion powder, garlic powder, pepper, and kale in a medium bowl. Pour half of the large beaten egg mixture into each ramekin and bake for 25 minutes or until the eggs are set. Serve and enjoy!

Per Serving: Calories 213, Fat 12g, Carbs 13g, Protein 17g

58. Lemon Cardamom Buckwheat Pancakes

Ingredients for 2 servings

- ½ cup of buckwheat flour
- ½ teaspoon of cardamom
- ½ teaspoon of baking powder
- ½ cup of milk
- ¼ cup of plain Greek yogurt
- 1 egg
- 1 teaspoon of lemon zest
- 1 tablespoon of honey

Directions and Total Time: approx. 20 minutes

Mix the buckwheat flour, cardamom, and baking powder in a medium bowl. Whisk the milk, yogurt, egg, lemon zest, and honey in another bowl. Add the listed wet ingredients above to the dry ingredients and stir until the batter is smooth. Spray a large-sized frying pan with non-stick cooking oil and cook the pancakes over medium heat until the edges begin to brown. Flip and also cook the dish on the other side for 3 more minutes. Serve.

Per Serving: Calories 196, Fat 6g, Carbs 27g, Protein 10g

59. Mediterranean Breakfast Panini

Ingredients for 4 servings

- 1 round of panini loaf
- 2 tablespoons of extra-virgin olive oil
- 8 large free-range eggs, hard-boiled, and sliced into rounds
- 1/2 cup of black olives, pitted and halved
- 2 heirloom tomatoes, thinly sliced into rounds
- 12 large, fresh basil leaves

Directions and Total Time: approx. 10 minutes

Slice the panini loaf in half horizontally, and use a basting brush to coat the inside of each slice with 1 tablespoon of olive oil. Begin building the panini by placing a single layer of boiled egg slices on one half of the panini, followed by the olives, tomato rounds, and finally, the basil leaves. Place the remaining panini slice on top. Slice the panini, and serve.

Per Serving: Calories 427, Fat 21g, Carbs 39g, Protein 23g

60. Milky Buckwheat Porridge

Ingredients for 4 servings

- 3 cups of water
- 2 cups of raw buckwheat groats
- Pinch of sea salt
- 1 cup of unsweetened almond milk

Directions and Total Time: approx. 45 minutes

In a medium saucepan, add the water, buckwheat groats, and sea salt and bring to a boil over medium-high heat. Once the water begins to actually boil, lower the heat to a low setting. Cook for about 20 minutes, stirring occasionally, or until most of the water is absorbed. Fold in the almond milk and whisk well. Continue cooking for about 15 minutes, or until the buckwheat groats are very softened. Pour the porridge into bowls and serve it while it's still warm.

Per Serving: Calories 120, Fat 0.9g, Carbs 21.4g, Protein 6.2g

61. Mini Frittatas

Ingredients for 8 servings

- 1 yellow onion, chopped
- 1 cup of Parmesan cheese, grated
- 1 yellow bell pepper, chopped
- 1 red bell pepper, chopped
- 1 zucchini, chopped
- Salt and black pepper
- A drizzle of olive oil
- 8 whisked eggs
- 2 tablespoons of chives, chopped

Directions and Total Time: approx. 29 minutes

Set a pan over medium-high heat. Add in oil to warm. Stir in all ingredients except chives and eggs. Sauté for around 5 minutes. Put the eggs on a muffin pan and top with the chives. Set oven to 350°F/176°C. Place the muffin pan into the oven to bake for about 10 minutes. Serve the eggs on a plate with sautéed vegetables.

Per Serving: Calories 55, Fat 3g, Carbs 21g, Protein 4.2g

62. Mozzarella and Olive Cakes

Ingredients for 6 servings

- 4 tablespoons of olive oil, softened
- ¼ cup of mozzarella, shredded
- ¼ cup of black olives, chopped
- ½ cup of milk
- 1 egg, beaten
- 1 cup of corn flour
- 1 teaspoon of baking powder
- 3 sun-dried tomatoes, chopped
- 2 tablespoons of fresh cilantro, chopped
- ¼ teaspoon of kosher salt

Directions and Total Time: approx. 25 minutes

Preheat oven to a heat of 360 F. In a bowl, whisk the egg with milk and olive oil. In a separate bowl, mix the salt, corn flour, cilantro, and baking powder. Combine the wet ingredients with the dry mixture. Stir in black olives, tomatoes, and mozzarella cheese. Pour the mixture into greased ramekins and bake for 18-20 minutes or until cooked and golden.

Per Serving: Calories 189, Fat 11.7g, Carbs 19g, Protein 4g

63. Mushroom and Zucchini Egg Muffins

Ingredients for 4 servings

- 2 tablespoons of olive oil
- 1 cup of Parmesan, grated
- 1 onion, chopped
- 1 cup of mushrooms, sliced
- 1 red bell pepper, chopped
- 1 zucchini, chopped
- Salt and black pepper to taste
- 8 eggs, whisked
- 2 tablespoons of chives, chopped

Directions and Total Time: approx. 20 minutes

Preheat the oven to 360 F. Warm the olive oil in a skillet over medium heat and sauté onion, bell pepper, zucchini, mushrooms, salt, and pepper for 5 minutes until tender. Mix with the whisked eggs and season with salt and pepper. Distribute the mixture across muffin cups and top with the Parmesan cheese. Sprinkle with chives and bake for 10 minutes. Serve.

Per Serving: Calories 60, Fat 4g, Carbs 4g, Protein 5g

64. Mushroom-Egg Casserole

Ingredients for 3 servings

- ½ cup of mushrooms, chopped
- ½ yellow onion, diced
- 4 eggs, beaten
- 1 tablespoon of coconut flakes
- ½ teaspoon of chili pepper
- 1 ounce of cheddar cheese, shredded
- 1 teaspoon of canola oil

Directions and Total Time: approx. 32 minutes

Pour canola oil into the skillet and preheat well. Add mushrooms and onion and roast for 5–8 minutes or until the vegetables are light brown. Transfer the cooked vegetables into the casserole mold. Add coconut flakes, chili pepper, and cheddar cheese. Then add eggs and stir well. Bake the casserole for 15 minutes at 360°F.

Per Serving: Calories 152, Fat 11.1g, Carbs 3g, Protein 10.4g

65. Napoli Scrambled Eggs with Anchovies

Ingredients for 4 servings

- 2 tablespoons of olive oil
- 1 green bell pepper, chopped
- 2 anchovy fillets, chopped
- 8 cherry tomatoes, cubed
- 2 spring onions, chopped
- 1 tablespoon of capers, drained
- 5 black olives, pitted and sliced
- 6 eggs, beaten
- Salt and black pepper to taste
- ¼ teaspoon of dried oregano
- 1 tablespoon of parsley, chopped

Directions and Total Time: approx. 20 minutes

Warm the olive oil in a large-sized skillet over medium heat and cook the bell pepper and spring onions for 3 minutes. Add in anchovies, cherry tomatoes, capers, and black olives and cook for another 2 minutes. Stir in eggs and sprinkle with salt, pepper, and oregano and scramble for 5 minutes. Serve sprinkled with parsley.

Per Serving: Calories 260, Fat 18g, Carbs 12g, Protein 12g

66. Nectarine Bruschetta

Ingredients for 2 servings

- 1 ½ tablespoon of white wine vinegar
- 1 teaspoon of honey
- 1 nectarine, sliced
- ¼ cup of olive oil
- 2 teaspoons of black pepper
- ⅓ cup of fresh ricotta cheese
- 2 slices of bread, toasted

Directions and Total Time: approx. 15 minutes

Mix the teaspoon of honey and the tablespoon of white wine vinegar in a medium-sized bowl. Stir in the sliced nectarine, mix it well and marinate for approximately about 10 minutes. Add the black pepper and olive oil, then mix well. Spread the cup of fresh ricotta cheese over the slices of toasted bread. Divide the nectarine and its juice on top of the bread. Serve.

Per Serving: Calories 347, Fat 29.1g, Carbs 18.5g, Protein 6.4g

67. Orange French Toast

Ingredients for 2 servings

- 1 cup of unsweetened almond milk
- 3 large eggs
- 2 teaspoons of grated orange zest
- 1 teaspoon of vanilla extract
- ⅛ teaspoon of ground cardamom
- ⅛ teaspoon of ground cinnamon
- 1 loaf of boule bread, sliced 1 inch thick (gluten-free preferred)
- 1 banana, sliced
- ¼ cup of Berry and Honey Compote

Directions and Total Time: approx. 20 minutes

Heat a nonstick skillet over medium-high heat. In a shallow dish, mix the milk, eggs, orange zest, vanilla, cardamom, and cinnamon. Working in batches, dredge the bread slices into the egg mixture and put them in the hot pan. Cook each side until golden brown. Serve, topped with banana and drizzled with honey compote.

Per Serving: Calories 394, Fat 6g, Carbs 68g, Protein 17g

68. Orzo and Veggie Bowls

Ingredients for 4 servings

- 2 ½ cups of whole-wheat orzo, cooked
- 14 ounces of canned cannellini beans
- 1 yellow bell pepper, cubed
- 1 green bell pepper, cubed
- A pinch of salt and black pepper
- 3 tomatoes, cubed
- 1 red onion, chopped
- 1 cup of mint, chopped
- 2 cups of feta cheese, crumbled
- 2 tablespoons of olive oil
- ¼ cup of lemon juice
- 1 tablespoon of lemon zest, grated
- 1 cucumber, cubed
- 1 ¼ cup of kalamata olives, sliced
- 3 garlic cloves, minced

Directions and Total Time: approx. 10 minutes

In a large-sized salad bowl, combine the orzo with the beans, bell peppers, and the rest of the ingredients, toss, divide the mix between plates and serve for breakfast.

Per Serving: Calories 411, Fat 17g, Carbs 51g, Protein 14g

69. Parsley Tomato Eggs

Ingredients for 6 servings

- 2 tablespoons of olive oil
- 1 onion, chopped
- 2 garlic cloves, minced
- 2 cans of tomatoes, diced
- 6 large eggs
- ½ cup of fresh chives, chopped

Directions and Total Time: approx. 25 minutes

Warm the olive oil in a large-sized skillet over medium heat. Add the onion and garlic and cook for 3 minutes, stirring occasionally. Pour in the tomatoes with their juices o and cook for 3 minutes until bubbling. Crack one egg into a small custard cup. With a large spoon, make six indentations in the tomato mixture. Gently pour the first cracked egg into one indentation and repeat, cracking the remaining eggs, one at a time, into the custard cup and pouring one into each indentation. Cover the skillet and cook for 6-8 minutes. Top with chives and serve.

Per Serving: Calories 123, Fat 8g, Carbs 4g, Protein 7g

70. Peanut Butter Banana Greek Yogurt Bowl

Ingredients for 4 servings

- 4 cups of vanilla Greek yogurt
- 2 medium bananas sliced
- ¼ cup of creamy natural peanut butter
- ¼ cup of flax seed meal
- 1 teaspoon of nutmeg

Directions and Total Time: approx. 20 minutes

Divide the yogurt into four dishes and top with the banana slices. Melt the peanut butter in a microwave-safe dish for 30-40 seconds, then pour one tablespoon on top of the bananas in each bowl. To serve, sprinkle with flax seed meal and grated nutmeg.

Per Serving: Calories 370, Fat 10.6g, Carbs 47.7g, Protein 22.7g

71. Pesto Salami and Cheese Egg Cupcakes

Ingredients for 6 servings

- ½ cup of roasted red peppers, chopped
- 1 tablespoon of olive oil
- 5 eggs, whisked
- 4 ounces of Italian dry salami, sliced
- 1/3 cup of spinach, chopped
- ¼ cup of ricotta cheese, crumbled
- Salt and black pepper to taste
- 1 ½ tablespoon of basil pesto

Directions and Total Time: approx. 25 minutes

Preheat the oven to 380 F. Brush 6 ramekin cups with olive oil and line them with dry salami slices. Top with spinach, ricotta cheese, and roasted peppers. Whisk the eggs with pesto, salt, and pepper in a bowl and pour over the peppers. Bake for 15 minutes and serve warm.

Per Serving: Calories 120, Fat 8g, Carbs 2g, Protein 10g

72. Pita with Greens, Fried Onions, and Bacon

Ingredients for 2 servings

- 2 pitas
- 3 ½ ounces of bacon
- 1 ½ ounces of red onion
- 1 bunch of green salad
- 3 ½ ounces of tomatoes
- 2 garlic cloves
- Sea salt to taste
- Ground black pepper to taste
- 2 tablespoons of vegetable oil
- ½ lemon juiced

Directions and Total Time: approx. 11 minutes

Cut the onion and tomato into slices, finely chop the garlic. Heat the oil and fry the onion and bacon until golden brown. Add the garlic, fry for 1 minute. Put the lettuce leaves on pita, put the tomatoes, fried onions, and bacon on top. Before serving, sprinkle with lemon juice, salt, pepper to taste.

Per Serving: Calories 470, Fat 21g, Carbs 41.8g, Protein 14.5g

73. Pork Loin Caramelized Onions

Ingredients for 4 servings

- 1 teaspoon of Seasoning mix (or use a mixture of any garlic, black pepper, salt, onion, and parsley)
- 1 ½ pound of Pork tenderloin (you can use chicken breasts or beef tenderloin)

Directions and Total Time: approx. 30 minutes

Preheat your oven to 400. Season both sides of the tenderloin. Over high heat, place the oven-safe pan on your oven and grease it with nonstick cooking spray. Once heated up, place the tenderloins in the pan without touching each other. Cook each side for about 3 minutes, or until it turns brown. Transfer the tenderloins to the oven and allow them to cook for about 25 minutes or until well cooked. Remove from the oven heat and allow it to cool down a bit for about 3 minutes. Slice the pork. Meanwhile, prepare the balsamic caramelize onions and serve with the sliced pork.

Per Serving: Calories 220, Fat 5g, Carbs 3.8g, Protein 37.5g

74. Potato Hash

Ingredients for 4 servings

- A drizzle of olive oil
- 2 Yukon Gold potatoes, cubed
- 2 garlic cloves, minced
- 1 yellow onion, chopped
- 1 cup of canned chickpeas, drained
- Salt and black pepper, to taste
- 1 ½ teaspoons of ground allspice
- 1 pound of baby asparagus, trimmed and chopped
- 1 teaspoon of sweet paprika
- 1 teaspoon of dried oregano
- 1 teaspoon of dried cilantro
- 2 tomatoes, cubed
- 1 cup of parsley, chopped
- ½ cup of feta cheese, crumbled

Directions and Total Time: approx. 25 minutes

Heat a large-sized pan with a drizzle of oil over medium-high heat, add the potatoes, onion, garlic, salt, and ground pepper and cook for 7 minutes. Add the rest of the ingredients except the tomatoes, parsley, and cheese. Toss together and then cook for seven more minutes. Transfer to a bowl. Add the remaining ingredients, toss and serve for breakfast.

Per Serving: Calories 535, Fat 20.8g, Carbs 34.5g, Protein 26.6g

75. Quinoa and Apple Porridge

Ingredients for 6 servings

- 1 ¼ cups of water
- 1 cup of fresh apple juice
- 1 ½ cups of uncooked quinoa, rinsed
- 1 tablespoon of honey
- 1 cinnamon stick
- Pinch of salt
- 2 apples, cored and chopped

Directions and Total Time: approx. 11 minutes

In the pot of Instant pot, place all ingredients except for apples and stir to combine well. Close the lid and adjust the vent in a sealed position. Select "Manual" and cook at "High Pressure" for 1 minute. After cooking time is completed, press "Cancel" and carefully do a "Quick" release. Open its lid and with a fork, fluff the quinoa. Transfer the porridge into serving bowls and serve immediately with the topping of apple slices.

Per Serving: Calories 225, Fat 28g, Carbs 45.1g, Protein 6.2g

76. Quinoa and Eggs Pan

Ingredients for 4 servings

- 4 bacon slices, cooked and crumbled
- A drizzle of olive oil
- 1 small red onion, chopped
- 1 red bell pepper, chopped
- 1 sweet potato, grated
- 1 green bell pepper, chopped
- 2 garlic cloves, minced
- 1 cup of white mushrooms, sliced
- ½ cup of quinoa
- 1 cup of chicken stock
- 4 eggs, fried
- Salt and ground black pepper

Directions and Total Time: approx. 33 minutes

Heat a pan with the oil over medium-low heat, add the onion, garlic, bell peppers, sweet potato, and mushrooms, toss and sauté for 5 minutes. Add the quinoa, toss and cook for 1 more minute. Add the stock, salt, and pepper, stir and cook for 15 minutes. Divide the mix between plates, top each serving with a fried egg, sprinkle some salt, pepper, and crumbled bacon, and serve for breakfast.

Per Serving: Calories 304, Fat 14g, Carbs 27.5g, Protein 17.8g

77. Quinoa and Yogurt Breakfast Bowls

Ingredients for 8 servings

- 2 cups of quinoa, rinsed and drained
- 4 cups of water
- 1 teaspoon of vanilla extract
- ¼ teaspoon of salt
- 2 cups of low-fat plain Greek yogurt
- 2 cups of blueberries
- 1 cup of toasted almonds
- ½ cup of pure maple syrup

Directions and Total Time: approx. 22 minutes

Place quinoa, water, vanilla, and salt in the Instant Pot®. Close lid and set steam release to Sealing. Press the Rice button and set time to 12 minutes. When the timer beeps, let pressure release naturally, about 20 minutes. Open its lid and fluff quinoa with a fork. Stir in yogurt. Serve warm, topped with berries, almonds, and maple syrup.

Per Serving: Calories 376, Fat 13g, Carbs 52g, Protein 16g

78. Quinoa Muffins

Ingredients for 12 servings

- 1 cup of quinoa, cooked
- 6 eggs, whisked
- Salt and black pepper, to taste
- 1 cup of Swiss cheese, grated
- 1 small yellow onion, chopped
- 1 cup of white mushrooms, sliced
- ½ cup of sun-dried tomatoes, chopped

Directions and Total Time: approx. 40 minutes

Combine the eggs with salt, pepper, and the rest of the ingredients in a bowl and whisk well. Divide this mixture into a silicone muffin pan, bake at 350°F for 30 minutes and serve for breakfast. Serve with yogurt. You can add other spices or seasonings or play with different veggie variations.

Per Serving: Calories 123, Fat 5.6g, Carbs 10.8g, Protein 7.5g

Ingredients for 1 serving

- ½ cup of fresh raspberries
- ¼ teaspoon of vanilla
- ¾ cup of unsweetened almond milk
- 1 teaspoon of honey
- 2 teaspoon of chia seeds
- ⅓ cup of rolled oats
- Pinch of salt

Directions and Total Time: approx. 15 minutes

Add raspberries into the bowl and mash using the fork. Transfer mash raspberries and remaining ingredients into the glass jar and stir everything well. Cover the glass jar with lid and place in refrigerator for overnight. Add little drizzle of milk and serve. Add one to two drops of almond extracts.

Per Serving: Calories 289, Fat 11.1g, Carbs 41.8g, Protein 8.5g

80. Raspberry Oats

Ingredients for 4 servings

- 2 cups of low-fat cottage cheese
- 2 tablespoons of chopped mixed herbs
- ½ teaspoon of ground black pepper
- 1 large tomato, chopped
- 1 small cucumber, peeled and chopped
- ¼ cup of pitted kalamata olives, halved
- 1 tablespoon of extra-virgin olive oil

Directions and Total Time: approx. 10 minutes

In a large-sized bowl, combine the cottage cheese, herbs, and pepper. Add the tomato, cucumber, and olives and gently stir to combine. Drizzle with the oil to serve.

Per Serving: Calories 181, Fat 10g, Carbs 8g, Protein 15g

81. Scrambled Eggs with Cheese and Pancetta

Ingredients for 4 servings

- 2 tablespoons of olive oil
- 4 eggs, whisked
- 1 red onion, chopped
- 3 ounces of pancetta, chopped
- 2 garlic cloves, minced
- 2 ounces of goat cheese, crumbled
- 1 tablespoon of basil, chopped
- Salt and black pepper to taste

Directions and Total Time: approx. 1 hour and 15 minutes

Warm half of oil in a skillet over medium heat and sauté onion, pancetta, and garlic for 3 minutes. Add in goat cheese and whisked eggs and cook for 5-6 minutes, stirring often. Season with salt and pepper. Sprinkle with basil and serve.

Per Serving: Calories 315, Fat 25.3g, Carbs 4g, Protein 18g

82. Seeds and Lentils Oats

Ingredients for 4 servings

- ½ cup of red lentils
- ¼ cup of pumpkin seeds, toasted
- 2 teaspoons of olive oil
- ¼ cup of rolled oats
- ¼ cup of coconut flesh, shredded
- 1 tablespoon of honey
- 1 tablespoon of orange zest, grated
- 1 cup of Greek yogurt
- 1 cup of blackberries

Directions and Total Time: approx. 60 minutes

Spread the lentils on a baking sheet lined with parchment paper, introduce them to the oven, and roast at 370°F for 30 minutes. Add the rest of the remaining ingredients except the yogurt and the berries, toss and bake at 370°F for 20 minutes more. Transfer this to a bowl, add the rest of the ingredients, toss, divide into smaller bowls and serve for breakfast.

Per Serving: Calories 204, Fat 7.1g, Carbs 27.6g, Protein 9.5g

83. Smoked Salmon Scrambled Eggs

Ingredients for 4 servings

- 2 tablespoons of olive oil
- 4 ounces of smoked salmon, flaked
- ½ red onion, finely chopped
- 8 eggs
- Salt and black pepper to taste
- ½ teaspoon of garlic powder
- 1 scallion, chopped
- 2 tablespoons of green olives, chopped

Directions and Total Time: approx. 15 minutes

Beat eggs, garlic powder, salt, and pepper in a bowl. Warm olive oil in a large-sized skillet over medium heat. Stir in onion and sauté for 1-2 minutes. Add in olives and salmon and cook for another minute. Pour in the eggs and stir-fry for 5-6 minutes until the eggs are set. Serve topped with scallion.

Per Serving: Calories 233, Fat 17.5g, Carbs 3g, Protein 18g

84. Spicy Wilted Greens with Garlic

Ingredients for 2 servings

- 1 tablespoon of olive oil
- 2 garlic cloves, minced
- 3 cups of sliced greens (spinach, chard, beet greens, dandelion greens, or a combination)
- Pinch of salt
- Pinch of red pepper flakes

Directions and Total Time: approx. 15 minutes

In a large-sized pan, heat the olive oil over medium-high heat until shimmering. Add garlic and sauté for 30 seconds, or just until fragrant. Add the greens, salt, and pepper flakes and stir to combine. Let the greens wilt, but do not overcook. Remove from the skillet and serve on a plate.

Per Serving: Calories 92, Fat 6.7g, Carbs 7.2g, Protein 1.1g

85. Spinach and Egg Scramble

Ingredients for 1 serving

- 1 tablespoon of olive oil
- 1 ½ cups of baby spinach
- 2 eggs, beaten
- Kosher salt and black pepper, to taste
- 1 slice of whole-grain bread, toasted
- ½ cup of raspberries, chopped

Directions and Total Time: approx. 25 minutes

Heat the oil in a large-sized non-stick skillet on medium-high heat. Add the spinach and cook for 5–7 minutes. Add the eggs to the same large-sized skillet and cook for 5 minutes, stirring every 2 minutes. Add salt and pepper to your taste. Serve with the toast and raspberries as a garnish. Serve and enjoy!

Per Serving: Calories 296, Fat 16g, Carbs 21g, Protein 18g

86. Spinach Frittata with Roasted Peppers

Ingredients for 4 servings

- 2 tablespoons of olive oil
- 1 cup of roasted peppers, chopped
- ½ cup of milk
- 8 eggs
- Salt and black pepper to taste
- 1 teaspoon of oregano, dried
- ½ cup of red onions, chopped
- 4 cups of baby spinach
- 1 cup of goat cheese, crumbled

Directions and Total Time: approx. 30 minutes

Beat the prepared eggs with salt, pepper, and oregano in a bowl. Warm the olive oil in a large-sized skillet over medium heat and sauté onions for 3 minutes until soft. Mix in spinach, milk, and goat cheese and pour over the eggs. Cook for 2-3 minutes until the base of the frittata is set. Place in preheated to 360 F oven and bake for 10-15 minutes until the top is golden. Top with roasted peppers.

Per Serving: Calories 260, Fat 5g, Carbs 5g, Protein 15g

87. Steel Cut Oats with Berries

Ingredients for 2 servings

- ½ unsweetened cocoa powder
- 1 tablespoon of peanut butter
- 1 cup of berries (blueberries and blackberries)
- 2 tablespoons of Chia seeds
- ½ tablespoon of butter
- ½ cup of steel cut oats
- 2 cups of water
- ½ teaspoon of vanilla extract
- 1.2 teaspoon of cinnamon powder
- 1 teaspoon of honey

Directions and Total Time: approx. 25 minutes

Take a skillet: add butter and melt on medium heat, then add the oats to saute. Stir to combine for about 3 minutes. Add water, vanilla, cinnamon and the rest of the ingredients; reduce heat and simmer and cook for about 20 minutes. Once ready, add the honey, mix to combine and pour the mixture in a container. Refrigerate overnight before consuming. Use some milk or almond mil to loosen the oats and heat in the microwave for a couple of minutes before serving.

Per Serving: Calories 189, Fat 2.7g, Carbs 27.7g, Protein 4g

88. Stuffed Pita Breads

Ingredients for 4 servings

- 1 and ½ tablespoons of olive oil
- 1 tomato, cubed
- 1 garlic clove, minced
- 1 red onion, chopped
- ¼ cup of parsley, chopped
- 15 ounces of canned fava beans, drained and rinsed
- ¼ cup of lemon juice
- Salt and black pepper to the taste
- 4 whole-wheat pita bread pockets

Directions and Total Time: approx. 20 minutes

In a medium-hot pan, heat the oil and sauté the onion for 5 minutes. Stir in the other ingredients and simmer for another 10 minutes. Serve the pita pockets stuffed with this mixture for breakfast.

Per Serving: Calories 382, Fat 1.8g, Carbs 66g, Protein 28.5g

89. Sweet Banana Pancakes with Strawberries

Ingredients for 4 servings

- 2 tablespoons of olive oil
- 1 cup of flour
- 1 cup + 2 tablespoons of milk
- 2 eggs, beaten
- ⅓ cup of honey
- 1 teaspoon of baking soda
- ¼ teaspoon of salt
- 1 sliced banana
- 1 cup of sliced strawberries
- 1 tablespoon of maple syrup

Directions and Total Time: approx. 15 minutes

Mix together the flour, milk, eggs, honey, baking soda, and salt in a bowl. Warm the olive oil in a large-sized skillet over medium heat and pour in ⅓ cup of the pancake batter. Cook for 2-3 minutes. Add half of the fresh fruit and flip to cook for 2-3 minutes on the other side until cooked through. Top with the remaining fruit, drizzle with maple syrup and serve.

Per Serving: Calories 415, Fat 24g, Carbs 46g, Protein 12g

90. Tasty Breakfast Donuts

Ingredients for 4 servings

- 43 grams of cream cheese
- 2 eggs
- 2 tablespoons of almond flour
- 2 tablespoons of erythritol
- 1 ½ tablespoons of coconut flour
- ½ teaspoon of baking powder
- ½ teaspoon of vanilla extract
- 5 drops of Stevia (liquid form)
- 2 strips of bacon, fried until crispy

Directions and Total Time: approx. 10 minutes

Rub coconut oil over the donut maker and turn it on. Mix all ingredients except bacon in a blender or food processor until smooth within 1 minute. Pour batter into donut maker, leaving 1/10 in each round for rising. Leave for 3 minutes before flipping each donut. Leave for another 2 minutes or until a fork comes out clean when piercing them. Take donuts out and let cool. Repeat all steps until all batter is used. Crumble bacon into bits and use it to top donuts.

Per Serving: Calories 60, Fat 5g, Carbs 1g, Protein 3g

91. Tempeh Bacon

Ingredients for 4 servings
- 2 tablespoons of soy sauce
- 2 tablespoons of grapeseed oil or canola
- 6 ounces of tempeh
- 1/2 teaspoon of (liquid) smoke

Directions and Total Time: approx. 35 minutes

The tempeh should be cooked for 25-30 minutes in a medium pot with simmering water over low heat. Allow it cool before patting dry and cutting into 1/8-inch strips. Heave the oil up to a medium in a big pan and wait for it to shimmer. Fry the tempeh slices until browned on both sides, approximately 3 minutes on each side. Drizzle the liquid smoke and soy sauce over the top, taking care not to spatter. Toss the tempeh to evenly coat it. Serve immediately.

Per Serving: Calories 320, Fat 14g, Carbs 25g, Protein 25g

92. Tomato and Prosciutto Sandwiches

Ingredients for 4 servings
- 1 large, ripe tomato, sliced into 8 rounds
- 8 whole-wheat bread slices
- 1 avocado, halved and pitted
- Salt and black pepper to taste
- 8 romaine lettuce leaves
- 8 thin prosciutto slices
- 1 tablespoon of cilantro, chopped

Directions and Total Time: approx. 10 minutes

Toast the bread and place on a large platter. Scoop the avocado flesh out of the skin into a small bowl. Season with pepper and salt. With a fork, gently mash the avocado until it resembles a creamy spread. Smear 4 bread slices with the avocado mix. Top with a layer of lettuce leaves, tomato slices, and prosciutto slices. Repeat the layers one more time, sprinkle with cilantro, then cover with the remaining bread slices. Serve and enjoy!

Per Serving: Calories 262, Fat 12.2g, Carbs 35g, Protein 8g

93. Tomato and Spinach Egg Wraps

Ingredients for 2 servings
- 1 tablespoon of parsley, chopped
- 1 tablespoon of olive oil
- ¼ onion, chopped
- 3 sun-dried tomatoes, chopped
- 3 large eggs, beaten
- 2 cups of baby spinach, torn
- 1 ounces of feta cheese, crumbled
- Salt to taste
- 2 whole-wheat tortillas, warm

Directions and Total Time: approx. 10 minutes

Warm the olive oil in a large-sized pan over medium heat. Sauté the onion and tomatoes for about 3 minutes. Add the prepared beaten eggs and stir to scramble them, about 4 minutes. Add the spinach and parsley stir to combine. Sprinkle the feta cheese over the eggs. Season with salt to taste. Divide the mixture between the tortillas. Roll them up and serve.

Per Serving: Calories 435, Fat 28g, Carbs 31g, Protein 17g

94. Tuna Breakfast Quiche

Ingredients for 4 servings
- 3 eggs
- 3 tablespoons of oats
- 3 tablespoons of cream cheese
- 1 tablespoon of dill
- 1 tablespoon of basil
- 1 cup of can tuna, drained
- ½ onion, chopped
- ½ carrot, grated
- ½ zucchini, grated
- Salt and pepper

Directions and Total Time: approx. 30 minutes

Preheat the oven to 350° F. In a bowl, whisk eggs with cream cheese, pepper, and salt. Add remaining ingredients and stir until well combined. Pour egg mixture into the greased quiche pan and bake in preheated oven for 20 minutes. Allow to cool then slice and serve.

Per Serving: Calories 151, Fat 6.6g, Carbs 6.4g, Protein 16.4g

95. Vanilla-Cream Morning Oatmeal

Ingredients for 4 servings
- 4 cups of water
- Pinch of sea salt
- 1 cup of steel-cut oats
- ¾ cup of unsweetened almond milk
- 2 teaspoons of pure vanilla extract

Directions and Total Time: approx. 45 minutes

Add the water and salt to a large saucepan over high heat and bring to a boil. Once its actually boiling, reduce the heat to low and add the oats. Mix well and cook for 30 minutes, stirring occasionally. Fold in the almond milk and vanilla and whisk to combine. Continue cooking for about 10 minutes, or until the oats are thick and creamy. Ladle the oatmeal into bowls and serve warm.

Per Serving: Calories 116, Fat 2.1g, Carbs 19g, Protein 4.2g

96. Vegetable and Hummus Bowl

Ingredients for 4 servings
- 2 tablespoons of butter
- 2 tablespoons of olive oil
- 3 cups of green cabbage, shredded
- 3 cups of kale, chopped
- 1 pound of asparagus, chopped
- ½ cup of hummus
- 1 avocado, sliced
- 4 boiled eggs, sliced
- 1 tablespoon of balsamic vinegar
- 1 garlic clove, minced
- 2 teaspoons of yellow mustard
- Salt and black pepper to taste

Directions and Total Time: approx. 15 minutes

Melt butter in a large-sized skillet over medium heat and sauté asparagus for 5 minutes. Mix the olive oil, balsamic vinegar, garlic, yellow mustard, salt, and pepper in a bowl. Spoon the hummus onto the center of a salad bowl and arrange in the asparagus, kale, cabbage, and avocado. Top with the egg slices. Drizzle with the dressing and serve.

Per Serving: Calories 392, Fat 31g, Carbs 22g, Protein 14g

Ingredients for 2 servings

- 4 ripe bananas
- 1/4 cup of maple syrup
- 1 tablespoon of apple cider vinegar
- 1 teaspoon of vanilla extract
- 1 1/2 cups of whole-wheat flour
- 1/2 teaspoon of ground cinnamon
- 1/2 teaspoon of baking soda
- 1/4 cup of walnut pieces (optional)

Directions and Total Time: approx. 1 hour and 35 minutes

Warm oven to 350 F. Use a fork or mixing spoon in a large bowl to mash the bananas until they reach a puréed consistency. Mix in your maple syrup, apple cider vinegar, plus vanilla. Stir in the flour, cinnamon, and baking soda. Fold in the walnut pieces (if using). Pour the batter into the loaf pan, just filling it about three-quarters full. Bake for 1 hour or you can stick a knife into the middle, and it comes out clean. Remove, and allow cooling on the countertop for a minimum of 30 minutes before serving.

Per Serving: Calories 125, Fat 1g, Carbs 40g, Protein 4g

98. Zoodle Carbonara

Ingredients for 6 servings

- 3 eggs
- 1 package of zucchini noodles
- 4 ounces of pancetta, diced
- 1 cup of Parmesan cheese, grated
- 1 handful of parsley, chopped

Directions and Total Time: approx. 10 minutes

To begin, place pancetta in a saucepan over medium-low heat and simmer for 1 to 2 minutes. In a separate bowl, whisk together cheese and eggs and cheese (until a creamy yellow texture develops) and put aside while the pancetta cooks. Raise the temperature to be high and toss the pancetta and zucchini noodles into the saucepan. 30 seconds of stirring. Turn off heat and add the cheese/egg mixture. Stir for 30 seconds, or until the sauce has thickened. Finally, garnish with parsley and serve.

Per Serving: Calories 174, Fat 8.2g, Carbs 7g, Protein 18g

99. Zucchini and Quinoa Pan

Ingredients for 4 servings

- 3 eggs
- 1 package of zucchini noodles
- 4 ounces of pancetta, diced
- 1 cup of Parmesan cheese, grated
- 1 handful of parsley, chopped

Directions and Total Time: approx. 30 minutes

Heat a pan with the oil over medium-high heat, add the garlic and quinoa, and brown for 3 minutes. Add the water, zucchinis, salt, and pepper, toss, bring to a simmer, and cook for 15 minutes. Add the rest of the remaining ingredients, toss, divide everything between plates and serve for breakfast.

Per Serving: Calories 310, Fat 11g, Carbs 42g, Protein 11g

Ingredients for 4 servings

- 3 tablespoons of olive oil
- ½ cup of ricotta cheese, crumbled
- 1 pound of zucchini, spiralized
- ¼ cup of sweet onion, chopped
- 4 large eggs
- ½ teaspoon of hot paprika
- 2 tablespoons of fresh parsley, chopped
- Salt and black pepper to taste

Directions and Total Time: approx. 20 minutes

Preheat oven to a heat of 350 F. Combine the zucchini and sweet onion with tablespoons of olive oil, teaspoons of salt, and black pepper in a bowl. Divide between greased muffin cups. Crack an egg in each one; scatter some salt and hot paprika. Bake for 12 minutes or until set. Serve topped with ricotta cheese and parsley.

Per Serving: Calories 226, Fat 4.6g, Carbs 6.6g, Protein 11g

101. Apple, Beet, Carrot and Kale Salad

Ingredients for 3 servings

- 1 cored apple julienned
- 2 peeled beets julienned
- 1 1/2 cups of carrots julienned
- 4 kale leaves curly, center vein taken out and chopped
- 1/3 cup of cranberries
- sunflower seeds
- 4 tablespoons of orange juice
- 1 tablespoon of vinegar apple cider
- 2 teaspoons of Dijon mustard
- 2 dashes of onion powder
- pinch of mineral salt
- black pepper

Directions and Total Time: approx. 15 minutes

Mix dressing ingredients in a bowl and place aside. In a separate medium-sized dish, combine the other ingredients, then pour the dressing over the top of the mixture. Toss and sprinkle with sunflower seeds.

Per Serving: Calories 205, Fat 4g, Carbs 42g, Protein 5g

102. Arugula and Chickpea Salad

Ingredients for 2 servings

- 1 large avocado, diced
- 8 sliced cherry tomatoes
- 1/4 cup of crumbled feta
- Half red onion, chopped
- 1 cup of canned chickpeas beans
- 1 cup of arugula
- 1/4 cup of sliced cucumbers
- 1/4 cup of cooked quinoa
- 1 tablespoon of lemon juice
- Salt and ground black pepper
- 1 teaspoon of balsamic vinegar

Directions and Total Time: approx. 15 minutes

Take the chickpeas, rinse and drain well. In a medium bowl: roughly mash together chickpeas and avocado. Add the onions and lemon juice. Season with salt and pepper. Stir to combine thoroughly. Take a serving plate: place 1/2 cup of the chickpea salad and top with the arugula, cucumbers, quinoa, tomatoes, feta and a drizzle of balsamic vinegar.

Per Serving: Calories 362, Fat 12g, Carbs 51g, Protein 13g

103. Baby Kale and Cabbage Salad

Ingredients for 6 servings

- 2 bunches of baby kale, thinly sliced
- ½ head of green savoy cabbage
- 1 medium red bell pepper, thinly sliced
- 1 garlic clove, thinly sliced
- 1 cup of toasted peanuts
- Juice of 1 lemon
- ¼ cup of apple cider vinegar
- 1 teaspoon of ground cumin
- ¼ teaspoon of smoked paprika

Directions and Total Time: approx. 10 minutes

In a medium-large mixing bowl, toss together the kale and cabbage. Make the dressing: whisk the lemon juice, vinegar, cumin, and paprika together in a small bowl. Put the dressing on the greens and massage with your hands. Add the pepper, garlic and peanuts to the mixing bowl. Toss to combine. Serve immediately.

Per Serving: Calories 199, Fat 12g, Carbs 17g, Protein 10g

104. Baked Cauliflower Mixed Salad

Ingredients for 4 servings

- 2 tablespoons of extra-virgin olive oil
- 1 teaspoon of dried mint
- 1 teaspoon of dried oregano
- 2 tablespoons of chopped parsley
- 1 red pepper, chopped
- 1 lemon, juiced
- 1 green onion, chopped
- 2 tablespoons of chopped cilantro
- Salt and pepper to taste

Directions and Total Time: approx. 40 minutes

Heat oven to 350°F. In a deep baking pan, combine olive oil, mint, cauliflower, and oregano, then bake for 15 minutes. Once cooked, pour into a salad bowl, and add the remaining ingredients, stirring together. Plate the salad and eat fresh and warm.

Per Serving: Calories 123, Fat 13g, Carbs 10g, Protein 12.5g

105. Basil Vinaigrette Salad

Ingredients for 4 servings

- ¼ cup of olive oil
- 1/2 cup of basil leaves
- 1 tablespoon of shallot
- 3 tablespoons of wine vinegar red
- 1 teaspoon of honey
- 2 teaspoons of Dijon mustard
- ¼ teaspoon of pepper
- ¼ teaspoon of salt
- 1 can of cannellini beans
- 10 cup of salad greens
- 1/2 cucumber
- 1 cup of cherry

Directions and Total Time: approx. 25 minutes

Add all the ingredients except veggies in a blender and blend. Once you get a smooth mixture, add veggies and blend again. You will obtain a texture that is creamy and silky. Transfer to a plate and enjoy.

Per Serving: Calories 246, Fat 15.3g, Carbs 21.5g, Protein 7.5g

106. Beet and Cheese Side Salad

Ingredients for 6 servings

- 2 pounds of beets, baked, peeled, and cubed
- 2 tablespoons of olive oil
- 1 tablespoon of lemon juice
- 2 tablespoons of red wine vinegar
- 1 cup of blue cheese, crumbled
- 3 small garlic cloves, minced
- 4 green onions, chopped
- 5 tablespoons of dill, chopped
- Salt and black pepper to taste

Directions and Total Time: approx. 15 minutes

Mix vinegar with oil, lemon juice, garlic, salt, and pepper, whisk well and leave aside in a bowl. Add green onions, cheese, beets, and dill, and toss to coat. Leave in the fridge for 15 minutes and then serve as a side dish.

Per Serving: Calories 180, Fat 2g, Carbs 2g, Protein 3g

107. Bell Pepper and Tomato Salad

Ingredients for 4 servings

- 8, sliced Roasted red bell pepper
- 2 tablespoons of extra virgin olive oil
- 1 pinch of Chili flakes
- 4 cloves of garlic, minced
- 2 tablespoons of Pine nuts
- 1 sliced Shallot
- 1 cup of halved Cherry tomatoes
- 2 tablespoons of Parsley chopped
- 1 tablespoon of Balsamic vinegar.
- Salt and pepper to taste

Directions and Total Time: approx. 25 minutes

Merge all Ingredients except salt and pepper in a salad bowl. Season with salt and pepper if you want, to suit your taste. Eat once freshly made.

Per Serving: Calories 112, Fat 11g, Carbs 10g, Protein 12g

108. Broccoli and Carrot Pasta Salad

Ingredients for 2 servings

- 8 ounces of whole-wheat pasta
- 2 cups of broccoli florets
- 1 cup of peeled and shredded carrots
- ¼ cup of plain Greek yogurt
- Juice of 1 lemon
- 1 teaspoon of red pepper flakes
- Salt and ground pepper

Directions and Total Time: approx. 15 minutes

Bring a medium-large pot of lightly salted water to a boil. Add the pasta to the boiling water and cook until al dente, about 8 to 10 minutes. Drain the pasta and let rest for a few minutes. When cooled, combine the pasta with the veggies, yogurt, lemon juice, and red pepper flakes in a large bowl, and stir to combine. Taste and season to taste with pepper and salt. Serve immediately.

Per Serving: Calories 428, Fat 2.9g, Carbs 84.6g, Protein 15.9g

109. Broccoli Salad

Ingredients for 6 servings

- 10 slices of bacon
- 1 cup of fresh broccoli
- ¼ cup of red onion, minced
- ½ cup of raisins
- 3 tablespoons of white wine vinegar
- 2 tablespoons of white sugar
- 1 cup of mayonnaise
- 1 cup of sunflower seeds

Directions and Total Time: approx. 25 minutes

Cook the bacon in a deep-frying pan over medium heat. Drain, crumble, and set aside. Combine broccoli, onion, and raisins in a medium bowl. Mix vinegar, sugar, and mayonnaise in a small bowl. Pour over the broccoli mixture and mix. Cool for at least two hours. Before serving, mix the salad with crumbled bacon and sunflower seeds.

Per Serving: Calories 559, Fat 1g, Carbs 31g, Protein 18g

110. Broccoli Salad with Caramelized Onions

Ingredients for 4 servings

- 3 tablespoons of extra-virgin olive oil
- 2 red onions, sliced
- 1 teaspoon of dried thyme
- 2 tablespoons of balsamic vinegar
- 1 pound of broccoli, cut into florets
- Salt and ground pepper to taste

Directions and Total Time: approx. 35 minutes

Heat the oil and add in sliced onions. Cook until the onions are caramelized. Stir in vinegar and thyme, and then remove from the stove. Mix together the broccoli and onion mixture in a bowl, adding salt and pepper if desired. Serve and eat salad as soon as possible.

Per Serving: Calories 113, Fat 9g, Carbs 13g, Protein 18g

111. Bulgur Salad

Ingredients for 4 servings

- 1/2 cup of bulgur wheat
- 1/4 cup of fresh parsley, chopped
- 1 tablespoon of fresh mint, chopped
- 1/3 cup of feta cheese, crumbled
- 2 tablespoons of fresh lemon juice
- 2 tablespoons of olives, chopped
- 1/4 cup of olive oil
- 1/2 cup of tomatoes, chopped
- 1/3 cup of cucumber, chopped
- 1/2 cup of water
- Salt

Directions and Total Time: approx. 11 minutes

Add the bulgur wheat, water, and salt into the instant pot. Cook on high for 1 minute. Once done, release pressure using quick release. Remove lid. Transfer bulgur wheat to the mixing bowl. Attach remaining ingredients to the bowl and mix well. Serve and enjoy.

Per Serving: Calories 430, Fat 32.2g, Carbs 31.5g, Protein 8.9g

112. Carrot and Broccoli Salad

Ingredients for 4 servings

- 8 ounces of whole-wheat pasta
- 2 cups of broccoli florets
- 1 cup of peeled and shredded carrots
- ¼ cup of plain Greek yogurt
- Juice of 1 lemon
- 1 teaspoon of red pepper flakes
- Salt and ground pepper, to taste

Directions and Total Time: approx. 15 minutes

Bring a large-sized pot of lightly salted water to a boil. Add the pasta to the boiling water and cook until al dente, about 8 to 10 minutes. Drain the pasta and let rest for a few minutes. When cooled, combine the pasta with the veggies, yogurt, lemon juice, and red pepper flakes in a large-sized bowl, and stir thoroughly to combine. Taste and season to taste with salt and pepper. Serve immediately.

Per Serving: Calories 428, Fat 2.9g, Carbs 84.6g, Protein 15.9g

113. Chicken and Mango Salad

Ingredients for 4 servings

- 2 cups of shredded cooked chicken breast
- 1 medium mango, sliced
- 6 cups of cabbage, chopped
- 1 cup of green peas
- 4 chopped fresh mint leaves
- ¼ cup of sliced scallions
- ⅓ cup of orange juice
- 3 tablespoons of rice vinegar
- 3 tablespoons of soy sauce
- 1 tablespoon of toasted sesame oil
- 2 tablespoons of toasted sesame seeds

Directions and Total Time: approx. 20 minutes

Combine sesame oil, orange juice, vinegar, and soy sauce in a small bowl. Set aside. In a large bowl add chicken, mango, peas, cabbage, mint and scallions; pour in gently the dressing and toss to coat. Serve the salad sprinkled with sesame seeds.

Per Serving: Calories 285, Fat 8.6g, Carbs 24.7g, Protein 27.2g

114. Chicken and Sunflower Seed Salad

Ingredients for 3 servings

- 1 chicken breast, skinless
- ¼ mayonnaise
- ¼ cup sour cream
- 2 tablespoons Cottage cheese, room temperature
- Salt and black pepper, to taste
- ¼ cup sunflower seeds, hulled and roasted
- ½ avocado, peeled and cubed
- ½ teaspoon fresh garlic, minced
- 2 tablespoons scallions, chopped

Directions and Total Time: approx. 30 minutes

Boil a pot of salted water. Turn off the heat in the pot, then cover, and let the chicken stand in the hot water for 15 minutes. Then drain the water and cut the chicken. Mix together the remaining ingredients. Place in the refrigerator for one and half hour. Serve well chilled. Enjoy!

Per Serving: Calories 401, Fat 35.2g, Carbs 5.7g, Protein 16.2g

115. Chicken Salad with Mustard Dressing

Ingredients for 4 servings

- 2 cups of chopped cooked chicken breasts
- 1 cup of canned artichoke hearts, chopped
- 2 hard-boiled eggs, chopped
- ½ cup of green olives, sliced
- 1 red bell pepper, chopped
- 8 cherry tomatoes, quartered
- 2 tablespoons of yellow mustard
- ½ cup of extra-virgin olive oil
- 3 tablespoons of lemon juice
- 1 green onion, chopped
- Salt and black pepper to taste
- ¼ teaspoon of red pepper flakes

Directions and Total Time: approx. 15 minutes

In a salad bowl, whisk the mustard, oil, lemon juice, salt, pepper, and red pepper flakes. Add the chicken, eggs, green olives, bell pepper, artichoke hearts, green onion, and cherry tomatoes toss to coat. Serve.

Per Serving: Calories 496, Fat 36g, Carbs 20g, Protein 28g

116. Chicken and Broccoli Salad

Ingredients for 6 servings

- ¼ cup of extra-virgin olive oil
- 10 ounces of broccoli florets, steamed
- 2 (14-ounces) cans of chickpeas
- 15 cherry tomatoes, halved
- ½ red onion, finely chopped
- 2 lemons, juiced and zested
- 2 cloves of garlic, minced
- 2 teaspoons of dried oregano
- Salt and black pepper to taste

Directions and Total Time: approx. 10 minutes

Mix the chickpeas, red onion, cherry tomatoes, and broccoli in a bowl. Combine the olive oil, lemon juice, lemon zest, oregano, garlic, salt, and pepper in another bowl. Pour over the mixed dressing in the salad and toss to combine. Serve immediately.

Per Serving: Calories 569, Fat 16g, Carbs 84g, Protein 26g

117. Chickpea and Zucchini Salad

Ingredients for 3 servings

- ¼ cup of balsamic vinegar
- 1/3 cup of chopped basil leaves
- 1 tablespoon of capers, drained and chopped
- ½ cup of crumbled feta cheese
- 1 can of chickpeas, drained
- 1 garlic clove, chopped
- ½ cup of Kalamata olives, chopped
- 1/3 cup of olive oil
- ½ cup of sweet onion, chopped
- ½ teaspoon of oregano
- 1 pinch of red pepper flakes, crushed
- ¾ cup of red bell pepper, chopped
- 1 tablespoon of chopped rosemary
- 2 cups of zucchini, diced
- salt and pepper

Directions and Total Time: approx. 10 minutes

Combine the vegetables in a bowl and cover well. Serve at room temperature. But for best results, refrigerate the bowl for a few hours before serving, to allow the flavors to blend.

Per Serving: Calories 258, Fat 12g, Carbs 19g, Protein 6g

118. Chickpea Tuna Salad

Ingredients for 4 servings

- 1 (6-ounces) can of solid white albacore tuna, drained
- ¼ cup of olive oil
- ¼ cup of balsamic vinegar
- ½ teaspoon of minced garlic
- ¼ teaspoon of dried oregano
- Salt and black pepper to taste
- 2 tablespoons of capers, drained
- 4 cups of baby greens
- 1 cup of canned chickpeas
- ¼ cup of olives, sliced
- 2 Roma tomatoes, chopped
- ¼ cup of feta cheese, crumbled

Directions and Total Time: approx. 15 minutes

In a bowl, whisk together the olive oil, balsamic vinegar, garlic, oregano, salt, and pepper until emulsified. Stir in capers. Place the baby greens in a salad bowl and top with tuna, chickpeas, olives, and tomatoes. Drizzle the vinaigrette overall and sprinkle with feta cheese. Serve immediately.

Per Serving: Calories 226, Fat 13g, Carbs 29g, Protein 5g

119. Chickpeas, Corn and Black Beans Salad

Ingredients for 4 servings

- 1 cup of canned black beans
- ½ teaspoon of garlic powder
- 2 teaspoons of chili powder
- salt and black pepper, to taste
- ½ can of chickpeas, drained and rinsed
- 1 cup of baby spinach
- 1 avocado, pitted, peeled and chopped
- 1 cup of corn kernels, chopped
- 2 tablespoons of lemon juice
- 1 tablespoon of EVO
- 1 tablespoon of apple cider vinegar
- 1 teaspoon of chives, chopped

Directions and Total Time: approx. 15 minutes

In a salad bowl, combine the black beans with the garlic powder, chili powder and the rest of the ingredients, toss and serve cold.

Per Serving: Calories 300, Fat 13.4g, Carbs 8.6g, Protein 13g

120. Collard Green and Rice Salad

Ingredients for 4 servings

- 1 tablespoon of olive oil
- 1 cup of white rice
- 10 ounces of collard greens, torn
- 4 tablespoons of walnuts, chopped
- 2 tablespoons of balsamic vinegar
- 4 tablespoons of tahini paste
- Salt and black pepper to taste
- 2 tablespoons of parsley, chopped

Directions and Total Time: approx. 10 minutes

Bring to a boil salted water over medium heat. Add in the rice and cook for 15-18 minutes. Drain and rest to cool. Whisk tahini, 4 tbsp of cold water, and vinegar in a bowl. In a separate bowl, combine cooled rice, collard greens, walnuts, salt, pepper, olive oil, and tahini dressing. Serve topped with parsley.

Per Serving: Calories 180, Fat 4g, Carbs 6g, Protein 4g

121. Coriander Mushroom Salad

Ingredients for 6 servings

- ½ pound of white mushrooms, sliced
- 1 tablespoon of olive oil
- 3 cloves of garlic, minced
- Salt and black pepper to the taste
- 1 tomato, diced
- 1 avocado, peeled, pitted and cubed
- 3 tablespoons of lime juice
- ½ cup of chicken stock
- 2 tablespoons of coriander, chopped

Directions and Total Time: approx. 12 minutes

Heat the oil in a small-sized skillet over medium heat until shimmering, then add the mushrooms and cook for approximately about 4 minutes, stirring occasionally. Add the rest of the remaining ingredients, toss, cook for 3-4 minutes more, divide into bowls and serve for breakfast.

Per Serving: Calories 73, Fat 4.8g, Carbs 5.3g, Protein 2.1g

122. Corn and Black Bean Salad

Ingredients for 4 servings

- 2 tablespoons of vegetable oil
- 1/4 cup of balsamic vinegar
- 1/2 teaspoon of salt
- 1/2 teaspoon of white sugar
- 1/2 teaspoon of ground cumin
- 1/2 teaspoon of ground black pepper
- 1/2 teaspoon of chili powder
- 3 tablespoons of chopped fresh coriander
- 1 can of black beans (15 oz)
- 1 can of sweetened corn (75 oz) drained

Directions and Total Time: approx. 10 minutes

Combine balsamic vinegar, oil, salt, sugar, black pepper, cumin and chili powder in a small bowl. Combine black corn and beans in a medium bowl. Mix with vinegar and oil vinaigrette and garnish with coriander. Cover and refrigerate overnight.

Per Serving: Calories 214, Fat 4g, Carbs 6g, Protein 5g

123. Corn and Shrimp Salad

Ingredients for 4 servings

- 4 ears of sweet corn, husked
- 1 avocado, peeled, pitted and chopped
- ½ cup of basil, chopped
- 1-pound of shrimp, peeled and deveined
- 1 and ½ cups of cherry tomatoes, halved

Directions and Total Time: approx. 20 minutes

Put the corn in a pot, boil water and cover, over medium heat for 6 minutes, drain, cool down, cut corn from the cob and put it in a bowl. Thread the shrimp onto skewers and brush with some of the oil. Situate the skewers on the prepared grill, cook over medium heat for 2 minutes on each side, remove from skewers and add over the corn. Place the rest of the ingredients to the bowl, toss, divide between plates and serve for breakfast.

Per Serving: Calories 371, Fat 22g, Carbs 26g, Protein 23g

124. Couscous Arugula Salad

Ingredients for 4 servings

- 1/2 cup couscous
- 1 cup vegetable stock
- 1 bunch, peeled asparagus
- 1 lemon, juiced
- 1 teaspoon dried tarragon
- 2 cups arugula
- Salt and pepper to taste

Directions and Total Time: approx. 35 minutes

Heat the vegetable stock in a pot until hot. Remove from heat and add in the couscous. Cover until the couscous is fully absorbed. Pour in a bowl and fluff with a fork and then set aside to cool. Peel asparagus with a vegetable peeler, making them into ribbons and put into a bowl with couscous. Merge the remaining ingredients and add salt and pepper to suit your taste. Serve the salad immediately.

Per Serving: Calories 100, Fat 6g, Carbs 25g, Protein 10g

125. Couscous Salad

Ingredients for 6 servings

- 1 cup of couscous
- 1 lemon juice
- ½ cucumber, sliced
- ¼ cup of fresh parsley, chopped
- ½ cup of onion, diced
- 1 cup of cherry tomatoes
- 15 ounces can of chickpeas, drained & rinsed
- 12 ounces of chicken broth
- Salt and pepper

Directions and Total Time: approx. 25 minutes

Add couscous and broth into the pot and cook over medium-high heat. Bring to boil. Turn heat to medium and simmer for 15 minutes. Remove pot from heat. In a large-sized mixing bowl, mix together cooked couscous and the remaining ingredients. Mix well and serve.

Per Serving: Calories 218, Fat 1.5g, Carbs 41.9g, Protein 9g

126. Creamy Barley Side Salad

Ingredients for 4 servings

- 1 cup of couscous
- 1 lemon juice
- ½ cucumber, sliced
- ¼ cup of fresh parsley, chopped
- ½ cup of onion, diced
- 1 cup of cherry tomatoes
- 15 ounces can of chickpeas, drained & rinsed
- 12 ounces of chicken broth
- Salt and pepper

Directions and Total Time: approx. 45 minutes

Put barley in a pan, add water and some salt, bring to a boil, cover, simmer for 25 minutes, drain, arrange on a baking sheet and leave aside. Mix yogurt with lemon juice, oil, salt, pepper, and mustard in a bowl and stir well. Add mint, apple, celery, barley, toss, coat, and serve.

Per Serving: Calories 132, Fat 2g, Carbs 3g, Protein 1g

127. Creamy Chicken Salad

Ingredients for 6 servings

- 20 ounces of chicken meat
- ½ cup of pecans, chopped
- 1 cup of green grapes
- ½ cup of celery, chopped
- 2 ounces of canned mandarin oranges, drained
- 1 cup of Greek yogurt cucumber, chopped garlic clove
- 1 teaspoon of lemon juice

Directions and Total Time: approx. 10 minutes

In a bowl, mix cucumber with salt, pepper to taste, lemon juice, garlic, and yogurt, and stir very well. In a salad bowl, mix chicken meat with grapes, pecans, oranges, and celery. Add cucumber salad dressing, toss to coat, and keep in the fridge until you serve it.

Per Serving: Calories 200, Fat 3g, Carbs 17g, Protein 8g

128. Creamy Salad with Broccoli

Ingredients for 3 servings

- 2 cups of steamed broccoli florets, sliced
- 2 tablespoons of extra-virgin olive oil
- 1/2 cup of cottage cheese
- 1/2 cup of mayonnaise
- 2 tablespoons of fresh lemon juice
- 1 cup of corn
- 1/3 teaspoon of salt
- 1/3 teaspoon of pepper

Directions and Total Time: approx. 35 minutes

Place the broccoli, corn, and mayonnaise in a large bowl. After that, drizzle the olive oil and lemon juice over the salad. Season with salt and pepper. Stir in the cottage cheese and combine well. Then, place in the refrigerator for approximately about 20 minutes to chill before serving. Serve and enjoy your Salad!

Per Serving: Calories 316, Fat 24.5g, Carbs 10.3g, Protein 15.7g

129. Cucumber and Garlic Salad

Ingredients for 4 servings

- 2 tablespoons of white vinegar
- ¼ cup of EVO
- ½ teaspoon of salt and pepper
- 1 tablespoon of oregano
- 1 cucumber, ala julienned (give shape of noodles)
- 1 red onion, sliced
- 1 cup of cherry tomatoes (about 12), halved
- ¼ cup of green olives, sliced
- 1/2 cup of feta cheese, crumbled

Directions and Total Time: approx. 20 minutes

Take the first 4 ingredients and add into a medium-sized mixing bowl and whisk until well-combined. Season with pepper and salt as per taste. In a large mixing bowl, combine the tomatoes, cucumbers noodles, onion, cheese, and olives. Toss the salad with the appropriate quantity of dressing until everything is well-combined. Serve.

Per Serving: Calories 149, Fat 13.4g, Carbs 4.9g, Protein 2.6g

130. Cucumber and Tomato Salad

Ingredients for 4 servings

- Salt and black pepper, to taste
- 1 tablespoon of fresh lemon juice
- 1 onion, chopped
- 1 cucumber, peeled and diced
- 2 tomatoes, chopped
- 4 cups of spinach

Directions and Total Time: approx. 10 minutes

In a salad bowl, mix the onions, cucumbers, and tomatoes. Season with pepper and salt to taste. Add the lemon juice and mix well. Add the spinach, toss to coat, serve and enjoy. Top with feta cheese and chickpeas.

Per Serving: Calories 70.3, Fat 0.3g, Carbs 8.9g, Protein 2.2g

131. Cucumber Avocado Salad

Ingredients for 4 servings

- 1 avocado, diced
- 2 tablespoons of olive oil
- 1 cup of cucumber, diced
- 1 cup of cherry tomatoes, halved
- 1 tablespoon of fresh parsley, chopped
- 1 teaspoon of garlic, minced
- ½ cup of onion, chopped
- Salt and pepper

Directions and Total Time: approx. 15 minutes

Add onion, cucumber, avocado, cherry tomatoes and garlic into the bowl and mix well. Drizzle with olive oil and season with pepper and salt. Garnish with parsley and serve. Add your choice of seasonings.

Per Serving: Calories 182, Fat 16.9g, Carbs 8.7g, Protein 1.8g

132. Egg Salad

Ingredients for 4 servings

- 5 hard-boiled eggs, peeled and diced
- 1 tablespoon of red onion, diced
- 1 green onion, sliced
- ¼ cup of cucumber diced
- ¼ cup of mixed olives chopped
- ¼ cup of crumbled feta cheese
- 5 ⅓ ounces of plain Greek yogurt
- ¼ cup of roasted red peppers chopped
- Salt and black pepper to taste

Directions and Total Time: approx. 10 minutes

In a salad bowl, ix the cucumber, yogurt, green onion, red onion, chopped olives, and feta. Stir in the eggs and adjust the seasoning with salt and black pepper. Toss in the roasted red peppers and mix evenly. Serve.

Per Serving: Calories 341, Fat 17.6g, Carbs 5.3g, Protein 42.2g

133. Eggplant and Sweet Potato Salad

Ingredients for 4 servings

- 1 tablespoon of olive oil
- 4 cups of arugula
- 2 baby eggplants, cubed
- 2 sweet potatoes, cubed
- 1 red onion, cut into wedges
- 1 teaspoon of hot paprika
- 2 teaspoons of cumin, ground
- Salt and black pepper to taste
- ¼ cup of lime juice

Directions and Total Time: approx. 25 minutes

Cook the eggplants and potatoes for approximately about 5 minutes in a pan over medium heat, until the eggplants and potatoes are soft. Stir in onion, paprika, cumin, salt, pepper, and lime juice and cook for approximately about another 10 minutes. Mix in arugula and serve.

Per Serving: Calories 210, Fat 9g, Carbs 13g, Protein 5g

134. Endive and Pear Salad

Ingredients for 4 servings

- 2 tablespoons of olive oil
- 1 tablespoon of balsamic vinegar
- 2 garlic cloves, minced
- 1 teaspoon of Dijon mustard
- 1 tablespoon of lemon juice
- Sea salt and pepper to taste
- 12 black olives, chopped
- 1 tablespoon of parsley, chopped
- 7 cups of baby spinach
- 2 endives, shredded
- 2 pears, sliced lengthwise
- 2 bulbs of fennel, shredded

Directions and Total Time: approx. 5 minutes

Place spinach, endives, pears, fennel, parsley, olives, salt, pepper, lemon juice, olive oil, mustard, garlic, and balsamic vinegar in a medium-sized bowl and toss to combine. Serve right away.

Per Serving: Calories 100, Fat 10g, Carbs 4g, Protein 2g

135. Endive and Tuna Salad with Pine Nuts

Ingredients for 6 servings

- 1 (5-ounces) can of tuna in olive oil, drained and flaked
- 1 endive head, chopped
- 1 shallot, sliced
- 3 tablespoons of chives, chopped
- 3 tablespoons of mayonnaise
- 1 teaspoon of Dijon mustard
- 1/2 lemon, juiced and zested
- Salt and black pepper to taste
- ¼ cup of toasted pine nuts

Directions and Total Time: approx. 10 minutes

In a salad bowl, toss endive, tuna, shallot, and chives. Whisk the mayonnaise, mustard, lemon zest, lemon juice, salt, and pepper in a small bowl. Spoon the mayonnaise mixture over the tuna salad and top with pine nuts. Serve.

Per Serving: Calories 128, Fat 8g, Carbs 5g, Protein 10g

136. Endives, Fennel and Orange Salad

Ingredients for 4 servings

- 1 tablespoon of balsamic vinegar
- 2 cloves of garlic, minced
- 1 teaspoon of Dijon mustard
- 2 tablespoons of olive oil
- 1 tablespoon of lemon juice
- Sea salt and black pepper to taste
- ½ cup of black olives, pitted and chopped
- 1 tablespoon of parsley, chopped
- 7 cups of baby spinach
- 2 endives, shredded
- 3 large oranges, cut into segments
- 2 bulbs of fennel, shredded

Directions and Total Time: approx. 5 minutes

In a salad bowl, combine the spinach with the endives, oranges, fennel, and the rest of the ingredients, toss and serve.

Per Serving: Calories 97, Fat 9.1g, Carbs 3.7g, Protein 1.9g

137. Feta and Olive Salad

Ingredients for 4 servings

- ½ cup of extra-virgin olive oil
- 1 head iceberg lettuce, torn
- 2 tomatoes, sliced
- 1 cucumber, sliced
- 1 red onion, thinly sliced
- ¼ cup of lemon juice
- Salt to taste
- 1 clove of garlic, minced
- 1 cup of Kalamata olives, pitted
- 6 ounces of feta cheese, crumbled
- 2 tablespoons of dill, chopped

Directions and Total Time: approx. 10 minutes

Place the lettuce in a medium-sized salad bowl. Add the tomatoes, cucumber, onion, and dill. In another small bowl, whisk together the olive oil, lemon juice, salt, and garlic. Pour dressing in the salad and toss lightly to coat. Sprinkle the salad with the Kalamata olives and feta cheese. Serve and enjoy!

Per Serving: Calories 539, Fat 50.2g, Carbs 18g, Protein 9g

138. Feta Cheese Tomato Salad

Ingredients for 4 servings

- 4 large tomatoes, chopped
- ¼ cup of fresh basil, chopped
- ¼ cup of fresh chives, chopped
- 1 cup of Feta cheese, crumbled
- 2 tablespoons of fresh lime juice
- ¼ cup of olive oil
- ¼ cup of fresh dill, chopped
- Salt and pepper

Directions and Total Time: approx. 15 minutes

Add tomatoes into the mixing bowl. In a large-sized bowl, whisk together lime juice, chives, dill, oil, basil, pepper and salt and pour over tomatoes. Sprinkle crumbled cheese on top of tomatoes. Mix well and serve. You can also use crumbled Goat cheese instead of Feta cheese.

Per Serving: Calories 254, Fat 21.2g, Carbs 12.3g, Protein 7.8g

139. Feta Garbanzo Bean Salad

Ingredients for 6 servings

- 1 1/2 (15 ounces) cans of garbanzo beans
- 1 1/2 (2-1/4 ounces) cans of sliced ripe olives, drained
- 1 1/2 medium tomatoes
- 6 tablespoons of thinly sliced red onions
- 2 1/4 cups of 1-1/2 coarsely chopped English cucumbers
- 6 tablespoons of chopped fresh parsley
- 4 1/2 tablespoons of olive oil
- 3/8 teaspoon of salt
- 1 1/2 tablespoons of lemon juice
- 3/16 teaspoon of pepper
- 7 1/2 cups of mixed salad greens
- 3/4 cup of crumbled feta cheese

Directions and Total Time: approx. 10 minutes

Transfer all of the listed ingredients to a large mixing basin and toss to incorporate. Toss in the parmesan cheese.

Per Serving: Calories 140, Fat 16g, Carbs 10g, Protein 24g

140. Freekeh, Chickpea, and Herb Salad

Ingredients for 6 servings

- 1 can of chickpeas, rinsed and drained
- 1 cup of cooked freekeh
- 1 cup of thinly sliced celery
- 1 bunch of scallions, chopped
- ½ cup of chopped fresh flat-leaf parsley
- ¼ cup of chopped fresh mint
- 3 tablespoons of chopped celery leaves
- ½ teaspoon of kosher salt
- 1/3 cup of extra-virgin olive oil
- ¼ cup of squeezed lemon juice
- ¼ teaspoon of cumin seeds
- 1 teaspoon of garlic powder

Directions and Total Time: approx. 15 minutes

In a large bowl, combine the chickpeas, freekeh, celery, scallions, parsley, mint, celery leaves, and salt and toss lightly. Mix the olive oil, lemon juice, cumin seeds, and garlic powder in a small bowl. Once combined, add to freekeh salad.

Per Serving: Calories 350, Fat 19g, Carbs 38g, Protein 9g

141. Fresh Salad with Carrot and Beetroot

Ingredients for 3 servings

- 2 cups of carrots, shredded
- 1 tablespoon of fresh parsley, finely chopped
- 1 cup of fresh beet, shredded
- 1/3 cup of cashew, finely chopped
- 1/3 teaspoon of pepper
- 2 tablespoons of fresh lemon juice
- 3 tablespoons of extra-virgin olive oil
- 1/3 teaspoon of salt
- 1 tablespoon of fresh orange juice
- 1 teaspoon of honey

Directions and Total Time: approx. 35 minutes

In a large-sized salad bowl mix the carrots, parsley, cashew, and fresh beet. Then, prepare the dressing by mixing the lemon juice, olive oil, salt, pepper, orange juice, and honey. Drizzle the dressing over your salad and serve. Bon appetite!

Per Serving: Calories 460, Fat 29g, Carbs 48.2g, Protein 8.5g

142. Fresh Shrimp Salad

Ingredients for 6 servings

- 25 shrimp, peeled and deveined
- 2 cloves of garlic, crushed
- ¼ teaspoon of salt
- ¼ teaspoon of ground pepper
- ¼ cup of lemon juice
- 1 cucumber, diced
- 3 small tomatoes, chopped
- 4 chopped fresh basil leaves
- ¼ cup of EVO
- 10 sprigs of fresh thyme

Directions and Total Time: approx. 25 minutes

Preheat oven to 350 degrees F. Sprinkle oil, thyme and garlic on the shrimps on a baking sheet. Bake for 10 minutes. Once cool, transfer them to a large bowl: stir in cucumber, tomatoes and basil, squeeze the lemon juice and stir to coat before serving.

Per Serving: Calories 290, Fat 15.1g, Carbs 10.2g, Protein 30.5g

143. Fresh Tortellini Salad

Ingredients for 8 servings

- 1 package of tortellini
- 1 can of black beans
- 1 cup of grape tomatoes, halved
- ¾ cup of crumbled feta cheese
- 1 cup of frozen chopped spinach
- 2 teaspoons of grated Parmesan cheese
- 2 teaspoons of EVO

Directions and Total Time: approx. 25 minutes

Cook the tortellini in a salted water boiling pot for about 7 minutes, when they start floating, they are ready. Drain and place them in a bowl. Meanwhile, microwave the spinach at high power for 7 minutes. Set aside. Once cool drain all moisture. Take the tortellini bowl and toss into beans, tomatoes and the spinach. Sprinkle oil, feta and parmesan cheese on top. Cool it in the refrigerator for about 20 minutes before serving.

Per Serving: Calories 341, Fat 9.3g, Carbs 49.1g, Protein 16.5g

144. Garbanzo and Arugula Salad with Blue Cheese

Ingredients for 4 servings

- 15 ounces of canned garbanzo beans, drained
- ½ cup of Gorgonzola cheese, crumbled
- 3 tablespoons of olive oil
- 1 cucumber, cubed
- 3 ounces of black olives, sliced
- 1 Roma tomato, slivered
- ¼ cup of red onion, chopped
- 5 cups of arugula
- Salt to taste
- 1 tablespoon of lemon juice
- 2 tablespoons of parsley, chopped

Directions and Total Time: approx. 10 minutes

Place the arugula in a salad bowl. Add in garbanzo beans, cucumber, olives, tomato, and onion and mix to combine. In another small bowl, whisk the lemon juice, olive oil, and salt. Serve the salad with the dressing and gorgonzola cheese and parsley.

Per Serving: Calories 280, Fat 17g, Carbs 25g, Protein 10g

145. Garbanzo Bean Salad

Ingredients for 4 servings

- 1 ½ cups of cucumber, cubed
- 15 ounces of canned garbanzo beans, drained and rinsed
- 3 ounces of black olives, pitted and sliced
- 1 tomato, chopped
- ¼ cup of red onion, chopped
- 5 cups of salad greens
- A pinch of salt and black pepper
- ½ cup of feta cheese, crumbled
- 3 tablespoons of olive oil
- 1 tablespoon of lemon juice
- ¼ cup of parsley, chopped

Directions and Total Time: approx. 10 minutes

In a salad bowl, combine the garbanzo beans with the cucumber, tomato, and the rest of the ingredients except the cheese and toss. Divide the mix into small bowls, sprinkle the cheese on top, and serve for breakfast.

Per Serving: Calories 268, Fat 16g, Carbs 24g, Protein 9g

146. Goat Cheese and Beet Salad with Nuts

Ingredients for 4 servings

- 3 steamed beets, cut into wedges
- 3 tablespoons of olive oil
- Salt and black pepper to taste
- 2 tablespoons of lime juice
- 4 ounces of goat cheese, crumbled
- 1/3 cup of hazelnuts, chopped
- 1 tablespoon of chives, chopped

Directions and Total Time: approx. 10 minutes

Over medium heat, roast the hazelnuts for 1-2 minutes, stirring the pan often, until they are golden brown. Remove and let cool. In a bowl, mix olive oil, lime juice, salt, and pepper. Arrange beets on a serving platter. Drizzle with the dressing. Sprinkle with goat cheese, hazelnuts, and chives and serve.

Per Serving: Calories 160, Fat 5g, Carbs 7g, Protein 5g

147. Grape and Walnut Garden Salad

Ingredients for 2 servings

- ½ cup of chopped walnuts, toasted
- 1 ripe persimmon
- ½ cup of red grapes halved lengthwise
- 1 shallot, minced
- 1 teaspoon of minced garlic
- 1 teaspoon of wholegrain mustard
- 2 tablespoons of fresh lemon juice
- 3 tablespoons of extra virgin olive oil
- 6 cups of baby spinach

Directions and Total Time: approx. 5 minutes

Cut persimmon and red pear into ½-inch cubes. Discard seeds. In a medium bowl, whisk garlic, shallot, olive oil, lemon juice, and mustard make the dressing. In a medium salad bowl, toss to mix spinach, pear, and persimmon. Pour in dressing and toss to coat well. Garnish with pecans. Serve and enjoy.

Per Serving: Calories 440, Fat 28.8g, Carbs 39.1g, Protein 6.1g

148. Horiatiki Salad

Ingredients for 4 servings

- 1 green bell pepper, cut into chunks
- 1 head of romaine lettuce, torn
- ½ red onion, cut into rings
- 2 tomatoes, cut into wedges
- 1 cucumber, thinly sliced
- 3 tablespoons of extra-virgin olive oil
- 2 tablespoons of lemon juice
- Garlic salt and pepper to taste
- ¼ teaspoon of dried Greek oregano
- 1 cup of feta cheese, cubed
- 1 handful of Kalamata olives

Directions and Total Time: approx. 10 minutes

In a medium-sized salad bowl, whisk the olive oil, lemon juice, pepper, garlic salt, and oregano. Add in the lettuce, red onion, tomatoes, cucumber, and bell pepper and mix with your hands to coat. Top with feta and olives and serve immediately.

Per Serving: Calories 226, Fat 19g, Carbs 9g, Protein 8g

Ingredients for 4 servings

- 2 cups of arugula
- ⅓ cup of cherry tomatoes, halved
- ⅓ cup of sliced cucumber
- 1 tablespoon of chopped red onion
- 1 ½ tablespoon of olive oil
- 2 teaspoons of red-wine vinegar
- ⅛ teaspoon of black pepper
- 1 tablespoon of feta cheese
- 1 4-inch of whole-wheat pita
- ¼ cup of hummus

Directions and Total Time: approx. 16 minutes

Mix the parsley, dry white wine, garlic, olive oil, lime zest, lime juice, salt, and black pepper in a bowl. Toss in the shrimp, mix well to coat and cover to refrigerate for 30 minutes. Assemble the shrimp onto the rosemary stems. Grill these skewers for 3 minutes on each side. Serve warm with lime wedges.

Per Serving: Calories 244, Fat 6.4g, Carbs 4.1g, Protein 39g

150. Lebanese Bean Salad

Ingredients for 4 servings

- 1 (15-ounce) can of fava beans, drained and rinsed
- 1 (15-ounce) can of chickpeas, drained and rinsed
- 1 can (15½-ounce) can of white beans, drained and rinsed
- ¼ cup of flat-leaf parsley, chopped
- 3 tablespoons of olive oil
- 2 cloves of garlic, minced
- 1 lemon, juiced
- Kosher salt and black pepper, to taste

Directions and Total Time: approx. 2 hours and 10 minutes

Thoroughly combine all the listed ingredients in a bowl. Refrigerate for two hours to marinate. Top with fresh cilantro. Add chili flakes for a hint of heat. Serve and enjoy!

Per Serving: Calories 312, Fat 9.3g, Carbs 44.7g, Protein 13.2g

151. Lemon and Mint-Topped Garden Salad

Ingredients for 4 servings

- 1/8 teaspoon of Himalayan salt
- 1 teaspoon of fresh mint, chopped
- 2 tablespoons of extra-virgin olive oil
- 1 small lemon, juiced
- 1/2 medium English cucumber, thinly sliced
- 1 heirloom tomato, roughly chopped
- 4-5 cups of mixed salad greens, shredded
- White pepper

Directions and Total Time: approx. 20 minutes

In a large-sized glass bowl, whisk together the salt, mint, olive oil, and lemon juice. Set aside. Place the cucumber, tomato, and salad greens in a bowl. Season it to taste with extra salt and pepper, if desired, and toss to combine. Drizzle with the lemon and mint mixture before serving.

Per Serving: Calories 80, Fat 7g, Carbs 2g, Protein 1g

152. Mediterranean Beef Salad

Ingredients for 5 servings

- 8 ounces of roast beef, thinly sliced
- 1 avocado, peeled and diced
- 2 tomatoes, diced
- 1 cucumber, peeled and diced
- 1 yellow pepper, sliced
- 2 carrots, shredded
- 1 cup of black olives, pitted and halved
- 2-3 fresh basil leaves, torn
- 2-3 fresh oregano leaves
- 1 tablespoon of balsamic vinegar
- 4 tablespoons of extra virgin olive oil
- salt and black pepper, to taste

Directions and Total Time: approx. 20 minutes

Combine the avocado and all vegetables in a large salad bowl. Add in basil and oregano leaves. Season with salt and pepper then sprinkle over the balsamic vinegar and olive oil and mix everything together. Top with roast beef and serve.

Per Serving: Calories 318, Fat 6.47g, Carbs 14.32g, Protein 10.04g

153. Mediterranean Broccoli Pasta Salad

Ingredients for 4 servings

- 8 ounces of whole-wheat farfalle pasta
- 6 cups of broccoli florets
- ½ cup of red bell pepper, chopped
- ¼ cup of red onion, chopped
- 2 tablespoons of fresh flat-leaf parsley, chopped
- 2 tablespoons of fresh basil, chopped
- ¾ cup of mayonnaise
- ½ cup of sun-dried tomatoes in oil, drained, chopped
- 1 teaspoon of lemon zest
- 1 teaspoon of dried oregano
- ½ teaspoon of salt
- ¼ teaspoon of crushed red pepper

Directions and Total Time: approx. 10 minutes

In a large-sized salad bowl, combine the spaghetti and chopped veggies. Add oregano and the rest of the ingredients. Toss well and serve.

Per Serving: Calories 401, Fat 5.5g, Carbs 32.6g, Protein 12.1g

154 Mediterranean Feta Salad

Ingredients for 2 servings

- 200 grams of feta cheese
- 200 grams of cocktail tomatoes
- 50 grams of almond slivers
- 100 grams of mixed salad
- 2 tablespoons of red wine vinegar
- 1 tablespoon of raspberry vinegar
- 1 tablespoon of green pesto
- 3 tablespoons of olive oil
- 1 teaspoon of mustard
- salt and pepper

Directions and Total Time: approx. 15 minutes

Drain and dice the feta. Clean the lettuce and spin dry. Quarter the cherry tomatoes and place everything in a salad bowl. Mix red wine vinegar, raspberry vinegar, olive oil, mustard and pesto. Season the mixed dressing with salt and pepper before pouring it over the salad. Finally add the almond slivers. Finished! Serve and enjoy.

Per Serving: Calories 959, Fat 91.88g, Carbs 15.44g, Protein 21.45g

Ingredients for 2 servings

- ½ cup of olive oil
- 6 tablespoons of red-wine vinegar
- 3 tablespoons of fresh oregano, chopped
- 1 ½ teaspoon of honey
- 1 ½ teaspoon of Dijon mustard
- ¼ teaspoon of crushed red pepper
- 3 cups of cooked quinoa, cooled
- 2 cups of English cucumber, sliced
- 1 ½ cups of red onion, sliced
- 1 cup o halved grape tomatoes
- ½ cup of Kalamata olives, halved, pitted
- 1 (15 ounces) can of chickpeas, rinsed
- 1 cup of crumbled feta
- 3 cups of baby spinach

Directions and Total Time: approx. 10 minutes

Place the quinoa and chopped vegetables in a salad bowl. Stir in the vinegar and the rest of the ingredients. Toss well and serve.

Per Serving: Calories 211, Fat 5.6g, Carbs 31.3g, Protein 10.3g

156. Mediterranean Romaine Wedge Salad

Ingredients for 4 servings

- 1 English cucumber, chopped
- 1 cup of quartered cherry tomatoes
- 1 cup of chopped fennel
- ½ cup of chopped roasted red peppers
- ¼ cup of pitted, halved Kalamata olives
- 1 scallion, chopped
- ½ cup of Pesto Vinaigrette, divided
- 2 romaine lettuce heads, cut in half lengthwise
- ¼ cup of grated Asiago cheese
- 2 tablespoons of chopped fresh basil

Directions and Total Time: approx. 15 minutes

In a large-sized bowl, stir together the cucumber, tomatoes, fennel, roasted red peppers, olives, scallion, and ¼ cup of pesto vinaigrette. Place each romaine half on a large plate. Evenly divide the vegetable mixture onto each wedge. Drizzle the remaining dressing over the romaine wedges. Serve topped with Asiago cheese and basil.

Per Serving: Calories 336, Fat 27g, Carbs 23g, Protein 11g

157. Mediterranean Salad

Ingredients for 2 servings

- 1 cup of diced tomatoes
- 1 diced cucumber
- ¼ cup of chopped parsley, fresh
- ¼ teaspoon of salt
- ¼ teaspoon of ground black pepper
- ¼ teaspoon of ground sumac
- 1 ½ teaspoon of olive oil
- 1 teaspoon of lemon juice

Directions and Total Time: approx. 15 minutes

Take a medium-sized bowl, add tomato, cucumber, salt, and parsley, toss until well mixed, and then set aside for approximately about 5 minutes. Then add sumac and oil, and then toss until combined. Divide the salad between two bowls and then serve.

Per Serving: Calories 62, Fat 4.9g, Carbs 4.8g, Protein 1g

Ingredients for 2 servings

- 200 grams of feta cheese
- 200 grams of cocktail tomatoes
- 50 grams of almond slivers
- 100 grams of mixed salad
- 2 tablespoons of red wine vinegar
- 1 tablespoon of raspberry vinegar
- 1 tablespoon of green pesto
- 3 tablespoons of olive oil
- 1 teaspoon of mustard
- salt and pepper

Directions and Total Time: approx. 15 minutes

Drain and dice the feta. Clean the lettuce and spin dry. Quarter the cherry tomatoes and place everything in a salad bowl. Mix red wine vinegar, raspberry vinegar, olive oil, mustard and pesto. Add salt and pepper and pour over salad. Finally add the almond slivers. Finished! Serve and enjoy.

Per Serving: Calories 959, Fat 91.88g, Carbs 15.44g, Protein 21.45g

159. Mediterranean Tortellini Salad

Ingredients for 6 servings

- 500 grams of tortellini
- 300 grams of dried tomatoes
- 2 onions
- 3 tablespoons of olive oil
- 3 tablespoons of white wine vinegar
- 1 teaspoon of thyme
- salt and pepper
- 200 grams of rocket

Directions and Total Time: approx. 42 minutes

Cook the tortellini, drain and set aside. Chop the onions and then sauté them in olive oil with the thyme. Add the chopped sun-dried tomatoes and fry for approximately about 2 minutes. Then add the tortellini and remove the pan from the heat. Season to taste with salt, pepper and white wine vinegar. Finally add the tomatoes and rocket. Finished! Serve and enjoy your Mediterranean Tortellini Salad.

Per Serving: Calories 343, Fat 12.93g, Carbs 45.03g, Protein 12.35g

160. Mediterranean Tuna Salad

Ingredients for 6 servings

- 1 clove of garlic
- 4 tomatoes
- 2 onions
- 200 grams of feta cheese
- 1 cucumber
- 3 tablespoons of olive oil
- 1 tin of tuna
- 1 teaspoon of rosemary
- 2 tablespoons of balsamic vinegar
- salt and pepper

Directions and Total Time: approx. 20 minutes

Wash and dice tomatoes and cucumber. Peel and chop the garlic and onions. Crumble the feta. Drain the tuna. Put the garlic, tomatoes, onions and cucumber in a bowl and season with rosemary and basil and add a little olive oil. Add the tuna and feta cheese. Season the salad with salt, pepper, and balsamic vinegar to taste, if desired. Finished! Serve and enjoy.

Per Serving: Calories 285, Fat 21.2g, Carbs 15.81g, Protein 9.35g

161. Melon Salad

Ingredients for 6 servings

- ¼ teaspoon of sea salt
- ¼ teaspoon of black pepper
- 1 tablespoon of balsamic vinegar
- 1 cantaloupe
- 12 watermelons
- 2 cups of mozzarella balls, fresh
- 1/3 cup of basil, fresh & torn
- 2 tablespoons of olive oil

Directions and Total Time: approx. 20 minutes

Spoon out balls of cantaloupe, then situate them in a colander over the bowl. Using a melon baller to cut the watermelon as well. Drain fruits for ten minutes, then chill the juice. Wipe the bowl dry, and then place your fruit in it. Mix in basil, oil, vinegar, mozzarella, and tomatoes before seasoning. Gently mix and serve.

Per Serving: Calories 218, Fat 13g, Carbs 49g, Protein 10g

162. Mozzarella Radish Salad

Ingredients for 2 servings

- 8 ounces of radish
- 4 ounces of Mozzarella
- 1 teaspoon of balsamic vinegar
- ½ teaspoon of salt
- 1 tablespoon of olive oil
- 1 teaspoon of dried oregano

Directions and Total Time: approx. 30 minutes

Wash the radish carefully and cut it into halves. Preheat the air fryer to 360 F. Put the radish halves in the air fryer basket. Sprinkle the radish with salt and olive oil. Cook the radish for 20 minutes. Shake the radish after 10 minutes of cooking. When the time is over – transfer the radish to the serving plate. Chop Mozzarella roughly. Sprinkle the radish with Mozzarella, balsamic vinegar, and dried oregano. Stir it gently with the help of 2 forks. Serve it immediately.

Per Serving: Calories 241, Fat 17.2g, Carbs 6.4g, Protein 16.9g

163. Mung Beans Salad

Ingredients for 6 servings

- 2 cups of tomatoes, chopped
- 2 cups of cucumber, chopped
- 3 cups of mixed greens
- 2 cups of mung beans, sprouted
- 2 cups of clover sprouts
- 1 tablespoon of cumin, ground
- 1 cup of dill, chopped
- 4 tablespoons of lemon juice
- 1 avocado, pitted, peeled and roughly chopped
- 1 cucumber, roughly chopped

Directions and Total Time: approx. 10 minutes

In a salad bowl, mix tomatoes with 2 cups of cucumber, greens, clover and mung sprouts. In your blender, mix cumin with dill, lemon juice, 1 cucumber and avocado, blend really well, add this to your salad, toss well and serve. Enjoy!

Per Serving: Calories 120, Fat 2g, Carbs 1g, Protein 6g

164. Mushroom and Bell Pepper Salad

Ingredients for 4 servings

- 2 tablespoons of olive oil
- ½ pound of mushrooms, sliced
- 3 cloves of garlic, minced
- Salt and black pepper to taste
- 1 tomato, diced
- 1 red bell pepper, sliced
- 3 tablespoons of lime juice
- ½ cup of chicken stock
- 2 tablespoons of cilantro, chopped

Directions and Total Time: approx. 15 minutes

Cook the mushrooms for approximately about 4 minutes in the olive oil in a pan over medium heat until they are soft. Stir in garlic, salt, pepper, tomato, bell pepper, lime juice, and chicken stock and sauté for another 4 minutes. Top with cilantro and serve right away.

Per Serving: Calories 89, Fat 7.4g, Carbs 5.6g, Protein 2.5g

165. Orange Celery Salad

Ingredients for 6 servings

- 1 tablespoon of lemon juice, fresh
- ¼ teaspoon of sea salt, fine
- ¼ teaspoon of black ground pepper
- 1 tablespoon of olive brine
- 1 tablespoon of olive oil
- ¼ cup of red onion, sliced
- ½ cup of green olives
- 2 oranges, peeled & sliced
- 3 celery stalks, sliced diagonally in ½ inch slices

Directions and Total Time: approx. 15 minutes

Put your oranges, olives, onion and celery in a medium-sized shallow bowl. In a different medium-sized bowl whisk your oil, your olive brine and lemon juice, pour this over to your salad. Before serving, season the dish with salt and pepper to your liking.

Per Serving: Calories 65, Fat 7g, Carbs 9g, Protein 2g

166. Panzanella Salad

Ingredients for 2 servings

- 2 cups of tomatoes
- 1 crushed garlic clove
- 1 tablespoon of drained capers rinsed
- 1 ripe stoned avocado peeled & chopped
- 1 small sliced red onion
- 2 slices of brown bread
- 2 tablespoons of olive oil
- 1 tablespoon of vinegar red wine
- small handful of basil leaves

Directions and Total Time: approx. 10 minutes

Dice the tomatoes and add to a bowl. Season and add rest of the ingredients. Mix and place aside for around 10 minutes. Form chunks of bread and add them to a bowl. Drizzle half amount of vinegar and olive oil. Scatter basil leaves and tomatoes when serving and drizzle rest of vinegar and oil. Stir and enjoy.

Per Serving: Calories 452, Fat 25g, Carbs 37g, Protein 6g

167. Party Summer Salad

Ingredients for 4 servings

- ½ cup of extra virgin olive oil
- 2 cucumbers, sliced
- 2 mixed bell peppers, sliced
- 2 tomatoes, sliced
- 2 green onions, thinly sliced
- 2 gem lettuces, sliced
- 1 cup of arugula
- 2 tablespoons of parsley, chopped
- Salt to taste
- 1 cup of feta cheese, crumbled
- 3 tablespoons of lemon juice

Directions and Total Time: approx. 10 minutes

In a bowl, mix the cucumbers, bell peppers, green onions, gem lettuce, and arugula. In a small bowl, whisk the olive oil, lemon juice, and salt. Pour the prepared mixed dressing over the salad and toss to combine. Scatter the feta over and top with tomato and parsley.

Per Serving: Calories 398, Fat 34g, Carbs 20g, Protein 19g

168. Pecan Salmon Salad

Ingredients for 4 servings

- 6 cups of mixed baby greens (spinach, kale, and Swiss chard)
- 2 large oranges, peeled, and cut into chunks
- 2 red grapefruits, peeled and cut into chunks
- 1 avocado, peeled, pitted, and chopped
- 2 (5-ounce) cans of boneless, skinless salmon, drained
- ½ cup of pecan halves
- ½ cup of pesto vinaigrette

Directions and Total Time: approx. 10 minutes

Prepare a large-sized dish by arranging the greens and topping them with the oranges, grapefruits, avocado, salmon, and pecans. Drizzle the prepared vinaigrette over the salad and serve immediately. Top with chopped cilantro. Swap the pecans for sunflower or pumpkin seeds.

Per Serving: Calories 459, Fat 34g, Carbs 28g, Protein 19g

169. Pesto Chicken Salad with Greens

Ingredients for 6 servings

- 1 pound of boneless chicken breast, trimmed
- ¼ cup of pesto
- ¼ cup of mayonnaise
- 3 tablespoons of red onion, chopped
- 2 tablespoons of olive oil
- 2 tablespoons of red-wine vinegar
- ¼ teaspoon of salt
- ¼ teaspoon of black pepper
- 1 5 ounces package of mixed salad greens
- 1-pint of grape tomatoes, halved

Directions and Total Time: approx. 25 minutes

Place the chicken in a medium-sized saucepan with enough water to cover it and cook for 15 minutes. Cut the chicken into small bite-sized pieces. Mix the chopped onion with the rest of the listed ingredients in a salad bowl. Top with the chicken and serve.

Per Serving: Calories 231, Fat 12.5g, Carbs 4.2g, Protein 21.7g

170. Pesto Ravioli Salad

Ingredients for 6 servings

- 1 cup of smoked mozzarella cheese, cubed
- ¼ teaspoon of lemon zest
- 1 cup of basil pesto
- ½ cup of mayonnaise
- 2 red bell peppers, chopped
- 18 ounces of cheese ravioli

Directions and Total Time: approx. 15 minutes

Bring to a boil salted water in a pot over high heat. Add the ravioli and cook, uncovered, for 4-5 minutes, stirring occasionally; drain and place them in a salad bowl to cool slightly. Blend the lemon zest, pesto, and mayonnaise in a large bowl and stir in mozzarella cheese and bell peppers. Pour the mixture over the ravioli and toss to coat. Serve.

Per Serving: Calories 447, Fat 32g, Carbs 24g, Protein 18g

171. Pine Nut Tuna Salad

Ingredients for 2 servings

- 1 tablespoon of tarragon
- 1 stalk of celery
- 1 medium shallot
- 3 tablespoons of chives
- 1 (5 ounces) can of tuna
- 1 teaspoon of Dijon mustard
- 2–3 tablespoons of mayonnaise
- ¼ teaspoon of salt
- ⅛ teaspoon of pepper
- ¼ cup of pine nuts, toasted

Directions and Total Time: approx. 10 minutes

Incorporate tuna, shallot, chives, tarragon, and celery. Blend mayonnaise, mustard, salt, and black pepper. Stir in mayonnaise mixture to a salad bowl; toss well to combine. Add pine nuts and toss again. Serve fresh.

Per Serving: Calories 276, Fat 12g, Carbs 8g, Protein 1g

172. Pita Chicken Salad

Ingredients for 4 servings

- 1 tablespoon of olive oil
- 1 piece of chicken breast
- 2 pieces of pita
- Dried basil to taste
- 3 tablespoons of natural yogurt
- 1 tablespoon of lemon juice
- 1 garlic clove
- 1 bunch of green salad
- 1 tomato
- 2 chives
- 1 cucumber
- Salt to taste
- Ground black pepper to taste

Directions and Total Time: approx. 23 minutes

Rub the chicken slices with salt, pepper, and dried basil, fry in a pan until cooked. Put the chicken, slices of tomato, cucumber, and onion in half the pits. Mix the yogurt with lemon juice and garlic, add to the salad in Pita. Garnish with chives then serve.

Per Serving: Calories 94, Fat 1.8g, Carbs 2.3g, Protein 6g

173. Pork and Greens

Ingredients for 4 servings

- 1-pound of pork chops
- 8 ounces of white mushrooms, sliced
- ½ cup of Italian dressing
- 6 cups of mixed salad greens
- 6 ounces of jarred artichoke hearts, drained
- Salt and black pepper to the taste
- ½ cup of basil, chopped
- 1 tablespoon of olive oil

Directions and Total Time: approx. 25 minutes

Heat a pan with the oil over medium-high heat, add the pork and brown for approximately about 5 minutes. Add the mushrooms, stir and sauté for approximately about 5 minutes more. Add the dressing, artichokes, salad greens, salt, pepper and basil, cook for approximately about 4-5 minutes, divide everything into bowls and serve.

Per Serving: Calories 235, Fat 6g, Carbs 21g, Protein 11g

174. Pork Chop and Arugula Salad

Ingredients for 4 servings

- 1 pound of pork chops
- 2 cups of goat cheese, crumbled
- 2 cloves of garlic, minced
- 2 teaspoons of lemon zest
- ½ teaspoon of thyme, chopped
- 2 cups of arugula
- 1 tablespoon of lemon juice

Directions and Total Time: approx. 50 minutes

Preheat your oven to a heat of 390 F. Rub the pork chops with garlic, lemon zest, thyme, and lemon juice and arrange them on a greased baking pan. Roast for 30 minutes. Sprinkle with goat cheese and bake for another 10 minutes. Place the cups of arugula on a platter and top with the pork chops to serve.

Per Serving: Calories 670, Fat 56g, Carbs 5g, Protein 44g

175. Potato Salad

Ingredients for 6 servings

- 4 russet potatoes, peeled and chopped
- 1 cup of frozen mixed vegetables, thawed
- 3 hard-boiled eggs, chopped
- ½ cup of Greek yogurt
- 10 pitted black olives
- ½ teaspoon of dried mustard seeds
- ½ teaspoon of lemon zest
- ½ tablespoon of lemon juice
- ½ teaspoon of dried dill
- Salt and black pepper to taste

Directions and Total Time: approx. 20 minutes

Put the potatoes in a large-sized spot of salted water, bring to a boil, and simmer until fork-tender, about 5-7 minutes. Drain and set aside to cool. In a large bowl, mix the eggs, vegetables, yogurt, olives, pepper, mustard, lemon juice, lemon zest, and dill. Season with salt and pepper. Mix in potatoes. Serve.

Per Serving: Calories 190, Fat 4.8g, Carbs 29.7g, Protein 9g

176. Quinoa and Eggs Salad

Ingredients for 4 servings

- 4 eggs, soft boiled, peeled and cut into wedges
- 2 cups of baby arugula
- 2 cups of cherry tomatoes, halved
- 1 cucumber, sliced
- 1 cup of quinoa, cooked
- 1 cup of almonds, chopped
- 1 avocado, peeled, pitted and sliced
- 1 tablespoon of olive oil
- ½ cup of mixed dill and mint, chopped
- A pinch of salt and black pepper
- Juice of 1 lemon

Directions and Total Time: approx. 5 minutes

In a large-sized salad bowl, add the eggs, arugula, and the rest of the ingredients; toss to blend. Divide the salad among plates and serve for breakfast as desired.

Per Serving: Calories 519, Fat 32.4g, Carbs 43.3g, Protein 19g

177. Quinoa Side Salad

Ingredients for 4 servings

- 1 cup of quinoa, cooked
- 1 avocado, chopped
- 1 medium bunch collard greens, chopped
- 1 handful of strawberries, sliced
- 4 tablespoons of walnuts, chopped
- 2 tablespoons of white wine vinegar
- 4 tablespoons of tahini
- 4 tablespoons of cold water
- 1 tablespoon of maple syrup

Directions and Total Time: approx. 10 minutes

Mix tahini with maple syrup, water, and vinegar in a bowl and pulse well. Mix collard green leaves with half of the salad dressing in a salad bowl and toss to coat. Add avocado, walnuts, quinoa, and strawberries and toss again. Add remaining dressing on top and serve.

Per Serving: Calories 175, Fat 3g, Carbs 5g, Protein 3g

178. Radish and Pecorino Salad

Ingredients for 6 servings

- 6 tablespoons of grated Pecorino Romano cheese
- ¼ cup of extra-virgin olive oil
- 6 cups of kale, chopped
- 2 tablespoons of lemon juice
- Salt to taste
- 2 cups of arugula
- ⅓ cup of shelled pistachios
- 20 radishes, sliced

Directions and Total Time: approx. 15 minutes

In a large-sized salad bowl, mix together the olive oil, lemon juice, and salt until well combined. Add the kale and gently massage the leaves with your hands for about 15 seconds until all are thoroughly coated. Let the kale sit for 5 minutes. Add in the arugula, radishes, and pistachios and toss. Sprinkle with Pecorino and serve.

Per Serving: Calories 105, Fat 9.2g, Carbs 3.8g, Protein 4g

Ingredients for 2 servings

- 1 mango, peeled, destoned, cubed
- ¼ of onion, chopped
- ½ cup of cherry tomatoes halved
- ½ of cucumber, deseeded, sliced
- ½ of green bell pepper, deseeded, sliced
- 1/3 teaspoon of salt
- ¼ teaspoon of cayenne pepper
- ¼ of key lime, juiced

Directions and Total Time: approx. 10 minutes

Take a medium bowl, place the mango pieces in it, add onion, tomatoes, cucumber, and bell pepper, and then drizzle with lime juice. Season with salt and cayenne pepper, toss until combined, and let the salad rest in the refrigerator for a minimum of 20 minutes.

Per Serving: Calories 108, Fat 1g, Carbs 3.3g, Protein 28.1g

180 Salmon and Shrimp Salad

Ingredients for 6 servings

- ½ cup of sour cream
- ½ cup of mayonnaise
- 2 tablespoons of lime juice
- 1 ounce of onion, minced
- 1 garlic of clove, minced
- Salt and ground white pepper, as required
- 1-pound of cooked salmon, bite-sized pieces
- 1-pound of cooked shrimp, chopped
- 1 avocado, peeled, pitted, and chopped
- 2 ½ ounces of tomatoes, chopped
- 1 ½ ounces of cucumber, chopped

Directions and Total Time: approx. 20 minutes

In a large-sized bowl, add the sour cream, mayonnaise, lime juice, onion, garlic, salt, and white pepper and beat until well combined. In a larger bowl, add the salmon, shrimp, avocado, tomato, and cucumber and mix well. Place the dressing over the salad and gently toss to coat. Refrigerate to chill for about 25-30 minutes before serving.

Per Serving: Calories 425, Fat 29.9g, Carbs 6.2g, Protein 33.4g

181. Seafood and Avocado Salad

Ingredients for 4 servings

- 6 tablespoons of grated Pecorino Romano cheese
- ¼ cup of extra-virgin olive oil
- 6 cups of kale, chopped
- 2 tablespoons of lemon juice
- Salt to taste
- 2 cups of arugula
- ⅓ cup of shelled pistachios
- 20 radishes, sliced

Directions and Total Time: approx. 10 minutes

Start by getting out a bowl and combine your garlic, salt, pepper, onion, mayonnaise, sour cream and lime juice. Get out a different bowl and mix together your salmon, shrimp, cucumber, and avocado. Add the mayonnaise mixture to your shrimp, and then allow it to sit for twenty minutes in the fridge before serving.

Per Serving: Calories 394, Fat 30g, Carbs 3g, Protein 27g

182. Shrimp and Greens Salad

Ingredients for 2 servings

- Non-stick cooking spray
- 1 garlic clove, crushed
- ½ pound of shrimp, peeled and deveined
- Salt and black pepper, as required
- 1 cup of baby arugula
- 1 cup of baby spinach
- ½ tablespoon of fresh lime juice

Directions and Total Time: approx. 21 minutes

Grease a wok with cooking spray and heat over medium heat. Add the garlic and sauté for about 1 minute. Add the shrimp with salt and black pepper and cook for about 3-5 minutes. Remove from the heat and set aside to cool. In a salad bowl, add the shrimp, arugula, spinach, lime juice, salt, and black pepper and gently toss to coat. Serve immediately.

Per Serving: Calories 143, Fat 2.1g, Carbs 3.2g, Protein 26.4g

183. Smoked Salmon Lentil Salad

Ingredients for 4 servings

- 1 cup of green lentils, rinsed
- 2 cups of vegetable stock
- ½ cup of chopped parsley
- 2 tablespoons of chopped cilantro
- 1 red pepper, chopped
- 1 red onion, chopped
- Salt and pepper to taste
- 4 ounces of smoked salmon, shredded
- 1 lemon, juiced

Directions and Total Time: approx. 30 minutes

In a saucepan, combine the stock and lentils. Cook for 20 minutes on low heat, or until all of the liquid has been absorbed. In a large salad plate, combine the lentils with the parsley, cilantro, red pepper, and onion. Season with salt and pepper to your actual liking. Combine the smoked salmon and lemon juice in a large mixing bowl. Serve the salad right away.

Per Serving: Calories 233, Fat 2g, Carbs 35.5g, Protein 18.7g

184. Spicy Leek and Green Cabbage Salad

Ingredients for 4 servings

- 4 tablespoons of extra-virgin olive oil
- 1 medium-sized leek, chopped
- ½ pound (227 g) green cabbage, shredded
- ½ teaspoon of caraway seeds
- Sea salt, to taste
- 4-5 black peppercorns
- 1 garlic clove, minced
- 1 teaspoon of yellow mustard
- 1 tablespoon of balsamic vinegar
- ½ teaspoon of Sriracha sauce

Directions and Total Time: approx. 55 minutes

Drizzle the olive oil over the leek and cabbage; sprinkle with caraway seeds, salt, black peppercorns. Roast in the preheated oven at 420°F (216°C) for 37 to 40 minutes. Place the roasted mixture in a salad bowl. Toss with the remaining olive oil garlic, mustard, vinegar, and Sriracha sauce. Serve immediately and enjoy.

Per Serving: Calories 116, Fat 10.1g, Carbs 6.5g, Protein 1g

185. Spicy Pea Salad

Ingredients for 8 servings

- 60 ounces of peas
- 1 yellow bell pepper, chopped
- 2 ounces of Cheddar cheese, grated
- ½ cup of mayonnaise
- 3 tablespoons of basil, dried
- 2 tablespoons of red onion, chopped
- 2 teaspoons of chili pepper, chopped
- 1 teaspoon of apple cider vinegar
- 1 teaspoon of sugar
- Salt and black pepper to taste
- 1 teaspoon of garlic powder
- A drizzle of hot sauce

Directions and Total Time: approx. 10 minutes

Mix bell pepper with cheese, onion, basil, chili pepper, salt, and pepper, and stir in a salad bowl. Add mayo, sugar, vinegar, hot sauce, and garlic powder and stir. Add peas, toss well, place in the fridge and serve cold as a side dish.

Per Serving: Calories 120, Fat 2g, Carbs 2g, Protein 3g

186. Spinach and Cherry Tomato Salad

Ingredients for 4 servings

- ¼ cup of olive oil
- 4 cups of baby spinach leaves
- 10 cherry tomatoes, halved
- Salt and black pepper to taste
- ¼ cup of pumpkin seeds
- ½ lemon, juiced

Directions and Total Time: approx. 15 minutes

Toast the pumpkin seeds in a dry sauté pan over medium heat for 2 minutes, shaking often. Let cool. Add the olive oil, lemon juice, salt, and pepper to a small container and shake well. Place the baby spinach on a salad platter and top with cherry tomatoes. Drizzle with the vinaigrette and sprinkle with toasted pumpkin seeds. Serve immediately.

Per Serving: Calories 199, Fat 14g, Carbs 36g, Protein 2g

187. Spinach and Grilled Feta Salad

Ingredients for 4 servings

- 8 ounces of feta cheese, sliced
- 1/4 cup of black olives, sliced
- 1/4 cup of green olives, sliced
- 4 cups of baby spinach
- 2 garlic cloves, minced
- 1 teaspoon of capers, chopped
- 2 tablespoons of extra-virgin olive oil
- 1 tablespoon of red wine vinegar

Directions and Total Time: approx. 35 minutes

Grill feta cheese slices over medium to high flame until brown on both sides. In a salad bowl, mix green olives, black olives, and spinach. In a separate bowl, mix vinegar, capers, and oil together to make a dressing. Top salad with the dressing and cheese, and it is ready to serve.

Per Serving: Calories 100, Fat 6g, Carbs 25g, Protein 10g

188. Spinach Salad with Strawberries and Goat Cheese

Ingredients for 3 servings

- 3 cups of fresh baby spinach, chopped
- 1 red onion, thinly sliced
- ½ cup of strawberries, sliced
- 1 cup of goat cheese, crumbled
- ½ cup of walnuts, chopped
- 1 tablespoon of mint, chopped
- 4 tablespoons of extra-virgin olive oil
- 2 tablespoons of red wine vinegar
- 1 tablespoon of lemon juice
- 1 tablespoon of Dijon mustard
- 1 tablespoon of honey
- 1/3 teaspoon of salt
- 1/3 teaspoon of pepper

Directions and Total Time: approx. 35 minutes

In a bowl combine the dressing ingredients and place them in your refrigerator. Then, in a salad bowl add the baby spinach, strawberries, mint, walnuts, goat cheese, and red onion. Combine well. Pour the mixed dressing over your salad and stir. Serve immediately and enjoy!

Per Serving: Calories 337, Fat 27.2g, Carbs 14.2g, Protein 10.6g

189. Spring Salad with Mustard Dressing

Ingredients for 4 servings

- 4 cups of spring mix salad greens
- ¼ cup of cherry tomatoes
- 1 tablespoon of fresh parsley, chopped
- 3 tablespoons of extra-virgin olive oil
- 1 tablespoon of wine vinegar
- 2 tablespoons of minced shallots
- ½ teaspoon of yogurt
- ½ teaspoon of Dijon mustard
- Salt and black pepper to taste

Directions and Total Time: approx. 5 minutes

Place parsley, vinegar, shallots, yogurt, mustard, salt, and pepper in a bowl and mix until smooth. While whisking continually, drip in the oil in a slow, steady stream until the mixture is emulsified. In a medium-sized bowl, combine the salad greens and tomatoes. Pour the dressing over and serve.

Per Serving: Calories 64, Fat 4.1g, Carbs 2.2g, Protein 0.6g

190. Strawberry Spinach Salad

Ingredients for 4 servings

- 2 tablespoons of sesame seeds
- 1 tablespoon of poppy seeds
- 1/2 cup of white sugar
- 1/2 cup of olive oil
- 1/4 cup of distilled white vinegar
- 1/4 teaspoon of paprika
- 1/4 teaspoon of Worcestershire sauce
- 1 tablespoon of minced onion
- 10 ounces of fresh spinach
- 1-quart of strawberries - cleaned, hulled and sliced
- 1/4 cup of almonds, blanched and slivered

Directions and Total Time: approx. 10 minutes

In a medium bowl, whisk together the same seeds, poppy seeds, sugar, olive oil, vinegar, paprika, Worcestershire sauce, and onion. Cover, and chill for one hour. In a large bowl, incorporate the spinach, strawberries, and almonds. Drizzle dressing over salad and toss. Refrigerate 10 to 15 minutes before serving.

Per Serving: Calories 491, Fat 2g, Carbs 9g, Protein 6g

191. Summer Fruit and Cheese Salad

Ingredients for 6 servings

- 1 cantaloupe, quartered and seeded
- 2 tablespoons of extra-virgin olive oil
- ½ small seedless watermelon
- 1 cup of grape tomatoes
- 2 cups of Goat cheese, crumbled
- ⅓ cup of mint leaves, torn into small pieces
- 1 tablespoon of balsamic vinegar
- Salt and black pepper to taste

Directions and Total Time: approx. 10 minutes

Scoop balls out of the cantaloupe melon using a melon-baller. Put the balls in a shallow bowl. Repeat the process with the watermelon. Add the watermelon balls to the cantaloupe bowl. Add the tomatoes, Goat cheese, mint, olive oil, vinegar, pepper, and salt, and gently mix until everything is incorporated. Serve and enjoy!

Per Serving: Calories 58, Fat 2.2g, Carbs 8.8g, Protein 1.1g

192. Three-Bean Salad with Black Olives

Ingredients for 6 servings

- 1 pound of green beans, trimmed
- 1 red onion, thinly sliced
- 2 tablespoons of marjoram, chopped
- ¼ cup of black olives, chopped
- ½ cup of canned cannellini beans
- ½ cup of canned chickpeas
- 2 tablespoons of extra-virgin olive oil
- ½ cup of balsamic vinegar
- ½ teaspoon of dried oregano
- Salt and black pepper to taste

Directions and Total Time: approx. 15 minutes

Steam the green beans for about 2 minutes or until just tender. Drain and place them in an ice-water bath. Drain thoroughly and pat them dry with paper towels. Put them in a large bowl and toss with the remaining ingredients. Serve.

Per Serving: Calories 187, Fat 6g, Carbs 27g, Protein 7g

193. Tomato and Bocconcini Side Salad

Ingredients for 4 servings

- 20 ounces of tomatoes, cut in wedges
- 2 tablespoons of olive oil
- 1 and ½ tablespoons of balsamic vinegar
- 1 teaspoon of sugar
- 1 clove of garlic, minced
- 3 ounces of baby bocconcini, drain and torn
- 1 cup of basil, chopped
- Salt and black pepper to taste

Directions and Total Time: approx. 12 minutes

Mix sugar with vinegar, garlic, oil, salt, and pepper, and whisk in a bowl very well. In a salad bowl, mix bocconcini with tomato and basil. Add dressing, toss to coat, and serve right away.

Per Serving: Calories 121, Fat 1g, Carbs 2g, Protein 2g

194. Tomato, Cucumber and White-Bean Salad

Ingredients for 4 servings

- ½ cup of packed fresh basil leaves
- ¼ cup of olive oil
- 3 tablespoons of red-wine vinegar
- 1 tablespoon of shallot, chopped
- 2 teaspoons of Dijon mustard
- 1 teaspoon of honey
- ¼ teaspoon of salt
- ¼ teaspoon of black pepper
- 10 cups of mixed salad greens
- 1 (15 ounces) can of cannellini beans, rinsed
- 1 cup of halved cherry tomatoes
- ½ cucumber, halved lengthwise and sliced

Directions and Total Time: approx. 10 minutes

Take a medium-sized salad bowl and add the chopped vegetables and beans. Sprinkle the black pepper and the rest of the ingredients on top. Toss well and serve.

Per Serving: Calories 280, Fat 23.9g, Carbs 14.1g, Protein 5.3g

195. Tomato, Mozzarella Salad

Ingredients for 4 servings

- ½ cup of fresh basil leaves
- 2 garlic cloves, peeled
- 4 tablespoons of olive oil
- 2 tablespoons of balsamic vinegar
- Salt and ground black pepper, to taste
- 2 cups of cherry tomatoes
- 3 ounces of mozzarella cheese balls
- 5 cups of fresh arugula
- 3 cherry tomatoes
- 3 ounces of mozzarella
- 5 cups of arugula

Directions and Total Time: approx. 15 minutes

For filling: In a small blender, add all the ingredients and pulse until smooth. For salad: In a large bowl, add all the ingredients and mix. Place the dressing over salad and toss to coat well. Serve well chilled and enjoy!

Per Serving: Calories 123, Fat 9.2g, Carbs 5.8g, Protein 4.6g

196. Tuscan Kale Salad with Anchovies

Ingredients for 4 servings

- 1 large bunch Lacinato
- ¼ cup of toasted pine nuts
- 1 cup of Parmesan cheese
- ¼ cup of extra-virgin olive oil
- 8 anchovy fillets
- 2 to 3 tablespoons of lemon juice
- 2 teaspoons of red pepper flakes (optional)

Directions and Total Time: approx. 45 minutes

Remove the rough center stems from the kale leaves and roughly tear each leaf into about 4-by-1-inch strips. Place torn kale in a medium-sized bowl and add the pine nuts and cheese. Blend the olive oil, anchovies, lemon juice, and red pepper flakes (if using). Sprinkle over the salad and toss to coat well. Let sit at room temperature 30 minutes before serving, tossing again just prior to serving.

Per Serving: Calories 337, Fat 25g, Carbs 32g, Protein 16g

197. Vegetable Patch Salad

Ingredients for 6 servings

- 1 bunch of cauliflower, cut into florets
- 1 zucchini, sliced
- 1 sweet potato, peeled and cubed
- 1/2 pounds of baby carrots
- Salt and pepper to taste
- 1 teaspoon of dried basil
- 2 red onions, sliced
- 2 eggplants, cubed
- 1 endive, sliced
- 3 tablespoons of extra-virgin olive oil
- 1 lemon, juiced
- 1 tablespoon of balsamic vinegar

Directions and Total Time: approx. 40 minutes

Preheat oven to 350°F. Mix together all vegetables, basil, salt, pepper, and oil in a baking dish and cook for 25-30 minutes. After cooked, pour into a salad bowl and stir in vinegar and lemon juice. Dish up and serve.

Per Serving: Calories 115, Fat 9g, Carbs 11g, Protein 15g

198. Veggie Salad

Ingredients for 4 servings

- 2 tomatoes, cut into wedges
- 2 red bell peppers, chopped
- 1 cucumber, chopped
- 1 red onion, sliced
- ½ cup of kalamata olives, pitted and sliced
- 2 ounces of feta cheese, crumbled
- ¼ cup of lime juice
- ½ cup of olive oil
- 2 cloves of garlic, minced
- 1 tablespoon of oregano, chopped
- Salt and black pepper to the taste

Directions and Total Time: approx. 5 minutes

In a large-sized salad bowl, combine the tomatoes with the peppers and the rest of the ingredients except the cheese and toss. Divide the salad into smaller bowls, sprinkle the cheese on top and serve for breakfast.

Per Serving: Calories 327, Fat 11.2g, Carbs 16.7g, Protein 6.4g

199. Vinegar with Mustardy Summer Salad

Ingredients for 4 servings

- ¼ cup of balsamic vinegar
- 2 tablespoons of Dijon mustard
- 1 tablespoon of sugar
- ½ teaspoon of garlic salt
- ½ teaspoon of pepper
- ¼ cup of extra-virgin olive oil
- 1 ½ cups of chopped orange, yellow, and red tomatoes
- ½ cucumber, peeled and diced
- 1 small red onion, thinly sliced
- ¼ cup of crumbled feta (optional)

Directions and Total Time: approx. 10 minutes

In a large-sized bowl, whisk the vinegar, mustard, sugar, pepper, and garlic salt. Then slowly whisk in the olive oil. In a large-sized bowl, add the tomatoes, cucumber, and red onion. Add the dressing. Toss once or twice, and serve with the feta crumbles (if desired) sprinkled on top.

Per Serving: Calories 245, Fat 17.9g, Carbs 18.9g, Protein 0.9g

200. Warm Kale Salad with Red Bell Pepper

Ingredients for 4 servings

- 1 tablespoon of olive oil
- 4 cups of kale, torn
- 2 cloves of garlic, minced
- 1 red bell pepper, diced
- Salt and black pepper to taste
- ½ lemon, juiced

Directions and Total Time: approx. 15 minutes

In a large-sized pan, heat the olive oil over medium heat until shimmering, then add the garlic. Cook for approximately about 1 minute, then add the bell pepper. Cook for approximately about 4-5 minutes until the pepper is tender. Stir in the kale. Cook for approximately about 3-4 minutes or just until wilted, then remove from heat. Place pepper and kale in a bowl and season with salt and black pepper. Drizzle with lemon juice.

Per Serving: Calories 123, Fat 4g, Carbs 22g, Protein 6g

201. Apple Pumpkin Soup

Ingredients for 8 servings

- 1 apple, chopped
- 1 kabocha pumpkin, peeled, seeded and cubed
- 1 cup of almond flour
- ¼ cup of ghee
- 1 pinch of cardamom powder
- 2 quarts of water
- ¼ cup of coconut cream
- 1 pinch of ground black pepper

Directions and Total Time: approx. 54 minutes

Heat ghee in the bottom of a heavy pot and add apples. Cook for about 5 minutes on a medium flame and add pumpkin. Sauté for about 3 minutes and add the almond flour. Sauté for about 1 minute and add water. Lower the flame and cook for approximately about 30 minutes. Transfer the soup into an immersion blender and blend until smooth. Top with coconut cream and serve.

Per Serving: Calories 186, Fat 14.9g, Carbs 10.4g, Protein 3.7g

202. Aromatic Tomato Soup

Ingredients for 2 servings

- 1 tablespoon of avocado oil
- 2 cloves of garlic, minced
- 2 ripe tomatoes, puréed
- 1/2 cup of cream cheese
- 1/3 cup of water
- 1/2 teaspoon of basil
- 1 teaspoon of dried sage
- Salt, to taste
- 1/4 teaspoon of ground black pepper
- 1/2 teaspoon of cayenne pepper
- 1/2 cup of Colby cheese, shredded

Directions and Total Time: approx. 10 minutes

Press the "Sauté" button to heat up the moment Pot; heat the oil. Once hot, cook the garlic until aromatic. Add the remaining of the prepared ingredients and stir to mix. Secure the lid. Choose "Manual" mode and Low pressure; cook for 3 minutes. Once cooking is complete, use a fast pressure release; carefully remove the lid. Ladle into individual bowls and serve immediately. Bon appétit!

Per Serving: Calories 339, Fat 29.5g, Carbs 9.1g, Protein 10.8g

203. Artichoke Soup

Ingredients for 4 servings

- 5 artichoke hearts, washed and trimmed
- 1 leek, sliced
- 5 tablespoons of butter
- 6 garlic cloves, peeled and minced
- ½ cup of shallots, chopped
- 8 ounces of Yukon gold potatoes, chopped
- 12 cups of chicken broth
- 1 herb
- Fresh parsley, chopped
- 2 thyme sprigs
- ¼ teaspoon of black peppercorns, crushed
- Salt, to taste
- ¼ cup of cream

Directions and Total Time: approx. 30 minutes

Set the moment Pot on Sauté mode, add the butter and melt it. Add the artichoke hearts, shallots, leek, and garlic, stir, and brown for 3-4 minutes. Add the potatoes, stock, bay leaf, thyme, parsley, peppercorns, and salt, stir, cover, and cook on the Soup setting for quarter-hour. Release the pressure, uncover the moment Pot, discard the herbs, blend well using an immersion blender, add salt to taste and therefore the cream, stir well, divide into bowls, and serve.

Per Serving: Calories 95, Fat 2g, Carbs 15g, Protein 4g

204. Basil and Tomato Soup

Ingredients for 2 servings

- 2 tablespoons of vegetable broth
- 1 garlic clove, minced
- ½ cup of white onion
- 1 celery stalk, chopped
- 1 carrot, chopped
- 3 cups of tomatoes, chopped
- Salt and pepper
- 2 bay leaves
- 1 ½ cup of unsweetened almond milk
- 1/3 cup of basil leaves

Directions and Total Time: approx. 30 minutes

Cook the vegetable broth in a large saucepan over medium heat. Add in the garlic and onions and cook for 4 minutes. Add in the carrots and celery. Cook for 1 more minute. Mix in the tomatoes and bring to a boil. Simmer for 15 minutes. Add the almond milk, basil, and bay leaves. Season and serve.

Per Serving: Calories 213, Fat 3.9g, Carbs 10g, Protein 6.9g

205. Basil Zucchini Soup

Ingredients for 4 servings

- 2 tablespoons of olive oil
- 3 garlic cloves, minced
- 1 yellow onion, chopped
- 4 zucchinis, cubed
- 4 cups of chicken stock
- Zest of 1 lemon, grated
- ½ cup of basil, chopped
- Salt and black pepper to the taste

Directions and Total Time: approx. 30 minutes

Heat the tablespoons of olive oil over medium heat in a large-sized saucepan, then add the chopped onion and minced garlic and simmer, stirring periodically, for 5 minutes. Combine the zucchinis with the other ingredients (except the basil), bring to a boil, and cook for 15 minutes over medium heat. Add the basil, stir, divide the soup into bowls and serve.

Per Serving: Calories 274, Fat 11.1g, Carbs 16.5g, Protein 4.5g

206. Beetroot and Carrot Soup

Ingredients for 6 servings

- 4 beets
- 2 carrots
- 2 potatoes
- 1 medium onion
- 4 cups of vegetable broth
- 2 cups of water
- 2 tablespoons of yogurt
- 2 tablespoons of olive oil

Directions and Total Time: approx. 44 minutes

Peel and chop the beets. Cook olive oil in a saucepan over medium high heat and sauté the onion and carrot until onion is tender. Add beets, potatoes, broth and water. Bring to the boil. Switch heat to medium and simmer, partially covered, for 30-40 minutes. Cool slightly. Blend the soup in batches until reached smooth. Return it to medium-sized pan over low heat and cook, stirring, for 4-5 minutes or until heated through. Season with salt and pepper. Serve soup topped with yogurt and sprinkled with spring onions.

Per Serving: Calories 301, Fat 21g, Carbs 36.1g, Protein 11g

207. Broccoli Fennel Soup

Ingredients for 4 servings

- 1 fennel bulb, white and green parts coarsely chopped
- 10 ounces of broccoli, cut into florets
- 3 cups of vegetable stock
- Salt and freshly ground black pepper
- 1 garlic clove
- 1 cup of dairy-free cream cheese
- 3 ounces of vegan butter
- ½ cup of chopped fresh oregano

Directions and Total Time: approx. 25 minutes

In a medium pot, combine the fennel, broccoli, vegetable stock, salt, and black pepper. Bring to a boil until the vegetables soften, 10 to 15 minutes. Stir in the remaining ingredients and simmer the soup for 3 to 5 minutes. Adjust the taste with salt and black pepper, and dish the soup. Serve warm.

Per Serving: Calories 240, Fat 10g, Carbs 20g, Protein 11g

208. Broccoli Soup

Ingredients for 6 servings

- 3 tablespoons of ghee
- 5 garlic cloves
- 1 teaspoon of sage
- ¼ teaspoon of ginger
- 2 cups of broccoli
- 1 small onion
- 1 teaspoon of oregano
- ½ teaspoon of parsley
- Salt and black pepper, to taste
- 6 cups of vegetable broth
- 4 tablespoons of butter

Directions and Total Time: approx. 52 minutes

Put ghee, onions, spices and garlic in a pot and cook for 3 minutes. Add broccoli and cook for about 4 minutes. Add vegetable broth, cover and allow it to simmer for approximately about 30 minutes. Transfer into a blender and blend until smooth. Add the butter to give it a creamy, delicious texture and flavor.

Per Serving: Calories 183, Fat 15.6g, Carbs 5.2g, Protein 6.1g

209. Bulgarian Lentil Soup

Ingredients for 10 servings

- 2 cups of brown lentils
- 2 onions, chopped
- 5-6 cloves of garlic, peeled
- 2-3 medium carrots, chopped
- 1-2 small tomatoes, ripe
- 4 tablespoons of olive oil
- 1 ½ teaspoon of paprika
- 1 teaspoon of summer savory

Directions and Total Time: approx. 23 minutes

Cook oil in a cooking pot, add the onions and carrots. Add the paprika and washed lentils with 4 cups of warm water; continue to simmer. Chop the tomatoes and stir in them to the soup about 15 minutes after the lentils have started to simmer. Add savory and peeled garlic cloves. Simmer soup. Salt to taste.

Per Serving: Calories 201, Fat 12g, Carbs 21g, Protein 5g

210. Cabbage Lentil Soup

Ingredients for 4 servings

- 1 cabbage head, chopped
- 12 ounces of baby carrots
- 3 celery stalks, chopped
- ½ Onion, peeled and chopped
- 1 packet of petite marmite mix
- 2 tablespoons of vegetable oil
- 12 ounces of soy burger
- 3 teaspoons of garlic, peeled and minced
- ¼ cup of cilantro, chopped
- 4 cups of chicken broth
- Salt and ground black pepper, to taste

Directions and Total Time: approx. 20 minutes

Within the Instant Pot, mix the cabbage with the celery, carrots, onion, soup mix, soy burger, stock, olive oil, and garlic, stir, cover, and cook on Soup mode for five minutes. Release the pressure, uncover the moment Pot, add the salt, pepper, and cilantro, stir again well, divide into soup bowls, and serve.

Per Serving: Calories 100, Fat 1g, Carbs 10g, Protein 10g

211. Carrot and Mushroom Soup

Ingredients for 4 servings

- 1 onion, diced
- 2 stalks of celery, sliced
- 2 carrots, sliced
- 1/4 cup of mushroom
- 4 cups of chicken stock

Directions and Total Time: approx. 30 minutes

Add the prepared 1 tablespoon of olive oil to the pot. Cook the onion, celery, carrots and mushroom for 5 minutes. Cover the pot. Choose manual function. Pour in the stock. Close the pot. Select manual mode. Cook at high pressure for 10 minutes. Release the pressure naturally.

Per Serving: Calories 71, Fat 1.2g, Carbs 13.4g, Protein 2.9g

212. Carrot Spread Soup

Ingredients for 4 servings

- 8 carrots, peeled and chopped
- 1 onion, chopped
- 3 garlic cloves, peeled
- 14 ounces of coconut milk
- 1 ½ cup of chicken broth
- ¼ cup of spread
- 1 tablespoons of curry paste
- Pepper
- Salt

Directions and Total Time: approx. 15 minutes

Add all ingredients into the moment pot and stir well. Seal large-sized pot with lid and cook on high for quarter-hour. Release pressure using an actual quick release method than open the lid. Puree the soup using an immersion blender just until smooth. Season soup with pepper and salt. Serve and luxuriate in.

Per Serving: Calories 316, Fat 34.2g, Carbs 25.3g, Protein 8.2g

Ingredients for 6 servings

- 2 teaspoons of thyme powder
- 1 head of cauliflower
- 3 cups of vegetable stock
- ½ teaspoon of matcha green tea powder
- 3 tablespoons of olive oil
- Salt and black pepper, to taste
- 5 garlic cloves, chopped

Directions and Total Time: approx. 28 minutes

Put the vegetable stock, thyme and matcha powder to a large pot over medium-high heat and bring to a boil. Add cauliflower and cook for approximately about 10 minutes. Meanwhile, put the olive oil and garlic in a small saucepan and cook for about 1 minute. Add the garlic, salt and black pepper and cook for about 2 minutes. Transfer into an immersion blender and blend until smooth. Dish out and serve immediately.

Per Serving: Calories 79, Fat 7.1g, Carbs 3.8g, Protein 1.3g

214. Cauliflower and Walnut Soup

Ingredients for 4 servings

- 1 pound of cauliflower, chopped
- 8 walnut halves, chopped
- 1 red onion, chopped
- 1 1/2 pints of vegetable stock (broth)
- 3 1/2 ounces of double cream (heavy cream)
- ½ teaspoon of turmeric
- 1 tablespoon of olive oil

Directions and Total Time: approx. 35 minutes

In a small-sized saucepan, heat the olive oil, then add the cauliflower and red onion and cook, stirring constantly, for 4 minutes. Pour in the stock (broth), bring to the boil and cook for 15 minutes. Stir in the walnuts, double cream, and turmeric. Process soup in a food processor until it is smooth and creamy. Serve into bowls and top off with a dash of chopped walnuts.

Per Serving: Calories 212, Fat 16.9g, Carbs 13g, Protein 3.3g

215. Cauliflower, Leek and Bacon Soup

Ingredients for 4 servings

- 4 cups of chicken broth
- ½ cauliflower head, chopped
- 1 leek, chopped
- Salt and black pepper, to taste
- 5 bacon strips

Directions and Total Time: approx. 1 hour and 46 minutes

Put the cauliflower, leek and chicken broth into the pot and cook for about 1 hour on medium heat. Transfer into an immersion blender and pulse until smooth. Return the soup into the pot and microwave the bacon strips for 1 minute. Cut the bacon into tiny/small pieces and put it into the soup. Cook on for about 30 minutes on low heat. Season with salt and pepper and serve.

Per Serving: Calories 185, Fat 12.7g, Carbs 5.8g, Protein 10.8g

216. Cauliflower Soup

Ingredients for 4 servings

- 4 tablespoons of butter, softened
- 1/2 cup of leeks, thinly sliced
- 2 cloves of garlic, minced
- 3/4 pound of cauliflower, broken into florets
- 1 cup of water
- 2 cups of chicken broth
- 1 cup of full-fat milk
- Kosher salt, to taste
- 1/3 teaspoon of ground black pepper

Directions and Total Time: approx. 10 minutes

Press the "Sauté" button to heat up your Instant Pot. Then, melt the butter; sauté the leeks until softened. Then, sauté the garlic until fragrant, about 30 seconds. Add the remaining prepared ingredients and gently stir to mix. Secure the lid. Choose "Manual" mode and Low pressure; cook for five minutes. Once cooking is complete, use a fast pressure release; carefully remove the lid. Ladle into individual bowls and serve warm. Bon appétit!

Per Serving: Calories 167, Fat 5.7g, Carbs 3.8g, Protein 3.1g

217. Cheesy Beet Soup

Ingredients for 4 servings

- 1 tablespoon of olive oil
- 6 large beets, peeled and chopped
- 1 fennel bulb, coarsely chopped
- 1 sweet onion, chopped
- 1 teaspoon of garlic, minced
- 6 cups of low-sodium chicken stock
- Sea salt and black pepper, to taste
- ½ cup goat's cheese, crumbled
- 1 tablespoon fresh parsley, chopped

Directions and Total Time: approx. 40 minutes

In a large-sized pot, heat the olive oil over medium-high heat. Sauté the beets, fennel, onion, and garlic until they soften, occasionally stirring, about 10 minutes. Add the chicken stock and bring the soup to a boil. Reduce the heat to low and simmer until the vegetables are very tender, about 20 minutes. Transfer the mixed soup to a food processor or, using an immersion blender, purée until smooth. Return the cooked soup to the saucepan and season with salt and pepper. Serve.

Per Serving: Calories 309, Fat 13g, Carbs 32g, Protein 17g

218. Cheesy Zucchini Soup

Ingredients for 2 servings

- ½ medium onion, peeled and chopped
- 1 cup of bone broth
- 1 tablespoon of coconut oil
- 1 ½ zucchinis, cut into chunks
- ½ tablespoon of nutritional yeast
- Dash of black pepper
- ½ tablespoon of parsley, chopped, for garnish
- ½ tablespoon of coconut cream, for garnish

Directions and Total Time: approx. 25 minutes

In a large-sized pot, heat the olive oil over medium-high heat. Sauté the beets, fennel, onion, and garlic until they soften, occasionally stirring, about 10 minutes. Add the chicken stock and bring the soup to a boil. Reduce the heat to low and simmer until the vegetables are very tender, about 20 minutes. Transfer the mixed soup to a food processor or, using an immersion blender, purée until smooth. Return the cooked soup to the saucepan and season with salt and pepper. Serve.

Per Serving: Calories 309, Fat 13g, Carbs 32g, Protein 17g

219. Chicken and Carrots Soup

Ingredients for 6 servings

- 1 whole chicken, dig medium pieces
- 3 carrots, sliced
- 4 eggs, whisked
- Juice of two lemons
- ¼ cup of dill, chopped
- Salt and black pepper to the taste
- 8 cups of water

Directions and Total Time: approx. 1 hour and 30 minutes

Put the chicken pieces during a pot, add the water, bring back an overboil medium heat, cover the large-sized pot and simmer for 1 hour. Transfer the chicken to a plate, calm down, discard bones, return the meat to the pot and warmth it up again over medium heat. Add the remainder of the prepared ingredients except the eggs, stir and simmer the soup for 10 minutes more. Add the eggs mixed with 2 cups of stock, stir the soup, cook for 2-3 minutes more, divide into bowls and serve.

Per Serving: Calories 264, Fat 17.5g, Carbs 28.7g, Protein 16.3g

220. Chicken and Leeks Soup

Ingredients for 6 servings

- 2 pounds of pigeon breast, skinless, boneless and cubed
- ½ cup of vegetable oil
- 2 leeks, sliced
- 4 spring onions, chopped
- 1 small green cabbage head, shredded
- 4 celery sticks, chopped
- 4 cups of veggie stock
- ½ teaspoon of sweet paprika
- A pinch of nutmeg, ground
- Salt and black pepper to the taste

Directions and Total Time: approx. 60 minutes

Heat up a large-sized pot with the oil over medium-high heat, add the chicken and brown for two minutes on all sides. Add the leeks, onions and celery and sauté for 1 minute more. Add the remainder of the prepared ingredients, bring back a simmer and cook over medium heat for 45 minutes. Ladle the soup into bowls and serve.

Per Serving: Calories 310, Fat 15.3g, Carbs 24.6g, Protein 18.4g

221. Chicken and Mushroom Soup

Ingredients for 8 servings

- 3 cups of chicken breasts, diced
- 1 cup of chicken broth
- 2 cups of hot water
- 1 can of diced Italian tomatoes
- 2 red bell peppers, sliced
- 1 red onion, diced
- ¾ cup of mushrooms, washed, dried, and sliced
- 4 cloves of garlic, minced
- 1 teaspoon of dried oregano
- 1 teaspoon of ground cumin
- Salt and pepper to taste
- 2 tablespoons of fresh parsley, chopped

Directions and Total Time: approx. 7 hours and 10 minutes

Preheat the slow cooker on low. Add all the ingredients, then cover and cook on low for 6 hours. Break up the chicken with a fork, cover the slow cooker again, and cook for an additional hour until ready. Serve it warm with top with fresh parsley.

Per Serving: Calories 129, Fat 4.3g, Carbs 5.5g, Protein 16.8g

222. Chicken and Orzo Soup

Ingredients for 4 servings

- ½ cup of carrot, chopped
- 1 yellow onion, chopped
- 12 cups of chicken broth
- 2 cups of kale, chopped
- 3 cups of chicken meat, cooked and shredded
- 1 cup of orzo
- ¼ cup of juice
- 1 tablespoon of vegetable oil

Directions and Total Time: approx. 21 minutes

Heat up a large-sized pot with the oil over medium heat, add the onion and sauté for 3 minutes. Add the carrots and therefore the remainder of the ingredients, stir, bring back a simmer and cook for 8 minutes more. Ladle into bowls and serve hot.

Per Serving: Calories 300, Fat 12.2g, Carbs 16.5g, Protein 12.2g

223. Chicken and Rice Soup

Ingredients for 4 servings

- 6 cups of chicken broth
- 1 and ½ cups of chicken meat, cooked and shredded
- 1 herb
- 1 yellow onion, chopped
- 2 tablespoons of vegetable oil
- 1/3 cup of polished rice
- 1 egg, whisked
- Juice of ½ lemon
- 1 cup of asparagus, trimmed and halved
- 1 cup of carrots, chopped
- ½ cup of dill, chopped
- Salt and black pepper to the taste

Directions and Total Time: approx. 45 minutes

Heat up a large-sized pot with the oil over medium heat, add the onions and sauté for five minutes. Add the stock, dill, the rice and therefore the herb, stir, bring back a overboil medium heat and cook for 10 minutes. Add the remainder of the prepared ingredients except the egg and therefore the juice, stir and cook for quarter-hour more. Add the egg whisked with the juice gradually, whisk the soup, cook for two minutes more, divide into bowls and serve.

Per Serving: Calories 263, Fat 18.5g, Carbs 19.8g, Protein 14.5g

224. Chicken Mulligatawny Soup

Ingredients for 10 servings

- 1 ½ tablespoons of curry powder
- 3 cups of celery root, diced
- 2 tablespoons of Swerve
- 10 cups of chicken broth
- 5 cups of chicken, chopped and cooked
- ¼ cup of apple cider
- ½ cup of sour cream
- ¼ cup of fresh parsley, chopped
- 2 tablespoons of butter
- Salt and black pepper, to taste

Directions and Total Time: approx. 15 minutes

Combine the broth, butter, chicken, curry powder, celery root and apple cider in a large soup pot. Bring to a very hot boil and simmer for just about 30 minutes. Stir in Swerve, sour cream, fresh parsley, salt and black pepper. Dish out and serve hot.

Per Serving: Calories 215, Fat 8.5g, Carbs 7.1g, Protein 26.4g

225. Chicken Noodle Soup

Ingredients for 6 servings

- 1 yellow onion, peeled and chopped
- 1 tablespoon of butter
- 1 celery stalk, chopped
- 4 carrots, peeled and sliced
- Salt and ground black pepper, to taste
- 6 cups of chicken broth
- 2 cups of chicken, already cooked and shredded
- Egg noodles, already cooked

Directions and Total Time: approx. 22 minutes

Set the moment Pot on Sauté mode, add the butter and warmth it up. Add the onion, stir, and cook 2 minutes. Add the celery and carrots, stir, and cook 5 minutes. Add the chicken and stock, stir, cover the moment Pot and cook on the Soup setting for five minutes. Release the pressure, uncover the moment Pot, add salt and pepper to taste, and stir. Divide the noodles into soup bowls, add the soup over them, and serve.

Per Serving: Calories 100, Fat 1g, Carbs 4g, Protein 7g

226. Chicken Rice Noodle Soup

Ingredients for 6 servings

- 6 cups of chicken, cooked and cubed
- 3 tablespoons of rice vinegar
- 2 ½ cups of cabbage, shredded
- 2 tablespoons of fresh ginger, grated
- 2 tablespoons of soy
- 3 garlic cloves, minced
- 8 ounces of rice noodles
- 1 bell pepper, chopped
- 1 large carrot, peeled and sliced
- 6 cups of chicken broth
- 2 celery stalks, sliced
- 1 onion, chopped
- ½ teaspoon of black pepper

Directions and Total Time: approx. 10 minutes

Add all ingredients into the moment pot and stir well. Seal large-sized pot with lid and cook on high for 10 minutes. Release the pressure using quick release method than open the lid. Stir well and serve.

Per Serving: Calories 306, Fat 5.1g, Carbs 18.7g, Protein 43.1g

227. Chicken Wild Rice Soup

Ingredients for 6 servings

- 2/3 cup of wild rice, uncooked
- 1 tablespoon of onion, chopped finely
- 1 tablespoon of fresh parsley, chopped
- 1 cup of carrots, chopped
- 8-ounces of chicken breast, cooked
- 2 tablespoons of butter
- 1/4 cup of all-purpose white flour
- 5 cups of low-sodium chicken broth
- 1 tablespoon of slivered almonds

Directions and Total Time: approx. 25 minutes

Start by adding rice and 2 cups broth along with ½ cup water to a cooking pot. Cook the chicken until the rice is "Al dente" and set it aside. Add butter to a saucepan and melt it. Stir in onion and sauté until soft, then add the flour and the remaining broth. Stir it and then cook for it 1 minute; add the chicken, cooked rice, and carrots. Cook for 5 minutes on simmer. Garnish with almonds. Serve fresh.

Per Serving: Calories 287, Fat 35g, Carbs 21.76g, Protein 21g

228. Chickpeas Soup

Ingredients for 4 servings

- 3 tomatoes, cubed
- 2 yellow onions, chopped
- 2 tablespoons vegetable oil
- 4 celery stalks, chopped
- ½ cup of parsley, chopped
- 2 garlic cloves, minced
- 16 ounces of canned chickpeas, drained and rinsed
- 6 cups of water
- 1 teaspoon of cumin, ground
- Juice of ½ lemon
- 1 teaspoon of turmeric powder
- ½ teaspoon of cinnamon powder
- ½ teaspoon of ginger, grated
- Salt and black pepper to the taste

Directions and Total Time: approx. 1 hour and 10 minutes

Heat up a large-sized pot with the oil over medium heat, add the onion and therefore the garlic and sauté for five minutes. Add the tomatoes, celery, cumin, turmeric, cinnamon and therefore the ginger, stir and sauté for five minutes more. Add the remaining ingredients, bring the soup to an overboil medium heat and simmer for 50 minutes. Ladle the soup into bowls and serve.

Per Serving: Calories 300, Fat 15.4g, Carbs 29.5g, Protein 15.4g

229. Chilled Cucumber Soup

Ingredients for 6 servings

- 2 large English cucumbers, peeled and coarsely chopped
- 1 medium yellow onion, coarsely chopped
- 5 cups of canned low-sodium, fat-free chicken broth
- 2 cups of plain low-fat yogurt
- 2 scallions, white and green parts, minced
- Salt to taste
- Freshly ground pepper to taste
- Fresh dill, finely chopped

Directions and Total Time: approx. 25 minutes

In a large saucepan, mix the cucumbers and the onion; add the chicken broth. Heat to a rapid boil on high heat, reduce to low immediately, cover and simmer until vegetables are tender. Remove from the sun, cool somewhat, and refrigerate for a few hours to cool. Mix in the cream, scallions, and salt to taste for the serving. Sprinkle with dill and seasoning.

Per Serving: Calories 316, Fat 24g, Carbs 8g, Protein 13g

230. Chorizo White Bean Stew

Ingredients for 8 servings

- 3 tablespoons of olive oil
- 4 chorizo links, sliced
- 2 sweet onions, chopped
- 4 garlic cloves, minced
- 2 celery stalks, sliced
- 2 carrots, sliced
- 2 red bell peppers, cored and diced
- 2 tablespoons of tomato paste
- 1 can of diced tomatoes
- 2 cans of white beans, drained
- 1 bay leaf
- 1 teaspoon of sherry vinegar
- ½ teaspoon of dried oregano
- 1 cup of chicken stock
- Salt and pepper to taste

Directions and Total Time: approx. 65 minutes

In a large saucepan, mix the cucumbers and the onion; add the chicken broth. Heat to a rapid boil on high heat, reduce to low immediately, cover and simmer until vegetables are tender. Remove from the sun, cool somewhat, and refrigerate for a few hours to cool. Mix in the cream, scallions, and salt to taste for the serving. Sprinkle with dill and seasoning.

Per Serving: Calories 316, Fat 24g, Carbs 8g, Protein 13g

Ingredients for 4 servings

- 1 pound of chicken thighs, boneless and dig chunks
- 2 cups of Swiss chard, chopped
- 1 ½ cups of celery stalks, chopped
- 1 teaspoon of turmeric
- 1 tablespoon of chicken stock base
- 10 ounces of can tomato
- 1 cup of coconut milk
- 1 tablespoon of ginger, grated
- 4 garlic cloves, minced
- 1 onion, chopped

Directions and Total Time: approx. 15 minutes

Add ½ cup of coconut milk, broth base, turmeric, tomatoes, ginger, garlic, and onion to the blender and blender and blend until smooth. Transfer blended the mixture to the moment pot along side Swiss chard, celery, and chicken. Stir well. Seal large-sized pot with lid and cook on high for five minutes. Allow to release pressure naturally for just about 10 minutes then release using quick release method. Add remaining copra oil and stir well. Serve and luxuriate in.

Per Serving: Calories 473, Fat 23.9g, Carbs 29.7g, Protein 39.5g

232. Cold Creamy Cucumber Soup

Ingredients for 6 servings

- Juice of 1 lemon
- ½ cup of chopped fresh parsley
- 2 medium cucumbers
- 1 ½ cups of low-sodium chicken broth
- 1 cup of fat-free plain yogurt
- 1 1/2 cups of fat-free half and half
- Salt and ground black pepper, to taste
- Chopped fresh dill

Directions and Total Time: approx. 20 minutes + chilling time

Combine the lemon juice, parsley, and cucumbers in a blender or food processor and puree until smooth. Switch to a plate with half of the puree and set aside. In a medium-size dish, mix the yogurt, half and half, and broth. In the blender, add half the yogurt mixture to the pureed mixture and puree until well blended. In a large-sized container, sprinkle with salt and pepper and refrigerate. With the remaining yogurt mixture and the puree, repeat the process. To eat, mix the soup and garnish it with fresh dill.

Per Serving: Calories 55, Fat 1g, Carbs 5g, Protein 8g

233. Corn Soup

Ingredients for 4 servings

- 2 leeks, chopped
- 2 tablespoons of butter
- 2 garlic cloves, peeled and minced
- 6 ears of corn, kernels stop, cobs reserved
- 2 bay leaves
- 4 tarragon sprigs, chopped
- 1-quart of chicken broth
- Salt and ground black pepper, to taste
- Extra virgin vegetable oil
- 1 tablespoon of fresh chives, chopped

Directions and Total Time: approx. 25 minutes

Set the moment Pot on Sauté mode, add the butter and melt it. Add the garlic and leeks, stir, and cook for 4 minutes. Add the corn, corn cobs, bay leaves, tarragon, and stock to hide everything, cover the moment pot and actually cook on the Soup setting for quarter-hour. Release the pressure, uncover the moment Pot, discard the bay leaves and corn cobs, and transfer everything to a blender. Pulse well to get a smooth soup, add the remainder of the stock and blend again. Add the salt and pepper, stir well, divide into soup bowls, and serve cold with chives and vegetable oil on top.

Per Serving: Calories 55, Fat 1g, Carbs 5g, Protein 8g

Ingredients for 4 servings

- 2 cups of cauliflower florets
- 1 teaspoon of pie spice
- 5 cups of chicken stock
- 3 tablespoons of vegetable oil
- 1 onion, chopped
- ¼ teaspoon of salt

Directions and Total Time: approx. 32 minutes

Add oil into the moment pot and set the pot on sauté mode. Add onion to the pot and sauté for five minutes. Add cauliflower and cook for a moment. Add broth and season with sea salt. Seal large-sized pot with lid and cook on high for twenty-four minutes. Release pressure using an actual quick release method than open the lid. Puree the soup using an immersion blender just until smooth. Add pie spice and stir well. Cook on sauté mode for two minutes. Serve and luxuriate in.

Per Serving: Calories 163, Fat 12.3g, Carbs 6.7g, Protein 7.4g

235. Creamy Chickpea Soup

Ingredients for 4 servings

- 2 tablespoons of olive oil
- 1 shallot, chopped
- 1 celery stalk, diced
- 1 can of chickpeas, drained
- 1 can of crushed tomatoes
- 2 cups of vegetable stock
- 2 cups of water
- Salt and pepper to taste
- ½ cup of Greek yogurt

Directions and Total Time: approx. 45 minutes

Heat oil in a soup pot and stir in the shallot and celery. Cook for 2 minutes until softened then add the chickpeas, tomatoes, stock and water, as well as salt and pepper. Cook on low heat for 15 minutes. Remove from heat and now, stir in the yogurt. Puree the soup with an immersion blender until creamy and smooth. Serve the soup fresh.

Per Serving: Calories 260, Fat 10.1g, Carbs 33.9g, Protein 10.7g

236. Creamy Jalapeno Soup

Ingredients for 10 servings

- 3 tablespoons of butter
- 2 cloves of garlic, minced
- ½ onion, chopped
- ½ bell pepper, chopped
- 2 jalapeño peppers, seeded and chopped
- 3 cups of vegetable stock
- ½ cup of heavy cream
- ¼ teaspoon of paprika
- 1 teaspoon of cumin
- 1 teaspoon of salt
- ½ teaspoon of freshly ground black pepper

Directions and Total Time: approx. 45 minutes

Heat butter in a heavy stockpot over medium-high heat. When the butter is melted, add onion, bell pepper, and jalapeños and sauté until the onion is soft about 5 minutes. Bring to a low/medium simmer and cook until the chicken is thoroughly cooked and the vegetables are tender about 30 minutes. Add water if necessary, during cooking. Stir in the cream, stirring to combine. Transfer to serving bowls and serve hot.

Per Serving: Calories 100, Fat 40g, Carbs 4g, Protein 41g

237. Creamy Squash Soup

Ingredients for 4 servings

- 4 pounds of butternut squash, cubed
- 4 cups of beef broth
- ½ teaspoon of sage
- 1 teaspoon of thyme
- 2 garlic cloves, minced
- 1 onion, chopped
- 2 tablespoons of vegetable oil
- Pepper
- Salt

Directions and Total Time: approx. 15 minutes

Add oil into the moment pot and set the pot on sauté mode. Add garlic and onion to the pot and sauté for five minutes. Add sage, thyme, pepper, and salt and stir for a moment. Add squash and stock. Stir well. Seal large-sized pot with lid and cook on high for 10 minutes. Release the pressure using quick release method than open the lid. Puree the combined soup using a blender until smooth and creamy. Serve and luxuriate in.

Per Serving: Calories 295, Fat 8.1g, Carbs 56.4g, Protein 7.7g

238. Delicious Cauliflower Soup

Ingredients for 4 servings

- 6 cups of cauliflower florets
- ¼ teaspoon of mustard powder
- 3 cups of vegetable stock
- 1 teaspoon of garlic, minced
- 4 ounces of Mascarpone cheese
- 1 ½ cup of Cheddar cheese, shredded
- Salt and pepper

Directions and Total Time: approx. 4 hours and 10 minutes

Add cauliflower, mustard powder, stock, and garlic into the slow cooker and stir well. Cover and cook on low for 4 hours. Stir in Mascarpone cheese and Cheddar cheese. Blend the mixed soup until it is actually smooth, using a blender. Season with pepper and salt. Garnish with parsley and serve.

Per Serving: Calories 96, Fat 6.6g, Carbs 3.8g, Protein 6.2g

239. Egg-Lemon Pasta Soup

Ingredients for 4 servings

- 4 cups of low-sodium, fat-free chicken broth
- 4 ounces of ditalini pasta
- ½ cup of egg substitute or two large whole eggs, if desired
- ½ cup of fresh lemon juice
- Salt and freshly ground pepper to taste
- 4 tablespoons of chopped fresh parsley for garnish
- 1 lemon, thinly sliced for garnish

Directions and Total Time: approx. 15 minutes

Boil the chicken broth in a medium saucepan. Add pasta; bring to a boil again. Remove from the flame. In a cup, pound the eggs, then beat in the lemon juice. Add to this mixture a ladle of broth and stir; switch to a soup pot. Low heat broth, careful not to curdle the eggs. To taste, apply salt and pepper. Divide the soup into four servings, garnish with slices of parsley and lemon, and eat.

Per Serving: Calories 435, Fat 23g, Carbs 20g, Protein 21g

240. Fagioli Pasta Soup

Ingredients for 8 servings

- 2 cups of onions, chopped
- 1 cup of carrots, chopped
- 1 cup of celery, chopped
- 1 pound of cooked chicken thighs, diced
- 4 cups of cooked rotini pasta
- 6 cups of chicken broth
- 4 teaspoons of dried Italian seasoning
- ¼ teaspoon of salt
- 1 can of white beans, rinsed
- 4 cups of baby spinach
- 4 tablespoons of basil, chopped
- 2 tablespoons of olive oil
- ½ cup of Parmigiano-Reggiano cheese, grated

Directions and Total Time: approx. 7 hours and 40 minutes

Add the celery, carrots, onions, pasta and the rest of the ingredients to a slow cooker. Cover and cook the soup for 7 ½ hour on Low heat. Serve warm.

Per Serving: Calories 235, Fat 17.1g, Carbs 12g, Protein 4.6g

241. Fish Soup

Ingredients for 4 servings

- 2 cups of onions, chopped
- 1 cup of carrots, chopped
- 1 cup of celery, chopped
- 1 pound of cooked chicken thighs, diced
- 4 cups of cooked rotini pasta
- 6 cups of chicken broth
- 4 teaspoons of dried Italian seasoning
- ¼ teaspoon of salt
- 1 can of white beans, rinsed
- 4 cups of baby spinach
- 4 tablespoons of basil, chopped
- 2 tablespoons of olive oil
- ½ cup of Parmigiano-Reggiano cheese, grated

Directions and Total Time: approx. 30 minutes

Heat up a small-sized pot with the oil over medium heat, add the onion and therefore the garlic and sauté for five minutes. Add the remainder of the ingredients, toss, simmer over medium heat for quarter-hour more, divide into bowls and serve for lunch.

Per Serving: Calories 198, Fat 8.1g, Carbs 4.2g, Protein 26.4g

242. French Cauliflower Soup

Ingredients for 4 servings

- 2 tablespoons of ghee, melted
- 1 medium-sized shallot, chopped
- 2 garlic cloves, minced
- 1 cup of cauliflower, small florets
- 1 celery stalk, chopped
- 1 cup of half-and-half
- 2 ½ cups of vegetable broth
- A pinch of grated nutmeg
- 1 dried chile negro
- 1/4 teaspoon of ground black pepper
- 1/3 teaspoon of sea salt
- 4 ounces of bleu, crumbled

Directions and Total Time: approx. 10 minutes

Press the "Sauté" button to heat up your Instant Pot. Once hot, melt the ghee. Sauté the shallot and garlic until aromatic or approximately 2 minutes. Now, add the cauliflower, celery stalk, half-and-half, vegetable broth, nutmeg, chile, pepper, and salt. Secure the lid. Choose "Manual" mode and Low pressure; cook for 3 minutes. Once cooking is complete, use a fast pressure release; carefully remove the lid. Ladle into soup bowls, top with bleu, and serve warm. Bon appétit!

Per Serving: Calories 221, Fat 15.7g, Carbs 5.9g, Protein 11.4g

243. Green Chili Soup

Ingredients for 8 servings

- ½ cup of dry navy beans, soaked for an hour in hot water
- 1 onion diced
- 3 New Mexico green chili peppers, chopped
- 5 cloves of garlic, minced
- 1 cup of cauliflower, diced
- 4 cups of vegetable stock
- ¼ cup of fresh cilantro, chopped
- 1 teaspoon of ground coriander
- 1 teaspoon of ground cumin
- 1 teaspoon of salt

Directions and Total Time: approx. 2 hours

Put the ingredients, into a medium/large, heavy stockpot. Bring to a low/medium simmer and cook until the beans are tender about 60 minutes. Add water if necessary, during cooking. Using an immersion blender, blend the soup. Return the soup to a simmer. Transfer the soup to serving bowls.

Per Serving: Calories 121, Fat 5g, Carbs 13g, Protein 22g

244. Grilled Tomatoes Soup

Ingredients for 4 servings

- 2 pounds of tomatoes
- ½ cup of shallot, chopped
- 1 tablespoon of avocado oil
- ½ teaspoon of ground black pepper
- ¼ teaspoon of minced garlic
- 1 tablespoon of dried basil
- 3 cups of low-sodium chicken broth

Directions and Total Time: approx. 20 minutes

Cut the tomatoes into halves and grill them in the preheated to 390F grill for 1 minute from each side. After this, transfer the grilled tomatoes to the blender and blend until smooth. Place the shallot and avocado oil in the saucepan and roast it until light brown. Add blended grilled tomatoes, ground black pepper, and minced garlic. Bring the soup to boil and sprinkle with dried basil. Simmer the soup for 2 minutes more.

Per Serving: Calories 72, Fat 0.9g, Carbs 13.4g, Protein 4.1g

245. Ground Beef Soup

Ingredients for 4 servings

- 1-pound of lean ground beef
- ½ cup of onion, chopped
- 2 teaspoons of lemon-pepper seasoning blend
- 1 cup of beef broth
- 2 cups of water
- 1/3 cup of white rice, uncooked
- 3 cups of frozen mixed vegetables
- 1 tablespoon of sour cream

Directions and Total Time: approx. 40 minutes

Spray a saucepan with cooking oil and place it over medium heat. Toss in onion and ground beef, then sauté until brown. Stir in broth and rest of the ingredients, then boil it. Reduce heat to a simmer, then cover the soup to cook for 30 minutes. Garnish with sour cream. Enjoy.

Per Serving: Calories 223, Fat 20g, Carbs 23g, Protein 20g

246. Ground Pork and Tomatoes Soup

Ingredients for 4 servings

- 1 pound of pork meat, ground
- Salt and black pepper to the taste
- 2 garlic cloves, minced
- 2 teaspoons of thyme, dried
- 2 tablespoons of vegetable oil
- 4 cups of beef broth
- A pinch of saffron powder
- 15 ounces of canned tomatoes, crushed
- 1 tablespoons of parsley, chopped

Directions and Total Time: approx. 50 minutes

Heat up a large-sized pot with the oil over medium heat, add the meat and therefore the garlic and brown for five minutes. Add the remainder of the prepared ingredients except the parsley, bring back a simmer and cook for 25 minutes. Divide the soup into bowls, sprinkle the parsley on top and serve.

Per Serving: Calories 372, Fat 17.3g, Carbs 28.4g, Protein 17.4g

247. Ham and Navy Bean Soup

Ingredients for 8 servings

- 1 pound of white beans, soaked for 1 hour and drained
- 1 carrot, peeled and chopped
- 1 tablespoon of extra virgin vegetable oil
- 1 yellow onion, peeled and chopped
- 3 garlic cloves, peeled and minced
- 1 tomato, cored, peeled and chopped
- 1 pound of ham, chopped
- Salt and ground black pepper, to taste
- 4 cups of water
- 4 cups of vegetable stock
- 1 teaspoon of dried mint
- 1 teaspoon of paprika
- 1 teaspoon of dried thyme

Directions and Total Time: approx. 25 minutes

Set the moment Pot on Sauté mode, add the oil, and warmth it up. Add the carrot, onion, garlic, tomato, stir, and cook for five minutes. Add the beans, ham, salt, pepper, water, stock, mint, paprika, and thyme, stir, cover, and cook on the Bean/Chili setting for quarter-hour. Release the pressure for just about 10 minutes, uncover the moment Pot, divide into soup bowls, and serve.

Per Serving: Calories 177, Fat 2g, Carbs 26g, Protein 14g

248. Italian Salsa Chicke Soup

Ingredients for 6 servings

- 1 pound of chicken breasts, boneless and cut into chunks
- 3 cups of chicken stock
- 8 ounces of cream cheese
- 1 1/2 cups of salsa
- 1 teaspoon of Italian seasoning
- 1 tablespoon of fresh parsley, chopped
- Pepper to taste
- Salt to taste

Directions and Total Time: approx. 35 minutes

Add all ingredients except cream cheese and parsley into the instant pot and stir well. Seal large-sized pot with lid and cook on high for 25 minutes. Once done, release pressure using quick release. Remove lid. Remove chicken from pot and shred using a fork. Return shredded chicken to the pot. Add cream cheese and stir well and cook in sauté mode until cheese is melted. Serve and enjoy.

Per Serving: Calories 301, Fat 19.4g, Carbs 5.6g, Protein 26.1g

249. Italian Shredded Pork Soup

Ingredients for 8 servings

- 2 medium sweet potatoes
- 2 cups of fresh kale, chopped
- 1 large onion, chopped
- 4 cloves of garlic, minced
- 1 2 ½–3 ½ pound of boneless pork shoulder butt roast
- 1 (14-ounce) can of cannellini beans
- 1½ teaspoons of Italian seasoning
- ½ teaspoon of salt
- ½ teaspoon of pepper
- 3 (14½-ounce) cans of chicken broth
- Sour cream (optional)

Directions and Total Time: approx. 8 hours and 20 minutes

Coat slow cooker with nonstick cooking spray or olive oil. Place the cubed sweet potatoes, kale, garlic, and onion into the slow cooker. Add the pork shoulder on top of the potatoes. Add the beans, Italian seasoning, salt, and pepper. Pour the chicken broth over the meat. Cook on low for 8 hours. Serve with sour cream, if desired.

Per Serving: Calories 283, Fat 13g, Carbs 24g, Protein 18g

250. Kale and Carrot Soup

Ingredients for 5 servings

- 2 tablespoons of extra-virgin olive oil
- 4 medium carrots, chopped
- 2 celery stalks, chopped
- 1 large red onion, chopped finely
- 2 garlic cloves, crushed
- ½ pound of fresh kale, tough ribs removed and chopped
- 4 ½ cups of vegetable broth
- Salt and ground black pepper, as required

Directions and Total Time: approx. 55 minutes

Heat the oil in a large-sized soup pan over medium heat and cook the carrot, celery, onion, and garlic for about 8-10 minutes, stirring frequently. Add the kale and cook for about 5 minutes, stirring twice. Add the prepared broth and bring it to a boil. Cook, partially covered for about 20 minutes. Stir in salt and black pepper and remove from the heat. With an immersion blender, blend the soup until smooth. Serve immediately.

Per Serving: Calories 140, Fat 6.9g, Carbs 13.8g, Protein 2.6g

251. Kale Beef Soup

Ingredients for 4 servings

- 1 pound of stew meat
- 1 teaspoon of cayenne pepper
- 3 garlic cloves, crushed
- 4 cups of chicken stock
- 2 tablespoons of vegetable oil
- 1 cup of kale, chopped
- 1 onion, sliced
- ¼ teaspoon of black pepper
- ½ teaspoon of salt

Directions and Total Time: approx. 43 minutes

Add oil into the moment pot and set the pot on sauté mode. Add garlic and onion and sauté for 3 minutes. Add meat and sauté for five minutes more. Add broth and season with cayenne pepper, pepper, and salt. Stir well. Seal large-sized pot with lid and cook on high for 25 minutes. Release pressure using an actual quick release method than open the lid. Add kale and stir well and let sit for 10 minutes. Stir well and serve.

Per Serving: Calories 333, Fat 15.6g, Carbs 6.3g, Protein 40.3g

252. Kale Pot Cheese Soup

Ingredients for 4 servings

- 5 cups of fresh kale, chopped
- 1 tablespoon of vegetable oil
- 1 cup of pot cheese, dig small chunks
- 3 cups of chicken stock
- ½ teaspoon of black pepper
- ½ teaspoon of sea salt

Directions and Total Time: approx. 5 minutes

Add all ingredients except pot cheese into the moment pot and stir well. Seal large-sized pot with lid and cook on high for five minutes. Release pressure using an actual quick release method than open the lid. Add pot cheese and stir well. Serve hot and luxuriate in.

Per Serving: Calories 152, Fat 5.6g, Carbs 11.7g, Protein 13.9g

253. Lamb and Potatoes Stew

Ingredients for 4 servings

- 2 pounds of lamb shoulder, boneless and cubed
- Salt and black pepper to the taste
- 1 yellow onion, chopped
- 3 tablespoons of olive oil
- 3 tomatoes, grated
- 2 cups of chicken stock
- 2 and ½ pounds of gold potatoes, cubed
- ¾ cup of green olives, pitted and sliced
- 1 tablespoon of cilantro, chopped

Directions and Total Time: approx. 1 hour and 30 minutes

Heat a pot with the oil over medium-high heat, add the lamb, and brown for 5 minutes on each side. Continue to sauté for approximately about another 5 minutes after adding the onion. Add the rest of the remaining listed ingredients, bring to a simmer, cook over medium heat, and cook for 1 hour and 10 minutes. Divide the stew into bowls and serve.

Per Serving: Calories 411, Fat 17.4g, Carbs 25.5g, Protein 34.3g

254. Lamb Stew

Ingredients for 4 servings

- 2 pounds of lamb, cut into chunks
- 1 teaspoon of dried oregano
- 1 tablespoon of olive oil
- 1 tablespoon of garlic, minced
- 1 cup of tomatoes, chopped
- 1 cup of olives, pitted and sliced
- 1 onion, chopped
- ½ cup of cilantro, chopped
- Pepper
- Salt

Directions and Total Time: approx. 40 minutes

Add oil into the instant pot and set pot on sauté mode. Add onion, garlic and oregano and cook for 5 minutes. Add meat and sauté for 5 minutes. Add remaining ingredients and stir well. Cover and cook on high temperature for approximately 20 minutes. Once done, allow to release pressure naturally. Remove the lid.

Per Serving: Calories 514, Fat 23.9g, Carbs 7.4g, Protein 64.9g

255 Leek, Rice and Potato Soup

Ingredients for 6 servings

- 1/3 cup of rice
- 4 cups of water
- 2-3 potatoes, diced
- 1 small onion, cut
- 1 leek, halved lengthwise and sliced
- 3 tablespoons of olive oil
- lemon juice, to serve

Directions and Total Time: approx. 26 minutes

Heat a soup pot over medium heat. Add olive oil and onion and sauté for 2 minutes. Add leeks and potatoes and stir for a few minutes more. Fill in three cups of water, boil, reduce heat and simmer for 5 minutes. Add the very well washed rice and simmer for 10 minutes. Serve with lemon juice to taste.

Per Serving: Calories 180, Fat 11g, Carbs 25g, Protein 5g

256. Leek Soup

Ingredients for 6 servings

- 2 gold potatoes, chopped
- 1 cup of cauliflower florets
- Black pepper to the taste
- 5 leeks, chopped
- 4 garlic cloves, minced
- 1 yellow onion, chopped
- 3 tablespoons of olive oil
- A handful of parsley, chopped
- 4 cups of low-sodium chicken stock

Directions and Total Time: approx. 1 hour and 25 minutes

Heat a pot with the oil over medium-high heat, add onion and garlic, stir, and cook for 5 minutes. Add potatoes, cauliflower, black pepper, leeks, and stock, stir, bring to a simmer, cook over medium heat for 30 minutes, blend using an immersion blender, add parsley, stir, ladle into bowls, and serve.

Per Serving: Calories 150, Fat 8g, Carbs 7g, Protein 8g

257. Lemon Orzo Chicken Soup

Ingredients for 8 servings

- 1 tablespoon of extra-virgin olive oil
- 1 cup of chopped onion
- ½ cup of chopped carrots
- ½ cup of chopped celery
- 3 garlic cloves, minced
- 9 cups of low-sodium chicken broth
- 2 cups of shredded cooked chicken breast
- ½ cup of freshly squeezed lemon juice
- Zest of 1 lemon, grated
- 1 to 2 teaspoons of dried oregano
- 8 ounces of cooked orzo pasta

Directions and Total Time: approx. 30 minutes

In a large-sized pot, heat the oil over medium heat and add the onion, carrots, celery, and garlic and cook for just about 5 minutes, until the onions are translucent. Add the broth and bring to a boil. Reduce to a simmer, then cover, and then cook for 10 more minutes, until the flavors meld. Then add the prepared shredded chicken, lemon juice and zest, and oregano. Plate the orzo in serving bowls first, then add the chicken soup.

Per Serving: Calories 215, Fat 5g, Carbs 27g, Protein 16g

258. Lemony Lamb Soup

Ingredients for 4 servings

- ½ cup of vegetable oil
- 2 pounds of lamb meat, cubed
- 5 cups of water
- 5 spring onions, chopped
- 2 tablespoons of dill, chopped
- Juice of 2 lemons
- Salt and black pepper to the taste
- 3 eggs, whisked
- 1 cup of baby spinach

Directions and Total Time: approx. 1 hour and 15 minutes

Heat up a large-sized pot with the oil over medium heat, add the lamb and brown for just about 10 minutes stirring from time to time. Add the chopped onions and sauté for 3 minutes more. Add the water, salt and pepper, stir and simmer over medium heat for half-hour. Add the spinach, eggs whisked with the juice and a few of the soup, whisk the soup well and cook for 20 minutes more. Add the dill, stir, ladle the soup into bowls and serve.

Per Serving: Calories 275, Fat 28.5g, Carbs 2.8g, Protein 5g

259. Lentil, Barley and Mushroom Soup

Ingredients for 6 servings

- 2 medium leeks
- 10 white mushrooms
- 3 garlic cloves
- 2 bay leaves
- 2 cans of tomatoes
- 3/4 cup of red lentils
- 1/3 cup of barley
- 3 tablespoons of olive oil
- 1 teaspoon of paprika
- 1 teaspoon of summer savory
- ½ teaspoon of cumin

Directions and Total Time: approx. 42 minutes

Cook oil in a large saucepan over medium-high heat. Sauté leeks and mushrooms for 3 to 4 minutes or until softened. Add cumin, paprika, savory and tomatoes, lentils, barley, and 5 cups cold water. Season with salt and pepper. Cover and bring to the boil. Reduce heat to low. Simmer for 37 minutes.

Per Serving: Calories 314, Fat 19g, Carbs 29g, Protein 5g

260. Lentils Soup

Ingredients for 6 servings

- 1 yellow onion, chopped
- 2 tablespoons of vegetable oil
- 2 celery stalks, chopped
- 1 carrot, sliced
- 1/3 cup of parsley, chopped
- ½ cup of cilantro, chopped
- 2 and ½ tablespoons of garlic, minced
- 2 tablespoons of ginger, grated
- 1 teaspoon of turmeric powder
- 2 teaspoons of sweet paprika
- 1 teaspoon of cinnamon powder
- 1 and ¼ cups of red lentils
- 15 ounces of canned chickpeas
- 28 ounces of canned tomatoes and juice, crushed
- 8 cups of chicken broth
- A pinch of salt and black pepper

Directions and Total Time: approx. 55 minutes

Heat up a large-sized pot with the oil over medium heat, add the onion, ginger, garlic, celery and carrots and sauté for five minutes. Add the remainder of the ingredients, stir, bring back a simmer over medium heat and cook for 35 minutes. Ladle the cooked soup into bowls and serve directly.

Per Serving: Calories 238, Fat 7.3g, Carbs 32g, Protein 14g

261. Loaded Tuscan Rapini Soup

Ingredients for 4 servings

- 2 tablespoons of butter, melted
- 1/2 cup of leeks, sliced
- 2 garlic cloves, minced
- 4 cups of broccoli rabe, broken into pieces
- 2 cups of water
- 2 cups of broth, preferably homemade
- 1 zucchini, shredded
- 1 carrot, trimmed and grated
- Sea salt, to taste
- 1/4 teaspoon of ground black pepper

Directions and Total Time: approx. 8 minutes

Press the "Sauté" button to heat up your Instant Pot; now, melt the butter. Cook the leeks for about 2 minutes or until softened. Add minced garlic and cook a further 40 seconds. Add the remaining ingredients. Secure the lid. Choose "Manual" mode and Low pressure; cook for 3 minutes. Once cooking is complete, use a fast pressure release; carefully remove the lid. Bon appétit!

Per Serving: Calories 95, Fat 6.7g, Carbs 5.2g, Protein 4.2g

262. Mediterranean Tomato Soup

Ingredients for 4 servings

- 2 red bell peppers, unseeded, chopped
- 2 medium onions, chopped
- 2-3 garlic cloves, minced
- 7–8 tomatoes, chopped
- 0.4 quarts of chicken broth
- Salt and pepper, to taste
- 3 tablespoons of olive oil
- 1 tablespoon of vinegar

Directions and Total Time: approx. 35 minutes

Heat oil in a large-sized saucepan and cook onion, garlic, and bell peppers for 5–6 minutes or until bell peppers are roasted well. Add tomatoes, salt, pepper, and vinegar; stir-fry for 4–5 minutes. Add chicken broth and cover with lid. Let it cook for about 20 minutes on low heat. When tomatoes are cooked well, puree the soup with the help of an electric beater. Simmer for 1–2 minutes. Add to a large-sized serving dish and top with desired herbs. Serve and enjoy.

Per Serving: Calories 318, Fat 97g, Carbs 60g, Protein 1.7g

263. Mediterranean Vegetable Soup

Ingredients for 6 servings

- 1 can of no-salt-added diced tomatoes
- 2 cups of low-sodium vegetable broth
- 1 green bell pepper, seeded and chopped
- 1 red or yellow bell pepper, chopped
- 4 ounces of mushrooms, sliced
- 2 zucchinis, chopped
- 1 small red onion, chopped
- 3 garlic cloves, minced
- 1 tablespoon of extra-virgin olive oil
- 2 teaspoons of dried oregano
- 1 teaspoon of paprika
- 1 teaspoon of sea salt
- ½ teaspoon of freshly ground black pepper
- Juice of 1 lemon

Directions and Total Time: approx. 8 hours and 20 minutes

In a slow cooker, combine the tomatoes, vegetable broth, green and red bell peppers, mushrooms, zucchini, onion, garlic, olive oil, oregano, paprika, salt, and black pepper. Stir to mix well. Cover the cooker and cook for 6 to 8 hours on Low heat. Stir in the lemon juice before serving.

Per Serving: Calories 91, Fat 3g, Carbs 16g, Protein 3g

264. Mixed Chicken Soup

Ingredients for 8 servings

- 1 whole chicken, cut into smaller pieces
- 1 sweet onion, chopped
- 2 celery stalks, sliced
- 2 carrots, sliced
- 2 red bell peppers, cored and diced
- 1 zucchini, cubed
- 2 potatoes, peeled and cubed
- 2 tomatoes, peeled and diced
- 2 cups of vegetable stock
- 8 cups of water
- Salt and pepper to taste
- 1 tablespoon of lemon juice
- 2 tablespoons of chopped parsley for serving

Directions and Total Time: approx. 1 hour and 45 minutes

Dissolve 2 tbsp. of butter in a large pot set on moderate heat. Mix in the thyme and halibut and cook.

Per Serving: Calories 103, Fat 1.6g, Carbs 15.4g, Protein 7.3g

265. Moroccan Pumpkin Soup

Ingredients for 6 servings

- 1 leek, white part only
- 3 cloves of garlic
- ½ teaspoon of ground ginger
- ½ teaspoon of ground cinnamon
- ½ teaspoon of ground cumin
- 2 carrots
- 2 pounds of pumpkin
- 1/3 cup of chickpeas
- 5 tablespoons of olive oil
- juice of ½ lemon

Directions and Total Time: approx. 61 minutes

Cook oil in a huge saucepan and sauté leek, garlic and 2 teaspoons of salt, stirring occasionally, until soft. Add cinnamon, ginger and cumin and stir. Add in carrots, pumpkin and chickpeas. Stir to combine. Add the prepared 5 cups of water and bring the soup to the boil, then reduce heat and simmer for 50 minutes. Pullout from heat, add lemon juice and blend the soup. Heat again over low heat for 4-5 minutes. Serve topped with parsley sprigs.

Per Serving: Calories 241, Fat 21g, Carbs 36g, Protein 4g

• Mushroom Spinach Soup

Ingredients for 4 servings

- 1 cup of spinach, cleaned and chopped
- 100 grams of mushrooms, chopped
- 1 onion
- 6 garlic cloves
- ½ teaspoon of red chili powder
- Salt and black pepper, to taste
- 3 tablespoons of buttermilk
- 1 teaspoon of almond flour
- 2 cups of chicken broth
- 3 tablespoons of butter
- ¼ cup of fresh cream for garnish

Directions and Total Time: approx. 25 minutes

Heat butter in a large-sized pan and add onions and garlic. Sauté for about 3 minutes and add spinach, salt and red chili powder. Sauté for about 4 minutes and add mushrooms. Transfer into a blender and blend to make a puree. Return to the pan and add buttermilk and almond flour for a creamy texture. Mix well and simmer for about 2 minutes. Garnish with fresh cream and serve hot.

Per Serving: Calories 160, Fat 13.3g, Carbs 7g, Protein 4.7g

267. Navy Bean Soup

Ingredients for 6 servings

- 1 cup of celery, chopped
- 1 cup of carrots, chopped
- 1 yellow onion, chopped
- 6 cups of veggie stock
- 4 garlic cloves, minced
- 2 cup of navy beans, dried
- ½ teaspoon of basil, dried
- ½ teaspoon of sage, dried
- 1 teaspoon of thyme, dried
- A pinch of salt and black pepper

Directions and Total Time: approx. 8 hours and 10 minutes

In your slow cooker, combine the beans with the stock and therefore the remainder of the prepared ingredients, put the lid on and cook on Low for 8 hours. Divide the soup into bowls and serve directly.

Per Serving: Calories 264, Fat 17.5g, Carbs 23.7g, Protein 11.5g

268. Old Styled Veggie Soup

Ingredients for 6 servings

- 3 tablespoons of butter
- 1 teaspoon of salt
- 3 stalks of diced celery
- 1 diced onion
- 2 large carrots diced
- 1 teaspoon of dried parsley
- 1 can of whole peeled tomatoes, chopped, and juice reserved
- 1/2 teaspoon of ground black pepper
- 1 teaspoon of paprika
- 1 tablespoon of Worcestershire sauce
- 3 tablespoons of soy sauce
- 2 quarts of beef broth

Directions and Total Time: approx. 30 minutes

In a large-sized saucepan on medium flame, melt the butter. Add the onion, celery, & carrots and sauté till they are transparent. Place the tomatoes, pepper, tomato juice, salt, Worcestershire sauce, parsley, soy sauce, & paprika. Pour in the beef broth. Bring to a simmer, then lower to a low flame and cook for another 25 minutes, just until the veggies are soft and the flavors are thoroughly combined.

Per Serving: Calories 123, Fat 6.8g, Carbs 11.4g, Protein 5.9g

269. Oyster Stew

Ingredients for 6 servings

- 2 garlic cloves, minced
- ¼ cup of jarred roasted red peppers
- 2 teaspoons of oregano, chopped
- 1-pound of lamb meat, ground
- 1 tablespoon of red wine vinegar
- Salt and black pepper to the taste
- 1 teaspoon of red pepper flakes
- 2 tablespoons of olive oil
- 1 and ½ cups of chicken stock
- 36 oysters, shucked
- 1 and ½ cups of canned black-eyed peas, drained

Directions and Total Time: approx. 1 hour and 20 minutes

Heat the oil in a large-sized saucepan over medium heat, add the meat and garlic and cook for 5 minutes. Add the peppers and the rest of the ingredients, bring to a simmer and cook for 15 minutes. Divide the stew into bowls and serve.

Per Serving: Calories 264, Fat 9.3g, Carbs 2.3g, Protein 1.2g

270. Red Clam Chowder

Ingredients for 10 servings

- 3 large stalks of celery, chopped
- 1 large white onion, chopped
- 4 (8-ounce) jars of clam juice
- 4 cloves of fresh garlic, chopped
- Creole seasoning of choice to taste
- Tabasco sauce to taste
- ¼ cup of Worcestershire sauce
- ¼ cup of freshly squeezed lemon juice
- 3 cups of water
- 1 ½ (14.5-ounce) cans of crushed tomatoes
- 6 cups of raw diced potatoes
- 4 (10-ounce) cans of whole baby clams
- Hot sauce
- Crusty country bread

Directions and Total Time: approx. 20 minutes

Combine all the ingredients in a big kettle, except the clams, the hot sauce, and the bread. For 25-30 minutes, bring to a low boil, cover, and prepare. Add the clams and proceed to cook for another 15–20 minutes on a medium simmer. Serve hot with hot sauce and crusty country bread, if desired.

Per Serving: Calories 226, Fat 4g, Carbs 22g, Protein 24g

271. Red Lentil Soup

Ingredients for 4 servings

- 2 tablespoons of nutritional yeast
- 1 cup of red lentil, washed
- ½ tablespoons of garlic, minced
- 4 cups of vegetable stock
- 1 teaspoon of salt
- 2 cups of kale, shredded
- 3 cups of mixed vegetables

Directions and Total Time: approx. 25 minutes

To start with, place all the ingredients needed to make the soup into a large pot. Heat the large-sized pot over medium-high heat and bring the mixture to a boil. Once it starts boiling, lower the heat to low. Allow the soup to simmer. Simmer it for 1o to 15 minutes or until cooked. Serve and enjoy.

Per Serving: Calories 212, Fat 11.9g, Carbs 31.7g, Protein 7.3g

272. Roasted Pepper Soup

Ingredients for 4 servings

- 2 tomatoes, halved
- 3 red bell peppers, halved and seeded
- 1 yellow onion, quartered
- 2 garlic cloves, peeled and halved
- 2 tablespoons of olive oil
- 2 cups of veggie stock
- A pinch of salt and black pepper
- 2 tablespoons of tomato paste
- ¼ cup of fresh parsley, chopped
- ¼ teaspoon of Italian seasoning
- ¼ teaspoon of sweet paprika

Directions and Total Time: approx. 65 minutes

To start with, place all the ingredients needed to make the soup into a large pot. Heat the large-sized pot over medium-hiSpread the bell peppers, tomatoes, onion, and garlic on a baking sheet lined with parchment paper. Add the oil, salt, and pepper and bake at 375°F for 45 minutes. Heat a pot with the stock over medium heat, add the roasted vegetables and the rest of the ingredients, stir, bring to a simmer and cook for 10 minutes. Blend the mix using an immersion blender. Divide the soup into bowls and serve.

Per Serving: Calories 273, Fat 11.2g, Carbs 15.7g, Protein 5.6g

273. Roasted Vegetable Soup

Ingredients for 4 servings

- 1 tablespoon of olive oil
- 5 garlic cloves, peeled
- 0.3 pounds of Potatoes diced (1 cm thick)
- 2 yellow bell peppers, diced
- ½ teaspoons of fresh rosemary, finely chopped
- 1 carrot, halved lengthwise piece
- 1 red onion, in chunks
- 0.4 quarts of carrot juice
- 0.3 pounds of Italian tomatoes, diced
- 1 teaspoon of fresh tarragon
- Salt and pepper, to taste

Directions and Total Time: approx. 35 minutes

Preheat the oven to 400° F. In a baking tray place potatoes, peppers, garlic, carrot, onion, and tomatoes. Drizzle with olive oil and roast for just about 10–15 minutes. In a saucepan add carrot juice, tarragon; let boil a little. Add all roasted vegetables and stir well. Let it simmer for a few minutes. Season with salt, pepper, and rosemary. Mix well. Serve and enjoy.

Per Serving: Calories 318, Fat 97g, Carbs 60g, Protein 1.7g

274. Sage Pork and Beans Stew

Ingredients for 4 servings

- 2 pounds of pork stew meat, cubed
- 2 tablespoons of olive oil
- 1 sweet onion, chopped
- 1 red bell pepper, chopped
- 3 garlic cloves, minced
- 2 teaspoons of sage, dried
- 4 ounces of canned white beans, drained
- 1 cup of beef stock
- 2 zucchinis, chopped
- 2 tablespoons of tomato paste
- 1 tablespoon of cilantro, chopped

Directions and Total Time: approx. 4 hours and 10 minutes

Brown the beef in the oil over medium heat for 10 minutes before transferring to the slow cooker. Add the other ingredients, except the cilantro, and simmer on high for 4 hours. Divide the stew into bowls, sprinkle the cilantro on top, and serve.

Per Serving: Calories 423, Fat 15.4g, Carbs 27.4g, Protein 43g

275. Sausage and Beans Soup

Ingredients for 4 servings

- 1 pound of Italian sausage, sliced
- ¼ cup of vegetable oil
- 1 carrot, chopped
- 1 yellow onion, chopped
- 1 celery stalk, chopped
- 2 garlic cloves, minced
- ½ pound of kale, chopped
- 4 cups of chicken broth
- 28 ounces of canned cannellini beans
- 1 herb
- 1 teaspoon of rosemary, dried
- Salt and black pepper to the taste
- ½ cup of parmesan, grated

Directions and Total Time: approx. 30 minutes

Heat up a large-sized pot with the oil over medium heat, add the sausage and brown for five minutes. Add the onion, carrots, garlic and celery and sauté for 3 minutes more. Add the remainder of the prepared ingredients except the parmesan, bring back a simmer and cook over medium heat for half-hour. Discard the herb, ladle the soup into bowls, sprinkle the parmesan on top and serve.

Per Serving: Calories 564, Fat 26.5g, Carbs 37.4g, Protein 26.6g

276. Shrimp and Halibut Stew

Ingredients for 6 servings

- 2 garlic cloves, minced
- 2 tablespoons of olive oil
- 1 yellow onion, chopped
- 14 ounces of canned tomatoes, chopped
- 1 tablespoon of orange zest, grated
- 4 and ½ cups of seafood stock
- 1-pound of halibut fillets, boneless, skinless, and cubed
- 20 shrimp, peeled and deveined
- 1 bunch of parsley, chopped
- Salt and white pepper to the taste

Directions and Total Time: approx. 40 minutes

Heat a pot with the oil over medium-high heat, add the onion and the garlic and sauté for 5 minutes. Add the tomatoes, orange zest, and the stock, stir, bring to a boil and simmer for 20 minutes over medium heat. Add the fish and the shrimp, cook for 5 minutes more, divide into bowls, sprinkle the parsley on top, and serve.

Per Serving: Calories 300, Fat 14.3g, Carbs 16.1g, Protein 11g

277. Slow Cooker Stew

Ingredients for 10 servings

- 2 cups of zucchini, cubed
- 2 cups of eggplant, cubed
- 1 can of tomato sauce
- 1 10 ounces of package frozen okra, thawed
- 1 butternut squash, peeled, seeded and diced
- 1 cup of onion, chopped
- 1 clove of garlic, chopped
- ½ cup of vegetable broth
- 1 carrot, thinly sliced
- 1 tomato, chopped
- ⅓ cup of raisins
- ¼ teaspoon of paprika
- ½ teaspoon of ground cumin
- ½ teaspoon of ground turmeric
- ¼ teaspoon of ground cinnamon
- ¼ teaspoon of crushed red pepper

Directions and Total Time: approx. 10 hours and 30 minutes

In a slow cooker, mix everything, cover and cook for 10 hours or until the vegetables are tender.

Per Serving: Calories 123, Fat 0.5g, Carbs 22g, Protein 2.7g

278. Spiced Lentil Soup

Ingredients for 8 servings

- 2 tablespoons of extra virgin olive oil
- 2 shallots, chopped
- 2 garlic cloves, chopped
- 2 red bell peppers, cored and diced
- 2 carrots, diced
- 1 celery stalk, diced
- ½ teaspoon of mustard seeds
- ½ teaspoon of cumin seeds
- 1 can of crushed tomatoes
- 3 cups of vegetable stock
- 3 cups of water
- 1 cup of green lentils
- Salt and pepper to taste
- Yogurt for serving

Directions and Total Time: approx. 45 minutes

Heat oil in a soup pot and stir in the shallots and garlic. Cook for 2 minutes then add the rest of the ingredients. Season to taste and simmer for 30 minutes on low heat. Serve the soup warm and fresh, topped with plain yogurt or freshly chopped parsley.

Per Serving: Calories 143, Fat 4g, Carbs 20.2g, Protein 7.3g

279. Spicy Mushroom Soup

Ingredients for 2 servings

- 1 cup of mushrooms, chopped
- ½ teaspoon of flavorer
- 2 teaspoons of garam masala
- 3 tablespoons of vegetable oil
- 1 teaspoon of fresh juice
- 5 cups of chicken broth
- ¼ cup of fresh celery, chopped
- 2 garlic cloves, crushed
- 1 onion, chopped
- ½ teaspoon of black pepper
- 1 teaspoon of sea salt

Directions and Total Time: approx. 11 minutes

Add oil into the moment pot and set the pot on sauté mode. Add garlic and onion to the pot and sauté for five minutes. Add flavorer and garam masala and cook for a moment. Add remaining ingredients and stir well. Seal large-sized pot with lid and cook on high for five minutes. Release pressure using an actual quick release method than open the lid. Puree the soup employing a blender and serve.

Per Serving: Calories 244, Fat 22.8g, Carbs 10.2g, Protein 3.9g

280. Spinach and Feta Cheese Soup

Ingredients for 4 servings

- 14 ounces of frozen spinach
- 1 ounce of feta cheese
- 1 large onion or 4-5 scallions
- 2-3 tablespoons of light cream
- 3-4 tablespoons of olive oil
- 1-2 cloves of garlic
- 4 cups of water

Directions and Total Time: approx. 32 minutes

Heat the oil in a cooking pot. Add the onion and spinach and sauté together for a few minutes, until just softened. Add garlic and stir for a minute. Remove from heat. Add about 2 cups of water, hot and season with salt and pepper. Bring back to the boil, then reduce the heat and simmer for around 30 minutes. Blend soup in a blender. Crumble the cheese with a fork. Stir in the crumbled feta cheese and the cream. Serve hot.

Per Serving: Calories 251, Fat 13g, Carbs 38g, Protein 5g

281. Spinach and Kale Soup

Ingredients for 4 servings

- 3 ounces of vegan butter
- 1 cup of fresh spinach, chopped coarsely
- 1 cup of fresh kale, chopped coarsely
- 1 large avocado
- 3 tablespoons of chopped fresh mint leaves
- 3 ½ cups of coconut cream
- 1 cup of vegetable broth
- Salt and black pepper to taste
- 1 lime, juiced

Directions and Total Time: approx. 10 minutes

Melt the ounces of vegan butter in a medium pot over medium heat and sauté the kale and spinach until wilted for 3 minutes. Turn the heat off. Stir in the remaining ingredients and using an immersion blender, puree the soup until smooth. Dish the soup and serve warm.

Per Serving: Calories 380, Fat 10g, Carbs 30g, Protein 20g

282. Spinach Chicken Stew

Ingredients for 4 servings

- 2 cups of spinach, chopped
- 1 pound of chicken breasts, skinless, boneless, and cut into chunks
- 1/2 cup of can tomato, crushed
- 1 cup of chicken stock
- 1 onion, chopped
- 1 tablespoon of olive oil
- Salt and pepper

Directions and Total Time: approx. 35 minutes

Set the instant pot into a sauté mode after adding oil to the inner pot. Add chicken and onion and sauté for 5 minutes. Add remaining ingredients and stir well. Seal pot with lid and cook on low for 20 minutes. Once done, allow the release of pressure naturally for approximately about 10 minutes, then release remaining using quick release. Remove lid. Stir well and serve.

Per Serving: Calories 266, Fat 12.2g, Carbs 4.2g, Protein 33.9g

283. Spinach Lentil Soup

Ingredients for 4 servings

- 4 cups of spinach
- 2 cups of green lentils
- 4 cups of vegetable stock
- 1 teaspoon of Italian seasoning
- 14 ounces can of tomato, chopped
- 2 teaspoons of thyme, chopped
- 1 teaspoon of garlic, minced
- 1 carrot, chopped
- 1 onion, chopped
- 1 celery stalks, chopped
- Pepper to taste
- Salt to taste

Directions and Total Time: approx. 40 minutes

Add all ingredients except spinach into the inner pot of the instant pot and stir well. Seal pot and cook on high for 25 minutes. Once done, allow to release pressure naturally for 10 minutes, then release remaining using quick release. Remove lid. Add spinach and stir well and cook on sauté mode for 5 minutes. Stir well and serve.

Per Serving: Calories 398, Fat 1.7g, Carbs 69.8g, Protein 27.5g

284. Spinach Soup

Ingredients for 6 servings

- 14 ounces of frozen spinach
- 1 large onion
- 1 carrot
- 4 cups of water
- 3-4 tablespoons of olive oil
- 1/4 cup of white rice
- 1-2 cloves of garlic, crushed

Directions and Total Time: approx. 31 minutes

Cook oil in a cooking pot, stir in onion and carrot and sauté together for a few minutes, until just softened. Add chopped garlic and rice and stir for a minute. Remove from heat. Add in the chopped spinach along with about 2 cups of hot water and season with salt and pepper. Bring back to an actual boil, then reduce the heat and simmer for around 30 minutes.

Per Serving: Calories 291, Fat 16g, Carbs 29g, Protein 7g

Ingredients for 6 servings

- 4 cups of low-sodium, fat-free chicken broth
- 2 cloves of fresh garlic, minced
- 4 scallions, chopped
- ¼ teaspoon of ground pepper
- 5 ounces of fresh cheese-filled tortellini
- 2 cups of coarsely chopped fresh spinach leaves
- Fresh grated Parmesan cheese

Directions and Total Time: approx. 20 minutes

Heat broth in a pot and add garlic, scallions, and pepper. Bring it to an actual boil, then you need to actually reduce to medium heat. Add tortellini and cook for 10 minutes. Add spinach and cook for approximately an additional 5 minutes or until pasta is tender. Transfer to 4 bowls and serve with a sprinkle of Parmesan cheese, if desired.

Per Serving: Calories 223, Fat 6g, Carbs 33g, Protein 11g

286. Split Pea Soup

Ingredients for 6 servings

- 1 tablespoon of olive oil
- 2 cups of onion, chopped
- 2 cups of carrot, chopped
- 2 cups of celery, chopped
- ½ tablespoon of garlic, minced
- 1 cup of yellow split peas
- 1 cup of green split peas
- 8 cups of chicken broth
- 1 ½ teaspoon of poultry seasoning blend
- 1 teaspoon of salt

Directions and Total Time: approx. 2 hours and 45 minutes

Sauté the garlic, celery, carrot and onion with oil in a Dutch oven until soft. Stir in the broth, split peas, seasoning and salt. Cover, cook to a boil then reduce the heat to a simmer and cook for 2 ½ hours. Puree this soup and serve warm.

Per Serving: Calories 257, Fat 8.8g, Carbs 40.1g, Protein 5.3g

287. Spring Vegetable Soup

Ingredients for 4 servings

- 1 cup of fresh green beans
- ¾ cup of celery
- ½ cup of onion
- ½ cup of carrots
- ½ cup of mushrooms
- ½ cup of frozen corn
- 1 medium Roma tomato
- 2 tablespoons of olive oil
- ½ cup of frozen corn
- 4 cups of vegetable broth
- 1 teaspoon of dried oregano leaves
- 1 teaspoon of garlic powder

Directions and Total Time: approx. 55 minutes

Place a suitably-sized cooking pot over medium heat and add olive oil to heat. Toss in onion and celery, then sauté until soft. Stir in the corn and rest of the ingredients and cook the soup to boil. Now reduce its heat to a simmer and cook for 45 minutes. Serve warm.

Per Serving: Calories 115, Fat 13g, Carbs 27g, Protein 3g

288. Squash and Turmeric Soup

Ingredients for 4 servings

- 4 cups of low-sodium vegetable broth
- 2 medium zucchini squash
- 2 medium yellow crookneck squash
- 1 small onion
- 1/2 cup of frozen green peas
- 2 tablespoons of olive oil
- 1/2 cup of plain non-fat yogurt
- 2 teaspoons of turmeric

Directions and Total Time: approx. 40 minutes

Warm the broth in a saucepan on medium heat. Toss in onion, squash, and zucchini. Let it simmer for approximately 25 minutes then add oil and green peas. Cook for another 5 minutes then allow it to cool. Puree the soup using a handheld blender then add Greek yogurt and turmeric. Refrigerate it overnight and serve fresh.

Per Serving: Calories 100, Fat 10g, Carbs 21g, Protein 4g

289. Squash Soup with Peppers

Ingredients for 2 servings

- ½ pound of butternut squash, chunks
- 1 cup of kale, torn
- 1 red bell pepper, chopped
- 1 cup of yellow bell pepper, chopped
- 5-6 green pitted olives
- 2 stalks of celery, chopped
- 4 cups of water
- 1 teaspoon of oregano
- 1 teaspoon of Dijon mustard
- Pinch of salt and white pepper

Directions and Total Time: approx. 25 minutes

Boil the prepared 4 cups of water in a large saucepan. Lower heat to medium. Add cubed squash, chopped bell peppers, kale, celery, olives, salt, and spices. Cover with its lid and let the soup simmer for 15 minutes. Cool and blend to a smooth paste. Top with chopped parsley leaves, spring onion, seeds, or nuts. Serve hot with toasted bread, baked nachos, or crackers.

Per Serving: Calories 51, Fat 0.3g, Carbs 9.7g, Protein 1.3g

290. Taco Cheese Soup

Ingredients for 8 servings

- 1 pound of hamburger
- 1 pound of ground pork
- ½ cup of Monterey Jack cheese, grated
- 2 tablespoons of parsley, chopped
- 4 cups of beef stock
- 20 ounces of can tomatoes
- 16 ounces of cheese
- 2 tablespoons of taco seasonings

Directions and Total Time: approx. 25 minutes

Add both the bottom meats within the instant pot and sauté for 10 minutes. Add taco seasonings, can tomatoes, and cheese and stir to mix. Seal large-sized pot with lid and cook on high for quarter-hour. Release pressure using an actual quick release method than open the lid. Add parsley and stir well. Top with cheese and serve.

Per Serving: Calories 445, Fat 28.1g, Carbs 5.7g, Protein 41.1g

291. Thick Herb Soup

Ingredients for 4 servings

- 2 ounces of mint leaves
- 2 ounces of celery leaves
- 4 tablespoons of butter or olive oil
- 2 tablespoons of flour
- 3 cups of water
- ½ cup of thick yogurt
- 1 juice of a lemon
- 2 egg yolks
- 1 teaspoon of salt

Directions and Total Time: approx. 34 minutes

Rinse the herbs, remove stalks and snip or chop finely. Cook butter or oil in a cooking pot, add prepared herbs, cover and simmer gently. When the herbs are tender, add in the flour and stir to combine. Cook for a few moments before slowly adding the water, stirring all the time. Simmer for about 10-15 min. Mix separately egg yolks, thick yogurt (or sour cream) and lemon juice. Add to the soup slowly, then stir well.

Per Serving: Calories 247, Fat 13g, Carbs 39g, Protein 7g

292. Tomato Soup

Ingredients for 8 servings

- 4 pounds of tomatoes, halved
- 2 tablespoons of vegetable oil
- 6 garlic cloves, minced
- 1 yellow onion, chopped
- Salt and black pepper to the taste
- 4 cups of chicken broth
- ½ teaspoon of red pepper flakes
- ½ cup of basil, chopped
- ½ cup of parmesan, grated

Directions and Total Time: approx. 65 minutes

Arrange the tomatoes during a roasting pan, add half the oil, salt and pepper, toss, and bake at a heat of 400 degrees F for 20 minutes. Heat up a pot with the remainder of the oil over medium heat, add the onion and sauté for five minutes. Add the tomatoes and therefore the refore the remainder of the ingredients except the basil and the parmesan, bring back a simmer and cook for half-hour. Blend the soup using an actual immersion blender, add the basil and therefore the parmesan, stir, divide into bowls and serve.

Per Serving: Calories 237, Fat 10g, Carbs 15.3g, Protein 7.4g

293. Tortellini and Spinach Soup

Ingredients for 2 servings

- 4 cups of low-sodium, fat-free chicken broth
- ¼ teaspoon of ground pepper
- 2 cups of coarsely chopped fresh spinach leaves
- 4 scallions, chopped
- 5 ounces of fresh cheese-filled tortellini
- 2 cloves of fresh garlic, minced
- freshly grated parmesan cheese

Directions and Total Time: approx. 25 minutes

Take a medium-sized pot and place it on medium heat. Add broth and stir for half a minute. Add garlic, scallions, and pepper and increase the heat to medium-high. Allow the broth to boil and when it starts boiling, bring the heat back to medium. Add the tortellini and cook for approximately 10 minutes. Toss in the spinach and cook for an additional 5 minutes, or until the pasta becomes tender. Transfer the soup equally to 4 bowls. Top it with parmesan cheese, if preferred.

Per Serving: Calories 97, Fat 4g, Carbs 14g, Protein 6g

294. Turnip Creamy Soup

Ingredients for 4 servings

- 1 peeled Granny Smith apple
- 3/4 teaspoon of Kosher salt
- 1 diced onion
- 1/2 teaspoon of curry powder
- 2 cups of chicken broth
- 1 peeled medium potato
- 1 tablespoon of olive oil extra-virgin
- 1/3 cup of light cream
- 1 1/2 pounds of peeled turnips

Directions and Total Time: approx. 35 minutes

Combine the olive oil & onions in a medium-sized skillet and sauté over medium flame until the onions are soft. In the meanwhile, cut the potato, turnips, & apple into 1" cubes. Combine all ingredients, except for the cream, in a saucepan. Bring to a boil, then lower to a low flame and simmer for 10 minutes, or until the veggies are completely soft. Using a hand blender, mix until smooth. After adding the cream, heat for another 2-3 minutes. Garnish with herbs and croutons if preferred.

Per Serving: Calories 149, Fat 7g, Carbs 21g, Protein 3g

295. Vegetable Broth

Ingredients for 4 servings

- 8 cups of water
- 1 onion, chopped
- 4 garlic cloves, crushed
- 2 celery stalks, chopped
- Pinch of salt
- 1 carrot, chopped
- Dash of pepper
- 1 potato, medium & chopped
- 1 tablespoon of soy sauce
- 3 bay leaves

Directions and Total Time: approx. 60 minutes

To make the vegetable broth, you need to place all the ingredients in a deep saucepan. Heat the pan over medium-high heat. Bring the vegetable mixture to a boil. Once it actually starts boiling, lower the heat to medium-low and allow it to simmer for at least an hour or so. Cover it with a lid. When the time is up, pass it through a filter and strain the vegetables, garlic, and bay leaves. Allow the stock to cool completely and store in an air-tight container.

Per Serving: Calories 44, Fat 0.6g, Carbs 9.7g, Protein 0.9g

296. Watercress Soup

Ingredients for 2 servings

- 2 teaspoons of native olive oil
- 30 grams of celery, smaller ties
- 30 grams of white onion, smaller rights
- 200 ml vegetable broth
- 50 grams of canned or homemade white beans such as cannellini or haricot
- 75 grams of watercress
- 1 tablespoon of chopped parsley

Directions and Total Time: approx. 23 minutes

Fill 1 teaspoon of olive oil in a small saucepan and cook the celery and onion gently for 2 minutes. Fill stock and beans, bring to a boil and cook over medium heat for 10 minutes. Chop roughly the watercress and parsley, add to the pan and cook for 1 minute. Remove from heat and stir until smooth. Serve the soup drizzled with the remaining teaspoon of olive oil.

Per Serving: Calories 130, Fat 11g, Carbs 23g, Protein 5g

Ingredients for 6 servings

- 1 cup of celery, chopped
- 1 cup of carrot, chopped
- 1 yellow onion, chopped
- 6 cups of veggie stock
- 4 garlic cloves, minced
- 2 cups of navy beans, dried
- ½ teaspoon of basil, dried
- ½ teaspoon of sage, dried
- 1 teaspoon of thyme, dried
- A pinch of salt and black pepper

Directions and Total Time: approx. 8 hours and 10 minutes

In your slow cooker, combine the beans with the stock and the rest of the ingredients. Put its lid on and cook on Low for 8 hours. Divide the soup into bowls and serve right away. Serve with roasted vegetables and crusty bread.

Per Serving: Calories 264, Fat 17.5g, Carbs 23.7g, Protein 11.5g

298. White Beans and Orange Soup

Ingredients for 4 servings

- 1 yellow onion, chopped
- 5 celery sticks, chopped
- 4 carrots, chopped
- 1 cup of vegetable oil
- ½ teaspoon of oregano, dried
- 1 herb
- 3 orange slices, peeled
- 30 ounces of canned white beans, drained
- 2 tablespoons of ingredient
- 2 cups of water
- 6 cups of chicken broth

Directions and Total Time: approx. 47 minutes

Heat up a large-sized pot with the oil over medium heat, add the onion, celery, carrots, the herb and therefore the oregano, stir and sauté for five minutes. Add the orange slices and cook for two minutes more. Add the remainder of the ingredients, stir, bring back a simmer and cook over medium heat for half-hour. Ladle the soup into bowls and serve.

Per Serving: Calories 273, Fat 16.3g, Carbs 15.6g, Protein 7.4g

299. Zesty Taco Soup

Ingredients for 2 servings

- 1 ½ pounds of chicken breast
- 15 ½ ounces of canned dark red kidney beans
- 15 ½ ounces of canned white corn
- 1 cup of canned tomatoes
- ½ cup of onion
- 15 ½ ounces of canned yellow hominy
- ½ cup of green bell peppers
- 1 garlic clove
- 1 medium jalapeno
- 1 tablespoon of package McCormick
- 2 cups of chicken broth

Directions and Total Time: approx. 7 hours and 10 minutes

Add drained beans, hominy, corn, onion, garlic, jalapeno pepper, chicken, and green peppers to a Crockpot. Cover the beans-corn mixture and cook for 1 hour on "high" temperature. Set heat to "low" and continue cooking for 6 hours. Shred the slow-cooked chicken and return to the taco soup. Serve warm.

Per Serving: Calories 191, Fat 20g, Carbs 59g, Protein 21g

Ingredients for 8 servings

- 2 and ½ pounds of zucchinis, roughly chopped
- 2 tablespoons of vegetable oil
- 1 yellow onion, chopped
- 4 garlic cloves, minced
- 4 cups of chicken broth
- ½ cup of basil, chopped
- Salt and black pepper to the taste

Directions and Total Time: approx. 30 minutes

Heat up a large-sized pot with the oil over medium heat, add the zucchinis and therefore the onion and sauté for five minutes. Add the garlic and therefore the remainder of the ingredients except the basil, stir, bring back a simmer and cook for quarter-hour over medium heat. Add the basil, blend the soup using an immersion blender, ladle into bowls and serve.

Per Serving: Calories 182, Fat 7.6g, Carbs 12.6g, Protein 2.3g

301. Baked Black-Eyed Peas

Ingredients for 3 servings

- 2 cans of black-eyed peas, rinsed
- 3 tablespoons of extra-virgin olive oil
- Salt, to taste
- 2 teaspoons of Za'atar
- 2 teaspoons of sumac
- 2 teaspoons of harissa

Directions and Total Time: approx. 50 minutes

Preheat the oven to 400°F. Place the black-eyed peas on a baking sheet and drizzle with the olive oil. Season with salt and toss to coat well. Bake for about 35 minutes, shaking the baking pan three times during the cooking time. Remove from the oven and season with the Za'atar, sumac, and harissa. Serve warm. Serve as a snack with tea.

Per Serving: Calories 478, Fat 18.5g, Carbs 66.1g, Protein 14.9g

302. Basil and Sun-Dried Tomatoes Rice

Ingredients for 4 servings

- 5 cups chicken stock
- 1 yellow onion, chopped
- ounces sun-dried tomatoes in olive oil, drained and chopped 2 cups Arborio rice
- Salt and black pepper to the taste
- 1 and ½ cup parmesan, grated
- 2 tablespoons olive oil
- ¼ cup basil leaves, chopped

Directions and Total Time: approx. 35 minutes

Heat a large-sized pan with the oil over medium heat, add the onion and the tomatoes and sauté for 5 minutes. Add the rice, stock, and the rest of the ingredients except the parmesan, bring to a simmer and cook over medium heat for 20 minutes. Add the parmesan, toss, divide the mix between plates and serve as a side dish.

Per Serving: Calories 426, Fat 8.4g, Carbs 56.3g, Protein 7.5g

303. Basmati Rice

Ingredients for 4 servings

- 1 cup basmati rice
- 2 tablespoons olive oil
- 1 teaspoon salt
- 2 ½ cup chicken stock

Directions and Total Time: approx. 22 minutes

Pour the tablespoons of olive oil into the skillet, and heat it. Add the basmati rice, and toast it for 3 minutes. Stir it occasionally. Then add the salt and chicken broth. Close its lid, and cook the rice for 12 minutes or until it absorbs all the liquid. Serve

Note: Basmati rice is great as a side dish for chicken curry and other meat or vegetable main courses.

Per Serving: Calories 235, Fat 7.7g, Carbs 37.4g, Protein 3.7g

304. Bean Patties

Ingredients for 3 servings

- ½ cup white beans, canned
- 1 egg, beaten
- 2 tablespoons semolina
- 1 teaspoon chili flakes
- 1 tablespoon almond meal
- 1 tablespoon olive oil

Directions and Total Time: approx. 20 minutes

Mash the white beans until you get pure. Then add egg, semolina, chili flakes, and almond meal. Mix the rest of the remaining ingredients with the help of a spoon until you get a smooth mass. Make the medium size ball. Press them in the shape of patties. After this, melt the olive oil in the skillet and add patties. Roast them for 3 minutes per side or until the patties are light brown.

Per Serving: Calories 157, Fat 19.3g, Carbs 33.4g, Protein 12.3g

305. Bean and Rice

Ingredients for 6 servings

- 1 tablespoon of olive oil
- 1 yellow onion, chopped
- 2 celery stalks, chopped
- 2 garlic cloves, minced
- 2 cups of brown rice
- 1 ½ cups of canned black beans, rinsed and drained
- 4 cups of water
- Salt and black pepper, to taste

Directions and Total Time: approx. 55 minutes

Heat a large-sized pan with the oil over medium heat. Add the celery, garlic, and onion, stir and cook for 10 minutes. Add the rest of the remaining ingredients, stir, and bring to a simmer. Cook over medium heat for 45 minutes. Divide between plates and serve.

Per Serving: Calories 224, Fat 8.4g, Carbs 15.3g, Protein 6.2g

306. Brown Rice

Ingredients for 2 servings

- 4 cups of canned low-sodium, low-fat chicken broth
- 2 cups of brown rice
- 6 cloves fresh garlic
- 1/2 cup of pine nuts
- 6 scallions, white and green parts, sliced
- 8 pitted large black olives, drained and coarsely chopped
- 1/2 tablespoon extra-virgin olive oil
- Salt and freshly ground pepper to taste
- Chopped chives for garnish

Directions and Total Time: approx. 20 minutes

In a saucepan, bring broth and rice to a boil; reduce heat to medium, cover, and continue boiling until all liquid is absorbed, occasionally stirring if needed. While rice is boiling, sauté garlic, pine nuts, scallions, and olives in olive oil until garlic is soft and pine nuts are lightly toasted. When rice is ready, fluff with a fork and stir in garlic and pine nut mixture; add salt and pepper to taste. Transfer to a large-sized serving platter and garnish with chives.

Per Serving: Calories 249, Fat 9g, Carbs 38g, Protein 7g

307. Brown Rice Pilaf with Golden Raisin

Ingredients for 6 servings

- 1 tbs. extra-virgin olive oil
- 1 cup chopped onion (about ½ medium onion)
- ½ cup shredded carrot (about 1 medium carrot)
- 1 teaspoon ground cumin
- ½ teaspoon ground cinnamon
- 2 cups instant brown rice
- 1 ¾ cups 100% orange juice
- ¼ cup water
- 1 cup golden raisins
- ½ cup shelled pistachios
- Chopped fresh chives (optional)

Directions and Total Time: approx. 20 minutes

In a large-sized saucepan over medium-high heat, heat the oil. Add the onion and cook for just about 5 minutes, stirring frequently. Add the carrot, cumin, and cinnamon, and cook for 1 minute, stirring frequently. Stir in the rice, orange juice, and water. Bring to a hot boil, cover, then lower the heat to medium-low. Simmer for 7 minutes, or until the rice is cooked through and the liquid is absorbed. Stir in the raisins, pistachios, and chives (if using) and serve.

Per Serving: Calories 320, Fat 7g, Carbs 61g, Protein 6g

308. Brown Rice Pilaf with Pistachios and Raisins

Ingredients for 6 servings

- 1 tablespoon extra-virgin olive oil
- 1 cup chopped onion
- ½ cup shredded carrot
- ½ teaspoon ground cinnamon
- 1 teaspoon ground cumin
- 2 cups brown rice
- 1¾ cups pure orange juice
- ¼ cup water
- ½ cup shelled pistachios
- 1 cup golden raisins
- ½ cup chopped fresh chives

Directions and Total Time: approx. 20 minutes

Heat the extra-virgin olive oil in a saucepan over medium-high heat until shimmering. Add the onion and sauté for 3-5 minutes or until translucent. Add the carrots, cinnamon, and cumin, then sauté for 1 minutes or until aromatic. Pour int the brown rice, orange juice, and water. Bring to a boil. Low the heat to medium-low and simmer for 7 minutes or until the liquid is almost absorbed. Transfer the rice mixture in a large serving bowl, then spread with pistachios, raisins, and chives. Serve immediately.

Per Serving: Calories 264, Fat 7.1g, Carbs 48.9g, Protein 5.2g

309. Brown Rice Pilaf with Raisins

Ingredients for 6 servings

- 1 tablespoon of extra-virgin olive oil
- 1 cup of onion, chopped
- ½ cup of carrot, shredded
- 1 teaspoon of ground cumin
- ½ teaspoon of ground cinnamon
- 2 cups of instant brown rice
- 1 ¾ cups of 100% orange juice
- ¼ cup of water
- 1 cup of golden raisins
- ½ cup of shelled pistachios
- Bunch of fresh chives, chopped (optional)

Directions and Total Time: approx. 25 minutes

In a large-sized saucepan over medium-high heat, heat the oil. Add the onion and cook for just about 5 minutes, stirring frequently. Add the carrot, cumin, and cinnamon, and cook for 1 minute, stirring frequently. Stir in the rice, orange juice, and water. Bring to a boil, then cover using its lid, then lower the heat to medium-low. Simmer for 7 minutes, or until the rice is cooked through and the liquid is absorbed. Stir in the raisins, pistachios, and chives (if using) and serve.

Per Serving: Calories 320, Fat 7g, Carbs 61g, Protein 6g

310. Brown Rice with Chicken and Scallions

Ingredients for 4 servings

- 1 ½ cups brown rice
- 3 cups chicken stock
- 1 tablespoon balsamic vinegar
- 1-pound chicken breast, boneless, skinless and cubed
- 6 scallions, chopped
- 1 tablespoon sweet paprika
- 2 tablespoons avocado oil
- Salt and black pepper to taste

Directions and Total Time: approx. 40 minutes

Heat a large-sized skillet with oil over medium-high heat. Add chicken and sauté for 5 minutes. Add shallots and sauté for another 5 minutes. Add the rice and the rest of the ingredients and bring to a boil. when it boils, lower the heat temperature to medium and cook for 20 minutes. Stir, divide among plates and serve.

Per Serving: Calories 300, Fat 9.2g, Carbs 18.6g, Protein 23.8g

311. Bulgur Pilaf with Almonds

Ingredients for 4 servings

- ⅔ cup uncooked bulgur
- 1 ⅓ cups water
- ¼ cup sliced almonds
- 1 cup small-diced red bell pepper
- ⅓ cup chopped fresh cilantro
- 1 tablespoon olive oil
- ¼ teaspoon salt

Directions and Total Time: approx. 25 minutes

Place the bulgur and water in a pot and bring the water to a boil. Once the water has actually reached a boil, cover the pot with a lid, turn off the heat temperature and let the covered pot sit for 20 minutes. Transfer the cooked bulgur to a large bowl, add the almonds, peppers, cilantro, oil, and salt and stir to combine. Divide the bulgur into 4 servings and serve.

Per Serving: Calories 17, Fat 7g, Carbs 25g, Protein 4g

312. Bulgur Pilaf with Garbanzo

Ingredients for 6 servings

- 3 tablespoons extra-virgin olive oil
- 1 large onion, chopped
- 1 (1-pound / 454-g) can garbanzo beans, rinsed and drained
- 2 cups bulgur wheat, rinsed and drained
- 1½ teaspoons salt
- ½ teaspoon cinnamon
- 4 cups water

Directions and Total Time: approx. 25 minutes

In a large-sized pot over medium heat, heat the olive oil. Add the onion and cook for just about 5 minutes. Add the garbanzo beans and cook for an additional 5 minutes. Stir in the remaining ingredients. Reduce the heat to low. Cover and cook for 10 minutes. When done, fluff the pilaf with a fork. Cover and let sit for another 5 minutes before serving.

Per Serving: Calories 462, Fat 13g, Carbs 76g, Protein 15g

313. Bulgur with Kale and Cheese

Ingredients for 6 servings

- 4 ounces bulgur
- 4 ounces kale, chopped
- 1 tablespoon mint, chopped
- 3 spring onions, chopped
- 1 cucumber, chopped
- A pinch of allspice, ground
- 2 tablespoons olive oil
- Zest, and juice of ½ lemon
- 4 ounces feta cheese, crumbled

Directions and Total Time: approx. 20 minutes

Place bulgur in a large-sized bowl, cover with hot water and set aside 10 minutes. Use a fork to shell it. Heat a skillet with the oil over medium heat. Add the onions and allspice, and cook for 3 minutes. Add the bulgur and the rest of the ingredients, and cook for 5 minutes. Serve.

Per Serving: Calories 200, Fat 6.7g, Carbs 15.4g, Protein 4.5g

314. Carrot and Caper Chickpeas

Ingredients for 4 servings

- 3 tablespoons of olive oil
- 3 tablespoons of capers, drained
- 1 lemon, juiced and zested
- 1 red onion, chopped
- 14 ounces of canned chickpeas
- 4 carrots, peeled and cubed
- 1 tablespoon of parsley, chopped
- Salt and black pepper to taste

Directions and Total Time: approx. 35 minutes

Warm the olive oil in a large-sized skillet over medium heat and cook onion, lemon zest, lemon juice, and capers for 5 minutes. Stir in chickpeas, carrots, parsley, salt, and pepper and cook for another 20 minutes. Serve and enjoy!

Per Serving: Calories 210, Fat 5g, Carbs 7g, Protein 4g

315. Cheese Basil Tomato Rice

Ingredients for 8 servings

- 1 ½ cups brown rice
- 1 cup parmesan cheese, grated
- ¼ cup fresh basil, chopped
- 2 cups grape tomatoes, halved
- 8 ounces can tomato sauce
- 1 ¾ cup vegetable broth
- 1 tablespoon garlic, minced
- ½ cup onion, diced
- 1 tablespoon olive oil
- Pepper and salt

Directions and Total Time: approx. 35 minutes

In a saucepan, heat olive oil. Add the garlic, onion, and sauté until tender. Add the rice, tomato sauce, broth, pepper, and salt, and cook for 22 minutes, stirring often. Add the remaining ingredients, and mix well. Serve, and enjoy.

Per Serving: Calories 208, Fat 5.6g, Carbs 32.1g, Protein 8.3g

316. Cherry, Apricot, and Pecan Brown Rice Bowl

Ingredients for 2 servings

- 2 tablespoons olive oil
- 2 green onions, sliced
- ½ cup brown rice
- 1 cup low -sodium chicken stock
- 2 tablespoons dried cherries
- 4 dried apricots, chopped
- 2 tablespoons pecans, toasted and chopped
- Sea salt and freshly ground pepper

Directions and Total Time: approx. 1 hour and 16 minutes

Preheat the olive oil in a medium-large saucepan over medium-high heat until shimmering. Add the green onions and sauté for 1 minute or until fragrant. Add the rice. Stir then after, mix well, then pour in the chicken stock. Bring to a boil. Reduce the heat to low. Cover and simmer for 48-50 minutes or until the brown rice is soft. Add the cherries, apricots, and pecans, and simmer for 10 more minutes or until the fruits are tender. Pour them in a large serving bowl. Fluff with a fork. Sprinkle with sea salt and pepper. Enjoy!

Per Serving: Calories 451, Fat 25.9g, Carbs 50.4g, Protein 8.2g

317. Cherry Tomatoes and Black Beans

Ingredients for 2 servings

- 1 (15-ounce) can of black beans, undrained
- 1 cup of cherry tomatoes, halved
- 1 teaspoon of salt
- 1 tablespoon of dried oregano
- 1 teaspoon of red pepper flakes

Directions and Total Time: approx. 25 minutes

Pour the can of black beans and their liquid into a large skillet and bring to a low boil over medium-high heat. Reduce the heat temperature to low heat and simmer for 5 minutes. Stir in the cherry tomatoes, salt, oregano, and red pepper flakes, and cook for 10 minutes. Serve and enjoy.

Per Serving: Calories 185, Fat 1g, Carbs 34g, Protein 12g

318. Chicken Curry Rice

Ingredients for 5 servings

- 1 tablespoon curry paste
- ¼ cup milk
- 1 cup wheatberries
- ½ cup of rice
- 1 teaspoon salt
- 4 tablespoons olive oil
- 6 cups chicken stock

Directions and Total Time: approx. 1 hour and 25 minutes

Place the wheat berries, and chicken broth in the pan. Close its lid, and cook the mixture for 1 hour over medium heat. After the time is up, add the rice, olive oil, and salt, and mix well. In a bowl, mix the milk, and curry paste, then add the liquid into the rice mixture, and mix well. Simmer on low heat for a heat of 15 minutes with the lid closed. Serve hot.

Per Serving: Calories 232, Fat 15g, Carbs 23.5g, Protein 3.9g

319. Chickpeas with Garlic and Parsley

Ingredients for 6 servings

- ¼ cup of extra-virgin olive oil
- 4 garlic cloves, thinly sliced
- ⅛ teaspoon of red pepper flakes
- 1 onion, chopped
- Salt and pepper, to taste
- 2 (15-ounce) cans of chickpeas, rinsed
- 1 cup of chicken broth
- 2 tablespoons of fresh parsley, minced
- 2 teaspoons of lemon juice

Directions and Total Time: approx. 30 minutes

Add the 3 tablespoons of the oil to a skillet and cook the garlic and pepper flakes for 3 minutes over medium heat. Stir in the onion and ¼ teaspoon of salt and cook for 5–7 minutes. Mix in the chickpeas and broth and bring to a simmer. Lower the heat temperature and then simmer on low for 7 minutes, covered. Uncover and set the heat to high and cook for 3 minutes, or until all the liquid has evaporated. Set aside and mix in the lemon juice and parsley. Season with salt and pepper to taste and serve.

Per Serving: Calories 611, Fat 17.6g, Carbs 89.5g, Protein 28.7g

320. Cranberry Wild Rice Pilaf

Ingredients for 8 servings

- ¾ cup wild rice
- 3 cups chicken broth
- ½ cup medium pearl barley
- ¼ cup dried currants
- 1 tablespoon butter
- 1/3 cup sliced almonds, toasted
- ¼ cup dried cranberries, chopped

Directions and Total Time: approx. 1 hour and 35 minutes

Preheat the oven to a heat of 325°, and grease a 1.5-quart baking dish. In a saucepan, combine the wild rice and broth, and bring to a boil. Reduce heat, and simmer covered for just about 10 minutes. Remove from heat, add barley, currants, and butter, stir, and transfer to the baking dish. Cook covered for 1 hour until wild rice and barley are tender. Strain, add almonds and cranberries and stir. Serve, and enjoy!

Per Serving: Calories 166, Fat 4g, Carbs 30g, Protein 5g

321. Creamy Lemon Rice

Ingredients for 4 servings

- ½ cups chicken broth
- 2-ounces cream cheese, cubed
- ½ teaspoon grated lemon zest
- 1 tablespoon lemon juice
- ¼ teaspoon salt
- ¼ teaspoon coarsely ground pepper
- 1 cup uncooked long-grain rice
- ¼ cup minced fresh basil

Directions and Total Time: approx. 25 minutes

In a large-sized saucepan, combine the first six ingredients. Bring to a boil, continue stirring with a whisk to combine. Add rice, then reduce the heat, and simmer, covered for about 15 minutes, until liquid is absorbed and tender rice. Plate, garnish with chopped basil, and serve.

Per Serving: Calories 246, Fat 6g, Carbs 42g, Protein 5g

322. Creamy Parmesan Polenta

Ingredients for 4 servings

- 1 (16-ounce) tube of polenta, cut into ½-inch dice
- 1 cup fat-free, less-sodium chicken broth
- ¼ cup (1 ounce) grated fresh Parmesan cheese
- ¼ teaspoon freshly ground pepper
- 2 teaspoons olive oil
- 3 cups cherry tomatoes
- 2 ounces very thin slices of prosciutto
- 3 garlic cloves, minced
- ¼ cup dry white wine
- Chopped fresh parsley

Directions and Total Time: approx. 35 minutes

In a large-sized saucepan, bring broth to a boil. Add polenta, and cook 5 minutes over medium heat, stirring with a whisk until smooth. Remove from heat; add cheese, and pepper, stir, then set aside. Heat olive oil in a large-sized nonstick skillet over medium heat. Add the tomato, ham, and garlic, and cook over medium-high heat for 2 minutes. Add the wine, and cook for just about 2 minutes to evaporate. Spread ¾ cup polenta in 4 bowls; top with ½ cup tomato mixture. Sprinkle with parsley, and serve immediately.

Per Serving: Calories 192, Fat 6g, Carbs 23g, Protein 10g

323. Cucumber Olive Rice

Ingredients for 8 servings

- 2 cups rice, rinsed
- 1/2 cup olives, pitted
- 1 cup cucumber, chopped
- 1 tablespoon red wine vinegar
- 1 teaspoon lemon zest, grated
- 1 tablespoon fresh lemon juice
- 2 tablespoons olive oil
- 2 cups vegetable broth
- 1/2 teaspoon dried oregano
- 1 red bell pepper, chopped
- 1/2 cup onion, chopped
- 1 tbsp olive oil
- Pepper
- Salt

Directions and Total Time: approx. 20 minutes

Add oil into the inner pot of instant pot and set the pot on sauté mode. Add onion and sauté for 3 minutes. Add bell pepper and oregano and sauté for 1 minute. Add rice and broth and stir well. Seal large-sized pot with lid and cook on high for 6 minutes. Once it's done, allow to release pressure naturally for just about 10 minutes then release remaining using quick release. Remove lid. Add remaining ingredients and stir everything well to mix. Serve immediately and enjoy it.

Per Serving: Calories 229, Fat 5.1g, Carbs 40.2g, Protein 4.9g

324. Cumin Beef Rice

Ingredients for 4 servings

- 1 green onion, chopped
- 2 cloves of garlic, minced
- ½-pound of ground beef
- 1 tablespoon of ground cumin
- 2 eggs
- 1 tablespoon of ginger, minced
- 3 cups of brown rice
- Salt, to taste
- 3 tablespoons of olive oil

Directions and Total Time: approx. 28 minutes

In a large-sized skillet on medium heat, add the olive oil. Once the oil is hot, add the cumin and allow it to toast. Add now the ground beef and break up the meat. Stir and cook until it's cooked through. Add the salt, ginger, and garlic and cook for another few minutes before adding the eggs. Swirl the yolk around so it mixes with the beef. Add the rice. Break up the bigger rice pieces until the rice is spread out evenly with the meat and egg. Remove from the heat and serve.

Per Serving: Calories 256, Fat 20.5g, Carbs 111.1g, Protein 31.2g

Ingredients for 5 servings

- 1 tablespoon curry paste
- ¼ cup milk
- 1 cup wheatberries
- ½ cup of rice
- 1 teaspoon salt
- 4 tablespoons olive oil
- 6 cups chicken stock

Directions and Total Time: approx. 1 hour and 25 minutes

Place the wheat berries and chicken broth in the pan. Close its lid, and cook the mixture for 1 hour over medium heat. After the time is up, add the rice, olive oil, and salt, and mix well. Mix the milk and curry paste in a bowl, add the liquid into the rice mixture, and mix well. Simmer on low heat for just about 15 minutes with the lid closed. Serve hot.

Per Serving: Calories 232, Fat 15g, Carbs 23.5g, Protein 3.9g

326. Earthy Lentil and Rice Pilaf

Ingredients for 6 servings

- ¼ cup of extra-virgin olive oil
- 1 large onion, chopped
- 6 cups of water
- 1 teaspoon of ground cumin
- 1 teaspoon of salt
- 2 cups of brown lentils
- 1 cup of basmati rice

Directions and Total Time: approx. 55 minutes

In a large-sized pot over medium heat, cook the olive oil and onions for 7 to 10 minutes until the edges are browned. Turn the heat to temperature of high, add the water, cumin, and salt, and bring this mixture to a boil, boiling for about 3 minutes. Add the lentils and turn the heat to medium-low. Cover the pot and cook for 20 minutes, stirring occasionally. Stir in the rice and cover; cook for an additional 20 minutes. Fluff the rice with a fork and serve warm.

Per Serving: Calories 397, Fat 11g, Carbs 60g, Protein 18g

327. Eggplant and Chickpea Casserole

Ingredients for 6 servings

- ¼ cup of olive oil
- 2 onions, chopped
- 1 green bell pepper, chopped
- Salt and black pepper to taste
- 3 garlic cloves, minced
- 1 teaspoon of dried oregano
- ½ teaspoon of ground cumin
- 1 pound of eggplants, cubed
- 1 can of tomatoes, diced
- 2 cans of chickpeas

Directions and Total Time: approx. 75 minutes

Preheat oven to a heat of 400 F. Warm the olive oil in a skillet over medium heat. Add the prepared chopped onions, bell pepper, salt, and pepper. Cook for about 5 minutes until softened. Stir in garlic, oregano, and cumin for about 30 seconds until fragrant. Transfer to a baking dish and add the eggplants, tomatoes, and chickpeas and stir. Place in the oven and bake for 45-60 minutes, shaking the dish twice during cooking. Serve.

Per Serving: Calories 260, Fat 12g, Carbs 8g, Protein 33.4g

328. Fennel Wild Rice

Ingredients for 6 servings

- 1 tablespoon of fresh parsley, chopped
- 2 cups of cooked wild rice
- 1 cup of fennel, diced
- 1 tablespoon of olive oil
- ½ cup of sweet onion, chopped
- ½ red bell pepper, finely diced
- ¼ teaspoon of fine sea salt
- ¼ teaspoon of black pepper

Directions and Total Time: approx. 35 minutes

Place a skillet over medium-high heat. Heat the olive oil and then add the onion, red bell pepper, and fennel. Sauté for 6 minutes. It should become tender. Stir in the pan the wild rice, and cook for 5 minutes, and then add in your parsley. Add salt and pepper for season, before serving warm.

Per Serving: Calories 222, Fat 3g, Carbs 43g, Protein 8g

329. Feta and Garbanzo Bowl

Ingredients for 4 servings

- 2 cups of canned garbanzo beans
- 2 tomatoes, diced
- 1 cucumber, thinly sliced
- 1 teaspoon of garlic, minced
- 1 red onion, chopped
- 2 green hot peppers, chopped
- 1 red bell pepper, sliced
- 2 tablespoons of fresh parsley, chopped
- 1 fresh lemon, juiced
- 1 cup of feta cheese, crumbled
- 1 teaspoon of harissa
- ¼ teaspoon of chili flakes
- Salt and black pepper to taste
- Fresh mint leaves, chopped

Directions and Total Time: approx. 10 minutes

In a bowl, combine the garbanzo beans with cucumber, garlic, onion, hot peppers, tomatoes, bell pepper, parsley, lemon juice, chili flakes, harissa, salt, and black pepper. Adjust the seasonings. Serve the dish with a topping of crumbled feta cheese and freshly chopped mint leaves.

Per Serving: Calories 330, Fat 11g, Carbs 43g, Protein 17g

330. Fiber Packed Chicken Rice

Ingredients for 6 servings

- 1 pound chicken breast, skinless, boneless, and cut into chunks
- 14.5 ounces can cannellini beans
- 4 cups chicken broth
- 2 cups wild rice
- 1 tablespoon Italian seasoning
- 1 small onion, chopped
- 1 tablespoon garlic, chopped
- 1 tablespoon olive oil
- Pepper
- Salt

Directions and Total Time: approx. 26 minutes

Add oil into the inner pot of instant pot and set the pot on sauté mode. Add garlic and onion and sauté for 2 minutes. Add chicken and cook for 2 minutes. Add remaining ingredients and stir well. Seal large-sized pot with lid and cook on high for 12 minutes. Once done, release pressure using quick release. Remove lid. Stir well and serve.

Per Serving: Calories 399, Fat 6.4g, Carbs 53.4g, Protein 31.6g

331. Fish and Chicken Rice

Ingredients for 8 servings

- 1 tablespoon olive oil
- 1 ½ cups brown rice (uncooked)
- 1 onion, diced
- 2 cloves garlic, minced
- 15 ounces diced tomatoes
- ¼ cup peas
- ½ pound chorizo, sliced into rounds
- 2 cups reduced-sodium chicken stock
- 1 ½ teaspoon paprika
- ½ teaspoon turmeric
- Salt and pepper to taste
- ¼ pound fish
- 2 pounds chicken thigh fillets

Directions and Total Time: approx. 4 hours and 45 minutes

Combine all the ingredients except fish and chicken in the slow cooker. Place the chicken on top of the mixture. Cover the pot. Cook on high for 4 hours. Stir in the fish to the mixture. Cook for 30 more minutes.

Per Serving: Calories 311, Fat 14g, Carbs 32.5g, Protein 13.7g

332. Flavors Herb Risotto

Ingredients for 4 servings

- 2 cups of rice
- 2 tablespoons parmesan cheese, grated
- 1 ounce heavy cream
- 1 tablespoon fresh oregano, chopped
- 1 tablespoon fresh basil, chopped
- ½ tablespoon sage, chopped
- 1 onion, chopped
- 2 tablespoons olive oil
- 1 teaspoon garlic, minced
- 4 cups vegetable stock
- Pepper, and Salt

Directions and Total Time: approx. 25 minutes

Heat the olive oil in a saucepan. Add the garlic, onion, and sauté for a couple of minutes. Add the rice, and toast for just about a couple of minutes. Add the oregano, basil, sage, and the hot vegetable stock a little at a time. Cook over high heat for 12 minutes, adding the broth from time to time as the rice absorbs it completely. Add the cream, grated Parmesan cheese, and stir at the end of cooking. Serve immediately.

Per Serving: Calories 173, Fat 14g, Carbs 20g, Protein 3g

333. Ful Medames

Ingredients for 5 servings

- ½ cup of water
- 2 cans of plain fava beans
- Kosher salt, to taste
- 2 hot peppers, chopped
- 1 large lemon, juiced
- 1 cup of parsley, chopped
- 1 teaspoon of ground cumin
- 2 garlic cloves, chopped
- 3 tablespoons of extra-virgin olive oil
- 1 tomato, diced

Directions and Total Time: approx. 25 minutes

Put the fava beans, salt, cumin, and water in a saucepan placed over medium-high heat. Cover and cook for about 15 minutes. Mash the fava beans with a fork. Smash the garlic and hot peppers in a mortar, and mix them with the fava beans. Squeeze in the prepared lemon juice and drizzle with the olive oil. Serve topped with the diced tomatoes and parsley.

Per Serving: Calories 218, Fat 9.1g, Carbs 25.3g, Protein 14.9g

334. Garbanzo and Kidney Bean Salad

Ingredients for 4 servings

- 1 (15 ounces) can kidney beans, drained
- 1 (15.5 ounces) can garbanzo beans, drained
- 1 lemon, zested and juiced
- 1 medium tomato, chopped
- 1 teaspoon capers, rinsed and drained
- 1/2 cup chopped fresh parsley
- 1/2 teaspoon salt, or to taste
- 1/4 cup chopped red onion
- 3 tablespoons extra virgin olive oil

Directions and Total Time: approx. 10 minutes

In a salad bowl, whisk well lemon juice, olive oil, and salt until dissolved. Stir in garbanzo, kidney beans, tomato, red onion, parsley, and capers. Toss well to coat. Allow flavors to mix for 30 minutes by setting them in the fridge. Mix again before serving.

Per Serving: Calories 329, Fat 12g, Carbs 46.6g, Protein 12.1g

335. Garlicky Lemon-Parsley Hummus

Ingredients for 8 servings

- ¼ cup tahini
- ¼ teaspoon fine grain sea salt
- ⅓ cup fresh lemon juice
- ¾ cup chopped parsley
- 1 tablespoon olive oil
- 1 ½ cans (15 ounces each) chickpeas, rinsed and drained
- 5 cloves garlic, peeled and roughly chopped
- Dash freshly ground black pepper

Directions and Total Time: approx. 10 minutes

Place all the prepared ingredients in a blender and puree until smooth and creamy. Transfer to a bowl and adjust seasoning if needed. If dip dries up, just add more olive oil and mix well. Serve and enjoy with carrot sticks.

Per Serving: Calories 131, Fat 7g, Carbs 13.8g, Protein 4.9g

336. Gigante Beans in Tomato Sauce

Ingredients for 2 servings

- 1 (12-ounce) jar of gigante beans, undrained
- 6 ounces of tomato paste
- ¾ cup of water
- ½ teaspoon of dried oregano

Directions and Total Time: approx. 15 minutes

Pour the gigante beans and their liquid into a small saucepan and bring to a boil over medium-high heat. Remove the medium-sized pan from the heat and drain the liquid. In another small saucepan, combine the tomato paste and water and bring to a simmer to heat through. Arrange the beans on a serving dish. Spoon over the tomato sauce and enjoy.

Per Serving: Calories 238, Fat 1g, Carbs 46g, Protein 15g

337. Grain Porridge

Ingredients for 4 servings

- 1 cup of spelt
- Salt and black pepper, to taste
- 1-ounces of Parmesan, grated
- 2 tablespoons of unsalted butter
- 4 large eggs, boiled
- 1 tablespoon of vegetable oil

Directions and Total Time: approx. 45 minutes

Chop the spelt in a food processor then add to a saucepan. Stir in the 4 cups of water with black pepper and salt and place over medium-high heat. Cook to a boil, reduce the heat, and let it simmer for 35 minutes. Stir in the butter, Parmesan and a splash of water. Peel and cut the eggs into slices. Serve the porridge with egg slices and oil on top. Enjoy.

Per Serving: Calories 242, Fat 14g, Carbs 21g, Protein 9g

338. Greek Beans Tortillas

Ingredients for 4 servings

- 1 red onion, chopped
- 2 garlic cloves, minced
- 1 tablespoon olive oil
- 1 green bell pepper, sliced
- 3 cups canned pinto beans
- 2 red chili peppers, chopped
- 4 tablespoon parsley, chopped
- 1 teaspoon cumin, ground
- A pinch of salt and black pepper
- 4 whole wheat Greek tortillas
- 1 cup cheddar cheese, shredded

Directions and Total Time: approx. 25 minutes

Heat up a large-sized pan with the oil over medium heat, add the onion and sauté for 5 minutes. Add the rest of the prepared ingredients except the tortillas and the cheese, stir and cook for 15 minutes. Divide the beans mix on each Greek tortilla, also divide the cheese, roll the tortillas and serve for breakfast.

Per Serving: Calories 673, Fat 14.9g, Carbs 75.4g, Protein 39g

339. Green Beans and Eggs

Ingredients for 2 servings

- ½ cup green beans
- ¼ teaspoon salt
- 5 eggs
- 1/3 cup skim milk
- 1 bell pepper, seeds removed
- 1 teaspoon olive oil

Directions and Total Time: approx. 25 minutes

Slice the bell pepper and combine it with the green beans. Pour the olive oil into a skillet and transfer the vegetable mixture to the skillet. Cook on medium heat for just about 3 minutes, stirring frequently. Meanwhile, beat the eggs in a mixing bowl. Sprinkle the egg mixture with salt and add skim milk. Whisk well. Pour the egg mixture over the vegetable mixture and cook for 3 minutes on medium heat. Stir the mixture carefully so that the eggs and vegetables are well combined. Cook for 4 minutes more. Stir again and close the lid. Cook the scrambled eggs for 5 minutes more. Stir the mixture again. Serve it.

Per Serving: Calories 231, Fat 13.4g, Carbs 9.3g, Protein 16.3g

340. Ground Beef, Tomato, and Kidney Bean Chili

Ingredients for 4 servings

- 1 tablespoon extra-virgin olive oil
- 1 pound extra-lean ground beef
- 1 onion, chopped
- 2 cans kidney beans
- 2 cans chopped tomatoes, juice reserved
- 1 teaspoon garlic powder
- 1 tablespoon chili powder
- ½ teaspoon sea salt

Directions and Total Time: approx. 25 minutes

Heat oil in until shimmering. Add the beef and onion to the pot and sauté for 5 minutes or until the onion is translucent and the beef is lightly browned. Add the remaining ingredients. Bring to a boil. Low the heat and cook for 10 more minutes. Keep stirring during the cooking. Pour them in a large serving bowl and serve immediately.

Per Serving: Calories 891, Fat 20.1g, Carbs 62.9g, Protein 116.3g

341. Herb Polenta

Ingredients for 6 servings

- 1 cup polenta
- 1/4 teaspoon nutmeg
- 3 tablespoons fresh parsley, chopped
- 1/4 cup milk
- 1/2 cup parmesan cheese, grated
- 4 cups vegetable broth
- 2 teaspoons thyme, chopped
- 2 teaspoons rosemary, chopped
- 2 teaspoons sage, chopped
- 1 small onion, chopped
- 2 tablespoons olive oil
- Salt

Directions and Total Time: approx. 22 minutes

Add oil into the inner pot of instant pot and set the pot on sauté mode. Add onion and herbs and sauté for 4 minutes. Add polenta, broth, and salt and stir well. Seal large-sized pot with lid and cook on high for 8 minutes. Once done, allow to release pressure naturally. Remove lid. Stir in remaining ingredients and serve.

Per Serving: Calories 196, Fat 7.8g, Carbs 23.5g, Protein 8.2g

342. Herbed Beans

Ingredients for 5 servings

- 4 teaspoons olive oil
- ½ teaspoon garlic powder
- ¼ cup chicken stock
- ½ white onion, sliced
- ¼ cup bell pepper, chopped
- 3 cups butter beans, canned
- ½ teaspoon dried thyme
- ¼ teaspoon ground coriander

Directions and Total Time: approx. 30 minutes

Heat oil in the pan and add the onion. Cook it until light brown and add garlic powder, chicken stock, bell pepper, thyme, and ground coriander. Simmer the ingredients for 5 minutes. Add butter beans, stir the meal, and cook for 5 minutes more.

Per Serving: Calories 146, Fat 19.3g, Carbs 33.4g, Protein 40.3g

343. Herbed Polenta

Ingredients for 4 servings

- 1 cup of stone-ground polenta
- 4 cups of low-sodium vegetable stock or low-sodium chicken stock
- 1 tablespoon of extra-virgin olive oil
- 1 small onion, minced
- 2 garlic cloves, minced
- 1 teaspoon of sea salt
- 1 teaspoon of dried parsley
- 1 teaspoon of dried oregano
- 1 teaspoon of dried thyme
- ½ teaspoon of freshly ground black pepper
- ½ cup of grated Parmesan cheese

Directions and Total Time: approx. 5 hours and 10 minutes

In a slow cooker, combine the polenta, vegetable stock, olive oil, onion, garlic, salt, parsley, oregano, thyme, and pepper. Stir to mix well. 2. Cover the cooker and cook for 3 to 5 hours on Low heat. 3. Stir in the Parmesan cheese for serving.

Per Serving: Calories 244, Fat 7g, Carbs 33g, Protein 9g

344. Herbed Rice

Ingredients for 4 servings

- 1 teaspoon of salt
- 2 tablespoons of butter
- 1 onion, chopped
- 1 teaspoon of black pepper
- 3 cups of chicken broth
- 1 teaspoon of garlic, minced
- ¼ cup of lemon juice
- ½ cup of basmati rice
- ½ teaspoon of each of dried rosemary, basil, dill, parsley, oregano, and thyme

Directions and Total Time: approx. 30 minutes

Melt the butter in a large-sized pan on moderate heat. Add the salt and black pepper. Add the chopped 1 onion and cook until it has softened. Add the garlic and cook for just approximately about a minute. Add the chicken broth and lemon juice, along with the dried herbs and rice. Keep stirring until mixed. Wait for the mixture to boil, then cover and lower the heat. Keep cooking until the rice is well softened. Serve and enjoy.

Per Serving: Calories 227, Fat 1g, Carbs 49g, Protein 4g

345. Italian Sauteed Cannellini Beans

Ingredients for 6 servings

- 2 teaspoons extra-virgin olive oil
- ½ cup minced onion
- ¼ cup red wine vinegar
- 1 can no-salt-added tomato paste
- 2 tablespoons raw honey
- ½ cup water
- ¼ teaspoon ground cinnamon
- 2 cans cannellini beans

Directions and Total Time: approx. 25 minutes

In a large-sized saucepan over medium heat, heat the olive oil until it shimmers. Add the onion and sauté for 5 minutes or until translucent. Pour in the red wine vinegar, tomato paste, honey, and water. Sprinkle with cinnamon. Stir to mix well. Reduce the heat to low, then pour all the beans into the saucepan. Cook for 10 more minutes. Stir constantly. Serve immediately.

Per Serving: Calories 435, Fat 2.1g, Carbs 19g, Protein 26.2g

346. Italian-Style Aromatic Risotto

Ingredients for 5 servings

- 1 ½ cups Arborio rice
- 1/4 teaspoon ground bay laurel
- 1/4 teaspoon mustard seeds
- 1/2 teaspoon oregano
- 1/2 teaspoon basil
- 1/2 teaspoon thyme
- 2 cups roasted vegetable broth
- 1 cup Parmigiano-Reggiano cheese, preferably freshly grated

Directions and Total Time: approx. 45 minutes

Place all ingredients, except for the Parmigiano-Reggiano cheese, in the inner pot of your Instant Pot. Secure the lid. Choose the "Rice" mode and cook for 12 minutes at high pressure. Once cooking is complete, use a natural pressure release for 10 minutes; carefully remove the lid. Ladle into serving bowls, garnish with cheese and serve immediately. Bon appétit!

Per Serving: Calories 295, Fat 8.1g, Carbs 44.1g, Protein 10.8g

347. Kidney Beans Meal

Ingredients for 6 servings

- 1 can of kidney beans, rinsed
- ½ English cucumber, chopped
- 1 medium heirloom tomato, chopped
- 1 bunch of cilantro
- 1 red onion, chopped
- 1 large lime, juiced
- 3 tablespoons of extra-virgin olive oil
- 1 teaspoon of Dijon mustard
- ½ teaspoon of fresh garlic paste
- 1 teaspoon of sumac
- Salt and pepper, to taste

Directions and Total Time: approx. 10 minutes

In a medium-sized bowl, add the kidney beans, chopped veggies, and cilantro. Take a small bowl and make the vinaigrette by adding the lime juice, oil, garlic paste, pepper, mustard, and sumac. Pour the mixed vinaigrette over the salad and give it a gentle stir. Add some salt and pepper. Cover the medium-sized bowl and allow it to chill for half an hour. Serve and enjoy!

Per Serving: Calories 74, Fat 0.7g, Carbs 16g, Protein 5.5g

348. Lemon Barley Salad

Ingredients for 6 servings

- 12-ounces whole wheat orzo pasta
- ¼ cup olive oil
- 1 lemon juice
- 1 cup fresh mint leaves, chopped
- 1 cup fresh basil leaves, chopped
- ½ small onion, diced
- 1 cucumber, diced
- 14.5 ounces can chickpeas
- 3 cups baby spinach, chopped
- Pepper, and salt

Directions and Total Time: approx. 25 minutes

In a pot, bring plenty of water to a boil. When it boils, pour in a handful of salt, and the pasta, and cook for the time indicated on the package. Drain the pasta, and transfer to a large-sized bowl. Add the remaining ingredients to the bowl, and mix well. Season with pepper, and salt. Serve and enjoy!

Per Serving: Calories 381, Fat 10.6g, Carbs 65.3g, Protein 11.7g

349. Lentils in Tomato Sauce

Ingredients for 4 servings

- 2 ½ cups of water
- 1 cup of green lentils
- 1 tablespoon of olive oil
- 1 zucchini, cubed
- ½ large onion, diced
- 2 cloves of garlic, minced
- 2 tablespoons of lovage, chopped
- 1 tablespoon of fresh thyme, chopped
- 2 cups of tomato sauce

Directions and Total Time: approx. 30 minutes

Add the water to a saucepan, add the lentils, and bring to a boil. Cover and simmer until the lentils are tender (about 20 minutes). Heat the tablespoon of olive oil in a skillet over high heat. Sauté the onion, garlic, and zucchini for 5–7 minutes. Add the lovage and thyme and cook until slightly wilted (about 10 seconds). Add the lentils and tomato sauce. Reduce the heat and cook for 3–5 minutes.

Per Serving: Calories 288, Fat 10.5g, Carbs 39g, Protein 11g

350. Mashed Fava Beans

Ingredients for 4 servings

- 3 pounds of fava beans, pods but unpeeled
- ¼ cup of water
- ¼ cup of extra-virgin olive oil
- 3 garlic cloves, chopped
- 1 tablespoon of fresh rosemary, finely chopped
- Salt and black pepper, to taste

Directions and Total Time: approx. 20 minutes

Bring a small-sized pot of water to a boil over high heat and cook the beans for 3 minutes. Drain the fava beans and rinse under cold running water to cool. Peel the outer skin off the beans. The inner bean should pop out easily. Put the fava beans in a food processor, add the water and salt, and puree. In a skillet, heat the olive oil over low heat. Add the fava bean puree, garlic, rosemary, and pepper. Stir to combine and cook for approximately about 5 minutes, until most of the water evaporates.

Per Serving: Calories 423, Fat 16g, Carbs 61g, Protein 27g

351. Mediterranean Brown Rice

Ingredients for 4 servings

- 1 pound of asparagus, steamed and chopped
- 2 tablespoons of olive oil
- 3 tablespoons of balsamic vinegar
- 1 cup of brown rice
- 2 teaspoons of mustard
- Salt and black pepper to taste
- 5 ounces of baby spinach
- ½ cup of parsley, chopped
- 1 tablespoon of tarragon, chopped

Directions and Total Time: approx. 20 minutes

Bring to a boil a large-sized pot of salted water over medium heat. Add in brown rice and cook for 7-9 minutes until al dente. Drain and place in a bowl. Add the asparagus to the same large-sized pot and blanch them for 4-5 minutes. Remove them to the rice bowl. Mix in spinach, olive oil, balsamic vinegar, mustard, salt, pepper, parsley, and tarragon. Serve.

Per Serving: Calories 330, Fat 12g, Carbs 17g, Protein 11g

352. Mediterranean Spiced Lentils

Ingredients for 6 servings

- 1 teaspoon of dried oregano
- ¾ cup of green lentils
- 1 teaspoon of dried basil
- ¼ teaspoon of ground sage
- 2 ¼ cups of water
- ½ teaspoon of dried parsley
- ¼ teaspoon of onion powder

Directions and Total Time: approx. 25 minutes

In a heavy saucepan placed over medium-high heat, add the lentils, water, and spices. Let the ingredients come to a boil, and then cover with a lid. Reduce the heat and simmer for just about 20 minutes. Stir well and serve hot.

Per Serving: Calories 258, Fat 0.9g, Carbs 44.1g, Protein 18.7g

353. Mediterranean Spinach and Beans

Ingredients for 4 servings

- 1 small onion, chopped
- 1 tablespoon of olive oil
- 2 garlic cloves, minced
- 2 tablespoons of Worcestershire sauce
- ¼ teaspoon of pepper
- 1 can (15 ounces) cannellini beans
- 8 cups of fresh baby spinach
- 1 can (14½-ounces) diced no-salt-added tomatoes, undrained
- ¼ teaspoon of salt
- ⅛ teaspoon of red pepper flakes, crushed
- 1 can (14 ounces) water-packed artichoke hearts, rinsed, drained, and quartered

Directions and Total Time: approx. 30 minutes

Heat the tablespoon of olive oil in a large-sized skillet placed over medium-high heat and sauté the minced garlic and chopped onion for about 5 minutes. Add the Worcestershire sauce, tomatoes, and seasonings, and let the mixture come to a boil. Reduce the heat and simmer for just about 8 minutes. Stir in the beans, spinach, and artichoke hearts, and cook for about 5 minutes.

Per Serving: Calories 241, Fat 4.3g, Carbs 39.5g, Protein 5.1g

354. Mediterranean Tomato Rice

Ingredients for 6 servings

- 1 cup of chopped onion
- 2 cloves of garlic, minced
- 2 tablespoons of olive oil
- 1 cup of celery, sliced
- 1 teaspoon of dried thyme
- 1/2 teaspoon of dried marjoram
- 1 cup of green bell pepper, diced
- 1 (15-ounces) can of tomatoes
- 1 tablespoon of tomato paste
- Salt and pepper, to taste
- 3 cups of cooked rice

Directions and Total Time: approx. 20 minutes

Sauté the garlic and onions in a skillet with oil for 5 minutes. Stir in the marjoram, thyme and celery then cook for 2 minutes. Add the bell pepper then sauté for 3 minutes. Stir in the tomato paste and drained tomatoes. Adjust the seasoning with black pepper and salt. Mix well and serve warm.

Per Serving: Calories 411, Fat 5.6, Carbs 81.5g, Protein 8g

355. Mediterranean White Beans

Ingredients for 4 servings

- ¼ cup of extra-virgin olive oil
- 1 (24-ounce) jar of white beans, drained and rinsed
- ½ cup of onion, chopped
- 1 large garlic clove, minced
- 1 teaspoon of salt
- ½ teaspoon of dried rosemary, crushed
- ½ cup of celery, chopped
- 1 (16-ounce) can of diced tomatoes, with juice
- 1 teaspoon of sugar
- ¼ cup of fresh Italian parsley, chopped

Directions and Total Time: approx. 30 minutes

Heat the cup of olive oil in a large-sized skillet placed over medium-high heat and sauté the minced garlic and chopped onion for about 5 minutes. Add the white beans, tomatoes, rosemary, salt, and sugar, and let the mixture come to a boil. Reduce the heat, then cover using its lid, and simmer for about 15 minutes. Stir in the parsley and serve.

Per Serving: Calories 346, Fat 8.3g, Carbs 60.2g, Protein 7.9g

356. Mexican Rice

Ingredients for 3 servings

- 1 cup of long-grain polished rice
- 1 tablespoon of Avocado oil
- 1/4 cup of onion; chopped
- 2 garlic cloves; finely chopped.
- 1/2 teaspoon of Salt
- 2 tablespoons of Crushed tomatoes
- 2 tablespoons of Cilantro; chopped.
- 2 tablespoons of Sun-dried tomatoes
- 2 cups of chicken broth
- 1/4 teaspoon of Cumin
- 1/4 teaspoon of Garlic powder
- 1/4 teaspoon of Smoked paprika

Directions and Total Time: approx. 21 minutes

Add oil, onion and garlic to Instant Pot. *Sauté* for 3 minutes. Stir in rice and blend well with the onion. Add all the remaining Ingredients to the cooker. Cover and secure the lid. Turn its pressure release handle to the sealing position. Cook on the *Manual* function with high for 8 minutes. When it beeps; do a Natural release, Stir and serve warm.

Per Serving: Calories 252, Fat 1.5g, Carbs 53.1g, Protein 5.6g

357. Milanese-Style Risotto

Ingredients for 4 servings

- 2 tablespoons of olive oil
- 2 tablespoons of butter, softened
- 1 cup of Arborio rice, cooked
- ½ cup of white wine
- 1 onion, chopped
- Salt and black pepper to taste
- 2 cups of hot chicken stock
- 1 pinch of saffron, soaked
- ½ cup of Parmesan, grated

Directions and Total Time: approx. 10 minutes

Warm the olive oil in a large-sized skillet over medium heat and sauté onion for 3 minutes. Stir in rice, salt, and pepper for 1 minute. Pour in white wine and saffron and stir to deglaze the bottom of the skillet. Gradually add in the chicken stock while stirring; cook for 15-18 minutes. Turn off the heat and mix in butter and Parmesan cheese. Serve immediately.

Per Serving: Calories 250, Fat 10g, Carbs 18g, Protein 5g

358. Minty Lamb Risotto

Ingredients for 4 servings

- 2 tablespoons of olive oil
- 2 garlic cloves, minced
- 1 onion, chopped
- 1 pound of lamb, cubed
- Salt and black pepper to taste
- 2 cups of vegetable stock
- 1 cup of arborio rice
- 2 tablespoons of mint, chopped
- 1 cup of Parmesan, grated

Directions and Total Time: approx. 90 minutes

Warm the olive oil in a large-sized skillet over medium heat and cook the onion for 5 minutes. Put in lamb and cook for another 5 minutes. Stir in garlic, salt, pepper, and stock and bring to a simmer; cook for 1 hour. Stir in rice and cook for 18-20 minutes. Top with Parmesan cheese and mint and serve.

Per Serving: Calories 310, Fat 14g, Carbs 17g, Protein 15g

359. Mung Beans Meatballs

Ingredients for 3 servings

- 1 cup mung beans, cooked
- 2 tablespoons flax meal
- ¼ cup onion, minced
- 1 teaspoon dried oregano
- 2 oz black olives, chopped
- 1 tablespoon olive oil
- ½ teaspoon cayenne pepper

Directions and Total Time: approx. 35 minutes

Mash the mung beans gently and mix with flax meal, minced onion, dried oregano, olives, and cayenne pepper. Make the balls from the mixture. Brush the large-sized baking pan with olive oil and put the mung beans balls inside. Cook them for 10 minutes at 355F. Flip the meatballs on another side and cook them for 5 minutes.

Per Serving: Calories 123, Fat 19.3g, Carbs 33.4g, Protein 12.3g

360. Mushroom and Green Onion Rice Pilaf

Ingredients for 4 servings

- 2 tablespoons of olive oil
- 1 cup of rice, rinsed
- 2 greens onions, chopped
- 2 cups of chicken stock
- 1 cup of mushrooms, sliced
- 1 garlic clove, minced
- Salt and black pepper to taste
- ½ cup of Parmesan cheese, grated
- 2 tablespoons of cilantro, chopped

Directions and Total Time: approx. 30 minutes

Warm the olive oil in a large-sized skillet over medium heat and cook onion, garlic, and mushrooms for 5 minutes until tender. Stir in rice, salt, and pepper for 1 minute. Pour in chicken stock and cook for 15-18 minutes. Transfer to a platter, scatter Parmesan cheese all over, and sprinkle with cilantro to serve.

Per Serving: Calories 250, Fat 10g, Carbs 28g, Protein 13g

361. Mushroom Chickpea Marsala

Ingredients for 4 servings

- 2 tablespoon olive oil
- 8 ouncces baby portobello mushrooms, sliced
- 2 garlic cloves, minced
- 1 cup dry Marsala wine
- 2 tablespoon lemon juice, or to taste
- 1 teaspoon rubbed sage
- 1/2 teaspoon black pepper
- 1/4 teaspoon salt
- 2 tablespoon chopped fresh parsley
- 1-14 ounces can or 1 3/4 cups cooked chickpeas, rinsed and drained

Directions and Total Time: approx. 30 minutes

On medium fire, place a large saucepan and heat oil. Add mushrooms, cover and cook for just about 5 minutes. Stir in garlic and cook for 2 minutes. Add wine, lemon juice, sage, salt and pepper. Deglaze pot. Simmer for 10 minutes while covered. Add chickpeas and mix well. Cook for 3 minutes. Remove pot from fire and stir in parsley. Serve and enjoy.

Per Serving: Calories 159, Fat 8.5g, Carbs 16.8g, Protein 6.1g

362. Mushroom Pilaf

Ingredients for 4 servings

- 2 tablespoons olive oil
- 1 shallot, chopped
- 2 garlic cloves, minced
- 1 pound button mushrooms
- 1 cup brown rice
- 2 cups chicken stock
- 1 bay leaf
- 1 thyme sprig
- Salt and pepper to taste

Directions and Total Time: approx. 55 minutes

Heat the oil in a skillet and stir in the shallot and garlic. Cook for 2 minutes until softened and fragrant. Add the mushrooms and rice and cook for 5 minutes. Add the stock, bay leaf and thyme, as well as salt and pepper and continue cooking for 20 more minutes on low heat. Serve the pilaf warm and fresh.

Per Serving: Calories 265, Fat 8.9g, Carbs 41.2g, Protein 7.6g

363. Mushroom Risotto

Ingredients for 4 servings

- 1 onion, chopped
- 1 teaspoon of olive oil
- 9 ounces of chestnut mushrooms, sliced
- 4 cups of vegetable stock
- 1 3/4 ounces of porcini
- 10 ½ ounces of wholegrain rice
- Small bunch of parsley, chopped
- Grated parmesan cheese, to serve

Directions and Total Time: approx. 3 hours and 30 minutes

Sauté the onion in a skillet with oil for 10 minutes. Stir in the mushroom slices and cook until soft. Pour the stock and porcini then let it simmer. Remove and set aside for 5-10 minutes to soak. Add the mushrooms, porcini, stock and onions to a slow cooker. Cook for 3 hours on high with rice. Garnish with parsley and parmesan. Serve warm.

Per Serving: Calories 363, Fat 3.8g, Carbs 76.9g, Protein 17g

364. Onion Green Beans

Ingredients for 2 servings

- 11 ounces green beans
- 1 tablespoon onion powder
- 1 tablespoon olive oil
- ½ teaspoon salt
- ¼ teaspoon chili flakes

Directions and Total Time: approx. 22 minutes

Wash the green beans carefully and place them in the bowl. Sprinkle the green beans with onion powder, salt, chili flakes, and olive oil. Shake the green beans carefully. Preheat the air fryer to 400 F. Put the green beans in the air fryer and cook for 8 minutes. After this, shake the green beans and cook them for 4 minutes more at 400 F. When the time is over – shake the green beans. Serve the side dish and enjoy!

Per Serving: Calories 120.5, Fat 7.2g, Carbs 13.9g, Protein 3.2g

365. Orzo-Veggie Pilaf

Ingredients for 6 servings

- 1-pint (2 cups) cherry tomatoes, cut in half
- 2 cups orzo
- 1 cup Kalamata olives
- 1 teaspoon salt
- 1/2 cup extra-virgin olive oil
- 1/2 cup fresh basil, finely chopped
- 1/2 teaspoon freshly ground black pepper
- 1/3 cup balsamic vinegar

Directions and Total Time: approx. 30 minutes

Bring a small-sized pot of water to a boil. Put the orzo and cook for 7 minutes. Using a strainer, drain and rinse the orzo with cold water. Once the orzo has cooled, put it in a huge bowl. Add the basil, olives, and tomatoes. Whisk together the salt, vinegar, olive oil, and pepper in a small bowl. Add this prepared dressing to the pasta and toss everything together. Serve chilled or at room temperature.

Per Serving: Calories 476, Fat 28g, Carbs 48g, Protein 8g

366. Paprika Spinach and Chickpea Bowl

Ingredients for 4 servings

- 2 tablespoons of olive oil
- 1 pound of canned chickpeas
- 10 ounces of spinach
- 1 teaspoon of coriander seeds
- 1 red onion, finely chopped
- 2 tomatoes, pureed
- 1 garlic clove, minced
- ½ tablespoon of rosemary
- ½ teaspoon of smoked paprika
- Salt and white pepper to taste

Directions and Total Time: approx. 20 minutes

Heat the olive oil in a large-sized pot over medium heat. Add in the onion, garlic, coriander seeds, salt, and pepper and cook for 3 minutes until translucent. Stir in tomatoes, rosemary, paprika, salt, and white pepper. Bring to a boil, then you can actually lower the heat, and simmer for 10 minutes. Add in chickpeas and spinach and cook covered until the spinach wilts. Serve.

Per Serving: Calories 512, Fat 1.8g, Carbs 76g, Protein 25g

367. Parmesan and Pork Rind Green Beans

Ingredients for 4 servings

- ½ pound fresh green beans
- 2 tablespoons crushed pork rinds
- 2 tablespoons olive oil
- 1 tablespoon grated Parmesan cheese
- Pink Himalayan salt
- Freshly ground black pepper

Directions and Total Time: approx. 20 minutes

Preheat the oven to 400°F. In a large-sized bowl, combine the green beans, pork rinds, olive oil, and Parmesan cheese. Season with pink Himalayan salt and pepper, and toss until the beans are thoroughly coated. Spread the bean mixture on a baking sheet in a single layer, and roast for about 15 minutes. At the halfway point, give the pan a little shake to move the beans around, or just give them a stir. Divide the beans between two plates and serve.

Per Serving: Calories 350, Fat 30g, Carbs 1.6g, Protein 8g

368. Parmesan Polenta

Ingredients for 6 servings

- 4 cups water
- 1 cup milk
- salt
- 1 cup coarse or medium-grind cornmeal
- 3 tablespoons butter
- ½ cup grated Parmesan cheese

Directions and Total Time: approx. 40 minutes

In a saucepan, pour the water, and milk, and bring to a boil. Add 1 ½ tsps. of salt, and stir. Gradually pour the polenta into the saucepan, whisking at the same time. Lower the heat to low, cover, and continue to cook the polenta for 25 to 30 minutes over low heat, until it is thick, fluffy, and begins to pull away from the sides of the pan. Stir occasionally so it doesn't stick to the bottom of the pot. When ready, remove from heat, and stir in the butter, cheese, and more salt to taste, if needed. Serve hot, sprinkling with more cheese if desired.

Per Serving: Calories 180, Fat 20g, Carbs 19g, Protein 6g

369. Pork Strips and Rice

Ingredients for 4 servings

- ½ pound pork loin, cut into strips
- Salt and black pepper to taste
- 2 tablespoons olive oil
- 2 carrots, chopped
- 1 red bell pepper, chopped
- 3 garlic cloves, minced
- 2 cups veggie stock
- 1 cup basmati rice
- ½ cup garbanzo beans
- 10 black olives, pitted and sliced
- 1 tablespoon parsley, chopped

Directions and Total Time: approx. 35 minutes

Heat a large-sized pan with the oil over medium-high heat. Add the pork fillets, stir, cook for 5 minutes and transfer them to a plate. Add the carrots, bell pepper and garlic, stir and cook for 5 more minutes. Add the rice, the stock, beans and the olives, stir, cook for 14 minutes, divide between plates, sprinkle the parsley on top as garnish and serve.

Per Serving: Calories 220, Fat 31g, Carbs 21g, Protein 23g

370. Pumpkin Rice

Ingredients for 3 servings

- 2 cups of pumpkin, cubed
- 1 cup of cauliflower rice
- Salt and black pepper, to taste
- 4 tablespoons of olive oil
- 2 cups of vegetable broth
- 1 cup of brown rice, presoaked
- 2 cloves of garlic, minced
- ¼ teaspoon of fresh ginger, minced
- 1 green onion, chopped

Directions and Total Time: approx. 30 minutes

Put an Instant Pot on sauté mode. Add the oil and sauté the green onions for 1 minute. Add the ginger and garlic and cook until fragrant. Add the cauliflower and pumpkin cubes. Sauté for approximately about a few minutes and then add salt, black pepper, and vegetable broth. Add the brown rice and lock the lid. Cook it at a natural high pressure for 15 minutes. Once the timer beeps, release the steam naturally. The rice should be fluffy, and the vegetables should be tender. Serve and enjoy.

Per Serving: Calories 470, Fat 20.9g, Carbs 66.3g, Protein 7.5g

371. Quinoa and Watercress Salad with Nuts

Ingredients for 4 servings

- 2 boiled eggs, cut into wedges
- 2 cups of watercress
- 2 cups of cherry tomatoes, halved
- 1 cucumber, sliced
- 1 cup of quinoa, cooked
- 1 cup of almonds, chopped
- 2 tablespoons of olive oil
- 1 avocado, peeled and sliced
- 2 tablespoons of fresh cilantro, chopped
- Salt to taste
- 1 lemon, juiced

Directions and Total Time: approx. 5 minutes

Place watercress, cherry tomatoes, cucumber, quinoa, almonds, olive oil, cilantro, salt, and lemon juice in a bowl and toss to combine. Top with egg wedges and avocado slices and serve immediately.

Per Serving: Calories 530, Fat 35g, Carbs 45g, Protein 20g

372. Quinoa with Peas and Onion

Ingredients for 2 servings

- 2 cups of water
- 1 cup of quinoa, rinsed
- 1 small onion, chopped
- 1 tablespoon of olive oil
- 1 ½ cup of frozen peas
- ½ teaspoon of salt
- ¼ teaspoon of black pepper
- 2 tablespoons of walnuts, chopped

Directions and Total Time: approx. 37 minutes

Bring the cup of quinoa and water to a boil in a saucepan. Reduce the heat, cover and let it simmer for 15 minutes. Sauté the onion with oil in a skillet until soft. Stir in the peas and cook for 2 minutes. Add the quinoa, black pepper, and salt then garnish with walnuts. Serve.

Per Serving: Calories 265, Fat 8.6g, Carbs 37.9g, Protein 10.2g

373. Rice with Pineapple, Raisins and Almonds

Ingredients for 4 servings

- 1 ½ cups of chicken broth
- ¾ cup of white rice, rinsed and drained
- ¼ cup of raisins
- ¼ cup of almond slivers
- 2 tablespoons of oil
- 2¼ teaspoons of soy sauce
- ¾ teaspoon of curry powder
- ½ teaspoon of ground turmeric
- ½ cup of canned pineapple chunks, drained

Directions and Total Time: approx. 40 minutes

In a pan, add broth over high heat and bring to a boil. Add the rice, raisins, almonds, oil, soy sauce, curry powder, and turmeric and stir to combine. Adjust the heat to low and simmer, covered for about 20 minutes or until all the liquid is absorbed. Stir in the chunks of pineapple and remove from the heat. Serve hot.

Per Serving: Calories 277, Fat 10.7g, Carbs 37.9g, Protein 6.2g

374. Rice with Pork Chops

Ingredients for 4 servings

- 1 cup of raw long-grain brown rice, rinsed
- 2 ½ cups of low-sodium chicken broth
- 1 cup of sliced tomato
- 8 ounces of fresh spinach, chopped
- 1 small onion, chopped
- 2 garlic cloves, minced
- 2 teaspoons of dried oregano
- 2 teaspoons of dried basil
- 1 teaspoon of sea salt
- ½ teaspoon of freshly ground black pepper
- 4 thick-cut pork chops
- ¼ cup of grated Parmesan cheese

Directions and Total Time: approx. 5 hours and 10 minutes

In a slow cooker, combine the rice, chicken broth, tomato, spinach, onion, garlic, oregano, basil, salt, and pepper. Stir to mix well. Place the thick-cut pork chops on top of the rice mixture. Cover the cooker and cook for 3 to 5 hours on Low heat. Top with the Parmesan cheese for serving.

Per Serving: Calories 375, Fat 10g, Carbs 43g, Protein 31g

375. Rice with Vermicelli

Ingredients for 6 servings

- 2 cups short-grain rice
- 3 ½ cups water, plus more for rinsing and soaking the rice
- ¼ cup olive oil
- 1 cup broken vermicelli pasta
- Salt

Directions and Total Time: approx. 55 minutes

Soak the rice under cold water until the water runs clean. Place the rice in a bowl, cover with water, and let soak for 10 minutes. Drain and set aside. Cook the olive oil in a medium pot over medium heat. Stir in the vermicelli and cook for 2 to 3 minutes, stirring continuously, until golden. Put the rice and cook for 1 minute, stirring, so the rice is well coated in the oil. Stir in the water and a pinch of salt and bring the liquid to a boil. Adjust heat and simmer for 20 minutes. Pull out from the heat and let rest for 10 minutes. Fluff with a fork and serve.

Per Serving: Calories 346, Fat 9g, Carbs 60g, Protein 2g

376. Riced Cauliflower

Ingredients for 8 servings

- 1 small head cauliflower, broken into florets
- ¼ cup extra-virgin olive oil
- 2 garlic cloves, finely minced
- 1 ½ teaspoons salt
- ½ teaspoon freshly ground black pepper

Directions and Total Time: approx. 15 minutes

Place the prepared cauliflower florets in a food processor and pulse several times, until the cauliflower is the consistency of rice or couscous. In a large-sized skillet, heat the olive oil over medium-high heat. Add the cauliflower, garlic, salt, and pepper and sauté for 5 minutes, just to take the crunch out but not enough to let the cauliflower become soggy. Remove the cauliflower from the skillet and place in a bowl until ready to use. Toss with chopped herbs and additional olive oil for a simple side, top with sautéed veggies and protein, or use in your favorite recipe.

Per Serving: Calories 92, Fat 9g, Carbs 3g, Protein 1g

377. Ricotta and Olive Rigatoni

Ingredients for 4 servings

- 2 tablespoons of extra-virgin olive oil
- 1 pound of rigatoni
- ½ pound of Ricotta cheese, crumbled
- 3⁄4 cup of black olives, chopped
- 10 sun-dried tomatoes, sliced
- 1 tablespoon of dried oregano
- Black pepper to taste

Directions and Total Time: approx. 25 minutes

Bring to a boil salted water in a pot over high heat. Add the rigatoni and small-sized saucepan over medium heat. Add the rigatoni, ricotta, olives, and sun-dried tomatoes. Toss mixture to combine and cook 2–3 minutes or until cheese just starts to melt. Season with oregano and pepper.

Per Serving: Calories 383, Fat 28g, Carbs 21g, Protein 15g

378. Rosemary Barley with Walnuts

Ingredients for 4 servings

- 2 tablespoons of olive oil
- ½ cup of diced onion
- ½ cup of diced celery
- 1 carrot, peeled and diced
- 3 cups of water
- 1 cup of barley
- ½ teaspoon of thyme
- ½ teaspoon of rosemary
- ¼ cup of pine nuts
- Salt and black pepper to taste

Directions and Total Time: approx. 45 minutes

Warm the olive oil in a large-sized saucepan over medium heat. Sauté the onion, celery, and carrot over medium heat until tender. Add the water, barley, and seasonings, and bring to a boil. Reduce the heat and simmer for 23 minutes or until tender. Stir in the pine nuts and season to taste. Serve warm.

Per Serving: Calories 276, Fat 9g, Carbs 41g, Protein 7g

Ingredients for 4 servings

- 5 cups of chicken stock
- 2 tablespoons of butter
- 1 tablespoon of olive oil
- 1 onion, chopped
- 12 ounces of arborio risotto rice
- ½ cup of sherry
- ½ teaspoon of saffron
- 3 ounces of parmesan, grated
- 1 egg yolk
- Rocket salad, to serve

Directions and Total Time: approx. 40 minutes

Warm the stock in a medium-sized saucepan over low heat. Sauté the onion with butter, olive oil and salt in a skillet for 5 minutes. Stir in the rice and mix well. Pour in the wine, stock and saffron then cook for 30 minutes. Stir in the egg yolk and parmesan to the rice and serve with rocket salad. Enjoy.

Per Serving: Calories 392, Fat 10g, Carbs 41g, Protein 16g

380. Sausage Fennel Risotto

Ingredients for 4 servings

- 4 sausages, sliced
- 1 tablespoon of butter
- 2 bulbs of fennel, sliced
- 1 teaspoon of fennel seeds
- 1 garlic clove, crushed
- 10 ½ ounces of risotto rice
- Glass of white wine
- 4 cups of chicken stock
- 2 ounces of parmesan, grated

Directions and Total Time: approx. 21 minutes

Sauté the sausage slices in a deep skillet until brown and set them aside. Add the fennel seeds, sliced fennel and butter into the same skillet and cook until the fennel slices soften. Stir in the garlic clove and sauté for 1 minute. Add the risotto rice, white wine, stock and cook on low heat until rice is soft. Garnish with sausage slices, parmesan and fennel fronds. Enjoy.

Per Serving: Calories 443, Fat 10.8g, Carbs 66.2g, Protein 13.8g

381. Seafood Risotto

Ingredients for 4 servings

- 6 cups vegetable broth
- 3 tablespoons extra-virgin olive oil
- 1 large onion, chopped
- 3 cloves garlic, minced
- ½ teaspoon saffron threads
- 1 ½ cups arborio rice
- 1 ½ teaspoon salt
- 8-ounces shrimp, peeled, and deveined
- 8-ounces scallops

Directions and Total Time: approx. 45 minutes

In a saucepan, heat the broth over medium-low heat. Meanwhile, in another large-sized saucepan, heat the olive oil over medium heat. Add the onion, garlic, and saffron, and season for 3 minutes. Add the rice, salt, and 1 cup of hot broth. Stir well, then after, cook over low heat until most of the liquid is absorbed. Add the prepared broth a little at a time as it is absorbed. Along with the last ½ cup of broth, add the shrimp, and scallops. Cover, and allow to cook for just about 10 minutes. Serve hot.

Per Serving: Calories 460, Fat 12g, Carbs 64g, Protein 24g

Ingredients for 2 servings

- 2 boneless pork chops
- Pink Himalayan salt
- Freshly ground black pepper
- 2 tablespoons toasted sesame oil, divided
- 2 tablespoons soy sauce
- 1 teaspoon Sriracha sauce
- 1 cup fresh green beans

Directions and Total Time: approx. 15 minutes

On a cutting board, pat the pork chops dry with a paper towel. Slice the chops into strips and season with pink Himalayan salt and pepper. In a large-sized skillet over medium-high heat, heat one tablespoon of sesame oil. Add the pork strips and cook for 7 minutes, stirring occasionally. In a large-sized bowl, mix the remaining one tablespoon of sesame oil, the soy sauce, and the Sriracha sauce. Pour into the skillet with the pork. Add the green beans to the skillet, reduce the heat to medium-low, and simmer for 3 to 5 minutes. Divide the pork, green beans, and sauce between two wide, shallow bowls and serve.

Per Serving: Calories 387, Fat 15.1g, Carbs 4.1g, Protein 18.1g

383. Spanish-Style Rice

Ingredients for 4 servings

- 1 ½ cups of white rice
- ¼ cup of olive oil
- 1 small onion, finely chopped
- 1 red bell pepper, seeded and diced
- 1 teaspoon of sweet paprika
- ½ teaspoon of ground cumin
- ½ teaspoon of ground cilantro
- 1 garlic clove, minced
- 3 tablespoons of tomato paste
- 3 cups of vegetable broth
- ⅛ teaspoon of salt

Directions and Total Time: approx. 35 minutes

Heat the cup of olive oil in a large heavy-bottomed skillet over medium heat. Stir in the onion and red bell pepper. Cook for 5 minutes or until softened. Add the rice, paprika, cumin, and cilantro and cook for 2 minutes, stirring often. Add the garlic, tomato paste, vegetable broth, and salt. Stir well and season, as needed. Allow the prepared mixture to come to a boil. Lower the heat and simmer for 20 minutes. Set aside for 5 minutes before serving.

Per Serving: Calories 414, Fat 14g, Carbs 63g, Protein 2g

384. Spicy Bean Rolls

Ingredients for 4 servings

- 1 tablespoon of olive oil
- 1 red onion, chopped
- 2 garlic cloves, minced
- 1 green bell pepper, sliced
- 2 cups of canned cannellini beans
- 1 red chili pepper, chopped
- 1 tablespoon of cilantro, chopped
- 1 teaspoon of cumin, ground
- Salt and black pepper to taste
- 4 whole-wheat tortillas
- 1 cup of mozzarella, shredded

Directions and Total Time: approx. 25 minutes

Warm the olive oil in a large-sized skillet over medium heat and sauté onion for 3 minutes. Stir in garlic, bell pepper, cannellini beans, red chili pepper, cilantro, cumin, salt, and pepper and cook for 15 minutes. Spoon bean mixture on each tortilla and top with cheese. Roll up and serve right away.

Per Serving: Calories 680, Fat 15g, Carbs 75g, Protein 38g

Ingredients for 4 servings

- 2 teaspoons olive oil
- 1 garlic clove, minced
- ½ teaspoon smoked paprika
- ¾ cup veggie stock
- 1 yellow onion, sliced
- 1 red bell pepper, chopped
- 15 ounces canned butter beans, drained
- 4 cups baby spinach
- ½ cup goats cheese, shredded
- 2 teaspoon sherry vinegar

Directions and Total Time: approx. 35 minutes

Heat a large-sized pan with the oil over medium heat, add garlic, stir and cook for 30 seconds. Add onion, paprika, and bell pepper and cook for 6 minutes. Add beans, spinach, and stock, and cook for 3 minutes more. Add cheese and vinegar, divide between plates and serve.

Per Serving: Calories 140, Fat 1g, Carbs 2g, Protein 2g

386. Spicy Cauliflower Steaks with Steamed Green Beans

Ingredients for 4 servings

- 2 heads cauliflower, sliced lengthwise into 'steaks.'
- 1/4 cup olive oil
- 1/4 cup chili sauce
- 2 teaspoons erythritol
- Salt and black pepper to taste
- 2 shallots, diced
- 1 bunch green beans, trimmed
- 2 tablespoons fresh lemon juice
- 1 cup of water Dried parsley to garnish

Directions and Total Time: approx. 35 minutes

In a bowl or container, mix the olive oil, chili sauce, and erythritol. Brush the cauliflower with the mixture. Grill for 6 minutes. Flip the cauliflower, cook further for 6 minutes. Let the water boil, place the green beans in a sieve, and set over the steam from the boiling water. Cover with a clean napkin to keep the steam trapped in the sieve. Cook for 6 minutes. After, remove to a bowl and toss with lemon juice. Remove the grilled caulis to a plate, sprinkle with salt, pepper, shallots, and parsley. Serve with the steamed green beans.

Per Serving: Calories 329, Fat 10.4g, Carbs 4.2g, Protein 8.4g

387. Spicy Rice Bowl with Broccoli and Spinach

Ingredients for 4 servings

- 2 tablespoons of olive oil
- 12 ounces of broccoli cuts
- 3 cups of fresh baby spinach
- 1 red chili, chopped
- 1 ½ cups of cooked brown rice
- 1 onion, chopped
- 1 garlic clove, minced
- 1 orange, juiced and zested
- 1 cup of vegetable broth
- Salt and black pepper to taste

Directions and Total Time: approx. 25 minutes

Warm olive oil in a large-sized pan over medium heat and sauté onion for 5 minutes, then add in broccoli cuts and cook for 4-5 minutes until tender. Stir-fry garlic and chili for 30 seconds. Pour in orange zest, orange juice, broth, salt, and pepper and bring to a boil. Stir in the rice and spinach and cook for 4 minutes until the liquid is reduced. Serve.

Per Serving: Calories 391, Fat 9.4g, Carbs 67.6g, Protein 9g

388. Spinach Rice

Ingredients for 2 servings

- 2 tablespoons olive oil
- ½ cup chopped onion
- ¾ cup water
- 1 tablespoon dried parsley flakes
- ¼ to ½ teaspoon salt
- 1/8 teaspoon pepper
- ½ cup uncooked instant rice
- 2 cups fresh baby spinach

Directions and Total Time: approx. 30 minutes

In a large-sized saucepan, heat oil over medium-high heat. Add onion, and sauté until tender. Add water, parsley, salt, and pepper, and bring to a boil. Add rice, and spinach, cover, remove from heat, and let stand for 10 minutes. Stir to combine, and serve immediately.

Per Serving: Calories 235, Fat 14g, Carbs 25g, Protein 3g

389. Stewed Borlotti Beans

Ingredients for 6 servings

- 3 tablespoons of olive oil
- 1 onion, chopped
- 1 (12-ounces) can of tomato paste
- ¼ cup of red wine vinegar
- 8 fresh sage leaves, chopped
- 2 garlic cloves, minced
- ½ cup of water
- 2 (15-ounces) cans of borlotti beans

Directions and Total Time: approx. 25 minutes

Warm the olive oil in a large-sized saucepan over medium heat. Sauté the onion and garlic for 5 minutes, stirring frequently. Add the tomato paste, vinegar, and 1 cup of water, and mix well. Turn the heat to low. Drain and rinse just one can of the beans in a colander and add to the saucepan. Pour the entire second can of beans (including the liquid) into the saucepan. Simmer for 10 minutes, stirring occasionally. Serve warm sprinkled with sage.

Per Serving: Calories 434, Fat 2g, Carbs 80g, Protein 26g

390. Sun-Dried Tomato and Basil Risotto

Ingredients for 4 servings

- 10 ounces of sundried tomatoes in olive oil, drained and chopped
- 2 tablespoons of olive oil
- 2 cups of chicken stock
- 1 onion, chopped
- 1 cup of Arborio rice
- Salt and black pepper to taste
- 1 cup of Pecorino cheese, grated
- ¼ cup of basil leaves, chopped

Directions and Total Time: approx. 35 minutes

Warm the olive oil in a large-sized skillet over medium heat and cook onion and sundried tomatoes for 5 minutes. Stir in rice, chicken stock, salt, pepper, and basil and bring to a boil. Cook for 20 minutes. Mix in Pecorino cheese and serve.

Per Serving: Calories 430, Fat 9g, Carbs 57g, Protein 8g

391. Tasty Greek Rice

Ingredients for 6 servings

- 1 3/4 cup brown rice, rinsed and drained
- 3/4 cup roasted red peppers, chopped
- 1 cup olives, chopped
- 1 teaspoon dried oregano
- 1 teaspoon Greek seasoning
- 1 3/4 cup vegetable broth
- 2 tablespoons olive oil
- Salt

Directions and Total Time: approx. 20 minutes

Add oil into the inner pot of instant pot and set the pot on sauté mode. Add rice and cook for 5 minutes. Add remaining ingredients except for red peppers and olives and stir well. Seal large-sized pot with lid and cook on high for 5 minutes. Once it's done, allow to release pressure naturally for just about 10 minutes then release remaining using quick release. Remove lid. Add red peppers and olives and stir well. Serve and enjoy.

Per Serving: Calories 285, Fat 9.1g, Carbs 45.7g, Protein 6g

392. Tomato Bean and Sausage Casserole

Ingredients for 4 servings

- 2 tablespoons of olive oil
- 1 pound of Italian sausages
- 1 (15-ounces) can of cannellini beans
- 1 carrot, chopped
- 1 onion, chopped
- 2 garlic cloves, minced
- 1 teaspoon of paprika
- 1 (14-ounces) can of tomatoes, diced
- 1 celery stalk, chopped
- Salt and black pepper to taste

Directions and Total Time: approx. 45 minutes

Preheat oven to a heat of 350 F. Warm olive oil in a pot over medium heat. Sauté onion, garlic, celery, and carrot for 3-4 minutes, stirring often until softened. Add in sausages and cook for another 3 minutes, turning occasionally. Stir in paprika for 30 seconds. Heat off. Mix in tomatoes, beans, salt, and pepper. Pour into a large-sized baking dish and bake for approximately about 30 minutes.

Per Serving: Calories 862, Fat 44g, Carbs 76g, Protein 43g

393. Traditional Yellow Rice

Ingredients for 4 servings

- Ground black pepper, to taste
- 1/2 teaspoon cayenne pepper
- 1/2 teaspoon celery seeds
- 1/2 teaspoon turmeric powder
- 1 bay laurel
- 1 cup vegetable broth
- 1 cup jasmine rice, rinsed
- 2 tablespoons ghee, melted

Directions and Total Time: approx. 25 minutes

Add all of the above prepared ingredients, except for the ghee, to the inner pot of your Instant Pot. Secure the lid. Choose the "Manual" mode and cook for 9 minutes at High pressure. Once cooking is complete, use a natural pressure release for 10 minutes; carefully remove the lid. Drizzle the melted ghee over each serving and enjoy!

Per Serving: Calories 158, Fat 12.3g, Carbs 5.7g, Protein 0.4g

394. Tunisian Style Green Beans

Ingredients for 3 servings

- 2 tablespoons organic canola oil
- 1 cup green beans
- ¼ teaspoon white pepper
- 1 teaspoon sesame seeds
- 1 tablespoon balsamic vinegar
- ¼ teaspoon dried tarragon
- 1 cup of water

Directions and Total Time: approx. 22 minutes

Bring the water to boil and put the green beans inside. Boil the beans for 7 minutes. Then cool the beans in ice water and chop roughly. Put the cooked green beans in the bowl, add white pepper, organic canola oil, sesame seeds, balsamic vinegar, and dried tarragon. Stir the meal well.

Per Serving: Calories 103, Fat 19.3g, Carbs 3.4g, Protein 9.3g

395. Valencian-Style Mussel Rice

Ingredients for 4 servings

- 1 pound of mussels, cleaned and debearded
- 2 tablespoons of olive oil
- 2 garlic cloves, minced
- 1 yellow onion, chopped
- 2 tomatoes, chopped
- 2 cups of fish stock
- 1 cup of white rice
- 1 bunch of parsley, chopped
- Salt and white pepper to taste

Directions and Total Time: approx. 40 minutes

Warm the olive oil in a pot over medium heat and cook onion and garlic for 5 minutes. Stir in rice for 1 minute. Pour in tomatoes and fish stock and bring to a boil. Add in the mussels and simmer for 20 minutes. Discard any unopened mussels. Adjust the taste according to you with salt and white pepper. Serve topped with parsley.

Per Serving: Calories 310, Fat 15g, Carbs 17g, Protein 12g

396. Veggie Brown Rice

Ingredients for 4 servings

- 2 cups brown rice
- 1 shallot, chopped
- A pinch of salt and black pepper
- 1 red bell pepper, chopped
- 1 zucchini, grated
- 1 carrot, grated
- ¼ cup parsley, chopped
- ¼ cup olive oil
- ½ teaspoon oregano, dried
- ¼ teaspoon sweet paprika
- ½ teaspoon thyme, dried
- 4 cups water

Directions and Total Time: approx. 50 minutes

Heat a pan with half the olive oil over medium heat. Add the shallot, bell pepper, zucchini, carrot, salt, and pepper, stir and cook for 2 minutes. Add oregano, paprika and thyme, stir and cook for 2 minutes more. Add the rice, parsley, and water, stir, bring to a simmer and cook for 35 minutes. Divide the rice between plates and serve as a side dish.

Per Serving: Calories 182, Fat 11g, Carbs 8g, Protein 5g

397. White Bean Dip

Ingredients for 4 servings

- 15 ounces canned white beans, drained and rinsed
- 6 ounces canned artichoke hearts, drained and quartered
- 4 garlic cloves, minced
- 1 tablespoon basil, chopped
- 2 tablespoons olive oil
- Juice of ½ lemon
- Zest of ½ lemon, grated
- Salt and black pepper to the taste

Directions and Total Time: approx. 10 minutes

In your food processor, combine the beans with the artichokes and the rest of the ingredients except the oil and pulse well. Add the oil gradually, pulse the mix again, divide into cups and serve as a party dip.

Per Serving: Calories 274, Fat 11.7g, Carbs 18.5g, Protein 16.5g

398. White Bean Dip with Garlic and Herbs

Ingredients for 16 servings

- 1 cup dried white beans
- 3 cloves garlic
- 8 cups water
- ¼ cup extra-virgin olive oil
- ¼ cup chopped fresh flat-leaf parsley
- 1 tablespoon fresh oregano
- 1 tablespoon fresh tarragon
- 1 teaspoon fresh thyme leaves
- 1 teaspoon lemon zest
- ¼ teaspoon salt
- ¼ teaspoon black pepper

Directions and Total Time: approx. 58 minutes

Place beans and garlic in the Instant Pot® and stir well. Add water, close lid, put steam release to Sealing, press the Manual, and adjust time to 30 minutes. When the timer beeps, release naturally, about 20 minutes. Open and check if beans are soft. Press the Cancel button, drain off excess water, and transfer beans and garlic to a food processor with olive oil. Add parsley, oregano, tarragon, thyme, lemon zest, salt, and pepper, and pulse 3–5 times to mix. Chill for 4 hours or overnight. Serve cold or at room temperature.

Per Serving: Calories 47, Fat 3g, Carbs 10g, Protein 2g

399. Wild Rice with Cheese and Mushrooms

Ingredients for 4 servings

- 2 cups of chicken stock
- 1 cup of wild rice
- 1 onion, chopped
- ½ pound of wild mushrooms, sliced
- 2 garlic cloves, minced
- 1 lemon, juiced and zested
- 1 tablespoon of chives, chopped
- ½ cup of mozzarella, grated
- Salt and black pepper to taste

Directions and Total Time: approx. 30 minutes

Warm chicken stock in a pot over medium heat and add in wild rice, onion, mushrooms, garlic, zested lemon juice, lemon zest, salt, and pepper. Bring to a simmer and then cook it for about 20 minutes. Transfer to a large-sized baking tray and top with mozzarella cheese. Place the tray under the broiler for 4 minutes until the cheese is melted. Sprinkle with chives and serve.

Per Serving: Calories 230, Fat 6g, Carbs 13g, Protein 6g

400. Zucchini Rice Pilaf

Ingredients for 4 servings

- ½ teaspoon dried basil
- 2 tablespoons butter
- 2 ¼ cups hot water
- 1 ¼ teaspoons chicken bouillon granules
- 1 cup uncooked long-grain rice
- ½ cup shredded carrot
- 1 small zucchini, halved, and thinly sliced

Directions and Total Time: approx. 30 minutes

In a large skillet, sauté basil in butter for 2 minutes. Add the water, and broth, and bring to a boil. Add the rice, and carrot, reduce heat, cover, and simmer for 10 minutes. After 10 minutes, add zucchini, cover, and simmer for 5 minutes until rice is tender. Plate, and serve immediately.

Per Serving: Calories 231, Fat 6g, Carbs 40g, Protein 4g

401. Algerian Vegetable Couscous

Ingredients for 4 servings

- 2 tablespoons extra-virgin olive oil
- 1 cup sliced cremini
- 1 small onion, chopped
- 1 carrot, grated
- 2 garlic cloves, minced
- 1 ¼ cups vegetable broth
- 1 cup couscous
- ¼ cup raisins
- Grated zest and juice of 1 lemon
- ½ teaspoon ground cumin
- ½ teaspoon ground coriander
- ½ teaspoon salt

Directions and Total Time: approx. 30 minutes

In a large-sized skillet, heat the olive oil over medium heat. Add the mushrooms, onion, and carrot and cook for about 5 minutes until they start to soften. Add the prepared minced garlic and cook for just about 1 minute. Stir in the broth, couscous, raisins, lemon zest and juice, cumin, coriander, and salt. Bring to a hot boil, then cover and remove the pan from heat. Let stand for 5 minutes before serving.

Per Serving: Calories 248, Fat 7g, Carbs 39g, Protein 7g

402. Angel Hair with Asparagus-Kale Pesto

Ingredients for 6 servings

- ¾ pound asparagus, woody ends removed, and coarsely chopped
- ¼ pound kale, thoroughly washed
- ½ cup grated Asiago cheese
- ¼ cup fresh basil
- ¼ cup extra-virgin olive oil
- Juice of 1 lemon
- Sea salt
- Freshly ground black pepper
- 1 pound angel hair pasta
- Zest of 1 lemon

Directions and Total Time: approx. 20 minutes

In a food processor, pulse the asparagus and kale until very finely chopped. Add the Asiago cheese, basil, olive oil, and lemon juice and pulse to form a smooth pesto. Season with sea salt and pepper and set aside. Cook the pasta al dente according to the package directions. Drain and transfer to a large bowl. Add the pesto, tossing well to coat. Sprinkle with lemon zest and serve.

Per Serving: Calories 283, Fat 12g, Carbs 33g, Protein 10g

403. Asparagus Pasta

Ingredients for 8 servings

- 8 ounces farfalle pasta, uncooked
- 1 ½ cups asparagus, fresh, trimmed & chopped into 1 inch pieces
- 1 pint grape tomatoes, halved
- 2 tablespoons olive oil
- Sea salt & black pepper to taste
- 2 cups mozzarella, fresh & drained
- 1/3 cup basil leaves, fresh & torn
- 2 tbs. balsamic vinegar

Directions and Total Time: approx. 25 minutes

Start by heating the oven to 400, and then get out a stockpot. Cook your pasta per package instructions, and reserve ¼ cup of pasta water. Get out a bowl and toss the tomatoes, oil, asparagus, and season with salt and pepper. Spread this mixture on a large-sized baking sheet, and bake for fifteen minutes. Stir twice in this time. Remove your vegetables from the oven, and then add the cooked pasta to your baking sheet. Mix with a few tablespoons of pasta water so that your sauce becomes smoother. Mix in your basil and mozzarella, drizzling with balsamic vinegar. Serve warm.

Per Serving: Calories 307, Fat 14g, Carbs 33g, Protein 18g

404. Baked Broccoli Cheese Pasta

Ingredients for 4 servings

- 1 ounce of butter
- 5 ounces of grated cheddar
- 10 ounces of penne
- 10 ounces of broccoli florets
- 1 ¼ cups of milk
- ¼ cup of flour
- 1 tablespoon of wholegrain mustard

Directions and Total Time: approx. 30 minutes

Cook the pasta according to the written and indicated instructions in the package. Add the broccoli and cook until tender. Heat the butter and stir in the flour, add the milk and bring to a boil. Simmer and add the mustard, cheese, and seasoning in. Mix the pasta, sauce, and broccoli and grill until golden.

Per Serving: Calories 539, Fat 21g, Carbs 5g, Protein 25g

405. Baked Pasta

Ingredients for 4 servings

- 8 ounces ziti pasta
- 1 can crushed tomatoes
- 1 clove minced garlic
- 1 cup grated mozzarella cheese
- ¾ cup ricotta cheese
- ¼ cup parmesan cheese
- 1 teaspoon salt, pepper, onion powder, oregano, and parsley

Directions and Total Time: approx. 45 minutes

Cook the ziti in salted water. In a large-sized saucepan, sauté the garlic in olive oil. Add the tomatoes, salt, pepper, onion powder, oregano, and parsley once the garlic becomes fragrant. In a bowl, combine the mozzarella, ricotta, and parmesan. Drain the pasta and add ¼ cup of pasta water to the cheeses. In a casserole dish, layer the pasta, sauce, and cheese. Bake at 375°F for 20 minutes.

Per Serving: Calories 276, Fat 6.4g, Carbs 39g, Protein 15.5g

406. Baked Tuna Pasta

Ingredients for 6 servings

- 2 ½ cups of milk
- 8-ounces can of sweet corn
- ½ cup of flour
- 20 ounces of rigatoni
- ¼ cup of butter
- 8 ounces of grated cheddar
- 2 cans of tuna steak, drained
- Some chopped parsley

Directions and Total Time: approx. 70 minutes

Cook the rigatoni, drain and set aside. Melt the cup of butter, stir the flour in and cook for 1 minute. Add in the milk and cook stirring to make a white sauce. Remove from the heat and stir ½ of the cheddar, tuna, pasta, 1 can of sweet corn, and parsley in. Season and transfer into a baking dish, then top with cheddar. Bake for about 22 minutes until the cheese is golden.

Per Serving: Calories 752, Fat 26g, Carbs 37g, Protein 4g

407. Basil Pesto Spaghetti

Ingredients for 4 servings

- 12 ounces spaghetti
- ¼ cup chopped white onion
- 2 tablespoons pesto
- 1 tablespoon olive oil
- ¼ cup parmesan cheese
- 1 teaspoon salt and pepper

Directions and Total Time: approx. 20 minutes

In a large-sized pot, cook the spaghetti in salted water. In a medium-heat skillet, saute the onion and pesto in olive oil, salt, and pepper for 5 minutes. Drain the spaghetti and save ¼ cup of pasta water. In the pot, combine the spaghetti, pesto mixture, and pasta water. Sprinkle the parmesan cheese and allow to cook for an additional 2-3 minutes.

Per Serving: Calories 314, Fat 8.9g, Carbs 47.8g, Protein 10.7g

408. Bean and Veggie Pasta

Ingredients for 4 servings

- 16 ounces of small whole-wheat pasta, such as penne, farfalle, or macaroni
- 5 cups of water
- 1 15-ounces of cannellini beans, drained and rinsed
- 1 14.5-ounces of diced (with juice) or crushed tomatoes 1 yellow onion, chopped
- 1 red or yellow bell pepper, chopped
- 2 tablespoons of tomato paste
- 1 tablespoon of olive oil
- 3 garlic cloves, minced
- ¼ teaspoon of crushed red pepper (optional)
- 1 bunch of kale, stemmed and chopped
- 1 cup of sliced basil
- ½ cup of pitted Kalamata olives, chopped

Directions and Total Time: approx. 30 minutes

In a saucepan, add the pasta, water, beans, tomatoes, onion, bell pepper, tomato paste, oil, garlic, and crushed red pepper (if desired). Stir well, and then now bring to a boil over a temperature of high heat. When it boils, reduce the heat, add the cabbage, and cook for about 10 minutes, stirring often. When the pasta is already al dente, remove from heat and rest for 5 minutes. Garnish with the basil and olives, and serve.

Per Serving: Calories 565, Fat 17.7g, Carbs 85.5g, Protein 18g

409. Blue Cheese Pasta

Ingredients for 4 servings

- 14.2-ounce of penne pasta
- 0.89-ounce of butter
- 1 onion, thinly sliced
- 1 garlic clove, crushed
- 1 tablespoon of fresh chopped sage or 1 tsp dried
- 3.5-ounces of stilton, cubed
- handful toasted walnuts, chopped

Directions and Total Time: approx. 20 minutes

In a large-sized saucepan, bring water to a boil. When it boils, add the salt, and pour in the pasta. Cook for just about the time listed on the package. Meanwhile, in a saucepan, melt butter, add onion, and sauté gently until golden brown. Add the garlic, sage, and sauté for another 2 minutes, then remove the pan from the heat. Drain the cooked pasta but keep some of the cooking water aside. Stir the onions into the butter, stilton, and 2 tbsps. Of the cooking water. Add the pasta to the cream cheese, and toss. Distribute the pasta onto serving plates, sprinkle with the toasted walnuts, and serve.

Per Serving: Calories 554, Fat 20g, Carbs 79g, Protein 19g

410. Broccoli and Carrot Pasta Salad

Ingredients for 2 servings

- 8 ounces whole-wheat pasta
- 2 cups broccoli florets
- 1 cup peeled and shredded carrots
- ¼ cup plain Greek yogurt
- Juice of 1 lemon
- 1 teaspoon red pepper flakes
- salt and ground pepper, to taste

Directions and Total Time: approx. 15 minutes

Bring a small-sized pot of lightly salted water to a boil. Add the whole-wheat pasta to the boiling water and cook until al dente. Drain and let rest for a few minutes. When cooled, combine the pasta with the veggies, yogurt, lemon juice, and red pepper flakes in a large-sized bowl, and stir thoroughly to combine. Taste and season to taste with salt and pepper. Serve immediately.

Per Serving: Calories 428, Fat 2.9g, Carbs 84.6g, Protein 15.9g

411. Broccoli and Orecchiette Pasta with Feta

Ingredients for 4 servings

- 1 pack (9 ounces) orecchiette
- 1 tablespoon feta, grated
- 16 ounces broccoli, roughly chopped
- 2 garlic cloves
- 1 teaspoon salt
- ¼ teaspoon black pepper
- 3 tablespoons olive oil

Directions and Total Time: approx. 24 minutes

Add broccoli and orecchiette into your instant pot. Cover with water and close the lid. Cook on High pressure for 10 minutes. Quick-release the pressure. Drain the broccoli and orecchiette. Set them aside and then heat the oil on sauté mode. Stir-fry garlic for 2 minutes. Stir in orecchiette, broccoli, salt and pepper. Cook for 2 minutes more. Once cooked, then press cancel and stir in grated feta. Serve and enjoy!

Per Serving: Calories 350, Fat 20g, Carbs 32g, Protein 15g

412. Broccoli and Tomato Pasta

Ingredients for 4 servings

- 3 quarts of water
- 8 ounces of spaghetti
- 2 cups of broccoli
- 2 tomatoes chopped
- 2 minced garlic cloves
- 1/2 teaspoon of red pepper
- 2 tablespoons of olive oil
- A quarter cup of Romano cheese grated
- 1/2 cup of olives sliced
- 1/2 cup of minced parsley
- 3/4 teaspoon of salt
- 1/8 teaspoon of pepper

Directions and Total Time: approx. 40 minutes

Boil water in a pan, add spaghetti and boil for 5 minutes. Transfer broccoli and boil for 3 to 4 minutes until pasta & broccoli gets tender. In a nonstick skillet, sauté tomatoes, garlic and pepper flakes, 2 minutes. Drain the pasta mixture, and add to the skillet. Now add remaining ingredients & toss to coat. Serve.

Per Serving: Calories 348, Fat 12g, Carbs 51g, Protein 12g

413. Broccoli Pesto Spaghetti

Ingredients for 4 servings

- 8 ounces spaghetti
- 1-pound broccoli, cut into florets
- 2 tablespoons olive oil
- 4 garlic cloves, chopped
- 4 basil leaves
- 2 tablespoons blanched almonds
- 1 lemon, juiced
- Salt and pepper to taste

Directions and Total Time: approx. 40 minutes

For the pesto, combine the broccoli, oil, garlic, basil, lemon juice and almonds in a blender and pulse until well mixed and smooth. Cook the spaghetti in a large-sized pot of salty water for 8 minutes or until al dente. Drain well. Mix the warm spaghetti with the broccoli pesto and serve right away.

Per Serving: Calories 284, Fat 10.2g, Carbs 40.2g, Protein 10.4g

414. Cajun Chicken Fettuccine

Ingredients for 6 servings

- 8 ounces fettuccine pasta
- 1 ½ pounds chicken breast
- ¼ cup butter
- 3 cups heavy cream
- 2 cloves of garlic
- ⅔ cup parmesan cheese
- 3 tablespoons each salt, pepper, paprika, garlic powder, onion powder, cayenne, and oregano

Directions and Total Time: approx. 30 minutes

Cook the fettuccine in salted water. Rinse and dice the breasts. Toss the breasts with cajun seasonings. In a medium-heat skillet, cook the breast chunks for 10 minutes. Add butter, garlic, and heavy cream and simmer for 8 minutes. Drain the fettuccine and save ¼ cup of pasta water. Add fettuccine, chicken, and pasta water to the pot and cook for 2-3 minutes. Sprinkle the cheese on top.

Per Serving: Calories 519, Fat 33.9g, Carbs 22.8g, Protein 30.2g

415. Cajun Seafood Pasta

Ingredients for 6 servings

- 2 cups thick whipped cream
- 1 tablespoon chopped fresh basil
- 1 tablespoon chopped fresh thyme
- 2 teaspoons salt
- 2 teaspoons ground black pepper
- 1 1/2 teaspoon ground red pepper flakes
- 1 teaspoon ground white pepper
- 1 cup chopped green onions
- 1 cup chopped parsley
- 1/2 shrimp, peeled
- 1/2 cup scallops
- 1/2 cup of grated Swiss cheese
- 1/2 cup grated Parmesan cheese
- 1 pound dry fettuccine pasta

Directions and Total Time: approx. 23 minutes

Cook the pasta in a large-sized pot with boiling salted water until al dente. Meanwhile, pour the cream into a large skillet. Cook over a heat of medium heat, constantly stirring until it boils. Reduce heat and add spices, salt, pepper, onions, and parsley. Let simmer for 7 to 8 minutes or until thick. Stir seafood and cook until shrimp are no longer transparent. Stir in the cheese and mix well. Drain the pasta. Serve the sauce over the noodles.

Per Serving: Calories 695, Fat 36.7g, Carbs 62.2g, Protein 31.5g

416. Caponata Pasta

Ingredients for 4 servings

- 4 tablespoons of olive oil
- 1 large onion, finely chopped
- 4 garlic cloves, finely sliced
- 8.8-ounces of chargrilled Mediterranean veg (peppers, and aubergines, if possible)
- 14.2-ounces can of chopped tomatoes
- 1 tablespoon of small capers
- 2 tablespoons of raisins
- 15.9-oz rigatoni, penne, or another short pasta shape bunch basil leaves, picked
- parmesan, to serve

Directions and Total Time: approx. 20 minutes

In a large-sized pot, bring water to a boil. When it boils, add the salt and pasta, and cook for the time indicated on the package. Meanwhile, heat the oil in a large-sized skillet, and sauté the onion for 8 minutes. Add the garlic, and cook another 2 minutes. Add the mixed greens, tomatoes, capers, and raisins. Stir well, and simmer, uncovered, for 10 minutes. Drain the pasta al dente reserving some of the cooking liquid, and add it to the pan with the vegetables. Sauté the pasta to flavor, and, if necessary, add the cooking water set aside. Serve on a plate, sprinkle with basil leaves, grated Parmesan cheese, and serve immediately.

Per Serving: Calories 542, Fat 14g, Carbs 85g, Protein 14g

417. Carbonara Spaghetti

Ingredients for 4 servings

- 13 ounces Whole wheat spaghetti
- 6 yolks
- 5 ounces pork cheek
- Pepper
- 2 ounces roman pecorino
- Salt

Directions and Total Time: approx. 45 minutes

Cut the pork cheek in 1/3 inches strips. In a pan, cook the pork cheek over medium heat for 10 minutes. Meanwhile, cook the spaghetti in salted boiling water. In a bowl beat the yolks, add most of the roman pecorino and some pepper. Mix everything. When the spaghetti are already cooked, drain them and pour it in the pork cheek pan with the heat off. Add the bowl compound and stir fast; the yolks must not cook. Serve the spaghetti seasoned with some more cheese.

Per Serving: Calories 186, Fat 8g, Carbs 38g, Protein 22g

418. Cauliflower Couscous

Ingredients for 4 servings

- 1 ½ cups of couscous cooked
- 3 cups of cauliflower florets
- 1 medium shallot peeled and sliced
- 2 tablespoons of chopped parsley
- 1 ½ teaspoon of salt
- ½ teaspoon of ground black pepper
- 1/8 teaspoon of cinnamon
- ¼ cup of chopped dates
- 2 tablespoons of olive oil
- 1 tablespoon of red wine vinegar

Directions and Total Time: approx. 12 minutes

Place a large-sized skillet pan over medium heat, add oil, and add shallots and cauliflower florets when hot. Cook for 3 minutes, then season with ½ teaspoon salt ¼ teaspoon black pepper cinnamon and add dates. Stir well, continue cooking for 2 minutes and then remove the pan from heat. Spoon this mixture into a bowl, add cooked couscous and remaining Ingredients: and toss until well mixed. Serve straightaway.

Per Serving: Calories 108, Fat 22g, Carbs 30g, Protein 19g

419. Chard and Couscous

Ingredients for 4 servings

- 10 ounces of couscous
- 1 and ½ cup of hot water
- 2 garlic cloves, minced
- 2 tablespoons of olive oil
- ½ cup of raisins
- 2 bunches of Swiss chard, chopped
- Salt and black pepper to the taste

Directions and Total Time: approx. 20 minutes

Toss the couscous with the water in a mixing basin, whisk to combine, cover, and set aside 10 minutes before fluffing with a fork. In a medium-hot pan, heat the oil and sauté the garlic for 1 minute. Add the couscous and the rest of the ingredients, toss, divide between plates and serve.

Per Serving: Calories 300, Fat 6.9g, Carbs 17.4g, Protein 6g

420. Cheesy Sicilian Tortellini

Ingredients for 4 servings

- ½ pound of ground beef
- ½ pound of Italian sausage, casings removed
- 1 16-ounce jar of marinara sauce
- 1 4.5-ounce can of sliced mushrooms
- 1 14.5-ounce can of Italian-style diced tomatoes, undrained
- 1 9-ounce package of cheese tortellini
- 1 cup of shredded mozzarella cheese
- ½ cup of shredded cheddar cheese

Directions and Total Time: approx. 7 hours and 38 minutes

Crumble the prepared Italian sausage and ground beef into a large skillet. Cook over medium-high heat until browned and drain. Combine the ground meats, marinara sauce, mushrooms, and tomatoes in a slow cooker. Cook it with lid covered on low heat for 7 hours. Stir the tortellini in. Sprinkle the cheddar and mozzarella cheese over the top. Cover and cook for an additional 14–18 minutes, or until the tortellini are tender.

Per Serving: Calories 132, Fat 14g, Carbs 10g, Protein 8g

421. Cheesy Spaghetti with Pine Nuts

Ingredients for 4 servings

- 8 ounces spaghetti
- 4 tablespoons (½ stick) unsalted butter
- 1 teaspoon freshly ground black pepper
- ½ cup pine nuts
- 1 cup fresh grated Parmesan cheese, divided

Directions and Total Time: approx. 20 minutes

Bring a small-sized pot of salted water to a boil. Add the pasta and cook for 8 minutes. In a large-sized saucepan over medium heat, combine the butter, black pepper, and pine nuts. Cook for 2 to 3 minutes or until the pine nuts are lightly toasted. Reserve ½ cup of the pasta water. Drain the pasta and put it into the pan with the pine nuts. Add ¾ cup of Parmesan cheese and the reserved pasta water to the pasta and toss everything together to coat the pasta evenly. Put the already cooked pasta in a serving dish and top with the remaining ¼ cup of Parmesan cheese.

Per Serving: Calories 238, Fat 6.3g, Carbs 3.4g, Protein 12.3g

422. Chicken Alfredo Pasta

Ingredients for 4 servings

- 8 ounces fettuccine pasta
- ½ pound chicken breasts
- 1 ½ cup spinach
- ½ cup butter
- 2 cup heavy cream
- 1 clove of chopped garlic
- ¼ cup parmesan cheese
- 1 teaspoon salt, pepper, and garlic powder

Directions and Total Time: approx. 15 minutes

Cook the fettuccine in salted water. Rinse and dice the chicken into 1-inch cubes. In a medium-heat skillet, sauté the chicken in butter and garlic. Add heavy cream, salt, pepper, and garlic after the breasts begin to brown. Cook for 10-15 minutes. Drain the pasta and save ¼ cup of the water. Add the pasta, chicken, and water to the pot and sprinkle cheese before serving.

Per Serving: Calories 688, Fat 51g, Carbs 33.4g, Protein 24.9g

423. Chicken Pasta

Ingredients for 6 servings

- 1 tablespoon of olive oil
- 1 tablespoon of butter
- 2 chicken breast (cut to 1/2 - inch pieces)
- 2 garlic cloves (chopped)
- 8-ounce of cremini mushrooms (halved)
- 2 cups of chicken stock
- 1 cup of heavy cream
- 1 pound of pasta (rotini)
- 8 ounces of cream cheese

Directions and Total Time: approx. 25 minutes

Turn your prepared Instant Pot to the sauté setting. Add the olive and garlic to the inner pot. Sauté for two minutes. Add the butter and mushroom to the pot and sauté for three minutes. Add the chicken and pasta, then pour in the chicken stock and heavy cream. Press cancel or stop. Secure its lid and set the pressure valve to seal. Choose the manual setting, and set the cooking time to five minutes. When it's done cooking, allow releasing for five minutes slowly. Then, quick release. Remove its lid, and add the cream cheese. Stir until the cream cheese is thoroughly incorporated. Serve warm.

Per Serving: Calories 532, Fat 29.1g, Carbs 24.3g, Protein 40.8g

424. Chicken Pasta Parmesan

Ingredients for 2 servings

- ¼ cup prepared marinara sauce
- ½ cup cooked whole-wheat spaghetti
- 1 ounce reduced-fat mozzarella cheese, grated
- 1 tablespoon olive oil
- 2 tablespoons seasoned dry breadcrumbs
- 4 ounces skinless chicken breast

Directions and Total Time: approx. 30 minutes

On medium-high fire, place an ovenproof skillet and heat oil. Pan fry chicken for 3 to 5 minutes per side or until cooked through. Pour marinara sauce, stir and continue cooking for 3 minutes. Turn off fire, add mozzarella and breadcrumbs on top. Pop into a preheated broiler on high and broil for 10 minutes or until breadcrumbs are browned and mozzarella is melted. Remove from broiler, serve and enjoy.

Per Serving: Calories 529, Fat 26.6g, Carbs 34.4g, Protein 38g

Ingredients for 4 servings

- 1 red onion, chopped
- 2 tablespoons of olive oil
- 2 garlic cloves, minced
- 28 ounces of canned chickpeas, rinsed
- 2 cups of veggie stock
- 2 cups of couscous, cooked
- 2 tablespoons of coriander, chopped
- ½ cup of figs, dried and chopped
- Salt and black pepper to the taste

Directions and Total Time: approx. 30 minutes

Heat a large-sized pan with the oil over medium heat, add the onion and the garlic, stir and sauté for 5 minutes. Add the canned chickpeas and the rest of the prepared ingredients except the couscous and cook over medium heat for approximately about 15 minutes, stirring often. Divide the couscous between plates, divide the chickpeas mix on top and serve.

Per Serving: Calories 263, Fat 11.5g, Carbs 22.4g, Protein 7.3g

426. Chickpeas with Couscous

Ingredients for 2 servings

- 1 1/2 cups of canned low-sodium, fat-free chicken broth
- 1/3 cup of couscous
- 1 (15-ounce) can chickpeas, rinsed and drained
- 1 medium tomato, chopped
- 10 medium pitted black olives, sliced
- 1 stalk celery, finely chopped
- 2 scallions, green and white parts, sliced into 1-inch pieces
- 1/4 cup of black seedless raisins
- 1/2 teaspoon of cumin
- 1/4 cup of non-fat plain yogurt for garnish
- Chopped fresh parsley (optional)

Directions and Total Time: approx. 30 minutes

Bring chicken broth to a hot boil, remove from heat, and add couscous. Cover it and after, let stand until the couscous is already tender and liquid is absorbed. Fluff with a small fork and transfer to a bowl. Add chickpeas, tomato, olives, celery, scallions, raisins, and cumin. Stir to mix well and garnish each serving with one tablespoon of yogurt and parsley.

Per Serving: Calories 207, Fat 3g, Carbs 38g, Protein 10g

427. Cinnamon Couscous

Ingredients for 2 servings

- 3 cups of warmed water
- Pinch of salt
- 1/2 tablespoon extra-virgin olive oil
- 6 ounces couscous
- 2 tablespoons of ground cinnamon
- A quarter cup of black seedless raisins
- A quarter cup of low-calorie baking sweetener
- 4 tablespoons of Mazahar (orange blossom water)
- Coarsely chopped walnuts for garnish

Directions and Total Time: approx. 29 minutes

Bring the prepared water to a boil; add salt and olive oil. Place couscous in an oiled oven-safe dish and pour the liquid over couscous. Add one tablespoon of cinnamon, raisins, sweetener, and Mazahar; let stand for about 10 minutes or until liquid is absorbed. Fluff couscous with fingers to separate grains. When ready to serve, top couscous with remaining cinnamon and walnuts.

Per Serving: Calories 87, Fat 1g, Carbs 19g, Protein 3g

428. Clams Spaghetti with Capers

Ingredients for 2 servings

- 2 cups spaghetti pasta
- 5 ounces clams
- 3 tablespoons capers
- 2 garlic cloves
- 1 chili pepper
- 1 cup of parsley
- Water
- Oil to taste

Directions and Total Time: approx. 25 minutes

Bring to a boil a large-sized pot of salted water and cook the spaghetti pasta for 7 to 8 minutes. In a pan in the meanwhile add the garlic, chili, and oil, and some parsley stems and stir for some minutes. Add the clams and cover using a lid and wait until they have opened up. Add the capers and the drained pasta. Let it cook for another 3 minutes with some pasta water.

Per Serving: Calories 193, Fat 10g, Carbs 70g, Protein 8.5g

429. Confetti Couscous

Ingredients for 6 servings

- 1 large onion, chopped
- 3 tablespoons extra-virgin olive oil
- 2 carrots, chopped
- 1 teaspoon salt
- 2 cups couscous
- 1 cup fresh peas
- 2 cups vegetable broth
- ½ cup golden raisins

Directions and Total Time: approx. 25 minutes

Using a medium-sized pot over medium heat, gently toss the onions, olive oil, carrots, raisins, and peas together and let cook for about 5 minutes. Add the broth and salt and stir to combine. Bring to a boil, and let ingredients boil for just about 5 minutes. Put the couscous. Stir, turn the heat temperature to low, cover, and let cook for about 10 minutes. Fluff with a fork and serve.

Per Serving: Calories 511, Fat 12g, Carbs 92g, Protein 14g

430. Couscous and Chickpea Bowls

Ingredients for 4 servings

- ¾ cup whole wheat couscous
- 1 yellow onion, chopped
- 1 tablespoon olive oil
- 1 cup water
- 2 garlic cloves, minced
- 15 ounces canned chickpeas, drained and rinsed
- A pinch of salt and black pepper
- 15 ounces canned tomatoes, chopped
- 14 ounces canned artichokes, drained and chopped
- ½ cup Greek olives, pitted and chopped
- ½ teaspoon oregano, dried
- 1 tablespoon lemon juice

Directions and Total Time: approx. 16 minutes

Put the water in a pot, bring to a boil over medium heat, add the couscous, stir, take off the heat, cover the pan, leave aside for 10 minutes and fluff with a fork. Heat up a large-sized pan with the oil over medium-high heat, add the onion and sauté for 2 minutes. Add the rest of the prepared ingredients, toss and cook for 4 minutes more. Add the couscous, toss, divide into bowls and serve for breakfast.

Per Serving: Calories 340, Fat 10g, Carbs 51g, Protein 11g

Ingredients for 4 servings

- 1 cup of whole-grain couscous.
- 400 ml of boiling water.
- 1 tablespoon of extra-virgin olive oil.
- 1/2 red onion, chopped.
- 1/2 teaspoon of ground ginger.
- 1/2 teaspoon of ground cinnamon.
- 1/2 teaspoon of ground coriander.
- 2 tablespoons of blanched almonds, toasted, and chopped

Directions and Total Time: approx. 15 minutes

Preheat the oven to 110°C. In a casserole, toss the couscous with the olive oil, onion, spices, salt, and pepper. Stir in the boiling water, cover, and bake for 10 minutes. Fluff using a fork. Scatter the nuts over the top and then serve.

Per Serving: Calories 8, Fat 1g, Carbs 37g, Protein 7g

432. Couscous Salad

Ingredients for 6 servings

- 1 ½ of couscous
- 1 cup of oil-free tuna
- 1 cucumber
- 1 cup of cherry tomatoes
- 1 cup of mozzarella cheese
- 1 handful of basil
- 2 tablespoons extra virgin olive oil
- Salt and pepper to taste
- Water

Directions and Total Time: approx. 20 minutes

Bring to a boil a large-sized pot of salted water. In a bowl add the couscous and stir it with the oil and cover with hot water and let it settle down for 10 minutes. Stir the couscous with a fork. In another bowl cut all the veggies, add the tuna, mozzarella, basil, and season with oil, salt, and pepper. Add the couscous to the vegetables and mix, serve cold.

Per Serving: Calories 270, Fat 10g, Carbs 44g, Protein 11g

433. Couscous with Chickpeas and Figs

Ingredients for 4 servings

- 1 red onion, chopped
- 2 tablespoons olive oil
- 2 garlic cloves, minced
- 28 ounces canned chickpeas drained and rinsed
- 2 cups veggie stock
- 2 cups couscous, cooked
- 2 tablespoons coriander, chopped
- ½ cup figs, dried and chopped
- Salt and black pepper to taste

Directions and Total Time: approx. 30 minutes

Heat a skillet with the oil over medium heat. Add the onion and garlic and sauté for 5 minutes. Add the prepared chickpeas and the rest of the prepared ingredients except the couscous and cook over medium heat for 15 minutes, stirring often. Divide the couscous among plates, spread the chickpea mixture on top, and serve.

Per Serving: Calories 263, Fat 11.5g, Carbs 22.4g, Protein 7.3g

434. Couscous with with Tuna and Pepperoncini

Ingredients for 4 servings

- 1 cup chicken broth or water
- ¾ teaspoon salt
- 1 ¼ cups couscous
- ⅓ cup fresh parsley, chopped
- 1 lemon, quartered
- 2 cans (5 ounces each) oil packed tuna
- 1 pint cherry tomatoes, halved
- Extra-virgin olive oil (for serving)
- ½ cup pepperoncini, sliced
- ¼ cup capers
- Salt, pepper, to taste

Directions and Total Time: approx. 25 minutes

Add the prepared 1 cup chicken broth or water to a small pot and boil it. Turn the heat off, stir in 1 ¼ cups of couscous, and cover it. Let it boil for 10 minutes. In the meantime, take about another bowl and add 1 pint of halved cherry tomatoes, ½ cup of sliced pepperoncini, ¼ cup capers, ⅓ cup fresh chopped parsley, and oil packed tuna; toss well. Fluff the couscous with a fork. Season with teaspoons of pepper and salt; drizzle with olive oil. Top with the mixture of tuna and serve your meal with lemon wedges.

Per Serving: Calories 226, Fat 10g, Carbs 44g, Protein 22g

435. Couscous with Vegetables

Ingredients for 3 servings

- 1 onion, chopped
- 1 red bell pepper, chopped
- 1 cup of carrot, grated
- 2 cups of couscous
- ½ tablespoon of lemon juice

Directions and Total Time: approx. 30 minutes

Pour the prepared 1 tablespoon of olive oil into the Instant Pot. Add the onion. Cook for 2 minutes. Add the red bell pepper and carrot. Cook for 3 minutes. Add the couscous and 2 cups water. Season with a little bit of salt. Cover the pot. Switch the pot to manual. Cook at high pressure for 2 minutes. Release the pressure naturally. Fluff the couscous. Stir in the lemon juice before serving.

Per Serving: Calories 477, Fat 0.9g, Carbs 99.4g, Protein 15.8g

436. Creamy Alfredo Fettuccine

Ingredients for 4 servings

- Grated parmesan cheese
- ½ cup freshly grated parmesan cheese
- 1/8 teaspoon freshly ground black pepper
- ½ teaspoon salt
- 1 cup whipping cream
- 2 tablespoons butter
- 8 ounces dried fettuccine, cooked and drained

Directions and Total Time: approx. 30 minutes

On medium high fire, place a big fry pan and heat butter. Add pepper, salt and cream and gently boil for three to five minutes. Once thickened, turn off fire and quickly stir in ½ cup of parmesan cheese. Toss in pasta, mix well. Top with another batch of parmesan cheese and serve.

Per Serving: Calories 202, Fat 10.2g, Carbs 21.1g, Protein 7.9g

437. Curry Apple Couscous with Leeks, and Pecans

Ingredients for 4 servings

- 2 teaspoons of extra-virgin olive oil
- 2 leeks, white parts only, sliced
- 1 apple, diced
- 1 cups of couscous
- 1 cups of water
- 2 tablespoons of curry powder
- ½ cup of chopped pecans

Directions and Total Time: approx. 23 minutes

Put the amount of water in a bowl, and couscous, add a tbsp. Extra virgin olive oil for each person, and the salt and spices. Let the couscous stand for just about 5 minutes until it has absorbed all the water, then crumble it with the tines of a fork, and finish crumbling it with your hands. Heat the olive oil in a small-sized skillet over medium heat. Add the leeks, and sauté for just 5 minutes until soft. Add the diced apple, and cook for approximately about another 3 minutes until tender. Add the cooked couscous, and curry powder, and mix well. Transfer to a large-sized serving bowl, then toss with pecans and serve.

Per Serving: Calories 254, Fat 11.9g, Carbs 34.3g, Protein 5.4g

438. Easy Couscous

Ingredients for 4 servings

- 10 ounces of couscous
- 1 ½ cup of hot water
- ½ cup of pine nuts
- 2 garlic cloves, minced
- 3 tablespoons of olive oil
- 15 ounces of canned chickpeas, rinsed
- ½ cup of raisins
- 2 bunches of Swiss chard
- Salt and black pepper to taste

Directions and Total Time: approx. 20 minutes

Put the couscous in a large-sized bowl, add water, stir, cover and leave aside for 10 minutes. Meanwhile, heat a large-sized pan over medium-high heat, add pine nuts, toast them for 4 minutes, transfer to a plate and leave aside. Return large-sized pan to medium heat, add oil and heat, add garlic, stir and cook for 1 minute. Add raisins, chickpeas, chard, salt, pepper, stir and cook for 5 Minutes. Fluff couscous, divide between plates, add chard and chickpeas mix, top with pine nuts, and serve.

Per Serving: Calories 153, Fat 2g, Carbs 6g, Protein 4g

439. Easy Tomato and Basil Spaghetti

Ingredients for 2 servings

- ¾ cup of spaghetti
- 1 can of tomato
- A handful of basil
- 1 garlic clove
- 1 tablespoon extra virgin olive oil
- Chili flakes to taste
- Salt and pepper to taste
- Water

Directions and Total Time: approx. 25 minutes

Bring to a boil some salted abundant water and cook the pasta al dente for 12 minutes circa. In the meanwhile let the smashed garlic, the chili flakes, and the olive oil fry for a minute then add the tomatoes. Stir it for some minutes then let it simmer with a quarter cup of water. Add the chopped basil, season it with salt and pepper and turn off the heat. Drain the already cooked pasta and add it to the sauce. Turn on the heat and stir it for a couple of seconds. Serve.

Per Serving: Calories 250, Fat 5g, Carbs 40g, Protein 15g

440. Escarole and Cannellini Beans on Pasta

Ingredients for 8 servings

- 1 can 14.5-ounces diced tomatoes with garlic and onion, drained
- 1 can 15.5-ounces cannellini beans, with liquid
- 1 head escarole chopped
- 1 package 16-ounces dry penne pasta

Directions and Total Time: approx. 45 minutes

Cook pasta according to package's instructions, then drain and rinse under cold running water. On medium-high fire, place skillet and cook diced tomatoes, cannellini beans with liquid and escarole. Season with pepper and salt and cook until boiling. Remove from fire and mix pasta. Serve and enjoy.

Per Serving: Calories 310, Fat 2g, Carbs 60.1g, Protein 13.7g

441. Garlic Shrimp Fettuccine

Ingredients for 6 servings

- 8 ounces fettuccine pasta
- ¼ cup extra-virgin olive oil
- 3 tablespoons garlic, minced
- 1 pound large shrimp, peeled and deveined
- ⅓ cup lemon juice
- 1 tablespoon lemon zest
- ½ teaspoon salt
- ½ teaspoon freshly ground black pepper

Directions and Total Time: approx. 25 minutes

Bring a small-sized pot of salted water to a boil. Add the fettuccine and cook for 8 minutes. Reserve ½ cup of the liquid cooking and drain the pasta. Heat the olive oil, in a medium/large saucepan over medium heat. Add the garlic and sauté for at least 1 minute. Add the shrimp to the large-sized saucepan and cook each side for 3 minutes. Remove the shrimp from the pan. Add the remaining ingredients to the saucepan. Stir in the cooking liquid. Add the pasta and toss together to evenly coat the pasta. Serve the pasta topped with the cooked shrimp.

Per Serving: Calories 615, Fat 17g, Carbs 89g, Protein 33g

442. Grains and Beans Beef and Pasta

Ingredients for 4 servings

- ½ cup of onion, chopped
- 1 tablespoon of dried garlic, minced
- 14 ounces of tomatoes, chopped
- 4 ounces of mushrooms, sliced
- 14 ounces of artichoke hearts, chopped
- 1 pound of beef stew meat
- 1 tablespoon of capers, drained
- 1 teaspoon of Italian seasoning
- 1 tablespoon of balsamic vinegar
- 1 teaspoon of sugar
- Salt to taste
- 1 tablespoon of olive oil
- 1 ½ cups of penne pasta, cooked
- ½ cup of Parmesan cheese, shredded
- Pepper to taste

Directions and Total Time: approx. 7 hours and 15 minutes

Spray your slow cooker with oil. Add all the ingredients except the oil, pasta, cheese, and pepper. Cover the pot. Cook on low for 7 hours. In the serving bowl, mix the pasta with the beef mixture and the rest of the ingredients. Serve.

Per Serving: Calories 560, Fat 21g, Carbs 58g, Protein 35g

443. Greek Pasta

Ingredients for 4 servings

- 3 cups of beef stock
- 1 beef steak, diced
- 2 tablespoons of olive oil
- 1 onion, diced
- 3 garlic cloves, sliced
- 2 cups of fresh spinach leaves
- 2 cups of tomato sauce
- Salt and pepper to taste
- ½ pound of whole wheat spaghetti pasta, cooked
- ½ cup of fat-free feta cheese, crumbled

Directions and Total Time: approx. 3 hours and 15 minutes

Pour the broth and beef cubes into the slow cooker. Cover the pot. Cook on high for 3 hours. Drain the beef and set it aside. Pour the oil into a large-sized pan over medium heat. Cook the onion and garlic for 3 minutes. Stir in the spinach and tomato sauce. Cook for another 3 minutes. Toss the pasta in the spinach mixture. Top with the beef cubes feta, and season with salt and pepper.

Per Serving: Calories 625, Fat 26.6g, Carbs 50.8g, Protein 45.3g

444. Hot Penne Pasta and Squash

Ingredients for 4 servings

- 12 ounces penne pasta
- 2 cups diced butternut squash
- 2 sliced cayenne peppers
- 4 cloves of chopped garlic
- 2 tablespoons olive oil
- 1 cup parmesan cheese
- 2 tablespoons fresh oregano and parsley
- 1 teaspoon salt and pepper

Directions and Total Time: approx. 25 minutes

In a large-sized pot, cook the pasta in salted water. In a medium-heat skillet, cook the butternut squash in olive oil. After 5 minutes, add the cayenne peppers and garlic. Drain the penne and save ¼ cup of pasta water. Add the penne, squash, peppers, and pasta water to the pot and simmer for 2-3 minutes. Sprinkle the parmesan, oregano, parsley, salt, and pepper on top while simmering before serving.

Per Serving: Calories 361, Fat 10.3g, Carbs 57.4g, Protein 12g

445. Lemon Cauliflower "Couscous" with Halloumi

Ingredients for 2 servings

- 4 ounces halloumi, sliced
- 1 cauliflower head, cut into small florets
- 1/4 cup chopped cilantro
- 1/4 cup chopped parsley
- 1/4 cup chopped mint
- 1/2 lemon juiced
- Salt and black pepper to taste
- Sliced avocado to garnish

Directions and Total Time: approx. 10 minutes

Heat the pan and add oil. Add the halloumi and fry it on both sides until golden brown, set aside. Turn the heat off. Next, pour the cauliflower florets in a food processor and pulse until it crumbles and resembles couscous. Transfer to a bowl and steam in the microwave for 2 minutes. They should be slightly cooked but crunchy. Stir in the cilantro, parsley, mint, lemon juice, salt, and black pepper. Garnish the couscous with avocado slices and serve with grilled halloumi and vegetable sauce.

Per Serving: Calories 312, Fat 9.4g, Carbs 1.2g, Protein 8.5g

446. Lemon Spaghetti

Ingredients for 2 servings

- ½ cup of Extra-virgin olive oil
- 2 teaspoons grated lemon zest
- 1/3 cup lemon juice
- 1 clove, minced to pate garlic
- Salt and pepper
- 2 ounces, grated Parmesan cheese
- 1 pound spaghetti
- 6 tablespoons shredded fresh basil

Directions and Total Time: approx. 25 minutes

In a large-sized pot, bring water to a boil. When it boils, add the salt, and pour in the spaghetti. Cook for approximately about the time written on the package. Drain, and reserve ½ cup of the cooking water. Meanwhile, in a bowl, whisk the garlic, oil, lemon zest, juice, ½ tablespoon salt, and ¼ teaspoon pepper. Add the Parmesan cheese, and mix until creamy. Add the lemon mixture to the pasta, and stir to combine (add a little pasta cooking water if needed). Serve and enjoy!

Per Serving: Calories 398, Fat 20.7g, Carbs 42.5g, Protein 11.9g

447. Linguine with Bottarga

Ingredients for 2 servings

- ½ cup of linguine pasta
- 1 tablespoon extra-virgin olive oil
- 1 tablespoon grated fresh Bottarga
- 1 lemon zest
- A pinch of chili flakes
- Salt and pepper to taste
- Water

Directions and Total Time: approx. 25 minutes

Bring to a boil a large-sized pot of water, season with salt and pepper, and add the linguine. Let them cook for 10 minutes or until "al dente." In a pan let the olive oil fry with the chili and add the rinsed pasta with a little bit of pasta water. Stir the pasta and add the Bottarga. Turn off the heat, stir it firmly and add the lemon zest. Serve immediately.

Per Serving: Calories 150, Fat 10g, Carbs 25g, Protein 5g

448. Linguine with an Easy Pesto

Ingredients for 4 servings

- 2 cups of linguine pasta
- 1 lemon zest
- 1 cup of pine nuts
- 1 teaspoon coarse salt
- 1 cup of basil
- 1 garlic clove
- ½ cup of Parmigiano cheese
- 2 tablespoons Pecorino cheese
- ½ cup of olive oil
- Salt and pepper to taste
- Water

Directions and Total Time: approx. 22 minutes

Cook the cups of linguine pasta in salted boiling water for 10-12 minutes. Meanwhile, In a blender, blend all the other ingredients together and create the pesto sauce. Drain the pasta and cook it with the pesto and a tablespoon of the pasta water. Serve with some more Parmigiano cheese and basil.

Per Serving: Calories 300, Fat 15g, Carbs 42g, Protein 6g

449. Linguine with Shrimp

Ingredients for 4 servings

- 3 tablespoons extra virgin olive oil
- 12 ounces linguine
- 1 tablespoon garlic, minced
- 30 large shrimp, peeled and deveined
- A pinch of red pepper flakes, crushed
- 1 cup green olives, pitted and chopped
- 3 tablespoons lemon juice
- 1 teaspoon lemon zest, grated
- ¼ cup parsley, chopped

Directions and Total Time: approx. 25 minutes

Put some water in a large saucepan, add water, bring to a boil over medium high heat, add linguine, cook according to instructions, take off heat, drain and put in a bowl and reserve ½ cup cooking liquid. Heat a pan with 2 tablespoons oil over medium high heat, add shrimp, stir and cook for 3 minutes. Add pepper flakes and garlic, stir and cook 10 seconds more. Add remaining oil, lemon zest and juice and stir well. Add pasta and olives, reserved cooking liquid and parsley, stir, cook for 2 minutes more, take off heat, divide between plates and serve.

Per Serving: Calories 500, Fat 20g, Carbs 45g, Protein 34g

450. Mediterranean Pasta with Tomato Sauce and Vegetables

Ingredients for 8 servings

- 8 ounces linguine or spaghetti, cooked
- 1 teaspoon garlic powder
- 1 can whole peeled tomatoes, drained and sliced
- 1 tablespoon olive oil
- 1 (8 ounces) can tomato sauce
- ½ teaspoon Italian seasoning
- 8 ounces mushrooms, sliced
- 8 ounces yellow squash, sliced
- 8 ounces zucchini, sliced
- ½ teaspoon sugar
- ½ cup grated Parmesan cheese

Directions and Total Time: approx. 40 minutes

Mix tomato sauce, tomatoes, sugar, Italian seasoning, and garlic powder in a medium saucepan. Bring to boil on medium heat. Reduce heat to low. Cover and simmer for 20 minutes. In a large-sized skillet, heat olive oil on medium-high heat. Add squash, mushrooms, and zucchini. Cook, stirring, for 4 minutes or until tender-crisp. Stir vegetables into the tomato sauce. Place pasta in a serving bowl. Spoon vegetable mixture over pasta and toss to coat. Top with grated Parmesan cheese.

Per Serving: Calories 154, Fat 2g, Carbs 28g, Protein 6g

451. Morning Couscous

Ingredients for 4 servings

- 3 cups low-fat milk
- 1 cup whole-wheat couscous, uncooked
- 1 cinnamon stick
- ½ chopped apricot, dried
- ¼ cup currants, dried
- 6 teaspoons brown sugar
- ¼ teaspoon salt
- 4 teaspoons melted butter

Directions and Total Time: approx. 18 minutes

Take a large saucepan and combine milk and cinnamon stick and heat over medium. Heat for 3 minutes or until microbubbles forms around edges of the pan. Do not boil. Remove from heat, stir in the couscous, apricots, currants, salt, and 4 tsps. brown sugar. Cover the mixture and allow it to sit for 15 minutes. Remove and throw away the cinnamon stick. Divide couscous among 4 bowls, and top each with 1 tsp. melted butter and ½ tsp. brown sugar. Ready to serve.

Per Serving: Calories 306, Fat 6g, Carbs 5g, Protein 9g

452. Moroccan-Style Couscous

Ingredients for 2 servings

- 1 tablespoon of olive oil
- ¾ cup of couscous
- ¼ teaspoon of garlic powder
- ¼ teaspoon of salt
- ¼ teaspoon of cinnamon
- 1 cup of water
- 2 tablespoons of raisins
- 2 tablespoons of minced dried apricots
- 2 teaspoons of minced fresh parsley

Directions and Total Time: approx. 15 minutes

Heat the tablespoon of olive oil in a saucepan over medium-high heat. Add the couscous, garlic powder, salt, and cinnamon. Stir for 1 minute to toast the couscous and spices. Add the water, raisins, and apricots and bring the mixture to a boil. Cover the large-sized pot and turn off the heat. Let the couscous sit for 4 to 5 minutes and then fluff it with a fork. Add parsley and season with additional salt or spices as needed.

Per Serving: Calories 338, Fat 8g, Carbs 59g, Protein 9g

453. Mushroom and Vegetable Penne Pasta

Ingredients for 4 servings

- 6 ounces penne pasta
- 6 ounces shitake mushrooms, chopped
- 1 small carrot, cut into strips
- 4 ounces baby spinach, finely chopped
- 1 teaspoon ginger, grounded
- 3 tablespoons oil
- 2 tablespoons soy sauce
- 6 ounces zucchini, cut into strips
- 6 ounces leek, finely chopped
- ½ teaspoon salt
- 2 garlic cloves, crushed
- 2 cups of water

Directions and Total Time: approx. 13 minutes

Heat the oil. Sauté and stir-fry carrot and garlic for 3-4 minutes. Add remaining ingredients and pour in 2 cups of water. Cook on High pressure for 4 minutes. Quick-release the pressure. Serve and enjoy!

Per Serving: Calories 429, Fat 8g, Carbs 64g, Protein 25g

454. Mushroom Couscous

Ingredients for 4 servings

- 1/2 cup couscous (uncooked)
- 1 cup of water
- 1 tablespoon butter
- 7 mushrooms (sliced)
- 2 carrots (sliced & cooked)
- 2 tablespoons chive (chopped)
- 1 teaspoon garlic powder
- 1 1/2 herb teaspoons (Italian, blend)
- 1 tablespoon lemon juice
- salt / pepper

Directions and Total Time: approx. 35 minutes

Add couscous and water in a medium saucepan. Bake for 5 - 10 minutes over medium heat until the couscous is cooked. Melt butter in a frying pan. Add sliced mushrooms and cook for just about 5 minutes. Add carrots, cooked couscous, chopped chives, garlic powder, Italian spice mix and lemon juice. Bake for about 5 - 10 minutes. Season with salt and pepper.

Per Serving: Calories 150, Fat 0.35g, Carbs 0.25g, Protein 0.5g

Ingredients for 4 servings

- 2 teaspoons olive oil
- ¼ cup minced shallot
- ½ cup squeezed orange juice
- ½ cup water
- ⅛ teaspoon ground cinnamon
- ¼ teaspoon kosher salt
- 1 cup whole-wheat couscous

Directions and Total Time: approx. 10 minutes

Heat the oil in a large-sized saucepan over medium heat. Once the oil is shimmering, add the shallot and cook for 2 minutes, stirring frequently. Add the orange juice, water, cinnamon, and salt, and bring to a boil. Once the liquid is actually boiling, add the couscous, cover the pan, and turn off the heat. Leave the couscous covered for 5 minutes. When the couscous is done, fluff with a fork. Place ¾ cup of couscous in each of 4 containers.

Per Serving: Calories 215, Fat 4g, Carbs 41g, Protein 8g

456. Orecchiette Pasta

Ingredients for 4 servings

- ½ pound orecchiette pasta
- 2 cups chopped broccoli
- 4 ounces guanciale
- 4 cloves of garlic
- ¼ cup olive oil
- ¼ cup white wine
- ¼ cup parmesan cheese
- 1 teaspoon salt, pepper, and chili flakes

Directions and Total Time: approx. 30 minutes

Boil the orecchiette in salted water. Dice the guanciale and sauté on medium-heat until fat is rendered. Add garlic and olive oil. Cook until garlic is fragrant. Add broccoli and sauté for 5 minutes. Drain the orecchiette and save 1 cup of the pasta water. Place the orecchiette, broccoli, guanciale, white wine, and pasta water in a low-heat pot for 5 minutes. Top with cheese, salt, pepper, and chili flakes.

Per Serving: Calories 321, Fat 21.3g, Carbs 20.1g, Protein 11.4g

457. Passion Fruit and Spicy Couscous

Ingredients for 4 servings

- 1 pinch of salt.
- 1 pinch of allspice.
- 1 teaspoon of mixed spice.
- 1 cup of boiling water.
- 2 teaspoons of extra-virgin olive oil.
- ½ cup of full-fat Greek yogurt.
- ½ cup of honey.
- 1 cup of couscous.
- 1 teaspoon of orange zest.
- 2 oranges peeled and sliced.
- 2 tablespoons of passion fruit pulp.
- ½ cup of blueberries.
- ½ cup of walnuts roasted and unsalted.
- 2 tablespoons of fresh mint

Directions and Total Time: approx. 30 minutes

In a mixing bowl, combine the salt, allspice, mixed spice, honey, couscous, and boiling water. Cover the bowl and allow to rest for 5 to 10 minutes, or until the water has been absorbed. Using a small fork, give the mixture a good stir, then add the diced walnuts. In a separate bowl, combine the passion fruit, yogurt, and orange zest. To serve, dish the couscous up into 4 bowls, add the yogurt mixture, and top with the sliced orange, blueberries, and mint leaves.

Per Serving: Calories 100, Fat 10.5g, Carbs 3.4g, Protein 2.1g

Ingredients for 4 servings

- 8 ounces rotini pasta
- 1 ½ cups chopped Brussel sprouts
- 2 cloves of crushed garlic
- 3 tablespoons olive oil
- ¾ cup parmesan cheese
- 1 teaspoon salt, pepper, and chili flakes

Directions and Total Time: approx. 35 minutes

In a large-sized pot, cook the pasta in salted water. On an olive oiled baking sheet place the Brussel sprouts with garlic and half of the parmesan cheese. Bake for 15 minutes in a 400°F oven. Drain the pasta and add it to the pot with the sprouts. Drizzle the olive oil, parmesan, salt, pepper, and chili flakes on top before serving.

Per Serving: Calories 275, Fat 12.3g, Carbs 34.6g, Protein 8.2g

459. Pasta and Chickpeas

Ingredients for 2 servings

- 1 ½ cup of broken pasta
- 1 carrot
- ½ golden onion
- 1 cup of canned chickpeas
- 1 sprig of rosemary
- 1 garlic clove
- 1 tablespoon extra-virgin olive oil
- 1 fresh chili pepper
- 1 cup of vegetable broth
- Salt and pepper to taste

Directions and Total Time: approx. 35 minutes

Finely chop the carrot and the onion. Add them to a pot with rosemary, oil, chili pepper, and garlic clove. Stir until they are golden and add the chickpeas. Add the broth and let it simmer for 10 minutes. Blend the mixture, without the rosemary, leaving some chickpeas integer. Add the cup of broken pasta and let it cook for 12 minutes, if the mixture is too thick add some broth. Season with salt and pepper and serve.

Per Serving: Calories 250, Fat 10g, Carbs 45g, Protein 10g

460. Pasta and Lentils

Ingredients for 4 servings

- 1 small onion
- 1 chili pepper
- 1 cup of canned tomato
- 1 cup of lentils
- 1 cup of mixed pasta
- 2 tablespoons olive oil
- 2 cups of broth
- Salt and pepper to taste

Directions and Total Time: approx. 40 minutes

In a pot fry the onion with the chili pepper and the oil until golden. Then add the tomato and the lentils. Add the 2 cups of broth and let it simmer for 30 minutes circa. Add the mixed pasta and stir until everything is cooked. Season in the end.

Per Serving: Calories 350, Fat 10g, Carbs 45g, Protein 18g

Ingredients for 4 servings

- 1 pound penne pasta
- 8 ounces baby bella mushrooms
- 1 cup heavy whipping cream
- 1 clove of garlic
- 3 tablespoons olive oil
- 2 tablespoons butter
- ½ cup parmesan cheese
- 1 teaspoon salt, pepper, and onion powder

Directions and Total Time: approx. 20 minutes

Cook the pasta in salted water. In a medium-heat skillet, cook the garlic and baby bell mushrooms in the olive oil for 5 minutes. Add heavy cream, salt, pepper, and onion powder and cook for 5 minutes. Drain the penne and save ¼ cup of pasta water. Add the penne, mushroom sauce, and pasta water to the pot and top with cheese. Simmer for 2-3 minutes before serving.

Per Serving: Calories 592, Fat 30.5g, Carbs 66.1g, Protein 15.5g

462. Pasta and White Beans

Ingredients for 2 servings

- 3 cups of whole-grain penne pasta
- 2 (15-ounce) cans of diced tomatoes with basil and oregano
- 4 cloves fresh garlic, minced
- 1 small white onion, diced
- 1 can of cannellini beans
- 1 bag of fresh spinach, cleaned and torn into pieces
- 1 log of fresh soft goat cheese, broken into small chunks
- Crusty bread

Directions and Total Time: approx. 30 minutes

Cook pasta according to package directions. In a large skillet, bring tomatoes, garlic, onion, and beans to a boil. Reduce heat to a low simmer and cook for roughly 10 minutes. Add spinach and continue to let simmer until leaves are wilted, stirring mixture occasionally. Drain cooked pasta and divide it onto plates. Top pasta with the tomato-spinach mixture and scatter on chunks of goat cheese. Serve with hearty crusty bread.

Per Serving: Calories 303, Fat 3g, Carbs 42g, Protein 14g

463. Pasta, Salmon, and Pesto

Ingredients for 4 servings

- 8 ounces penne pasta
- 1 pound salmon
- ⅓ cup pesto
- 2 tablespoons olive oil
- 1 teaspoon lemon juice
- ¼ cup parmesan cheese
- ½ cup fresh basil
- 1 teaspoon salt, pepper, and garlic powder

Directions and Total Time: approx. 35 minutes

Cook the penne in salted water. On an oiled baking sheet, add the salmon, lemon juice, and half of the pesto. Bake at 450°F for 15 minutes. Drain the pasta and save ¼ cup of water. Add the pasta to the water, olive oil, parmesan cheese, salt, pepper, and garlic powder. Slice the salmon into bite-sized pieces and combine with the pasta. Top with fresh basil.

Per Serving: Calories 467, Fat 24.2g, Carbs 32.5g, Protein 30.8g

464. Pasta with Greek Olive and Feta Cheese

Ingredients for 4 servings

- 2 cloves of finely minced fresh garlic
- 2 large tomatoes, seeded and diced
- 3 ounces feta cheese, crumbled
- ½ diced red bell pepper
- 10 small-sized Greek olives, coarsely chopped and pitted
- ½ diced yellow bell pepper
- ¼ cup basil leaves, coarsely chopped
- 1 tablespoon Olive oil
- ¼ teaspoon hot pepper, finely chopped
- 4 ½ ounces of ziti pasta

Directions and Total Time: approx. 40 minutes

In a large-sized pot, bring water to a boil over high heat. When it boils, add the salt, and pour in the pasta, and cook for the time indicated on the package. Meanwhile, in a large bowl, mix olives, feta cheese, bell peppers, basil, garlic, and red pepper. Add cooked pasta, and a drizzle of oil, and mix well. Refrigerate for half an hour. Stir before serving.

Per Serving: Calories 235, Fat 10g, Carbs 27g, Protein 7g

465. Pasta with Ham

Ingredients for 4 servings

- 1 fresh onion
- 4 tablespoons EVO oil
- 1 cup of ham (cut into cubes)
- 3 cups of short pasta
- 1 cup of Quartirolo cheese
- Salt and pepper to taste
- Mint to taste
- Water

Directions and Total Time: approx. 40 minutes

In a pan fry the sliced fresh onion with oil and the cubes of ham. Cooked the pasta in a pot with salted water for 10 minutes. Drain it and pour it in the large-sized pan for another 2 minutes. Serve hot with some Quartirolo cheese, salt, pepper, and mint on top.

Per Serving: Calories 190, Fat 5g, Carbs 44g, Protein 5.7g

466. Pasta Lemon and Artichokes

Ingredients for 4 servings

- 16 ounces of linguine or angel hair pasta
- 1/4 cup of extra-virgin olive oil
- 8 garlic cloves, finely minced or pressed
- 2 (15-ounce) jars water-packed artichoke hearts, drained and quartered
- 2 tablespoons of freshly squeezed lemon juice
- 1/4 cup of thinly sliced fresh basil
- 1 teaspoon of sea salt
- Freshly ground black pepper

Directions and Total Time: approx. 25 minutes

Boil water on high heat and cook the pasta. While the pasta is cooking, heat the oil in a skillet over medium heat and cook the garlic, stirring often, for 1 to 2 minutes until it just begins to brown. Toss the garlic with the artichokes in a large bowl. Gently stir and serve.

Per Serving: Calories 423, Fat 14g, Carbs 57g, Protein 15g

467. Pasta with Peas and Ham

Ingredients for 4 servings

- 2 cups of pasta
- 1 cup of ham
- 1 cup of fresh peas
- Basil to taste
- 2 tablespoons olive oil
- 1 garlic cloves
- 2 tablespoons pecorino Romano cheese
- 1 cup of water

Directions and Total Time: approx. 20 minutes

In a large-sized pot bring to a boil the water, salt it, and pour it into the pasta. Cook al dente. In a large-sized pan fry the olive oil, garlic, basil, and ham, after 5 minutes add the peas and cover with 1 cup of water. Let it cook for another 5 minutes then cover with water and let it simmer. When the cup of water is almost absorbed add the pasta and the cheese and mix with the strength to combine all the ingredients well.

Per Serving: Calories 260, Fat 20g, Carbs 43g, Protein 7.8g

468. Pasta with Shrimps, Lemon, and Basil

Ingredients for 4 servings

- 2 cups baby spinach
- ½ teaspoon salt
- 2 tablespoons fresh lemon juice
- 2 tablespoons extra virgin olive oil
- 3 tablespoons drained capers
- ¼ cup chopped fresh basil
- 1 pound peeled, and deveined large shrimp
- 8 ounces uncooked spaghetti
- ¾ water

Directions and Total Time: approx. 15 minutes

In a pot, bring 3 quarts of water to a boil. When it actually boils, add the salt, and pasta cook for the time indicated on the package. Meanwhile, in a frying pan pour a drizzle of oil, and heat over medium heat. Add the shrimp, and cook a minute and a half per side. Drain pasta, and add shrimp, salt, lemon juice, olive oil, capers, and basil. Mix well, then plate in serving dishes with ½ cup spinach around it. Serve and enjoy!

Per Serving: Calories 151, Fat 7.4g, Carbs 18.9g, Protein 4.3g

469. Pasta with Tomatoes and Spinach

Ingredients for 3 servings

- 4 ounces of pasta (whole wheat)
- ½ teaspoon of olive oil (extra virgin)
- 2 ounces of tin tomatoes, drained
- 2 ounces of spinach, frozen
- 1/3 cup of feta cheese, crumbled
- ½ teaspoon of salt
- 1 teaspoon of pepper, ground

Directions and Total Time: approx. 35 minutes

Cook the whole-wheat pasta until al dente according to package directions in a saucepan of boiling water. Meanwhile, heat the prepared teaspoon of olive oil in a pan over medium heat, add the onion and cook for three minutes. Simmer for around ten minutes after adding the tomatoes. Cook until the spinach is cooked thoroughly. Drain the cooked pasta and mix it in the sauce until it is well covered. Add salt and pepper, then top with feta cheese.

Per Serving: Calories 333, Fat 8g, Carbs 55g, Protein 15g

470. Pecorino Pasta with Fresh Tomato

Ingredients for 4 servings

- ¼ cup torn fresh basil leaves
- 1/8 teaspoon black pepper
- ¼ teaspoon salt
- 6 tablespoons grated fresh pecorino Romano cheese, divided
- 1 ¼ pounds tomatoes, chopped
- 2 teaspoons minced garlic
- 1 cup vertically sliced onions
- 2 teaspoons olive oil
- 8 ounces uncooked penne, cooked and drained

Directions and Total Time: approx. 20 minutes

On medium high fire, place a nonstick fry pan with oil and cook for five minutes onion. Stir in garlic and continue cooking for two minutes more. Add tomatoes and cook for another two minutes. Remove pan from fire, season with pepper and salt. Mix well. Stir in 2 tbsp cheese and pasta. Toss well. Transfer the cooked dish to a serving dish, garnish with basil and remaining cheese before serving.

Per Serving: Calories 376, Fat 11.6g, Carbs 50.8g, Protein 17.8g

471. Penne Pasta and Shrimp

Ingredients for 4 servings

- 8 ounces penne pasta
- 1 pound jumbo shrimp
- 3 tablespoons lemon juice
- 4 tablespoons butter
- 3 cloves of garlic
- ¼ cup white wine
- 2 tablespoons fresh parsley
- 1 teaspoon salt and pepper

Directions and Total Time: approx. 25 minutes

Cook the pasta in salted water. Remove the shells, devein, and rinse the shrimp. In a medium-heat skillet, add butter and shrimp. Sauté for 3 minutes, turn off the heat and add the white wine and garlic. Cook for 3 minutes and add the lemon juice and parsley. Drain the pasta and save ¼ cup of pasta water. Return the penne to the pot and simmer 3-5 minutes before serving.

Per Serving: Calories 365, Fat 12.9g, Carbs 32.5g, Protein 27.1g

472. Penne Pasta with Tomato Sauce and Mizithra Cheese

Ingredients for 5 servings

- 2 tablespoons olive oil
- 2 scallion stalks, chopped
- 2 green garlic stalks, minced
- 10 ounces penne
- 1/3 teaspoon ground black pepper, to taste
- Sea salt, to taste
- 1/4 teaspoon cayenne pepper
- 1/4 teaspoon dried marjoram
- 1/2 teaspoon dried oregano
- 1/2 teaspoon dried basil
- 1/2 cup marinara sauce
- 2 cups vegetable broth
- 2 overripe tomatoes, pureed
- 1 cup Mitzithra cheese, grated

Directions and Total Time: approx. 35 minutes

Heat the oil in your pot until sizzling. Now, sauté the scallions and garlic until just tender and fragrant. Stir in the penne pasta, spices, marinara sauce, broth, and pureed tomatoes; do not stir, but your pasta should be covered with the liquid. Secure the lid and cook for 7 minutes at high heat. Once cooking is complete, carefully remove the lid. Fold in the cheese and seal the lid. Let it sit in the residual heat until the cheese melts. Bon appetite!

Per Serving: Calories 395, Fat 15.6g, Carbs 51.8g, Protein 14.9g

473. Pesto Pasta

Ingredients for 6 servings

- 1 pound spaghetti
- 4 cups fresh basil leaves, stems removed
- 3 cloves garlic
- 1 teaspoon salt
- ½ teaspoon freshly ground black pepper
- ½ cup toasted pine nuts
- ¼ cup lemon juice
- ½ cup grated Parmesan cheese
- 1 cup extra-virgin olive oil

Directions and Total Time: approx. 18 minutes

Bring a large-sized pot water to a boil and then add the salt. Add spaghetti to the pot and cook for 8 minutes. In a food processor, place the remaining ingredients, except for the olive oil, and pulse. While the processor is running, slowly drizzle the olive oil through the top opening. Process until all the olive oil has been added. Reserve ½ cup of the cooking liquid. Drain the pasta and put it into a large bowl. Add the pesto and cooking liquid to the bowl of pasta and toss everything together. Serve immediately.

Per Serving: Calories 106.7, Fat 7.2g, Carbs 9.1g, Protein 2.3g

474. Pork and Sage Couscous

Ingredients for 4 servings

- 2 pounds pork loin boneless and sliced
- ¾ cup veggie stock
- 2 tablespoons olive oil
- ½ tablespoon chili powder
- 2 teaspoon sage, dried
- ½ tablespoon garlic powder
- Salt and black pepper to the taste
- 2 cups couscous, cooked

Directions and Total Time: approx. 7 hours

In a slow cooker, combine the pork with the stock, the oil and the other ingredients except the couscous, put the lid on and cook on Low for 7 hours. Divide the mix between plates, add the couscous on the side, sprinkle the sage on top and serve.

Per Serving: Calories 272, Fat 14.5g, Carbs 16.3g, Protein 14.3g

475. Pork with Couscous

Ingredients for 6 servings

- 2 and ½ pounds pork loin boneless and trimmed
- ¾ cup chicken stock
- 2 tablespoons olive oil
- ½ tablespoon sweet paprika
- 2 and ¼ teaspoon sage, dried
- ½ tablespoon garlic powder
- ¼ teaspoon rosemary, dried
- ¼ teaspoon marjoram, dried
- 1 teaspoon basil, dried
- 1 teaspoon oregano, dried
- Salt and black pepper to taste
- 2 cups couscous, cooked

Directions and Total Time: approx. 7 hours and 10 minutes

In a bowl, mix oil with stock, paprika, garlic powder, sage, rosemary, thyme, marjoram, oregano, salt and pepper to taste and whisk well. Put pork loin in your crock pot. Add stock and spice mix, stir, cover and cook on Low for 7 hours. Slice pork return to pot and toss with cooking juices. Divide between plates and serve with couscous on the side.

Per Serving: Calories 320, Fat 31g, Carbs 21g, Protein 23g

476. Quick Tomato Spaghetti

Ingredients for 4 servings

- 8 ounces spaghetti
- 3 tablespoons olive oil
- 4 garlic cloves, sliced
- 1 jalapeno, sliced
- 2 cups cherry tomatoes
- Salt and pepper to taste
- 1 teaspoon balsamic vinegar
- ½ cup grated Parmesan

Directions and Total Time: approx. 20 minutes

Heat a large pot of water on medium flame. Add a pinch of salt and bring to a boil then add the pasta. Cook for just about 8 minutes or until al dente. While the pasta cooks, heat the oil in a skillet and add garlic and jalapeno. Cook for approximately 1 minute then stir in the tomatoes, as well as salt and pepper. Cook for 5-7 minutes until the tomatoes' skins burst. Add the vinegar and remove off heat. Drain the already cooked pasta well and mix it with the tomato sauce. Sprinkle with cheese and serve right away.

Per Serving: Calories 298, Fat 13.5g, Carbs 36g, Protein 9.7g

477. Raisins, Garbanzos, and Spinach Pasta

Ingredients for 6 servings

- 8 ounces of farfalle (bow-tie) pasta
- 2 tablespoons of olive oil (extra virgin)
- 4 smashed garlic cloves
- ½ cup of broth de poulet (unsalted)
- ½ washed and drained garbanzo beans
- 4 cups of fresh spinach, chopped
- ½ cup of raisin golden
- 2 tablespoons of Parmigiano-Reggiano black peppercorns, cracked

Directions and Total Time: approx. 40 minutes

Fill a saucepan three full with salted water and bring to a boil over high heat. Cook for just about 12 minutes, or until pasta is al dente; drain and put aside. In a large-sized pan, heat extra virgin olive oil and sauté garlic till fragrant; pour chicken broth and beans and mix to cook thoroughly. Cook for just about 3 minutes, or until spinach is wilted, after adding the spinach and raisins. Distribute the pasta among the dishes and top with approximately a sixth sauce, peppercorns, and Parmesan cheese. Serve immediately.

Per Serving: Calories 446, Fat 8g, Carbs 15g, Protein 15g

478. Rigatoni Pasta with Capers and Ricotta Cheese

Ingredients for 4 servings

- 3 cups of rigatoni
- 2 ½ cup of ricotta cheese
- ¾ cup of Taggiasche olives
- ½ cup of capers
- 15 dried tomatoes
- 2 tablespoons olive oil
- 8 capers fruits
- Salt and pepper to taste
- Water

Directions and Total Time: approx. 20 minutes

Cut the tomato into slices and let it soak in water for 5 minutes. Drain them and set them aside. Wash the capers. Boil the pasta in salted water meanwhile, blend the ricotta, the capers, oil, salt, and pepper together. Add the tomatoes to the mixture. Pour the mixture into a large-sized bowl and add the pasta to it, add the olive and mix well. Serve with some capers fruits.

Per Serving: Calories 450, Fat 20g, Carbs 42g, Protein 19g

479. Roasted Eggplant Red Pepper Penne

Ingredients for 4 servings

- 8 ounces penne
- 2 eggplants
- 4 roasted red bell peppers, sliced
- ½ teaspoon dried oregano
- 2 tablespoons olive oil
- Salt and pepper to taste

Directions and Total Time: approx. 45 minutes

Heat a large pot of water on medium flame. Add a pinch of salt and bring it to a boil. Add the penne and cook them until al dente, not more than 8 minutes. Cut the eggplants in half, season them with salt and pepper and place them in a baking tray. Cook in the preheated oven at a heat of 400°F for 15 minutes. When done, scoop out the flesh and chop it into fine bits. Mix with the sliced bell peppers, oregano and oil then adjust the taste with salt and pepper. Stir in the cooked penne and serve the pasta right away.

Per Serving: Calories 292, Fat 8.8g, Carbs 47.3g, Protein 9.1g

480. Roasted Pepper Pasta

Ingredients for 6 servings

- 1 pound of whole wheat penne pasta
- 1 tablespoon of Italian seasoning
- 4 cups of vegetable broth
- 1 tablespoon of garlic, minced
- ½ onion, chopped
- 14 ounces jar of roasted red peppers
- 1 cup of feta cheese, crumbled
- 1 tablespoon of olive oil
- Pepper and salt

Directions and Total Time: approx. 23 minutes

In a large-sized pot, bring plenty of water to a boil. When it boils, add the salt, pour in the pasta, and cook for the time indicated on the package. Meanwhile, add the roasted bell pepper to the blender, and blend until smooth. In a skillet, pour a drizzle of oil, add the garlic, onion, and sauté for 2-3 minutes. Add the roasted bell pepper cream, and cook for 2 minutes, stirring. Add the prepared broth, Italian seasoning, salt, and pepper, and mix well. Drain the already cooked pasta, and add it to the skillet, stirring well over high heat to season. Finally, add the feta cheese, plate, and serve.

Per Serving: Calories 459, Fat 10.6g, Carbs 68.1g, Protein 21.3g

481. Robust Mediterranean Sausage and Pasta

Ingredients for 4 servings

- Sausage, Italian links, cut into half - 4 ounces each Undrained tomatoes and chilies chopped – 10 ounces Italian sausage spaghetti sauce - 25.6 ounces
- 1 medium onion, chopped
- 1 large green pepper, julienned
- 1 teaspoon of Italian seasoning
- 2 cups of spiral pasta, uncooked
- 2 cloves of garlic, minced

Directions and Total Time: approx. 6 hours and 45 minutes

Brown the sausages in a large non-stick skillet. Transfer the brown sausages into a 4-quarter slow cooker. Now put tomatoes, onion, green pepper, garlic, spaghetti sauce, Italian seasoning, and combine. Close the lid and slow cook for 6 hours. Add pasta. Cover and cook again high for 30 minutes to tender the pasta. Serve hot.

Per Serving: Calories 529, Fat 22g, Carbs 60g, Protein 23g

482. Saffron Chickpea and Zucchini Pasta

Ingredients for 4 servings

- 3 cups of mezze maniche pasta
- 2 cups of pre-cooked chickpeas
- 2 cups of grated zucchini
- ½ cup of olive oil
- Parsley to taste
- 1 teaspoon saffron pistils
- 1 garlic clove
- Salt and pepper to taste
- 1 cup of hot water

Directions and Total Time: approx. 35 minutes

Add the pistils to 1 cup of hot water and let it settle for 40 minutes. Wash and grate the zucchini and cook them with oil and garlic in a pan for 10 minutes. Add 1 cup of saffron water and add the chickpeas, cook for another minute and turn off the heat. Add parsley, salt, and pepper. Boil the pasta to an al dente, drain it, and add it to the zucchini pan and the rest of the saffron water. Cook until the pasta results creamy, 2 minutes, and serve with parsley and olive oil.

Per Serving: Calories 498, Fat 10g, Carbs 56g, Protein 19g

483. Seafood Garlic Couscous

Ingredients for 8 servings

- 8 scallions, sliced
- 4 (5.4-ounces) boxes garlic-flavored couscous, boiled and drained
- 1-pound raw shrimp, peeled, deveined and coarsely chopped
- 1 cup fresh parsley, chopped
- 4 tablespoons olive oil
- 2 pounds codfish, cut into 1-inch pieces
- 1 cup fresh chives, chopped
- Hot sauce, to taste
- 1-pound bay scallops
- Salt and black pepper, to taste

Directions and Total Time: approx. 30 minutes

Mix shrimps, scallions, codfish, scallops, parsley, chives, salt and black pepper in a bowl. Heat oil in a deep large-sized skillet and add the seafood mixture. Sauté until golden and pour in the hot sauce. Lower the heat temperature and cover with a lid. Divide the couscous into the serving plates and top evenly with the seafood mixture. Dish out and serve immediately.

Per Serving: Calories 476, Fat 9g, Carbs 68g, Protein 32.9g

484. Simple Penne Anti-Pasto

Ingredients for 4 servings

- ¼ cup pine nuts, toasted
- ½ cup grated Parmigiano-Reggiano cheese, divided
- 8-ounces penne pasta, cooked and drained
- 1 6-ounces jar drained, sliced, marinated and quartered artichoke hearts
- 1 7-ounces jar drained and chopped sun-dried tomato halves packed in oil
- 3 ounces chopped prosciutto
- 1/3 cup pesto
- ½ cup pitted and chopped Kalamata olives
- 1 medium red bell pepper

Directions and Total Time: approx. 15 minutes

Slice bell pepper, discard membranes, seeds and stem. On a foiled lined baking sheet, place bell pepper halves, press down by hand and broil in oven for eight minutes. Remove from oven, put in a sealed bag for 5 minutes before peeling and chopping. Place chopped bell pepper in a bowl and mix in artichokes, tomatoes, prosciutto, pesto and olives. Toss in ¼ cup cheese and pasta. Transfer it to a medium-sized serving dish and garnish with ¼ cup cheese and pine nuts. Serve and enjoy!

Per Serving: Calories 606, Fat 27.6g, Carbs 70.3g, Protein 27.2g

485. Small Pasta and Beans Pot

Ingredients for 4 servings

- 1 pound small whole wheat pasta
- 1 can diced tomatoes, juice reserved
- 1 can cannellini beans, drained and rinsed
- 2 tablespoons no-salt-added tomato paste
- 1 red or yellow bell pepper, chopped
- 1 yellow onion, chopped
- 1 tablespoon Italian seasoning mix
- 3 garlic cloves, minced
- ¼ teaspoon crushed red pepper flakes, optional
- 1 tablespoon extra-virgin olive oil
- 5 cups water
- 1 bunch kale, stemmed and chopped
- ½ cup pitted Kalamata olives, chopped
- 1 cup sliced basil

Directions and Total Time: approx. 30 minutes

Except for the kale, olives, and basil, combine all the ingredients in a pot. Stir to mix well. Bring to a boil over high heat. Stir constantly. Reduce the heat temperature to medium-high and add the kale. Cook for 10 minutes or until the pasta is al dente. Stir constantly. Transfer all of them on a large plate and serve with olives and basil on top.

Per Serving: Calories 357, Fat 7.6g, Carbs 64.5g, Protein 18.2g

486. Spaghetti and Meatballs

Ingredients for 4 servings

- 8 ounces spaghetti
- 1 can crushed tomatoes
- 1 pound ground beef
- 1 large egg
- 2 cloves of minced garlic
- ½ cup chopped white onion
- ⅓ cup breadcrumbs
- ½ cup parmesan cheese
- 1 teaspoon salt, pepper, and red pepper flakes

Directions and Total Time: approx. 30 minutes

Cook the spaghetti in salted water. In a large-sized mixing bowl, combine the ground beef, egg, garlic, onion, breadcrumbs, half of the parmesan cheese, salt, pepper, and also red pepper flakes. Form the meatballs into 2-inch-thick circles. In a medium-heat saucepan, add the meatballs and cook for 10 minutes. Drain the spaghetti and add to the crushed tomatoes. Heat the sauce and pasta for 3-5 minutes before serving. Top with fresh basil.

Per Serving: Calories 466, Fat 10.5g, Carbs 44.5g, Protein 45.9g

487. Spaghetti Bolognese

Ingredients for 4 servings

- 17.6-ounces of beef mince
- 7-ounces of red onions
- 14.2-ounces tin of tomatoes
- 4 cloves of garlic
- 1-ounce of tomato puree
- 1 teaspoon of oregano
- 10.6-ounces of dried spaghetti
- 1-ounce of parmesan
- Salt and pepper to taste

Directions and Total Time: approx. 60 minutes

Heat a skillet with oil, add the onions, and sauté them. When they turn golden, add the ground beef and brown. When the beef turns brown, add the minced garlic, tomatoes, tomato puree, oregano, salt, and a little water, and simmer for 30 minutes. Meanwhile, bring plenty of water to a boil in a large pot. Add the salt spaghetti, and cook for 8 minutes when it boils. Drain the spaghetti, add some sauce, and toss to season. Plate, garnish with plenty of meat sauce, Parmesan cheese, and serve.

Per Serving: Calories 455, Fat 10g, Carbs 61g, Protein 38g

488. Spaghetti in Lemon Avocado White Sauce

Ingredients for 6 servings

- Freshly ground black pepper
- Zest and juice of 1 lemon
- 1 avocado, pitted and peeled
- 1-pound spaghetti
- Salt
- 1 tablespoon Olive oil
- 8 ounces small shrimp, shelled and deveined
- ¼ cup dry white wine
- 1 large onion, finely sliced

Directions and Total Time: approx. 30 minutes

Let a big pot of water boil. Once boiling add the spaghetti or pasta and cook following manufacturer's instructions until al dente. Drain and set aside. In a large fry pan, over medium fire sauté wine and onions for ten minutes or until onions are translucent and soft. Add the shrimps into the fry pan and increase fire to high while constantly sautéing until shrimps are cooked around five minutes. Turn the fire off. Season with salt and add the oil right away. Then quickly toss in the cooked pasta, mix well. In a blender, until smooth, puree the lemon juice and avocado. Pour into the fry pan of pasta, combine well. Garnish with pepper and lemon zest then serve.

Per Serving: Calories 206, Fat 8g, Carbs 26.3g, Protein 10.2g

489. Spaghetti with Anchovies

Ingredients for 2 servings

- 160 grams of spaghetti
- 4 anchovy fillets, chopped
- 2 cloves of garlic, minced or pressed
- 3 tablespoons of olive oil
- 1 pinch of salt
- ground pepper to taste

Directions and Total Time: approx. 15 minutes

In a saucepan, bring plenty of water to a boil. When it boils, add salt and pasta, and cook for the time indicated on the package. Meanwhile, heat the oil in a small-sized saucepan over low heat. Sauté the crushed or minced garlic for 1-2 minutes. Chop the anchovies, add them to the pan, and stir until crumbled. Set aside. Drain the spaghetti, and transfer to the skillet with the anchovies. Sauté the spaghetti to season, then plate, and serve.

Per Serving: Calories 450, Fat 17g, Carbs 61g, Protein 13g

490. Spaghetti with Pine Nut and Cheese

Ingredients for 4 servings

- 8 ounces of spaghetti
- 4 tablespoons of almond butter
- 1 teaspoon of freshly ground black pepper
- ½ cup of pine nuts
- 1 cup of fresh grated Parmesan cheese, divided

Directions and Total Time: approx. 26 minutes

Bring a small-sized pot of salted water to a boil. Add the pasta, and cook for the time indicated on the package. Meanwhile, heat a medium-sized saucepan over medium heat. Add the butter, black pepper, pine nuts, and toast for a couple of minutes. Drain the pasta al dente but reserve ½ cup of the cooking water. Place the pasta in the skillet with the pine nuts, add ¾ cup of the Parmesan cheese and the before reserved cooking water, and toss to coat the pasta evenly. Plate, top with grated Parmesan cheese, and serve immediately.

Per Serving: Calories 542, Fat 32g, Carbs 46g, Protein 20g

Ingredients for 4 servings

- 3 cups cooked whole-wheat fusilli
- 2 cups cherry tomatoes, halved
- ½ cup vegan cheese, shredded
- 4 cups spinach, chopped
- 2 cups edamame, thawed
- 1 large red onion, finely chopped
- 2 tablespoons white wine vinegar
- ½ teaspoon dried dill
- 2 tablespoons extra-virgin olive oil
- Salt to taste
- Pepper to taste

Directions and Total Time: approx. 5 minutes

To make dressing: Add all the rest of the prepared ingredients for dressing into a bowl and whisk well. Set aside for about a while for the flavors to set in. To make salad: Add all the ingredients of the salad in a bowl. Toss well. Drizzle dressing on top. Toss well. Divide into 4 plates and serve.

Per Serving: Calories 684, Fat 33.6g, Carbs 69.5g, Protein 31.7g

492. Spinach and Gorgonzola Penne

Ingredients for 4 servings

- 8 ounces penne pasta
- ¾ cup baby spinach
- 2 ounces gorgonzola cheese
- ¼ cup chopped walnuts
- ¾ cup heavy cream
- 2 cloves of chopped garlic
- 1 teaspoon salt and pepper

Directions and Total Time: approx. 30 minutes

In a large-sized pot, cook the penne in salted water. On a lined large-sized baking sheet, toast the walnuts for 5-10 minutes at 350°F. In a medium-heat saucepan, add the gorgonzola, heavy cream, salt, and pepper. Stir until thick and add the spinach. Drain the penne and save ¼ cup of water. Add the penne and pasta water to the saucepan. Add the toasted walnuts until well combined.

Per Serving: Calories 341, Fat 18.3g, Carbs 34g, Protein 12.1g

493. Spinach Pesto Fusili

Ingredients for 2 servings

- 1 ½ cup of fusilli pasta
- 4 cups of fresh spinach
- 2 tablespoons pine nuts
- 2 tablespoons olive oil
- 1 garlic clove
- 2 chili peppers
- 2 tablespoons Parmigiano cheese
- Salt and pepper to taste
- Water

Directions and Total Time: approx. 45 minutes

Boil a pot of salted water and meanwhile blend all the ingredients except for the pasta. Pour the spinach mixture into a pan and let it cook for 5 minutes. Add the pasta to the water and let it cook for 10 minutes. Drain the already cooked pasta and add it to the spinach sauce. Serve with some basil and some more Parmigiano cheese.

Per Serving: Calories 350, Fat 10g, Carbs 45g, Protein 8.6g

Ingredients for 4 servings

- 8 ounces of whole-grain pasta
- 1/3 cup of mozzarella cheese, grated
- 1/2 cup of pesto
- 5 ounces of fresh spinach
- 1 3/4 cup of water
- 8 ounces of mushrooms, chopped
- 1 tablespoon of olive oil
- Salt and pepper

Directions and Total Time: approx. 20 minutes

Add oil into the inner pot of instant pot and set the pot on sauté mode. Add mushrooms and sauté for 5 minutes. Add water and pasta and stir well. Seal pot with its lid and cook on high for approximately about 5 minutes. Once done, release pressure using quick release. Remove lid. Stir in the rest of the remaining ingredients and lastly, serve.

Per Serving: Calories 213, Fat 17.3g, Carbs 9.5g, Protein 7.4g

495. Vegan Olive Pasta

Ingredients for 4 servings

- 4 cups whole grain penne pasta
- ½ cup olives, sliced
- 1 tablespoon capers
- ¼ teaspoon red pepper flakes
- 4 cups pasta sauce, homemade
- 1 tablespoon garlic, minced
- Olive oil
- Pepper, and salt
- Fresh Basil to garnish

Directions and Total Time: approx. 15 minutes

In a pot pour plenty of water, and bring to a boil. When it boils, pour in the salt, and pasta, and cook for the time stated on the package. Meanwhile, in a frying pan, pour a drizzle of oil, and heat over medium heat. Add the garlic, and brown. Pour in the tomato sauce, olives, capers, red pepper flakes, and salt, and cook for about 12 minutes. Drain the pasta, pour into the sauce, and mix well. Plate, garnish with a basil leaf and serve immediately.

Per Serving: Calories 441, Fat 10.1g, Carbs 77.3g, Protein 11.8g

496. Vegan Patras Pasta

Ingredients for 6 servings

- 4 quarts of salted water
- 10 ounces of whole-grain pasta
- 5 cloves of garlic, minced
- 1 cup of hummus
- Salt and pepper
- 1/3 cup of water
- ½ cup of walnuts
- ½ cup of olives
- 2 tablespoons of dried cranberries

Directions and Total Time: approx. 15 minutes

Bring the salted water to a boil for cooking the pasta. Prepare for the hummus sauce. Combine the garlic, hummus, salt, and pepper with water in a mixing bowl. Add the walnuts, olive, and dried cranberries, if desired. Set aside. Add the pasta in the boiling water. Cook the pasta following the manufacturer's specifications until attaining an al dente texture. Drain the pasta. Transfer the pasta to a bowl and combine with the sauce.

Per Serving: Calories 329, Fat 13g, Carbs 43g, Protein 12g

Ingredients for 4 servings

- 1 kilogram of thin zucchini
- 20 grams of fresh ginger
- 350 grams smoked tofu
- 1 lime
- 2 cloves of garlic
- 2 tablespoons sunflower oil
- 2 tablespoons of sesame seeds
- Pinch of salt and pepper
- 4 tablespoons fried onions

Directions and Total Time: approx. 30 minutes

Wash and clean the zucchini and, using a julienne cutter, cut the pulp around the kernel into long thin strips (noodles). Ginger peel and finely chop. Crumble tofu. Halve lime, squeeze juice. Peel and chop garlic. Warm-up 1 tbsp of oil in a large pan and fry the tofu for about 5 minutes. After about 3 minutes, add ginger, garlic, and sesame. Season with soy sauce. Remove from the pan and keep warm. Wipe out the pan, then warm 2 tablespoons of oil in it. Stir fry zucchini strips for about 4 minutes while turning. Season with salt, pepper, and lime juice. Arrange pasta and tofu. Sprinkle with fried onions.

Per Serving: Calories 262, Fat 17.7g, Carbs 17.1g, Protein 15.4g

498. Very Vegan Patras Pasta

Ingredients for 6 servings

- 4 quarts salted water
- 10 ounces gluten-free and whole grain pasta
- 5 cloves garlic, minced
- 1 cup hummus
- Salt and pepper
- ⅓ cup water
- ½ cup walnuts
- ½ cup olives
- 2 tablespoons dried cranberries (optional)

Directions and Total Time: approx. 15 minutes

Bring the salted water to a boil for cooking the pasta. In the meantime, prepare for the hummus sauce. Combine the garlic, hummus, salt, and pepper with water in a mixing bowl. Add the walnuts, olive, and dried cranberries, if desired. Set aside. Add the pasta in the boiling water. Cook the pasta in accordance with the manufacturer's specifications until attaining an al dente texture. Drain the pasta. Transfer the pasta to a large-sized serving bowl and combine with the sauce.

Per Serving: Calories 329, Fat 12.6g, Carbs 43.3g, Protein 12g

499. Zucchini Pasta Salad

Ingredients for 15 servings

- 5 tablespoons olive oil
- 2 teaspoons Dijon mustard
- 3 tablespoons red-wine vinegar
- 1 clove garlic, grated
- 2 tablespoons fresh oregano, chopped
- 1 shallot, chopped
- ¼ teaspoon red pepper flakes
- 16 ounces zucchini noodles
- ¼ cup Kalamata olives, pitted
- 3 cups cherry tomatoes, sliced in half
- ¾ cup Parmesan cheese, shaved

Directions and Total Time: approx. 5 minutes

Mix the olive oil, Dijon mustard, red-wine vinegar, garlic, oregano, shallot and red pepper flakes in a bowl. Stir in the zucchini noodles. Sprinkle on top the olives, tomatoes and Parmesan cheese.

Per Serving: Calories 299, Fat 24.7g, Carbs 11.6g, Protein 7g

500. Zucchini Pasta with Mango-Kiwi Sauce

Ingredients for 2 servings

- 1 teaspoon dried herbs – optional
- ½ cup Raw Kale leaves, shredded
- 2 small dried figs
- 3 medjool dates
- 4 medium kiwis
- 2 big mangos, seed discarded
- 2 cup zucchini, spiralized
- ¼ cup roasted cashew

Directions and Total Time: approx. 25 minutes

On a salad bowl, place kale then topped with zucchini noodles and sprinkle with dried herbs. Set aside. In a food processor, grind to a powder the cashews. Add figs, dates, kiwis and mangoes then puree to a smooth consistency. Pour over zucchini pasta, serve and enjoy.

Per Serving: Calories 530, Fat 18.5g, Carbs 95.4g, Protein 8g

501. Artichoke and Curly Kale Flatbread

Ingredients for 4 servings

- 3 tablespoons of olive oil
- 1 cup of curly kale, chopped
- 1 tablespoon of garlic powder
- 2 tablespoons of parsley, chopped
- 2 flatbread wraps
- 4 tablespoons of Parmesan cheese, grated
- ½ cup of mozzarella, grated
- 14 ounces of canned artichokes
- 12 cherry tomatoes, halved
- Salt and black pepper to taste

Directions and Total Time: approx. 25 minutes

Preheat the oven to a temperature of a heat of 390 F. Line a baking sheet with parchment paper. Brush the flatbread wrap with some olive oil and sprinkle with garlic, salt, and pepper. Top with half of the prepared Parmesan and mozzarella cheeses. Combine artichokes, tomatoes, salt, pepper, and remaining olive oil in a bowl. Spread the mixture on the top of the wraps and top with the remaining Parmesan cheese. Transfer to the large-sized baking sheet and bake for 15 minutes. Top with curly kale and parsley.

Per Serving: Calories 230, Fat 12g, Carbs 16g, Protein 8g

502. Asparagus with Greek Aioli

Ingredients for 6 servings

- 1 pound asparagus spears
- salt and black pepper, to taste
- Homemade aioli sauce:
- 1 teaspoon garlic, minced
- 1 ingredient
- 1/2 cup vegetable oil
- salt and black pepper, to your liking
- 1/4 cup Greek yogurt
- 2 teaspoons freshly squeezed juice

Directions and Total Time: approx. 10 minutes

Start by adding the prepared 1 cup of water and a steamer basket to the moment Pot. Place the asparagus within the steamer basket. Secure the lid. Choose "Manual" mode and High pressure; cook for 1 minute. Once cooking is complete, use a fast pressure release; carefully remove the lid. Season your asparagus with salt and pepper; reserve. During a blender or a kitchen appliance, mix garlic, egg yolk, and oil until well incorporated. Now, add the salt, ground black pepper, and Greek yogurt. Afterwards, add the juice and blend until your aioli is thickened and emulsified. Serve the reserved asparagus spears with this homemade aioli on the side. Enjoy!

Per Serving: Calories 194, Fat 19.2g, Carbs 4.5g, Protein 2.6g

503. Avocado and Salmon Stuffed Cucumbers

Ingredients for 4 servings

- 1 tablespoon of extra-virgin olive oil
- 2 large cucumbers, peeled
- 1 (4-ounces) can of red salmon
- 1 ripe avocado, mashed
- 2 tablespoons of chopped fresh dill
- Salt and black pepper to taste

Directions and Total Time: approx. 10 minutes

Cut the cucumber into 1-inch-thick segments, and using a spoon, scrape seeds out of the center of each piece and stand up on a plate. In a bowl, mix the salmon, avocado, olive oil, lime zest and juice, dill, salt, and pepper, and blend until creamy. Spoon the prepared salmon mixture into the center of each cucumber segment and serve chilled.

Per Serving: Calories 159, Fat 11g, Carbs 8g, Protein 9g

504. Avocado Caprese Wrap

Ingredients for 2 servings

- 2 tortillas
- Balsamic vinegar, as needed
- 1 ball of mozzarella cheese, grated
- ½ cup of arugula
- 1 tomato, sliced
- 2 tablespoons of fresh basil leaves, chopped
- Kosher salt, to taste
- 1 avocado, sliced
- Olive oil, as required
- Black pepper, to taste

Directions and Total Time: approx. 10 minutes

Divide the tomato slices and cheese evenly among the tortilla wraps. Then add the avocado and basil. Drizzle olive oil and also the vinegar over the top. Season to your taste with salt and pepper. Wrap the tortilla and serve. Garnish with parsley.

Per Serving: Calories 791, Fat 47g, Carbs 71g, Protein 23g

505. Avocado Chickpea Pizza

Ingredients for 2 servings

- 1 and ¼ cup chickpea flour.
- A pinch salt and black pepper.
- 1 and ¼ cup water.
- 2 tablespoons olive oil.
- 1 teaspoon onion powder.
- 1 teaspoon garlic, minced.
- 1 tomato, sliced.
- 1 avocado, peeled, pitted and sliced.
- 2 ounces Gouda sliced.
- ¼ cup tomato sauce.
- 2 tablespoons green onions, chopped.

Directions and Total Time: approx. 40 minutes

In a large-sized bowl, mix the chickpea flour with salt, pepper, water, the oil, onion powder and the garlic, stir well until you obtain a dough, knead a bit, put in a bowl, cover and leave aside for 20 minutes. Transfer the dough to a working surface, shape a bit circle, transfer it to a baking sheet lined with parchment paper and then now bake at 425°F for 10 minutes. Spread the tomato sauce over the pizza, also spread the rest of the ingredients, and bake at 400°F for 10 minutes more. Cut and serve.

Per Serving: Calories 416, Fat 24.5g, Carbs 36.6g, Protein 15.4g

506. Baked Apples Mediterranean Style

Ingredients for 4 servings

- ½ lemon, squeezed for juice
- 1 ½ pounds of peeled and sliced apples
- ¼ teaspoon cinnamon

Directions and Total Time: approx. 25 minutes

Set the temperature of your oven to a heat of 350 degrees Fahrenheit so it can preheat. Take at least a piece of parchment paper and lay on top of a baking pan. Combine your lemon juice, cinnamon, and apples into a medium bowl and mix well. Pour the apples onto the baking pan and arrange them so they are not doubled up. Place the large-sized pan in the oven and set your timer to 25 minutes. The apples should be tender but not mushy. Remove from the oven, plate and enjoy!

Per Serving: Calories 90, Fat 0.3g, Carbs 24g, Protein 0.5g

507. Baked Balsamic Beet Rounds

Ingredients for 6 servings

- 4 tablespoons of olive oil
- 4 beets, peeled, cut into wedges
- Salt and black pepper to taste
- 3 teaspoons of fresh thyme
- ⅓ cup of balsamic vinegar
- 1 tablespoon of fresh dill, chopped

Directions and Total Time: approx. 45 minutes

Preheat oven to a heat of 400 F. Place the beets into a large bowl. Add 2 tbsp of olive oil, salt, and thyme and toss to combine. Spread the beets onto a baking sheet. Bake for approximately about 35-40 minutes, turning once or twice until the beets are tender. Remove and let them cool for 10 minutes. In a large-sized bowl, whisk together the remaining olive oil, vinegar, dill, and black pepper. Transfer the beets into a serving bowl, spoon the vinegar mixture over the beets, and serve.

Per Serving: Calories 111, Fat 7g, Carbs 11g, Protein 2g

508. Baked Eggplant Fries

Ingredients for 8 servings

- 2 eggs
- 2 cups of almond flour
- 2 tablespoons of coconut oil spray
- 2 eggplants, peeled and cut thinly
- Salt and pepper, to taste

Directions and Total Time: approx. 25 minutes

Preheat the oven to 400°F. Put the almond flour with a little salt and pepper in a shallow bowl. Beat the eggs until frothy in a bowl. Dip the pieces of eggplants into the egg, then coat them in the flour mixture. Add another layer of flour and egg. Take at least one baking sheet and grease it with the coconut oil spray. Arrange the coated eggplant on the sheet. Bake for about 15 minutes. Serve and enjoy.

Per Serving: Calories 119, Fat 8.2g, Carbs 9.7g, Protein 4.2g

509. Baked Italian Fries

Ingredients for 4 servings

- 12 baby red potatoes, cut into wedges
- 1 tablespoon Italian seasoning
- 3 tablespoons olive oil
- 1 teaspoon turmeric
- ½ teaspoon of sea salt
- ½ teaspoon dried rosemary
- 1 tablespoon dried dill

Directions and Total Time: approx. 50 minutes

Preheat the oven to 375°F. Put the red potato wedges in a large bowl. Add the Italian seasoning, olive oil, turmeric, sea salt, dried rosemary, and dried dill. Toss well to coat the wedges. Line a baking tray with parchment paper. Place the potatoes wedges in the tray in a single layer. Bake in the oven for 40 minutes, occasionally gently stirring the wedges using a spatula. Garnish with rosemary sprigs.

Per Serving: Calories 122, Fat 11.6g, Carbs 4.5g, Protein 0.6g

510. Baked Zucchini Boats Stuffed with Feta

Ingredients for 4 servings

- 2 zucchinis, halved lengthwise
- 2 tablespoons of olive oil
- 1 egg
- 2 garlic cloves, minced
- 2 tablespoons of oregano, chopped
- Salt and black pepper to taste
- 1 cup of feta cheese, crumbled

Directions and Total Time: approx. 50 minutes

Preheat the oven to a temperature of a heat of 390 F. Line a baking sheet with parchment paper. Scoop the flesh from the zucchini halves to make shells and place them on the baking sheet. In a bowl, mix egg, feta cheese, garlic, oregano, salt, pepper, and olive oil and bake for 40 minutes. Remove to a plate and serve.

Per Serving: Calories 200, Fat 16.5g, Carbs 7g, Protein 8.3g

511. Balsamic Strawberry Caprese Skewers

Ingredients for 6 servings

- 1 tablespoon of olive oil
- 1 cup of balsamic vinegar
- 24 whole, hulled strawberries
- 24 basil leaves, halved
- 12 fresh mozzarella balls

Directions and Total Time: approx. 15 minutes + cooling time

Pour the balsamic vinegar into a large-sized saucepan and simmer for 10 minutes or until it's reduced by half and is actually thick enough to coat the back of a spoon. Set aside to cool completely. Thread the strawberries onto wooden skewers, followed by basil leaves folded in half and mozzarella balls. Drizzle with cup of balsamic glaze and olive oil and serve.

Per Serving: Calories 206, Fat 10g, Carbs 17g, Protein 10g

512. BBQ Chicken Pizza

Ingredients for 4 servings

- Dairy Free Pizza Crust
- 6 tablespoons Parmesan cheese
- 6 large eggs
- 3 tablespoons psyllium husk powder
- Salt and black pepper, to taste
- 1 ½ teaspoons Italian seasoning
- 6 ounces rotisserie chicken, shredded
- 4 ounces cheddar cheese
- 1 tablespoon mayonnaise
- 4 tablespoons tomato sauce
- 4 tablespoons BBQ sauce

Directions and Total Time: approx. 30 minutes

Preheat the oven to a heat of 400 degrees F and grease a baking dish. Place all Pizza Crust ingredients in an immersion blender and blend until smooth. Spread dough mixture onto the baking dish and transfer in the oven. Bake for about 10 minutes and top with favorite toppings. Bake for about 3 minutes and dish out.

Per Serving: Calories 356, Fat 24.5g, Carbs 2.9g, Protein 24.5g

513. Bread Machine Pizza Dough

Ingredients for 6 servings

- 1 cup of beer
- 2 tablespoons butter
- 2 tablespoons sugar
- 1 teaspoon of salt
- 2 1/2 cups of all-purpose flour
- 2 1/4 teaspoons of yeast

Directions and Total Time: approx. 39 minutes

Place beer, butter, sugar, salt, flour, and yeast in a bread maker in the order recommended by the manufacturer. Select the Paste setting and press Start. Remove the dough from the bread maker once the cycle is complete. Roll or press the dough to cover a prepared pizza dish. Brush lightly with olive oil. Cover and let stand for 15 minutes. Preheat the oven to 250 degrees (400 degrees F). Spread the sauce and garnish on the dough. Bake until the crust is a bit brown and crispy on the outside, about 24 minutes.

Per Serving: Calories 101, Fat 2g, Carbs 18g, Protein 3g

514. Broccoli and Pecorino Flat Bread Pizzas

Ingredients for 8 servings

- 4 oval, trans fat-free whole grain flatbreads
- 30 fresh broccoli florets, thinly sliced
- 2 tablespoons olive oil
- 3 cloves fresh garlic, thinly sliced
- ½ teaspoon crushed red hot pepper flakes nor
- To taste Salt and pepper to taste
- 1 cup shaved fresh Pecorino Romano (about 4 ounces)

Directions and Total Time: approx. 40 minutes

Preheat the oven to 400°F. On two rimmed baking sheets, put the flatbreads. Toss broccoli, olive oil, garlic, hot pepper flakes, salt, and pepper together in a bowl to taste. Scatter equally on flatbreads with broccoli mixture and scatter with Pecorino shavings. Bake until the flatbreads are crispy and broccoli brown, about 15 minutes, at 400° F.

Per Serving: Calories 298, Fat 15g, Carbs 29g, Protein 12g

515. Bruschetta with Tomato and Basil

Ingredients for 4 servings

- 1 ciabatta loaf, halved lengthwise
- 2 tablespoons of olive oil
- 3 tablespoons of basil, chopped
- 4 tomatoes, cubed
- 1 shallot, sliced
- 2 garlic cloves, minced
- Salt and black pepper to taste
- 1 tablespoon of balsamic vinegar
- ½ teaspoon of garlic powder

Directions and Total Time: approx. 20 minutes

Preheat the oven to a heat of 380 F. Line a baking sheet with parchment paper. Cut in half each half of the ciabatta loaf. Place them on the sheet and sprinkle with some olive oil. Bake for 10 minutes. Mix tomatoes, shallot, basil, garlic, salt, pepper, olive oil, vinegar, and garlic powder in a bowl and let sit for 10 minutes. Apportion the mixture among bread pieces.

Per Serving: Calories 170, Fat 5g, Carbs 30g, Protein 5g

516. Brussels Sprouts with Pistachios

Ingredients for 4 servings

- 1-pound of Brussels sprouts, tough bottoms trimmed, halved lengthwise
- 4 shallots, peeled and quartered
- 1 tablespoon of extra-virgin olive oil
- Sea salt
- Freshly ground black pepper
- ½ cup of chopped roasted pistachios
- Zest of ½ lemon
- Juice of ½ lemon

Directions and Total Time: approx. 30 minutes

Preheat the oven to 400°F. In a large-sized bowl, toss the Brussels sprouts and shallots with the olive oil until well coated. Season with sea salt and pepper, and then spread the vegetables evenly on the sheet. Bake for 15 minutes, or until tender and lightly caramelized. Take away from the oven and transfer to a serving bowl. Toss with the pistachios, lemon zest, and lemon juice. Serve warm.

Per Serving: Calories 126, Fat 7g, Carbs 14g, Protein 6g

517. Burrata Caprese Stack

Ingredients for 4 servings

- 1 large organic tomato
- ½ teaspoon salt
- ¼ teaspoon black pepper
- 1 (4-ounce) ball burrata cheese
- 8 fresh basil leaves
- 2 tablespoons extra-virgin olive oil
- 1 tablespoon red wine

Directions and Total Time: approx. 5 minutes

Slice the tomato into 4 thick slices, removing any rigid center core and sprinkle with salt and pepper. Place the tomatoes, seasoned-side up, on a plate. Slice the burrata into 4 thick slices on a separate rimmed plate and place one slice on top of each tomato slice. Top each with one-quarter of the basil and pour any reserved burrata cream from the rimmed plate over the top. Drizzle with the prepared olive oil and vinegar and serve with a fork and knife.

Per Serving: Calories 153, Fat 13g, Carbs 6g, Protein 7g

518. Butternut Squash Fries

Ingredients for 2 servings

- 1 butternut squash, seeded
- 1 tablespoon of extra-virgin olive oil
- ½ tablespoon of grapeseed oil
- Sea salt, to taste

Directions and Total Time: approx. 30 minutes

Preheat the oven to a heat of 425°F. Cut the squash into thin slices and place the slices into a bowl. Coat the slices with the extra-virgin olive oil and grapeseed oil. Add a sprinkle of salt and toss to coat well. Arrange the squash slices onto three baking sheets and bake for approximately about 20 minutes, tossing halfway through. Serve with your preferred sauce.

Per Serving: Calories 153, Fat 10g, Carbs 10g, Protein 1.5g

519. Calamari Mediterranean

Ingredients for 2 servings

- 1 tablespoon Italian parsley
- 1 teaspoon ancho chili, chopped
- 1 teaspoon cumin
- 1 teaspoon red pepper flakes
- 1/2 cup white wine
- 2 cups calamari
- 2 medium plum tomatoes, diced
- 2 tablespoons capers
- 2 tablespoons garlic cloves, roasted
- 2 tablespoons olive oil
- 2 tablespoons extra virgin olive oil
- 3 tablespoons lime juice
- Salt

Directions and Total Time: approx. 10 minutes

Heat a sauté pan. Add the oil, garlic, and the calamari; sauté for 1 minute. Add the capers, red pepper flakes, cumin, ancho chili and the diced tomatoes; cook for 1 minute. Add the wine and the lime juice; simmer for 4 minutes. Stir in the extra virgin olive oil, parsley, and the salt; continue cooking until the sauce is thick. Serve with whole-wheat French bread.

Per Serving: Calories 308.8, Fat 25.7g, Carbs 10.2g, Protein 1.9g

520. Carrot Cake Balls

Ingredients for 22 servings

- ½ cup of old-fashioned rolled oats
- 1 cup of dates, pitted
- ¼ teaspoon of turmeric
- ½ teaspoon of ground cinnamon
- 1 teaspoon of vanilla
- 2 medium carrots, grated
- ¼ cup of chia seeds
- ¼ cup of pecans, chopped
- ¼ teaspoon of salt

Directions and Total Time: approx. 20 minutes

Add dates, chia seeds, pecans, and oats into the food processor and process until well combined. Add the rest of the remaining ingredients and process until just combined. Make small balls from oat mixture and place onto the dish then place dish in the refrigerator for 20 minutes. Serve chilled and enjoy.

Per Serving: Calories 54, Fat 2g, Carbs 9g, Protein 1g

521. Carrot Snack

Ingredients for 14 servings

- ½ teaspoon of cinnamon powder
- 1 cup of water
- 1 albumen, whisked
- 1 cup of baby carrots, grated
- ¾ cup of pecans, chopped
- 1 tablespoon of honey
- 2 tablespoons of coconut flour
- 2 tablespoons of flax meal

Directions and Total Time: approx. 16 minutes

In a bowl, mix baby carrots with albumen, cinnamon, pecans, honey,

and flax meal and coconut flour, stir well and shape 14 balls out of this mix. Add the water to your instant pot, add the steamer basket, add carrot balls, cover and cook on High for six minutes. Arrange carrot balls on a platter and serve. Enjoy!

Per Serving: Calories 120, Fat 2g, Carbs 2g, Protein 3g

522. Carrot Sticks with Blue-Cheese Sauce

Ingredients for 8 servings

- 1 pound carrots, dig sticks
- Himalayan salt and white pepper, to taste
- 1/4 teaspoon red pepper flakes, crushed
- 1 cup water
- 6 ounces bleu
- 1/2 cup full-fat yogurt
- 1/2 cup mayonnaise
- 1 teaspoon deli mustard
- 1 tablespoon fresh chives, chopped
- 3 tablespoons water

Directions and Total Time: approx. 10 minutes

Simply add carrots, salt, white pepper, red pepper and 1 cup of water to your Instant Pot. Secure the lid. Choose "Manual" mode and High pressure; cook for two minutes. Once cooking is complete, use a fast pressure release; carefully remove the lid. Meanwhile, thoroughly combine the remaining ingredients during a bowl. Serve the prepared carrot sticks with the sauce on the side. Bon appétit!

Per Serving: Calories 202, Fat 16.8g, Carbs 7.1g, Protein 6.1g

523. Cheese Plate with Fruit and Crackers

Ingredients for 8 servings

- 8 fresh figs, quartered
- 2 cups of red and/or green grapes
- 8 ounces of goat cheese
- 8 ounces of Gorgonzola cheese
- 8 ounces of Manchego cheese
- 8 ounces of Parmigiano-Reggiano cheese
- Rosemary and thyme sprigs
- 1 cup of pistachios
- 1 cup of hazelnuts
- 1 cup of almonds
- 2 cups of red, green, and/or black olives
- 1 package of whole wheat crackers
- 1 baguette, sliced

Directions and Total Time: approx. 45 minutes

Arrange the fruits and cheeses artfully on a wooden board. Scatter the herb sprigs here and there. Put the nuts and olives in small bowls and the crackers and baguette slices on a plate or in a basket.

Per Serving: Calories 990, Fat 66g, Carbs 64g, Protein 42g

524. Cherry Tomato Bruschetta

Ingredients for 4 servings

- 8 ounces of assorted cherry tomatoes, halved
- ⅓ cup of fresh herbs, chopped (such as basil, parsley, tarragon, dill)
- 1 tablespoon of extra-virgin olive oil
- ¼ teaspoon of kosher salt
- ⅛ teaspoon of freshly ground black pepper
- ¼ cup of ricotta cheese
- 4 slices of whole-wheat bread, toasted

Directions and Total Time: approx. 15 minutes

Combine the tomatoes, herbs, olive oil, salt, and black pepper in a medium bowl and mix gently. Spread the prepared 1 tablespoon of ricotta cheese onto each slice of toast. Spoon one-quarter of the tomato mixture onto each bruschetta. If desired, garnish with more herbs.

Per Serving: Calories 147, Fat 6g, Carbs 17g, Protein 6g

525. Chicken Pizza

Ingredients for 4 servings

- 2 flatbreads.
- 1 tablespoon Greek vinaigrette.
- ½ cup feta cheese, crumbled.
- ¼ cup Parmesan cheese, grated.
- ½ cup water-packed artichoke hearts, rinsed, drained and chopped.
- ½ cup olives pitted and sliced.
- ½ cup cooked chicken breast strips, chopped.
- 1/8 teaspoon dried basil.
- 1/8 teaspoon dried oregano.
- Pinch ground black pepper.
- 1 cup part-skim mozzarella cheese, shredded

Directions and Total Time: approx. 11 minutes

Preheat the oven to 400°F. Arrange the flatbreads onto a large ungreased baking sheet and coat each with vinaigrette. Top with feta, followed by the Parmesan, veggies and chicken. Sprinkle with dried herbs and black pepper. Top with mozzarella cheese evenly. Bake for just about 8-10 minutes or until cheese is melted. Remove from the oven and set aside for about 1-2 minutes before slicing. Cut the bread into 2 pieces and serve.

Per Serving: Calories 393, Fat 22g, Carbs 20.6g, Protein 28.9g

526. Chicken Skewers

Ingredients for 4 servings

- 1 pound of chicken breast, boneless
- 1 tablespoon of fresh lemon juice
- 1 ¾ cups of green grapes, seedless, rinsed
- 1 teaspoon of lemon zest
- 1 tablespoon of fresh rosemary, minced
- 1 tablespoon of fresh oregano, minced
- ½ teaspoon of chili flakes, crushed
- 1 teaspoon of garlic, minced
- ¼ cup of olive oil
- ½ teaspoon of salt

Directions and Total Time: approx. 20 minutes

Add chicken and remaining ingredients into the zip-lock bag. Seal bag and place in refrigerator for overnight. Thread marinated chicken pieces onto the soaked wooden skewers. Preheat the grill. Arrange chicken skewers onto the hot grill and cook for 3-5 minutes on each side. Drizzle with lemon juice and serve.

Per Serving: Calories 273, Fat 15.9g, Carbs 8.6g, Protein 24.5g

527. Chickpea Spinach Fritters

Ingredients for 12 servings

- 1 egg
- 2 cups of can chickpeas, rinsed & drained
- 1 teaspoon of ground cumin
- 1 tablespoon of paprika
- 1 teaspoon of garlic, minced
- ½ onion, chopped
- 1 carrot, grated
- 1 cup of baby spinach, cooked & drained
- Salt and pepper

Directions and Total Time: approx. 20 minutes

Add chickpeas into the mixing bowl and mash using the fork. Add remaining ingredients into the bowl and mix until well combined. Spray medium-sized pan with the cooking spray and heat over medium-high heat. Make patties from chickpea mixture and place onto the hot pan and cook for 4-5 minutes on each side or until golden brown.

Per Serving: Calories 60, Fat 1g, Carbs 10.6g, Protein 2.7g

528. Chili and Lemon Shrimp

Ingredients for 6 servings

- 24 large shrimp, peeled and deveined
- ½ cup of olive oil
- 5 garlic cloves, minced
- 1 teaspoon of red pepper flakes
- 1 lemon, juiced and zested
- 1 teaspoon of dried dill
- 1 teaspoon of dried thyme
- Salt and black pepper to taste

Directions and Total Time: approx. 10 minutes

Warm the olive oil in a large-sized skillet over medium heat. Add the garlic and red pepper flakes and cook for 1 minute. Add the shrimp and cook an approximately additional 3 minutes, stirring frequently. Remove from the pan, and sprinkle with lemon juice, lemon zest, thyme, dill, salt, and pepper. Serve.

Per Serving: Calories 198, Fat 6g, Carbs 28g, Protein 9g

529. Chili Grilled Eggplant Rounds

Ingredients for 4 servings

- 1 cup of roasted peppers, chopped
- 4 tablespoons of olive oil
- 2 eggplants, cut into rounds
- 12 Kalamata olives, chopped
- 1 teaspoon of red chili flakes, crushed
- Salt and black pepper to taste
- 2 tablespoons of basil, chopped
- 2 tablespoons of Parmesan cheese, grated

Directions and Total Time: approx. 25 minutes

Combine roasted peppers, half of the olive oil, olives, red chili flakes, salt, and pepper in a bowl. Rub each eggplant slice with remaining olive oil and salt grill them on the preheated grill for 14 minutes on both sides. Remove to a platter. Distribute the pepper mixture across the eggplant rounds and top with basil and Parmesan cheese to serve.

Per Serving: Calories 220, Fat 11g, Carbs 16g, Protein 6g

530. Citrus Cups

Ingredients for 4 servings

- ½ cup of water
- 1 tablespoon of orange juice
- 3 cups of full-fat Greek yogurt
- 1 vanilla bean
- 1 ruby grapefruit
- 2 mandarins
- 1 orange
- 6 strips of mandarin rind
- 1/3 cup of powdered sugar
- 1 small handful of fresh mint leaves

Directions and Total Time: approx. 30 minutes

Slice open the vanilla bean lengthways and transfer the seeds into a medium saucepan. Add the pod to the saucepan, followed by the water, sugar, and mandarin rind. Bring the mixed mixture to a boil, turn it down to a simmer, and cook for five minutes or until the syrup thickens. Allow to cool, remove the pod, and stir in the orange juice. Pour the syrup over the sliced citrus fruits and allow to rest. Dish the yogurt up into four bowls, top with the citrus and syrup, sprinkle with a bit of mint, then serve.

Per Serving: Calories 217, Fat 16g, Carbs 3.2g, Protein 4g

531. Coconut Flour Pizza

Ingredients for 4 servings

- 2 tablespoons psyllium husk powder
- ¾ cup coconut flour
- 1 teaspoon garlic powder
- ½ teaspoon salt
- ½ teaspoon baking soda
- 1 cup boiling water
- 1 teaspoon apple cider vinegar
- 3 eggs
- 3 tablespoons tomato sauce
- 1 ½ ounce Mozzarella cheese
- 1 tablespoon basil, freshly chopped

Directions and Total Time: approx. 35 minutes

Preheat the oven to a heat of 350 degrees F and grease a baking sheet. Mix coconut flour, salt, psyllium husk powder, and garlic powder until fully combined. Add eggs, apple cider vinegar, and baking soda and knead with boiling water. Place the dough out on a baking sheet and top with the toppings. Transfer in the prepared preheated oven and bake for about 20 minutes. Dish out and serve warm.

Per Serving: Calories 173, Fat 7.4g, Carbs 16.8g, Protein 10.4g

532. Creamy Panini

Ingredients for 4 servings

- 1 jar of 7 ounces roasted red peppers, drained and sliced
- 4 slices provolone cheese
- 1 small zucchini, thinly sliced
- 8 slices rustic whole grain bread
- 2 tablespoons finely chopped oil-cured black olives
- ¼ cup chopped fresh basil leaves
- ½ cup Mayonnaise dressing with olive oil, divided

Directions and Total Time: approx. 16 minutes

In a small bowl, mix together olives, basil and mayonnaise dressing. Spread the dressing evenly on 4 slices of whole grain bread. Then top it with zucchini, peppers and provolone before covering with another slice of bread. Spread the remaining mayonnaise mixture around the bread and cook over medium heat on a nonstick skillet for about approximately 2 minutes on each side or until bread is golden brown on both sides and cheese is melted.

Per Serving: Calories 350, Fat 21.8g, Carbs 24.2g, Protein 14.4g

533. Crispy and Yummy Beef Bites

Ingredients for 6 servings

- 2 tablespoons vegetable oil
- 1 pound beef steak, dig cubes
- Salt and ground black pepper, to taste
- 1 teaspoon cayenne pepper
- 1/2 teaspoon dried marjoram
- 1 cup beef bone broth
- 1/4 cup dry wine

Directions and Total Time: approx. 25 minutes

Press the "Sauté" button and warmth the vegetable oil. Once hot, cook the meat for two to three minutes, stirring periodically. Add the remaining ingredients to the moment Pot. Secure the lid. Choose "Manual" mode and High pressure; cook for 20 minutes. Once cooking is complete, use a natural pressure release; carefully remove the lid. Arrange beef cubes on a pleasant serving platter and serve with sticks. Bon appétit!

Per Serving: Calories 169, Fat 9.9g, Carbs 1.1g, Protein 17.9g

534. Easy Toasted Almonds

Ingredients for 2 servings

- 1 tablespoon extra-virgin olive oil
- 1 teaspoon salt
- 2 cups skin-on raw whole almonds

Directions and Total Time: approx. 20 minutes

Heat the tablespoon of olive oil in a 12-inch non-stick frying pan on moderate to high heat until it barely starts to shimmer. Put in the almonds, salt, and pepper and reduce the heat to moderate to low. Cook, frequently stirring, until the almonds become aromatic and their color becomes somewhat deep, approximately 8 minutes. Move the almonds to a plate lined with paper towels and allow them to cool before serving.

Per Serving: Calories 230, Fat 22g, Carbs 6g, Protein 6g

535. Eggplant and Pepper Spread on Toasts

Ingredients for 4 servings

- 1 red bell pepper, roasted and chopped
- 1 pound of eggplants, baked, peeled and chopped
- ¾ cup of olive oil
- 1 lemon, zested
- 1 red chili pepper, chopped
- 1 ½ teaspoon of capers
- 1 garlic clove, minced
- Salt and black pepper to taste
- 1 baguette, sliced and toasted

Directions and Total Time: approx. 10 minutes

In a food processor, place the eggplants, lemon zest, red chili pepper, bell pepper, garlic, salt, and pepper. Blend while actually gradually adding the olive oil until smooth. Spread each baguette slice with the spread and top with capers to serve.

Per Serving: Calories 364, Fat 38g, Carbs 9.3g, Protein 1.5g

536. Eggplant Bites

Ingredients for 8 servings

- 2 eggplants, cut into 20 slices
- 2 tablespoons olive oil
- ½ cup roasted peppers, chopped
- ½ cup kalamata olives, pitted and chopped
- 1 tablespoon lime juice
- 1 teaspoon red pepper flakes, crushed
- Salt and black pepper to the taste
- 2 tablespoons mint, chopped

Directions and Total Time: approx. 15 minutes

In a large-sized bowl, mix the roasted peppers with the olives, half of the oil and the rest of the ingredients except the eggplant slices and stir well. Brush eggplant slices with the rest of the olive oil on both sides, place them on the preheated grill over medium high heat, cook for 7 minutes on each side and transfer them to a platter. Top each eggplant slice with roasted peppers mix and serve.

Per Serving: Calories 214, Fat 10.6g, Carbs 15.4g, Protein 5.4g

537. Eggplant Pie

Ingredients for 6 servings

- 2 eggplants
- 1 tablespoon olive oil
- 3 ½ ounces feta cheese
- 3 ½ ounces provolone cheese, grated
- 1 potato, cooked and mashed
- 2 eggs

Directions and Total Time: approx. 45 minutes

Preheat the oven to 350°F. Place the 2 eggplants on a baking sheet and roast them until evenly charred. Cut a slit at the bottom of each eggplant and place them in a sieve. Leave them to drain. Once it is already cool enough to handle, peel the burnt skin off the eggplants, remove the dark seeds, and roughly chop. Mix the chopped eggplants with the olive oil, cheeses, mashed potato, and eggs until thoroughly combined. Put in a baking pan and bake for 35 minutes, until lightly browned on the top. Remove from the prepared preheated oven and cool for a few minutes before serving.

Per Serving: Calories 210, Fat 12.1g, Carbs 16.8g, Protein 10.8g

538. Eggplant Pizza with Tofu

Ingredients for 4 servings

- 2 eggplants, sliced
- 1/3 cup of butter, melted
- 2 garlic cloves, minced
- 1 Red onion
- 12 ounces of tofu, chopped
- 2 Ounces of tomato sauce
- Salt and black pepper to taste
- 1/2 teaspoon of cinnamon powder
- 1 cup of parmesan cheese, shredded
- 1/4 cup of dried oregano

Directions and Total Time: approx. 55 minutes

Let the oven heat to 400°F. Lay the slices of eggplants on a baking sheet and brush with some butter. Bake in the oven until lightly browned about 20 minutes. Heat the remaining butter in a skillet; sauté garlic and onion until fragrant and soft about 3 minutes. Stir in the chopped tofu and cook for 3 minutes. Add the tomato sauce, salt, and black pepper. Simmer for 10 minutes. Sprinkle with Parmesan cheese and oregano. Bake for 10 minutes.

Per Serving: Calories 321, Fat 11.3g, Carbs 4.3g, Protein 10.1g

539. Energy Granola Bites

Ingredients for 5 servings

- ¾ cup of diced dried figs
- ½ cup of chopped walnuts
- ¼ cup of old-fashioned oats
- 2 tablespoons of ground flaxseed
- 2 tablespoons of peanut butter
- 2 tablespoons of honey

Directions and Total Time: approx. 10 minutes

In a medium-sized bowl, mix together the figs, walnuts, oats, flaxseed, and peanut butter. Drizzle with the honey, and mix everything with a wooden spoon. Freeze the dough for 5 minutes. Divide the dough evenly into four sections in the bowl. Dampen your hands with water —but don't get them too wet, or the dough will stick to them. With hands, roll three bites out of each of the four sections of dough, making 10 energy bites. Store in the fridge for approximately up to a week.

Per Serving: Calories 158, Fat 8g, Carbs 23g, Protein 3g

540. Fig Relish Panini

Ingredients for 4 servings

- Grated parmesan cheese, for garnish
- Olive oil
- Arugula
- Basil leaves
- Toma cheese, grated or sliced
- Sweet extra virgin olive oil
- 4 ciabatta slices
- 1 teaspoon dry mustard
- Pinch of salt
- 1 teaspoon mustard seed
- ½ cup apple cider vinegar
- ½ cup honey
- ½ pound Mission figs, stemmed and peeled

Directions and Total Time: approx. 40 minutes

Create fig relish by mincing the figs. Then put in all ingredients, except for the dry mustard, in a small pot and simmer for 30 minutes until it becomes jam like. Season with dry mustard according to taste and let cool before refrigerating. Spread sweet extra virgin olive oil on two slices of ciabatta rolls and layer on the following: cheese, basil leaves, arugula and fig relish then cover with the remaining bread slice. Grill in a Panini press just until the cheese is actually melted and bread is crisped and ridged.

Per Serving: Calories 264, Fat 4.2g, Carbs 55.1g, Protein 6g

541. Fresh Basil and Mozzarella Cheese Pizza

Ingredients for 8 servings

- 1 flat wrap
- 1 teaspoon of finely minced fresh garlic
- ¼ cup of fresh Traditional Pizza Sauce or a market sauce like Dei Fratelli
- ¼ cup of shredded part-skim mozzarella cheese
- 4 slices of fresh tomato
- 4–6 fresh whole basil leaves

Directions and Total Time: approx. 45 minutes

Preheat the oven to 350°F. Place the wrap on a baking sheet. Combine the garlic with the pizza sauce and scatter uniformly over the wrap. Cover the sauce with the mozzarella cheese first, then the tomato and basil slices. Bake until the cheese melts at 350° F. Remove and serve from the oven.

Per Serving: Calories 264, Fat 4.2g, Carbs 55.1g, Protein 6g

542. Fresh Bell Pepper Basil Pizza

Ingredients for 3 servings

- ½ cup almond flour
- 2 tablespoons cream cheese
- 1 teaspoon Italian seasoning
- ½ teaspoon black pepper
- 6 ounces mozzarella cheese
- 2 tablespoons psyllium husk
- 2 tablespoons fresh Parmesan cheese
- 1 large egg
- ½ teaspoon salt
- 4 ounces cheddar cheese, shredded
- ¼ cup Marinara sauce
- 2/3 medium bell pepper
- 1 medium vine tomato
- 3 tablespoons basil, fresh chopped

Directions and Total Time: approx. 25 minutes

Preheat the oven to a heat of 400 degrees F and grease a baking dish. Microwave mozzarella cheese for about 30 seconds and top with the remaining pizza crust. Add the remaining pizza ingredients to the cheese and mix together. Flatten the dough and transfer in the oven. Bake for about 10 minutes and remove pizza from the oven. Top the half-baked pizza with your choice of toppings and bake for another 10 minutes. Remove the cooked pizza from the oven and allow to cool.

Per Serving: Calories 411, Fat 31.3g, Carbs 6.4g, Protein 22.2g

Ingredients for 8 servings

- 8 slices of 1/2-inch thick of a French baguette
- 11/2 teaspoons of minced fresh garlic
- 11/4 cups of chopped plum tomatoes
- 1 teaspoon of extra-virgin olive oil
- 1 teaspoon of balsamic vinegar
- 1/2 teaspoon of dried basil
- 1/4 teaspoon of non-caloric sweetener
- 1/4 teaspoon of freshly ground pepper

Directions and Total Time: approx. 10 minutes

Preheat the oven to a heat of 500 F. Take out a baking tray. Add olive oil to all sides of the baguette. Bake it for about 4 minutes. Combine the rest of the remaining ingredients in a small bowl. Mix well. Add the mixture to the baguette.

Per Serving: Calories 57, Fat 1g, Carbs 11g, Protein 2g

544. Goat Cheese-Mackerel Pâté

Ingredients for 4 servings

- 4 ounces of olive oil-packed wild-caught mackerel
- 2 ounces of goat cheese
- Zest and juice of 1 lemon
- 2 tablespoons of chopped fresh parsley
- 2 tablespoons of chopped fresh arugula
- 1 tablespoon of extra-virgin olive oil
- 2 teaspoons of chopped capers
- 1 to 2 teaspoons of fresh horseradish (optional)
- Crackers, cucumber rounds, endive spears, or celery, for serving (optional)

Directions and Total Time: approx. 10 minutes

In a food processor, blender, or large bowl with immersion blender, combine the mackerel, goat cheese, lemon zest and juice, parsley, arugula, olive oil, capers, and horseradish (if using). Process or blend until smooth and creamy. Serve with crackers, cucumber rounds, endive spears, or celery.

Per Serving: Calories 118, Fat 8g, Carbs 1g, Protein 9g

545. Green Beans with Pine Nuts and Garlic

Ingredients for 6 servings

- 1-pound of green beans, trimmed
- 1 head garlic (10 to 12 cloves), smashed
- 2 tablespoons of extra-virgin olive oil
- 1/2 teaspoon of kosher salt
- 1/4 teaspoon of red pepper flakes
- 1 tablespoon of white wine vinegar
- 1/4 cup of pine nuts, toasted

Directions and Total Time: approx. 30 minutes

Preheat the oven to 425°F. In a large bowl, blend the green beans, garlic, olive oil, salt, and red pepper flakes and mix—put it in a single layer on the baking sheet. Roast for 10 minutes, stir, and roast for another 10 minutes, or until golden brown. Mix the cooked green beans with the vinegar and top with the pine nuts.

Per Serving: Calories 165, Fat 13g, Carbs 12g, Protein 4g

Ingredients for 2 servings

- 2 pieces of Bacon
- 1 Shallot
- 230 grams of Green String Beans
- 2 teaspoons of White wine vinegar

Directions and Total Time: approx. 30 minutes

Please, cook the beans, chopped into small pieces, in boiling salted water until soft, about 8 minutes. Drain and transfer to a bowl. Meanwhile, sauté the chopped bacon in a well-heated skillet over medium heat until crisp. Put on a paper towel. Put the finely chopped shallots into the pan and sauté for 30 seconds. Remove from heat and cool slightly. Add vinegar, salt, and pepper. Pour beans with warm dressing and lay on top slices of bacon.

Per Serving: Calories 140, Fat 9.2g, Carbs 7.3g, Protein 7.3g

547. Ground Meat Pizza

Ingredients for 4 servings

- 7 ounces of ground beef
- 1 teaspoon of tomato paste
- 1/2 teaspoon of ground black pepper
- 2 egg whites, whisked
- 1/2 cup of Mozzarella cheese, shredded
- 1 teaspoon of fresh basil, chopped

Directions and Total Time: 50 minutes

Line the baking tray with baking paper. Preheat the oven to 370 F. Mix all ingredients except Mozzarella in the mixing bowl. Then place the mixture in the tray and flatten it to get a thick layer. Top the meat pizza with Mozzarella cheese and bake in the oven for 35 minutes. Then cut the cooked pizza into the servings.

Per Serving: Calories 113, Fat 3.8g, Carbs 0.7g, Protein 18g

548. Healthy Tuna Stuffed Zucchini Rolls

Ingredients for 4 servings

- 5 ounces of canned tuna, drained and mashed
- 2 tablespoons of olive oil
- 1/2 cup of mayonnaise
- 2 tablespoons of capers
- 2 zucchinis, sliced lengthwise
- Salt and black pepper to taste
- 1 teaspoon of lime juice

Directions and Total Time: approx. 5 minutes

Heat a grill pan over medium heat. Season the zucchini lengthwise slices with salt and pepper after they have been drizzled with olive oil. Grill for 5-6 minutes on both sides. In a bowl, mix the tuna, capers, lime juice, mayonnaise, salt, and pepper until well combined. Spread the tuna mixture onto zucchini slices and roll them up. Transfer the actual rolls you made to a plate and serve.

Per Serving: Calories 210, Fat 7g, Carbs 8g, Protein 4g

549. Hot Lager Chicken Wings

Ingredients for 6 servings

- 2 tablespoons butter, melted
- 1 pound chicken thighs
- salt and ground black pepper, to taste
- 1 teaspoon cayenne pepper
- 1 teaspoon shallot powder
- 1 teaspoon garlic powder
- 1 teaspoon sauce
- 1/2 cup lager
- 1/2 cup water

Directions and Total Time: approx. 15 minutes

Press the "Sauté" button and melt the butter. Once hot, brown the chicken thighs for two minutes per side. Add the remaining ingredients to your Instant Pot. Secure the lid. Choose "Poultry" mode and High pressure; cook for six minutes. Once cooking is complete, use a fast pressure release; carefully remove the lid. Serve at temperature and enjoy!

Per Serving: Calories 216, Fat 16.4g, Carbs 2.2g, Protein 0.5g

550. Jalapeno Chickpea Hummus

Ingredients for 4 servings

- 1 cup dry chickpeas, soaked overnight and drained
- 1 teaspoon ground cumin
- 1/4 cup jalapenos, diced
- 1/2 cup fresh cilantro
- 1 tablespoon tahini
- 1/2 cup olive oil
- Pepper
- Salt

Directions and Total Time: approx. 35 minutes

Add chickpeas into the instant pot and cover with vegetable stock. Seal pot with lid and cook on high for 25 minutes. Once done, allow to release pressure naturally. Remove lid. Drain chickpeas well and transfer into the food processor along with remaining ingredients and process until smooth. Serve and enjoy.

Per Serving: Calories 425, Fat 30.4g, Carbs 31.8g, Protein 10.5g

551. Kohlrabi Sticks with Hungarian Mayo

Ingredients for 6 servings

- 1 pound kohlrabi, dig sticks
- 1 cup water
- Salt and pepper, to taste
- 1/2 cup mayonnaise
- 1 teaspoon whole-grain mustard
- 1/2 teaspoon Hungarian paprika
- 1 teaspoon shallot powder
- 1/4 teaspoon porcini powder
- 1 teaspoon granulated garlic

Directions and Total Time: approx. 10 minutes

Add kohlrabi sticks and water to your Instant Pot. Now, season with salt and pepper. Secure the lid. Choose "Manual" mode and Low pressure; cook for 3 minutes. Once cooking is complete, use a fast pressure release; carefully remove the lid. Within the meantime, mix the remaining ingredients until everything is well incorporated. Serve with the prepared kohlrabi sticks. Bon appétit!

Per Serving: Calories 148, Fat 13.8g, Carbs 1.5g, Protein 2.6g

552. Lamb Ragu Tagliatelle

Ingredients for 4 servings

- 2 tablespoons of olive oil
- 16 ounces of tagliatelle
- 1 teaspoon of paprika
- 1 teaspoon of cumin
- Salt and black pepper to taste
- 1 pound of ground lamb
- 1 cup of onions, chopped
- 1/4 cup of parsley, chopped
- 2 garlic cloves, minced

Directions and Total Time: approx. 25 minutes

Boil the tagliatelle in a pot over medium heat for 9-11 minutes or until "al dente". Drain and set aside. Warm the olive oil in a large-sized skillet over medium heat and sauté lamb, onions, and garlic until the meat is browned, about 10-15 minutes. Stir in cumin, paprika, salt, and pepper for 1-2 minutes. Spoon tagliatelle on a platter and scatter lamb over. Top with parsley and serve.

Per Serving: Calories 140, Fat 10g, Carbs 7g, Protein 6g

553. Light and Creamy Garlic Hummus

Ingredients for 12 servings

- 1 1/2 cups dry chickpeas, rinsed
- 2 1/2 tablespoon fresh lemon juice
- 1 tablespoon garlic, minced
- 1/2 cup tahini
- 6 cups of water
- Pepper
- Salt

Directions and Total Time: approx. 50 minutes

Add water and chickpeas into the instant pot. Seal pot with a lid and select manual and set timer for 40 minutes. Once done, allow to release pressure naturally. Remove lid. Drain chickpeas well and reserved 1/2 cup chickpeas liquid. Transfer chickpeas, reserved liquid, lemon juice, garlic, tahini, pepper, and salt into the food processor and process until smooth. Serve and enjoy.

Per Serving: Calories 152, Fat 6.9g, Carbs 17.6g, Protein 6.6g

554. Manchego Crackers

Ingredients for 4 servings

- 4 tablespoons of butter, at room temperature
- 1 cup of Manchego cheese
- 1 cup of almond flour
- 1 teaspoon of salt, divided
- 1/4 teaspoon of black pepper
- 1 large egg

Directions and Total Time: approx. 30 minutes

Using an electric mixer, scourge butter and shredded cheese. Mix almond flour with 1/2 teaspoon salt and pepper. Mix almond flour mixture to the cheese, mixing constantly to form a ball. Place onto plastic wrap and roll into a cylinder log about 1½ inches thick. Wrap tightly and cool for at least 1 hour. Preheat the oven to 350°F. Prepare two baking sheets with parchment paper. For egg wash, blend egg and remaining ½ teaspoon salt. Slice the refrigerated dough into small rounds, about ¼ inch thick and place it on the lined baking sheets. Egg wash the tops of the crackers and bake for 15 minutes. Pull out from the oven and place in a wire rack. Serve.

Per Serving: Calories 243, Fat 23g, Carbs 25g, Protein 8g

Ingredients for 2 servings

- 4 ounces of traditional Greek feta, cut into ½-inch cubes
- 4 ounces of drained artichoke hearts, quartered lengthwise
- 1/3 cup of extra-virgin olive oil
- Zest and juice of 1 lemon
- 2 tablespoons of roughly chopped fresh rosemary
- 2 tablespoons of roughly chopped fresh parsley
- ½ teaspoon of black peppercorns

Directions and Total Time: approx. 20 minutes

In a glass bowl combine the feta and artichoke hearts. Add the olive oil, lemon zest and juice, rosemary, parsley, and peppercorns and toss gently to coat, being sure not to crumble the feta. Cool for 4 hours, or up to 4 days. Take out of the refrigerator 30 minutes before serving.

Per Serving: Calories 235, Fat 23g, Carbs 1g, Protein 4g

556. Mozzarella Bean Pizza

Ingredients for 6 servings

- 2 tablespoons cornmeal
- 1 cup mozzarella
- 1/3 cup barbecue sauce
- 1 Roma tomato, diced
- 1 cup black beans
- 1 cup corn kernels
- 1 medium whole-wheat pizza crust

Directions and Total Time: approx. 25 minutes

Preheat your oven to 400°F. Take a baking sheet, line it with parchment paper. Grease it with some avocado oil. Spread some cornmeal over the baking sheet. In a bowl, mix the tomatoes, corn and beans. Place the pizza crust on the baking sheet. Spread the sauce on top; add the topping, and top with the cheese and bake until the cheese melts and the crust edges are golden-brown for 12-15 minutes. Slice and serve warm.

Per Serving: Calories 223, Fat 14g, Carbs 41g, Protein 8g

557. No-Mayo Tuna Salad Cucumber Bites

Ingredients for 3 servings

- 1 (5 ounces) can water-packed tuna, drained
- 1/3 cup full-fat Greek yogurt
- ½ teaspoons extra virgin olive oil
- 1 tablespoon finely chopped spring onion (white parts only)
- 1 tablespoon chopped fresh dill
- Pinch of coarse sea salt
- ¼ teaspoons freshly ground black pepper
- 1 medium cucumber, cut into 15 (¼-inch/.5cm) thick slices
- 1 teaspoon red wine vinegar

Directions and Total Time: approx. 5 minutes

In a medium bowl, combine the tuna, yogurt, olive oil, spring onion, dill, sea salt, and black pepper. Mix well. Arrange the prepared cucumber slices on a plate and sprinkle the vinegar over the slices. Place 1 heaping teaspoon of the tuna salad on top of each cucumber slice 4. Serve promptly. Store the tuna salad mixture covered in the refrigerator for up to 1 day.

Per Serving: Calories 50, Fat 3g, Carbs 13g, Protein 1g

Ingredients for 2 servings

- 1/4 cup steel cut oats
- 2 tablespoons pure maple syrup
- 1 teaspoon chia seeds
- 1 cup fresh fruits
- 1/2 cup almonds, chopped

Directions and Total Time: approx. 30 minutes

Add all the ingredients along with a cup of water inside a mason jar. Shake well. Seal the jar. Place the jar inside the steamer rack. Pour the prepared cup of water into the Instant Pot. Add the jar on top of the rack. Cook at high pressure for 20 minutes.

Per Serving: Calories 517, Fat 26.4g, Carbs 63.2g, Protein 14.1g

559. Open Face Egg and Tomato Sandwich

Ingredients for 2 servings

- ¼ ounce reduced fat cheddar, shredded
- ½ small jalapeno, thinly sliced
- ½ whole grain English muffin, split
- 1 large organic egg
- 1 thick slice of tomato
- 2 thin slices red onion
- 4-5 sprigs fresh cilantro
- Cooking spray
- Pepper to taste

Directions and Total Time: approx. 20 minutes

In same skillet, drain oils, and place ½ of English muffin and heat for at least a minute per side. Transfer muffin to a serving plate. Coat the same large-sized skillet with cooking spray and fry egg to desired doneness. Once cooked, place egg on top of muffin. Add cilantro, tomato, onion and jalapeno op of egg. Serve and enjoy.

Per Serving: Calories 245, Fat 11g, Carbs 24.7g, Protein 11.8g

560. Oregano Crackers

Ingredients for 8 servings

- ½ cup wheat flour, whole grain
- ¼ cup Feta cheese, crumbled
- ¾ cup of water
- 1 teaspoon dried oregano
- 1 teaspoon salt
- ½ teaspoon sesame seeds

Directions and Total Time: approx. 15 minutes

Mix up together water and flour. Add dried oregano, salt, and Feta cheese. Knead the non-sticky dough. After this, roll up the dough into the thick sheet and cut the sheet on the crackers. Line the baking tray with baking paper. Arrange the uncooked crackers in the tray and bake for 14 minutes at 365F. After this, flip the crackers on another side and cook for 1 minute more. Chill the cooked crackers well.

Per Serving: Calories 38, Fat 1.1g, Carbs 5.6g, Protein 1.4g

561. Panini with Chicken-Fontina

Ingredients for 2 servings

- ¼ Cup Arugula
- 2 ounces sliced cooked chicken
- 3 ounces fontina cheese thinly sliced
- 1 tablespoon Dijon mustard
- 1 ciabatta roll
- ¼ cup water
- 1 tablespoon + 1 teaspoon olive oil
- 1 large onion, diced

Directions and Total Time: approx. 45 minutes

On medium low fire, place a skillet and heat 1 tbsp oil. Sauté onion and cook for 5 minutes. Pour in water while stirring and cooking continuously for 30 minutes until onion is golden brown and tender. Slice bread roll lengthwise and spread the following on one bread half, on the cut side: mustard, caramelized onion, chicken, arugula and cheese. Cover with the remaining bread half. Place the already prepared sandwich in a Panini maker and grill for 5 to 8 minutes or just about until cheese is melted and bread is ridged and crisped.

Per Serving: Calories 216, Fat 24.5g, Carbs 18.7g, Protein 22.3g

562. Parsley Nachos

Ingredients for 3 servings

- 3 ounces tortilla chips
- ¼ cup Greek yogurt
- 1 tablespoon fresh parsley, chopped
- ¼ teaspoon garlic, minced
- 2 kalamata olives, chopped
- 1 teaspoon paprika
- ¼ teaspoon ground thyme

Directions and Total Time: approx. 10 minutes

Combine all the prepared ingredients except for the tortilla chips in a bowl. Add the tortilla chips and mix up gently. Garnish with fresh chopped parsley. Serve immediately.

Per Serving: Calories 81, Fat 1.6g, Carbs 14.1g, Protein 3.5g

563. Pita Pizza with Shrimp

Ingredients for 2 servings

- 2 tablespoons spaghetti sauce
- Olive oil cooking spray
- 1 tablespoon pesto sauce
- 2 tablespoons mozzarella cheese, shredded
- ⅛ cup bay shrimp
- Pinch of dried basil
- 1 (6-inch) pita bread
- 5 cherry tomatoes, halved
- Pinch of garlic powder

Directions and Total Time: approx. 25 minutes

Preheat the oven to 330°F. Grease a baking sheet lightly with the cooking spray. Combine the spaghetti sauce and pesto in a bowl. Layer the pesto mixture thinly over the pita bread. Arrange the cheese, tomatoes, and shrimp over the pita bread. Dust with the garlic powder and basil. Place the prepared pita bread onto the baking sheet and bake for about 10 minutes. Take out from the oven and set aside for about 5 minutes. Cut into the desired size of slices and serve.

Per Serving: Calories 571, Fat 18.8g, Carbs 73.4g, Protein 31.9g

564. Pizza Bianca

Ingredients for 2 servings

- 2 tablespoons of olive oil
- 4 eggs
- 2 tablespoons of water
- 1 jalapeño pepper, diced
- ¼ cup of mozzarella cheese, shredded
- 2 chives, chopped
- 2 cups of egg Alfredo sauce
- ½ teaspoon of oregano
- ½ cup of mushrooms, sliced

Directions and Total Time: approx. 20 minutes

Preheat the oven to 360°F. In a bowl, whisk eggs, water, and oregano. Heat the olive oil in a large skillet. The egg mixture must be poured in then let it cook until set, flipping once. Remove and spread the Alfredo sauce and jalapeño pepper all over. Top with mozzarella cheese, mushrooms, and chives. Let it bake for 10 minutes.

Per Serving: Calories 314, Fat 15.6g, Carbs 5.9g, Protein 10.4g

565. Pizza Margherita

Ingredients for 8 servings

- Thin Crust Pizza Dough
- 4 Roma tomatoes, thinly sliced
- Salt and freshly ground pepper to taste
- ½ cup yellow sweet pepper, thinly sliced
- ¾ cup shredded part-skim mozzarella cheese, about
- 3 ounces 4–5 snipped fresh basil leaves
- ¼ cup freshly grated Parmesan cheese
- 1 tablespoon extra-virgin olive oil

Directions and Total Time: approx. 45 minutes

Preheat the oven to 450°C. Place dough on a pizza pan that is scarcely oiled. For pizza dough, follow instructions and roll out to a 12-15-inch round. Range the tomatoes nearly to the edge of the crust on the rolled-out dough. Sprinkle with pepper and salt to taste. Cover with yellow pepper tomatoes, mozzarella cheese, basil cheese, parmesan cheese, and drizzle over the top with olive oil. Bake for just about 8 to 10 minutes at 450 F or until the crust is crisp and the cheeses are melted.

Per Serving: Calories 353, Fat 15g, Carbs 17g, Protein 19g

566. Quinoa Pizza Muffins

Ingredients for 4 servings

- 1 cup uncooked quinoa
- 2 large eggs
- ½ medium onion, diced
- 1 cup diced bell pepper
- 1 cup shredded mozzarella cheese
- 1 tablespoon dried basil
- 1 tablespoon dried oregano
- 2 teaspoons garlic powder
- 1/8 teaspoon salt
- 1 teaspoon crushed red peppers
- ½ cup roasted red pepper, chopped*
- Pizza Sauce, about 1-2 cups

Directions and Total Time: approx. 30 minutes

Preheat oven to 350°F. Cook quinoa according to directions. Combine all ingredients (except sauce) into bowl. Mix all ingredients well. Scoop quinoa pizza mixture into muffin tin evenly. Makes 12 muffins. Bake for 30 minutes until muffins turn golden in color and the edges are getting crispy. Top with 1 or 2 tbsp pizza sauce and enjoy!

Per Serving: Calories 303, Fat 6.1g, Carbs 41.3g, Protein 21g

567. Red Pepper Hummus

Ingredients for 6 servings

- 6 ounces of roasted red peppers, peeled and chopped
- 16 ounces of canned chickpeas, drained and rinsed
- ¼ cup of Greek yogurt
- 3 tablespoons of tahini paste
- Juice of 1 lemon
- 3 garlic cloves, minced
- 1 tablespoon of olive oil
- A pinch of salt and black pepper
- 1 tablespoon of parsley, chopped

Directions and Total Time: approx. 10 minutes

In your food processor, combine the red peppers with the rest of the ingredients. Do not include the oil and the parsley and pulse well. Add the oil, pulse again, divide into cups, sprinkle the parsley on top, and serve as a party spread.

Per Serving: Calories 255, Fat 11.4g, Carbs 17.4g, Protein 6.5g

568. Roasted Eggplant Hummus

Ingredients for 4 servings

- 1 pound of eggplants, peeled and sliced
- 1 lemon, juiced
- 1 garlic clove, minced
- ¼ cup of tahini
- ¼ teaspoon of ground cumin
- Salt and black pepper to taste
- 2 tablespoons of fresh parsley, chopped
- ½ cup of mayonnaise

Directions and Total Time: approx. 25 minutes

Preheat oven to a heat of 350 F. Arrange the eggplant slices on a baking sheet and bake for 15 minutes until tender. Let cool slightly before chopping. In a food processor, mix eggplants, salt, lemon juice, tahini, cumin, garlic, and pepper for 30 seconds. Remove to a bowl. Stir in mayonnaise. Serve topped with parsley.

Per Serving: Calories 235, Fat 18g, Carbs 17g, Protein 4.1g

569. Roasted Parmesan Broccoli

Ingredients for 4 servings

- 2 heads of broccoli, small florets
- 2 tablespoons of extra-virgin olive oil
- 2 teaspoons of minced garlic
- Zest of 1 lemon
- Juice of 1 lemon
- Pinch sea salt
- ½ cup of grated Parmesan cheese

Directions and Total Time: approx. 20 minutes

Preheat the oven to 400°F. Lightly grease a baking sheet using olive oil and set it aside. In a large bowl, toss the broccoli with two tablespoons of olive oil, garlic, lemon zest, lemon juice, and sea salt. Spread the combination on the baking sheet in a single layer and sprinkle with the Parmesan cheese. Bake for about 10 minutes, or until tender. Transfer the broccoli to a serving dish and serve.

Per Serving: Calories 154, Fat 11g, Carbs 10g, Protein 9g

570. Roasted Pumpkin Seeds

Ingredients for 4 servings

- 1 cup of pumpkin seeds, washed and dried
- 1/3 teaspoon of red chili powder
- ¼ teaspoon of ground turmeric
- Salt, as required
- 3 tablespoons of coconut oil, melted
- ½ tablespoon of fresh lemon juice

Directions and Total Time: approx. 30 minutes

Preheat your oven to 350 °F. Add all the listed ingredients except lemon juice to a bowl, and toss to coat well. Transfer the pumpkin seed mixture onto a baking sheet. Roast for 20 minutes, flipping occasionally. Remove from the prepared preheated oven and set aside to cool completely before serving. Drizzle with lemon juice and serve.

Per Serving: Calories 276, Fat 26.1g, Carbs 6.4g, Protein 8.6g

571. Sage and Walnut Pizza

Ingredients for 8 servings

- 1 loaf of white bread dough, thawed
- 6 ounces of Brie cheese, cut into ½-inch pieces
- 3 tablespoons of walnuts, chopped
- 2 teaspoons of fresh sage leaves, shredded

Directions and Total Time: approx. 35 minutes

Preheat your oven to 400 °F. Place the prepared pizza dough onto a baking sheet and roll into 12-inch diameter. With your fingers, crimp the edges to form a rim. With a small fork, pierce the surface of the dough. Arrange the Brie cheese pieces over the dough and top with walnuts and sage. Bake for approximately about 20 minutes, or until golden brown. Remove from the oven and set the pizza aside for about 5 minutes before slicing. Cut into desired-sized slices and serve.

Per Serving: Calories 356, Fat 25.1g, Carbs 22.3g, Protein 8.4g

572. Salmon Patties

Ingredients for 4 servings

- 1 pound of salmon, ground
- 2 tablespoons of lemon peel
- Black pepper to the taste
- A pinch of sea salt
- 1 teaspoon of vegetable oil
- ½ cup of flax meal

Directions and Total Time: approx. 20 minutes

In your kitchen appliance, mix salmon with flax meal, salt, pepper and lemon peel, pulse well, shape 4 patties out of this mix and place them on a plate. Set your instant pot on Sauté mode, add the oil and warmth it up. Add patties, cover pot and cook on High for 10 minutes. Arrange patties on a platter and serve. Enjoy!

Per Serving: Calories 142, Fat 3g, Carbs 3g, Protein 4g

Ingredients for 4 servings

- 1-pound of salmon fillet, cooked and flaked
- 1 carrot, diced
- 1 celery stalk, diced
- 3 tablespoons of fresh dill, chopped
- 1 small red onion, diced
- 2 tablespoons of capers
- 1 ½ tablespoons of extra-virgin olive oil
- 1 tablespoon of aged balsamic vinegar
- Sea salt and black pepper, to taste
- 4 whole-wheat tortillas

Directions and Total Time: approx. 10 minutes

Mix the salmon, carrots, celery, dill, red onion, capers, oil, vinegar, pepper, and salt in a large bowl. Divide the salmon salad among the flatbreads. Fold up the bottoms of each of the tortillas, then roll them up and serve. Garnish with chopped cilantro.

Per Serving: Calories 336, Fat 16g, Carbs 23g, Protein 20.3g

574. Sandwich Hummus

Ingredients for 4 servings

- 4 cups alfalfa sprouts
- 1 cup cucumber sliced 1/8 inch thick
- 4 red onion sliced ¼-inch thick
- 8 tomatoes sliced ¼-inch thick
- 2 cups shredded Bibb lettuce
- 12 slices 1-ounce whole wheat bread
- 1 can 15.5-ounces chickpeas, drained
- 2 garlic cloves, peeled
- ¼ teaspoon salt
- ½ teaspoon ground cumin
- 1 tablespoon tahini
- 1 tablespoon lemon juice
- 2 tablespoons water
- 3 tablespoons plain fat free yogurt

Directions and Total Time: approx. 5 minutes

In a food processor, blend chickpeas, garlic, salt, cumin, tahini, lemon juice, water and yogurt until smooth to create hummus. On 1 slice of bread, spread 2 tbsp hummus, top with 1 onion slice, 2 tomato slices, ½ cup lettuce, another bread slice, 1 cup sprouts, ¼ cup cucumber and cover with another bread slice. Repeat the whole procedure for the rest of the ingredients.

Per Serving: Calories 407, Fat 6.8g, Carbs 67.7g, Protein 18.8g

575. Sandwich with Spinach and Tuna Salad

Ingredients for 4 servings

- 1 cup fresh baby spinach
- 8 slices 100% whole wheat sandwich bread
- ¼ teaspoon freshly ground black pepper
- ½ teaspoon salt free seasoning blend
- Juice of one lemon
- 2 tablespoons olive oil
- ½ teaspoon dill weed
- 2 ribs celery, diced

Directions and Total Time: approx. 5 minutes

In a medium bowl, mix well dill weed, celery, onion, cucumber and tuna. Add lemon juice and olive oil and mix thoroughly. Season with pepper and salt-free seasoning blend. To assemble sandwich, you can toast bread slices, on top of one bread slice layer ½ cup tuna salad, top with ¼ cup spinach and cover with another slice of bread. Repeat procedure to remaining ingredients, serve and enjoy.

Per Serving: Calories 272.5, Fat 9.7g, Carbs 35.9g, Protein 10.4g

576. Sauteed Apricots

Ingredients for 4 servings

- 2 tablespoons olive oil
- 1 cup almonds, blanched, skinless, and unsalted
- ½ teaspoon fine sea salt
- ⅛ teaspoon red pepper flakes
- ⅛ teaspoon ground cinnamon
- ½ cup dried apricots, chopped

Directions and Total Time: approx. 25 minutes

Place a large-sized frying pan over high heat, adding in your almonds, salt, and olive oil. Sauté until the almonds turn light gold, which will take five to ten minutes. Make sure to stir often because they can burn easily. Spoon your almonds into a serving dish, adding the cinnamon, red pepper flakes, and chopped apricot. Allow the mixture to cool before serving.

Per Serving: Calories 207, Fat 19g, Carbs 7g, Protein 5g

577. Savory Lentil Dip

Ingredients for 16 servings

- 2 tablespoons olive oil
- ½ medium yellow onion, peeled and diced
- 3 cloves garlic, peeled and minced
- 2 cups dried red lentils
- 4 cups water
- 1 teaspoon salt
- ¼ teaspoon ground black pepper
- 2 tablespoons minced fresh flat-leaf parsley

Directions and Total Time: approx. 42 minutes

Press the Sauté button on the Instant Pot® and heat oil. Add onion and cook for just about 2–3 minutes, or until translucent. Add teh prepared garlic and cook until fragrant, about 30 seconds. Add lentils, water, and salt to pot, and stir to combine. Close lid, set steam release to Sealing, press the Bean button, and cook for the default time of 30 minutes. When the timer beeps, let pressure release naturally for 10 minutes. Quick-release any of the remaining pressure until the float valve drops, then open lid. Transfer lentil mixture to a food processor and blend until smooth. Season with pepper and garnish with parsley. Serve warm.

Per Serving: Calories 76, Fat 2g, Carbs 11g, Protein 5g

578. Sheet Pan Sweet Potatoes

Ingredients for 4 servings

- 4 sweet potatoes, pricked with a fork
- 4 tablespoons of olive oil
- 1 cup of arugula
- 1 garlic clove, minced
- 1 red onion, sliced
- 1 lemon, juiced and zested
- 2 tablespoons of dill, chopped
- 2 tablespoons of Greek yogurt
- 2 tablespoons of tahini paste
- Salt and black pepper to taste

Directions and Total Time: approx. 70 minutes

Preheat oven to a heat of 340 F. Line a baking sheet with parchment paper. Arrange potatoes on the sheet and bake for 1 hour. Peel them and slice into wedges. Remove to a large-sized bowl and combine with garlic, olive oil, onion, arugula, lemon juice, lemon zest, dill, Greek yogurt, tahini paste, salt, and pepper.

Per Serving: Calories 220, Fat 6g, Carbs 7g, Protein 4g

579. Simple Tomato and Cream Cheese Dip

Ingredients for 6 servings

- 12 ounces of Greek cream cheese
- 1 big tomato, cut into quarters
- ¼ cup of mayonnaise
- 2 garlic cloves, minced
- 2 tablespoons of yellow onion, chopped
- 1 celery stalk, chopped
- 1 teaspoon of sugar
- 2 tablespoons of lemon juice
- Salt and black pepper to taste
- Drops of hot sauce

Directions and Total Time: approx. 10 minutes

In a blender, mix cream cheese with tomato, onion, garlic and celery and pulse a few times. Add mayo, lemon juice, sugar, salt, pepper and hot sauce, blend again well. Transfer to a bowl and serve.

Per Serving: Calories 74, Fat 3g, Carbs 3g, Protein 4g

580. Skillet Pesto Pizza

Ingredients for 2 servings

- 1 tablespoon of butter
- 2 pieces of focaccia bread
- 2 tablespoons of pesto
- 1 medium tomato, sliced
- 2 large eggs

Directions and Total Time: approx. 10 minutes

Place a large skillet over medium heat. Place the focaccia in the skillet and let it warm for about 4 minutes on both sides until softened and just starting to turn golden. Remove to a platter. Spread 1 tablespoon of the pesto on one side of each slice. Cover with tomato slices. Melt the butter in the large-sized skillet over medium heat. Crack in the eggs, keeping them separated, and cook until the whites are no longer translucent and the yolk is actually cooked to desired doneness. Spoon one egg onto each pizza. Serve and enjoy!

Per Serving: Calories 427, Fat 17g, Carbs 10g, Protein 17g

581. Spiced Baked Pita Chips

Ingredients for 6 servings

- 2 tablespoons of extra-virgin olive oil
- 1 teaspoon of dried oregano
- 1/2 teaspoon of paprika
- 1/2 teaspoon of salt
- 1/4 teaspoon of ground black pepper
- 1/4 teaspoon of cayenne pepper
- 3 pita breads, each cut into 8 triangles

Directions and Total Time: approx. 20 minutes

Preheat the oven to 350F. Prepare a sheet with rim by actually lining it with parchment paper. Merge the olive oil, oregano, paprika, salt, black pepper, and cayenne. Mix well. Spread out the pita triangles on the prepared baking sheet. Brush with the oil mixture. Flip over and brush the other side. Bake until golden and crisp.

Per Serving: Calories 78, Fat 5g, Carbs 8g, Protein 1g

582. Spiced Fries

Ingredients for 6 servings

- 2 pounds of red potatoes, cut into wedges
- ¼ cup of olive oil
- 3 tablespoons of garlic, minced
- ½ teaspoon of smoked paprika
- Salt and black pepper to taste
- ½ cup of fresh cilantro, chopped
- ¼ teaspoon of cayenne pepper

Directions and Total Time: approx. 35 minutes

Preheat oven to a heat of 450 F. Place the potatoes into a bowl. Add the garlic, salt, pepper, and olive oil and toss everything together to coat evenly. Spread the potato mixture onto a baking sheet; bake for 25 minutes, flipping them halfway through the cooking time until golden and crisp. Sprinkle the potatoes with cilantro, cayenne pepper, and smoked paprika. Serve warm and enjoy!

Per Serving: Calories 203, Fat 11g, Carbs 24g, Protein 3g

583. Spicy Mediterranean Tapenade

Ingredients for 16 servings

- 1/4 teaspoon of dried thyme
- 3 teaspoons of crushed garlic
- 1 tablespoon of capers, drained
- 1 tablespoon of fresh parsley, chopped
- 2 tablespoons of extra-virgin olive oil
- 2 tablespoons of freshly squeezed lime juice
- 1/4 cup of chopped poblano peppers
- 1/2 cup of black olives, pitted
- 1/2 cup of red bell peppers
- 16 thin slices of French baguette, lightly toasted

Directions and Total Time: approx. 10 minutes

In a food processor, combine the thyme, garlic, capers, parsley, olive oil, lime juice, poblano peppers, olives, and bell peppers. Spread about 1 tablespoon of the tapenade over each slice of lightly toasted baguette, and serve.

Per Serving: Calories 63, Fat 3g, Carbs 7g, Protein 1g

584. Spicy Sweet Pepper Pizza

Ingredients for 8 servings

- Whole Wheat Pizza Dough
- 1 tablespoon extra-virgin olive oil
- 3 large red bell peppers, thinly sliced
- 3 large yellow bell peppers, seeded and thinly sliced
- 2 cloves fresh garlic, minced
- 1 tablespoon chopped fresh thyme
- Salt and pepper to taste
- crushed red hot pepper flakes to taste
- 1 cup shredded part-skim mozzarella cheese

Directions and Total Time: approx. 45 minutes

Preheat the oven to 500°F. Ignore the pizza dough instructions and roll out to a 12-15-inch round. Place the dough on a completely oiled pizza pan. In a heavy-bottomed skillet, heat the olive oil and sauté the red and yellow bell peppers and garlic until tender, about 10 minutes. Incorporate thyme, salt and pepper to taste, and flakes of sweet pepper. Spread the pepper mixture over the pizza dough, scatter the mozzarella cheese over the pepper mixture, and bake for 20-25 minutes at 500 F until the crust is crisp and the cheese melts.

Per Serving: Calories 662, Fat 30g, Carbs 74g, Protein 29g

585. Spinach and Sausage Pizza

Ingredients for 8 servings

- 1 Tablespoon olive oil
- 1 cup lean ground beef
- 2 cups spicy pork sausage
- 2 garlic cloves, minced
- 1 Tablespoon dry, fried onions
- Salt and pepper to taste
- 1 ¾ cups sugarless ready-made pizza sauce
- 3 cups fresh spinach
- ½ cup sliced pepperoni
- ¼ cup pitted black olives, sliced
- ¼ cup sun-dried tomatoes, chopped
- ½ cup spring onions, chopped
- 3 cups shredded mozzarella

Directions and Total Time: approx. 6 hours and 5 minutes

In a pan, heat the olive oil. Brown the beef, then the pork. Drain the oil off both meats mix. Pour the meat into the crockpot. Spread evenly and press down. Alternate in layers: pizza sauce, toppings, and cheese. Cover and cook on low for just about 4-6 hours.

Per Serving: Calories 50, Fat 37g, Carbs 5g, Protein 30g

586. Stuffed Baby Bell Peppers

Ingredients for 5 servings

- 10 baby bell peppers, seeded and sliced lengthwise
- 1 tablespoon vegetable oil
- 4 ounces cheese
- 4 ounces Monterey-Jack cheese, shredded
- 1 teaspoon garlic, minced
- 2 tablespoons scallions, chopped
- 1/4 teaspoon of black pepper, or more to taste
- 1/2 teaspoon of cayenne pepper

Directions and Total Time: approx. 10 minutes

Start by adding the prepared 1 cup of water and a steamer basket to the moment Pot. During a bowl, thoroughly combine all ingredients, apart from bell peppers. Then, stuff the peppers with cheese mixture. Place the dish within the steamer basket. Secure the lid. Choose "Manual" mode and High pressure; cook for five minutes. Once cooking is complete, use a fast pressure release; carefully remove the lid. Serve at temperature and enjoy!

Per Serving: Calories 224, Fat 17.5g, Carbs 9g, Protein 8.7g

587. Stuffed Cucumber Bites

Ingredients for 4 servings

- ¼ cup of extra-virgin olive oil
- 2 cucumbers
- Salt to taste
- 6 basil leaves, chopped
- 1 tablespoon of fresh mint, minced
- 1 garlic clove, minced
- ¼ cup of walnuts, ground
- ¼ cup of feta cheese, crumbled
- ½ teaspoon of paprika

Directions and Total Time: approx. 10 minutes

Cut cucumbers lengthwise. With a spoon, remove the seeds and hollow out a shallow trough in each piece. Lightly salt each piece and set aside on a platter. In a bowl, combine the basil, mint, garlic, walnuts, feta, and olive oil and blend until smooth. Spoon the mixture into each cucumber half and sprinkle with paprika. Cut each half into 4 pieces. Serve.

Per Serving: Calories 176, Fat 3g, Carbs 18g, Protein 5g

588. Sun-Dried Tomato and Anchovy Pizza

Ingredients for 8 servings

- Crispy Thin Whole Wheat Pizza Dough
- 1 red onion, thinly sliced
- 8 sundried tomatoes in oil, chopped
- 1 tablespoon fresh basil leaves, broken into pieces
- 1 tin (2 ounces) anchovy
- fillets, chopped, oil reserved
- 1 clove fresh garlic, minced
- 1 cup fresh part-skim mozzarella cheese, shredded
- Salt and freshly ground pepper to taste
- Finely chopped fresh parsley for garnish (optional)

Directions and Total Time: approx. 45 minutes

Preheat oven to 425 F. Follow directions for pizza dough; when ready, roll out to a 15-inch round. Place on scantly oiled pizza pan. Top pizza crust dough with onion, sundried tomatoes, basil, anchovies, garlic, and mozzarella cheese. Season with the teaspoons of salt and pepper to taste and bake at 425 F until crust is crisp and cheese is melted. Garnish with parsley, if desired.

Per Serving: Calories 285, Fat 4g, Carbs 49g, Protein 12g

589. Sweet and Spicy Cashews

Ingredients for 8 servings

- 2 cups of cashews
- 2 teaspoons of raw honey
- 1 ½ teaspoons of smoked paprika
- ½ teaspoon of chili flakes
- Salt, as required
- 1 tablespoon of fresh lemon juice
- 1 teaspoon of olive oil

Directions and Total Time: approx. 30 minutes

Preheat your oven to 350 °F. Line a baking dish with parchment paper. In a bowl, add all ingredients and toss to coat well. Transfer the cashew mixture into the prepared baking dish in a single layer. Roast for approximately 20 minutes, flipping once halfway through. Remove from the prepared preheated oven and set aside to cool completely before serving.

Per Serving: Calories 209, Fat 16.5g, Carbs 11.7g, Protein 5.3g

590. Tempeh Snack

Ingredients for 6 servings

- 11 ounces of soy tempeh, cut into sticks
- 1 teaspoon of olive oil
- ½ teaspoon of ground black pepper
- ¼ teaspoon of garlic powder

Directions and Total Time: approx. 35 minutes

Preheat the oven to 400°F. Line a baking sheet with parchment paper. Toss the tempeh sticks in the salt, black pepper, garlic powder, and olive oil. Spread the sticks out evenly onto the prepared baking sheet and bake in the oven for 25 minutes. When ready, the cooked tempeh sticks will be golden and crispy. Serve with ginger soy dressing.

Per Serving: Calories 88, Fat 2.5g, Carbs 10.2g, Protein 6.5g

591. Thin Crust Low Carb Pizza

Ingredients for 6 servings

- 2 tablespoons tomato sauce
- 1/8 teaspoon black pepper
- 1/8 teaspoon chili flakes
- 1 piece low-carb pita bread
- 2 ounces low-moisture mozzarella cheese
- 1/8 teaspoon garlic powder

Directions and Total Time: approx. 25 minutes

Preheat the oven to a heat of 450 degrees F and grease a baking dish. Mix together tomato sauce, black pepper, chili flakes, and garlic powder in a bowl and keep aside. Place the low-carb pita bread in the oven and bake for about 2 minutes. Remove from oven and spread the tomato sauce on it. Add mozzarella cheese and top with your favorite toppings. Bake again for 3 minutes and dish out.

Per Serving: Calories 254, Fat 16g, Carbs 12.9g, Protein 19.3g

592. Tomato and Pine Nuts Pizza

Ingredients for 6 servings

- ½ cup of pesto
- ½ cup of pizza sauce
- 1 (12-inch) refrigerated pizza crust
- 4-6 plum tomatoes, sliced
- 1 cup of mozzarella cheese, shredded
- 1 cup of Havarti cheese, shredded
- ½ cup of refrigerated Parmesan cheese, shredded
- 1 (4-ounce) package of goat cheese, crumbled
- 2 tablespoons of pine nuts

Directions and Total Time: approx. 25 minutes

Preheat your oven to 425 °F. Place the pizza dough onto a large-sized baking sheet. Spread pesto over dough, followed by and pizza sauce. Top with tomato slices, followed by cheeses, and sprinkle with pine nuts. Bake for about approximately 10 minutes or until cheese is melted and bubbly. Remove from the oven and set the pizza aside for about 5 minutes before slicing. Cut into desired-sized slices and serve.

Per Serving: Calories 461, Fat 25.7g, Carbs 36.5g, Protein 22.7g

593. Tuna Cucumber Roll-Ups

Ingredients for 6 servings

- 1 big cucumber, sliced lengthwise
- 1 tablespoon of cilantro, chopped
- 1 tablespoon of cranberries, dried
- 3 ounces of canned sardines, drained and flaked
- 3 ounces of canned tuna pate
- Salt and black pepper to taste
- 1 teaspoon of lemon juice

Directions and Total Time: approx. 10 minutes

Arrange cucumber slices on a working surface. In a bowl, mix sardines with tuna paste, salt and pepper to taste and lemon juice and mash everything well. Spoon this mix on each cucumber slice, add cilantro and cranberries on top, roll, arrange on a platter and serve.

Per Serving: Calories 80, Fat 1g, Carbs 2g, Protein 1g

594. Tuna Melt Panini

Ingredients for 4 servings

- 2 tablespoons extra virgin olive oil
- 16 pieces of 1/8-inch kosher dill pickle
- 8 pieces of ¼ inch thick cheddar or Swiss cheese
- Mayonnaise and Dijon mustard
- 4 ciabatta rolls, split
- Pepper and salt
- ½ teaspoon crushed red pepper
- 1 tablespoon minced basil
- 1 tablespoon balsamic vinegar
- ¼ cup extra virgin olive oil
- ¼ cup finely diced red onion
- 2 cans of 6 ounces albacore tuna

Directions and Total Time: approx. 10 minutes

Combine thoroughly the following in a bowl: salt pepper, crushed red pepper, basil, vinegar, olive oil, onion and tuna. Smear with mayonnaise and mustard the cut sides of the bread rolls then layer on: cheese, tuna salad and pickles. Cover with the remaining slice of roll. Grill in a Panini press ensuring that cheese is melted and bread is crisped and ridged.

Per Serving: Calories 539, Fat 38.5g, Carbs 27.7g, Protein 21.6g

595. Vegetarian Spinach-Olive Pizza

Ingredients for 4 servings

- ½ cup almond flour
- ¼ teaspoon salt
- 2 tablespoons ground psyllium husk
- 1 tablespoon olive oil
- 1 cup lukewarm water
- ½ cup tomato sauce
- ½ cup baby spinach
- 1 cup grated mozzarella cheese
- 1 teaspoon dried oregano
- 3 tablespoons sliced black olives

Directions and Total Time: approx. 40 minutes

Preheat the oven to a heat of 400 F. Line a baking sheet with parchment paper. In a large-sized bowl, mix the almond flour, salt, psyllium powder, olive oil, and water until dough forms. Spread the mixture on the pizza pan and bake in the oven until crusty, 10 minutes. When ready, remove the crust and spread the tomato sauce on top. Add the spinach, mozzarella cheese, oregano, and olives. Bake until the cheese melts, 15 minutes. Take out of the hot oven, slice, and serve warm.

Per Serving: Calories 95, Fat 4.3g, Carbs 1.8g, Protein 9.7g

596. Wax Beans with Pancetta

Ingredients for 6 servings

- 1 tablespoon of groundnut oil
- 1/2 cup of shallots, chopped
- 4 slices of pancetta, diced
- 1 teaspoon of roasted garlic paste
- 1 pound of yellow wax beans, cut in half
- Kosher salt and ground black pepper, to your liking
- 1 cup of water

Directions and Total Time: approx. 10 minutes

Press the "Sauté" button to heat up your Instant Pot. Now, heat the groundnut oil and sauté the shallot until softened. Now, add pancetta and still cook for an extra 3 to 4 minutes; reserve. Add the opposite ingredients; stir to mix Secure the lid. Choose "Manual" mode and Low pressure; cook for 3 minutes. Once cooking is complete, use a fast pressure release; carefully remove the lid. Serve warm, garnished with the reserved shallots and pancetta. Bon appétit!

Per Serving: Calories 194, Fat 8.7g, Carbs 58g, Protein 24.3g

Ingredients for 4 servings

- ½ cup of olive oil
- 1 garlic clove
- 1 (15-ounces) can of cannellini beans
- 1 lemon, zested and juiced
- Salt to taste
- ½ teaspoon of oregano
- 4 pitas, cut into wedges
- 5 black olives

Directions and Total Time: approx. 25 minutes

Preheat the oven to a heat of 350 F. Arrange the pita wedges on a baking sheet and sprinkle with salt and oregano; drizzle them with some olive oil. Bake for 10-12 minutes until the pita beginning to brown. Place the beans, garlic, lemon juice, lemon zest, and salt and purée, drizzling in as much cup of olive oil as needed until the beans are smooth. Transfer the dip to a bowl and serve the toasted pita bread.

Per Serving: Calories 209, Fat 17g, Carbs 12g, Protein 4g

598. White Pizza with Prosciutto and Arugula

Ingredients for 4 servings

- 1 pound (454 g) prepared pizza dough
- ½ cup ricotta cheese
- 1 tablespoon garlic, minced
- 1 cup grated mozzarella cheese
- 3 ounces prosciutto, thinly sliced
- ½ cup fresh arugula
- ½ teaspoon freshly ground black pepper

Directions and Total Time: approx. 25 minutes

Preheat the oven to a heat of 450°F (235°C). Roll out the prepared pound of pizza dough on a floured surface. Put the prepared pizza dough on a parchment-lined baking sheet or pizza sheet. Put the dough in the oven and bake for 8 minutes. In a small-sized bowl, mix together the ricotta, garlic, and mozzarella. Remove the pizza dough from the oven and spread the cheese mixture over the top. Bake for another 5 to 6 minutes. 5. Top the pizza with prosciutto, arugula, and pepper; serve warm.

Per Serving: Calories 435, Fat 17g, Carbs 51g, Protein 20g

599. Zingy Zucchini Bites

Ingredients for 6 servings

- 2 tablespoons vegetable oil
- 1 red chili pepper, chopped
- 1 pound zucchini, dig thick slices
- 1 teaspoon garlic powder
- 1 cup chicken stock
- salt and ground black pepper, to taste
- 1/2 teaspoon paprika
- 1/2 teaspoon ground coriander

Directions and Total Time: approx. 10 minutes

Press the "Sauté" button and warmth the vegetable oil. Once hot, cook chili pepper for 1 minute. Add the remaining ingredients. Secure the lid. Choose "Manual" mode and Low pressure; cook for 3 minutes. Once cooking is complete, use a fast pressure release; carefully remove the lid. Bon appétit!

Per Serving: Calories 70, Fat 5.1g, Carbs 4.4g, Protein 3.2g

600. Zucchini Chips

Ingredients for 4 servings

- 1 zucchini, thinly sliced
- A pinch of sea salt
- Black pepper, to taste
- 1 teaspoon of dried thyme
- 1 egg
- 1 teaspoon of garlic powder
- 1 cup of almond flour

Directions and Total Time: approx. 22 minutes

Preheat the oven to 450°F. In a bowl, whisk the egg with a pinch of salt. Put the flour in another bowl and mix it with the thyme, black pepper, and garlic powder. Dredge the zucchini slices in the egg mix and then in the flour. Arrange the chips on a lined baking sheet, place the sheet in the oven, and bake for 6 minutes on each side. Serve and enjoy.

Per Serving: Calories 67, Fat 8.2g, Carbs 3.9g, Protein 3.6g

601. Almond-Crusted Tilapia

Ingredients for 4 servings

- ¼ cup of ground flax seeds
- 1 cup of almonds, finely chopped and divided
- 4 (6-ounce) tilapia fillets
- 2 tablespoons of olive oil
- Salt and black pepper, to taste

Directions and Total Time: approx. 25 minutes

Mix half a cup of the almonds with the ground flax seeds in a large shallow dish. Season the pieces of tilapia fillets with salt and black pepper. Rub the tilapia fillets in the almond mixture and coat evenly. In a heavy skillet placed over medium heat, heat the oil and cook the tilapia fillets for about 4 minutes per side. Put the tilapia fillets onto a serving plate. In the same heavy skillet, add the remaining almonds and cook for about 1 minute, frequently stirring. Remove the almonds from the heat and sprinkle over the fish. Serve warm.

Per Serving: Calories 374, Fat 22.6g, Carbs 7.1g, Protein 38g

602. Asparagus Smoked Salmon

Ingredients for 6 servings

- 1 tablespoon of extra-virgin olive oil
- 6 large eggs
- 1 cup of heavy (whipping) cream
- 2 teaspoons of fresh dill, chopped
- ½ teaspoon of kosher salt
- ¼ teaspoon of freshly ground black pepper
- 1 1/2 cups of shredded Havarti or Monterey Jack cheese
- 12 ounces of asparagus, trimmed and sliced
- 6 ounces of smoked salmon, flaked

Directions and Total Time: approx. 5 hours and 15 minutes

Brush butter into a cooker. Whisk in the heavy cream with eggs, dill, salt, and pepper. Stir in the cheese and asparagus. Gently fold in the salmon and then pour the mixture into the prepared insert. Cover and cook on low or 3 hours on high. Serve warm, garnished with additional fresh dill.

Per Serving: Calories 388, Fat 19g, Carbs 1g, Protein 21g

603. Baked Cod in Parchment

Ingredients for 1 serving

- 1-2 potatoes, sliced
- 5 cherry tomatoes, halved
- 5 pitted olives
- Juice of ½ lemon
- ½ tablespoon of olive oil
- 4 ounces of cod
- 20 inches of long parchment
- Sea salt and black pepper

Directions and Total Time: approx. 15 minutes

Set your oven to preheat at a heat of 350°F/176.6°C. Spread the olive oil on parchment and arrange potato on it. In separate bowl combine the tomatoes, olives, and lemon juice. Put the fish fillet on potatoes and top with tomato mixture. Add salt and pepper. Fold the filled parchment squares and bake for approximately about 20 minutes.

Per Serving: Calories 330, Fat 8g, Carbs 35g, Protein 25g

604. Baked Dijon Salmon

Ingredients for 2 servings

- 1 ½ pound of salmon
- ⅓ cup of Dijon mustard
- 1 tablespoon of olive oil
- 2 tablespoons of lemon juice
- ¼ teaspoon of salt
- 1 tablespoon of fresh dill chopped
- 4 cloves of garlic minced
- 1 tablespoon of caper
- 1 lemon sliced

Directions and Total Time: approx. 33 minutes

Preheat your oven at 400°F. Line a baking sheet with parchment paper. Place the salmon onto the sheet with the skin facing down. Mix the capers with the garlic, dill, salt, lemon juice, oil, and Dijon mustard in a small bowl. Spread this mixture over the salmon and bake for 23 minutes until it is flaky. Serve warm.

Per Serving: Calories 552, Fat 29.9g, Carbs 4.7g, Protein 68.4g

605. Baked Halibut with Eggplants

Ingredients for 4 servings

- 2 tablespoons of olive oil
- ¼ cup of tomato sauce
- 4 halibut fillets, boneless
- 2 eggplants, sliced
- Salt and black pepper to taste
- 2 tablespoons of balsamic vinegar
- 2 tablespoons of chives, chopped

Directions and Total Time: approx. 35 minutes

Preheat the oven to 380F. Warm the olive oil in a large-sized skillet over medium heat and fry the eggplant slices for 5-6 minutes, turning once; reserve. Add the tomato sauce, salt, pepper, and vinegar to the skillet and cook for 5 minutes. Return the eggplants to the skillet and cook for 2 minutes. Remove to a plate. Place the halibut fillets on a greased baking tray and bake for 12-15 minutes. Serve the halibut over the eggplants sprinkled with chives.

Per Serving: Calories 300, Fat 13g, Carbs 19g, Protein 16g

606. Baked Trout with Dill

Ingredients for 4 servings

- 3 teaspoons of olive oil, divided
- 2 (8-ounce) whole trout, cleaned
- Sea salt and black pepper, to taste
- 1 lemon, thinly sliced into about 6 pieces
- 1 tablespoon of fresh dill, finely chopped
- 1 tablespoon of fresh parsley, chopped
- ½ cup of low-sodium fish stock

Directions and Total Time: approx. 30 minutes

Preheat the oven to 400°F. Lightly grease a 9x13" baking dish with one teaspoon of olive oil. Rinse the trout, pat dry with paper towels, and coat with the remaining two teaspoons of olive oil. Season with salt and pepper. Stuff the interior of the trout with the lemon slices, dill, and parsley and place it into the prepared baking dish. Bake the fish for 10 minutes, then add the fish stock to the dish. Continue to bake until the fish flakes easily with a fork, about 10 minutes. Serve.

Per Serving: Calories 194, Fat 10g, Carbs 1g, Protein 25g

Ingredients for 4 servings

- ½ cup of balsamic vinegar
- 1 tablespoon of honey
- 4 salmon fillets
- Sea salt and freshly ground pepper
- 1 tablespoon of olive oil

Directions and Total Time: approx. 10 minutes

Heat a skillet over medium-high heat. Mix the vinegar and honey in a small bowl. Season the salmon fillets with sea salt and freshly ground pepper; brush with the honey-balsamic glaze. Add olive oil to the skillet, then sear the salmon fillets, cooking for 3 to 4 minutes on every side until lightly browned and medium-rare in the center. Let sit for 5 minutes before serving.

Per Serving: Calories 454, Fat 17.3g, Carbs 9.7g, Protein 65.3g

608. Barbecued Sardines with Walnut Pesto

Ingredients for 4 servings

- 24 whole sardines
- 8 to 9 pieces of sourdough bread
- A pinch of sea salt
- Walnut pesto:
- 2 1/2 ounces of Manchego cheese
- 1 garlic clove, minced
- 210 ml of extra virgin olive oil
- 2 1/2 ounces of walnuts
- A handful of parsley

Directions and Total Time: approx. 15 minutes

Preheat the barbecue pan over a medium flame. It can take about 10 minutes. To prepare walnut pesto, put all the items inside a food processor machine, then blend until well combined. Now cook the fish over the hot barbecue pan or grill for 4 minutes on both sides. Sprinkle with a pinch of salt, then serve over a few toasted slices of sourdough bread, including a tablespoonful of walnut pesto.

Per Serving: Calories 439, Fat 10g, Carbs 75g, Protein 13g

609. Beer-Batter Fish

Ingredients for 4 servings

- 1 ¼ tablespoon of salt
- 1 ½ cups of dark beer, cold
- ¾ cup of all-purpose flour
- 1 tablespoon of baking powder
- ¾ cup of cornstarch
- 4 of 6 ounces of cod fillets
- 3-4 pieces of sunflower oil

Directions and Total Time: approx. 65 minutes

Mix cornstarch, ½ tablespoon of salt, baking powder, and flour in a bowl. Then put it inside the fridge. Put the fish on parchment paper, add half tbsp of salt. Put oil inside a frying pan, put the fish inside the oil, and fry it till it is golden in color. Remove the fish after frying, and put it inside oil to soak. Add the remaining half tbsp of salt and serve.

Per Serving: Calories 250, Fat 12g, Carbs 20g, Protein 14g

Ingredients for 4 servings

- ½ teaspoon of lemon zest
- 1 and ½ teaspoons of coriander seeds, toasted
- 2 tablespoons of lemon juice
- 1 lemon cut in wedges
- 1 cup of cornmeal
- 4 cod pieces
- 3 ounces of butter, melted
- 3 cups of water
- Salt and black pepper to the taste
- 2 tablespoons of harissa paste
- 2 teaspoons of cilantro, chopped

Directions and Total Time: approx. 50 minutes

In a pot, mix the water with lemon zest, salt and pepper, bring to a boil, add the cornmeal, stir, cook for 20 minutes stirring often and take off the heat. Place fish in a medium-sized baking dish, season with salt and pepper, add harissa, lemon juice and melted butter, stir, place in the oven at 400 degrees F and bake for 15 minutes. Take fish out of the oven, divide it between plates, top with cilantro and serve with the polenta and with lemon wedges on the side.

Per Serving: Calories 450, Fat 23g, Carbs 30g, Protein 30g

611. Caper and Herring Stuffed Eggs

Ingredients for 6 servings

- 1/3 cup of aioli
- 1 tablespoon of capers, drained
- 12 eggs
- 1 tablespoon of tarragon, chopped
- 2 pickled jalapenos, minced
- Salt and black pepper to taste
- 1 (6.7-ounces) can of smoked herring
- 1 teaspoon of paprika

Directions and Total Time: approx. 20 minutes

Fill a pot over medium heat with water by 1 inch. Bring to a boil. Carefully add the eggs, one at a time to the pot, cover, and boil them for 10 minutes. Cool the eggs in cold water. Peel the 12 eggs and slice them accordingly in half lengthwise; mix the yolks with the aioli, herring, paprika, capers, tarragon, jalapenos, salt, and pepper. Divide the mixture between the egg whites. Arrange the deviled eggs on a large-sized serving platter.

Per Serving: Calories 205, Fat 13g, Carbs 4g, Protein 18g

612. Cheesy Tilapia

Ingredients for 7 servings

- ¼ cup of flour
- 1 tablespoon of olive oil
- 1 teaspoon of dried dill
- 2 pounds of tilapia fillet
- 7 ounces of parmesan cheese, grated
- 1 tablespoon of paprika
- 1 teaspoon of dried oregano

Directions and Total Time: approx. 25 minutes

Combine the paprika, dried dill, dried oregano, and flour. Mix well. Pour the tablespoon of olive oil into a medium-sized skillet and heat over medium heat. Rub the tilapia fillets with the oregano mixture. Sear the tilapia for 10 minutes in the skillet on both sides. Sprinkle the grated cheese over the fish and cover it with a lid. Cook the tilapia for 2 minutes more. Serve hot!

Per Serving: Calories 235, Fat 9.4g, Carbs 5.2g, Protein 33.9g

613. Citrus Clams

Ingredients for 4 servings

- 2 ¼ pounds of clams
- ½ cup of olive oil
- 4 cloves of garlic, minced
- 1 cup of parsley, chopped
- ¾ cup of cilantro, chopped
- 2 tablespoons of lemon juice
- Salt and pepper, to taste

Directions and Total Time: approx. 2 hours and 25 minutes

Soak the clams in water for 2 hours. Rinse well and drain. Heat the oil in a small-sized skillet over medium heat and sauté the garlic until slightly browned (about 2 minutes). Add the pounds of clams and the rest of the ingredients. Cook until the clams are done or until they open (about 10 minutes). Discard any unopened clams.

Per Serving: Calories 514, Fat 26.6g, Carbs 67.4g, Protein 4.3g

614. Citrus Scallops

Ingredients for 4 servings

- 1 sweet pepper, sliced
- 1 pound of sea scallops
- 5 green onions, chopped
- Salt and black pepper, to taste
- 3 tablespoons of olive oil
- ¼ teaspoon of red pepper flakes
- 4 medium oranges, peeled and sectioned
- 2 teaspoons of fresh cilantro or parsley, diced
- 3 tablespoons of lime juice
- 4 cloves of garlic, minced

Directions and Total Time: approx. 28 minutes

In a large skillet, lightly fry the onions, garlic, and pepper in olive oil until the vegetables are soft. Add the scallops and sprinkle with pepper, black pepper, and salt. Cook until the scallops are cooked through. Add the lime juice. Reduce the heat before adding the orange slices and fresh cilantro. Cook until the scallops are lightly golden. Remove from the heat and serve.

Per Serving: Calories 275, Fat 11.7g, Carbs 23.7g, Protein 21.1g

615. Clams Toscano

Ingredients for 6 servings

- 36 clams in the shell, scrubbed
- 3 tablespoons of olive oil
- 5 cloves of garlic, minced
- 2 cups of fish broth
- 1 tablespoon of dried oregano
- 1 tablespoon of dried parsley
- 1 teaspoon of red pepper flakes (optional)

Directions and Total Time: approx. 25 minutes

Stir fry your garlic in olive oil for a minute, then add the pepper flakes, broth, parsley, and oregano. Add in the clams and stir the mix. Place a lid on the pan and let everything cook until the clams open. Divide the mix between serving bowls. Enjoy.

Per Serving: Calories 227, Fat 15.7g, Carbs 4.4g, Protein 3.2g

616. Classic Prawn Scampi

Ingredients for 4 servings

- 1 pound of prawns, peeled and deveined
- 2 tablespoons of olive oil
- 1 onion, chopped
- 6 garlic cloves, minced
- 1 lemon, juiced and zested
- ½ cup of dry white wine
- Salt and black pepper to taste
- 2 cups of fusilli, cooked
- ½ teaspoon of red pepper flakes

Directions and Total Time: approx. 25 minutes

Warm olive oil in a large-sized pan over medium heat and sauté onion and garlic for 3 minutes, stirring often, until fragrant. Stir in prawns and cook for 3-4 minutes. Mix in lemon juice, lemon zest, salt, pepper, wine, and red flakes. Bring to a boil, then you can actually decrease the heat, and simmer for 2 minutes until the liquid is reduced by half. Turn the heat off. Stir in pasta and serve.

Per Serving: Calories 388, Fat 9g, Carbs 38.2g, Protein 32g

617. Cod and Brussels Sprouts

Ingredients for 4 servings

- 1 teaspoon of garlic powder
- 1 teaspoon of smoked paprika
- 2 tablespoons of olive oil
- 2 pounds of Brussels sprouts
- 4 boneless of cod fillets
- ½ cup of tomato sauce
- 1 teaspoon of Italian seasoning
- 1 tablespoon of chives, chopped

Directions and Total Time: approx. 40 minutes

In a roasting pan, combine the sprouts with the garlic powder and the other ingredients except for the cod, and then toss. Put the cod on top, cover the pan with tin foil and bake at 450°F for 20 minutes. Divide between plates and serve.

Per Serving: Calories 188, Fat 12.8g, Carbs 22.2g, Protein 16.8g

618. Cod Fettuccine

Ingredients for 4 servings

- 1 pound of cod fillets, cubed
- 16 ounces of fettuccine
- 3 tablespoons of olive oil
- 1 onion, finely chopped
- Salt and lemon pepper to taste
- 1 ½ cups of heavy cream
- 1 cup of Parmesan cheese, grated

Directions and Total Time: approx. 30 minutes

Boil salted water in a large-sized pot over medium heat and stir in fettuccine. Cook according to package directions and drain. Heat the olive oil in a small-sized saucepan over medium heat and add the onion. Stir-fry for 3 minutes until tender. Sprinkle cod with salt and lemon pepper and add to saucepan; cook for 4–5 minutes until fish fillets and flakes easily with a fork. Stir in heavy cream for 2 minutes. Add in the pasta, tossing gently to combine. Cook for approximately about 3–4 minutes until sauce is slightly thickened. Sprinkle with Parmesan cheese.

Per Serving: Calories 431, Fat 36g, Carbs 97g, Protein 42g

619. Creamy Swordfish

Ingredients for 6 servings

- 28 ounces of canned tomatoes, chopped
- 1 shallot, chopped
- 1 small fennel bulb, chopped
- 2 tablespoons of tomato paste
- 1 tablespoon of rosemary
- 1 teaspoon of fennel seeds
- Salt and black pepper to taste
- 1 teaspoon of garlic, minced
- ¼ cup of heavy cream
- 1 and ½ pounds of swordfish steaks

Directions and Total Time: approx. 2 hours and 40 minutes

In a slow cooker, mix fennel with and the other ingredients except the fish, stir, cover and cook on High for 2 hours. Add fish, cover it with some sauce and cook on High for 30 minutes more. Divide into bowls and serve.

Per Serving: Calories 340, Fat 14g, Carbs 15g, Protein 32g

620. Crispy Fried Sardines

Ingredients for 4 servings

- 1 teaspoon of freshly ground black pepper
- 2 cups of flour
- Avocado oil, as needed
- 1 ½ pounds of whole fresh sardines, scales removed
- 1 teaspoon of salt

Directions and Total Time: approx. 10 minutes

Preheat a deep skillet over medium heat. Pour in just enough oil as needed to cover the bottom of the pan by approximately an inch. Season the fish with salt and pepper. Dip the fish in the flour so that it is completely covered. Slowly dip 1 fish at a time, being careful not to overcrowd the pan. Cook for approximately about 3 minutes on each side or until the fish begins to brown on all sides. Serve hot.

Per Serving: Calories 794, Fat 47g, Carbs 44g, Protein 48g

621. Curry Salmon with Mustard

Ingredients for 4 servings

- ¼ teaspoon of ground red pepper or chili powder
- ¼ teaspoon of ground turmeric
- ¼ teaspoon of salt
- 1 teaspoon of honey
- 1/8 teaspoon of garlic powder
- 2 teaspoons of whole grain mustard
- 4 pieces of salmon fillets

Directions and Total Time: approx. 18 minutes

In a small bowl, mix well salt, garlic powder, red pepper, turmeric, honey, and mustard. Preheat oven to broil and grease a baking dish with cooking spray. Place salmon on a baking dish with skin side down and spread evenly mustard mixture on top of the salmon. Pop in the oven and broil until flaky around 8 minutes.

Per Serving: Calories 324, Fat 18.9g, Carbs 2.9g, Protein 34g

622. Date and Hazelnut Crusted Barramundi

Ingredients for 2 servings

- 2 tablespoons of olive oil
- 2 barramundi fillets, boneless
- 1 shallot, sliced
- 4 lemon slices
- ½ lemon, zested and juiced
- 1 cup of baby spinach
- ¼ cup of hazelnuts, chopped
- 4 dates, pitted and chopped
- Salt and black pepper to taste

Directions and Total Time: approx. 25 minutes

Preheat oven to 380 F. Sprinkle barramundi with salt and pepper and place on 2 parchment paper pieces. Top each fillet with lemon slices, lemon juice, shallot, lemon zest, spinach, hazelnuts, dates, and parsley. Sprinkle each fillet with 1 tbsp of oil and fold the paper around it. Place them on a baking sheet and bake for 12 minutes. Serve and enjoy!

Per Serving: Calories 240, Fat 17g, Carbs 26g, Protein 7g

623. Dijon Mustard and Lime Marinated Shrimp

Ingredients for 8 servings

- ½ cup of fresh lime juice, plus lime zest as garnish
- ½ cup of rice vinegar
- ½ teaspoon of hot sauce
- 1 bay leaf
- 1 cup of water
- 1 pound of uncooked shrimp, deveined
- 1 medium red onion, chopped
- 2 tablespoons of capers
- 2 tablespoons of Dijon mustard
- 3 whole cloves

Directions and Total Time: approx. 20 minutes

Mix hot sauce, mustard, capers, lime juice, and onion in a shallow baking dish and set aside. Bring to a boil in a large-sized saucepan bay leaf, cloves, vinegar, and water. Once boiling, add shrimps and cook for a minute while stirring continuously. Drain shrimps and pour shrimps into the onion mixture. For an hour, refrigerate while covered the shrimps. Then serve shrimps cold and garnished with lime zest.

Per Serving: Calories 232.2, Fat 3g, Carbs 15g, Protein 17.8g

624. Dill Baked Sea Bass

Ingredients for 6 servings

- ¼ cup of olive oil
- 2 pounds of sea bass
- Salt and freshly ground pepper, to taste
- 1 garlic clove, minced
- ¼ cup of dry white wine
- 3 teaspoons of fresh dill
- 2 teaspoons of fresh thyme

Directions and Total Time: approx. 15 minutes

Preheat the oven to 425ºF. Brush the bottom of a large-sized roasting pan with the olive oil. Place the fish in the pan and brush the fish with oil. Season the pounds of sea bass with sea salt and freshly ground pepper. Combine the rest of the remaining ingredients and pour over the fish. Bake in the prepared preheated oven for 10 to 15 minutes, depending on the size of the fish. Serve hot.

Per Serving: Calories 224, Fat 12.1g, Carbs 0.9g, Protein 28.1g

625. Dill Smoked Salad and Eggplant Rolls

Ingredients for 4 servings

- 2 eggplants, lengthwise cut into thin slices
- 2 tablespoons of olive oil
- 1 cup of ricotta cheese, soft
- 4 ounces of smoked salmon, chopped
- 2 teaspoons of lemon zest, grated
- 1 small red onion, sliced
- Salt and pepper to the taste

Directions and Total Time: approx. 20 minutes

Mix salmon, cheese, lemon zest, onion, salt, and pepper in a bowl. Grease the eggplant with olive oil and grill them on a preheated grill pan for 3-4 minutes per side. Set aside to cool. Spread the cooled eggplant slices with the salmon mixture. Roll out and secure with toothpicks and serve.

Per Serving: Calories 310, Fat 25g, Carbs 16g, Protein 12g

626. Fennel and Bell Pepper Salmon

Ingredients for 4 servings

- 2 tablespoons of olive oil
- 4 salmon fillets, boneless
- 1 fennel bulb, sliced
- Salt and black pepper to taste
- ½ teaspoon of chili powder
- 1 yellow bell pepper, diced
- 1 red bell pepper, chopped
- 1 green bell pepper, chopped

Directions and Total Time: approx. 30 minutes

Warm olive oil in a large-sized skillet over medium heat. Season the salmon with chili powder, salt, and pepper and cook for 6-8 minutes, turning once. Remove to a serving plate. Add fennel and peppers to the skillet and cook for another 10 minutes until tender. Top the salmon with the mixture.

Per Serving: Calories 580, Fat 19g, Carbs 73g, Protein 35g

627. Garlic Shrimp Kabobs

Ingredients for 4 servings

- 1 pound of frozen shrimp, thawed and peeled
- ¼ cup of olive oil
- 1 tablespoon of garlic, minced
- 2 teaspoons of lemon juice
- ¼ teaspoon of black pepper
- 1 pinch of parsley, chopped

Directions and Total Time: approx. 20 minutes

Mix the parsley, black pepper, lemon juice, garlic and olive oil in a bowl. Place this mixture into a plastic bag along with the shrimp, then seal the bag, shake well and refrigerate for 2 hours. Set an outdoor grill over medium heat and grease its grilling grate with cooking oil. Assemble 5 shrimps onto each skewer and grill them for 5 minutes on each side. Serve warm.

Per Serving: Calories 233, Fat 14.7g, Carbs 1.8g, Protein 23.3g

628. Garlic Steamed Clams

Ingredients for 4 servings

- 5 tablespoons of unsalted butter
- 1 tablespoon of fresh garlic, minced
- 1 cup of white wine
- 1 tablespoon of lemon juice
- 3 dozen little neck clams
- ⅓ cup of fresh parsley, chopped
- wedges from 1 lemon for garnish

Directions and Total Time: approx. 19 minutes

Sauté the garlic with 2 ½ tsp of butter in a large skillet for 30 seconds. Stir in the lemon juice and wine then cook to a boil. Add the remaining butter and clams, cover and cook for 8 minutes. Discard the unopened clams and serve the rest with parsley and lemon wedges on top. Enjoy.

Per Serving: Calories 242, Fat 15.3g, Carbs 4.8g, Protein 10.8g

629. Garlicky Shrimp

Ingredients for 4 servings

- 2 tablespoons of olive oil
- 3 garlic cloves, sliced
- 1-pound of shrimp, peeled and deveined
- 1 tablespoon of fresh rosemary, chopped
- ½ teaspoon of red pepper flakes, crushed
- Salt and ground black pepper, as required
- 1 tablespoon of fresh lemon juice

Directions and Total Time: approx. 21 minutes

In a large-sized skillet, heat oil over medium heat and sauté the garlic slices or about 2 minutes or until golden brown. With a slotted spoon, transfer the garlic slices into a bowl. In the same skillet, add the shrimp, rosemary, red pepper flakes. salt and black pepper and cook for about 3-4 minutes, stirring frequently. Stir in the lemon juice and remove from the heat. Serve hot with a topping of the garlic slices.

Per Serving: Calories 202, Fat 9.1g, Carbs 3.2g, Protein 26.1g

630. Grilled Oysters

Ingredients for 4 servings

- 12 large oysters
- 1/2 cup of tarragon leaves
- 8 ounces of butter
- 1 shallot, diced
- 1 tablespoon of white wine vinegar
- 1/8 teaspoon of salt

Directions and Total Time: approx. 25 minutes

Add the butter, shallot, tarragon, vinegar, and sea salt and process on high until well blended in a food processor. Set the grill to medium heat. Shuck the oysters and save as much juice as possible.2 tsp. prepared tarragon butter on top of each oyster. Place the oysters on the grill cup-side down. Cover the grill and cook the oysters for about 10 minutes, or until the butter has melted and the liquids have started to bubble. Remove the cooked hot skewers from the grill and serve immediately.

Per Serving: Calories 80, Fat 5g, Carbs 5g, Protein 4g

631. Grilled Salmon

Ingredients for 6 servings

- 1 ½ pounds of salmon fillet
- 1 tablespoon of garlic powder
- 1/3 cup of soy sauce
- 1/3 cup of brown sugar
- 1/3 cup of water
- ¼ cup of olive oil
- Salt and pepper, to taste
- 1 lemon, juiced

Directions and Total Time: approx. 37 minutes

Season the salmon fillets with lemon, pepper, salt, and garlic powder. Mix the soy sauce, brown sugar, water, and olive oil in a small bowl until the sugar is dissolved. Place the fish in a big resealable plastic bag with the soy sauce mixture, seal, and let marinate for at least 2 hours. Preheat the broiler on medium heat. Lightly oil a griddle pan. Set the salmon on the pan and discard the marinade. Broil the salmon for 7 minutes per side or until the fish flakes easily with a fork.

Per Serving: Calories 318, Fat 20.1g, Carbs 13.2g, Protein 20.5g

632. Grilled Salmon with Lemon and Soy Sauce

Ingredients for 4 servings

- 2 tablespoons of olive oil
- 2 Salmon fillets
- Lemon juice
- 1/3 cup of water
- 1/3 cup of Gluten-free soy sauce
- 1/3 cup of honey
- Scallion slices
- Cherry tomato
- Freshly ground black pepper, garlic powder, kosher salt to taste

Directions and Total Time: approx. 20 minutes

Season salmon with pepper and salt. In a large-sized bowl, mix honey, soy sauce, lemon juice, water, oil. Add salmon in this marinade and let it rest for least two hours. Let the air fryer preheat at 180°C. Place fish in the air fryer and cook for 8 minutes. Move to a dish and top with scallion slices.

Per Serving: Calories 211, Fat 9g, Carbs 4.9g, Protein 15g

633. Grilled Salmon with Lemon and Wine

Ingredients for 4 servings

- 1 big lemon
- 1 ½ cup of olive oil
- ½ teaspoon of pepper
- 3 teaspoons of vegetable oil
- 4 of 6 ounces of salmon fillets
- 1 teaspoon of lime zest
- 1 ½ tablespoon of salt

Directions and Total Time: approx. 20 minutes

Prepare the grill and rub the fillets with oil. Put lime zest, lemon zest, salt, and pepper on both sides of the fillets. Brush oil on the grill, put the salmon and the fillets on the grill, and allow it to grill for about 7 minutes. Turn it to the other side and grill for about 3 minutes. The salmon can now be served with lemon wedges.

Per Serving: Calories 270, Fat 14.2g, Carbs 11.5g, Protein 28.1g

634. Grilled Shrimp Skewers

Ingredients for 4 servings

- 1 pound of large shrimp
- ¼ cup of olive oil
- ¼ cup of cilantro, chopped
- ¼ cup of parsley, chopped
- 4 garlic cloves, minced
- 1 tablespoon of lemon juice
- ½ teaspoon of salt
- ¼ teaspoon of black pepper
- Pinch of cayenne pepper

Directions and Total Time: approx. 16 minutes

In a mixing dish, combine the herbs and spices. Place the shrimp and ¾ of the prepared marinade in a large bowl. Mix well to coat and cover. Refrigerate for 30 minutes. Assemble the shrimp onto the skewers. Place a grill over medium-high heat and grease its grates. Grill the shrimp skewers for 3 minutes on each side. Serve warm with the remaining marinade on top.

Per Serving: Calories 206, Fat 12.7g, Carbs 3.5g, Protein 21.6g

635. Grilled Swordfish

Ingredients for 4 servings

- 10 garlic cloves
- 2 tablespoons of lemon juice
- 1/3 cup of olive oil
- 1 teaspoon of Spanish paprika
- ¾ teaspoon of cumin
- ¾ teaspoon of salt
- 4 swordfish steaks
- ½ teaspoon of black pepper
- Crushed red pepper, to taste

Directions and Total Time: approx. 18 minutes

Blend the olive oil, pepper, garlic, salt, cumin, paprika, and lemon juice in a blender to obtain a smooth mixture. Coat the swordfish with the blended mixture and set it aside for 15 minutes. Heat a skillet with some oil on high heat. Add the fish and cook for approximately about five minutes on each side. Sprinkle with the lemon juice and crushed red pepper and serve.

Per Serving: Calories 398, Fat 30.7g, Carbs 3.1g, Protein 28.4g

636. Grilled White Fish with Fresh Basil Pesto

Ingredients for 4 servings

- 1 cup of basil leaves
- 4 tablespoons of olive oil
- ¼ cup of grated parmesan
- ¼ cup of toasted pine nuts
- Juice of ½ lemon
- Salt & pepper
- 4 white fish fillets

Directions and Total Time: approx. 30 minutes

Place the first six pesto ingredients into a food processor and blitz until smooth. Place the pesto into a bowl, and add the fish filets, ensuring each one is coated in pesto. Place a griddle pan onto a high heat. Place the pesto-coated fish filets onto the hot griddle pan and grill on both sides until slightly charred, and the fish cooked well but still juicy. Serve the fish with the leftover pesto on top.

Per Serving: Calories 488, Fat 24g, Carbs 3g, Protein 61.9g

637. Grilled Whole Fish

Ingredients for 4 servings

- 2 teaspoons of chopped tarragon
- 1 big onion
- 2 teaspoons of chopped rosemary
- 2 teaspoons of oregano
- 4 of ½ pounds of whole fish
- ½ cup of olive oil
- 4 tablespoons of salt
- 2 teaspoons of thyme
- ½ cup of ladolemono
- 1 big lemon
- 3 teaspoons of vegetable oil

Directions and Total Time: approx. 20 minutes

Wash and rinse the fish, put it on parchment paper. Brush olive oil all over the fish, add salt, pepper. Put the fish inside the refrigerator for about 30 minutes to chill. Put the lemon slices and herbs inside the fish. Use oil to wipe the grill, grill the fish for about 5 minutes. Serve with the ladolemono sauce.

Per Serving: Calories 280, Fat 12.5g, Carbs 5g, Protein 29g

638. Halibut Pan

Ingredients for 4 servings

- 4 halibut fillets, boneless
- 1 red bell pepper, chopped
- 2 tablespoons of olive oil
- 1 yellow onion, chopped
- 4 garlic cloves, minced
- ½ cup of chicken stock
- 1 teaspoon of basil, dried
- ½ cup of cherry tomatoes, halved
- ⅓ cup of kalamata olives, pitted & halved
- Salt and black pepper to the taste

Directions and Total Time: approx. 30 minutes

Heat up a large-sized pan with the oil over medium heat, add the fish, cook for just about 5 minutes on each side, and divide between plates. Add the onion, bell pepper, garlic, and tomatoes to the pan, stir and sauté for 3 minutes. Add salt, pepper, and the rest of the ingredients, toss, cook for 3 minutes more, divide next to the fish and serve.

Per Serving: Calories 159, Fat 5g, Carbs 10g, Protein 26g

639. Halibut with Kale

Ingredients for 4 servings

- 3 tablespoons of olive oil, divided
- 3 cups of kale, coarsely chopped
- 2 cups of cherry tomatoes, halved
- 4 (4-ounce) boneless, skinless halibut fillets
- Juice and zest of 1 lemon
- Sea salt and black pepper, to taste
- 1 tablespoon of fresh basil, chopped

Directions and Total Time: approx. 25 minutes

Preheat the oven to 375°F. Lightly grease an 8x8" baking dish with two teaspoons of olive oil. Arrange the kale in the bottom of the baking dish and top with the cherry tomatoes and the halibut. Drizzle over the rest of the remaining olive oil and the lemon juice, lemon zest, basil, salt, and pepper. Bake until the bunch of fish flakes easily and the greens are wilted (about 15 minutes). Serve and enjoy.

Per Serving: Calories 228, Fat 10g, Carbs 9g, Protein 28g

640. Herb-Crusted Halibut

Ingredients for 4 servings

- ⅓ cup of fresh parsley
- ¼ cup of fresh dill
- ¼ cup of fresh chives
- 1 teaspoon of lemon zest
- ¾ cup of panko breadcrumbs
- 1 tablespoon of olive oil
- ¼ teaspoon of cracked black pepper
- 1 teaspoon of sea salt
- 4–6 ounces of halibut fillets

Directions and Total Time: approx. 25 minutes

Chop the fresh dill, chives, and parsley. Line a baking tray with foil. Set the oven to 400°F. Combine the salt, pepper, lemon zest, olive oil, chives, dill, parsley, and breadcrumbs in a mixing bowl. Rinse the halibut thoroughly. Use paper towels to dry it before baking. Arrange the fish on the baking sheet. Spoon the crumbs over the fish and press them into each of the fillets. Bake until the top is browned and easily flaked (about 10-15 minutes).

Per Serving: Calories 273, Fat 7g, Carbs 5.1g, Protein 38g

641. Herby Cod Skewers

Ingredients for 4 servings

- 1 pound of cod fillets, cut into chunks
- 2 sweet peppers, cut into chunks
- 2 tablespoons of olive oil
- 2 oranges, juiced
- 1 tablespoon of Dijon mustard
- 1 teaspoon of dried dill
- 1 teaspoon of dried parsley
- Salt and black pepper to taste

Directions and Total Time: approx. 30 minutes

Mix olive oil, orange juice, dill, parsley, mustard, salt, and pepper in a bowl. Stir in cod to coat. Allow sitting for 10 minutes. Heat the grill over medium heat. Thread the cod and peppers onto skewers. Grill for 7-8 minutes, turning regularly until the fish is cooked through.

Per Serving: Calories 244, Fat 8g, Carbs 15.5g, Protein 27g

642. Honey Garlic Shrimp

Ingredients for 4 servings

- ⅓ cup of honey
- ¼ cup of soy sauce
- 2 garlic cloves, minced
- 1 teaspoon of minced fresh ginger
- 1 pound of medium uncooked shrimp, deveined and peeled
- 2 teaspoons of olive oil
- Chopped green onion, for garnish

Directions and Total Time: approx. 16 minutes

Mix the ginger, garlic, soy sauce and honey in a medium bowl. Half of the marinade should be poured over the shrimp. Cover and marinate the shrimp in the refrigerator for 15 minutes. Assemble the shrimp onto the skewers. Place a grill over medium-heat and grease its grates. Grill the shrimp for approximately about 2-3 minutes. Pour the remaining marinade on top and garnish with green onion. Serve.

Per Serving: Calories 198, Fat 2.4g, Carbs 25.3g, Protein 19.3g

Ingredients for 4 servings

- 24 ounces of halibut fillets
- 2 garlic cloves, crushed
- 2 tablespoons of olive oil
- 2 teaspoons of capers, drained
- 3 tablespoons of fresh basil, sliced
- 2 ½ tablespoons of fresh lemon juice

Directions and Total Time: approx. 18 minutes

In a small bowl, mix together garlic, lemon juice, olive oil, 2 tablespoons of basil, pepper and salt. Preheat the grill over medium-high heat. Season fish fillets with pepper and salt and brush with garlic mixture. Place fish fillets onto the grill and cook for 4 minutes on each side.

Per Serving: Calories 254, Fat 11.1g, Carbs 0.8g, Protein 36.1g

644. Lemon-Garlic Baked Halibut

Ingredients for 2 servings

- 1 large garlic clove, minced
- 1 tablespoon of chopped flat-leaf parsley
- 1 teaspoon of olive oil
- 2 5-ounces of boneless, skin-on halibut fillets
- 2 teaspoons of lemon zest
- Juice of ½ lemon, divided
- Salt and pepper to taste

Directions and Total Time: approx. 25 minutes

Grease a large-sized baking dish with cooking spray and preheat the oven to 400°F. Place halibut with skin touching the dish and drizzle with olive oil. Season with pepper and salt. Pop into the oven and bake until flaky around 12-15 minutes. Remove from oven and drizzle with remaining lemon juice, serve and enjoy with a side of salad greens.

Per Serving: Calories 315.3, Fat 10.5g, Carbs 36.6g, Protein 14.1g

645. Lemon-Parsley Swordfish

Ingredients for 5 servings

- 1 cup of fresh Italian parsley
- ¼ cup of lemon juice
- ¼ cup of extra-virgin olive oil
- ¼ cup of fresh thyme
- 1 clove of garlic
- ½ teaspoon of salt
- 2 swordfish steaks
- Olive oil spray

Directions and Total Time: approx. 30 minutes

Preheat the oven to 450F. Grease a large pan with olive oil spray. Place the parsley, lemon juice, olive oil, thyme, garlic, and salt in a food processor and pulse until smoothly blended. Arrange the swordfish steaks in the greased baking dish and spoon the parsley mixture over the top. Bake for 18 minutes until flaky. Serve the fish among two plates and serve hot.

Per Serving: Calories 396, Fat 21.7g, Carbs 2.9g, Protein 44.2g

Ingredients for 4 servings

- 1 pound of shrimp, peeled and deveined
- 3 tablespoons of olive oil
- 1 lemon, juiced
- 1 tablespoon of flour
- 1 cup of fish stock
- Salt and black pepper to taste
- 1 cup of black olives, halved
- 1 tablespoon of rosemary, chopped

Directions and Total Time: approx. 25 minutes

Warm the olive oil in a large-sized skillet over medium heat and sear shrimp for 4 minutes on both sides; set aside. In the same large-sized skillet over low heat, stir in the flour for 2-3 minutes. Gradually pour in the fish stock and lemon juice while stirring and simmer for 3-4 minutes until the sauce thickens. Adjust the seasoning of the dish according to your taste with salt and pepper and mix in shrimp, olives, and rosemary. Serve immediately.

Per Serving: Calories 240, Fat 16g, Carbs 16g, Protein 9g

647. Lemony Salmon

Ingredients for 2 servings

- 1 cup of water
- ¼ cup of fresh lemon juice
- 2 (5-6-ounce) frozen salmon fillets
- Non-stick cooking spray
- Salt and ground black pepper, as required

Directions and Total Time: approx. 14 minutes

Arrange the trivet in the actual bottom of instant pot and pour water and lemon juice. Spray the salmon fillets with cooking spray evenly. Place the pieces of salmon fillets on top of the trivet in a single layer, skin-side down. Close the lid and adjust the vent in a sealed position. Select "Steam" and just use the default time of 3-4 minutes. After cooking time is completed, press "Cancel" and carefully do a "Quick" release. Open the lid and transfer the salmon fillets onto a platter. Sprinkle with salt and black pepper and serve.

Per Serving: Calories 232, Fat 10.7g, Carbs 0.6g, Protein 33.2g

648 Mahi-Mahi and Mushrooms

Ingredients for 4 servings

- 3 tablespoons of olive oil, divided
- ¼ cup of lemon juice
- ¼ cup of fresh chives, minced
- ¼ cup of pine nuts or any nuts
- 1 large onion, chopped
- 5 pounds of portobello mushrooms, chopped
- Salt and black pepper, to taste
- ¾ cup of bell pepper, chopped
- 4 (6 ounces) mahi-mahi fillets

Directions and Total Time: approx. 35 minutes

In a large-sized skillet on medium heat, lightly fry the fish for 8 minutes in olive oil until the fish begins to flake. Remove from the heat. Add the bell peppers, onions, lemon juice, and mushrooms into the remaining oil. Season with salt and pepper. Cook until the peppers are tender. Add the fish on top and season the fillets with salt and black pepper. Cook for a bit longer until the fish is cooked through.

Per Serving: Calories 444, Fat 16.6g, Carbs 27g, Protein 53.9g

649 Mahi-Mahi and Olives

Ingredients for 4 servings

- 4 mahi-mahi fillets, skinless
- 2 tablespoons of olive oil
- 1 yellow onion, chopped
- Salt and black pepper to taste
- ¾ cup of dry white wine
- 1 garlic clove, crushed
- 1 teaspoon of oregano, dried
- ½ cup of green olives, pitted and chopped
- 14 ounces of canned tomatoes, chopped
- 1 tablespoon of capers, drained
- ¼ cup of parsley, chopped

Directions and Total Time: approx. 30 minutes

Heat a pan with 1 tablespoon oil over medium high heat, add fish fillets, salt and pepper to taste, cook for just about 5 minutes on each side and transfer to a platter. Heat up the pan again with the rest of the oil, add the onion, garlic, oregano and wine, stir and cook for 7 minutes. Add tomatoes, olives, capers, salt and pepper, stir, cook for 5 minutes and drizzle over fish. Sprinkle parsley at the end and serve.

Per Serving: Calories 300, Fat 11g, Carbs 7g, Protein 22g

650. Marinated Tuna Steak

Ingredients for 4 servings

- 2 tablespoons of olive oil
- ½ cup of orange juice
- ½ cup of soy sauce
- 1 tablespoon of lemon juice
- 2 tablespoons of fresh parsley
- 1 garlic clove
- ½ teaspoon of ground black pepper
- ½ teaspoon of fresh oregano
- 4 (4 ounces) tuna steaks

Directions and Total Time: approx. 24 minutes

Mince the garlic and also the chopped oregano and parsley. In a glass container, mix the pepper, oregano, garlic, parsley, lemon juice, soy sauce, olive oil, and orange juice. Warm the grill using the high heat setting. Grease the grate with oil. Add the tuna steaks and cook for 5–6 minutes. Turn and baste with the marinated sauce. Cook another 5 minutes or until it's the way you like it. Discard the remaining marinade.

Per Serving: Calories 200, Fat 8g, Carbs 4g, Protein 27g

651. Mediterranean Salmon

Ingredients for 4 servings

- ¼ teaspoon of salt
- ¼ teaspoon of black pepper
- 4 (6-ounces) skinless salmon fillets
- Cooking spray
- 2 cups of cherry tomatoes, halved
- ½ cup of chopped zucchini
- 2 tablespoons of capers, undrained
- 1 tablespoon of olive oil
- 1 (2 ¼-ounces) can of sliced ripe olives, drained

Directions and Total Time: approx. 32 minutes

Preheat your oven at 425°F. Mix the fish with black pepper and salt. Grease a baking dish with cooking spray. Place the fish in this baking dish. Combine the tomatoes and the other ingredients in a bowl and distribute over the fish. Bake the fish for 22 minutes at 425 degrees° F. Serve warm.

Per Serving: Calories 341, Fat 17.6g, Carbs 5.3g, Protein 42.2g

652. Mediterranean Tuna Capellini

Ingredients for 4 servings

- 1-pound of capellini pasta
- 3 lemons, zested and juiced
- ¼ cup of olive oil
- ½ cup of Parmesan cheese
- 2 tablespoons of parsley, minced
- 2 garlic cloves, minced
- ½ teaspoon of salt
- Pinch of crushed red pepper flakes
- 1 (5-ounces) can of tuna
- ½ (15 ½-ounces) can of cannellini beans

Directions and Total Time: approx. 15 minutes

Add the pasta into a pot will filled with boiling water. Cook for 5 minutes then drain. Mix the lemon juice, olive oil, red pepper flakes, salt, garlic, lemon zest, parsley, and Parmesan cheese in a bowl. Stir in the tuna and cannellini beans then mix well. Fold in the pasta then mix again. Serve.

Per Serving: Calories 410, Fat 15.4g, Carbs 53.1g, Protein 19g

653. Minty-Cucumber Yogurt Topped Grilled Fish

Ingredients for 4 servings

- ¼ cup of 2% plain Greek yogurt
- ¼ teaspoon + 1/8 teaspoon of salt
- ¼ teaspoon of black pepper
- ½ green onion, finely chopped
- ½ teaspoon of dried oregano
- 1 tablespoon of finely chopped mint leaves
- 3 tablespoons of finely chopped English cucumber
- 4 5-ounces of cod fillets
- Cooking oil as needed

Directions and Total Time: approx. 12 minutes

Brush large-sized grill grate with oil and preheat grill to high. Season cod fillets on both sides with pepper, ¼ teaspoon salt, and oregano. Grill cod for 3 minutes per side or until cooked to desired doneness. Mix thoroughly 1/8 teaspoon salt, onion, mint, cucumber, and yogurt in a small bowl. Serve cod with a dollop of the dressing. This dish can be paired with salad greens or brown rice.

Per Serving: Calories 253.5, Fat 1g, Carbs 5g, Protein 25.5g

654. Mustard Sardine Cakes

Ingredients for 4 servings

- 3 tablespoons of olive oil
- 1 teaspoon of mustard powder
- 1 teaspoon of chili powder
- 20 ounces of canned sardines, mashed
- 2 garlic cloves, minced
- 2 tablespoons of dill, chopped
- 1 onion, chopped
- 1 cup of panko breadcrumbs
- 1 egg, whisked
- Salt and black pepper to taste
- 2 tablespoons of lemon juice

Directions and Total Time: approx. 20 minutes

Combine sardines, garlic, dill, onion, breadcrumbs, egg, mustard powder, chili powder, salt, pepper, and lemon juice in a bowl and form medium patties out of the mixture. Warm the olive oil in a skillet over medium heat and fry the cakes for 10 minutes on both sides. Serve with aioli.

Per Serving: Calories 300, Fat 14g, Carbs 23g, Protein 7g

Ingredients for 4 servings

- 2 teaspoons of lemon juice
- 4 of 6 ounces of cod fillets
- 3 cups of olive oil
- 1 teaspoon of lemon zest
- 1 tablespoon of salt

Directions and Total Time: approx. 15 minutes

Wash the fillets and put them on a paper towel. Put oil inside a big pot, add the fish's fillets to poach for about 6 minutes, or the fish color changes opaque. Take the prepared fish out of the oil and add salt to it. Put some of the left-over warm oil on the fish, add lemon juice with it. Add zest by sprinkling. It is ready to be served.

Per Serving: Calories 305, Fat 15g, Carbs 10g, Protein 31g

656. Oven-Baked Spanish Salmon

Ingredients for 4 servings

- 15 green pimiento-stuffed olives
- 2 small red onions, sliced
- 1 cup of fennel bulbs shaved
- 1 cup of cherry tomatoes
- Salt and black pepper to taste
- 1 teaspoon of cumin seeds
- ½ teaspoon of smoked paprika
- 4 salmon fillets
- ½ cup of chicken broth
- 3 tablespoons of olive oil
- 2 cups of cooked farro

Directions and Total Time: approx. 30 minutes

Preheat oven to a heat of 375 F. In a bowl, combine the onions, fennel, tomatoes, and olives. Season with salt, pepper, cumin, and paprika and mix well. Spread out on a greased baking dish. Arrange the fish fillets over the vegetables, season with salt, and gently pour the broth over. Drizzle with olive oil and bake for 20 minutes. Serve over farro.

Per Serving: Calories 475, Fat 18g, Carbs 26g, Protein 50g

657. Pan-Fried Chili Sea Scallops

Ingredients for 4 servings

- 1 ½ pound of large sea scallops, tendons removed
- 3 tablespoons of olive oil
- 1 garlic clove, finely chopped
- ½ red pepper flakes
- 2 tablespoons of chili sauce
- ¼ cup of tomato sauce
- 1 small shallot, minced
- 1 tablespoons of minced fresh cilantro
- Salt and black pepper to taste

Directions and Total Time: approx. 25 minutes

Warm the olive oil in a large-sized skillet over medium heat. Add the scallops and cook for 2 minutes without moving them. Flip them and continue to cook for 2 more minutes, without moving them, until golden browned. Set aside. Add the shallot and minced garlic to the skillet and sauté for 3-5 minutes until softened. Pour in the chili sauce, tomato sauce, and red pepper flakes and stir for 3-4 minutes. Add the scallops back and warm through. Adjust the taste and top with cilantro.

Per Serving: Calories 204, Fat 14.1g, Carbs 5g, Protein 14g

Ingredients for 4 servings

- 1 cucumber, grated and squeezed
- 3 tablespoons of olive oil
- 4 trout fillets, boneless
- ½ lime, juiced
- Salt and black pepper to taste
- 1 garlic clove, minced
- 1 teaspoon of sweet paprika
- 4 garlic cloves, minced
- 2 cups of Greek yogurt
- 1 tablespoon of dill, chopped

Directions and Total Time: approx. 20 minutes

Warm the prepared 2 tablespoons of the olive oil in a skillet over medium heat. Sprinkle the trout with salt, pepper, lime juice, garlic, and paprika and sear for 8 minutes on all sides. Remove to a paper towel–lined plate. Combine cucumber, garlic, remaining olive oil, yogurt, salt, and dill in a bowl. Share trout into plates and serve with tzatziki.

Per Serving: Calories 400, Fat 19g, Carbs 19g, Protein 41g

659. Paprika Butter Shrimps

Ingredients for 2 servings

- ¼ tablespoon of smoked paprika
- 1/8 cup of sour cream
- ½ pound of tiger shrimps
- 1/8 cup of butter
- Salt and black pepper, to taste

Directions and Total Time: approx. 37 minutes

Prep the oven to a heat of 390 F and grease a baking dish. Mix together all the ingredients in a large bowl and transfer into the baking dish. Situate in the oven and bake for approximately about 15 minutes. Place paprika shrimp in a dish and set aside to cool for meal prepping. Divide it in 2 containers and cover the lid. Refrigerate for 1-2 days and reheat in microwave before serving.

Per Serving: Calories 330, Fat 21.5g, Carbs 71.4g, Protein 32.6g

660. Parchment Orange and Dill Salmons

Ingredients for 4 servings

- 2 tablespoons of butter, melted
- 4 salmon fillets
- Salt and black pepper to taste
- 1 orange, juiced and zested
- 4 tablespoons of fresh dill, chopped

Directions and Total Time: approx. 25 minutes

Preheat oven to 375 F. Coat the salmon fillets on both sides with butter. Season with salt and pepper and divide them between 4 pieces of parchment paper. Drizzle the orange juice over each piece of fish and top with orange zest and dill. Wrap the prepared paper around the fish to make packets. Place on a large-sized baking sheet and bake for 15-20 minutes until the cod is cooked through. Serve and enjoy!

Per Serving: Calories 481, Fat 21g, Carbs 4.2g, Protein 65g

661. Parsley Littleneck Clams in Sherry Sauce

Ingredients for 4 servings

- 2 tablespoons of olive oil
- 1 cup of dry sherry
- 3 shallots, minced
- 4 garlic cloves, minced
- 4 pounds of littleneck clams, scrubbed
- 2 tablespoons of minced fresh parsley
- ½ teaspoon of cayenne pepper
- 1 Lemon, cut into wedges

Directions and Total Time: approx. 20 minutes

Bring the sherry wine, shallots, and garlic to a simmer in a large saucepan and cook for 3 minutes. Add clams, cover, and cook, stirring twice, until clams open, about 7 minutes. With a small-sized slotted spoon, transfer clams to a serving bowl, discarding any that refuse to open. Stir in olive oil, parsley, and cayenne pepper. Pour sauce over clams and serve with lemon wedges.

Per Serving: Calories 333, Fat 9g, Carbs 14g, Protein 44.9g

662. Parsley Salmon Bake

Ingredients for 4 servings

- 2 tablespoons of olive oil
- 1 pound of salmon fillets
- ¼ fresh parsley, chopped
- 1 garlic clove, minced
- ¼ teaspoon of dried dill
- ¼ teaspoon of chili powder
- ¼ teaspoon of garlic powder
- 1 lemon, grated
- Salt and black pepper to taste

Directions and Total Time: approx. 20 minutes

Preheat oven to 350 F. Sprinkle the salmon with dill, chili powder, garlic powder, salt, and pepper. Warm olive oil in a large-sized pan over medium heat and sear salmon skin-side down for 5 minutes. Transfer to the oven and bake for another 4-5 minutes. Combine parsley, lemon zest, garlic, and salt in a bowl. Serve salmon topped with the mixture.

Per Serving: Calories 212, Fat 14g, Carbs 0.5g, Protein 22g

663. Pecan Salmon Fillets

Ingredients for 6 servings

- 3 tablespoons of olive oil
- 3 tablespoons of mustard
- 5 teaspoons of honey
- 1 cup of pecans, chopped
- 6 salmon fillets, boneless
- 1 tablespoon of lemon juice
- 3 teaspoons of parsley, chopped
- Salt and pepper to the taste

Directions and Total Time: approx. 25 minutes

In a bowl, mix the oil with the mustard and honey and whisk well. Put the pecans and the parsley in another bowl. Season the boneless, salmon fillets with salt and pepper, arrange them on a baking sheet lined with parchment paper, brush with the honey and mustard mix and top with the pecans mix. Place in oven at a heat of 400 F, bake for 15 minutes, divide between plates, drizzle the lemon juice on top and serve.

Per Serving: Calories 282, Fat 15.5g, Carbs 20.9g, Protein 16.8g

664. Peppercorn-Seared Tuna Steaks

Ingredients for 2 servings

- 2 ahi tuna steaks
- 1 teaspoon of kosher salt
- ¼ teaspoon of cayenne pepper
- 2 tablespoons of olive oil
- 1 teaspoon of whole peppercorns

Directions and Total Time: approx. 10 minutes

On a plate, Season the tuna steaks on both sides with salt and cayenne pepper. In a large-sized skillet, heat the olive oil over medium-high heat until it shimmers. Add the peppercorns and cook for about 5 minutes, or until they soften and pop. Carefully put the tuna steaks in the skillet and sear for 1 to 2 minutes per each side of tuna steak, depending on the thickness of the tuna steaks, or until the fish is cooked to the desired level of doneness. Cool for 5 minutes before serving.

Per Serving: Calories 260, Fat 14.3g, Carbs 0.2g, Protein 33.4g

665. Pesto Fish Fillet

Ingredients for 2 servings

- 2 halibut fillets
- 1/2 cup of water
- 1 tablespoon of lemon zest, grated
- 1/2 tablespoon of capers
- 1/2 cup of basil, chopped
- 1/2 tablespoon of garlic, chopped
- 1/2 avocado, peeled and chopped
- Salt and black pepper to taste

Directions and Total Time: approx. 18 minutes

Add lemon zest, capers, basil, garlic, avocado, pepper, and salt into the blender and blend until smooth. Place fish fillets on aluminum foil and spread the blended mixture on fish fillets. Fold foil around the fish fillets. Pour the prepared half-cup of water into the pot and place the trivet in the pot. Place the fish foil on the trivet. Cover the medium-sized pan with a lid and cook over high heat for 8 minutes. Once done, remove the lid. Serve and enjoy.

Per Serving: Calories 426, Fat 16.6g, Carbs 5.5g, Protein 61.8g

666. Pesto Shrimp Skewers

Ingredients for 4 servings

- 1 cup of basil leaves, chopped
- 1 garlic clove
- ¼ cup of Parmigiano Reggiano, grated
- 3 tablespoons of olive oil
- 1 ½ pounds of shrimp, peeled and deveined
- Salt and pepper, to taste

Directions and Total Time: approx. 18 minutes

Blend the black pepper, salt parmesan cheese, garlic and basil in a food processor. Slowly add the olive oil and mix. Toss the shrimp with pesto in a bowl, cover and marinate in the refrigerator for 4 hours. Assemble the shrimp onto the 7 wooden skewers. Place an outdoor grill over medium-low heat and grease its grates. Grill the shrimp skewers for 4 minutes on each side. Serve warm.

Per Serving: Calories 234, Fat 12g, Carbs 0.4g, Protein 32.6g

Ingredients for 4 servings

- 1 tablespoons of olive oil
- 4 salmon steaks
- Salt and black pepper to taste
- ¼ mustard powder
- ½ teaspoon of garlic powder
- 2 Roma tomatoes, chopped
- ¼ cup of green olives, chopped
- 1 teaspoon of capers
- ½ cup of breadcrumbs
- 1 lemon, cut into wedges

Directions and Total Time: approx. 25 minutes

Preheat oven to 375 F. Arrange the salmon fillets on a greased baking dish. Season with salt, pepper, garlic powder, and mustard powder and coat with the breadcrumbs. Drizzle with olive oil. Scatter the tomatoes, green olives, garlic, and capers around the fish fillets. Bake for 15 minutes until the salmon steaks flake easily with a fork. Serve with lemon wedges.

Per Serving: Calories 504, Fat 18g, Carbs 14g, Protein 68g

668. Roasted Shrimp Skewers with Lemon

Ingredients for 5 servings

- 1 1/2 pound of shrimps
- Salt and pepper, to taste
- 2 tablespoons of fresh cilantro, finely chopped
- 3 tablespoons of lemon juice
- 3 tablespoons of fresh parsley, finely chopped
- 1//3 cup of olive oil

Directions and Total Time: approx. 30 minutes

Add the lemon juice, olive oil, parsley, cilantro, salt, and pepper to a large bowl. Then, place the shrimps in the bowl and coat well. Marinade for 20 minutes. Thread the shrimps on skewers and heat your grill pan. Grill for approximately about 2 minutes on each side or until the shrimps are pink. Serve warm and enjoy!

Per Serving: Calories 334, Fat 24.6g, Carbs 13.7g, Protein 3.7g

669. Rosemary Wine Poached Haddock

Ingredients for 4 servings

- 4 haddock fillets
- Salt and black pepper to taste
- 2 garlic cloves, minced
- ½ cup of dry white wine
- ½ cup of seafood stock
- 4 rosemary sprigs for garnish

Directions and Total Time: approx. 40 minutes

Preheat oven to 380 F. Sprinkle haddock fillets with salt and black pepper and arrange them on a baking dish. Pour in the wine, garlic, and stock. Bake covered for 20 minutes until the fish is tender; remove to a serving plate. Pour the cooking liquid into a pot over high heat. Cook for 10 minutes until reduced by half. Place on serving dishes and top with the reduced poaching liquid. Serve garnished with rosemary.

Per Serving: Calories 215, Fat 4g, Carbs 3g, Protein 35g

670. Salmon and Peach Pan

Ingredients for 4 servings

- 1 tablespoon of balsamic vinegar
- 1 teaspoon of thyme, chopped
- 1 tablespoon of ginger, grated
- 2 tablespoons of olive oil
- Sea salt and black pepper to the taste
- 3 peaches, cut into medium wedges
- 4 salmon fillets, boneless

Directions and Total Time: approx. 21 minutes

Heat up a large-sized pan with the oil over medium-high heat, add the salmon and cook for 3 minutes on each side. Add the vinegar, the peaches, and the rest of the ingredients, cook for 5 minutes more, divide everything between plates and serve.

Per Serving: Calories 450, Fat 8g, Carbs 68g, Protein 2g

671. Salmon Packets

Ingredients for 4 servings

- 2 tablespoons of olive oil
- ½ cup of apple juice
- 4 salmon fillets
- 4 teaspoons of lemon zest
- 4 tablespoons of chopped parsley
- Salt and black pepper to taste

Directions and Total Time: approx. 25 minutes

Preheat oven to 380F. Brush salmon with tablespoons of olive oil and season with salt and pepper. Cut four pieces of nonstick baking paper and divide the salmon between them. Top each one with apple juice, lemon zest, and parsley. Wrap the paper to make packets and arrange them on a baking sheet. Cook for 15 minutes until the salmon is cooked through. Remove the packets to a serving plate, open them, and drizzle with cooking juices to serve.

Per Serving: Calories 495, Fat 21g, Carbs 5g, Protein 55g

672. Salmon Stuffed Peppers

Ingredients for 4 servings

- 4 bell peppers
- 10 ounces of canned salmon, drained
- 12 black olives, chopped
- 1 red onion, finely chopped
- ½ teaspoon of garlic, minced
- 1/3 cup of mayonnaise
- 1 cup of cream cheese
- 1 teaspoon of Mediterranean seasoning
- Salt and pepper flakes to taste

Directions and Total Time: approx. 25 minutes

Preheat oven to 390 F. Cut the peppers into halves and remove the seeds. In a mixing bowl, combine the salmon, onion, garlic, mayonnaise, olives, salt, red pepper, Mediterranean spice mix, and cream cheese. Divide the mixture between the peppers and bake them in the oven for 10-12 minutes or until cooked through. Serve and enjoy!

Per Serving: Calories 272, Fat 14g, Carbs 5g, Protein 29g

673. Salmon with Dill Sauce

Ingredients for 4 servings

- 1 ½ pounds of salmon
- 4 teaspoons of olive oil
- ½ cup of non-fat Greek yogurt
- ½ cup of light sour cream
- 2 tablespoons of dill, finely chopped
- Pinch of sea salt

Directions and Total Time: approx. 43 minutes

Preheat your air fryer to 270°Fahrenheit. Cut salmon into four 6-ounce portions and drizzle 1 teaspoon of olive oil over each piece. Season with sea salt. Place salmon into cooking basket and cook for 23-minutes. Make dill sauce. In a mixing bowl, mix sour cream, yogurt, chopped dill and sea salt. Top cooked salmon with sauce and garnish with additional dill and serve.

Per Serving: Calories 303, Fat 10.2g, Carbs 8.9g, Protein 14.8g

674. Salmon with Lemon and Dill

Ingredients for 4 servings

- Cooking spray
- 1 teaspoon of olive oil
- 2 pounds of salmon
- 1 tablespoon of fresh dill, chopped
- Salt and pepper to taste
- 1 clove of garlic, minced
- 1 lemon, sliced

Directions and Total Time: approx. 2 hours and 15 minutes

Spray your slow cooker with oil. Brush both of each side of salmon with olive oil. Season the salmon with salt, pepper, dill and garlic. Add to the slow cooker. Put the lemon slices on top. Cover the pot and cook on a heat of high heat for 2 hours.

Per Serving: Calories 313, Fat 15.2g, Carbs 0.7g, Protein 44.2g

675. Saucy Cod with Calamari Rings

Ingredients for 4 servings

- 1 pound of cod, skinless and cubed
- 2 tablespoons of olive oil
- 1 mango, peeled and cubed
- ½ pound of calamari rings
- 1 tablespoon of garlic chili sauce
- ¼ cup of lime juice
- ½ teaspoon of smoked paprika
- ½ teaspoon of cumin, ground
- 2 garlic cloves, minced
- Salt and black pepper to taste

Directions and Total Time: approx. 20 minutes

Warm the olive oil in a large-sized skillet over medium heat and cook chili sauce, lime juice, paprika, cumin, garlic, salt, pepper, and mango for 3 minutes. Stir in cod and calamari and cook for another 7 minutes. Serve warm.

Per Serving: Calories 290, Fat 13g, Carbs 12g, Protein 16g

676. Seafood Paella

Ingredients for 4 servings

- 2 tablespoons of olive oil
- 1 onion, finely chopped
- 3 garlic cloves, minced
- 1 red bell pepper, chopped
- ½ pound of squid rings
- 1 teaspoon of saffron
- 1 teaspoon of paprika
- 1 cup of Spanish rice
- 1 cup of peeled shrimp
- 1 pound of mussels, cleaned
- ½ cup of green peas
- 2 tablespoons of parsley, chopped
- 1 lemon, cut into wedges
- Salt and black pepper to taste

Directions and Total Time: approx. 22 minutes

Warm the olive oil in a large-sized saucepan over medium heat. Sauté the onion, bell pepper, and garlic for 3 minutes. Add squid and fry for 5-6 minutes until golden. Stir in paprika, rice, saffron, and 2 cups of water. Bring to a boil and actually simmer for just approximately about 15-18 minutes. Stir in shrimp, mussels, and green peas for 5-8 minutes. Season with salt and pepper. Sprinkle with tablespoons of chopped parsley and then serve with lemon wedges.

Per Serving: Calories 507, Fat 11g, Carbs 51g, Protein 49g

677. Shrimp Alfredo

Ingredients for 4 servings

- 12 shrimps, shells removed
- 1 tablespoon of garlic, minced
- ¼ cup of parmesan cheese, grated
- 2 cups of whole-wheat fettuccini pasta
- 1 cup of fish broth
- 15 ounces of alfredo sauce
- 1 onion, chopped
- Salt and black pepper, to taste

Directions and Total Time: approx. 14 minutes

Add the listed ingredients above except the parmesan cheese to the Instant Pot. Stir well. Seal the pot with the lid and cook on High for 4 minutes. Once done, release the pressure using quick release Remove the lid and serve.

Per Serving: Calories 669, Fat 23.1g, Carbs 76g, Protein 37.8g

678. Shrimp Quinoa Bowl with Black Olives

Ingredients for 4 servings

- 10 black olives, pitted and halved
- ¼ cup of olive oil
- 1 cup of quinoa
- 1 lemon, cut in wedges
- 1 pound of shrimp, peeled and cooked
- 2 tomatoes, sliced
- 2 bell peppers, thinly sliced
- 1 red onion, chopped
- 1 teaspoon of dried dill
- 1 tablespoon of fresh parsley, chopped
- Salt and black pepper to taste

Directions and Total Time: approx. 20 minutes

Place the quinoa in a large-sized pot and cover with 2 cups of water over medium heat. Bring to a boil, you can actually reduce the heat, and simmer for 12-15 minutes or until tender. Remove from the heat temperature and fluff it with a fork. Mix in the quinoa with olive oil, dill, parsley, salt, and black pepper. Stir in tomatoes, bell peppers, olives, and onion. Serve decorated with shrimp and lemon wedges.

Per Serving: Calories 662, Fat 21g, Carbs 38g, Protein 79g

679. Shrimp Scampi

Ingredients for 6 servings

- 4 tablespoons of butter
- 2 tablespoons of olive oil
- 6 garlic cloves, minced
- 3/4 cup of dry white wine
- ½ teaspoon of salt
- ½ teaspoon of crushed red pepper flakes
- 1 ½ pounds of large shrimp, shelled and deveined
- ¼ cup of fresh parsley, chopped
- 2 tablespoons of lemon juice

Directions and Total Time: approx. 21 minutes

Sauté the garlic with butter and olive oil in a large skillet for 1 minute. Stir in the wine and let it simmer for 6 minutes. Add the black pepper, red pepper flakes and salt. Stir in the shrimp and sauté for 4 minutes. Add the lemon juice and parsley then serve with bread. Enjoy.

Per Serving: Calories 231, Fat 12.5g, Carbs 4.2g, Protein 21.7g

680. Shrimp with Endives

Ingredients for 4 servings

- 30 big shrimp, peeled and deveined
- Salt and black pepper to taste
- A pinch of cayenne pepper
- ¼ cup olive oil
- 2 tablespoons shallots, chopped
- 1 teaspoon lime zest
- 4 teaspoons lime juice
- ½ pound frisee or curly endive, torn into small pieces
- 1 honeydew melon, peeled, seeded and chopped
- ¼ cup mint, chopped
- 8 ounces feta cheese, crumbled
- 1 tablespoon coriander seeds

Directions and Total Time: approx. 14 minutes

Heat a pan with 2 tablespoons oil over medium high heat, add shrimp, lime zest, 1 teaspoon lime juice, shallots, salt and pepper, stir cook for 2 minutes and take off the heat. In a medium-sized bowl, mix the remaining oil with the rest of the lime juice, salt and pepper to taste, honeydew and endives, toss and divide between plates. Add shrimp, coriander seeds, mint and feta on top and serve.

Per Serving: Calories 245, Fat 23g, Carbs 23g, Protein 45g

681. Simple Fried Cod Fillets

Ingredients for 4 servings

- ½ cup of all-purpose flour
- 1 teaspoon of garlic powder
- 1 teaspoon of salt
- 4 pieces of cod fillets
- 1 tablespoon of extra-virgin olive oil

Directions and Total Time: approx. 15 minutes

Mix together the flour, garlic powder, and salt in a shallow dish. Season the flour with salt and pepper and coat each piece of fish until it's equally covered. Heat the olive oil in a small-sized skillet over medium-high heat. Once hot, add the cod fillets and fry for 6 to 8 minutes, flipping the fish halfway through, or until the fish is opaque and flakes easily. Remove from the heat and serve on plates.

Per Serving: Calories 332, Fat 18.7g, Carbs 19g, Protein 21.1g

682. Simple Salmon with Balsamic Haricots Vert

Ingredients for 4 servings

- 2 tablespoons of olive oil
- 3 tablespoons of balsamic vinegar
- 1 garlic clove, minced
- ½ teaspoon of red pepper flakes
- 1 ½ pound of haricots vert, chopped
- Salt and black pepper to taste
- 1 red onion, sliced
- 4 salmon fillets, boneless

Directions and Total Time: approx. 25 minutes

Warm half of oil in a skillet over medium heat and sauté vinegar, onion, garlic, red pepper flakes, haricots vert, salt, and pepper for 6 minutes. Share into plates. Warm the remaining oil. Sprinkle salmon according to you with salt and pepper and sear for 8 minutes on all sides. Serve with haricots vert.

Per Serving: Calories 230, Fat 16g, Carbs 23g, Protein 17g

683. Sole Fillets with Lemon Sauce

Ingredients for 2 servings

- 3 tablespoons of olive oil
- 1/3 teaspoon of Kosher salt
- 4 tablespoons of lemon juice
- ½ pound of petrale sole fillets
- ½ teaspoon oregano
- Salt and pepper, to taste
- 4 tablespoons melted ghee

Directions and Total Time: approx. 20 minutes

Heat the olive oil in a small-sized saucepan over medium-high heat, season the sole fillets with salt and pepper. Fry for 2-3 minutes per side and set aside. In a small skillet add the melted ghee. Then, stir in the lemon juice, oregano, and Kosher salt. Combine well and cook for 2 minutes. Serve the fish fillets and top with the lemon sauce. Bon appetite!

Per Serving: Calories 275, Fat 22.6g, Carbs 14.5g, Protein 2.3g

684. Spaghetti with Tuna and Capers

Ingredients for 4 servings

- 1 tablespoon of olive oil
- 1 small red onion, sliced
- 1 (5-ounces) can of tuna
- 1 tablespoon of capers, drained
- ¼ teaspoon of crushed red pepper flakes
- ½ pound of spaghetti
- ½ tablespoon of parsley, chopped

Directions and Total Time: approx. 32 minutes

Set a large pan with olive oil over medium heat. Add the onion and sauté for 10 minutes. Stir in the red pepper flakes, capers, tuna and oil. Put the spaghetti in a saucepan of boiling water. Boil for 10 minutes and drain. Set aside ½ cup of the cooking liquid. Add this liquid to the tuna mixture then sauté for 2 minutes. Serve heated with minced parsley.

Per Serving: Calories 698, Fat 23.6g, Carbs 88g, Protein 31.6g

685. Spiced Lemon-Baked Salmon

Ingredients for 4 servings

- ¼ teaspoon of dried thyme
- Zest and juice of ½ lemon
- ¼ teaspoon of salt
- ½ teaspoon of freshly ground black pepper
- 1 pound of salmon fillet
- Nonstick cooking spray

Directions and Total Time: approx. 25 minutes

Preheat the oven to a heat of 425°F (220°C). Coat a baking sheet with nonstick cooking spray. Mix together the thyme, lemon zest and juice, salt, and pepper in a small bowl and stir to incorporate. Arrange the salmon, skin-side down, on the coated baking sheet. Spoon the thyme mixture over the salmon and spread it all over. Bake in the preheated oven for about 15 to 20 minutes, or until the fish flakes apart easily. Serve warm.

Per Serving: Calories 161, Fat 6.9g, Carbs 0.9g, Protein 23g

686. Spicy Cod Fillets

Ingredients for 4 servings

- 2 tablespoons of olive oil
- 1 teaspoon of lime juice
- Salt and black pepper to taste
- 1 teaspoon of sweet paprika
- 1 teaspoon of chili powder
- 1 onion, chopped
- 2 garlic cloves, minced
- 4 cod fillets, boneless
- 1 teaspoon of ground coriander
- ½ cup of fish stock
- ½ pound of cherry tomatoes, cubed

Directions and Total Time: approx. 35 minutes

Warm olive oil in a large-sized skillet over medium heat. Season the cod with salt, pepper, and chili powder and cook in the skillet for 8 minutes on all sides; set aside. In the same large-sized skillet, cook onion and garlic for 3 minutes. Stir in lime juice, paprika, coriander, fish stock, and cherry tomatoes and bring to a boil. Simmer for 10 minutes. Serve topped with cod fillets.

Per Serving: Calories 240, Fat 17g, Carbs 26g, Protein 17g

687. Steamed Mussels with Spaghetti

Ingredients for 4 servings

- 2 pounds of mussels, cleaned and beards removed
- 1 pound of cooked spaghetti
- 3 tablespoons of butter
- 2 garlic cloves, minced
- 1 carrot, diced
- 1 onion, chopped
- 2 celery sticks, chopped
- 1 cup of white wine
- 2 tablespoons of parsley, chopped
- ½ teaspoon of red pepper flakes
- 1 lemon, juiced

Directions and Total Time: approx. 30 minutes

Melt butter in a large-sized saucepan over medium heat and sauté the garlic, carrot, onion, and celery for 4-5 minutes, stirring occasionally until softened. Add the mussels, white wine, and lemon juice, cover, and bring to a boil. Reduce the heat and steam the for 4-6 minutes. Discard any unopened mussels. Stir in spaghetti to coat. Sprinkle with parsley and red pepper flakes to serve.

Per Serving: Calories 669, Fat 16g, Carbs 77g, Protein 41g

688. Steamed Trout with Lemon Herb Crust

Ingredients for 2 servings

- 3 tablespoons of olive oil
- 3 garlic cloves, chopped
- 2 tablespoons of fresh lemon juice
- 1 tablespoon of chopped fresh mint
- 1 tablespoon of chopped fresh parsley
- ¼ teaspoon of dried ground thyme
- 1 teaspoon of sea salt
- 1 pound of fresh trout (2 pieces)
- 2 cups of fish stock

Directions and Total Time: approx. 25 minutes

Stir well the olive oil, lemon juice, mint, garlic, parsley, thyme, and salt in a small bowl. Brush the marinade onto the fish. Insert a trivet in the Instant Pot. Pour in the fish stock and place the fish on the trivet. Secure the lid. Select the Steam mode and set the cooking time for 15 minutes at High Pressure. Once cooking is complete, do a quick pressure release. Carefully open the lid. Serve warm.

Per Serving: Calories 477, Fat 29.6g, Carbs 3.6g, Protein 51.7g

689. Stewed Mussels and Scallops

Ingredients for 4 servings

- 2 cups of mussels
- 1 cup of scallops
- 2 cups of fish stock
- 2 bell peppers, diced
- 2 cups of cauliflower rice
- 1 onion, chopped
- 1 tablespoon of olive oil
- Pepper
- Salt

Directions and Total Time: approx. 21 minutes

Add oil into the inner pot of instant pot and set the pot on sauté mode. Add onion and peppers and sauté for 3 minutes. Add scallops and cook for 2 minutes. Add remaining ingredients and stir well. Seal the large-sized pot with lid and cook on high for 6 minutes. Once done, allow to release pressure naturally. Remove lid. Stir and serve.

Per Serving: Calories 191, Fat 7.4g, Carbs 13.7g, Protein 18g

690. Tangy Tilapia Fish Fillets with Crusty Coating

Ingredients for 4 servings

- ¼ cup of ground flaxseed
- 1 cup of almonds, finely chopped (divided)
- 4-6 ounces of tilapia fillets
- ½ teaspoon of salt
- 2 tablespoons of olive oil

Directions and Total Time: approx. 15 minutes

Combine the flaxseed with half of the almonds in a shallow mixing bowl to serve as a crusty coating instead of a flour mixture. Sprinkle the tilapia fillets evenly with salt. Dredge the fillet in the flaxseed-almond mixture. Set aside. Heat the olive oil in a heavy, thick-bottomed skillet placed over medium heat. Add the coated fillets, and cook for 4 minutes on each side until golden brown, flipping once. Remove the fillets, and transfer them to a serving plate. In the same skillet, add the remaining almonds. Toast for a minute until turning golden brown, stirring frequently. Sprinkle the toasted almonds over the fish fillets.

Per Serving: Calories 258, Fat 21.3g, Carbs 7.1g, Protein 11.6g

Ingredients for 4 servings

- 1 ½ teaspoons of paprika
- 1 ½ teaspoons of ground cumin
- 2 shallots, finely chopped
- 2 tablespoons of fresh lemon juice
- 1 pound of tilapia, cut into 8 pieces
- Salt and black pepper, to taste
- 3 garlic cloves, minced
- 1 ½ tablespoons of unsalted butter, melted
- ¼ cup of capers

Directions and Total Time: approx. 30 minutes

Preheat the oven to a heat of 375°F and line a baking sheet with parchment paper. Combine the paprika, cumin, salt, and black pepper in a small bowl and toss well. Mix the butter, garlic, shallots, butter, and lemon juice in another small bowl and mix well. Dust the tilapia fillets evenly with the spice mixture and coat generously with the butter mixture. Arrange the pieces of tilapia fillets in a single layer onto the baking sheet and top with the capers. Bake for approximately about 15 minutes and serve hot.

Per Serving: Calories 151, Fat 5.8g, Carbs 3.8g, Protein 22.2g

692. Tilapia with with Smoked Gouda

Ingredients for 6 servings

- 1 shallot
- 1 cup of fish stock
- 2 turnips
- 1 leek
- 3 cloves of garlic
- 1 ¼ pound of tilapia
- 6 medium-sized tomatoes
- ¼ bunch of parsley
- ¼ cup of red wine
- 1 teaspoon of Olive oil
- 3 ounces of smoked gouda

Directions and Total Time: approx. 45 minutes

Wash and rinse the fish in ice water. Dice all the tomatoes, remove the covering of the turnips. Slice leek, mince all the shallot and the garlic, make the parsley chopped, and the cheese should be grated. Put the olive oil inside the baking dish, place shallot, garlic, fish, turnip. Add the wine and stock, also bake for 30 minutes. Open the cover and add cheese, tomatoes. Put it back inside the oven until the cheese has melted. It is ready to be served.

Per Serving: Calories 100, Fat 2g, Carbs 52g, Protein 20g

693. Traditional Tuscan Scallops

Ingredients for 4 servings

- 2 tablespoons of olive oil
- 1 pound of sea scallops, rinsed
- 4 cups of Tuscan kale
- 1 orange, juiced
- Salt and black pepper to taste
- ¼ teaspoon of red pepper flakes

Directions and Total Time: approx. 25 minutes

Sprinkle scallops with salt and pepper. Warm olive oil in a large-sized skillet over medium heat and brown scallops for 6-8 minutes on all sides. Remove to a large-sized plate and keep warm, covering with foil. In the same skillet, add the kale, red pepper flakes, orange juice, salt, and pepper and cook approximately until the kale wilts, about 4-5 minutes. Share the kale mixture into 4 plates and top with the scallops. Serve warm.

Per Serving: Calories 214, Fat 8g, Carbs 15.2g, Protein 21g

694. Trout Fillets with Horseradish Sauce

Ingredients for 4 servings

- 3 tablespoons of olive oil
- 2 tablespoons of horseradish sauce
- 1 onion, sliced
- 2 teaspoons of Italian seasoning
- 4 trout fillets, boneless
- ¼ cup of panko breadcrumbs
- ½ cup of green olives, pitted and chopped
- Salt and black pepper to taste
- 1 lemon, juiced

Directions and Total Time: approx. 35 minutes

Preheat the oven to 380F. Line a baking sheet with parchment paper. Sprinkle trout fillets with salt and pepper and dip in breadcrumbs. Arrange them along with the onion on the sheet. Sprinkle with olive oil, Italian seasoning, and lemon juice and bake for 15-18 minutes. Transfer to a medium-sized serving plate and top with horseradish sauce and olives. Serve right away.

Per Serving: Calories 310, Fat 10g, Carbs 25g, Protein 6g

695. Tuna and Couscous

Ingredients for 4 servings

- 1 cup of chicken stock
- 1 ¼ cups of couscous
- A pinch of salt and black pepper
- 10 ounces of canned tuna, drained and flaked
- 1-pint of cherry tomatoes, halved
- ½ cup of pepperoncini, sliced
- ⅓ cup of parsley, chopped
- 1 tablespoon of olive oil
- ¼ cup of capers, drained
- ½ lemon, juiced

Directions and Total Time: approx. 10 minutes

Put the stock in a medium-sized pan and bring to a boil over medium-high heat. Add the couscous, stir, take off the heat, cover, and set aside for 10 minutes. Fluff it using a fork and transfer to a bowl. Add the tuna and the rest of the ingredients, toss and serve right away.

Per Serving: Calories 253, Fat 11.5g, Carbs 16.5g, Protein 23.2g

696. Tuna Gyros with Tzatziki

Ingredients for 4 servings

- 4 ounces of tzatziki
- ½ pound of canned tuna, drained
- ½ cup of tahini
- 4 sundried tomatoes, diced
- 2 tablespoons of warm water
- 2 garlic cloves, minced
- 1 tablespoon of lemon juice
- 4 pita wraps
- 5 black olives, chopped
- Salt and black pepper to taste

Directions and Total Time: approx. 15 minutes

In a bowl, combine the tahini, water, garlic, lemon juice, salt, and black pepper. Warm the pita wraps in a grilled pan for a few minutes, turning once. Spread the tahini and tzatziki sauces over the warmed pitas and top with tuna, sundried tomatoes, and olives. Fold in half and serve immediately.

Per Serving: Calories 334, Fat 24g, Carbs 9g, Protein 21.3g

697. Tuna Patties

Ingredients for 6 servings

- 1 egg, lightly beaten
- 10 ounces of can tuna, drained
- 3 tablespoons of flax meal
- ½ cup of Feta cheese, crumbled
- ½ teaspoon of lemon zest
- 1 teaspoon of dried oregano
- 2 tablespoons of fresh mint, chopped
- 3 tablespoons of olive oil
- 1 garlic clove, minced
- 1 tablespoon of lemon juice
- 2 tablespoons of green onion, minced

Directions and Total Time: approx. 20 minutes

Add all ingredients except oil into the mixing bowl and mix until well combined. Make small patties from the tuna mixture and set them aside. Heat oil in a medium-sized pan over medium heat. Place patties onto the hot pan and cook for 10 minutes. Turn patties halfway through.

Per Serving: Calories 177, Fat 121g, Carbs 2.3g, Protein 15.7g

698. Tuna with Tomatoes

Ingredients for 4 servings

- 4 tuna steaks, boneless and skinless
- 2 tablespoons of extra virgin olive oil
- Salt and black pepper to taste
- 2 cups of cherry tomatoes, yellow and red, cut in halves
- 1 shallot, chopped
- ½ cup of green olives, pitted and chopped
- ½ tablespoon of lemon juice
- 2 tablespoons of basil, chopped

Directions and Total Time: approx. 16 minutes

Heat a large-sized pan with the oil over medium high heat, add tuna steaks, salt and pepper, cook for about 4 minutes and transfer to a platter. Heat the large-sized pan again over medium heat, add shallots, olives and the rest of the ingredients, stir, cook for approximately 3 minutes and take off the heat. Divide this mix into serving plates, add tuna on the side and serve.

Per Serving: Calories 300, Fat 14g, Carbs 4g, Protein 42g

699. Vinegary Honey-Balsamic Glazed Salmon

Ingredients for 4 servings

- ½ cup of balsamic vinegar
- 1 tablespoon of honey
- 4 pieces of salmon fillets
- Salt and ground pepper, to taste
- 1 tablespoon of olive oil

Directions and Total Time: approx. 10 minutes

Heat a skillet over medium-high heat. In a large-sized mixing bowl, combine the vinegar and honey. Season the salmon fillets with the sea salt and freshly ground pepper; brush with the honey-balsamic glaze. Cook the salmon fillets for 3 to 4 minutes on each side, or until they are lightly browned on the outside and medium rare in the interior, in a pan with olive oil over medium heat. Let sit for 5 minutes before serving.

Per Serving: Calories 453, Fat 17.2g, Carbs 9.6g, Protein 65.2g

700. Walnut-Crusted Salmon

Ingredients for 4 servings

- 2 tablespoons of olive oil
- 4 salmon fillets, boneless
- 2 tablespoons of mustard
- 5 teaspoons of honey
- 1 cup of walnuts, chopped
- 1 tablespoon of lemon juice
- 2 teaspoons of parsley, chopped
- Salt and pepper to the taste

Directions and Total Time: approx. 25 minutes

Preheat the oven to 380F. Line a baking tray with parchment paper. In a large-sized bowl, whisk the olive oil, mustard, and honey. In a separate bowl, combine walnuts and parsley. Sprinkle salmon according to you with salt and pepper and place them on the tray. Rub each fillet with mustard mixture and scatter with walnut mixture; bake for 15 minutes. Drizzle with lemon juice.

Per Serving: Calories 300, Fat 16g, Carbs 22g, Protein 17g

701. Asparagus and Chicken Skillet

Ingredients for 4 servings

- 2 tablespoons of olive oil
- 1 pound of chicken breasts, sliced
- Salt and black pepper to taste
- 1 pound of asparagus, chopped
- 6 sundried tomatoes, diced
- 3 tablespoons of capers, drained
- 2 tablespoons of lemon juice

Directions and Total Time: approx. 30 minutes

Warm the olive oil in a large-sized skillet over medium heat. Cook asparagus, tomatoes, salt, pepper, capers, and lemon juice for 10 minutes. Remove to a bowl. Brown chicken in the same skillet for 8 minutes on both sides. Put veggies back to skillet and cook for another 2-3 minutes. Serve and enjoy!

Per Serving: Calories 560, Fat 29g, Carbs 34g, Protein 45g

702. Baked Root Veggie and Chicken

Ingredients for 6 servings

- 2 sweet potatoes, peeled and cubed
- ½ cup of green olives, pitted and smashed
- ¼ cup of olive oil
- 2 pounds of chicken breasts, sliced
- 2 tablespoons of harissa seasoning
- 1 lemon, zested and juiced
- Salt and black pepper to taste
- 2 carrots, chopped
- 1 onion, chopped
- ½ cup of feta cheese, crumbled
- ½ cup of parsley, chopped

Directions and Total Time: approx. 50 minutes

Preheat the oven to 390 F. Place chicken, harissa seasoning, lemon juice, lemon zest, olive oil, salt, pepper, carrots, sweet potatoes, and onion in a roasting pan and mix well. Bake for 40 minutes. Combine feta cheese and green olives in a bowl. Share chicken mixture into plates and top with olive mixture. Top with parsley and parsley and serve immediately.

Per Serving: Calories 310, Fat 10g, Carbs 23g, Protein 15g

703. Basil Turkey

Ingredients for 4 servings

- 1 pound of turkey breast, skinless, and cut into strips
- 1 cup of coconut cream
- 1 cup of chicken stock
- 2 tablespoons of parsley, chopped
- 1 teaspoon of chili powder
- 1 bunch of asparagus, trimmed and halved
- 2 tablespoons of olive oil
- A pinch of salt and pepper

Directions and Total Time: approx. 50 minutes

Heat up a large-sized pan with the oil over medium-high heat, add the turkey and some black pepper, toss and cook for 5 minutes. Add the chili powder, asparagus, and the other ingredients, toss, bring to a simmer and cook over medium heat for 30 minutes more. Divide everything between plates and serve.

Per Serving: Calories 290, Fat 12.1g, Carbs 12.7g, Protein 24g

704. Basil Turkey and Zucchinis

Ingredients for 4 servings

- 2 tablespoons of avocado oil
- 1-pound of turkey breast, skinless, boneless and sliced
- Salt and black pepper to the taste
- 3 garlic cloves, minced
- 2 zucchinis, sliced
- 1 cup of chicken stock
- ¼ cup of heavy cream
- 2 tablespoons of basil, chopped

Directions and Total Time: approx. 70 minutes

Heat a pot with the oil over medium-high heat, add the turkey and brown for 5 minutes on each side. Add the garlic and cook everything for 1 minute. Add the rest of the ingredients except the basil, toss gently, bring to a simmer and cook over medium-low heat for 50 minutes. Add the basil, toss, divide the mix between plates and serve.

Per Serving: Calories 262, Fat 9.8g, Carbs 25.8g, Protein 14.6g

705. Bruschetta Chicken Breasts

Ingredients for 4 servings

- 4 (6-ounce) chicken breasts
- Olive oil cooking spray
- Salt and black pepper, to taste
- ¼ cup of fresh basil leaves, chopped
- 1 teaspoon of balsamic vinegar
- 5 small tomatoes, chopped
- 1 garlic clove, minced
- 1 teaspoon of olive oil

Directions and Total Time: approx. 55 minutes

Preheat the oven to a heat of 375°F and grease a baking dish with the olive oil cooking spray. Season the pieces of chicken breasts with the salt and black pepper. Arrange the chicken breasts in a single layer in the baking dish. Cover the baking dish and bake for about 40 minutes. In the meantime, in a bowl, add the tomatoes, garlic, basil, vinegar, oil, and salt. Mix well and refrigerate until using. Remove the pieces of chicken breasts from the oven and transfer them to serving plates. Serve topped with the tomato mixture.

Per Serving: Calories 355, Fat 14g, Carbs 4.7g, Protein 50.3g

706. Buttered Creamy Chicken

Ingredients for 4 servings

- ½ cup of heavy whipping cream
- 1 tablespoon of salt
- ½ cup of bone broth
- Salt and black pepper, to taste
- 4 tablespoons of cashew butter
- 4 chicken breast halves

Directions and Total Time: approx. 30 minutes

Place a pan with one tablespoon of the cashew butter on medium heat. Once the cashew butter is warm and melted, place the chicken in and cook for 7 minutes on each side. Once the chicken is actually cooked through and golden, place it on a plate. Add the bone broth, heavy whipping cream, salt, and pepper into the warm pan, and let the sauce simmer. In about 5 minutes, the sauce should thicken up. Add the rest of the cashew butter and the chicken back into the pan. Spoon the prepared sauce over the chicken and cover it completely. Serve and enjoy!

Per Serving: Calories 350, Fat 25g, Carbs 17g, Protein 25g

707. Cannellini Bean and Chicken Cassoulet

Ingredients for 4 servings

- 1 pound of chicken thighs
- 2 tablespoons of olive oil
- 2 tablespoons of tomato paste
- 1 celery stalk, chopped
- 1 sweet onion, chopped
- 2 garlic cloves, chopped
- ½ cup of chicken stock
- 14 ounces of canned cannellini beans
- Salt and black pepper to taste

Directions and Total Time: approx. 40 minutes

Warm the olive oil in a pot over medium heat. Cook onion, celery, and garlic for 3 minutes. Put in chicken and cook for 6 minutes on all sides. Stir in tomato paste, stock, beans, salt, and pepper and bring to a boil. Cook for 30 minutes.

Per Serving: Calories 260, Fat 11g, Carbs 26g, Protein 25g

708. Caprese Chicken

Ingredients for 4 servings

- 2 boneless chicken breasts, sliced
- Salt and black pepper, to taste
- 1 tablespoon of olive oil
- 1 tablespoon of extra-virgin olive oil
- 6 ounces of pesto
- 8 tomatoes, chopped
- 6 mozzarella cheese, grated
- Balsamic glaze, as needed
- Kosher salt, to taste
- Fresh basil, as required

Directions and Total Time: approx. 30 minutes

Preheat the oven to 400°F. Mix the salt, sliced chicken, and pepper in a bowl. Set aside for 10 minutes. Melt the olive oil in a skillet over medium heat. Cook the chicken pieces in the melted olive oil for 5 minutes on each side. Remove from the heat. Spread the pesto over the chicken and place the mozzarella cheese and tomatoes on top. Bake in the preheated oven for 12 minutes. Serve and enjoy.

Per Serving: Calories 232, Fat 15g, Carbs 5g, Protein 18g

709. Cardamon Chicken Breasts

Ingredients for 4 servings

- 2 tablespoons of olive oil
- 2 chicken breasts, halved
- Juice of ½ lemon
- Zest of ½ lemon, grated
- 2 teaspoons of cardamom, ground
- Salt and black pepper to taste
- 2 spring onions, chopped
- 2 tablespoons of tomato paste
- 2 garlic cloves, minced
- 1 cup of pineapple juice
- ½ cup of chicken stock
- ¼ cup of cilantro, chopped

Directions and Total Time: approx. 8 hours and 10 minutes

Place chicken, lemon juice, lemon zest, cardamom, salt, pepper, olive oil, spring onions, tomato paste, garlic, pineapple juice, and stock in your slow cooker. Cover with the lid and cook for 8 hours on Low. Garnish with cilantro.

Per Serving: Calories 340, Fat 13g, Carbs 25g, Protein 18g

710. Carrot, Potato and Chicken Bake

Ingredients for 4 servings

- 2 tablespoons of olive oil
- 1 pound of chicken breasts, cubed
- 1 carrot, chopped
- 2 garlic cloves, minced
- Salt and black pepper to taste
- 2 teaspoons of thyme, dried
- 1 baby potatoes, halved
- 1 onion, sliced
- ¾ cup of chicken stock
- 2 tablespoons of basil, chopped

Directions and Total Time: approx. 60 minutes

Preheat the oven to 380 F. Grease a baking dish with oil. Put carrot, potatoes, chicken, garlic, salt, pepper, thyme, onion, stock, and basil in the dish and bake for 50 minutes. Serve.

Per Serving: Calories 290, Fat 10g, Carbs 23g, Protein 15g

711. Cheesy Bean and Chicken Bake

Ingredients for 4 servings

- 1 ½ pound of skinless, boneless chicken thighs, cubed
- ½ cup of canned artichokes, drained and chopped
- 2 tablespoons of olive oil
- 2 garlic cloves, minced
- 1 tablespoon of oregano, chopped
- 2 shallots, sliced
- 1 teaspoon of paprika
- 1 cup of canned white beans
- ½ cup of parsley, chopped
- 1 cup of mozzarella, shredded
- Salt and black pepper to taste

Directions and Total Time: approx. 40 minutes

Preheat the oven to 390 F. Warm the olive oil in a skillet over medium heat and sauté the chicken for 5 minutes. Transfer to a baking pan and garlic, oregano, artichokes, paprika, shallots, beans, parsley, salt, and pepper. Top with mozzarella cheese and bake for 25 minutes.

Per Serving: Calories 200, Fat 7g, Carbs 13g, Protein 13g

712. Chicken and Artichokes

Ingredients for 4 servings

- 2 pounds of chicken breast, skinless, boneless, and sliced
- A pinch of salt and black pepper
- 4 tablespoons of olive oil
- 8 ounces of canned roasted artichoke hearts, drained
- 6 ounces of sun-dried tomatoes, chopped
- 3 tablespoons of capers, drained
- 2 tablespoons of lemon juice

Directions and Total Time: approx. 30 minutes

Heat up a large-sized pan with half of the oil over medium-high heat, add the artichokes and the other ingredients except the chicken, stir and sauté for 10 minutes. Transfer the mix to a bowl, heat up the pan again with the rest of the oil over medium-high heat temperature, add the meat and cook for 4 minutes on each side. Return the veggie mix to the pan, toss, cook everything for 2-3 minutes more, divide between plates, and serve.

Per Serving: Calories 552, Fat 28g, Carbs 33g, Protein 43g

Ingredients for 6 servings

- 5 ounces of cooking chorizo
- 2 red onions, sliced into wedges
- 4 chicken drumsticks
- 4 garlic cloves, whole
- 4 chicken thighs
- 4 medium potatoes, cut into wedges
- 2 rosemary sprigs
- 2 tablespoons of olive oil

Directions and Total Time: approx. 55 minutes

Set your oven to 375 F. Slice the chorizo into coin-sized pieces. Place the garlic cloves and onion wedges in a large roasting tin. Spread the chorizo, chicken pieces, rosemary, potato and black pepper on top. Drizzle with olive oil, then bake for approximately about 45 minutes. Halfway through, thoroughly toss everything in the pan and continue baking. Serve warm.

Per Serving: Calories 551, Fat 29.4g, Carbs 28.1g, Protein 43.4g

714. Chicken and Olives

Ingredients for 4 servings

- 4 chicken breasts, skinless and boneless
- 2 tablespoons of garlic, minced
- 1 tablespoon of oregano, dried
- Salt and black pepper to taste
- 2 tablespoons of olive oil
- ½ cup of chicken stock
- Juice of 1 lemon
- 1 cup of red onion, chopped
- 1 ½ cup of tomatoes, cubed
- ¼ cup of green olives, pitted and sliced
- A handful of parsley, chopped

Directions and Total Time: approx. 25 minutes

Heat up a large-sized pan with the oil over medium-high heat, add the chicken, garlic, salt, pepper, and brown for approximately 2 minutes on each side. Add the rest of the ingredients, toss, bring the mix to a simmer and cook over medium heat for 13 minutes. Divide the mix between plates and serve.

Per Serving: Calories 135, Fat 5.8g, Carbs 12.1g, Protein 9.6g

715. Chicken and Olives Tapenade

Ingredients for 4 servings

- 2 chicken breasts, boneless, skinless and halved
- 1 cup of black olives, pitted
- ½ cup of olive oil
- Salt and black pepper to taste
- ½ cup of mixed parsley, chopped
- ½ cup of rosemary, chopped
- 4 garlic cloves, minced
- Juice of ½ lime

Directions and Total Time: approx. 35 minutes

In a blender, combine the olives with half of the oil and the rest of the ingredients except the chicken and pulse well. Heat up a pan with the rest of the oil over medium-high heat, add the chicken and brown for approximately about 4 minutes on each side. Add the olives mix, and cook for 20 minutes more tossing often.

Per Serving: Calories 291, Fat 12.9g, Carbs 15.8g, Protein 34.2g

716. Chicken and Spinach Dish

Ingredients for 4 servings

- 2 tablespoons of olive oil
- 2 cups of baby spinach
- 1 pound of chicken sausage, sliced
- 1 red bell pepper, chopped
- 1 onion, sliced
- 2 tablespoons of garlic, minced
- Salt and black pepper to taste
- ½ cup of chicken stock
- 1 tablespoon of balsamic vinegar

Directions and Total Time: approx. 60 minutes

Preheat oven to 380 F. Warm olive oil in a skillet over medium heat. Cook sausages for 6 minutes on all sides. Remove to a bowl. Add the bell pepper, onion, garlic, salt, pepper to the skillet and sauté for 5 minutes. Pour in stock and vinegar and return the sausages. Bring to a hot boil and cook for approximately about 10 minutes. Add in the spinach and cook until wilts, about 4 minutes. Serve and enjoy!

Per Serving: Calories 300, Fat 15g, Carbs 18g, Protein 27g

717. Chicken and Tomato Quinoa

Ingredients for 8 servings

- 1 tablespoon of olive oil
- 2 pounds of skinless chicken breasts, boneless and halved
- 1 teaspoon of rosemary, ground
- A pinch of salt and black pepper
- 2 shallots, chopped
- 1 tablespoon of olive oil
- 3 tablespoons of tomato passata
- 2 cups of quinoa, already cooked

Directions and Total Time: approx. 45 minutes

Heat up a large-sized pan with the oil over medium-high heat, add the meat and shallots and brown for approximately 2 minutes on each side. Add the rosemary and the other ingredients, toss, introduce in the oven and cook at 370 degrees F for 30 minutes. Divide the mix between plates and serve.

Per Serving: Calories 406, Fat 14.5g, Carbs 28.1g, Protein 39g

718. Chicken Bake

Ingredients for 4 servings

- 1 ½ pound of chicken thighs, skinless, boneless, and cubed
- 2 garlic cloves, minced
- 1 tablespoon of oregano, chopped
- 2 tablespoons of olive oil
- 1 tablespoon of red wine vinegar
- ½ cup of canned artichokes, drained and chopped
- 1 red onion, sliced
- 1-pound of whole-wheat fusilli pasta, cooked
- ½ cup of canned white beans
- ½ cup of parsley, chopped
- 1 cup of mozzarella, shredded
- Salt and black pepper to taste

Directions and Total Time: approx. 40 minutes

Heat up a large-sized pan with half of the oil over medium-high heat, add the meat, and brown for 5 minutes. Grease a baking pan with the rest of the oil, add the browned chicken, and the rest of the ingredients except the pasta and the mozzarella. Spread the pasta all over and toss gently. Sprinkle the shredded cup of mozzarella on top and bake at 425°F for 25 minutes. Divide the bake between plates and serve.

Per Serving: Calories 195, Fat 5.8g, Carbs 12.1g, Protein 11.6g

719. Chicken Drumsticks with Grapes

Ingredients for 4 servings

- 4 (5-ounce) chicken drumsticks
- 3 teaspoons of olive oil, divided
- 1 ½ teaspoons of fresh rosemary, chopped
- Salt and ground black pepper, as needed
- 1 cup of red seedless grapes

Directions and Total Time: approx. 45 minutes

Preheat your oven to 425 °F. Line a small-sized baking sheet with a piece of foil. In a bowl, place chicken, 2 teaspoons of oil, rosemary, salt, and black pepper and toss to coat well. Arrange the chicken drumsticks onto the prepared baking sheet. Roast for 10 minutes. Meanwhile, in a bowl, place grapes, remaining oil, and a pinch of salt and toss to coat well. Remove the large-sized baking sheet from the oven and arrange the grapes around chicken drumsticks. Roast for 25 minutes. Serve hot.

Per Serving: Calories 297, Fat 11.7g, Carbs 6.6g, Protein 39.3g

720. Chicken Drumsticks with Peach Glaze

Ingredients for 4 servings

- 2 tablespoons of olive oil
- 8 chicken drumsticks, skinless
- 3 peaches, peeled and chopped
- ¼ cup of honey
- ¼ cup of cider vinegar
- 1 sweet onion, chopped
- 1 teaspoon of minced fresh rosemary
- Salt to taste

Directions and Total Time: approx. 35 minutes

Warm the olive oil in a large-sized skillet over medium heat. Sprinkle chicken with salt and pepper and brown it for about 7 minutes per side. Remove to a plate. Add onion and rosemary to the skillet and sauté for 1 minute or until lightly golden. Add honey, vinegar, salt, and peaches and cook for 10-12 minutes or until peaches are softened. Add the chicken back to the large-sized skillet and heat just until warm, brushing with the sauce. Serve chicken thighs with peach sauce. Enjoy!

Per Serving: Calories 492, Fat 26g, Carbs 27g, Protein 54g

721. Chicken Fajita Platter

Ingredients for 4 servings

- 1 pound of skinless, boneless chicken breasts, thin strips
- 1/2 of green bell pepper, strips
- 1/2 of red bell pepper, strips
- 1 medium onion, sliced
- 2 tablespoons of olive oil
- 1/2 teaspoon of dried oregano
- 2 teaspoons of chili powder
- 11/2 teaspoon of ground cumin
- 1 teaspoon of garlic powder
- Salt, to taste

Directions and Total Time: approx. 50 minutes

Preheat the oven to 400 degrees F. In a large-sized mixing bowl, combine all listed ingredients. Place the chicken mixture into a 9x13-inch baking dish and spread in an even layer. For about 4-5 minutes, or until chicken is cooked through. Serve hot.

Per Serving: Calories 306, Fat 15.9g, Carbs 6.5g, Protein 33.9g

722. Chicken in Wine Sauce

Ingredients for 4 servings

- 4 chicken breasts, fillets
- 2 shallots, diced
- 1 cup of white wine
- 3 tablespoons of almond butter
- 1 cup of half-and-half cream
- 2 tablespoons of Dijon mustard
- 3 tablespoons of tarragon leaves
- 3 garlic cloves, minced

Directions and Total Time: approx. 20 minutes

Melt the butter in a skillet. Place the chicken in the pan and sauté until golden brown. Transfer the chicken into a bowl and set it aside. Sauté the shallots and garlic in the same butter until soft, then add the white wine, Dijon mustard, and chicken. Stir for 1 minute then add the half and half cream. Cook for 2 minutes then add the salt and tarragon leaves. Mix well and cook until the leaves change their color. Serve warm.

Per Serving: Calories 462, Fat 13.8g, Carbs 19g, Protein 29g

723. Chicken Kebabs

Ingredients for 4 servings

- 2 chicken breasts, skinless, boneless, and cubed
- 1 red bell pepper, cut into squares
- 1 red onion, roughly cut into squares
- 2 teaspoons of sweet paprika
- 1 teaspoon of nutmeg, ground
- 1 teaspoon of Italian seasoning
- ¼ teaspoon of smoked paprika
- A pinch of salt and black pepper
- ¼ teaspoon of cardamom, ground
- Juice of 1 lemon
- 3 garlic cloves, minced
- ½ cup of olive oil

Directions and Total Time: approx. 50 minutes

In a large-sized bowl, combine the chicken with the onion, the bell pepper, and the other ingredients, toss well, cover the bowl and keep in the fridge for 30 minutes. Assemble skewers with chicken, peppers, and onions, place them on your preheated grill and cook over medium heat for just about 8 minutes on each side. Divide the kebabs between plates and serve with a side salad.

Per Serving: Calories 262, Fat 14g, Carbs 14g, Protein 20g

724. Chicken Lentils with Artichokes

Ingredients for 4 servings

- 2 tablespoons of olive oil
- 4 chicken breasts, halved
- 1 lemon, juiced and zested
- 2 garlic cloves, crushed
- 1 tablespoon of thyme, chopped
- 6 ounces of canned artichokes hearts
- 1 cup of canned lentils, drained
- 1 cup of chicken stock
- 1 teaspoon of cayenne pepper
- Salt and black pepper to taste

Directions and Total Time: approx. 50 minutes

Warm the olive oil in a large-sized skillet over medium heat and cook chicken for 5-6 minutes until browned, flipping once. Mix in lemon zest, garlic, lemon juice, salt, pepper, thyme, artichokes, lentils, stock, and cayenne pepper and bring to a boil. Cook for 35 minutes. Serve immediately.

Per Serving: Calories 300, Fat 16g, Carbs 25g, Protein 25g

725. Chicken Meatballs with Peach Chutney

Ingredients for 4 servings

- 1 pound of ground chicken
- 2 peaches, cubed
- ½ red onion, finely chopped
- 1 lemon, juiced
- 1 garlic clove, minced
- ½ jalapeño pepper, minced
- 2 tablespoons of chopped fresh cilantro
- 2 tablespoons of olive oil
- Salt and black pepper to taste

Directions and Total Time: approx. 23 minutes

Season the pound of ground chicken with salt and pepper. Shape the mixture into meatballs. Warm olive oil in a pan over medium heat and brown fry the meatballs for 8-10 minutes per on all sides until golden brown. Meanwhile, in a bowl combine peaches, lemon juice, garlic, red onion, jalapeño pepper, cilantro, and salt. Top the meatballs with the salsa and serve.

Per Serving: Calories 312, Fat 15.6g, Carbs 8.7g, Protein 33.7g

726. Chicken Pesto Pasta

Ingredients for 4 servings

- 8 ounces of whole-wheat penne
- 1 pound of asparagus, cut into 2-inch pieces
- 3 cups of cooked chicken breast, shredded
- 1 (7-oz.) container basil pesto
- 1 teaspoon of salt
- ¼ teaspoon of black pepper
- 1 ounces of Parmesan cheese, grated
- Small fresh basil leaves for garnish

Directions and Total Time: approx. 25 minutes

Cook the pasta in salted water. Add the asparagus into the pasta liquid and cook for 2 minutes. Drain and keep ½ cup of cooking liquid. Add the pasta mixture into the pot then add in the black pepper, salt, pesto, cooking liquid, and chicken. Cook for 1 minute then garnish with basil and parmesan. Enjoy.

Per Serving: Calories 521, Fat 5.8g, Carbs 85.6g, Protein 40.2g

727. Chicken Sausages with Pepper Sauce

Ingredients for 4 servings

- 2 tablespoons of olive oil
- 4 chicken sausage links
- 2 garlic cloves, minced
- 1 onion, thinly sliced
- 1 red bell pepper, sliced
- 1 green bell pepper, sliced
- ½ cup of dry white wine
- Salt and black pepper to taste
- ½ dried chili pepper, minced

Directions and Total Time: approx. 30 minutes

Warm the olive oil in a large-sized pan over medium heat and brown the sausages for 6 minutes, turning periodically. Set aside. In the same pan, sauté onion and bell peppers and garlic for 5 minutes until tender. Deglaze with the wine and stir in salt, pepper, and chili pepper. Simmer for 4 minutes until the sauce reduces by half. Serve sausages topped with bell peppers.

Per Serving: Calories 193, Fat 10g, Carbs 12g, Protein 6.2g

728. Chicken Shawarma

Ingredients for 8 servings

- 2 pounds of chicken breast, strips
- 1 teaspoon of paprika
- 1 teaspoon of ground cumin
- 1/4 teaspoon of granulated garlic
- 1/2 teaspoon of turmeric
- 1/4 teaspoon of ground allspice

Directions and Total Time: approx. 23 minutes

Season the chicken with spices and a little salt and pepper. Pour 1 cup chicken broth into the skillet. Seal the skillet. Choose a poultry setting. Cook for 15 minutes. Release the pressure naturally. Serve with flatbread.

Per Serving: Calories 481, Fat 9g, Carbs 21g, Protein 18g

729. Chicken Sicilian Style

Ingredients for 4 servings

- 1 Chicken cut into 4 pieces
- 2 cups of Water
- ½ cup of Cherry Tomatoes, halved
- ½ cup of Black olives, pitted
- 3 tablespoons of Capers in vinegar
- 2 fresh mint leaves, finely chopped
- ½ cup of white wine
- 2 Garlic cloves
- 2 Fresh chili peppers, thinly chopped
- 1 tablespoon of EVO
- ½ teaspoon of salt and pepper

Directions and Total Time: approx. 40 minutes

Take a large skillet, heat the EVO, garlic, chopped chili peppers, and when it starts to sizzle add the chicken pieces. Cook the chicken on medium heat for 2/3 minutes turning them each side, then add cherry tomatoes, capers and olives. Sprinkle the mint and pour the wine until evaporated and pour slowly the water too. Cover with a lid, reduce to low heat and let it cook for 20 minutes stirring occasionally. Once ready, remove the garlic and serve on a platter.

Per Serving: Calories 497, Fat 31.7g, Carbs 3.8g, Protein 24.4g

730. Chicken Souvlaki

Ingredients for 4 servings

- 1 red bell pepper, cut into chunks
- 2 chicken breasts, cubed
- 2 tablespoons of olive oil
- 2 cloves of garlic, minced
- 8 ounces of cipollini onions
- ½ cup of lemon juice
- Salt and black pepper to taste
- 1 teaspoon of rosemary, chopped
- 1 cup of tzatziki sauce

Directions and Total Time: approx. 20 minutes + cooling time

In a bowl, mix oil, garlic, salt, pepper, and lemon juice and add the chicken, cipollini, rosemary, and bell pepper. Refrigerate for 2 hours. Preheat your grill to high heat. Thread chicken, bell pepper, and cipollini onto skewers and grill them for 6 minutes per side. Serve with tzatziki sauce.

Per Serving: Calories 363, Fat 14.1g, Carbs 8g, Protein 32g

731. Chicken Stir-Fry

Ingredients for 2 servings

- 1/2 cup of chicken broth, low sodium
- 12 ounces of skinless chicken breasts, cut into strips
- 1 cup of red bell pepper, seeded and chopped
- 8 ounces of broccoli, cut into florets
- 1 teaspoon of crushed red pepper

Directions and Total Time: approx. 25 minutes

Place a small amount of the cup of chicken broth in a saucepan. Heat over medium flame and stir in the chicken. Water sautés the chicken for at least 5 minutes while stirring constantly. Place the rest of the ingredients and stir. Cover the large-sized pan with the lid and cook for another 5 minutes.

Per Serving: Calories 137, Fat 1.2g, Carbs 15.4g, Protein 15g

732. Chicken with Bell Peppers

Ingredients for 4 servings

- 2 tablespoons of olive oil
- 2 pounds of chicken breasts, cubed
- 2 garlic cloves, minced
- 1 red onion, chopped
- 2 red bell peppers, chopped
- ¼ teaspoon of cumin, ground
- 2 cups of corn
- ½ cup of chicken stock
- 1 teaspoon of chili powder

Directions and Total Time: approx. 65 minutes

Warm the olive oil in a large-sized skillet over medium heat and sear chicken for 8 minutes on both sides. Put in onion and garlic and cook for another 5 minutes. Stir in bell peppers, cumin, corn, stock, and chili powder. Cook for 45 minutes. Serve.

Per Serving: Calories 340, Fat 17g, Carbs 27g, Protein 19g

733. Chicken with Carrots

Ingredients for 4 servings

- 1 pound of chicken breast, skinless, boneless and cubed
- 2 tablespoons of olive oil
- 2 carrots, peeled and grated
- 1 teaspoon of sweet paprika
- ½ cup of veggie stock
- 1 red cabbage head, shredded
- 1 yellow onion, chopped
- Black pepper to the taste

Directions and Total Time: approx. 35 minutes

Heat up a large-sized pan with the oil over medium heat, add the onion, stir and sauté for 5 minutes. Add the meat, and brown it for 5 minutes more. Add the carrots and the other ingredients, toss, bring to a simmer and cook over medium heat for 15 minutes. Divide everything between plates and serve.

Per Serving: Calories 370, Fat 22.2g, Carbs 44.2g, Protein 24.2g

734. Chicken with Coconut Veggie

Ingredients for 4 servings

- 2 chicken breasts, boneless, skinless, and cubed
- 1 red onion, chopped
- 2 tablespoons of olive oil
- 1 eggplant, cubed
- 1 red bell pepper, cubed
- 1 yellow bell pepper, cubed
- Black pepper to the taste
- 2 cups of coconut milk

Directions and Total Time: approx. 35 minutes

Heat up a large-sized pan with the oil over medium-high heat, add the onion, stir and cook for 3 minutes. Add the bell peppers, toss and cook for 2 minutes more. Add the chicken and the other ingredients, toss, bring to a simmer and cook over medium heat for 20 minutes more. Divide everything between plates and serve.

Per Serving: Calories 310, Fat 14.7g, Carbs 14.5g, Protein 12.6g

735. Chicken with Farro and Carrots

Ingredients for 4 servings

- 2 tablespoons of olive oil
- 3 carrots, chopped
- 1 cup of farro, soaked
- 1 pound of chicken breasts, cubed
- 1 red onion, chopped
- 4 garlic cloves, minced
- 2 tablespoons of dill, chopped
- 2 tablespoons of tomato paste
- 2 cups of vegetable stock
- Salt and black pepper to taste

Directions and Total Time: approx. 50 minutes

Warm olive oil in your pressure cooker on Sauté and sear the chicken for 10 minutes on all sides, stirring occasionally. Remove to a plate. Add onion, garlic, and carrots to the cooker and sauté for 3 minutes. Stir in tomato paste, farro, and vegetable stock and return the chicken. Seal the lid, select Pressure Cook, and cook for 30 minutes on High. Do a natural pressure release for approximately about 10 minutes. Adjust the taste with salt and pepper. Sprinkle with dill and serve.

Per Serving: Calories 317, Fat 13g, Carbs 18g, Protein 8g

736. Chicken with Yogurt-Mint Sauce

Ingredients for 4 servings

- 1 cup of low-fat plain Greek yogurt
- 1 onion, finely chopped
- 1 tablespoon of fresh mint, chopped
- 1 teaspoon of fresh dill, chopped
- 1 teaspoon of garlic, minced
- 1 teaspoon of ground cumin
- Pinch of red pepper flakes
- 4 (3-ounce) boneless, skinless chicken breasts

Directions and Total Time: approx. 50 minutes

In a large-sized bowl, whisk together the yogurt, onion, mint, dill, garlic, cumin, and red pepper flakes until blended. Transfer ½ cup of the yogurt to a small bowl. Set aside, covered, in the refrigerator. Add the chicken to the remaining yogurt mixture, turning to coat. Cover and actually place the chicken in the refrigerator to marinate for 3 hours. Preheat the oven to 400°F. Transfer the pieces of chicken breasts to a baking sheet and roast until the chicken is cooked through, 25 minutes. Serve with the reserved yogurt-mint sauce.

Per Serving: Calories 136, Fat 7.6g, Carbs 5.7g, Protein 26g

737. Citrus Grilled Chicken

Ingredients for 4 servings

- 4 chicken breasts, boneless, skinless
- 2 teaspoons of olive oil
- 4 teaspoons of cumin, ground
- 1 lemon, juiced
- 1 lime, juiced
- 1 orange, juiced
- ½ teaspoon of salt
- ¼ teaspoon of black pepper, cracked

Directions and Total Time: approx. 25 minutes

Pound the chicken breasts with a mallet. Prepare and preheat the grill. Preheat your oven at a heat of 350°F. Rub the pounded chicken with olive oil, black pepper, salt, cumin, and citrus juices. Grill the chicken for approximately about 5 minutes on each side. Place it on a dish with a clean surface and leave it aside for approximately about 5 minutes. Slice and serve.

Per Serving: Calories 316, Fat 13.2g, Carbs 6.4g, Protein 41.3g

738. Cloves Chicken

Ingredients for 4 servings

- 1 pound of chicken breast, cubed
- 1 cup of chicken stock
- 1 tablespoon of avocado oil
- 2 teaspoons of cloves, ground
- 1 yellow onion, chopped
- 2 teaspoons of sweet paprika
- 3 tomatoes, cubed
- ½ cup of parsley, chopped
- A pinch of salt and black pepper

Directions and Total Time: approx. 40 minutes

Heat up a large-sized pan with the oil over medium heat, add the onion and sauté for 5 minutes. Add the cubed chicken breasts and brown for 5 minutes more. Add the stock and the rest of the ingredients, bring to a simmer and cook over medium heat for 20 minutes more. Divide the mix between plates and serve.

Per Serving: Calories 324, Fat 12.3g, Carbs 33.g, Protein 22.4g

739. Cream Zucchini and Chicken Dish

Ingredients for 4 servings

- 3 tablespoons of canola oil
- 1 pound of turkey breast, sliced
- Salt and black pepper to taste
- 3 garlic cloves, minced
- 2 zucchinis, sliced
- 1 cup of chicken stock
- ¼ cup of heavy cream
- 2 tablespoons of parsley, chopped

Directions and Total Time: approx. 70 minutes

Warm the olive oil in a pot over medium heat. Cook the turkey for 10 minutes on both sides. Put in garlic and cook for 1 minute. Season with salt and pepper. Stir in zucchinis for 3-4 minutes and pour in the chicken stock. Bring to a boil and cook for just approximately about 40 minutes. Stir in heavy cream and parsley.

Per Serving: Calories 270, Fat 11g, Carbs 27g, Protein 16g

740. Creamy Chicken Ball with Almonds

Ingredients for 4 servings

- 2 tablespoons of olive oil
- 1 pound of ground chicken
- 2 teaspoons of toasted chopped almonds
- 1 egg, whisked
- 2 teaspoons of turmeric powder
- 2 garlic cloves, minced
- Salt and black pepper to taste
- 1 ¼ cups of heavy cream
- ¼ cup of parsley, chopped
- 1 tablespoon of chives, chopped

Directions and Total Time: approx. 30 minutes

Place chicken, almonds, egg, turmeric powder, garlic, salt, pepper, parsley, and chives in a bowl and toss to combine. Form meatballs out of the mixture. Warm olive oil in a large-sized skillet over medium heat. Brown meatballs for 8 minutes on all sides. Stir in cream and cook for another 10 minutes.

Per Serving: Calories 290, Fat 10g, Carbs 26g, Protein 36g

741. Creamy Chicken Breast

Ingredients for 4 servings

- 1 tablespoon of olive oil
- A pinch of black pepper
- 2 pounds of chicken breasts, skinless, boneless, and cubed
- 4 garlic cloves, minced
- 2 ½ cups of low-sodium chicken stock
- 2 cups pf coconut cream
- ½ cup of low-fat parmesan, grated
- 1 tablespoon of basil, chopped

Directions and Total Time: approx. 30 minutes

Heat-up a pan with the oil over medium-high heat, add chicken cubes, and brown them for 3 minutes on each side. Add garlic, black pepper, stock, and cream, toss, cover the pan and cook everything for 10 minutes more. Add cheese and basil, toss, divide between plates and serve for lunch. Enjoy!

Per Serving: Calories 221, Fat 6g, Carbs 14g, Protein 7g

742. Eggplant and Chicken Skillet

Ingredients for 4 servings

- 2 tablespoons of olive oil
- 1 pound of eggplants, cubed
- Salt and black pepper to taste
- 1 onion, chopped
- 2 garlic cloves, minced
- 1 teaspoon of hot paprika
- 1 tablespoon of oregano, chopped
- 1 cup of chicken stock
- 1 pound of chicken breasts, cubed
- 1 cup of half and half
- 3 teaspoons of toasted chopped almonds

Directions and Total Time: approx. 40 minutes

Warm the olive oil in a large-sized skillet over medium heat and sauté chicken for 8 minutes, stirring often. Mix in eggplants, onion, and garlic and cook for another 5 minutes. Season with salt, pepper, hot paprika, and oregano and pour in the stock. Bring the dish to a boil and simmer for 16 minutes. Stir in half and half for 2 minutes. Serve topped with almonds.

Per Serving: Calories 400, Fat 13g, Carbs 22g, Protein 26g

743. Feta Chicken and Cabbage

Ingredients for 4 servings

- 2 chicken breasts, skinless, boneless and cut into strips
- 1 red cabbage, shredded
- 2 tablespoons of olive oil
- Salt and black pepper to the taste
- 2 tablespoons of balsamic vinegar
- 1 and ½ cups of tomatoes, cubed
- 1 tablespoon of chives, chopped
- ¼ cup of feta cheese, crumbled

Directions and Total Time: approx. 35 minutes

Heat up a large-sized pan with the oil over medium-high heat, add the chicken and brown for 5 minutes. Add the rest of the prepared ingredients except the cheese, and cook over medium heat for 20 minutes stirring often. Add the cheese, toss, divide everything between plates and serve.

Per Serving: Calories 277, Fat 15g, Carbs 14.9g, Protein 14.2g

744. Feta Turkey Meatballs

Ingredients for 6 servings

- 1 egg, lightly beaten
- 2 pounds of ground turkey
- 4 ounces of Feta cheese, crumbled
- 1 tablespoon of fresh mint, chopped
- ¼ teaspoon of cumin
- ½ teaspoon of onion powder
- ½ cup of almond flour
- ¼ cup of fresh parsley, chopped
- 1 cup of spinach, chopped
- ½ teaspoon of oregano
- ½ teaspoon of pepper
- Salt

Directions and Total Time: approx. 30 minutes

Preheat the oven to 450° F. Add ground turkey and remaining ingredients into the large bowl and mix until well combined. Make small balls from the meat mixture and place onto the baking sheet. Bake for 20 minutes. Allow to cool completely and serve.

Per Serving: Calories 373, Fat 22.6g, Carbs 2.2g, Protein 45.8g

745. Five Spice Chicken

Ingredients for 4 servings

- 1 cup of tomatoes, crushed
- 1 teaspoon of five spice
- 2 chicken breast halves, skinless, boneless and halved
- 1 tablespoon of avocado oil
- 2 tablespoons of coconut aminos
- Black pepper to the taste
- 1 tablespoon of hot pepper
- 1 tablespoon of cilantro, chopped

Directions and Total Time: approx. 40 minutes

Heat up a large-sized pan with the oil over medium heat, add the meat and brown it for 2 minutes on each side. Add the tomatoes, five spice and the other ingredients, bring to a simmer and cook over medium heat for 30 minutes. Divide the whole mix between plates and serve.

Per Serving: Calories 244, Fat 8.4g, Carbs 4.5g, Protein 31g

746. French Chicken Cassoulet

Ingredients for 4 servings

- 1 tablespoon of olive oil
- ½ cup of heavy cream
- 4 chicken breasts, halved
- 1/3 cup of yellow mustard
- Salt and black pepper to taste
- 1 onion, chopped
- 1 ½ cups of chicken stock
- ¼ teaspoon of dried oregano

Directions and Total Time: approx. 40 minutes

Warm stock in a saucepan over medium heat and stir in mustard, onion, salt, pepper, and oregano. Bring to a boil and cook for just approximately 8 minutes. Warm olive oil in a large-sized skillet over medium heat. Sear chicken for 6 minutes on both sides. Transfer to the saucepan and simmer for another 12 minutes. Stir in heavy cream for 2 minutes. Serve warm.

Per Serving: Calories 260, Fat 12g, Carbs 18g, Protein 27g

747. Garlic Chicken and Endives

Ingredients for 4 servings

- 1-pound of chicken breasts, skinless, boneless and cubed
- 2 endives, sliced
- 2 tablespoons of olive oil
- 4 garlic cloves, minced
- ½ cup of chicken stock
- 2 tablespoons of parmesan, grated
- 1 tablespoon of parsley, chopped
- Salt and black pepper to the taste

Directions and Total Time: approx. 25 minutes

Heat up a large-sized pan with the oil over medium-high heat, add the chicken and cook for 5 minutes. Add the endives, garlic, the stock, salt and pepper, stir, bring to a simmer and cook over medium-high heat for 10 minutes. Add the parmesan and the parsley, toss gently, divide everything between plates and serve.

Per Serving: Calories 280, Fat 9.2g, Carbs 21.6g, Protein 33.8g

748. Garlic Chicken Balls

Ingredients for 4 servings

- 2 cups of ground chicken
- 1 teaspoon of minced garlic
- 1 teaspoon of dried dill
- 1/3 carrot, grated
- 1 egg, beaten
- 1 tablespoon of olive oil
- 1/4 cup of coconut flakes
- 1/2 teaspoon of salt

Directions and Total Time: approx. 25 minutes

Mix up ground chicken, minced garlic, dried dill, carrot, egg, and salt in the mixing bowl. Stir the chicken mixture with the help of the fingertips until homogenous. Then make medium balls from the mixture. Coat every chicken ball in coconut flakes. Heat olive oil in the skillet. Add chicken balls and cook them for 3 minutes from each side. The cooked chicken balls will have a golden-brown color.

Per Serving: Calories 200, Fat 11.5g, Carbs 1.7g, Protein 21.9g

749. Garlic Turkey and Spring Onions

Ingredients for 4 servings

- ½ tablespoon of black peppercorns
- 1 tablespoon of olive oil
- 1 pound of turkey breast, boneless, skinless, and cubed
- 1 cup of chicken stock
- 3 garlic cloves, minced
- 2 tomatoes, cubed
- A pinch of black pepper
- 2 tablespoons of spring onions, chopped

Directions and Total Time: approx. 40 minutes

Heat up a large-sized pan with the oil over medium heat, add the garlic and the turkey and brown for 5 minutes. Add the peppercorns and the rest of the ingredients, bring to a simmer and cook over medium heat for 25 minutes. Divide the mix between plates and serve.

Per Serving: Calories 313, Fat 13.3g, Carbs 23.4g, Protein 16g

750. Greek Penne and Chicken

Ingredients for 4 servings

- 16-ounce package of penne pasta
- 1-pound of chicken breast halves
- 1/2 cup of chopped red onion
- 1 1/2 tablespoons of butter
- 2 cloves of minced garlic
- 14-ounce can of artichoke hearts
- 1 chopped tomato
- 3 tablespoons of chopped fresh parsley
- 1/2 cup of crumbled feta cheese
- 2 tablespoons of lemon juice
- 1 teaspoon of dried oregano
- ground black pepper
- salt

Directions and Total Time: approx. 20 minutes

In a large-sized skillet over medium-high heat, melt your butter. Add your garlic and onion. Cook approximately 2 minutes. Add your chopped chicken and continue to cook until golden brown. It should take approximately 5 to 6 minutes. Stir occasionally. Reduce your heat to a medium-low. Drain and chop your artichoke hearts. Add them to your skillet along with your chopped tomato, fresh parsley, feta cheese, dried oregano, lemon juice, and drained pasta. Cook for 2 to 3. Season. Serve!

Per Serving: Calories 411, Fat 14g, Carbs 20g, Protein 8g

751. Greek Roasted Pepper Chicken

Ingredients for 4 servings

- 2 pounds of chicken thighs, boneless
- ½ cup of chicken stock
- ¾ cup of olives
- 1 teaspoon of oregano
- 1 cup of roasted red peppers, chopped
- 1 tablespoon of garlic, minced
- 1 tablespoon of capers
- 1 teaspoon of rosemary
- 1 teaspoon of dried thyme
- 1 tablespoon of olive oil
- ½ cup of onion, sliced
- Pepper
- Salt

Directions and Total Time: approx. 4 hours and 10 minutes

Heat oil in a small-sized pan over medium-high heat. Add chicken and cook until browned. Add garlic and onion and cook for 5 minutes. Transfer the chicken mixture into the slow cooker along with the remaining ingredients. Cover and cook on low for 4 hours.

Per Serving: Calories 344, Fat 15.5g, Carbs 4.8g, Protein 44.5g

752. Grilled Chicken Breasts with Spinach Pesto

Ingredients for 4 servings

- 4 boneless, skinless chicken breasts
- ¼ cup + 1 tablespoon of olive oil
- 1 cup of spinach
- ¼ cup of grated Pecorino cheese
- Salt and black pepper to taste
- ¼ cup of pine nuts
- 1 garlic clove, minced

Directions and Total Time: approx. 25 minutes

Rub chicken with salt and black pepper. Grease a grill pan with 1 tablespoon of olive oil and place over medium heat. Grill the chicken for 8-10 minutes, flipping once. Mix spinach, garlic, Pecorino cheese, and pine nuts in a food processor. Slowly, pour in the remaining oil; pulse until smooth. Spoon 1 tablespoon of pesto on each breast and cook for an additional 5 minutes.

Per Serving: Calories 493, Fat 27g, Carbs 4g, Protein 53g

753. Grilled Harissa Chicken

Ingredients for 2 servings

- Juice of 1 lemon
- 1 red onion, sliced
- 1 ½ teaspoons of ground coriander
- 1 ½ teaspoons of smoked paprika
- 1 teaspoon of cumin
- 2 teaspoons of cayenne pepper
- 3 tablespoons of olive oil
- Kosher salt, to taste
- 8 boneless chicken thighs
- 2 tablespoons of harissa paste

Directions and Total Time: approx. 22 minutes

In a medium-sized bowl, add the chicken, olive oil, salt, onion, garlic, coriander, cumin, cayenne, lemon juice, and harissa paste, then mix well until the chicken is fully coated. Place the oven rack 4 inches from the heat source. Preheat the broiler. Place the chicken on a broiler pan. Broil each of the side of the chicken for about 7 minutes. The thickest part of the cooked chicken's temperature should read as 165°F on a thermometer.

Per Serving: Calories 142, Fat 4.7g, Carbs 1.7g, Protein 22.1g

754. Grilled Lemon Chicken

Ingredients for 4 servings

- 24 ounces of skinless, boneless chicken breast halves
- ½ cup of fresh lemon juice
- ½ cup of soy sauce
- ½ teaspoon of ground ginger
- ¼ teaspoon of ground black pepper

Directions and Total Time: approx. 40 minutes

Rinse and wipe dry the chicken breasts with paper towels after removing them from the refrigerator. In a bowl, stir the lemon juice, ginger, soy sauce, and black pepper, then pour it into a resealable plastic bag. Add the chicken breast into the bag and sell. Massage to coat the chicken with lemon juice. Refrigerate the marinated chicken for at least 20 minutes and up to 24 hours. Preheat the oven to 400°F/ 204°C. Lightly grease a grill grate and place about 4 inches from the heat source. Retrieve the chicken breasts from the marinade and prepare a grill. Sauté chicken for 6–8 minutes each side or until cooked through.

Per Serving: Calories 214.1, Fat 4.1g, Carbs 5.3g, Protein 37.6g

755. Herb and Pistachio Turkey Breasts

Ingredients for 4 servings

- ½ cup of pistachios, toasted and chopped
- 1 tablespoon of olive oil
- 1 pound of turkey breast, cubed
- 1 cup of chicken stock
- 1 tablespoon of basil, chopped
- 1 tablespoon of rosemary, chopped
- 1 tablespoon of oregano, chopped
- 1 tablespoon of parsley, chopped
- 1 tablespoon of tarragon, chopped
- 3 garlic cloves, minced
- 3 cups of tomatoes, chopped

Directions and Total Time: approx. 50 minutes

Warm the olive oil in a large-sized skillet over medium heat and cook turkey and garlic for 5 minutes. Stir in stock, basil, rosemary, oregano, parsley, tarragon, pistachios, and tomatoes and bring to a simmer. Cook for 35 minutes. Serve immediately.

Per Serving: Calories 310, Fat 12g, Carbs 20g, Protein 25g

756. Herb Roasted Turkey Breast

Ingredients for 6 servings

- 2 tablespoons of extra-virgin olive oil
- 4 garlic cloves, minced
- Zest of 1 lemon
- 1 tablespoon of fresh thyme leaves
- 1 tablespoon of fresh rosemary leaves
- 2 tablespoons of fresh Italian parsley leaves
- 1 teaspoon of ground mustard
- 1 teaspoon of sea salt
- ¼ teaspoon of black pepper
- 1 (6-pound) bone-in, skin-on turkey breast
- 1 cup of dry white wine

Directions and Total Time: approx. 50 minutes

Preheat the oven to 325°F. Scourge olive oil, garlic, lemon zest, thyme, rosemary, parsley, mustard, sea salt, and pepper. Layout herb mixture evenly over the surface of the turkey breast, and loosen the skin, and rub underneath as well. Situate turkey breast in a roasting pan on a rack, skin-side up. Pour the wine into the pan. Roast for 1 to 1½ hours. Before carving, take it out from the oven and rest for 20 minutes, tented with aluminum foil to keep it warm.

Per Serving: Calories 392, Fat 6g, Carbs 49.4g, Protein 84g

757. Herbed Almond Turkey

Ingredients for 4 servings

- 1 turkey breast, skinless, boneless and cubed
- 1 tablespoon of olive oil
- ½ cup of chicken stock
- 1 tablespoon of basil, chopped
- 1 tablespoon of rosemary, chopped
- 1 tablespoon of oregano, chopped
- 1 tablespoon of parsley, chopped
- 3 garlic cloves, minced
- ½ cup of almonds, toasted and chopped
- 3 cups of tomatoes, chopped

Directions and Total Time: approx. 55 minutes

Heat a pan with the oil over medium-high heat, add the turkey and the garlic and brown for 5 minutes. Stir in the 1/2 cup chicken stock and the other ingredients, then reduce to a low heat and cook for 35 minutes. Divide the mix between plates and serve.

Per Serving: Calories 297, Fat 11.2g, Carbs 19.4g, Protein 23.6g

758. Herbed Chicken

Ingredients for 4 servings

- 2 chicken breasts, skinless, boneless and sliced
- 2 red onions, chopped
- 2 tablespoons of olive oil
- 2 garlic cloves, minced
- ½ cup of chicken stock
- 1 teaspoon of oregano, dried
- 1 teaspoon of basil, dried
- 1 teaspoon of rosemary, dried
- 1 cup of canned tomatoes, chopped
- Salt and black pepper to the taste

Directions and Total Time: approx. 50 minutes

Heat a pot with the oil over medium-high heat, add the chicken and brown for 4 minutes on each side. Add the garlic and the onions and sauté for 5 minutes more. Add the rest of the ingredients, bring to a simmer and cook over medium heat for 25 minutes. Divide everything between plates and serve.

Per Serving: Calories 251, Fat 11.6g, Carbs 15.6g, Protein 9.1g

759. Juicy Almond Turkey

Ingredients for 4 servings

- 2 tablespoons of canola oil
- ¼ cup of almonds, chopped
- 1 pound of turkey breast, sliced
- Salt and black pepper to taste
- 1 lemon, juiced and zested
- 1 grapefruit, juiced
- 1 tablespoon of rosemary, chopped
- 3 garlic cloves, minced
- 1 cup of chicken stock

Directions and Total Time: approx. 40 minutes

Warm the olive oil in a large-sized skillet over medium heat and cook garlic and turkey for 8 minutes on both sides. Stir in salt, pepper, lemon juice, lemon zest, grapefruit juice, rosemary, almonds, and stock and bring to a boil. Cook for 20 minutes.

Per Serving: Calories 300, Fat 13g, Carbs 19g, Protein 25g

760. Lemon Chicken

Ingredients for 4 servings

- 4 chicken breast fillets
- 1 large lemon
- 2 teaspoons of fresh thyme leaves
- 1 ½ tablespoon of honey

Directions and Total Time: approx. 25 minutes

Preheat your grill at a high temperature and grease a shallow baking dish. Placed the chicken in the dish with the skin side facing down. Season chicken breast fillets with salt and black pepper and grill it for 5 minutes. Meanwhile, thinly slice the lemon. Turn the chicken pieces and place the lemon slice on top of each. Season the chicken with honey, lemon juice, 2 tbsp of water, seasoning and thyme. Return the baking dish to the grill and grill the chicken for 10 minutes. Serve warm.

Per Serving: Calories 359, Fat 10.5g, Carbs 25.5g, Protein 40.8g

Ingredients for 4 servings

- 4 sweet potatoes, sliced
- 2 chicken breasts, boneless, skinless
- ½ cup of lemon juice
- ¼ cup of olive oil
- 2 garlic, minced
- 1 tablespoon of Dijon mustard
- 1 teaspoon of oregano
- 1 teaspoon of turmeric
- ½ teaspoon of salt
- ½ teaspoon of black pepper
- 1 cup of chicken broth
- 1 lemon, sliced

Directions and Total Time: approx. 60 minutes

Slice the sweet potatoes and place them in a baking pan. In a bowl, mix the lemon juice, mustard, turmeric, salt, black pepper, broth, garlic, olive oil and oregano. Set the chicken breasts over the sweet potatoes. Pour the lemon broth mixture over the chicken. Bake the chicken for 60 minutes approximately. Serve fresh.

Per Serving: Calories 355, Fat 18.8g, Carbs 23.3g, Protein 23.3g

762. Lemon Garlic Thighs with Asparagus

Ingredients for 4 servings

- 1 ¾ pounds of bone-in, skinless chicken thighs
- 2 tablespoons of lemon juice
- 2 tablespoons of minced fresh oregano
- 2 cloves of garlic, minced
- 1/4 teaspoon of pepper
- 1/4 teaspoon of salt
- 2 pounds of asparagus, trimmed

Directions and Total Time: approx. 45 minutes

Preheat the oven to 350°F. Toss all the ingredients except the asparagus in a mixing bowl until combined. Roast the chicken thighs in the preheated oven for about 40 minutes or until it reaches an internal temperature of 165°F. When cooked, remove the chicken thighs from the oven and set them aside to cool. Meanwhile, steam the asparagus in the microwave to the desired doneness. Serve the asparagus with roasted chicken thighs.

Per Serving: Calories 197, Fat 14g, Carbs 14g, Protein 9g

763. Lemony Turkey and Pine Nuts

Ingredients for 4 servings

- 1 turkey breast, boneless, skinless and halved
- A pinch of salt and black pepper
- 1 tablespoon of avocado oil
- Juice of 1 lemon
- 1 tablespoon of rosemary, chopped
- 2 garlic cloves, minced
- ¼ cup of pine nuts, chopped
- 1 cup of chicken stock

Directions and Total Time: approx. 35 minutes

Heat a pan with the oil over medium-high heat, add the garlic and the turkey and brown for 4 minutes on each side. Add the rest of the remaining ingredients, bring to a simmer and cook over medium heat for 20 minutes. Divide the mix between plates and serve with a side salad.

Per Serving: Calories 293, Fat 12.4g, Carbs 17.8g, Protein 34g

Ingredients for 4 servings

- 2 pounds of chicken breasts
- ½ teaspoon of red pepper flakes
- 1 teaspoon of dried oregano
- 2 tablespoons of fresh lemon juice
- 1 tablespoon of garlic, minced
- 3 tablespoon of olive oil
- 1 tablespoon of Balsamic vinegar
- ½ teaspoon of onion powder
- ½ teaspoon of pepper
- ½ teaspoon of Kosher salt

Directions and Total Time: approx. 24 minutes

Add chicken and remaining ingredients into the zip-lock bag. Seal bag and place in refrigerator for overnight. Preheat the grill. Place marinated chicken onto the grill and cook for 5-7 minutes on each side.

Per Serving: Calories 530, Fat 27.5g, Carbs 1.7g, Protein 65.9g

765. Mediterranean Chicken Stir Fry

Ingredients for 4 servings

- ½ cup of pitted green olives, sliced
- 2 small tomatoes, chopped
- 1 onion, chopped
- 1 zucchini, chopped
- ¼ teaspoon of red pepper flakes
- 3 cloves of garlic, minced
- 1 cup of brown rice
- 2 teaspoons of olive oil
- 1 teaspoon of dried oregano
- 1 teaspoon of dried basil
- 3 cups of water
- 1-pound of boneless chicken breasts, cubed
- Salt and pepper, to taste

Directions and Total Time: approx. 35 minutes

In a large-sized pot on the stove, bring the water to a boil. Add the rice and cook as per the package instructions. Remove from the heat. Add the olive oil to a skillet. Lightly fry the chicken until it's fully cooked. Remove from the heat. Add the onion to the same skillet. Add the garlic, red pepper, basil, zucchini, and oregano. Stir fry until the vegetables become softer, then season with salt and pepper. Add the cooked chicken, cooked rice, and tomatoes, and olives.

Per Serving: Calories 401, Fat 13.3g, Carbs 44.1g, Protein 38g

766. Mustardy Turkey Ham Stuffed Peppers

Ingredients for 4 servings

- 1 cup of Greek yogurt
- 1 pound of turkey ham, chopped
- 2 tablespoons of mustard
- Salt and black pepper to taste
- 1 celery stalk, chopped
- 2 tablespoons of balsamic vinegar
- 1 bunch of scallions, sliced
- ¼ cup of parsley, chopped
- 1 cucumber, sliced
- 1 red bell peppers, halved and deseeded
- 1 tomato, sliced

Directions and Total Time: approx. 10 minutes

Preheat the oven to 360 F. Combine turkey ham, celery, balsamic vinegar, salt, pepper, mustard, yogurt, scallions, parsley, cucumber, and tomatoes in a bowl. Fill bell peppers with the mixture and arrange them on a greased baking dish. Bake in the oven for approximately about 20 minutes. Serve warm.

Per Serving: Calories 280, Fat 13g, Carbs 16g, Protein 4g

767. Nutty Chicken Breasts

Ingredients for 4 servings

- 2 tablespoons of canola oil
- 1 pound of chicken breasts, halved
- ½ teaspoon of hot paprika
- 1 cup of chicken stock
- 2 tablespoons of hazelnuts, chopped
- 2 spring onions, chopped
- 2 garlic cloves, minced
- ¼ cup of Parmesan cheese, grated
- 2 tablespoons of cilantro, chopped
- 2 tablespoons of parsley, chopped
- Salt and black pepper to taste

Directions and Total Time: approx. 65 minutes

Preheat the oven to 370 F. Combine chicken, canola oil, hot paprika, stock, hazelnuts, spring onions, garlic, salt, and pepper in a greased baking pan and bake for 40 minutes. Sprinkle with Parmesan cheese and bake for an additional 5 minutes until the cheese melts. Top with cilantro and parsley.

Per Serving: Calories 230, Fat 10g, Carbs 22g, Protein 19g

768. Oregano Chicken and Zucchini Pan

Ingredients for 4 servings

- 2 cups of tomatoes, peeled and crushed
- 1 and ½ pounds of chicken breast, boneless, skinless and cubed
- 2 tablespoons of olive oil
- Salt and black pepper to the taste
- 1 small yellow onion, sliced
- 2 garlic cloves, minced
- 2 zucchinis, sliced
- 2 tablespoons of oregano, chopped
- 1 cup of chicken stock

Directions and Total Time: approx. 40 minutes

Heat up a large-sized pan with the oil over medium-high heat, add the chicken and brown for 3-minute son each side. Add the onion and the garlic and sauté for 4 minutes more. Add the rest of the remaining ingredients except the oregano, bring to a simmer and cook over medium heat and cook for 20 minutes. Divide the mix between plates, sprinkle the oregano on top and serve.

Per Serving: Calories 228, Fat 9.5g, Carbs 15.6g, Protein 18.6g

769. Oregano Grilled Chicken

Ingredients for 4 servings

- ½ cup of lemon juice
- ½ cup of extra-virgin olive oil
- 3 tablespoons of garlic, minced
- 2 teaspoons of dried oregano
- 1 teaspoon of red pepper flakes
- 1 teaspoon of salt
- 2 pounds of boneless, skinless chicken breasts

Directions and Total Time: approx. 30 minutes

Combine the minced garlic, lemon juice, olive oil, oregano, red pepper flakes, and salt in a medium bowl. Divide a chicken breast horizontally to get two thin pieces. Repeat this same actual process with the rest of the chicken breasts. Put the chicken in the bowl with the marinade and let it sit for at least 10 minutes before cooking. Place a medium-sized skillet on high heat and add some oil. Cook each side of the breasts for 10 minutes, turning regularly. Serve warm.

Per Serving: Calories 479, Fat 32g, Carbs 5g, Protein 47g

770. Paprika Chicken with Caper Dressing

Ingredients for 4 servings

- 2 tablespoons of canola oil
- 4 chicken breast halves
- Salt and black pepper to taste
- 1 tablespoon of sweet paprika
- 1 onion, chopped
- 1 tablespoon of balsamic vinegar
- 2 tablespoons of parsley, chopped
- 1 avocado, peeled and cubed
- 2 tablespoons of capers

Directions and Total Time: approx. 35 minutes

Preheat the grill over medium heat. Rub chicken halves with half of the canola oil, paprika, salt, and pepper and grill them for 14 minutes on both sides. Share into plates. Combine onion, remaining oil, vinegar, parsley, avocado, and capers in a bowl. Pour the prepared mixed sauce over the chicken and serve.

Per Serving: Calories 300, Fat 13g, Carbs 25g, Protein 15g

771. Parmesan Chicken Breasts

Ingredients for 4 servings

- 1 tablespoon of olive oil
- 1 ½ pound of chicken breasts, cubed
- 1 teaspoon of ground coriander
- 1 teaspoon of parsley flakes
- 2 garlic cloves, minced
- 1 cup of heavy cream
- Salt and black pepper to taste
- ¼ cup of Parmesan cheese, grated
- 1 tablespoon of basil, chopped

Directions and Total Time: approx. 35 minutes

Warm the olive oil in a large-sized skillet over medium heat and brown chicken, salt, and pepper for 6 minutes on all sides. Add in garlic and cook for approximately about another minute. Stir in coriander, parsley, and cream and cook for an additional 20 minutes. Serve scattered with basil and Parmesan cheese.

Per Serving: Calories 260, Fat 18g, Carbs 26g, Protein 27g

772. Peppery Chicken Bake

Ingredients for 4 servings

- 3 tablespoons of olive oil
- 1 pound of chicken breasts, sliced
- 2 pound of cherry tomatoes, halved
- 1 onion, chopped
- 3 garlic cloves, minced
- 3 red chili peppers, chopped
- ½ lemon, zested
- Salt and black pepper to taste

Directions and Total Time: approx. 70 minutes

Warm the olive oil in a large-sized skillet over medium heat and brown chicken for 8 minutes on both sides. Remove to a roasting pan. In the same large-sized skillet, add onion, garlic, and chili peppers and cook for 2 minutes. Pour the prepared mixture over the chicken and toss to coat. Add in tomatoes, lemon zest, 1 cup of water, salt, and pepper. Bake for 45 minutes. Serve and enjoy!

Per Serving: Calories 280, Fat 14g, Carbs 25g, Protein 34g

773. Picante Green Pea and Chicken

Ingredients for 4 servings

- 2 tablespoons of olive oil
- 1 pound of chicken breasts, halved
- 1 teaspoon of chili powder
- Salt and black pepper to taste
- 1 teaspoon of garlic powder
- 1 tablespoon of smoked paprika
- ½ cup of chicken stock
- 2 teaspoons of sherry vinegar
- 3 teaspoons of hot sauce
- 2 teaspoons of cumin, ground
- 1 cup of green peas
- 1 carrot, chopped

Directions and Total Time: approx. 35 minutes

Warm the olive oil in a large-sized skillet over medium heat and cook chicken for 6 minutes on both sides. Sprinkle with chili powder, salt, pepper, garlic powder, and paprika. Pour in the chicken stock, vinegar, hot sauce, cumin, carrot, and green peas and bring to a boil; cook for an additional 15 minutes.

Per Serving: Calories 240, Fat 19g, Carbs 16g, Protein 14g

774. Portuguese-Style Chicken Breasts

Ingredients for 4 servings

- 2 tablespoons of avocado oil
- 1 pound of chicken breasts, cubed
- Salt and black pepper to taste
- 1 red onion, chopped
- 15 ounces of canned chickpeas
- 15 ounces of canned tomatoes, diced
- 1 cup of Kalamata olives, halved
- 2 tablespoons of lime juice
- 1 teaspoon of cilantro, chopped

Directions and Total Time: approx. 45 minutes

Warm the olive oil in a pot over medium heat and sauté chicken and onion for 5 minutes. Put in salt, pepper, chickpeas, tomatoes, olives, lime juice, cilantro, and 2 cups of water. Cover with its lid and then bring to a boil, then reduce the heat and simmer for 30 minutes. Serve warm.

Per Serving: Calories 360, Fat 16g, Carbs 26g, Protein 28g

775. Quinoa and Chicken Bowl

Ingredients for 4 servings

- 4 chicken thighs, skinless and boneless
- 2 tablespoons of olive oil
- Salt and black pepper to taste
- 1 celery stalk, chopped
- 2 leeks, chopped
- 2 cups of chicken stock
- 2 tablespoons of cilantro, chopped
- 1 cup of quinoa
- 1 teaspoon of lemon zest

Directions and Total Time: approx. 50 minutes

Warm the olive oil in a pot over medium heat and cook the chicken for 6-8 minutes on all sides. Stir in leeks and celery and cook for another 5 minutes until tender. Season with salt and pepper. Stir in quinoa and lemon zest for 1 minute and pour in the chicken stock. Bring to a boil and simmer for 35 minutes. Serve topped with cilantro.

Per Serving: Calories 250, Fat 14g, Carbs 17g, Protein 35g

776. Rice with Red Beans and Chicken

Ingredients for 4 servings

- 10 ounces of skinless, boneless chicken breast, 1-inch pieces
- 1 green sweet pepper chopped
- 1 onion chopped
- 2 cloves of garlic, minced
- 1 can of no-salt added red beans, rinsed and drained
- 1 package of cooked brown rice
- ½ teaspoon of ground cumin
- ¼ cup of reduced-sodium chicken broth
- ¼ teaspoon of salt and pepper
- 1 tablespoon of EVO

Directions and Total Time: approx. 35 minutes

Preheat EVO in a large skillet, sprinkle salt and pepper on the chicken bites and add the chicken, sweet pepper, onion and garlic; cook and gently stir for about 10 minutes, i.e., chicken is no longer pink and vegetables are tender. Slowly stir in rice, beans, broth, and cumin. Heat for another 10 minutes on low heat. Take a platter and place the chicken and vegetables. You can eat warm or cooled.

Per Serving: Calories 272, Fat 15g, Carbs 30g, Protein 25g

777. Rosemary Tomato Chicken

Ingredients for 4 servings

- 2 tablespoons of olive oil
- 1 pound of chicken breasts, sliced
- 1 onion, chopped
- 1 carrot, chopped
- 2 garlic cloves, minced
- ½ cup of chicken stock
- 1 teaspoon of oregano, dried
- 1 teaspoon of tarragon, dried
- 1 teaspoon of rosemary, dried
- 1 cup of canned tomatoes, diced
- Salt and black pepper to taste

Directions and Total Time: approx. 50 minutes

Warm the olive oil in a pot over medium heat and cook the chicken for 8 minutes on both sides. Put in carrot, garlic, and onion and cook for an additional 3 minutes. Season with salt and pepper. Pour in stock, oregano, tarragon, rosemary, and tomatoes and bring to a boil; simmer for 25 minutes. Serve.

Per Serving: Calories 260, Fat 12g, Carbs 16g, Protein 10g

778. Saucy Green Pea and Chicken

Ingredients for 4 servings

- 2 tablespoons of olive oil
- 1 teaspoon of dried thyme
- 1 pound of chicken breasts, cubed
- Salt and black pepper to taste
- 1 cup of chicken stock
- ½ cup of tomato sauce
- 1 cup of green peas
- 2 tablespoons of chives, chopped

Directions and Total Time: approx. 40 minutes

Warm the olive oil in a pot over medium heat and sauté the chicken for 8 minutes, stirring occasionally. Season with thyme, salt, and pepper. Pour in chicken stock and tomato sauce and bring to a boil. Simmer for 20 minutes. Add in green peas and cook for 4-5 minutes. Top with chives.

Per Serving: Calories 316, Fat 16g, Carbs 7g, Protein 35g

779. Sicilian Olive Chicken

Ingredients for 4 servings

- 1 (14-oz.) can of petite diced tomatoes with garlic
- 1 ½ cups of frozen spinach, chopped, thawed
- ⅓ cup of halved Sicilian olives
- 1 tablespoon of capers, rinsed
- ¼ teaspoon of crushed red pepper
- 4 4-ounces of chicken cutlets
- ¼ teaspoon of black pepper
- 1 tablespoon of olive oil

Directions and Total Time: approx. 22 minutes

In a suitable bowl, mix the tomatoes, red pepper, capers, olives and spinach. Rub the chicken with black pepper. Sear the chicken with oil in a skillet over medium-high heat for 4 minutes on each side. Add the tomato mixture on top, cover and cook for 5 minutes. Serve warm.

Per Serving: Calories 280, Fat 12.1g, Carbs 7.4g, Protein 34g

780. Simple Chicken with Olive Tapenade

Ingredients for 4 servings

- ½ cup of olive oil
- 2 tablespoons of capers, canned
- 2 chicken breasts
- 1 cup of black olives, pitted
- Salt and black pepper to taste
- ½ cup of parsley, chopped
- ½ cup of rosemary, chopped
- Salt and black pepper to taste
- 2 garlic cloves, minced
- ½ lemon, juiced and zested

Directions and Total Time: approx. 35 minutes

In a food processor, blend olives, capers, half of the oil, salt, pepper, parsley, rosemary, garlic, lemon zest, and zested lemon juice until smooth; set aside. Warm the remaining oil in a large-sized skillet over medium heat. Brown the chicken for 8-10 minutes on both sides. Top with tapenade. Serve and enjoy!

Per Serving: Calories 300, Fat 14g, Carbs 17g, Protein 35g

781. Slow Cooker Brussel Sprout and Chicken

Ingredients for 4 servings

- 2 tablespoons of olive oil
- 1 pound of Brussels sprouts, halved
- 2 pounds of chicken breasts, cubed
- 1 ½ cups of veggie stock
- 2 red onions, sliced
- 2 garlic cloves, minced
- 1 tablespoon of sweet paprika
- ½ cup of tomato sauce
- Salt and black pepper to taste

Directions and Total Time: approx. 8 hour and 20 minutes

Warm the olive oil in a large-sized skillet over medium heat and sear the chicken for 10 minutes on all sides. Remove to your slow cooker. Add in onions, stock, garlic, paprika, Brussels sprouts, tomato sauce, salt, pepper, and dill. Cover the lid and cook for approximately about 8 hours on Low. Serve immediately.

Per Serving: Calories 302, Fat 15g, Carbs 17g, Protein 16g

782. Spanish Chicken Skillet

Ingredients for 4 servings

- 2 tablespoons of olive oil
- ½ cup of chicken stock
- 4 chicken breasts
- 2 garlic cloves, minced
- 1 celery stalk, chopped
- 1 tablespoon of oregano, dried
- Salt and black pepper to taste
- 1 white onion, chopped
- 1 ½ cups of tomatoes, cubed
- 10 green olives, sliced

Directions and Total Time: approx. 25 minutes

Warm the olive oil in a large-sized skillet over medium heat. Season the chicken with salt and pepper and cook for 4 minutes on both sides. Stir in garlic, oregano, stock, onion, celery, tomatoes, and olives and bring to a boil. Simmer for 13-15 minutes.

Calories 140 Fat 7g, Carbs 13g, Protein 11g

783. Spiced Chicken Meatballs

Ingredients for 2 servings

- 0.5-pound of chicken meat, ground
- 1/2 tablespoon of pine nuts, toasted and chopped
- 1 egg, whisked
- 1 teaspoon of turmeric powder
- 1 garlic clove, minced
- Salt and black pepper to taste
- 1 cup of heavy cream
- 1 tablespoon of olive oil
- ¼ cup of parsley, chopped
- 1 tablespoon of chives, chopped

Directions and Total Time: approx. 30 minutes

In a bowl, combine the pine nuts with the chicken and the rest of the ingredients except the oil and the cream; stir well and shape medium meatballs out of this mix. Heat a pan with the oil over medium-high heat, add the meatballs and cook them for 4 minutes on each side. Add the cream, toss gently, cook everything over medium heat for 10 minutes more, divide between plates and serve.

Per Serving: Calories 283, Fat 9.2g, Carbs 24.4g, Protein 34.5g

784. Spinach Chicken with Chickpeas

Ingredients for 4 servings

- 2 tablespoons of olive oil
- 1 pound of chicken breasts, cubed
- 10 ounces of spinach, chopped
- 1 cup of canned chickpeas
- 1 onion, chopped
- 2 garlic cloves, minced
- ½ cup of chicken stock
- 2 tablespoons of Parmesan cheese, grated
- 1 tablespoon of parsley, chopped
- Salt and black pepper to taste

Directions and Total Time: approx. 25 minutes

Warm the olive oil in a large-sized skillet over medium heat and brown chicken for 5 minutes. Season with salt and pepper. Stir in onion and garlic for 3 minutes. Pour in stock and chickpeas and bring to a boil. Cook for 20 minutes. Mix in ounces of spinach and cook until wilted, about 5 minutes. Top with Parmesan cheese and parsley. Serve and enjoy!

Per Serving: Calories 290, Fat 10g, Carbs 22g, Protein 35g

785. Spinach Pesto Chicken Breasts

Ingredients for 4 servings

- ¼ cup + 1 tablespoon of olive oil
- 4 chicken breasts
- 1 cup of spinach
- ¼ cup of grated Pecorino cheese
- Salt and black pepper to taste
- ¼ cup of pine nuts
- 1 garlic clove, minced

Directions and Total Time: approx. 25 minutes

Rub chicken with salt and black pepper. Grease a grill pan with 1 tbsp of olive oil and place over medium heat. Grill the chicken for 8-10 minutes, flipping once. Mix spinach, garlic, Pecorino cheese, and pine nuts in a food processor. Slowly, pour in the remaining oil; pulse until smooth. Spoon 1 tbsp of pesto on each breast and cook for an additional 5 minutes.

Per Serving: Calories 493, Fat 27g, Carbs 4g, Protein 53g

786. Tasty Chicken Pot

Ingredients for 4 servings

- 1 pound of chicken thighs, skinless and boneless
- 2 tablespoons of olive oil
- 1 onion, chopped
- 2 garlic cloves, minced
- 1 teaspoon of smoked paprika
- 1 teaspoon of chili powder
- ½ teaspoon of fennel seeds, ground
- 2 teaspoons of oregano, dried
- 14 ounces of canned tomatoes, diced
- ½ cup of capers

Directions and Total Time: approx. 35 minutes

Warm the olive oil in a large-sized skillet over medium heat and sauté the onion, garlic, paprika, chili powder, fennel seeds, and oregano for 3 minutes. Put in chicken, tomatoes, 1 cup of water, and capers. Bring to a boil and simmer for 20-25 minutes.

Per Serving: Calories 160, Fat 9g, Carbs 10g, Protein 13g

787. Thyme Zucchini and Chicken Stir-Fry

Ingredients for 4 servings

- 2 tablespoons of olive oil
- 2 cups of tomatoes, crushed
- 1 pound of chicken breasts, cubed
- Salt and black pepper to taste
- 2 shallots, sliced
- 3 garlic cloves, minced
- 2 zucchinis, sliced
- 2 tablespoons of thyme, chopped
- 1 cup of chicken stock

Directions and Total Time: approx. 40 minutes

Warm the olive oil in a large-sized skillet over medium heat. Sear chicken for 6 minutes, stirring occasionally. Add in sliced shallots and garlic and cook for another 4 minutes. Stir in tomatoes, salt, pepper, zucchinis, and stock and bring to a boil; simmer for 20 minutes. Garnish with thyme and serve.

Per Serving: Calories 240, Fat 10g, Carbs 17g, Protein 19g

788. Turkey and Cilantro

Ingredients for 4 servings

- 1 cup of lentils, cooked
- 1 cup of chicken stock
- 1 pound of turkey breast, boneless, skinless, and cubed
- A pinch of black pepper
- 1 teaspoon of oregano, dried
- 1 teaspoon of nutmeg, ground
- 2 tablespoons of olive oil
- 1 yellow onion, chopped
- 1 green bell pepper, chopped
- 1 cup of cilantro, chopped

Directions and Total Time: approx. 50 minutes

Heat up a large-sized pan with the oil over medium heat. Then, add the meat, onion, and bell pepper and cook for 10 minutes stirring often. Add the rest of the prepared ingredients, toss, bring to a simmer and cook over medium heat for 30 minutes. Divide the mix between plates and serve.

Per Serving: Calories 304, Fat 11.2g, Carbs 22.2g, Protein 17g

789. Turkey and Cilantro Broccoli

Ingredients for 4 servings

- 1 red onion, chopped
- 1 pound of turkey breast, boneless, skinless, and cubed
- 2 cups of broccoli florets
- 1 teaspoon of cumin, ground
- 3 garlic cloves, minced
- 2 tablespoons of olive oil
- 14 ounces of coconut milk
- A pinch of black pepper
- ¼ cup of cilantro, chopped

Directions and Total Time: approx. 40 minutes

Heat up a large-sized pot with the oil over medium heat, add the onion and the garlic, stir and sauté for 5 minutes. Add the turkey, toss and brown for 5 minutes. Add the broccoli and the rest of the ingredients, bring to a simmer over medium heat and cook for 20 minutes. Divide the mix between plates and serve.

Per Serving: Calories 438, Fat 32.9g, Carbs 16.8g, Protein 23.5g

790. Turkey and Mango

Ingredients for 4 servings

- 2 pounds of turkey breasts, skinless, boneless and cubed
- 1 tablespoon of olive oil
- 1 red onion, chopped
- 1 cup of mango, peeled and cubed
- 1 cup of chicken stock
- ¼ cup of cilantro, chopped
- Black pepper to the taste

Directions and Total Time: approx. 45 minutes

Heat up a large-sized pot with the oil over medium-high heat, add the onion, stir and sauté for 5 minutes. Add the meat, berries and the other ingredients, bring to a simmer and cook over medium heat for 30 minutes more. Divide the mix between plates and serve.

Per Serving: Calories 293, Fat 7.3g, Carbs 14.7g, Protein 39.3g

791. Turkey Curry

Ingredients for 3 servings

- 1 pound of turkey breasts, chopped
- 3 ½ ounces of fresh rocket (arugula) leaves
- 2 cloves of garlic, chopped
- 1 teaspoon of medium curry powder
- 1 teaspoon of turmeric powder
- 1 tablespoon of fresh coriander (cilantro), finely chopped
- bird's eye chilies, chopped
- 2 red onions, chopped
- 400ml full-fat coconut milk
- 1 tablespoon of olive oil

Directions and Total Time: approx. 45 minutes

Cook the red onions in the olive oil for 5 minutes until tender. Stir in the garlic and the turkey and cook it for 7-8 minutes. Stir in the turmeric, chilies, and curry powder, then add the coconut milk and coriander cilantro). Bring to an actual boil, then you need to reduce to a simmer for 10 minutes. Scatter the rocket (arugula) onto plates and spoon the curry on top. Serve alongside brown rice.

Per Serving: Calories 400, Fat 6g, Carbs 3g, Protein 14g

792. Turkey, Leeks and Carrots

Ingredients for 4 servings

- 1 big turkey breast, cubed
- 2 tablespoons of avocado oil
- Salt and black pepper to the taste
- 1 tablespoon of sweet paprika
- ½ cup of chicken stock
- 1 leek, sliced
- 1 carrot, sliced
- 1 yellow onion, chopped
- 1 tablespoon of lemon juice
- 1 teaspoon of cumin, ground
- 1 tablespoon of basil, chopped

Directions and Total Time: approx. 1 hour and 10 minutes

Heat up a large-sized pan with the oil over medium-high heat, add the turkey and brown for 4 minutes on each side. Add the leeks, carrot and the onion and sauté everything for 5 minutes more. Add the rest of the ingredients, bring to a simmer and cook over medium heat for 40 minutes. Divide the mix between plates and serve.

Per Serving: Calories 249, Fat 10.7g, Carbs 22.3g, Protein 17.3g

793. Turkey Meatballs

Ingredients for 2 servings

- 1 yellow onion, diced
- 14 ounces of artichoke hearts, diced
- 1-pound of ground turkey
- 1 teaspoon of dried parsley
- 1 teaspoon of olive oil
- 4 tablespoons of basil, chopped
- Salt and pepper, to taste

Directions and Total Time: approx. 35 minutes

Preheat the oven to 350°F. Grease a baking sheet. Place the artichokes in a pan, add the oil, and sauté with the diced onions over medium heat for approximately about 5 minutes or until the onions are soft. Meanwhile, mix the parsley, basil, and ground turkey with your hands in a big bowl. Season to taste. Once the prepared onion mixture has cooled, add it into the bowl and mix thoroughly. With an ice cream scooper, scoop the ground turkey mixture and form balls. Place the balls on the prepared baking sheet, pop in the oven, and bake until cooked (around 17 minutes). Serve and enjoy.

Per Serving: Calories 283, Fat 12g, Carbs 30g, Protein 12g

794. Turkey Tortillas

Ingredients for 4 servings

- 4 whole wheat tortillas
- ½ cup of yogurt
- 1 pound of turkey, breast, boneless, skinless, and cut into strips
- 1 tablespoon of olive oil
- 1 red onion, sliced
- 1 zucchini, cubed
- 2 tomatoes, cubed
- Black pepper to the taste

Directions and Total Time: approx. 30 minutes

Heat up a large-sized pan with the oil over medium heat, add the onion, stir and sauté for 5 minutes. Add the zucchini and tomatoes, toss and cook for 2 minutes more. Add the turkey meat, toss and cook for 13 minutes more. Spread the yogurt on each tortilla, add divide the turkey and zucchini mix, roll, divide between plates and serve.

Per Serving: Calories 290, Fat 13.4g, Carbs 12.5, Protein 6.9g

795. Tzatziki Chicken Loaf

Ingredients for 4 servings

- 1 pound of ground chicken
- 1 onion, chopped
- 1 teaspoon of garlic powder
- 1 cup of tzatziki sauce
- ½ teaspoon of dried Greek oregano
- ½ teaspoon of dried cilantro
- ½ teaspoon of sweet paprika
- Salt and black pepper to taste

Directions and Total Time: approx. 70 minutes + chilling time

Preheat oven to 350 F. In a bowl, add chicken, paprika, onion, Greek oregano, cilantro, garlic, salt, and pepper and mix well with your hands. Shape the mixture into a greased loaf pan and bake in the oven for 55-60 minutes. Let sit for 15 minutes and slice. Serve topped with tzatziki sauce.

Per Serving: Calories 240, Fat 9g, Carbs 3.6g, Protein 33.2g

796. Vegetable and Chicken Skewers

Ingredients for 4 servings

- 2 tablespoons of olive oil
- 1 chicken breast, cubed
- 1/2 red bell pepper
- 1/2 red onion, cut into squares
- 1/2 cup of mushrooms, quartered
- 1 teaspoon of sweet paprika
- 1 teaspoon of ground nutmeg
- 1 teaspoon of Italian seasoning
- ¼ teaspoon of smoked paprika
- Salt and black pepper to taste
- ¼ teaspoon of ground cardamom
- 1 lemon, juiced
- 2 garlic cloves, minced
-

Directions and Total Time: approx. 25 minutes

Combine chicken, onion, bell pepper, paprika, nutmeg, Italian seasoning, paprika, salt, pepper, cardamom, lemon juice, garlic, and olive oil in a bowl. Transfer to the fridge covered for 30 minutes. Preheat your grill to high. Alternate chicken cubes, peppers, mushrooms, and onions on each of 4 metal skewers. Grill them for 16 minutes on all sides, turning frequently. Serve with salad.

Per Serving: Calories 270, Fat 15g, Carbs 15g, Protein 21g

Ingredients for 4 servings

- 2 tablespoons of olive oil
- 1 pound of turkey breast, cubed
- 1 head of broccoli, cut into florets
- 2 ounces of cherry tomatoes, halved
- 2 tablespoons of cilantro, chopped
- 1 lemon, zested
- Salt and black pepper to taste
- 2 spring onions, chopped

Directions and Total Time: approx. 80 minutes

Preheat the oven to 360 F. Warm the olive oil in a skillet over medium heat and sauté spring onions and lemon zest for 3 minutes. Add in turkey and cook for another 5-6 minutes, stirring occasionally. Transfer to a medium-sized baking dish, pour in 1 cup of water and bake for 30 minutes. Add in broccoli and tomatoes and bake for another 10 minutes. Top with cilantro.

Per Serving: Calories 310, Fat 10g, Carbs 21g, Protein 15g

798. Walnut Turkey and Peaches

Ingredients for 4 servings

- 2 turkey breasts, skinless, boneless and sliced
- ¼ cup of chicken stock
- 1 tablespoon of walnuts, chopped
- 1 red onion, chopped
- Salt and black pepper to the taste
- 2 tablespoons of olive oil
- 4 peaches, pitted and cut into quarters
- 1 tablespoon of cilantro, chopped

Directions and Total Time: approx. 70 minutes

In a roasting pan greased with the oil, combine the turkey and the onion and the rest of the ingredients except the cilantro, introduce in the oven and bake at 390 degrees F for 1 hours. Divide the mix between plates, sprinkle the cilantro on top and serve.

Per Serving: Calories 500, Fat 14g, Carbs 15g, Protein 10g

799. Yogurt-Marinated Chicken

Ingredients for 6 servings

- 1 cup of Greek yogurt
- 1 cup of cilantro, chopped
- 2 tablespoons of lemon juice
- 3 garlic cloves, minced
- 1 teaspoon of cayenne
- 1 teaspoon of ground cumin
- salt and pepper, to taste
- 3 ½ pounds of chicken, halved
- Vegetable oil, for brushing
- Cooking spray

Directions and Total Time: approx. 40 minutes

In a large-sized bowl, mix the yogurt with the lemon juice, cayenne, salt, black, garlic, and cilantro. Place the chicken into the mixture and coat well. Cover the chicken ad marinate it for 3 hours in the refrigerator. Prepare and preheat a grill over medium-high heat. Grease its grates with cooking spray. Place the chicken in the grill over indirect heat. Grill for 25 minutes, turning it every 5 minutes. Serve.

Per Serving: Calories 243, Fat 5.1g, Carbs 2.4g, Protein 44.2g

800. Zesty Turkey Breast

Ingredients for 4 servings

- 2 tablespoons of olive oil
- 1 pound of turkey breast
- 2 garlic cloves, minced
- ½ cup of chicken broth
- 1 lemon, zested
- ¼ teaspoon of dried thyme
- ¼ teaspoon of dried tarragon
- ½ teaspoon of red pepper flakes
- 2 tablespoons of chopped fresh parsley
- 1 teaspoon of ground mustard
- Salt and black pepper to taste

Directions and Total Time: approx. 1 hour and 40 minutes + chilling time

Preheat oven to 325 F. Mix the olive oil, garlic, lemon zest, thyme, tarragon, red pepper flakes, mustard, salt, and pepper in a bowl. Rub the breast with the mixture until well coated and transfer onto a roasting pan skin-side up. Pour in the chicken broth. Roast in the oven for 60-90 minutes. Allow to sit for 10 minutes covered with foil, then remove from the roasting tin and carve. Serve topped with parsley.

Per Serving: Calories 286, Fat 16g, Carbs 0.9g, Protein 34g

801. Baked Lamb Patties

Ingredients for 4 servings

- 1 pound of ground lamb
- 1 teaspoon of cinnamon
- 1 teaspoon of coriander
- 1 tablespoon of garlic, minced
- ¼ teaspoon of pepper
- 1 teaspoon of ground cumin
- ¼ cup of fresh parsley, chopped
- ¼ cup of onion, minced
- ¼ teaspoon of Cayenne
- ½ teaspoon of allspice
- 1 teaspoon of Kosher salt

Directions and Total Time: approx. 25 minutes

Preheat the oven to 450° F. Add ground meat and remaining ingredients into the bowl and mix until well combined. Make patties from the meat mixture and place onto the baking sheet. Bake for 12-15 minutes.

Per Serving: Calories 223, Fat 8.5g, Carbs 2.6g, Protein 32.3g

802. BBQ and Thyme Pork Bites

Ingredients for 5 servings

- ½ cup of BBQ sauce
- 12 ounces of pork sirloin, roughly chopped
- 1 tablespoon of coconut oil
- 1 teaspoon of dried thyme
- ½ teaspoon of dried dill

Directions and Total Time: approx. 25 minutes

Sprinkle the pork sirloin with dried thyme and dried dill. Place the tablespoon of coconut oil in the skillet and heat it up. Add pork sirloin and roast it for 15 minutes over the medium heat. Stir it from time to time. After this, add BBQ sauce and mix it up well. Close its lid and cook the meal for 10 minutes.

Per Serving: Calories 193, Fat 7.3g, Carbs 9.3g, Protein 21.2g

803. Beef Blue Cheese Crostini

Ingredients for 12 servings

- 1 1/4 pounds of roast deli beef shaved
- 1 French bread baguette
- 2 tablespoons of minced chives
- Additional minced chives
- 1/4 teaspoon of salt
- 1 tablespoon of horseradish
- Olive oil cooking spray
- 1/3 cup of crumbled blue cheese
- 1/2 cup of sour cream low-fat

Directions and Total Time: approx. 40 minutes

Preheat your oven to 375°F. Cut the French baguette into 36 equal pieces. Place on a cookie sheet that has not been buttered. Using olive oil cooking spray, coat the pan. Garnish baguettes with pepper & bake for around 4–6 minutes, or till golden brown. Combine the minced chives, horseradish, low-fat sour cream, & salt in a small-sized mixing dish. Place the pounds of beef on top of the bread. Spread the sour cream mixture on top and garnish with more chives and cheese. In the oven, broil for around 2 minutes.

Per Serving: Calories 48, Fat 1g, Carbs 5g, Protein 4g

804. Beef Bourguignon

Ingredients for 4 servings

- 1 ½ pounds of beef chuck roast, cut into chunks
- 2/3 cup of beef stock
- 2 tablespoons of fresh thyme
- 1 bay leaf
- 1 teaspoon of garlic, minced
- 8 ounces of mushroom, sliced
- 2 tablespoons of tomato paste
- 2/3 cup of dry red wine
- 1 onion, sliced
- 4 carrots, cut into chunks
- 1 tablespoon of olive oil
- Salt and pepper, to taste

Directions and Total Time: approx. 30 minutes

Add the oil to an Instant Pot and set the pot on Sauté mode. Add the meat and sauté until brown. Add the onion and sauté until softened. Add the remaining ingredients and stir well. Seal the pot with the lid and cook on High for 12 minutes. Once done, allow to release the pressure naturally. Remove the lid. Stir well and serve.

Per Serving: Calories 744, Fat 51.3g, Carbs 14.5g, Protein 48.1g

805. Beef Chili Verde

Ingredients for 2 servings

- ½ pound of beef stew meat, cut into cubes
- ¼ teaspoon of chili powder
- 1 tablespoon of olive oil
- 1 cup of chicken broth
- 1 serrano pepper, chopped
- 1 teaspoon of garlic, minced
- 1 small onion, chopped
- ¼ cup of grape tomatoes, chopped
- ¼ cup of tomatillos, chopped
- Salt and black pepper, to taste

Directions and Total Time: approx. 33 minutes

Add the oil to an Instant Pot and set the pot on Sauté mode. Add the garlic and onion and sauté for 3 minutes. Add the remaining ingredients and stir well. Seal the pot with the lid and cook on High for 20 minutes. Once done, allow to release the pressure naturally. Remove the lid. Stir well and serve.

Per Serving: Calories 317, Fat 15.1g, Carbs 6.4g, Protein 37.8g

806. Beef Chuck Roast

Ingredients for 6 servings

- 2 pounds of beef chuck roast
- ¼ cup of olives, sliced
- 1 teaspoon of Italian seasoning
- 2 tablespoons of Balsamic vinegar
- ½ cup of beef broth
- ¼ cup of sun-dried tomatoes, chopped
- 15 garlic cloves, peeled

Directions and Total Time: approx. 10 hours and 10 minutes

Place meat into the slow cooker. Pour remaining ingredients over meat. Cover and cook on low temperature for 10 hours. Shred the meat using the fork. Garnish with cilantro and serve.

Per Serving: Calories 574, Fat 43.1g, Carbs 3.3g, Protein 40.6g

807. Beef Roll-Up

Ingredients for 4 servings

- 2 pounds beef flank steak
- Salt and pepper to taste
- ¾ cup baby spinach, fresh
- 3-ounces red bell peppers, roasted
- 6 slices provolone cheese
- 3 tablespoons Pesto

Directions and Total Time: approx. 14 minutes

Open the steak and spread the pesto evenly over the meat. Layer the cheese, roasted red peppers and spinach ¾ of the way down the meat. Roll up and secure with toothpicks. Season with sea salt and pepper. Preheat air fryer to 400°Fahrenheit. Place the roll-ups in the fry basket and into the air fryer and cook it for 14-minutes. Halfway through the cook time rotate the meat. When cook time is completed, allow the meat to rest for 10-minutes before cutting and serving.

Per Serving: Calories 282, Fat 12.3g, Carbs 9.8g, Protein 16.3g

808. Beef Shawarma

Ingredients for 2 servings

- 1/2 pound ground beef
- 1/4 teaspoon cinnamon
- 1/2 teaspoon dried oregano
- 1 cup cabbage, cut into strips
- 1/2 cup bell pepper, sliced
- 1/4 teaspoon ground coriander
- 1/4 teaspoon cumin
- 1/4 teaspoon cayenne pepper
- 1/4 teaspoon ground allspice
- 1/2 cup onion, chopped
- 1/2 teaspoon salt

Directions and Total Time: approx. 20 minutes

Set instant pot on sauté mode. Add meat to the pot and sauté until brown. Add remaining ingredients and stir well. Seal pot using the lid and cook on high for 5 minutes. Once done, release pressure using quick release. Remove lid. Stir and serve.

Per Serving: Calories 245, Fat 7.4g, Carbs 7.9g, Protein 35.6g

809. Beef Steak Tartare

Ingredients for 6 servings

- 1 pound of minced beef tenderloin
- 4 teaspoons of EVO
- ½ cup of capers
- ½ red onion, chopped
- ½ lemon, juiced
- 1 egg
- 1 tablespoon of fresh parsley, chopped
- 1 tablespoon of Worcestershire sauce
- ½ teaspoon of salt and black pepper
- 1 teaspoon of mustard

Directions and Total Time: approx. 40 minutes

Take a medium bowl, add in beef, mustard, Worcestershire sauce, salt, pepper and egg and mix together until well blended. Arrange the minced meat in a neat pile on a serving platter, and cover with aluminum foil. Refrigerate for 30 minutes. Before serving the dish, season with a pinch of salt and pepper and sprinkle a bit of EVO on top. Serve as a spread or eat pure and simple like it is.

Per Serving: Calories 231, Fat 18.2g, Carbs 0.4g, Protein 14.5g

810. Beef Stew with Eggplants

Ingredients for 2 servings

- 10 ounces of the beef neck, or another tender cut, chopped into bite-sized pieces
- 1 large eggplant, sliced
- 2 cups of fire-roasted tomatoes
- ½ cup of fresh green peas
- 1 cup of beef broth
- 4 tablespoons of olive oil
- 2 tablespoons of tomato paste
- 1 tablespoons of Cayenne pepper, ground
- ½ teaspoon of chili pepper, ground (optional)
- ½ teaspoon of salt
- Parmesan cheese

Directions and Total Time: approx. 10 hours and 15 minutes

Grease the bottom of your prepared slow cooker with olive oil. Toss all ingredients and add about 1-1 ½ cup of water. Cook within 8-10 hours on low, or until the meat is fork-tender. Sprinkle with Parmesan cheese before serving, but this is optional.

Per Serving: Calories 195, Fat 11.1g, Carbs 9.6g, Protein 15.3g

811. Beef with Mushroom and Herbs

Ingredients for 6 servings

- 1/2 cup of garlic cloves, sliced
- 1 cup of mushrooms
- 2 pounds of beef chuck steak, sliced into cubes
- 1 cup of tomatoes with tomato sauce
- 4 tablespoons of mixed dried herbs (rosemary, sage, and parsley)

Directions and Total Time: approx. 8 hours and 30 minutes

Pour 1 tablespoon olive oil into the Instant Pot. Add the minced onion and mushrooms and cook for 5 minutes. Add the chuck of beef and cook until brown on both sides. Pour in the rest of the ingredients. Season with salt and pepper. Seal the pot. Set it to slow cook. Cook for 8 hours.

Serving: Calories 400, Fat 17g, Carbs 11.9g, Protein 48.8g

812. Braised Lamb Shanks with Veggies

Ingredients for 6 servings

- 6 lamb shanks
- 1 onion, chopped
- 1 pound of frozen carrots and potatoes, chopped
- Seasoning mixture (2 1/4 teaspoons of garlic powder,
- 1 teaspoon of sweet Spanish paprika and 3/4 teaspoon of ground nutmeg)
- 28 ounces of canned tomatoes with juice

Directions and Total Time: approx. 60 minutes

Season the lamb shanks with the seasoning mixture. Pour 2 tablespoons olive oil into the Instant Pot. Set it to sauté. Brown the lamb shanks for 8 minutes. Add the rest of the ingredients. Mix well. Cover the pot. Set it to manual. Cook at high pressure for 20 minutes. Release the pressure naturally.

Per Serving: Calories 839, Fat 29.9g, Carbs 26.6g, Protein 97.5g

813. Brie-Stuffed Meatballs

Ingredients for 5 servings

- 2 eggs, beaten
- 1 pound ground pork
- 1/3 cup double cream
- 1 tablespoon fresh parsley
- Kosher salt and ground black pepper
- 1 teaspoon dried rosemary
- 10 (1-inch) cubes of brie cheese
- 2 tablespoons scallions, minced
- 2 cloves garlic, minced

Directions and Total Time: approx. 25 minutes

Mix all ingredients, except for the brie cheese, until everything is well incorporated. Roll the mixture into 10 patties; place a piece of cheese in the center of each patty and roll into a ball. Roast in the preheated oven at 380 degrees F for about 20 minutes. Place the meatballs in airtight containers or Ziploc bags; keep in your refrigerator for up to 3 to 4 days. Freeze the meatballs in airtight containers or heavy-duty freezer bags. Freeze up to 3 to 4 months. To defrost, slowly reheat in a saucepan. Bon appétit!

Per Serving: Calories 302, Fat 17.3g, Carbs 1.9g, Protein 33.4g

814. Buttered Lamb Chops

Ingredients for 4 servings

- 8 (1-inch thick) bone-in lamb loin chops
- Salt, as required
- 1 teaspoon of ground black pepper
- 2 tablespoons of olive oil
- 4 tablespoons of salted butter
- 4 garlic cloves, minced
- 1 tablespoon of fresh thyme, chopped
- 1 tablespoon of fresh rosemary, chopped

Directions and Total Time: approx. 23 minutes

Season the prepared lamb chops with salt and black pepper evenly. In a large cast-iron wok, heat the oil over medium-high heat and cook the lamb chops for about 3-4 minutes per side. Stir in the butter, garlic, and fresh herbs and adjust the heat to medium-low. Cook for about 5 minutes, spooning the butter sauce over chops occasionally. Serve hot.

Per Serving: Calories 594, Fat 35.4g, Carbs 2.3g, Protein 64.2g

815. Buttered Pork Chops

Ingredients for 4 servings

- 4 pork chops.
- 1 teaspoon of salt.
- 2 tablespoons of bacon grease.
- 4 tablespoons of butter.
- 1 teaspoon of pepper

Directions and Total Time: approx. 30 minutes

You will want to start off this recipe by taking out your pork chops and seasoning them on either side. If you need more than 1 teaspoon of salt and pepper, season as desired. Next, you are going to want to place your skillet over high heat and place the bacon grease and butter into the bottom. Once the butter is melted and the grease is sizzling, pop the pork chops into the skillet and sear on both of each side for about 3–4 minutes. In the end, the pork should be a nice golden color. When the meat is cooked as desired, remove the skillet from the heat and enjoy your meal!

Per Serving: Calories 450, Fat 30g, Carbs 10g, Protein 45g

816. Cayenne Pork

Ingredients for 4 servings

- 8 ounces beef sirloin
- 1 poblano pepper, grinded
- 1 teaspoon minced garlic
- ½ cup of water
- 1 tablespoon extra-virgin olive oil
- 1 teaspoon ground black pepper
- 1 teaspoon salt
- ½ teaspoon paprika
- 1 teaspoon cayenne pepper

Directions and Total Time: approx. 50 minutes

Toss the extra virgin olive oil in the saucepan and melt it. Meanwhile rub the beef sirloin with minced garlic, salt, ground black pepper, paprika, and cayenne pepper. Put the meat in the hot extra virgin olive oil and roast for 5 minutes from each side over the medium heat. After this, add water and poblano pepper. Cook the meat for 50 minutes over the medium heat. Then transfer the beef sirloin on the cutting board and shred it with the help of the fork.

Per Serving: Calories 97, Fat 5.5g, Carbs 3g, Protein 9.5g

817. Cheesy Meat Bake

Ingredients for 4 servings

- 6 ounces pork butt, chopped
- 3 ounces veal stew meat, chopped
- 1 potato, peeled
- ¼ cup cauliflower, shredded
- ¼ cup carrot, grated
- 1 teaspoon tomato paste
- 2 ounces Provolone cheese, grated
- ¼ cup cream
- 1 teaspoon extra virgin olive oil
- 1 teaspoon salt
- ½ teaspoon chili flakes

Directions and Total Time: approx. 40 minutes

Melt extra virgin olive oil in the saucepan and add all meat. Sprinkle it with salt, chili flakes, and carrot. Mix up well and cook for 10 minutes. Then add tomato paste and mix up well. Add shredded cauliflower and roughly chopped potato. Then add cream and top it with cheese. Cover the saucepan with foil and transfer it in the preheated to the 365F oven. Bake the casserole for 30 minutes.

Per Serving: Calories 211, Fat 9g, Carbs 9.5g, Protein 22.4g

818. Cheesy Pork Macaroni

Ingredients for 2 servings

- 1/4 pound of Ground pork
- 1/4 cup of grated cheddar
- 1/4 cup of cooked macaroni
- 1 tablespoon of vegetable oil
- 2 tablespoons of diced' mushroom
- 2 eggs
- 2 teaspoons of garlic powder
- 1/2 teaspoon of pepper

Directions and Total Time: approx. 25 minutes

Combine the whole ingredients except cheese in a bowl then mix well. Transfer the mixture in a disposable aluminum pan then spread evenly. Sprinkle grated cheddar on top then put aside. Pour water into the moment Pot and place a trivet in it. Place the disposable aluminum pan on the trivet then cover and seal the moment Pot properly. Select *Manual* setting on the moment Pot and cook the pork on high for 20 minutes. Once it's done; naturally release the moment Pot then open the lid. Take the disposable aluminum pan out of the moment Pot and let it sit for a jiffy

Per Serving: Calories 368, Fat 30.7g, Carbs 3.8g, Protein 19.2g

819. Chipotle Sirloin Steak

Ingredients for 4 servings
- 6 ounces of Greek yogurt plain
- 1/2 teaspoon of ground cumin
- 4 beef sirloin
- 1 chipotle Chile in adobo sauce
- 1/4 teaspoon of dried dill
- 1/4 cup of cilantro chopped
- 2 tablespoons of olive oil extra-virgin
- Kosher salt, to taste

Directions and Total Time: approx. 40 minutes

In a mixing cup, combine the Greek yoghurt, cilantro, chipotle, dill, & cumin. Salt the chipotle sauce mixture & place it in a zip lock bag. Toss the steak in the marinade to evenly coat both sides. Allow 2 hours for the bag to be refrigerated. Coat the nonstick pan with 2 tablespoons of olive oil. Preheat the pan on medium flame and cook the steaks for about 15 minutes, turning halfway through.

Per Serving: Calories 283, Fat 19.2g, Carbs 2g, Protein 24.2g

820. Cumin Pork

Ingredients for 4 servings
- 1 red onion, chopped
- 1 tablespoon of olive oil
- 1 ½ teaspoons of fresh ginger, grated
- 3 garlic cloves, chopped
- Salt and black pepper, to taste
- 2 teaspoons of ground cumin
- 1 ½ pounds of pork meat, roughly cubed
- 2 cups of chicken stock
- 2 tablespoons of lime juice

Directions and Total Time: approx. 55 minutes

Heat a pot with the oil over medium heat. Add the meat and brown for 5 minutes. Add the chopped onion and chopped cloves of garlic and cook for 5 minutes more. Add the rest of the ingredients, bring to a simmer and cook over medium heat for 35 minutes. Divide between plates and serve.

Per Serving: Calories 292, Fat 16.5g, Carbs 10.7g, Protein 14.5g

821. Delicious Beef Chili

Ingredients for 4 servings
- 2 pounds of ground beef
- 1 teaspoon of olive oil
- 1 teaspoon of garlic, minced
- 1 small onion, chopped
- 2 tablespoons of chili powder
- 1 teaspoon of oregano
- 1/2 teaspoon of thyme
- 28 ounces can of tomato, crushed
- 2 cups of beef stock
- 2 carrots, chopped
- 3 sweet potatoes, peeled and cubed
- Pepper and salt to taste

Directions and Total Time: approx. 35 minutes

Add oil into the instant pot and set the pot on sauté mode. Add meat and cook until brown. Add the remaining ingredients and stir well. Seal large-sized pot with the lid and cook on high for 35 minutes. Once done, allow releasing pressure naturally. Remove the lid. Stir well and serve.

Per Serving: Calories 302, Fat 8.2g, Carbs 19.2g, Protein 37.1g

822. Dijon and Herb Pork Tenderloin

Ingredients for 6 servings
- ½ cup of fresh Italian parsley leaves
- 3 tablespoons of fresh rosemary leaves
- 3 tablespoons of fresh thyme leaves
- 3 tablespoons of Dijon mustard
- 1 tablespoon of extra-virgin olive oil
- 4 garlic cloves, minced
- ½ teaspoon of sea salt
- ¼ teaspoon of freshly ground black pepper
- 1 (1½-pound) pork tenderloin

Directions and Total Time: approx. 40 minutes

Preheat the oven to 400°F. In a blender, pulse parsley, rosemary, thyme, mustard, olive oil, garlic, sea salt, and pepper. Spread the mixture evenly over the pork and place it on a rimmed baking sheet. Bake for about 20 minutes. Pull out from the oven and put aside for 10 minutes before slicing and serving.

Per Serving: Calories 393, Fat 12g, Carbs 74g, Protein 23g

823. Dill Beef Brisket

Ingredients for 4 servings
- 2 1/2 pounds of beef brisket, cut into cubes
- 2 1/2 cups of beef stock
- 2 tablespoons of dill, chopped
- 1 celery stalk, chopped
- 1 onion, sliced
- 1 tablespoon of garlic, minced
- Pepper to taste
- Salt to taste

Directions and Total Time: approx. 60 minutes

Add all the rest of the ingredients into the inner pot of the instant pot and stir well. Seal large-sized pot with the lid and cook on high for 50 minutes. Once done, allow releasing pressure naturally for 10 minutes then release the rest using the quick release. Remove the lid. Serve and enjoy.

Per Serving: Calories 556, Fat 18.1g, Carbs 4.3g, Protein 88.5g

824. Fall-Apart Tender Beef

Ingredients for 12 servings
- 4 pounds of boneless beef chuck roast, trimmed
- 2 large onions, sliced into thin strips
- 4 celery stalks, sliced
- 4 garlic cloves, minced
- 1 ½ cup of catsup
- 1 cup of BBQ sauce
- ¼ cup of molasses
- ¼ cup of apple cider vinegar
- 2 tablespoons of prepared yellow mustard
- ¼ teaspoon of red chili powder
- Fresh ground black pepper, to taste

Directions and Total Time: approx. 11 hours and 10 minutes

In a slow cooker, place all the ingredients and stir to combine. Set the slow cooker on a heat of "Low" and cook, covered for about 8-10 hours. Uncover the slow cooker and with 2 forks, shred the meat. Stir the meat with pan sauce. Set the slow cooker on a heat of "Low" and cook, covered for about 1 hour. Serve hot.

Per Serving: Calories 454, Fat 10g, Carbs 43.4g, Protein 48.3g

825. Feta Stuffed Pork Chops

Ingredients for 4 servings

- 4 pork chops
- 1 teaspoon of dried oregano
- 1 teaspoon of dried basil
- 2 tablespoons of fresh dill, chopped
- 1 tablespoon of parsley, chopped
- 4 ounces of feta cheese, crumbled
- 1 pinch of chili flakes

Directions and Total Time: approx. 40 minutes

Season the pork chops with oregano and basil, then cut a small pocket into each of them. Mix the dill, parsley, feta, and chili in a bowl. Stuff the pork chops with the feta mixture. Heat a grill pan over medium heat and place the pork chops in it. Cook on each side for 13 minutes. Serve immediately.

Per Serving: Calories 336, Fat 26g, Carbs 2.3g, Protein 22.4g

826. Garlic Meatballs

Ingredients for 5 servings

- 1 pound of lean ground beef
- 7 ounces of rice
- 2 small onions, peeled and chopped
- 2 garlic cloves, crushed
- 1 egg, beaten
- 1 large potato, peeled and sliced
- 3 tablespoons of extra virgin olive oil
- 1 teaspoon of salt

Directions and Total Time: approx. 8 hours and 15 minutes

Mix the lean ground beef with rice, finely chopped onions, crushed garlic, one beaten egg, and salt in a large bowl. Shape the batter into 15-20 meatballs. Oiled the bottom of your slow cooker with three tablespoons of olive oil. Make the first layer with sliced potatoes and top with meatballs. Cook low within 6-8 hours.

Per Serving: Calories 468, Fat 15.3g, Carbs 47g, Protein 33g

827. Garlic Pork Rinds

Ingredients for 2 servings

- 1/2 pound of Pork rinds
- 1/4 teaspoon of ginger
- 3 teaspoons of minced' garlic
- 1/2 cup of water
- 3 tablespoons of soy
- 1/4 teaspoon of salt
- 1/2 teaspoon of pepper

Directions and Total Time: approx. 20 minutes

Cut the pork rinds into medium cubes then rub with minced' garlic, soy sauce, salt, pepper and ginger. Let it sit for about 10 minutes. Pour the prepared cup of water into the inner pot of a moment Pot then place the seasoned pork rinds in it. Cover the moment Pot with the lid and seal it properly. Close the steam valve. Select *Manual* setting on the moment Pot and cook the pork rinds on high. Set the time to fifteen minutes. Once it's done; naturally release the moment Pot and open the lid. Transfer the cooked pork rinds to a dish then serve

Per Serving: Calories 621, Fat 37.6g, Carbs 3.7g, Protein 69.4g

828. Garlic Veal

Ingredients for 6 servings

- 6 garlic cloves, crushed
- 3 pounds of veal, cubed
- 1 cup of broth
- 1 glass of wine
- A handful of chives and parsley
- Sea salt, to taste
- Ground black pepper, to taste
- 3 tablespoons of sour cream
- 4 tablespoons of olive oil

Directions and Total Time: approx. 50 minutes

Sear the veal cubes for several minutes in olive oil while constantly stirring until brown. Add some chives and parsley, then sauté for several minutes. Add salt and pepper as desired. Add the cup of broth. Slowly cook until the meat becomes tender. Add more broth as needed. When the meat is actually tender and cooked through, add the sour cream and a glass of wine, then cook for 5 more minutes. Serve.

Per Serving: Calories 508, Fat 27.9g, Carbs 1.9g, Protein 56.4g

829. Glazed Pork Chops

Ingredients for 4 servings

- ¼ cup of apricot preserves
- 4 pork chops, boneless
- 1 tablespoon of thyme, chopped
- ½ teaspoon of cinnamon powder
- 2 tablespoons of olive oil

Directions and Total Time: approx. 20 minutes

Heat up a large-sized pan with the oil over medium-high heat, add the apricot preserves and cinnamon, whisk, bring to a simmer, cook for 10 minutes and take off the heat. Heat up your grill over medium-high heat, brush the pork chops with some of the apricot glaze, place them on the grill and cook for 10 minutes. Flip the chops, brush them with more apricot glaze, cook for 10 minutes more and divide between plates. Sprinkle the thyme on top and serve.

Per Serving: Calories 225, Fat 11g, Carbs 6g, Protein 23g

830. Glazed Ribs

Ingredients for 4 servings

- 1 rack of pork ribs, ribs separated
- 1 and ¼ cups of tomato sauce
- ¼ cup of white vinegar
- 3 tablespoons of spicy mustard
- 2 tablespoons of coconut sugar
- 3 tablespoons of water
- ¼ teaspoon of hot sauce
- 1 teaspoon of onion powder
- Cooking spray

Directions and Total Time: approx. 1 hour and 30 minutes

Cover the pork ribs with foil and bake for 1 hour at 400°F. Combine the tomato sauce, mustard, sugar, vinegar, water, onion powder, and hot sauce in a skillet, swirl to combine, and simmer for 10 minutes. Brush half of the sauce over the ribs put them on a prepared grill over medium-high heat, spray with cooking spray, cook for 4 minutes on each side, split into plates, and serve with the remaining created sauce on the side. Enjoy!

Per Serving: Calories 287, Fat 5g, Carbs 16g, Protein 15g

831. Greek Pork

Ingredients for 8 servings

- 3 pounds of pork roast, sliced into cubes
- 1/4 cup of chicken broth
- 1/4 cup of lemon juice
- 2 teaspoons of dried oregano
- 2 teaspoons of garlic powder

Directions and Total Time: approx. 1 hour and 10 minutes

Put the pork in the Instant Pot. In a large-sized bowl, mix all the remaining ingredients. Pour the mixture over the pork. Toss to coat evenly. Secure the pot. Choose manual mode. Cook at high pressure for 50 minutes. Release the pressure naturally.

Per Serving: Calories 478, Fat 21.6g, Carbs 1.2g, Protein 65.1g

832. Greek Pork Chops

Ingredients for 8 servings

- 8 pork chops, boneless
- 4 teaspoons of dried oregano
- 2 tablespoons of Worcestershire sauce
- 3 tablespoons of fresh lemon juice
- ¼ cup of olive oil
- 1 teaspoon of ground mustard
- 2 teaspoons of garlic powder
- 2 teaspoons of onion powder
- Pepper
- Salt

Directions and Total Time: approx. 16 minutes

Whisk together oil, garlic powder, onion powder, oregano, Worcestershire sauce, lemon juice, mustard, pepper, and salt. Place pork chops in a dish, pour marinade over pork chops, and coat well. Place in refrigerator overnight—preheat the grill. Put the boneless pork chops on the grill and cook within 3-4 minutes on each side. Serve and enjoy.

Per Serving: Calories 324, Fat 26.5g, Carbs 2.5g, Protein 18g

833. Grilled Kefta

Ingredients for 4 servings

- 1 medium onion
- ⅓ cup of fresh Italian parsley
- 1-pound of ground beef
- ¼ teaspoon of ground cumin
- ¼ teaspoon of cinnamon
- 1 teaspoon of salt
- ½ teaspoon of freshly ground black pepper

Directions and Total Time: approx. 15 minutes

Warm a grill or grill pan to high. Mince the onion plus parsley in a food processor until finely chopped. Combine the beef with the onion mix, ground cumin, cinnamon, salt, and pepper in a large bowl using your hands. Divide the meat into 6 portions. Form each portion into a flat oval. Put the patties on the grill or grill pan and cook for 3 minutes on each side.

Per Serving: Calories 203, Fat 10g, Carbs 3g, Protein 24g

834. Grilled Pork Chops

Ingredients for 2 servings

- 2 pork chops
- Salt and black pepper, to taste
- 1 teaspoon of garlic powder
- 1 teaspoon of oregano
- ½ cup of feta cheese, cubed
- 2 tablespoons of olive oil
- 2 tablespoons of black olives, sliced
- Splash of lemon juice

Directions and Total Time: approx. 24 minutes

Rub the pork chops with black pepper, oregano, garlic powder and salt. Set a grill pan greased with oil over medium heat. Sear the pork chops for approximately about 5-7 minutes on each side until tender. Mix the lemon juice, oil, olives and cheese in a bowl. Serve the grilled chops with cheese mixture. Enjoy.

Per Serving: Calories 492, Fat 42.9g, Carbs 3.6g, Protein 23.7g

835. Herb Pork Chops

Ingredients for 4 servings

- 4 pork chops, bone-in
- 1 teaspoon of fennel seed, crushed
- 1 teaspoon of dried thyme
- 2 teaspoons of dried rosemary, crumbled
- ⅓ cup of olive oil
- 1 bay of leaf, crushed
- 2 teaspoons of dried sage, crumbled
- 1 ½ teaspoon of salt

Directions and Total Time: approx. 18 minutes

In a bowl, mix together sage, oil, bay leaf, thyme, rosemary, fennel seed and salt. Add herb mixture and pork chops into the zip-lock bag, seal bag, and place in refrigerator for overnight. Preheat the grill. Place marinated pieces of pork chops on the grill and cook for 4 minutes on each side or until cooked.

Per Serving: Calories 406, Fat 36.9g, Carbs 1.1g, Protein 18.2g

836. Honey Glazed Pork Loins

Ingredients for 4 servings

- 4 small pork loin chops
- 1 tablespoon of honey
- 2 teaspoons of mustard
- 1 teaspoon of cider vinegar
- ½ cup of chicken stock
- Spray oil
- Salt and black pepper, to taste

Directions and Total Time: approx. 40 minutes

Place a pan greased with oil spray over medium high heat. Sear the pork loins until golden brown on both the sides. Adjust the seasoning with salt and pepper. In a suitable bowl, mix the stock with the vinegar, mustard and honey. Pour this prepared mixture over the pork chops and cook until the sauce is reduced to half. Garnish with parsley. Serve warm.

Per Serving: Calories 281, Fat 20.4g, Carbs 5g, Protein 18.5g

Ingredients for 4 servings

- 10 ounces pork chops
- 1 teaspoon liquid honey
- 1 teaspoon tomato sauce
- 1 teaspoon sunflower oil
- ½ teaspoon sage
- ½ teaspoon mustard

Directions and Total Time: approx. 8 minutes

Cut the pork chops on the strips and place in the bowl. Add liquid honey, tomato sauce, sunflower oil, sage, and mustard. Mix up the meat well and leave for 15-20 minutes to marinate. Meanwhile, preheat the grill to 385F. Arrange the pork strips in the grill and roast them for 4 minutes from each side. Sprinkle the meat with remaining honey liquid during to cooking to make the taste of meat juicier.

Per Serving: Calories 245, Fat 18.9g, Carbs 1.7g, Protein 16.1g

838. Hot Pork Meatballs

Ingredients for 2 servings

- 4 ounces pork loin, grinded
- ½ teaspoon garlic powder
- ¼ teaspoon chili powder
- ¼ teaspoon cayenne pepper
- ¼ teaspoon ground black pepper
- ¼ teaspoon white pepper
- 1 tablespoon water
- 1 teaspoon olive oil

Directions and Total Time: approx. 10 minutes

Mix up together grinded meat, garlic powder, cayenne pepper, ground black pepper, white pepper, and water. With the help of the fingertips make the small meatballs. Heat up olive oil in the skillet. Arrange the kofte in the oil and cook them for 10 minutes totally. Flip the kofte on another side from time to time.

Per Serving: Calories 162, Fat 10.3g, Carbs 1g, Protein 15.7g

839. Italian Pork Medallions

Ingredients for 2 servings

- 7 ounces of pork tenderloin, sliced
- 1 teaspoon of Italian seasonings
- 1 teaspoon of jam
- 1 tablespoon of sunflower oil

Directions and Total Time: approx. 10 minutes

Heat up sunflower oil in the skillet. Rub one side of the pork tenderloins with Italian spices and place them in the hot oil. Sprinkle now the second side of the meat with remaining Italian seasoning. Cook the pork tenderloins for 3 minutes from each side. Then add jam and wait till it is melted. Cook the meat for 2 minutes from each side more over the medium-low heat. Serve the meat with the hot jam sauce from the skillet.

Per Serving: Calories 220, Fat 11.2g, Carbs 2.6g, Protein 26g

840. Jalapeno Lamb Patties

Ingredients for 4 servings

- 1 pound of ground lamb
- 1 jalapeno pepper, minced
- 5 basil leaves, minced
- 10 mint leaves, minced
- 1/4 cup of fresh parsley, chopped
- 1 cup of feta cheese, crumbled
- 1 tablespoon of garlic, minced
- 1 teaspoon of dried oregano
- 1/4 teaspoon of pepper
- 1/2 teaspoon of kosher salt
- Cooking spray

Directions and Total Time: approx. 18 minutes

Add all the rest of ingredients into the mixing bowl and mix until well combined. Preheat the grill to 450°F. Spray grill with cooking spray. Make four equal shape patties from the meat mixture and place them on a hot grill and cook for 3 minutes. Turn patties to another side and cook for 4 minutes. Serve and enjoy.

Per Serving: Calories 317, Fat 16g, Carbs 3g, Protein 37.5g

841. Kale and Ground Beef Casserole

Ingredients for 4 servings

- 4-ounces of mozzarella, shredded
- 2 cups of marinara sauce
- 10-ounces of kale, fresh
- 1 teaspoon of oregano
- 1 teaspoon of onion powder
- ½ teaspoon of sea salt
- 1 pound of lean ground beef
- 2 tablespoons of olive oil

Directions and Total Time: approx. 26 minutes

In a deep large-sized skillet, heat the olive oil for 2-minutes, add in the ground beef, and cook for an additional 8-minutes or until meat is browned. In a mixing dish, combine the salt and pepper. In batches, stir the kale into beef mixture, cooking for another 2-minutes. Add the marinara sauce and simmer for another 2 minutes. Mix in half the cheese into the mixture. Transfer mixture into the air fryer baking dish. Sprinkle the remaining cheese on top. Broil in the air fryer at 400°Fahrenheit for 2-minutes. Allow resting for 5-minutes before serving.

Per Serving: Calories 312, Fat 13.2g, Carbs 9.2g, Protein 43.2g

842. Lamb and Coconut

Ingredients for 4 servings

- 1 ounce of shredded coconut
- 1 ounce of almond flour
- 1 tablespoon of salt
- 1 egg (small)
- 4 ounces of boneless, skinless chicken breast
- ½ teaspoon of coconut oil

Directions and Total Time: approx. 30 minutes

Mix grated coconut, almond flour, and sea salt in a mixing bowl. In a second dish, whisk the egg; put the lamb into the egg, then turn in the flour mixture until well coated. In a large-sized skillet, heat the coconut oil and cook the chicken until the coating is brown. Place the skinless chicken breast in the oven and bake for almost 10 minutes at 350°F.

Per Serving: Calories 506, Fat 40g, Carbs 8g, Protein 28g

843. Lamb and Tomato Sauce

Ingredients for 3 servings

- 9 ounces lamb shanks
- 1 onion, diced
- 1 carrot, diced
- 1 tablespoon olive oil
- 1 teaspoon salt
- 1 teaspoon ground black pepper
- 1 ½ cup chicken stock
- 1 tablespoon tomato paste

Directions and Total Time: approx. 55 minutes

Sprinkle the lamb shanks with salt and ground black pepper. Heat up olive oil in the saucepan. Add lamb shanks and roast them for 5 minutes from each side. Transfer meat in the plate. After this, add onion and carrot in the saucepan. Roast the vegetables for 3 minutes. Add tomato paste and mix up well. Then add chicken stock and bring the liquid to boil. Add lamb shanks, stir well, and close the lid. Cook the meat for 40 minutes over the medium-low heat.

Per Serving: Calories 232, Fat 11.3g, Carbs 7.3g, Protein 25.1g

844. Lamb Chops

Ingredients for 4 servings

- 1 tablespoon of oregano, dry
- 1 tablespoon of minced garlic
- 1/4 teaspoon of black pepper
- 1/2 tablespoon of salt
- 2 tablespoons of lemon juice, freshly squeezed
- 8 fat-trimmed lamb loin chops
- Spray for cooking

Directions and Total Time: approx. 25 minutes

Preheat the oven to broil. Combine all of the spices, herbs, and lemon juice in a small dish and rub the mix on each side of the lamb chops. Grill the lamb chops for four minutes on every side or until done to your liking on a large-sized broiler pan sprayed with cooking spray. Cover the grilled lamb chops with foil and set aside for five minutes before serving.

Per Serving: Calories 465, Fat 38g, Carbs 12g, Protein 14g

845. Lamb Kofta

Ingredients for 6 servings

- 2 tablespoons of fat-free plain Greek yogurt
- 1 pound of ground lamb
- 2 tablespoons of onion, grated
- 2 tablespoons of fresh cilantro, minced
- 1 teaspoon of ground cumin
- Salt and black pepper, to taste
- 2 teaspoons of garlic, minced
- 1 teaspoon of ground cilantro
- 1 teaspoon of ground turmeric
- 1 tablespoon of olive oil

Directions and Total Time: approx. 30 minutes

Combine all the rest of the prepared ingredients in a large bowl and mix well. Make 12 equal-sized oblong patties out of the mixture. Heat the tablespoons of olive oil in a large non-stick skillet placed over medium-high heat. Add the patties and cook for about 10 minutes until browned on both sides, flipping occasionally. Dish out and serve.

Per Serving: Calories 169, Fat 8g, Carbs 1.2g, Protein 21.9g

846. Lamb Shanks with Red Wine

Ingredients for 4 servings

- 2 tablespoons of olive oil
- 2 tablespoons of flour
- 4 lamb shanks, trimmed
- 1 onion, chopped
- 2 garlic cloves, crushed
- 2/3 cup of red wine
- 3 cups of tomato sauce

Directions and Total Time: approx. 5 hours and 20 minutes

Heat a skillet over high heat. Add the olive oil. Season the lamb shanks, then roll in the flour. Shake off excess flour and place the shanks in the skillet to brown on all sides. Spray the slow cooker with olive oil and place the browned shanks in the slow cooker. Add the crushed garlic to the red wine. Mix with the tomato sauce and then pour the mixture over the lamb shanks and cook on low for 5–6 hours.

Per Serving: Calories 354, Fat 12g, Carbs 43g, Protein 16g

847. Lamb with Black Olives

Ingredients for 6 servings

- 2 tablespoons of extra-virgin olive oil
- 3 garlic cloves, peeled and smashed
- fresh parsley, 1–2 sprigs
- 2-pounds of lean ground lamb
- 2 peeled and sliced tomatoes
- ½ teaspoon of rosemary (dried)
- 12 black olives pitted and halved
- 1 cup of white wine (dry)

Directions and Total Time: approx. 55 minutes

In a large-sized pan, heat the olive oil, add the garlic and parsley and cook until golden brown. Continue to cook, often stirring, until the lamb is browned. Tomatoes, rosemary, olives, and wine are added to the pan. Stir in the lamb, cover, and simmer for 3–5 minutes, or until most of the liquid has evaporated. Serve with a side of rice.

Per Serving: Calories 720, Fat 53g, Carbs 9g, Protein 48g

848. Lebanese Beef and Green Beans

Ingredients for 4 servings

- 1 pound of beef stew meat, cubed
- 1 pound of fresh green beans, 2-inch pieces
- 1 medium onion, chopped
- 1 (32-ounces) can of crushed tomatoes
- 1 tablespoon of ground cinnamon
- Salt and black pepper, to taste
- ¼ cup of fresh parsley, chopped

Directions and Total Time: approx. 4 hours and 15 minutes

Place all the rest of the prepared ingredients except for the parsley and stir to combine in a slow cooker. Set the slow cooker on a heat of "High" and cook, covered for about 4 hours. Serve hot with the garnishing of parsley.

Per Serving: Calories 353, Fat 7.3g, Carbs 30.4g, Protein 42.4g

849. Lime and Mustard Lamb

Ingredients for 2 servings

- 8 ounces lamb ribs, trimmed
- 1 tablespoon olive oil
- 1 tablespoon lime juice
- ½ teaspoon lime zest, grated
- ¼ teaspoon mustard
- ½ teaspoon salt

Directions and Total Time: approx. 25 minutes

In the shallow bowl combine together olive oil, lime juice, lime zest, mustard, and salt. Rub the lamb ribs with the lime mixture well and place in the skillet. Roast the meat for 5 minutes from each side. Then add remaining lime mixture and close the lid. Cook the lamb ribs for 20 minutes over the medium heat. You can flip the ribs on another side during cooking.

Serving: Calories 325, Fat 22.2g, Carbs 0.2g, Protein 29.8g

850. Meat Cakes

Ingredients for 4 servings

- 1 cup broccoli, shredded
- ½ cup ground pork
- 2 eggs, beaten
- 1 teaspoon salt
- 1 tablespoon Italian seasonings
- 1 teaspoon olive oil
- 3 tablespoons wheat flour, whole grain
- 1 tablespoon dried dill

Directions and Total Time: approx. 10 minutes

In the mixing bowl combine together shredded broccoli and ground pork. Add salt, Italian seasoning, flour, and dried dill. Mix up the mixture until homogenous. Then add eggs and stir until smooth. Heat up olive oil in the skillet. With the help of the spoon make latkes and place them in the hot oil. Roast the latkes for 4 minutes from each side over the medium heat. The cooked latkes should have a light brown crust. Dry the latkes with the paper towels if needed.

Per Serving: Calories 143, Fat 6g, Carbs 7g, Protein 15.1g

851. Meat Pie with Yogurt

Ingredients for 4 servings

- 2 pounds of lean ground beef
- 5-6 garlic cloves, crushed
- 1 teaspoon of salt
- ½ teaspoon of freshly ground black pepper
- 1 pack of yufka dough
- ½ cup of butter, melted
- 1 cup of sour cream
- 3 cups of liquid yogurt

Directions and Total Time: approx. 25 minutes

Mix the ground beef with garlic cloves, salt, and pepper in a large bowl. Mix well until fully incorporated. Lay a sheet of yufka on a work surface and brush with melted butter. Line with the meat mixture and roll up. Repeat the process until all fixing is used. Gently place in a lightly greased slow cooker and close the lid. Cook for 4-6 hours on low, remove from the cooker and allow it to cool. Meanwhile, combine sour cream with yogurt. Spread the mixture over the pie and serve cold.

Per Serving: Calories 503, Fat 32.8g, Carbs 2.6g, Protein 47.4g

852. Mediterranean Beef

Ingredients for 6 servings

- 3 tablespoons of all-purpose flour mixed with 1/2 teaspoon dried oregano
- 2 pounds of beef chuck shoulder (boneless), trimmed and sliced into cubes
- 1 onion, chopped
- 1/2 cup of beef broth
- 1/4 cup of balsamic vinegar

Directions and Total Time: approx. 1 hour and 10 minutes

Add the prepared little salt and pepper to the flour mixture. Coat the beef cubes with the flour mixture. Set your Instant Pot to a sauté mode and add a teaspoon of oil. Cook the beef, onion and garlic for 5 minutes. Pour in the broth and vinegar. Seal the pot. Choose manual. Cook at high pressure for 40 minutes. Release the pressure naturally.

Per Serving: Calories 357, Fat 14.3g, Carbs 5.4g, Protein 46.9g

853. Mediterranean Flank Steak

Ingredients for 6 servings

- 2 tablespoons of fragrant herbs, chopped (marjoram, rosemary, sage, thyme, or a combination)
- 2 garlic cloves, minced
- 2 tablespoons of olive oil (extra virgin)
- 1 teaspoon of salt
- 1 tablespoon of black pepper, ground
- 2 pounds of trimmed flank steak
- 1/2 cup of vinaigrette (Greek)

Directions and Total Time: approx. 60 minutes

Combine herbs, garlic, extra virgin olive oil, sea salt, and pepper in a small bowl; rub over the steak and set aside for twenty minutes. Meanwhile, preheat your gas grill over medium-high heat. Cook the steak for fifteen minutes on the grill, flipping it after four minutes to ensure equal grilling. Transfer the prepared grilled steak to a cutting board and set aside for five minutes to rest before slicing it into tiny pieces and plating. Serve immediately with vinaigrette drizzled over the top.

Per Serving: Calories 240, Fat 15g, Carbs 1g, Protein 23g

854. Mediterranean Grilled Pork with Tomato Salsa

Ingredients for 4 servings

- 4 pork chops
- 1 teaspoon dried oregano
- 1 teaspoon dried basil
- 1 teaspoon dried marjoram
- Salt and pepper to taste
- 4 tomatoes, peeled and diced
- 1 jalapeno, chopped
- 1 shallot, chopped
- 2 garlic cloves, minced
- 1 green onion, chopped
- 2 tablespoons chopped parsley
- 1 tablespoon lemon juice

Directions and Total Time: approx. 60 minutes

Season with salt and pepper, oregano, basil and marjoram. Heat a grill pan over medium flame and place the pork chops on the grill. Cook on each side for 5-6 minutes. For the salsa, mix the tomatoes, jalapeno, shallot, garlic, onion and parsley. Add salt and pepper to taste. Add the lemon juice as well. Serve the pork chops with salsa.

Per Serving: Calories 286, Fat 20.3g, Carbs 6.3g, Protein 19.4g

855. Lamb Chop Traybake

Ingredients for 4 servings

- 2 tablespoons of fresh mint, chopped
- 1 teaspoon of fresh rosemary, chopped
- 3 cloves of garlic, minced
- 2 tablespoons of olive oil
- 4 lean lamb chops
- 1 butternut squash, diced
- 4 zucchinis, diced

Directions and Total Time: approx. 45 minutes

Preheat your oven at a heat of 360°F. Blend the mint, garlic, 1 tablespoon of olive oil and rosemary in a blender. Liberally rub this mixture over the lamb chops. Spread the squash and zucchini onto a baking sheet. Drizzle remaining oil over them and place the lamb chops on top. Roast these chops and veggies for approximately about 35 minutes. Serve warm.

Per Serving: Calories 296, Fat 15.5g, Carbs 11.8g, Protein 28g

856. Mediterranean Lamb Chops

Ingredients for 4 servings

- 4 lean lamb chops
- 1 tablespoon of mint
- 1 tablespoon of rosemary
- 2 cloves of garlic
- 2 tablespoons of olive oil
- 1 small eggplant, sliced
- 1 zucchini, sliced
- 1 red pepper, large chunks
- 2 ounces of feta cheese
- 9 ounces of cherry tomatoes

Directions and Total Time: approx. 45 minutes

At 360°F preheat your oven. Mash the garlic with the rosemary, 1 tablespoon of oil and mint using a mortar and pestle. Rub this mixture over the lamb chops. Spread pepper, zucchini and eggplant onto a baking sheet. Drizzle 1 tablespoon of oil over the lamb and bake for 25 minutes. Add the cherry tomatoes and feta cheese on top. Roast the pork for 10 minutes Serve warm.

Per Serving: Calories 317, Fat 18.4g, Carbs 8.7g, Protein 28.8g

857. Mediterranean Pork Cacciatore

Ingredients for 4 servings

- 2 tablespoons of olive oil
- 1 sliced onion
- 4 boneless pork chops
- 1 jar of pasta sauce
- 1 can of diced tomatoes
- 1 green bell pepper, strips
- 1 package of fresh mushrooms, sliced
- 2 large cloves garlic, minced
- 1 teaspoon of Italian seasoning
- 1/2 teaspoon of dried basil
- 1/2 cup of dry white wine
- 4 slices of mozzarella cheese

Directions and Total Time: approx. 8 hours and 15 minutes

Cook the pork chops over medium-high heat in a large skillet, then transfer it to your slow cooker. Cook onion in oil on medium heat in the same pan. Mix in mushrooms plus bell pepper until they are soft. Mix in pasta sauce, diced tomatoes, plus white wine. Season with Italian seasoning, basil, and garlic. Pour over pork chops in the slow cooker. Cook on low within 7 to 8 hours. Put cheese slices on each chop and cover with sauce to serve.

Per Serving: Calories 252, Fat 6g, Carbs 23g, Protein 26g

858. Moist Shredded Beef

Ingredients for 4 servings

- 2 pounds of beef chuck roast, chunks
- 1/2 tablespoon of dried red pepper
- 1 tablespoon of Italian seasoning
- 1 tablespoon of garlic, minced
- 2 tablespoons of vinegar
- 14 ounces of can fire-roasted tomatoes
- 1/2 cup of bell pepper, chopped
- 1/2 cup of carrots, chopped
- 1 cup of onion, chopped
- 1 teaspoon of salt

Directions and Total Time: approx. 30 minutes

Add all the rest of the ingredients into the inner pot of the instant pot and set the pot on sauté mode. Seal large-sized pot with the lid and cook on high for 20 minutes. Once done, release pressure using quick release. Remove the lid. Shred the meat using a fork. Stir well and serve.

Per Serving: Calories 456, Fat 32.7g, Carbs 7.7g, Protein 31g

859. Moroccan Lamb

Ingredients for 6 servings

- 2 pounds of stew lamb meat, diced
- 3 cloves of garlic, diced
- Seasoning mixture (1/2 teaspoon cinnamon, 1 teaspoon dried oregano, 1/2 teaspoon chili flakes, 1 teaspoon paprika, 1 teaspoon mild curry, 1 teaspoon coriander seed powder)
- 1 cup of canned tomatoes, undrained
- 1 cup of beef stock

Directions and Total Time: approx. 60 minutes

Choose sauté in the Instant Pot. Pour in 1 tablespoon of olive oil. Cook the onion and season with a pinch of salt. Add the remaining ingredients. Lock the lid in place. Set it to manual and cook at high pressure for 20 minutes. Release the pressure naturally.

Per Serving: Calories 321, Fat 13.7g, Carbs 3.9g, Protein 43.6g

860. Mustard and Rosemary Pork Tenderloin

Ingredients for 4 servings

- ½ cup of fresh parsley leaves.
- ¼ cup of Dijon mustard.
- 6 garlic cloves.
- 3 tablespoons of fresh rosemary leaves.
- 3 tablespoons of extra-virgin olive oil.
- ½ teaspoon of sea salt.
- ¼ teaspoon of freshly ground black pepper.
- 1 (1½-pound) pork tenderloin

Directions and Total Time: approx. 30 minutes

Preheat the oven to 400°F. In a food processor, combine the parsley, mustard, garlic, rosemary, olive oil, salt, and pepper. Pulse in 1-second pulses, about 20 times, until a paste form. Rub this paste all over the tenderloin and put the pork on a rimmed baking sheet. Bake the pork for about 15 minutes or until it registers 165°F on an instant-read meat thermometer. Let rest for just about 5 minutes, slice, and serve.

Per Serving: Calories 362, Fat 18g, Carbs 5g, Protein 2g

861. Parmesan Pork Chops

Ingredients for 6 servings

- 1 tablespoon of salt
- 1 teaspoon of ground black pepper
- 1 teaspoon of chili flakes
- 2 pounds of pork loin
- 1 cup of breadcrumbs
- 2 tablespoons of Italian seasoning
- 3 tablespoons of olive oil
- 5 ounces of parmesan, grated

Directions and Total Time: approx. 25 minutes

Slice the pork loin into the serving chops. Then rub the pork chops with salt and ground black pepper. Add chili flakes. Combine the breadcrumbs with the Italian seasoning and stir the mixture with the help of the fork. Add the grated parmesan and stir. Pour the tablespoons of olive oil into a skillet and heat it over medium heat. Coat the pork chops in the breadcrumb mixture carefully. Fry the pork chops in the preheated olive oil for 10 minutes on both sides. Chill the cooked pork chops.

Per Serving: Calories 574, Fat 34.1g, Carbs 14.1g, Protein 51.3g

862. Pepper Meat

Ingredients for 6 servings

- 2 pounds of beef fillet or another tender cut
- 5 medium-sized onions, peeled and finely chopped 3 tbsp. of tomato paste
- 2 tablespoons of oil
- 1 tablespoon of butter, melted
- 2 tablespoons of fresh parsley, finely chopped
- ½ teaspoon of freshly ground black pepper
- 1 teaspoon of salt

Directions and Total Time: approx. 10 hours and 15 minutes

Oil the bottom of your slow cooker with some oil. About two tablespoons will be enough. Slice the meat into bite-sized and place them in the cooker. Add finely chopped onions, tomato paste, fresh parsley, salt, and pepper. Mix and put about 2 cups of water. Cook on low for 8-10 hours. Stir in one tablespoon of melted butter and serve warm.

Per Serving: Calories 382, Fat 16g, Carbs 10.3g, Protein 47.3g

863. Pepper Pork Rack

Ingredients for 6 servings

- ¼ cup of pepper.
- 1 Pork Rib Rack

Directions and Total Time: approx. 1 hour and 30 minutes

You'll want to start off by heating your oven only to 375°F. As the oven heat, you will want to prepare your rib rack. Be sure that you coat the roast with the pepper seasoning. While a quarter of 1 cup pepper may seem like a lot, you will want this much for maximum flavor. When the meat is coated, place the roast into a baking dish, bones up. If you are ready to cook your meal, pop it into the oven for 1 hour and 30 minutes. Once it is cooked through until the inside, you can remove it from the oven and allow it to rest for just around about 10 minutes.

Finally, cut the meat between the rib bones, and your meal is ready to be served!

Per Serving: Calories 400, Fat 15g, Carbs 28g, Protein 30g

864. Pitas with Mediterranean Beef

Ingredients for 4 servings

- 1 pound of beef, ground
- Black pepper, freshly ground
- 1/2 teaspoon of sea salt
- 1/2 teaspoon of oregano, dry
- 1/4 small red onion, sliced
- 2 tablespoons extra virgin olive oil, split
- 3/4 cup of store-bought hummus
- 2 tablespoons of flat-leaf parsley, fresh
- 4 pita bread
- 4 slices of lemon

Directions and Total Time: approx. 15 minutes

Season beef with 1/4 teaspoon ground pepper, 1/2 teaspoon sea salt, oregano, and shape into 16 patties. In a large-sized pan set over medium heat, add one tablespoon extra-virgin olive oil and fry the beef patties for around two minutes per side, or until lightly browned. To serve, layer the beef patties, hummus, parsley, and onion on top of pitas, then sprinkle with the extra olive oil and lemon wedges.

Per Serving: Calories 368, Fat 10g, Carbs 42g, Protein 27g

865. Pork and Cheese Stuffed Peppers

Ingredients for 2 servings

- 2 sweet Italian peppers, deveined and halved.
- 1/2 Spanish onion, finely chopped.
- 1 cup of marinara sauce.
- 1/2 cup of cheddar cheese, grated.
- 4 ounces of pork, ground

Directions and Total Time: approx. 55 minutes

Heat 1 tablespoon of canola oil in a large-sized saucepan over a moderate heat. Then, sauté the onion for 3–4 minutes until tender and fragrant. Add in the ground pork; cook for 3–4 minutes more. Add in Italian seasoning mix. Spoon the mixture into the pepper halves. Spoon the marinara sauce into a lightly greased baking dish. Arrange the stuffed peppers in the baking dish. Bake in the prepared preheated oven at a temperature of 395°F for 17–20 minutes. Top with cheddar cheese and continue to bake for about 5 minutes or until the top is golden brown. Bon appétit!

Per Serving: Calories 21.3, Fat 5.7g, Carbs 20.2g, Protein 1.9g

866. Pork and Orzo

Ingredients for 2 servings

- 1 ½ pounds of pork tenderloin, diced
- 1 teaspoon of black pepper
- 2 tablespoons of olive oil
- 3 quarts of water
- 1-¼ cup of uncooked orzo pasta
- ¼ teaspoon of salt
- 1 package (6 oz.) fresh baby spinach
- 1 cup of grape tomatoes, halved
- 3/4 cup of feta cheese, crumbled

Directions and Total Time: approx. 29 minutes

Season the pork cubes with black pepper. Sauté the pork with oil in a skillet for 10 minutes until brown. Meanwhile, cook the orzo in salted water in a Dutch oven for 8 minutes. Cook for approximately about 1 minute once you've added the spinach. Drain and add this orzo mixture, cheese and tomatoes to the pork. Serve warm.

Per Serving: Calories 396, Fat 1.1g, Carbs 18.7g, Protein 43.7g

867. Pork and Peas

Ingredients for 4 servings

- 4 ounces of snow peas
- 2 tablespoons of avocado oil
- 1-pound of boneless pork loin, cubed
- ¾ cup of beef stock
- ½ cup of red onion, chopped
- Salt and white pepper, to taste

Directions and Total Time: approx. 30 minutes

Heat a pan with the oil over medium-high heat. Add the pork and brown for 5 minutes. Add the prepared peas and the rest of the ingredients, toss, bring to a simmer and cook over medium heat for 15 minutes. Divide between plates and serve right away.

Per Serving: Calories 332, Fat 16.5g, Carbs 20.7g, Protein 26.5g

868. Pork and Tomato Meatloaf

Ingredients for 8 servings

- 2 cups ground pork
- 1 egg, beaten
- ¼ cup crushed tomatoes
- 1 teaspoon salt
- 1 teaspoon ground black pepper
- 1 oz Swiss cheese, grated
- 1 teaspoon minced garlic
- 1/3 onion, diced
- ¼ cup black olives, chopped
- 1 jalapeno pepper, chopped
- 1 teaspoon dried basil
- Cooking spray

Directions and Total Time: approx. 55 minutes

Spray the loaf mold with cooking spray. Then combine together ground pork, egg, crushed tomatoes, salt, ground black pepper. Grated Swiss cheese, minced garlic, onion, olives, jalapeno pepper, and dried basil. Stir the mass until it is homogenous and transfer it in the prepared loaf mold. Flatten the surface of meatloaf well and cover with foil. Bake the meatloaf for 40 minutes at 375F. Then discard the foil and bake the meal for 15 minutes more. Chill the cooked meatloaf to the room temperature and then remove it from the loaf mold. Slice it on the servings.

Per Serving: Calories 265, Fat 18.3g, Carbs 1.9g, Protein 22.1g

869. Pork Bruschetta

Ingredients for 4 servings

- 1 teaspoon of extra virgin olive oil, split
- 1 pork breast, boneless and skinless
- 3 ounces of cherry tomatoes
- 2 teaspoons of balsamic vinegar
- Basil leaves, fresh
- 1 small garlic clove, minced
- 1 small sliced onion

Directions and Total Time: approx. 30 minutes

Cook the pork in half of the oil in a pan over medium heat. Meanwhile, prepare the veggies and chop basil leaves into slivers. Sauté the prepared minced garlic and onion in the remaining oil for around 3 minutes. For approximately 5 minutes, stir in the basil and tomatoes. Add the vinegar and mix well. Cook until the pork is well cooked, then serve with the tomato and onion mixture on top.

Per Serving: Calories 60, Fat 2g, Carbs 10g, Protein 2g

870. Pork Cacciatore

Ingredients for 6 servings

- 1 ½ pound of pork chops
- 1 teaspoon of dried oregano
- 1 cup of beef broth
- 3 tablespoons of tomato paste
- 14 ounces can of tomato, diced
- 2 cups of mushrooms, sliced
- 1 small onion, diced
- 1 garlic clove, minced
- 2 tablespoons of olive oil
- ¼ teaspoon of pepper
- ½ teaspoon of salt

Directions and Total Time: approx. 6 hours and 10 minutes

Warm-up oil in your pan over medium heat. Add the pound of pork chops to the pan and cook until brown on both sides. Transfer pork chops into the pot. Pour remaining ingredients over the pork chops. Cook on low heat within 6 hours. Serve and enjoy.

Per Serving: Calories 440, Fat 33g, Carbs 6g, Protein 28g

871. Pork Chops and Relish

Ingredients for 6 servings

- 6 pork chops, boneless
- 7 ounces marinated artichoke hearts, chopped and their liquid reserved
- A pinch of salt and black pepper
- 1 teaspoon hot pepper sauce
- 1 and ½ cups tomatoes, cubed
- 1 jalapeno pepper, chopped
- ½ cup roasted bell peppers, chopped
- ½ cup black olives, pitted and sliced

Directions and Total Time: approx. 14 minutes

In a bowl, mix the chops with the pepper sauce, reserved liquid from the artichokes, cover and keep in the fridge for 15 minutes. Heat up a grill over medium-high heat, add the pork chops and cook for 7 minutes on each side. In a large-sized bowl, combine the artichokes with the peppers and the remaining ingredients, toss, divide on top of the chops and serve.

Per Serving: Calories 215, Fat 6g, Carbs 6g, Protein 35g

872. Pork Chops and Sauce

Ingredients for 6 servings

- 6 chops of pork loin
- 1 tablespoon of olive oil
- 2 tablespoons of tapioca, crushed
- 1 minced yellow onion
- Low-sodium 10-ounce mushroom soup cream
- 1/2 cup of juice for apples
- 2 teaspoons thyme, diced
- 1 and 1/2 cups of cut mushrooms
- 1/4 teaspoon of crushed garlic

Directions and Total Time: approx. 9 hours and 39 minutes

In a hot skillet, sear the pork chops for four minutes on each side, then transfer to a slow cooker. Include the crushed tapioca, onion, mushroom soup sauce, apple juice, thyme, mushrooms, and ground garlic.

Per Serving: Calories 229, Fat 4g, Carbs 16g, Protein 17g

873. Pork Chops and Tomato Sauce

Ingredients for 4 servings

- 4 pork chops, boneless
- 1 tablespoon of soy sauce
- ¼ teaspoon of sesame oil
- 1 and ½ cups of tomato paste
- 1 yellow onion
- 8 mushrooms, sliced

Directions and Total Time: approx. 30 minutes

Toss pork chops in a dish with soy sauce and sesame oil, then set aside for 10 minutes. Set and prepare your instant pot to sauté mode, add the pork chops, and brown them on all sides for 5 minutes. Stir in onion, and cook for 1-2 minutes more. Toss in the tomato paste and mushrooms, cover, and simmer for 8-9 minutes on high. Divide everything between plates and serve. Enjoy!

Per Serving: Calories 300, Fat 7g, Carbs 18g, Protein 4g

874. Pork Chops with Cinnamon

Ingredients for 2 servings

- 1/2 pound of Pork chops
- 1/4 teaspoon of cinnamon
- 1/2 apple
- 1 teaspoon of sugar
- 1 tablespoon of butter
- 1/4 teaspoon of nutmeg
- 1/2 cup of water
- 1/4 teaspoon of salt
- 1/4 teaspoon of pepper

Directions and Total Time: approx. 25 minutes

Rub the pound of pork chops with salt and pepper then let it sit. Meanwhile, cut the apple into slices then place in a bowl. Sprinkle sugar, cinnamon and nutmeg over the sliced apple then toss to mix. Now, pour water into the inner pot of a moment Pot then sprinkle the sliced apple in it. After that; place the seasoned pork chops on top then cover and seal the moment Pot properly. Close the steam valve. Select *Manual* setting on the moment Pot and cook the pork chops on high for 20 minutes. Once it's done; naturally release the moment Pot and open the lid. Transfer the cooked pork chops to a dish then garnish with the apples

Per Serving: Calories 267, Fat 16.6g, Carbs 8.5g, Protein 21.1g

875. Pork Chops with Cumin

Ingredients for 2 servings

- 4-ounces of pork chop with a lean center cut
- 1/8 tablespoon of salt
- 1/8 teaspoon of cumin powder
- Spray with olive oil
- 2 tablespoons of avocado mashed
- 2 teaspoons of cilantro leaves, fresh

Directions and Total Time: approx. 30 minutes

Preheat the oven to 400 Fahrenheit. Over medium heat, heat a large skillet. Meanwhile, season the pork chop with salt and cumin. Add the seasoned pork chop to the pan after spraying it with extra virgin olive oil. Place the large-sized skillet in the oven for around ten minutes, flip the pork chop and distribute the avocado on the charred side. Bring to the oven & cook for another ten minutes, or until the pork is cooked through. Over mashed potatoes, serve the pork topped with cilantro.

Per Serving: Calories 278, Fat 22g, Carbs 5g, Protein 16g

876. Pork Gyros

Ingredients for 8 servings

- 4 pounds of pork shoulder, sliced into cubes
- 3 teaspoons of garlic powder
- 4 teaspoons of dried mixed herbs (oregano, coriander, thyme)
- 1 teaspoon of paprika
- 1 cup of chicken broth

Directions and Total Time: approx. 1 hour and 10 minutes

Press the sauté setting in the Instant Pot. Add the pork shoulder and the rest of the ingredients. Season with celery salt. Mix well. Cover the pot. Set it to manual. Cook at high pressure for 35 minutes. Release the pressure naturally. Drain the liquid. Set the Instant Pot to sauté. Add 2 tablespoons of avocado oil and brown the pork on both sides.

Per Serving: Calories 677, Fat 18g, Carbs 1.5g, Protein 53.7g

877. Pork Kebabs Grilled with Plum Glaze

Ingredients for 6 servings

- 2 pork tenderloins (3/4 pound each)
- 1 garlic clove minced
- 1 sweet red pepper medium
- 1/2 teaspoon of ground ginger
- 1 medium green pepper
- 2 tablespoons of soy sauce
- 1 small red onion
- 1/3 cup of plum jam
- Olive oil cooking spray

Directions and Total Time: approx. 35 minutes

To make the glaze, combine the jam, soy sauce, garlic, & ginger in a small-sized dish. Using a sharp knife, cut the veggies and meat into 1-inch pieces. Thread meat and veggies alternately onto six metal or wet wooden skewers. Coat an outside grill with olive oil cooking spray before transferring to it. Grill for about 15 minutes, rotating halfway through and coating with 1/4 cup glaze for the last 5 minutes. Before serving, drizzle the remaining glaze over the top.

Per Serving: Calories 196, Fat 4g, Carbs 15g, Protein 24g

878. Pork Larb

Ingredients for 4 servings

- 1 tablespoon of olive oil
- 1-pound of ground pork
- ¼ cup of Thai Dressing
- 3 shallots of thinly sliced
- ½ cup of chopped fresh cilantro.
- 24 Bibb lettuce leaves

Directions and Total Time: approx. 25 minutes

In a large-sized skillet over medium heat, heat the olive oil. When the oil is shimmering, add the ground pork and cook for 10-12 minutes, until browned, using a small-sized wooden spoon to break it up. Remove from heat and drain any liquid. Allow the pork to cool for just about 10 minutes. Pour the Thai Dressing into a medium bowl. Add the cooked pork and toss to blend. Add the shallots and cilantro, and gently stir to incorporate. Scoop 2 tbsp. meat into each of 24 lettuce leaves. Serve warm.

Per Serving: Calories 402, Fat 33g, Carbs 6g, Protein 22g

879. Pork Skewers

Ingredients for 6 servings

- 2 pounds of pork tenderloin, 1-inch cubes
- ½ cup of olive oil
- ½ cup of vinegar
- 3 tablespoons of fresh parsley, chopped
- 1 tablespoon of garlic, chopped
- 1 onion, chopped
- Pepper
- Salt

Directions and Total Time: approx. 18 minutes

Add meat and remaining ingredients into the zip-lock bag, seal bag and place in refrigerator for overnight. Thread marinated meat pieces onto soaked wooden skewers. Preheat the grill. Place meat skewers onto the grill and cook for 4 minutes on each side.

Per Serving: Calories 375, Fat 22.2g, Carbs 2.5g, Protein 39.9g

880. Pork Tenderloin with Orzo

Ingredients for 6 servings

- 1-1/2 pound of pork tenderloin
- 1 teaspoon of coarsely ground pepper
- 2 tablespoons of extra virgin olive oil
- 3 quarts of wate.
- 1 1/4 cup of uncooked Orzo pasta
- 1/4 teaspoon of salt
- 6 ounces of fresh baby spinach
- 1 cup of grape tomatoes, halved
- 3/4 cup of crumbled feta cheese

Directions and Total Time: approx. 30 minutes

Place the pork onto a flat surface and rub with the pepper. Cut into the 1" cubes. Place a skillet over a medium heat and add the oil. Add the pork and cook for 10 minutes until no longer pink. Fill a Dutch oven with water and place over a medium heat. Bring to a boil. Stir in the orzo and cook uncovered for 8–10 minutes. Stir through the spinach then drain. Add the tomatoes to the pork, heat through then stir through orzo and cheese. Serve and enjoy.

Per Serving: Calories 372, Fat 11g, Carbs 34g, Protein 31g

881. Pork with Green Beans and Potatoes

Ingredients for 6 servings

- 1 pound of lean pork, sliced into cubes
- 1 onion, chopped
- 2 carrots, sliced thinly
- 2 cups of canned crushed tomatoes
- 2 potatoes, cubed

Directions and Total Time: approx. 45 minutes

Set the Instant Pot to sauté. Add ½ cup of olive oil. Cook the pork for 5 minutes, stirring frequently. Add the rest of the ingredients. Mix well. Seal the pot. Choose manual setting. Cook at high pressure for 17 minutes. Release the pressure naturally.

Per Serving: Calories 428, Fat 24.4g, Carbs 27.6g, Protein 26.7g

882. Pork with Tomato and Olives

Ingredients for 6 servings

- 6 pork chops, thick slices
- 1/8 teaspoon of ground cinnamon
- 1/2 cup of olives, pitted and sliced
- 8 ounces of can tomato, crushed
- 1/4 cup of beef broth
- 2 garlic cloves, chopped
- 1 large onion, sliced
- 1 tablespoon of olive oil

Directions and Total Time: approx. 40 minutes

Heat olive oil in a small-sized pan over medium-high heat. Place pork chops in a large-sized pan and cook until lightly brown and set aside. Cook the chopped garlic and onion in the same pan over medium heat, until onion is softened. Add the prepared broth and bring to boil over high heat. Return pork to the pan and stir in crushed tomatoes and remaining ingredients. Cover and simmer for 20 minutes. Serve and enjoy.

Per Serving: Calories 321, Fat 23g, Carbs 7g, Protein 19g

883. Rack of Lamb

Ingredients for 6 servings

- 2 (1 ½ pounds) racks of lamb
- ¼ cup of lemon zest, grated
- ¼ cup of minced fresh oregano
- 6 cloves of garlic, minced
- 1 tablespoon of olive oil
- ¼ teaspoon of salt
- ¼ teaspoon of black pepper
- Fresh oregano and lemon slices

Directions and Total Time: approx. 50 minutes

Preheat your oven at a heat of 375˚F. Add the lamb to a shallow roasting pan. Mix the black pepper, salt, oil, garlic, oregano and lemon zest in a small bowl. Spread this mixture over the lamb and rub well. Bake the lamb for 40 minutes in the oven. Garnish with lemon slices and oregano. Enjoy.

Per Serving: Calories 393, Fat 16.5g, Carbs 3.3g, Protein 55.1g

884. Roasted Rack of Lamb with Macadamia Crust

Ingredients for 4 servings

- 1 garlic clove, minced
- 1 1/3 pounds rack of lamb
- 1 tablespoon olive oil
- Salt and pepper to taste
- 3-ounces macadamia nuts, raw and unsalted
- 1 egg, beaten
- 1 tablespoon fresh rosemary, chopped
- 1 tablespoon breadcrumbs

Directions and Total Time: approx. 35 minutes

In a small mixing bowl, mix garlic and olive oil. Brush all over lamb and season with salt and pepper. In your food processor, chop macadamia nuts and mix with breadcrumbs and rosemary. Be careful not to make the nuts into a paste. Stir in egg. Coat lamb with nut mixture. Preheat your air fryer to 220˚Fahrenheit. Place the lamb in air fryer and cook for 30-minutes. Raise the temperature to 390˚Fahrenheit and cook for an additional 5-minutes. Remove the meat, cover it loosely with foil for 10-minutes. Serve warm.

Per Serving: Calories 306, Fat 11.4g, Carbs 10.7g, Protein 16.5g

885. Rosemary Meatballs

Ingredients for 5 servings

- 1 pound of lean ground beef
- 3 garlic cloves, crushed
- ¼ cup of all-purpose flour
- 1 tablespoon of fresh rosemary, crushed
- 1 large egg, beaten
- ½ teaspoon of salt
- 3 tablespoons of extra virgin olive oil
- 2 cups of liquid yogurt
- 1 cup of Greek yogurt
- 2 tablespoons of fresh parsley
- 1 garlic clove, crushed

Directions and Total Time: approx. 6 hours and 15 minutes

Mix the ground beef with crushed garlic, rosemary, one egg, and salt in a large bowl. Lightly dampen hands and shape 1 ½ inch balls transferring into the greased cooker as you work. Slowly add about ½ cup of water. Cook on low for 4-6 hours. Remove from the cooker and cool completely. Meanwhile, combine liquid yogurt with Greek yogurt, parsley, and crushed garlic. Stir well and drizzle over meatballs.

Per Serving: Calories 477, Fat 21.4g, Carbs 17.8g, Protein 49g

886. Shredded Beef

Ingredients for 8 servings

- 2 pounds of beef chuck roast
- 1 cup of onion, chopped
- 1 cup of mixed frozen vegetables (carrots, bell pepper), chopped
- 14 ounces of canned fire roasted tomatoes
- 2 tablespoons of red wine vinegar

Directions and Total Time: approx. 30 minutes

Season the beef with salt. Add to the Instant Pot. Top with the onion and frozen vegetables. Pour the tomatoes and vinegar. Mix well. Seal the pot. Choose manual setting. Cook at high pressure for 20 minutes. Release the pressure quickly. Let cool for 5 minutes. Shred the beef. Season with salt and pepper or Italian blend seasoning.

Per Serving: Calories 431, Fat 31.6g, Carbs 4.3g, Protein 30.2g

887. Simple Meat Loaf

Ingredients for 4 servings

- 1 1/2 pounds of ground beef
- 1/2 cup of Baked bread crumbs
- 1/2 cup of flat-leaf parsley, chopped
- 1 onion, grated
- A single big egg
- 1/2 cup of Parmesan cheese
- 1/4 cup of tomato paste
- Sea salt to taste
- Black pepper, freshly ground

Directions and Total Time: approx. 60 minutes

Preheat the oven to 400 Fahrenheit. Combine minced beef bread crumbs, parsley, tomato paste egg, Parmesan cheese, onion, sea salt, and pepper in a large mixing bowl. To make an 8-inch loaf, prepare a baking sheet with foil and put the meat mixture, pushing it down. Bake for about 50 minutes or till well done in a preheated oven.

Per Serving: Calories 631, Fat 39g, Carbs 13g, Protein 56g

888. Slow-Cooked Mediterranean Pork Casserole

Ingredients for 4 servings

- 2 pounds of pork loin, cubes
- 1 large onion, chopped
- 2 cups of white button mushrooms, cut
- 1-2 garlic cloves, finely chopped
- 1 green pepper, cut into strips
- 1 red pepper, cut into strips
- 1 small eggplant, peeled and diced
- 1 zucchini, peeled and diced
- 2 tomatoes, diced
- 1 cup of chicken broth
- 1/2 teaspoon of cumin
- 1 tablespoon of paprika
- salt and black pepper, to taste

Directions and Total Time: approx. 10 hours and 15 minutes

Spray the slow cooker with nonstick spray. Place the pork in the slow cooker. Put in all other fixings and stir to combine. Cook on low within 8-10 hours.

Per Serving: Calories 265, Fat 9g, Carbs 5g, Protein 2g

889. Smoky Pork and Cabbage

Ingredients for 6 servings

- 3 pounds of pork roast
- 1/2 cabbage head, chopped
- 1 cup of water
- 1/3 cup of liquid smoke
- 1 tablespoon of kosher salt

Directions and Total Time: approx. 8 hours and 10 minutes

Rub pork with kosher salt and place it into the pot. Pour liquid smoke over the pork. Add water. Cook on low within 7 hours. Remove pork from the crockpot and add cabbage to the bottom of the pot. Place pork on top of the cabbage. Cook again within 1 more hour. Shred pork with a fork and served.

Per Serving: Calories 484, Fat 21.5g, Carbs 4g, Protein 66g

890. Spanish Pepper Steak

Ingredients for 4 servings

- 1-pound of beef fillet
- 1 tablespoon of smoked paprika
- ¼ cup of extra-virgin olive oil
- 3 tablespoons of garlic, minced
- 1 ½ teaspoon of salt
- 1 large onion, sliced
- 2 large bell peppers, any color, sliced

Directions and Total Time: approx. 30 minutes

Cut the beef into thin strips. Season with paprika. Cook the olive oil, garlic, beef, and salt for 7 minutes in a large skillet over medium heat, using tongs to toss. Adjust your heat to low then add in the onion. Cook for 7 minutes. Add the bell peppers and cook for 6 minutes.

Per Serving: Calories 441, Fat 32g, Carbs 12g, Protein 28g

Ingredients for 8 servings

- 2 pounds of stewing beef, ½" pieces
- 2 x 15 ounces cans of chili-seasoned diced tomatoes, undrained.
- 1 cup of assorted olives, pitted and halved.
- 1/2 teaspoon of salt.
- 1/4 teaspoon of pepper.
- 2 cup of cooked basmati rice.
- 1/2 cup of crumbled feta cheese

Directions and Total Time: approx. 10 hours

Open its lid of your slow cooker and add the beef, tomatoes and olives. Stir well. Cover and then cook on a heat of high for 5–6 hours or low for 8–9 hours until tender. Season well then serve with the rice and feta cheese. Serve and enjoy.

Per Serving: Calories 380, Fat 19g, Carbs 14g, Protein 36g

892. Spicy Pork Ribs

Ingredients for 3 servings

- 2-pounds of pork ribs
- 1/2 teaspoon of garlic powder
- 1/4 teaspoon of coriander powder
- 1/4 cup of catsup
- 1/4 teaspoon of black pepper
- 1/2 teaspoon of onion powder
- 1/4 teaspoon of liquid smoke
- 3/4 tablespoon of wine vinegar
- 1/2 teaspoon of ground mustard
- 3/4 teaspoon of erythritol
- 1/2 teaspoon of allspice
- 1/2 teaspoon of salt

Directions and Total Time: approx. 55 minutes

Add all the dry spices to the pork and marinate for 1 hour. In a different bowl; mix the mustard, vinegar, ketchup and liquid smoke to organize a sauce. Place the marinated ribs within the instant pot and pour the sauce over it. Secure the lid and choose the *Manual* function. Cook for 35 minutes at *HIGH* pressure. Natural release the steam for five minutes then remove the lid. Transfer the ribs to a platter, Cook the remaining sauce within the pot on the *Sauté* setting for five minutes, to serve; drizzle the sauce over the ribs.

Per Serving: Calories 852, Fat 53.8g, Carbs 7.3g, Protein 80.7g

893. Sriracha Lamb Chops

Ingredients for 4 servings

- 4 (4-ounce) loin lamb chops with bones, trimmed
- Sea salt and black pepper, to taste
- 1 tablespoon of olive oil
- 2 tablespoons of sriracha sauce
- 1 tablespoon of fresh cilantro, chopped

Directions and Total Time: approx. 20 minutes

Preheat the oven to 450°F. Lightly season the trimmed lamb chops with salt and pepper. In a large-sized ovenproof skillet, heat the olive oil over medium-high heat. Brown the chops on both sides, approximately about 2 minutes per side, and then spread the chops with sriracha. Place the medium-sized skillet in the oven and roast until the desired doneness, 4–5 minutes for medium. Serve.

Per Serving: Calories 223, Fat 14g, Carbs 1g, Protein 23g

Ingredients for 6 servings

- 2 large onions sliced
- 2 sliced green onions
- 2 cups of teriyaki sauce
- 2 tablespoons of olive oil extra-virgin
- 2 Pork Tenderloin (1 pound each), Cut in 4-5 pieces each
- For garnishing sesame seeds

Directions and Total Time: approx. 35 minutes

Cut 4-5 pork tenderloins into 12" thick slices using a sharp knife. Marinate the tenderloins for around 4-6 hours in teriyaki sauce with onion pieces. Cook the pork tenderloin and onions in a nonstick pan with two tablespoons of olive oil for around 15 to 20 minutes on medium flame, rotating halfway through.

Per Serving: Calories 315, Fat 5g, Carbs 37g, Protein 26g

895. Thyme Ginger Garlic Beef

Ingredients for 2 servings

- 1 pound beef roast
- 2 whole cloves
- 1/2 teaspoon ginger, grated
- 1/2 cup beef stock
- 1/2 teaspoon garlic powder
- 1/2 teaspoon thyme
- 1/4 teaspoon pepper
- 1/4 teaspoon salt

Directions and Total Time: approx. 55 minutes

Mix together ginger, cloves, thyme, garlic powder, pepper, and salt and rub over beef. Place meat into the instant pot. Pour stock around the meat. Seal pot using the lid and cook on high for 45 minutes. Once done, release pressure using quick release. Remove lid. Shred meat using a fork and serve.

Per Serving: Calories 452, Fat 15.7g, Carbs 5.2g, Protein 70.1g

896. Thyme Lamb

Ingredients for 2 servings

- 8 ounces of lamb shanks
- 1 tablespoon of thyme
- 1 teaspoon of garlic, minced
- 1 tablespoon of balsamic vinegar
- Salt and black pepper, to taste
- 1 tablespoon of olive oil
- ½ cup of water
- 1 tablespoon of fresh dill, chopped

Directions and Total Time: approx. 30 minutes

Rub the lamb shanks with thyme, minced garlic, balsamic vinegar, salt, and ground black pepper. Sprinkle the meat with olive oil and leave for 15 minutes to marinate. Transfer the marinated lamb to an Instant Pot or pressure cooker and add the fresh dill. Add the water and close the lid. Cook for 20 minutes on high pressure. Do a natural pressure release and transfer the meat to a platter. Serve and enjoy!

Per Serving: Calories 284, Fat 15.5g, Carbs 2.6g, Protein 32.4g

Ingredients for 4 servings

- 4 pork chops, bone-in
- 1 tablespoon of garlic, minced
- ½ small onion, chopped
- 6 ounces can of tomato paste
- 1 bell pepper, chopped
- ¼ teaspoon of red pepper flakes
- 1 teaspoon of Worcestershire sauce
- 1 tablespoon of dried Italian seasoning
- 14 1/2 ounces can of tomato, diced
- 2 teaspoons of olive oil
- ¼ teaspoon of pepper
- 1 teaspoon of kosher salt

Directions and Total Time: approx. 6 hours and 10 minutes

Heat-up oil in a pan over medium heat. Season pork chops with pepper and salt. Sear pork chops in the pan until brown from both sides. Transfer pork chops into the pot. Add remaining ingredients over pork chops. Cook on low heat within 6 hours. Serve and enjoy.

Per Serving: Calories 325, Fat 23.4g, Carbs 10g, Protein 20g

898. Turkey Burgers

Ingredients for 6 servings

- 1 ½ pounds of ground turkey breast
- 1 teaspoon of sea salt, divided
- ¼ teaspoon of freshly ground black pepper
- 2 tablespoons of extra-virgin olive oil
- 2 mangos, peeled, pitted, and cubed
- ½ red onion, finely chopped
- Juice of 1 lime
- 1 garlic clove, minced
- ½ jalapeño pepper, seeded and finely minced
- 2 tablespoons of chopped fresh cilantro leaves

Directions and Total Time: approx. 25 minutes

Form the turkey breast into 4 patties and season with ½ teaspoon of sea salt and pepper. Using a nonstick skillet over medium-high heat, heat the olive oil until it shimmers. Add the turkey patties and cook for about 5 minutes per side until browned. While the patties cook, mix the mango, red onion, lime juice, garlic, jalapeño, cilantro, and remaining ½ teaspoon of sea salt in a small bowl. Spoon the salsa over the turkey patties and serve.

Per Serving: Calories 384, Fat 16g, Carbs 44g, Protein 3g

899. Worcestershire Pork Chops

Ingredients for 3 servings

- 2 tablespoons of Worcestershire sauce
- 8 ounces of pork loin chops
- 1 tablespoon of lemon juice
- 1 teaspoon of olive oil

Directions and Total Time: approx. 15 minutes

Mix up together Worcestershire sauce, lemon juice, and olive oil. Brush the pork loin chops with the sauce mixture from each side. Preheat the grill to 395F. Place the pork chops in the grill and cook them for 5 minutes. Then flip the pork chops on another side and brush with remaining sauce mixture. Grill the meat for 7-8 minutes more.

Per Serving: Calories 267, Fat 20.4g, Carbs 2.1g, Protein 17g

Ingredients for 6 servings

- 2 Pork Tenderloins, 10-12 Ounces Each
- Sea Salt & Black Pepper
- ¼ cup Greek Yogurt, 2%
- 1 tablespoon Rosemary, Fresh & Chopped
- Tzatziki Sauce
- 2 Tablespoons Mint, Fresh & Chopped

Directions and Total Time: approx. 30 minutes

Start by heating the oven to 500. Get a large baking sheet and then line it with foil with a wire rack on top. Spray the rack down with oil. Put both pieces of pork on the rack, and season with salt and pepper. Get out a bowl and mix your yogurt and rosemary. Make sure it's coated on all sides. Roast for ten minutes. Remove it from the oven, and then turn it over. Roast for ten to twelve more minutes. Remove the pork from the rack and cut. Allow it to rest for five minutes before slicing. Serve with tzatziki and mint leaves.

Per Serving: Calories 183, Fat 10g, Carbs 4g, Protein 22g

901. Artichoke and Bean Pot

Ingredients for 4 servings

- 2 tablespoons of olive oil
- 10 artichoke hearts, halved
- 1 onion, sliced
- 12 whole baby carrots
- ½ cup of chopped celery
- 1 lemon, juiced
- 2 tablespoons of chopped fresh basil
- 1 red chili, sliced
- ¾ cup of frozen fava beans
- Salt and black pepper to taste

Directions and Total Time: approx. 40 minutes

Warm olive oil in a large-sized pot over medium heat and sauté onion, carrots, and celery for 7-8 minutes until tender. Stir in lemon juice, butter, and 1 cup of water. Bring the dish to a hot boil, then lower the heat and simmer for 10-15 minutes. Add in artichoke hearts, fava beans, salt, and pepper and cook covered for another 10 minutes. Top with basil and red chili and serve.

Per Serving: Calories 353, Fat 4.1g, Carbs 68g, Protein 22g

902. Artichoke with Garlic and Cream Sauce

Ingredients for 6 servings

- Cooking spray
- 30 ounces of canned diced tomatoes
- 6 cloves of garlic, crushed and minced
- 28 ounces of canned artichoke hearts, rinsed, drained, and sliced into quarters
- ½ cup of whipping cream
- 1 teaspoon of dried basil
- ½ teaspoon of dried oregano
- Feta cheese

Directions and Total Time: approx. 8 hours and 15 minutes

Spray the slow cooker with oil. Add the tomatoes with juice, garlic, and artichoke hearts. Season with basil and oregano. Mix well. Cover the pot. Cook on low for 8 hours. Stir in the cream. Let's sit for 5 minutes. Top with the crumbled cheese.

Per Serving: Calories 403, Fat 5g, Carbs 38g, Protein 13g

903. Artichoke Provencal

Ingredients for 4 servings

- ½ of a medium white onion chopped
- 2 medium tomatoes
- 18 ounces frozen artichoke hearts
- 1 teaspoon minced garlic
- ¾ teaspoon salt
- ½ teaspoon ground black pepper
- 1 tablespoon olive oil
- ½ cup white wine
- ½ teaspoon lemon zest
- 3 tablespoons water

Directions and Total Time: approx. 25 minutes

Place a medium skillet pan over medium heat, add oil, add onion, garlic, and ¼ teaspoon salt when hot. Cook for just about 5 minutes or until softened, stir in wine, and cook for 3 minutes or reduce by half. Add tomatoes, artichoke hearts, salt, lemon zest, and water and continue cooking for 6 minutes, covering the pan and stirring occasionally. Season with rest of the remaining salt and black pepper, add basil and olives and cook for 1 minute. Remove pan from heat and serve straightaway.

Per Serving: Calories 200, Fat 16g, Carbs 40g, Protein 15g

904. Authentic Mushroom Gratin

Ingredients for 4 servings

- 2 pound of Button mushrooms, cleaned
- 2 tablespoons of olive oil
- 2 tomatoes, sliced
- 2 tomato paste
- ½ cup of Parmesan cheese, grated
- ½ cup of dry white wine
- ¼ teaspoon of sweet paprika
- ½ teaspoon of dried basil
- ½ teaspoon of dried thyme
- Salt and black pepper to taste

Directions and Total Time: approx. 25 minutes

Preheat oven to 360 F. Combine tomatoes, tomato paste, wine, oil, mushrooms, paprika, black pepper, salt, basil, and thyme in a baking dish. Bake for 15 minutes. Top with grated Parmesan cheese and continue baking for 5 minutes until the cheese melts.

Per Serving: Calories 162, Fat 8.6g, Carbs 12.3g, Protein 9g

905. Baby Corn in Chili-Turmeric Spice

Ingredients for 5 servings

- ¼ cup of water
- ¼ teaspoon baking soda
- ¼ teaspoon salt
- ¼ teaspoon turmeric powder
- ½ teaspoon curry powder
- ½ teaspoon red chili powder
- 1 cup chickpea flour or besan
- 10 pieces' baby corn, blanched

Directions and Total Time: approx. 13 minutes

Preheat the air fryer to 400F. Position the air fryer basket with aluminum foil and brush with oil. In a mixing bowl, mix all ingredients except for the corn. Whisk until well combined. Dip the corn in the batter and place it inside the air fryer. Cook for 8 minutes until golden brown.

Per Serving: Calories 89, Fat 1.54g, Carbs 14.35g, Protein 4.75g

906. Baked Asparagus with Cheesy Sauce

Ingredients for 5 servings

- 1 cup of cream half-and-half
- 1 pound of fresh asparagus trimmed
- 2 teaspoons of cornstarch
- 1/2 cup of grated Parmesan cheese
- 1 cup of shredded mozzarella cheese
- 1/2 teaspoon of ground mustard
- 1 teaspoon of Italian seasoning
- 1/4 teaspoon of red pepper flakes

Directions and Total Time: approx. 13 minutes

Arrange asparagus in a small-sized baking dish. In a mixing dish, combine the half-and-half, ground mustard, shredded mozzarella, red pepper flakes, cornstarch, & grated parmesan cheese. In a baking dish, pour the mixture over the asparagus. Preheat oven at 350°F and bake for approximately 10 minutes.

Per Serving: Calories 113, Fat 7.3g, Carbs 4.9g, Protein 7.6g

907. Baked Goat Cheese with Green Pepper

Ingredients for 4 servings

- 6 cups of green peppers
- 4 cups of goat cheese
- ¾ cup of taggiasche olives
- 1 garlic clove
- 1 tablespoon of honey
- 2 basil leaves to garnish
- 1 rosemary branch
- Salt and pepper to taste
- Oil to taste

Directions and Total Time: approx. 1 hour and 20 minutes

Wash and cut the bell peppers into slices. Cut the garlic into slices. Place both in a baking sheet with oil, salt, and pepper. Bake for 20 minutes at 180°. Take the large-sized pan out of the oven and place the cheese in the middle of the peppers. Drizzle with the rest of the oil, honey, rosemary, olives and bake again for 15 minutes at 180°. Garnish with basil and rosemary and serve.

Per Serving: Calories 562, Fat 27g, Carbs 4g, Protein 20g

908. Baked Omelet Square

Ingredients for 8 servings

- 1/4 cup butter
- 1 small onion, minced meat
- 1 1/2 cups grated cheddar cheese
- 1 can of sliced mushrooms
- 1 can slice black olives cooked ham (optional)
- sliced jalapeno peppers (optional)
- 12 eggs, scrambled eggs
- 1/2 cup of milk
- salt and pepper, to taste

Directions and Total Time: approx. 45 minutes

Prepare the oven to 205°C (400 ° F). Grease a 9 x 13-inch baking dish. Cook the cup of butter in a frying pan over medium heat and cook the onion until done. Lay out the Cheddar cheese on the bottom of the prepared baking dish. Layer with mushrooms, olives, fried onion, ham, and jalapeno peppers. Stir the eggs in a bowl with milk, salt, and pepper. Pour the egg mixture over the ingredients, but do not mix. Bake in the uncovered and preheated oven, until no more liquid flows in the middle and is light brown above. Allow to cool a little, then cut it into squares and serve.

Per Serving: Calories 344, Fat 3g, Carbs 2g, Protein 9g

909. Baked Potato with Veggie Mix

Ingredients for 4 servings

- 4 tablespoons of olive oil
- 1 pound of potatoes, peeled and diced
- 2 red bell peppers, halved
- 1 pound of mushrooms, sliced
- 2 tomatoes, diced
- 8 garlic cloves, peeled
- 1 eggplant, sliced
- 1 yellow onion, quartered
- ½ teaspoon of dried oregano
- ¼ teaspoon of caraway seeds
- Salt to taste

Directions and Total Time: approx. 45 minutes

Preheat the oven to a temperature of a heat of 390 F. In a bowl, combine the bell peppers, mushrooms, tomatoes, eggplant, onion, garlic, salt, olive oil, oregano, and caraway seeds. Set aside. Arrange the potatoes on a large-sized baking dish and bake for 15 minutes. Top with the veggies mixture and bake for 15-20 minutes until tender.

Per Serving: Calories 302, Fat 15g, Carbs 39g, Protein 8.5g

910. Baked Ricotta with Tomatoes

Ingredients for 4 servings

- 6 cups of mixed tomatoes
- 3 cups of fresh ricotta cheese
- 1 garlic clove
- Rosemary to taste
- 1 tablespoon of oregano
- ½ tablespoon of thyme
- Basil to taste
- 6 tablespoons of olive oil
- Salt and pepper to taste

Directions and Total Time: approx. 60 minutes

Pat dry the ricotta and divide it into 4 pieces. Season it with oil, salt, and pepper and set aside. Wash and cut the tomatoes in halves and season them with salt, pepper, oil, oregano, thyme, garlic, and ground rosemary. Bake the tomatoes in a sheet pan for 20 minutes with the garlic at 180 °. Add the ricotta and bake again for 20 minutes. Garnish with basil and serve.

Per Serving: Calories 320, Fat 20g, Carbs 12g, Protein 20g

911. Baked Sweet Potato Fries with Basil Pesto

Ingredients for 2 servings

- 2 (6-ounce) sweet potatoes
- 1 tablespoon of fresh Basil Pesto Sauce or market-fresh basil pesto
- Salt and freshly ground pepper to taste
- Low-fat or fat-free sour cream, for garnish (optional)

Directions and Total Time: approx. 20 minutes

Clean the skins of sweet potatoes under cold running water and pat potatoes dry with paper towels. Cut the prepared potatoes in half and then each half into fry strips. Place fries in a single layer on a non-stick baking sheet and brush with pesto sauce. Add salt and pepper to taste. Place baking sheet in oven and bake fries at 400 degrees F until tender and lightly browned around edges. Divide fries into two servings and garnish with a dollop of sour cream, if desired.

Per Serving: Calories 221, Fat 7g, Carbs 34g, Protein 4g

912. Baked Veggie Medley

Ingredients for 4 servings

- 2 tablespoons of olive oil
- ½ pound of green beans, trimmed
- 1 tomato, chopped
- 1 potato, sliced
- ½ tablespoon of tomato paste
- 2 tablespoons of chopped fresh parsley
- 1 teaspoon of sweet paprika
- 1 onion, sliced
- 1 cup of mushrooms, sliced
- 1 celery stalk, chopped
- 1 red bell pepper, sliced
- 1 eggplant, sliced
- ½ cup of vegetable broth
- Salt and black pepper to taste

Directions and Total Time: approx. 70 minutes

Preheat oven to a heat of 375 F. Warm oil in a skillet over medium heat and sauté onion, bell pepper, celery, and mushrooms for 5 minutes until tender. Stir in paprika and tomato paste for 1 minute. Pour in the vegetable broth and stir. Combine the remaining ingredients in a baking pan and mix in the sautéed vegetable. Bake covered with foil for 40-50 minutes.

Per Serving: Calories 175, Fat 8g, Carbs 25.2g, Protein 5.2g

913. Balsamic Brussels Sprouts

Ingredients for 6 servings
- 2 tablespoons brown sugar
- ½ cup balsamic vinegar
- 2 pounds Brussels sprouts, trimmed and sliced in half
- 2 tablespoons olive oil
- 2 tablespoons butter, cut into cubes
- Salt and pepper to taste
- ¼ cup Parmesan cheese, grated

Directions and Total Time: approx. 4 hours and 20 minutes

Put the brown sugar and vinegar in a saucepan over medium heat. Mix and bring to a boil. Reduce heat and simmer for 8 minutes. Let cool and set aside. Mix the Brussel sprouts in olive oil plus butter. Season with salt and pepper. Cover the pot. Cook low for 4 hours. Drizzle the balsamic vinegar on top of the Brussels sprouts. Sprinkle the Parmesan cheese on top.

Per Serving: Calories 193, Fat 10g, Carbs 21.9g, Protein 6.9g

914. Bell Pepper-Corn Wrapped in Tortilla

Ingredients for 4 servings
- 1 small red bell pepper, chopped
- 1 small yellow onion, diced
- 1 tablespoon water
- 2 cobs grilled corn kernels
- 4 large tortillas
- 4 pieces' commercial vegan nuggets, chopped
- mixed greens for garnish

Directions and Total Time: approx. 20 minutes

Preheat the air fryer to 400F. Water sautés vegan nuggets and onions, bell peppers, and corn kernels in a skillet heated over medium heat. Set aside. Place filling inside the corn tortillas. Fold the tortillas, place them inside the air fryer, and cook for 15 minutes until the tortilla wraps are crispy. Serve with mixed greens on top.

Per Serving: Calories 548, Fat 20.76g, Carbs 43.5g, Protein 46.7g

915. Black Bean Burger with Garlic-Chipotle

Ingredients for 3 servings
- ½ cup corn kernels
- ½ teaspoon chipotle powder
- ½ teaspoon garlic powder
- ¾ cup of salsa
- 1 ¼ teaspoon chili powder
- 1 ½ cup rolled oats
- 1 can black beans, rinsed and drained
- 1 tablespoon soy sauce

Directions and Total Time: approx. 30 minutes

In a mixing container, mix all components using your hands. Form small patties and set them aside. Brush patties with oil if desired. Place the grill pan in the air fryer and place the patties on the grill pan accessory. Conceal the lid and cook for twenty minutes on each side at 330F.

Per Serving: Calories 395, Fat 5.8g, Carbs 52.2g, Protein 24.3g

916. Buttered Carrot-Zucchini with Mayo

Ingredients for 4 servings
- 1 tablespoon grated onion
- 2 tablespoons butter, melted
- 1/2-pound carrots, sliced
- 1-1/2 zucchinis, sliced
- 1/4 cup water
- 1/4 cup mayonnaise
- 1/4 teaspoon prepared horseradish
- 1/4 teaspoon salt
- 1/4 teaspoon ground black pepper
- 1/4 cup Italian bread crumbs

Directions and Total Time: approx. 40 minutes

Lighten skillet with cooking spray. Add the carrots. Cook for 360 minutes at 360°F. Put the zucchini and continue cooking for another five minutes. Meanwhile, whisk together the pepper, salt, horseradish, onion, mayonnaise, and water in a bowl. Pour into a vegetable skillet. Pull well over the coat. In a small container, mix the melted butter and breadcrumbs. Sprinkle over the vegetables. Cook for 10 minutes at 390 F until tops are lightly browned. Serve and enjoy.

Per Serving: Calories 223, Fat 17.4g, Carbs 13.8g, Protein 2.7g

917. Buttery Garlic Green Beans

Ingredients for 6 servings
- 2 tablespoons butter
- 1 pound green beans, trimmed
- 4 cups water
- 6 garlic cloves, minced
- 1 shallot, chopped
- Celery salt to taste
- ½ teaspoon red pepper flakes

Directions and Total Time: approx. 25 minutes

Pour the prepared 4 cups of water in a pot over high heat and bring to a boil. Cut the green beans in half crosswise. Reduce the heat and add in the green beans. Simmer for 6-8 minutes until crisp-tender but still vibrant green. Drain beans and set aside. Melt the butter in a large-sized pan over medium heat and sauté garlic and shallot for 3 minutes until the garlic is slightly browned and fragrant. Stir in the beans and season with celery salt. Cook for 2-3 minutes. Serve topped with red pepper flakes.

Per Serving: Calories 65, Fat 4g, Carbs 7g, Protein 2g

918. Carrot Potato Medley

Ingredients for 6 servings
- 4 pounds baby potatoes, clean and cut in half
- 1 1/2 pounds carrots, cut into chunks
- 1 teaspoon Italian seasoning
- 1 1/2 cups vegetable broth
- 1 tablespoon garlic, chopped
- 1 onion, chopped
- 2 tablespoons olive oil
- Pepper
- Salt

Directions and Total Time: approx. 25 minutes

Add oil into the inner pot of instant pot and set the pot on sauté mode. Add onion and sauté for 5 minutes. Add carrots and cook for 5 minutes. Add remaining ingredients and stir well. Seal large-sized pot with lid and cook on high for 5 minutes. Once done, allow to release pressure naturally for 10 minutes then release remaining using quick release. Remove lid. Stir and serve.

Per Serving: Calories 283, Fat 5.6g, Carbs 51.3g, Protein 10.2g

919. Cauliflower Curry

Ingredients for 4 servings

- 2 tablespoons of olive oil
- ½ cauliflower, chopped into florets
- ¼ teaspoon of salt
- 1 teaspoon of curry paste
- 1 cup of unsweetened coconut milk
- ¼ cup of fresh cilantro, chopped
- 1 tablespoon of lime juice

Directions and Total Time: approx. 35 minutes

Sauté the cauliflower in heated olive oil over medium heat for 10 minutes. Mix the coconut milk and curry powder, add to the cauliflower, and simmer for ten minutes. Add the lime juice and cilantro and toss well. Serve and enjoy!

Per Serving: Calories 243, Fat 24g, Carbs 9g, Protein 3g

920. Cauliflower Hash with Carrots

Ingredients for 4 servings

- 3 tablespoons of extra-virgin olive oil
- 1 large onion, chopped
- 1 tablespoon of minced garlic
- 2 cups of diced carrots
- 4 cups of cauliflower florets
- ½ teaspoon of ground cumin
- 1 teaspoon of salt

Directions and Total Time: approx. 10 minutes

In a large-sized skillet, heat the olive oil over medium heat. Add the onion and garlic and sauté for 1 minute. Stir in the carrots and stir-fry for 3 minutes. Add the cauliflower florets, cumin, and salt and toss to combine. Cover and cook for 3 minutes until lightly browned. Stir well and cook, uncovered, for 3 to 4 minutes, until softened. Remove from the heat and serve warm.

Per Serving: Calories 158, Fat 10.8g, Carbs 14.9g, Protein 3.1g

921. Celery Carrot Brown Lentils

Ingredients for 6 servings

- 2 cups dry brown lentils
- 2 1/2 cups vegetable stock
- 2 tomatoes, chopped
- 1/2 teaspoon red pepper flakes
- 1/2 teaspoon ground cinnamon
- 1 bay leaf
- 1 tablespoon tomato paste
- 2 celery stalks, diced
- 2 carrots, grated
- 1 tablespoon garlic, minced
- 2 onions, chopped
- 1/4 cup olive oil
- Pepper
- Salt

Directions and Total Time: approx. 35 minutes

Add oil into the inner pot of instant pot and set the pot on sauté mode. Add celery, carrot, garlic, onion, pepper, and salt and sauté for 3 minutes. Add remaining ingredients and stir everything well. Seal large-sized pot with lid and cook on high for 22 minutes. Once done, release pressure using quick release. Remove lid. Stir well and serve.

Per Serving: Calories 137, Fat 8.8g, Carbs 12.3g, Protein 3.1g

922. Chargrilled Vegetable Kebabs

Ingredients for 4 servings

- 2 red bell peppers, cut into squares
- 2 zucchinis, sliced into half-moons
- 6 portobello mushroom caps, quartered
- ¼ cup of olive oil
- 1 teaspoon of Dijon mustard
- 1 teaspoon of fresh rosemary, chopped
- 1 garlic clove, minced
- Salt and black pepper to taste
- 2 red onions, cut into wedges

Directions and Total Time: approx. 26 minutes

Preheat your grill to High. Mix the olive oil, mustard, rosemary, garlic, salt, and pepper in a bowl. Reserve half of the oil mixture for serving. Thread the vegetables in alternating order onto metal skewers and brush them with the remaining oil mixture. Grill them for about 15 minutes until browned, turning occasionally. Transfer the kebabs to a serving platter and remove the skewers. Drizzle with reserved oil mixture and serve.

Per Serving: Calories 96, Fat 9.2g, Carbs 3.6g, Protein 1.1g

923. Chickpeas, Zucchini and Carrot Medallions

Ingredients for 6 servings

- 3 cups of chickpeas
- 1 cup of ricotta
- 1 potato
- 1 carrot
- 1 zucchini
- 1 egg
- 1 teaspoon of curry
- 1 tablespoon of olive oil
- Salt and pepper to taste
- 1 cup of mixed seeds
- Water

Directions and Total Time: approx. 1 hour and 40 minutes

Wash and cook the potato for 30 minutes in hot water. Smash it and add it to the chickpeas and blend together. Add the egg, the ricotta, and mix. Cut the zucchini and the carrot into little pieces on a pan with a little bit of oil. Add the vegetables to the potato mixture. Add the curry, salt, mixed seeds, and pepper. Form medallion shapes with the hands and bakes them for 25 minutes at 180°.

Per Serving: Calories 316, Fat 15g, Carbs 38.9g, Protein 19g

924. Chilled Avocado with Paprika

Ingredients for 2 servings

- 2 tablespoons of lemon juice
- 2 tablespoons of tahini sauce
- 1 ripe avocado, cut in half, pitted and peeled
- 1/4 cup of parsley, freshly chopped
- 1 tablespoon of extra-virgin olive oil
- 1/8 cup of onion, chopped
- 3 garlic cloves, peeled and chopped
- 3 tablespoons of mayonnaise (low calorie)
- 1/8 teaspoon of cayenne pepper
- To taste, season with salt and freshly ground pepper.
- A pinch of paprika

Directions and Total Time: approx. 10 minutes

Add parsley, cayenne olive oil, garlic, avocado mayonnaise, onion, and salt and pepper to taste after blending lemon juice and tahini paste. Blend until smooth, then refrigerate in a serving dish. Sprinkle with paprika when ready to serve.

Per Serving: Calories 194, Fat 16g, Carbs 14g, Protein 3g

925. Clams Spaghetti with Capers

Ingredients for 5 servings

- 2 cups spaghetti pasta
- 5 ounces clams
- 3 tablespoons capers
- 2 garlic cloves
- 1 chili pepper
- 1 cup of parsley
- Water
- Oil to taste

Directions and Total Time: approx. 25 minutes

Bring to a boil a large-sized pot of salted water and cook the spaghetti pasta for 7 to 8 minutes. In a pan in the meanwhile add the garlic, chili, and oil, and some parsley stems and stir for some minutes. Add the ounces of clams and cover with a lid and wait until they have opened up. Add the capers and the drained pasta. Let it cook for another 3 minutes with some pasta water.

Per Serving: Calories 193, Fat 10g, Carbs 70g, Protein 8.5g

926. Crunchy Roasted Chickpeas

Ingredients for 4 servings

- 15 ounces of can chickpeas, drained, rinsed and pat dry
- 1/4 teaspoon of paprika
- 1 tablespoon of olive oil
- 1/4 teaspoon of pepper
- Pinch of salt

Directions and Total Time: approx. 35 minutes

Preheat the oven to 450° F. Spray a large-sized baking tray with cooking spray and set it aside. In a large bowl, toss chickpeas with olive oil and spread chickpeas onto the prepared baking tray. Roast chickpeas in preheated oven for 25 minutes. Shake after every 10 minutes. Once chickpeas are done, then immediately toss with paprika, pepper, and salt. Serve and enjoy.

Per Serving: Calories 157, Fat 4.7g, Carbs 24.2g, Protein 5.3g

927. Cucumber Salad with Onion and Garlic

Ingredients for 3 servings

- 2 cups cucumber, peeled and seeded, coarsely diced
- 1/2 cup red onion, thinly diced
- 1/2 cup fresh cilantro, chopped
- 1 fresh garlic clove, minced
- 1 jalapeno pepper, coarsely diced
- 3 tbsp lime juice, freshly squeezed
- 1 tbsp extra-virgin olive oil
- To taste, season with salt and freshly ground black pepper

Directions and Total Time: approx. 10 minutes

Mix cucumber, onion, cilantro, garlic, and jalapeno in a medium mixing bowl. Toss to combine the said ingredients, then season to taste with lime juice, olive oil, and salt and pepper. Toss once more and chill for 15 minutes to let flavors meld. Before serving, allow it cool to room temperature. Serve as a delicious topping over grilled tuna or swordfish.

Per Serving: Calories 23, Fat 1g, Carbs 5g, Protein 1g

928. Eggplant with Yogurt and Dill

Ingredients for 4 servings

- 1 pound of chopped eggplant
- 3 shallots unpeeled
- 3 cloves of garlic unpeeled
- 1/4 cup of olive oil
- 1 1/2 teaspoon of salt
- 1/2 teaspoon of ground black pepper
- 2 tablespoons of chopped walnuts
- 1/2 cup of yogurt
- 1 teaspoon of dried dill

Directions and Total Time: approx. 48 minutes

Set oven to 400 degrees F and let preheat. In the meantime, place eggplant shallots and garlic cloves on a baking sheet, drizzle with oil, and season with 3/4 teaspoon salt and 1/4 teaspoon black pepper. Place this baking sheet into the oven and roast for 30 minutes. Then add walnuts and continue baking for 8 minutes. When done, remove the baking sheet from the oven, let cool slightly, peel shallots, and squeeze garlic from their skins. Chop onion and garlic and place them into a large bowl. Add walnuts, dill remaining salt, black pepper, yogurt, and toss until well combined. Serve straightaway.

Per Serving: Calories 271, Fat 30g, Carbs 25g, Protein 13g

929. Eggs over Kale Hash

Ingredients for 4 servings

- 4 large eggs
- 1 bunch chopped kale
- Dash of ground nutmeg
- 2 sweet potatoes, cubed
- 1 14.5-ounce can of chicken broth

Directions and Total Time: approx. 20 minutes

In a large-sized non-stick skillet, bring the chicken broth to a simmer. Add the sweet potatoes and season slightly with salt and pepper. Add a dash of nutmeg to improve the flavor. Cook until the sweet potatoes become soft, around 10 minutes. Add the chopped kale and then season with salt and pepper. Continue cooking for four minutes or until kale has wilted. Set aside. Using the same large-sized skillet, heat 1 tablespoon of olive oil over medium high heat. Cook the eggs sunny side up until the whites become opaque and the yolks have set. Top the kale hash with the eggs. Serve immediately.

Per Serving: Calories 158, Fat 5.6g, Carbs 18.5g, Protein 9.8g

930. Eggs with Zucchini Noodles

Ingredients for 4 servings

- 2 tablespoons of extra-virgin olive oil
- 3 zucchinis, cut with a spiralizer
- 4 eggs
- Salt and black pepper to taste
- A pinch of red pepper flakes
- Cooking spray
- 1 tablespoon basil, chopped

Directions and Total Time: approx. 21 minutes

In a bowl, combine the zucchini noodles with salt, pepper, and olive oil and toss well. Grease a large-sized baking sheet with cooking spray and divide the zucchini noodles into 4 nests. Crack one of the eggs on top of each nest, sprinkle salt, pepper, and pepper flakes on top and bake at a heat of 350°F for 11 minutes. Divide the mix between plates, sprinkle the basil on top, and serve.

Per Serving: Calories 296, Fat 23.6g, Carbs 10.6g, Protein 14.7g

Ingredients for 4 servings

- 10 ½ ounces farfalle pasta
- 5 ounces champignons
- 1 bunch radish
- 1-piece avocado
- 1 ounce parsley
- 6 ounces canned tuna
- 6 tablespoons vegetable broth
- 1 tablespoon mustard
- Salt to taste
- Ground black pepper to taste

Directions and Total Time: approx. 20 minutes

Boil the pasta. Prepare the champignons by cutting them into thin plates and frying them. Using a sharp knife, cut the radish into 6-8 pieces. Avocado should be cut into wedges. Chop the parsley finely. Pour the pasta on top of the broth, which has been mixed with mustard, salt, and pepper. Add the tuna, champignons, radishes, avocados, and parsley (after draining the liquid). Combine all of the ingredients and steep for half an hour in a cool area.

Per Serving: Calories 125, Fat 3.2g, Carbs 15g, Protein 7g

932. Feta and Zucchini Rosti Cakes

Ingredients for 4 servings

- 5 tablespoons of olive oil
- 1 pound of zucchini, shredded
- 4 spring onions, chopped
- Salt and black pepper to taste
- 4 ounces of feta cheese, crumbled
- 1 egg, lightly beaten
- 2 tablespoons of minced fresh dill
- 1 garlic clove, minced
- ¼ cup of flour
- Lemon wedges for serving

Directions and Total Time: approx. 25 minutes

Preheat oven to a heat of 380 F. In a large bowl, mix the zucchini, spring onions, feta cheese, egg, dill, garlic, salt, and pepper. Sprinkle cup of flour over the mixture and stir to incorporate. Warm the oil in a skillet over medium heat. Cook the rosti mixture in small flat fritters for about 4 minutes per side until crisp and golden on both sides, pressing with a fish slice as they cook. Serve with lemon wedges.

Per Serving: Calories 239, Fat 19.8g, Carbs 9g, Protein 7.8g

933. Flavors Basil Lemon Ratatouille

Ingredients for 8 servings

- 1 small eggplant, cut into cubes
- 1 cup fresh basil
- 2 cups grape tomatoes
- 1 onion, chopped
- 2 summer squash, sliced
- 2 zucchini, sliced
- 2 tablespoons vinegar
- 2 tablespoons tomato paste
- 1 tablespoon garlic, minced
- 1 fresh lemon juice
- 1/4 cup olive oil
- Salt

Directions and Total Time: approx. 20 minutes

Add basil, vinegar, tomato paste, garlic, lemon juice, oil, and salt into the blender and blend until smooth. Add eggplant, tomatoes, onion, squash, and zucchini into the instant pot. Pour blended basil mixture over vegetables and stir well. Seal large-sized pot with lid and cook on high for 10 minutes. Once done, allow to release pressure naturally. Remove lid. Stir well and serve.

Per Serving: Calories 103, Fat 6.8g, Carbs 10.6g, Protein 2.4g

Ingredients for 4 servings

- 14 ounces zucchini, sliced
- 1/4 cup fresh basil, chopped
- 1/2 teaspoon red pepper flakes
- 14 ounces can tomatoes, chopped
- 1 teaspoon garlic, minced
- 1/2 onion, chopped
- 1/4 cup feta cheese, crumbled
- 1 tablespoon olive oil
- Salt

Directions and Total Time: approx. 18 minutes

Add oil into the inner pot of instant pot and set the pot on sauté mode. Add onion and garlic and sauté for 2 minutes. Add remaining ingredients except feta cheese and stir well. Seal large-sized pot with lid and cook on high for 6 minutes. Once done, allow to release pressure naturally. Remove lid. Top with feta cheese and serve.

Per Serving: Calories 99, Fat 5.7g, Carbs 10.4g, Protein 3.7g

935. Garlicky Rosemary Potatoes

Ingredients for 4 servings

- 1-pound potatoes, peeled and sliced thinly
- 2 garlic cloves
- ½ teaspoon salt
- 1 tablespoon olive oil
- 2 sprigs of rosemary

Directions and Total Time: approx. 5 minutes

Place a steamer basket in your prepared Instant Pot and pour in a cup of water. In a large-sized baking dish that can fit inside the Instant Pot, combine all ingredients and toss to coat everything. Cover the large-sized baking dish with aluminum foil and place on the steamer basket. Close the lid and press the Steam button. Adjust the cooking time to 30 minutes. Do quick pressure release. Once cooled, evenly divide into serving size, keep in your preferred container, and refrigerate until ready to eat.

Per Serving: Calories 119, Fat 3.48g, Carbs 20.3g, Protein 2.3g

936. Garlicky Zucchini Cubes with Mint

Ingredients for 4 servings

- 3 large green zucchinis, cut into ½-inch cubes
- 3 tablespoons of extra-virgin olive oil
- 1 large onion, chopped
- 3 cloves of garlic, minced
- 1 teaspoon of salt
- 1 teaspoon of dried mint

Directions and Total Time: approx. 10 minutes

Heat the olive oil in a small-sized skillet over medium heat. Add the onion and garlic and sauté for 3 minutes, stirring constantly, or until softened. Stir in the zucchini cubes and salt and cook for 5 minutes, or until the zucchini is browned and tender. Add the mint to the skillet and toss to combine, then continue cooking for 2 minutes. Serve warm.

Per Serving: Calories 146, Fat 10.6g, Carbs 11.8g, Protein 4.2g

937. Ginger Vegetable Stir-Fry

Ingredients for 4 servings

- 1 tablespoon oil
- 3 cloves of garlic, minced
- 1 onion, chopped
- 1 thumb-size ginger, sliced
- 1 tablespoon water
- 1 large carrots, peeled and julienned
- 1 large green bell pepper
- 1 large yellow bell pepper
- 1 large red bell pepper
- 1 zucchini, julienned
- Salt and pepper to taste

Directions and Total Time: approx. 5 minutes

Heat oil in a large-sized skillet over medium flame and sauté the garlic, onion, and ginger until fragrant. Stir in the rest of the prepared ingredients and adjust the flame to high. Keep on stirring for at least 5 minutes until vegetables are half-cooked. Place in individual containers. Put a label and store in the fridge. Allow to thaw at room temperature before heating in the microwave oven.

Per Serving: Calories 102, Fat 2g, Carbs 13.6g, Protein 1g

938. Glazed Cinnamon Honey Carrots

Ingredients for 4 servings

- 1/4 pound Carrots
- 1/2 tablespoon butter
- 1 tablespoon honey
- 1/4 cup vegetable broth
- 1/2 teaspoon cinnamon
- 1/4 teaspoon salt

Directions and Total Time: approx. 5 minutes

Pell the carrots then set aside. Pour vegetable broth into the Instant Pot then place a trivet in it. Rub the carrots with salt then put on the trivet. Cover your prepared Instant Pot with the lid and seal it properly. Select the *Manual* setting on your prepared Instant Pot and cook the carrots for 2 minutes. Once it is done; naturally release the Instant Pot then open the lid. Take the cooked carrots out of the Instant Pot then place on a plate. Clean and wipe the Instant Pot then put butter in it. Return the carrots back to the Instant Pot then drizzle honey and sprinkle cinnamon on top. Select *Sauté* setting and cook the carrots for 1 minute. Stir well. Transfer the carrots to a serving dish then serve

Per Serving: Calories 50, Fat 0.4g, Carbs 6.2g, Protein 3.9g

939. Grilled Avocado with Tomatoes

Ingredients for 6 servings

- 3 avocados, halved and pitted
- 3 limes, wedged
- 1 ½ cup grape tomatoes
- 1 cup fresh corn
- 1 cup onion, chopped
- 3 serrano peppers
- 2 garlic cloves, peeled
- ¼ cup cilantro leaves, chopped
- 1 tablespoon olive oil
- Salt and black pepper to taste

Directions and Total Time: approx. 25 minutes

Prepare and set a grill over medium heat. Brush the avocado with oil and grill it for 5 minutes per side. Meanwhile, toss the garlic, onion, corn, tomatoes, and pepper in a baking sheet. At 550 degrees F, roast the vegetables for 5 minutes. Toss the veggie mix and stir in salt, cilantro, and black pepper. Mix well then fill the grilled avocadoes with the mixture. Garnish with lime. Serve.

Per Serving: Calories 56, Fat 6g, Carbs 3g, Protein 1g

940. Grilled Eggplant Caprese

Ingredients for 4 servings

- 1 eggplant aubergine, small/ medium
- 1 tomato large
- 2 basil leaves
- 4-ounces mozzarella
- good quality olive oil
- Pepper and salt to taste

Directions and Total Time: approx. 10 minutes

Cut the ends of the eggplant aubergine and then cut it lengthwise into ¼-inch thick slices. Discard the smaller pieces that's mostly skin and short. Slice the tomatoes and the mozzarella cheese into thin slices just like the eggplant. On medium-high the fire, place a griddle and let it heat up. Brush the prepared eggplant slices with olive oil and place on grill. Grill for 3 minutes. Turnover and grill for a minute. Add a slice of mozzarella cheese on one side and tomato on the other side. Continue cooking for another 2 minutes. Sprinkle with basil leaves. Season with pepper and salt. Fold eggplant in half and skewer with a cocktail stick. Serve and enjoy.

Per Serving: Calories 59, Fat 3g, Carbs 4g, Protein 3g

941. Hard-Boiled Egg

Ingredients for 8 servings

- 1 tablespoon of salt
- 1/4 cup distilled white vinegar
- 6 cups of water
- 8 eggs

Directions and Total Time: approx. 20 minutes

Place the salt, vinegar, and water in a large saucepan and bring to a boil over high heat. Stir in the prepared 8 eggs one by one, and be careful not to split them. Lower the heat temperature and cook over low heat and cook for 14 minutes. Pull out the eggs from the hot water and place them in a container filled with ice water or cold water. Cool completely, approximately 15 minutes.

Per Serving: Calories 72, Fat 5g, Carbs 4g, Protein 3g

942. Kale and Red Pepper Frittata

Ingredients for 4 servings

- Salt and pepper to taste
- ½ cup almond milk
- 8 large eggs
- 2 cups kale, rinsed and chopped
- 1/3 cup onion, chopped
- ½ cup red pepper, chopped
- 1 tablespoon coconut oil

Directions and Total Time: approx. 23 minutes

Preheat the oven to 350F. In a large-sized bowl, combine the eggs and almond milk. Season with salt and pepper. Set aside. In a large-sized skillet, heat the coconut oil over medium flame and sauté the onions and red pepper for three minutes or until the onion is translucent. Add in the kale and cook for 5 minutes more. Add the eggs into the mixture and cook for four minutes or until the edges start to set. Continue cooking the frittata in the oven for 15 minutes.

Per Serving: Calories 242, Fat 16.45g, Carbs 7g, Protein 16.5g

943. Lemon Herb Potatoes

Ingredients for 6 servings

- 1 1/2 pounds baby potatoes, rinsed and pat dry
- 1/2 fresh lemon juice
- 1 teaspoon dried oregano
- 1/2 teaspoon garlic, minced
- 1 tablespoon olive oil
- 1 cup vegetable broth
- 1/2 teaspoon sea salt

Directions and Total Time: approx. 21 minutes

Add broth and potatoes into the instant pot. Seal large-sized pot with lid and cook on high for 8 minutes. Once done, release pressure using quick release. Remove lid. Drain potatoes well and clean the instant pot. Add oil into the inner pot of instant pot and set the pot on sauté mode. Add potatoes, garlic, oregano, lemon juice, and salt and cook for 3 minutes. Serve and enjoy.

Per Serving: Calories 94, Fat 2.7g, Carbs 14.6g, Protein 3.8g

944. Lemon-Rosemary Beets

Ingredients for 7 servings

- 2 pounds of beets, slice into wedges
- 2 tablespoons of fresh lemon juice
- 2 tablespoons of extra-virgin olive oil
- 2 tablespoons of honey
- 1 tablespoon of apple cider vinegar
- ¾ teaspoon of sea salt
- ½ teaspoon of black pepper
- 2 sprigs of fresh rosemary
- ½ teaspoon of lemon zest

Directions and Total Time: approx. 8 hours and 15 minutes

Place the beets in the slow cooker. Whisk the lemon juice, extra-virgin olive oil, honey, apple cider vinegar, salt, and pepper in a small bowl. Pour over the beets. Add the sprigs of rosemary to the slow cooker. Cover and cook on low within 8 hours or until the beets are tender. Remove and discard the rosemary sprigs. Stir in the lemon zest. Serve hot.

Per Serving: Calories 112, Fat 4g, Carbs 18g, Protein 2g

945. Lentil and Tomato Collard Wraps

Ingredients for 4 servings

- 2 cups of cooked lentils
- 5 Roma tomatoes, diced
- ½ cup of crumbled feta cheese
- 10 large fresh basil leaves, thinly sliced
- ¼ cup of extra-virgin olive oil
- 1 tablespoon of balsamic vinegar
- 2 garlic cloves, minced
- ½ teaspoon of raw honey
- ½ teaspoon of salt
- ¼ teaspoon of freshly ground black pepper
- 4 large collard leaves, stems removed

Directions and Total Time: approx. 5 minutes

Combine the lentils, tomatoes, cheese, basil leaves, olive oil, vinegar, garlic, honey, salt, and black pepper in a large-sized bowl and stir until well blended. Lay the collard leaves on a flat work surface. Spoon the equal-sized amounts of the lentil mixture onto the edges of the leaves. Roll them up and slice in half to serve.

Per Serving: Calories 318, Fat 17.6g, Carbs 27.5g, Protein 13.2g

946. Marinara Zoodles

Ingredients for 4 servings

- 2 (14-ounces) cans crushed tomatoes
- 2 tablespoons of olive oil
- 16 ounces of zucchini noodles
- 1 (14-ounces) can diced tomatoes,
- 1 onion, chopped
- 4 garlic cloves, minced
- 1 tablespoon of dried Italian seasoning
- 1 teaspoon of dried oregano
- Sea salt to taste
- ¼ teaspoon of red pepper flakes
- ¼ cup of Romano cheese, grated

Directions and Total Time: approx. 65 minutes

Warm olive oil in a large-sized pot over medium heat and sauté onion and garlic for 5 minutes, stirring frequently until fragrant. Pour in tomatoes, oregano, Italian seasoning, salt, and red pepper flakes. Bring the dish to a hot, boil, then lower the heat, and simmer for 10-15 minutes. Stir in the ounces of zucchini noodles and cook for 3-4 minutes until the noodles are slightly softened. Scatter with Romano cheese and serve.

Per Serving: Calories 209, Fat 9g, Carbs 27.8g, Protein 8.1g

947. Mediterranean Kale and White Kidney Beans

Ingredients for 6 servings

- 1 onion, chopped
- 4 cloves of garlic, crushed
- ¼ cup of celery, chopped
- 2 carrots, sliced
- 1 cup of farro, rinsed and drained
- 14 ounces of canned roasted tomatoes
- 4 cups of low-sodium vegetable broth
- ½ teaspoon of red pepper, crushed
- Salt to taste
- 3 tablespoons of freshly squeezed lemon juice
- 15-ounces of white kidney beans, drained
- 4 cups of kale
- ½ cup of feta cheese, crumbled
- Fresh parsley, chopped

Directions and Total Time: approx. 3 hours and 30 minutes

Put the onion, garlic, celery, carrots, farro, tomatoes, broth, red pepper, and salt in your slow cooker. Seal the pot. Cook on high for 2 hours. Stir in the lemon juice, beans, and kale. Cover and cook for 1 more hour. Sprinkle the cheese and parsley before serving.

Per Serving: Calories 274, Fat 9g, Carbs 46g, Protein 14g

948. Mediterranean Zucchini and Eggplant

Ingredients for 4 servings

- 1 tablespoon of olive oil
- 1 onion, diced
- 4 cloves of garlic, minced
- 1 red bell pepper, chopped
- 4 tomatoes, diced
- 1 zucchini, chopped
- 1 pound of eggplant, sliced into cubes
- Salt and pepper to taste
- 2 teaspoons of dried basil
- 4 ounces of feta cheese

Directions and Total Time: approx. 3 hours and 15 minutes

Coat your slow cooker with olive oil. Mix all the fixing except cheese in the pot. Cook on high within 3 hours. Sprinkle feta cheese on top and serve.

Per Serving: Calories 341, Fat 12g, Carbs 51g, Protein 13g

949. Mixed Tomato Quiche

Ingredients for 4 servings

- 1 brisée pastry sheet
- 1 ½ cup of ricotta cheese
- 2 cups of Stracciatella cheese
- 3 cups of mixed tomatoes (cheery, beef, ramato, pachino)
- 1 tablespoon olive paste
- 4 tablespoons Parmigiano cheese
- 2 eggs
- 2 tablespoons olive oil
- 1 branch of basil
- Salt and pepper to taste

Directions and Total Time: approx. 65 minutes

Roll out the brisée pastry and place it in a folded round baking pan. Make some holes on the bottom of the pastry with the ribbons of a fork and cook it in the oven at a heat of 180° for 10 minutes. In a blender, blend together the Stracciatella cheese, ricotta, and Parmigiano cheese. Add the prepared eggs to the mixture and whisk well. Season with salt and pepper and pour the mixture into the pastry shell. Before pouring the mixture spread on top of the pastry the olive paste. Pour the mixture and dip inside of it the washed and pitted tomatoes. Drizzle with tablespoons of olive oil and bake at 180° for approximately 40 minutes. Let it cool down and serve at room temperature with some basil.

Per Serving: Calories 539, Fat 20g, Carbs 40g, Protein 12g

950. Mushroom and Cauliflower Roast

Ingredients for 4 servings

- 2 tablespoons of olive oil
- 4 cups of cauliflower florets
- 1 celery stalk, chopped
- 1 cup of mushrooms, sliced
- 10 cherry tomatoes, halved
- 1 yellow onion, chopped
- 2 garlic cloves, minced
- 2 tablespoons of dill, chopped
- Salt and black pepper to taste

Directions and Total Time: approx. 35 minutes

Preheat the oven to a heat of 340 F. Line a baking sheet with parchment paper. Place in cauliflower florets, olive oil, mushrooms, celery, tomatoes, onion, garlic, salt, and pepper and mix to combine. Bake for 25 minutes. Serve topped with dill.

Per Serving: Calories 380, Fat 15g, Carbs 17g, Protein 12g

951. Mushroom with a Soy Sauce Glaze

Ingredients for 2 servings

- 2 tablespoons butter
- 1(8 ounces) package sliced white mushrooms
- 2 cloves garlic, minced
- 2 teaspoons soy sauce
- ground black pepper to taste

Directions and Total Time: approx. 15 minutes

Cook the tablespoons of butter in a frying pan over medium heat; stir in the mushrooms; cook and then continue to stir until the mushrooms are soft and released about 5 minutes. Stir in the garlic; keep cooking and stir for 1 minute. Pour the soy sauce; cook the mushrooms in the soy sauce until the liquid has evaporated, about 4 minutes.

Per Serving: Calories 135, Fat 9g, Carbs 4g, Protein 2g

952. Olives and Swiss Chard

Ingredients for 4 servings

- ¼ pound of Swiss chard, cut and washed
- 1 teaspoon of olive oil (extra virgin)
- 1/3 cup of Kalamata olives (brine-cured), halved and coarsely chopped
- ½ cup of water
- 2 garlic cloves, cut
- 1 medium yellow onion, sliced
- 1 jalapeño pepper, chopped

Directions and Total Time: approx. 30 minutes

Separate Swiss chard stems from leaves; chop stems into tiny bits and coarsely slice leaves; set aside in a Dutch oven or a big pan, heat extra virgin olive oil over medium heat. Sauté for approximately 6 minutes, or until onion is soft and translucent, adding garlic, onion, and jalapeño as needed. Cook, covered, for 3 minutes with the olives, Swiss chard stems, and water. Add the chard leaves and simmer, covered, for another four minutes or when the leaves & stems are soft. Serve right away.

Per Serving: Calories 93, Fat 6g, Carbs 8g, Protein 4g

953. Orange Roasted Brussels Sprouts

Ingredients for 4 servings

- 2 tablespoons of olive oil
- ½ teaspoon of salt
- 1 pound of Brussels sprouts, quartered
- 2 garlic cloves, minced
- 1 orange, cut into rings

Directions and Total Time: approx. 15 minutes

Warm the air fryer to 360°F (182°C). In a large bowl, mix the quartered Brussels sprouts with garlic, olive oil, and salt until well coated. Pour the quartered Brussels sprouts into the air fryer, place the orange slices on top, and roast for 10 minutes. Remove from the deep fryer and set orange slices aside. Sauté the Brussels sprouts before serving.

Per Serving: Calories 111, Fat 7g, Carbs 11g, Protein 4g

954. Paprika and Chives Potatoes

Ingredients for 4 servings

- 4 potatoes, scrubbed and pricked with a fork
- 1 tablespoon olive oil
- 1 celery stalk, chopped
- 2 tomatoes, chopped
- 1 teaspoon sweet paprika
- Salt and black pepper to the taste
- 2 tablespoons chives, chopped

Directions and Total Time: approx. 1 hour and 23 minutes

Arrange the scrubbed potatoes on a baking tray lined with parchment paper, place them in the oven and bake at 180°F within 1 hour. Cool the potatoes, peel them and cut them into larger cubes. Heat up a large-sized pan with oil over medium heat, add celery and tomatoes and sauté for 2 minutes. Add the potatoes and the rest of the ingredients, mix, cook for 6 minutes, divide the mixture into plates and serve.

Per Serving: Calories 223, Fat 8.7g, Carbs 14.4g, Protein 6.4g

955. Parmesan Omelet

Ingredients for 2 servings

- 1 tablespoon cream cheese
- 2 eggs, beaten
- ¼ teaspoon paprika
- ½ teaspoon dried oregano
- ¼ teaspoon dried dill
- 1 ounces Parmesan, grated
- 1 teaspoon coconut oil

Directions and Total Time: approx. 15 minutes

Combine cream cheese, eggs, dried oregano, and dill in a mixing bowl. Heat the coconut oil in the skillet until it covers the whole pan. Then, in the same skillet, add the egg mixture and flatten it. Close the cover and add the grated Parmesan. Over low heat, cook the omelet for 10 minutes. After that, place the cooked omelet on a serving tray and top with paprika.

Per Serving: Calories 148, Fat 11.5g, Carbs 1.4g, Protein 10.6g

956. Parmesan Stuffed Zucchini Boats

Ingredients for 4 servings

- 1 cup canned low-sodium chickpeas, drained and rinsed
- 1 cup no-sugar-added spaghetti sauce
- 2 zucchinis
- ¼ cup shredded Parmesan cheese

Directions and Total Time: approx. 15 minutes

Preheat the oven to 425°F. In a large-sized bowl, stir together the chickpeas and spaghetti sauce. Cut the 2 zucchinis in half lengthwise and scrape a spoon gently down the length of each half to remove the seeds. Fill each zucchini half with the chickpea sauce and top with one-quarter of the Parmesan cheese. Place the pieces of zucchini halves on a baking sheet and roast in the oven for 15 minutes. Transfer to a plate. Let rest for 5 minutes before serving.

Per Serving: Calories 139, Fat 4g, Carbs 20g, Protein 8g

957. Pea and Carrot Noodles

Ingredients for 4 servings

- 2 tablespoons of olive oil
- 4 carrots, spiralized
- 1 sweet onion, chopped
- 2 cups of peas
- 2 garlic cloves, minced
- ¼ cup of chopped fresh parsley
- Salt and black pepper to taste

Directions and Total Time: approx. 25 minutes

Warm the prepared 2 tablespoons of olive oil in a pot over medium heat and sauté the onion and garlic for approximately about 3 minutes until just tender and fragrant. Add in spiralized carrots and cook for 4 minutes. Mix in peas, salt, and pepper and cook for 4 minutes. Drizzle with the remaining olive oil and sprinkle with parsley.

Per Serving: Calories 157, Fat 7g, Carbs 19.6g, Protein 4.8g

958. Peaches Caprese

Ingredients for 4 servings

- 4 peaches
- 3 cups of mozzarella
- 4 sprigs of basil
- Olive oil to taste
- 1 tablespoon balsamic vinegar
- Salt and pepper to taste
- A pinch of oregano

Directions and Total Time: approx. 15 minutes

Slice the peaches and grill them on a grill pan for a couple of minutes on each side. Slice the mozzarella at the same thickness as the peaches. Season the peaches and the mozzarella with salt, pepper, oregano, and oil and place them on a serving plate alternating them with a basil leaf. Drizzle with fresh balsamic vinegar.

Per Serving: Calories 250, Fat 18g, Carbs 10g, Protein 28g

959. Peas and Spinach Medallions

Ingredients for 4 servings

- 1 cup of peas
- ½ cup of spinach
- 2 boiled potatoes
- 1 zucchini
- 1 fresh onion
- 3 spoons of olive oil
- 1 cup of Parmigiano cheese
- 1 ½ cup of breadcrumbs
- Salt and pepper to taste

Directions and Total Time: approx. 1 hour and 40 minutes

Smash the potatoes in a puree. Boil the spinach in hot water, drain them, and squeeze them. Slice the onion and cut the zucchini into little cubes. Cook them in a pan with a little bit of olive oil. Add the vegetables to the potato mixture and mix. Create some medallions and roll them in the breadcrumbs with Parmigiano. Cook them in a pan with a little bit of oil for 15 minutes and season with salt and pepper.

Per Serving: Calories 298, Fat 10g, Carbs 35g, Protein 14g

960. Potato and Green Beans Flan

Ingredients for 4 servings

- 2 pre-cooked potatoes
- 2 cups of pre-cooked green beans
- 2 eggs
- 2 cups of ricotta cheese
- 2 tablespoons of Parmigiano cheese
- 1 branch of basil
- ½ cup of milk
- Salt and pepper to taste
- Oil to taste

Directions and Total Time: approx. 60 minutes

In a blender, blend the ricotta, Parmigiano, potatoes, milk, salt, pepper, and basil all together. Add the eggs and whisk well together. Add to the mixture the cut green beans and mix. Flour one rounded baking pan and pour the mixture inside. Level with a spoon and drizzle with oil. Bake at 180° for 40 minutes. Serve at room temperature.

Per Serving: Calories 350, Fat 25g, Carbs 45g, Protein 20g

961. Pumpkin Cauliflower Curry

Ingredients for 4 servings
- ½ cup pumpkin puree
- 4 cups cauliflower florets
- ½ chopped yellow onion
- 2 cloves minced garlic
- 2 cups coconut milk
- 2 tablespoons olive oil
- 2 teaspoons coriander, ginger, and cilantro
- 1 teaspoons salt, pepper, paprika, turmeric, cumin, and chili powder

Directions and Total Time: approx. 35 minutes

In a medium-heat saucepan, heat the onions and garlic in olive oil until fragrant. Add the ginger and sauté for 5 minutes. Add the coconut milk, coriander, salt, pepper, paprika, turmeric, cumin, and chili powder to the saucepan and stir until combined. Add the cauliflower florets and pumpkin puree and simmer for 10 minutes. Top with cilantro before serving.

Per Serving: Calories 379, Fat 35.8g, Carbs 16.2g, Protein 5.3g

962. Rigatoni Pasta with Capers and Ricotta Cheese

Ingredients for 4 servings
- 3 cups of rigatoni
- 2 ½ cup of ricotta cheese
- ¾ cup of Taggiasche olives
- ½ cup of capers
- 15 dried tomatoes
- 2 tablespoons of olive oil
- 8 capers fruits
- Salt and pepper to taste
- Water

Directions and Total Time: approx. 20 minutes

Cut the tomato into slices and let it soak in water for 5 minutes. Drain them and set them aside. Wash the capers. Boil the pasta in salted water meanwhile, blend the ricotta, the capers, oil, salt, and pepper together. Add the tomatoes to the mixture. Pour the mixture into a large-sized bowl and add the pasta to it, add the olive and mix well. Serve with some capers fruits.

Per Serving: Calories 450, Fat 20g, Carbs 42g, Protein 19g

963. Roasted Asian Green Beans

Ingredients for 2 servings
- 8 ounces of fresh green beans
- 1 tablespoon of tamari
- 1 teaspoon of Olive oil extra-virgin

Directions and Total Time: approx. 20 minutes

Snap the green beans in half after cutting off the ends. In a resealable plastic bag or a jar with a cover, place the green beans. Give it an actual thorough shake to combine the tamari and olive oil. Place the fresh green beans in the air fryer basket. Cook at 390°F for about 10 minutes, tossing halfway through.

Per Serving: Calories 58, Fat 2g, Carbs 8g, Protein 3g

964. Roasted Asparagus with Hazelnuts

Ingredients for 4 servings
- 2 tablespoons of olive oil
- 1 pound of asparagus, trimmed
- ¼ cup of hazelnuts, chopped
- 1 lemon, juiced and zested
- Salt and black pepper to taste
- ½ teaspoon of red pepper flakes

Directions and Total Time: approx. 25 minutes

Preheat oven to a heat of 425 F. Arrange the asparagus on a baking sheet. Combine olive oil, lemon zest, lemon juice, salt, hazelnuts, and black pepper in a bowl and mix well. Pour the mixture over the asparagus. Place in the prepared preheated oven and roast for approximately about 15-20 minutes until tender and lightly charred. Serve topped with red pepper flakes.

Per Serving: Calories 112, Fat 10g, Carbs 5.2g, Protein 3.2g

965. Roasted Bell Peppers

Ingredients for 4 servings
- 3 sliced red bell peppers
- 2 sliced russet potatoes
- ½ cup Kalamata olives
- 3 cloves of garlic
- ½ can tomato paste
- ⅓ cup fresh basil
- 2 tablespoons olive oil
- 1 teaspoon salt, pepper, and oregano

Directions and Total Time: approx. 25 minutes

In a medium-heat saucepan, cook the cloves of garlic in the olive oil until fragrant. Add the bell peppers, potatoes, tomato paste, salt, pepper, and oregano to the saucepan and cook for 10 minutes. Add the Kalamata olives 2 minutes before the dish is done cooking. Top with the fresh basil before serving.

Per Serving: Calories 203, Fat 9.3g, Carbs 29.3g, Protein 4g

966. Roasted Cabbage Steaks

Ingredients for 3 servings
- 1 small head of cabbage
- 2 small tomatoes sliced
- 6 marinated artichoke halves
- 1 tablespoon Mediterranean seasoning
- 4-ounce basil pesto
- 1 cup shredded parmesan cheese
- 2-ounce feta cheese crumbled
- 2 tablespoons basil leaves

Directions and Total Time: approx. 30 minutes

Set oven to 400 degrees F and let preheat. In the meantime, cut the cabbage into ½ inch thick steaks and place it in a single layer onto a greased sheet pan. Season with seasoning, then spread pesto generously on top of steaks, top with cheeses, tomatoes, and artichoke hearts, and place the sheet pan into the heated oven. Bake for 20 minutes or until steaks are cooked through and cheese bubbles. When done, top steaks with basil leaves and basil pesto and serve.

Per Serving: Calories 278, Fat 20g, Carbs 40g, Protein 15g

967. Roasted Tomatoes and Feta Cheese

Ingredients for 4 servings

- 2 tablespoons extra virgin olive oil
- 2 garlic cloves, peeled and minced
- To taste, season with salt and freshly ground pepper
- 6 plum tomatoes, deseeded and half
- 1/3 of a cup of panko bread crumbs
- 1/2 cup feta cheese, crumbled
- Garnish with chopped fresh parsley

Directions and Total Time: approx. 15 minutes

Combine the olive oil, garlic, and salt & pepper to taste in a mixing bowl. Fill a resealable baggie with tomato halves and the olive oil mixture. Mix to coat tomatoes and set aside for 20 minutes to marinate. Preheat the oven to 350 Fahrenheit. In a large-sized bowl, combine bread crumbs with feta cheese. Fill tomato halves with cheese mixture and place on a baking pan. Bake for just about 30 minutes, or until tomatoes are tender and cheese has melted. Serve with a sprinkling of freshly chopped parsley.

Per Serving: Calories 60, Fat 4g, Carbs 1g, Protein 5g

968. Root Vegetable Tagine

Ingredients for 8 servings

- 1-pound of parsnips, peeled and chopped into bite-size pieces
- 1-pound turnips, peeled and chopped into bite-size pieces
- 2 medium yellow onions, chopped into bite-size pieces
- 1-pound carrots, peeled and chopped into bite-size pieces
- 6 dried apricots, chopped
- 6 figs, chopped
- 1 teaspoon of ground turmeric
- 1 teaspoon of ground cumin
- ½ teaspoon of ground ginger
- ½ teaspoon of ground cinnamon
- ¼ teaspoon of cayenne pepper
- 1 tablespoon of dried parsley
- 1 tablespoon of dried cilantro (or 2 tablespoons chopped fresh cilantro)
- 1 ¾ cups of vegetable stock

Directions and Total Time: approx. 9 hours and 15 minutes

The slow cooker combines parsnips, turnips, onions, carrots, apricots, and figs. Sprinkle with turmeric, cumin, ginger, cinnamon, cayenne pepper, parsley, and cilantro. Pour in the vegetable stock. Cover and cook within 9 hours on low. Serve hot.

Per Serving: Calories 131, Fat 1g, Carbs 31g, Protein 3g

969. Sandwich with Tongue, Arugula, and Champignons

Ingredients for 2 servings

- 1 piece of pitta bread
- 1 piece of tomatoes flame
- 1 bunch of arugula
- 5 ounces of Fresh champignons
- 1 teaspoon of truffle oil
- 2 tablespoons of olive oil
- Dried thyme, to taste
- Ground black pepper, to taste
- Salt, to taste
- 3 ½ ounces of veal tongue

Directions and Total Time: approx. 20 minutes

Cut the tongue into long thin slices and fry in olive oil, salt, pepper, and add thyme to taste. Lightly fry the champignons in olive oil and put in a clean bowl, trying to leave excess fat in a pan. Drizzle with truffle oil to give mushrooms a flavor. Put the arugula, thin slices of tomato, mushrooms, and tongue evenly on the unfolded pita bread. Wrap tightly, if necessary, cut off excess pita bread along the edges. Cut into two and serve.

Per Serving: Calories 200, Fat 13.6g, Carbs 13g, Protein 7.5g

970. Sauté of Green Beans and Zucchini

Ingredients for 4 servings

- ½ teaspoon of extra virgin olive oil, split
- 2 ounces of green beans, trimmed and chopped into little pieces
- 1/2 finely sliced tiny zucchini
- 2 tablespoons of red chili powder
- Lemon juice (1/2 teaspoon)
- 2 ounces of scallions, sliced
- 1 teaspoon of red chili powder
- A sprinkling of parmesan flakes
- ½ teaspoon of pepper
- ½ teaspoon of salt

Directions and Total Time: approx. 15 minutes

Heat half of the prepared oil in a medium-sized skillet. Stir in the green beans, zucchini, salt, and pepper, and cook for approximately nine minutes, occasionally turning, until the veggies are crisp-tender. Take the large-sized pan off the heat and add the lemon juice and scallions. Serve with cheese and red chili flakes on top.

Per Serving: Calories 111, Fat 7g, Carbs 12g, Protein 3g

971. Sauteed Collard Greens

Ingredients for 4 servings

- 1 pound of collard greens, 2-inch pieces
- 1 pinch of red pepper flakes
- 3 cups of chicken broth
- 1 teaspoon of pepper
- 1 teaspoon of salt
- 2 cloves of garlic, minced
- 1 large onion, chopped
- 3 slices bacon
- 1 tablespoon olive oil

Directions and Total Time: approx. 10 minutes

Using a large skillet, heat oil on medium-high heat. Sauté bacon until crisp. Remove it from the pan and crumble it once cooled. Set it aside. Using the same pan, sauté onion and cook until tender. Add garlic until fragrant. Add the pound of collard greens and cook until they start to wilt. Pour in the cups of chicken broth and season with pepper, salt, and red pepper flakes. Reduce the heat temperature to low and simmer for 45 minutes.

Per Serving: Calories 20, Fat 1g, Carbs 3g, Protein 1g

972. Savoy Cabbage with Coconut Cream Sauce

Ingredients for 4 servings

- 3 tablespoons of olive oil
- 1 onion, chopped
- 4 cloves of garlic, minced
- 1 head of savoy cabbage, chopped finely
- 2 cups of bone broth
- 1 cup of coconut milk, freshly squeezed
- 1 bay leaf
- Salt and pepper to taste
- 2 tablespoons of chopped parsley

Directions and Total Time: approx. 25 minutes

Heat oil in a pot for 2 minutes. Stir in the onions, bay leaf, and garlic until fragrant, around 3 minutes. Add the rest of the prepared ingredients, except for the parsley, and mix well. Cover pot, bring to a boil, and let it simmer for 5 minutes or until cabbage is tender to taste. Stir in parsley and serve.

Per Serving: Calories 195, Fat 19.7g, Carbs 12.3g, Protein 2.7g

973. Scrambled Eggs

Ingredients for 2 servings

- 1 yellow bell pepper, chopped
- 8 cherry tomatoes, cubed
- 2 spring onions, chopped
- 1 tablespoon olive oil
- 1 tablespoon caper, drained
- 2 tablespoons black olives, pitted and sliced
- 4 eggs
- A pinch of salt and black pepper
- ¼ teaspoon oregano, dried
- 1 tablespoon parsley, chopped

Directions and Total Time: approx. 20 minutes

Over a temperature of medium-high heat, heat the oil in a skillet, then add the bell pepper and spring onions and cook for 3 minutes. Sauté for another 2 minutes with the tomatoes, capers, and olives. Scramble the eggs in the large-sized pan, season with salt, pepper, and oregano, and cook for another 5 minutes. Serve the scramble by dividing it amongst dishes and garnishing it with parsley.

Per Serving: Calories 249, Fat 17g, Carbs 13.3g, Protein 13.5g

974. Slow Cooker Caponata

Ingredients for 8 servings

- 1-pound of plum tomatoes, chopped
- 1 eggplant, not peeled, cut into ½-inch pieces
- 2 medium zucchinis, cut into ½-inch pieces
- 1 large yellow onion, finely chopped
- 3 stalks of celery, sliced
- ½ cup of chopped fresh parsley
- 2 tablespoons of red wine vinegar
- 1 tablespoon of brown sugar
- ¼ cup of raisins
- ¼ cup (4 ounces) tomato paste
- 1 teaspoon of sea salt
- ¼ teaspoon of black pepper
- ¼ cup of pine nuts
- 2 tablespoons of capers, drained
- 3 tablespoons of oil-cured black olives (optional)

Directions and Total Time: approx. 5 hours and 45 minutes

In the slow cooker, combine the tomatoes, eggplant, zucchini, onion, celery, and parsley. Add the vinegar, brown sugar, raisins, and tomato paste. Sprinkle with salt and pepper. Cover and cook on low within 5½ hours, or until thoroughly cooked. Stir in the pine nuts, capers, and olives (if using). Serve hot.

Per Serving: Calories 68, Fat 4g, Carbs 6g, Protein 1g

975. Spicy Kale with Almonds

Ingredients for 4 servings

- 2 tablespoons of olive oil
- ¼ cup of slivered almonds
- 1 pound of chopped kale
- ¼ cup of vegetable broth
- 1 lemon, juiced and zested
- 1 garlic clove, minced
- 1 tablespoon of red pepper flakes
- Salt and black pepper to taste

Directions and Total Time: approx. 25 minutes

Warm olive oil in a large-sized pan over medium heat and sauté garlic, kale, salt, and pepper for 8-9 minutes until soft. Add in lemon juice, lemon zest, red pepper flakes, and vegetable broth and continue cooking until the liquid evaporates, about 3-5 minutes. Garnish with almonds and serve.

Per Serving: Calories 123, Fat 8.1g, Carbs 10.8g, Protein 4g

976. Spinach Frittata

Ingredients for 4 servings

- 2 ounces of cheddar grated
- 1 cup of cherry tomatoes halved
- Kosher salt and ground black pepper
- 8 ounces of spinach leaves
- 1 medium onion chopped
- 6 eggs whole
- 2 tablespoons of olive oil extra-virgin

Directions and Total Time: approx. 35 minutes

In a mixing dish, whisk together the 6 eggs and add salt and pepper to taste. In a large-sized pan, heat the olive oil on medium flame. Cook for another 3 minutes, occasionally stirring, before adding the spinach leaves & cherry tomatoes. Cook for around 3 minutes while constantly stirring. Place the veggies on top. Pour the beaten eggs into the pan. On top, there's a sprinkling of cheddar cheese. Cook on low flame for about 10 minutes with the lid on.

Per Serving: Calories 215, Fat 12.9g, Carbs 8.5g, Protein 14.2g

977. Spinach Ricotta Lasagna

Ingredients for 4 servings

- 16 ounces phyllo dough
- 2 cups chopped spinach
- 1 ¼ cup ricotta
- 1 chopped yellow onion
- 2 cloves minced garlic
- 4 large eggs
- 2 tablespoons olive oil
- 2 tablespoons parsley
- 2 teaspoons salt, pepper, and dill

Directions and Total Time: approx. 1 hour and 15 minutes

Rinse and drain the spinach. In a large-sized mixing bowl, combine the spinach, ricotta, onion, garlic, eggs, olive oil, parsley, salt, pepper, and dill. In a baking dish, layer a sheet of phyllo, brush with olive oil, and add a layer of the filling. Repeat this process and top with a sheet of phyllo. Bake at 325°F for 1 hour or until the phyllo is golden brown.

Per Serving: Calories 437, Fat 25.7g, Carbs 28.1g, Protein 21g

978. Sprout Crackers with Cheese and Lemon

Ingredients for 12 servings

- 12 whole grain crackers, 12 oz.
- 1/2 quarts of hummus
- 12 low-fat cheddar cheese slices
- 12 tablespoons of sprouted alfalfa
- pepper, freshly ground
- Garnish with lemon wedges

Directions and Total Time: approx. 15 minutes

Place crackers on a serving plate. On top of the crackers, evenly distribute the hummus. Add a piece of cheddar cheese, sprout, and a pinch of pepper to each cracker. Before serving, garnish the plate with lime wedges to drizzle over the crackers.

Per Serving: Calories 130, Fat 5g, Carbs 20g, Protein 2g

979. Steamed Zucchini-Paprika

Ingredients for 4 servings

- 4 tablespoons olive oil
- 3 cloves of garlic, minced
- 1 onion, chopped
- 3 medium-sized zucchinis, sliced thinly
- A dash of paprika
- Salt and pepper to taste

Directions and Total Time: approx. 45 minutes

Place all the rest of the prepared ingredients in the Instant Pot. Give a good stir to combine all the ingredients. Close its lid and make sure that the steam release valve is set to "Venting." Press the "Slow Cook" button and adjust the cooking time to 4 hours. Halfway through the required cooking time, open the lid and give a good stir to brown the other side.

Per Serving: Calories 93, Fat 10.2g, Carbs 3.1g, Protein 0.6g

980. Stir-Fried Bok Choy

Ingredients for 4 servings

- 3 tablespoons coconut oil
- 4 cloves of garlic, minced
- 1 onion, chopped
- 2 heads bok choy, rinsed and chopped
- 2 teaspoons coconut aminos
- Salt and pepper to taste
- 2 tablespoons sesame oil
- 2 tablespoons sesame seeds, toasted

Directions and Total Time: approx. 18 minutes

Heat the oil in a pot for 2 minutes. Sauté the garlic and onions until fragrant, around 3 minutes. Stir in the bok choy, coconut aminos, salt and pepper. Cover pan and cook for 5 minutes. Stir and continue cooking for just about another 3 minutes. Drizzle with sesame oil and sesame seeds on top before serving.

Per Serving: Calories 358, Fat 28.4g, Carbs 5.2g, Protein 21.5g

981. Stir-Fried Brussels Sprouts and Carrots

Ingredients for 4 servings

- 1 tablespoon of cider vinegar
- 1/3 cup of water
- 1 pound of Brussels sprouts halved lengthwise
- 1 pound of carrots cut diagonally into ½-inch thick lengths
- 3 tablespoons of unsalted butter, divided
- 2 tablespoons of chopped shallot
- ½ teaspoon of pepper
- ¾ teaspoon of salt

Directions and Total Time: approx. 25 minutes

On medium-high temperature fire, place a nonstick medium fry pan and heat 2 tablespoons of butter. Add shallots and cook until softened, around 1–2 minutes while occasionally stirring. Add pepper, salt, Brussels sprouts, and carrots. Stir-fry until vegetables start to brown on the edges, around 3 to 4 minutes. Add water, cook, and cover. After approximately about 5 to 8 minutes, or when veggies are already soft, add the remaining butter. Season with more teaspoons of pepper and salt to taste. Turn off the fire, transfer to a platter, serve and enjoy.

Per Serving: Calories 98, Fat 4.2g, Carbs 13.9g, Protein 3.5g

982. Stir-Fried Kale with Mushrooms

Ingredients for 4 servings

- 1 cup of cremini mushrooms, sliced
- 4 tablespoons of olive oil
- 1 small red onion, chopped
- 2 cloves of garlic, thinly sliced
- 1 ½ pound of curly kale
- 2 tomatoes, chopped
- 1 teaspoon of dried oregano
- 1 teaspoon of dried basil
- ½ teaspoon of dried rosemary
- ½ teaspoon of dried thyme
- Salt and black pepper to taste

Directions and Total Time: approx. 10 minutes

Warm the olive oil in a medium-sized saucepan over medium heat. Sauté the onion and garlic for about 3 minutes or until they are softened. Add in the mushrooms, kale, and tomatoes, stirring to promote even cooking. Turn the heat to a simmer, add in the spices and cook for 5-6 minutes until the kale wilt.

Per Serving: Calories 221, Fat 16g, Carbs 19g, Protein 9g

983. Stir-Fried Spicy Cauliflower

Ingredients for 4 servings

- 5 cloves of garlic finely sliced
- 1 tablespoon of Sriracha
- 3/4 cup of onion white thinly sliced
- 1/2 teaspoon of sugar
- 1 tablespoon of rice vinegar
- 1 1/2 tablespoons of tamari
- 2 tablespoons of olive oil extra-virgin
- 1 head of cauliflower, cut into florets

Directions and Total Time: approx. 35 minutes

In a nonstick skillet, add two teaspoons of olive oil, the cauliflowers, then cook for about 10 minutes on medium flame. Cook for about a further 5 minutes after adding the sliced onion. After adding the garlic, cook for another 5 minutes. In a small-sized cup, combine rice vinegar, soy sauce, sugar, Sriracha, pepper, & salt. Spoon the sauce over all the cauliflower mixture and simmer for an additional 5 minutes.

Per Serving: Calories 93, Fat 3g, Carbs 12g, Protein 4g

984. Stuffed Acorn Squash

Ingredients for 4 servings

- 1 acorn squash
- 1 tablespoon of honey
- 1 tablespoon of olive oil (not extra-virgin)
- ¼ cup of chopped pecans or walnuts
- ¼ cup of chopped dried cranberries
- sea salt

Directions and Total Time: approx. 6 hours and 15 minutes

Cut the squash in half. Discard the seeds and pulp from the middle. Cut the halves in half again to make it into quarters. Place the squash quarters cut-side up in the slow cooker. Combine the honey, olive oil, pecans, and cranberries in a small bowl. Spoon the pecan mixture into the center of each squash quarter. Season the squash with salt. Cook on low within 5 to 6 hours, or until the squash is tender. Serve hot.

Per Serving: Calories 387, Fat 19g, Carbs 42g, Protein 12g

985. Sweet Mustard Cabbage Hash

Ingredients for 4 servings

- 1 head of Savoy cabbage, shredded
- 3 tablespoons of olive oil
- 1 onion, finely chopped
- 2 garlic cloves, minced
- ½ teaspoon of fennel seeds
- ¼ cup of red wine vinegar
- 1 tablespoon of mustard powder
- 1 tablespoon of honey
- Salt and black pepper to taste

Directions and Total Time: approx. 30 minutes

Warm olive oil in a large-sized pan over medium heat and sauté onion, fennel seeds, cabbage, salt, and pepper for 8-9 minutes. In a bowl, mix vinegar, mustard, and honey; set aside. Sauté garlic in the pan for 30 seconds. Pour in vinegar mixture and cook for 10-15 minutes until the liquid reduces by half.

Per Serving: Calories 181, Fat 12g, Carbs 19g, Protein 3.4g

986. Sweet Potatoes Oven Fried

Ingredients for 4 servings

- 1 small garlic clove, minced
- 1 teaspoon of grated orange rind
- 1 tablespoon of fresh parsley, chopped finely
- ¼ teaspoon of pepper
- ¼ teaspoon of salt
- 1 tablespoon of olive oil
- 4 medium sweet potatoes, ¼-inch thickness

Directions and Total Time: approx. 40 minutes

In a large bowl mix well pepper, salt, olive oil, and sweet potatoes. In a greased baking sheet, in a single layer arrange sweet potatoes. Pop in a preheated 400ºF oven and bake for 15 minutes, turnover potato slices, and return to oven. Bake for another 15 minutes or until tender. Meanwhile, mix well in a small bowl, garlic, orange rind, and parsley, sprinkle over cooked potato slices, and serve. You can store the baked sweet potatoes in a lidded container and just microwave whenever you want to eat them. Consume within 3 days.

Per Serving: Calories 176, Fat 2.5g, Carbs 36.6g, Protein 2.5g

987. Tasty Avocado Sauce over Zoodles

Ingredients for 4 servings

- 1 zucchini peeled and spiralized into noodles
- 4 tablespoons of pine nuts
- 2 tablespoons of lemon juice
- 1 avocado peeled and pitted
- 12 sliced cherry tomatoes
- 1/3 cup of water
- 1 1/4 cup of basil
- Pepper and salt to taste

Directions and Total Time: approx. 20 minutes

Make the sauce in a blender by adding pine nuts, lemon juice, avocado, water, and basil. Pulse until smooth and creamy. Season with pepper and salt to taste. Mix well. Place zoodles in the salad bowl. Pour over the avocado sauce and toss well to coat. Add cherry tomatoes, serve, and enjoy.

Per Serving: Calories 313, Fat 26.8g, Carbs 18.7g, Protein 6.8g

988. Tofu Hoagie Rolls

Ingredients for 6 servings

- ½ cup vegetable broth
- ¼ cup hot sauce
- 1 tablespoon vegan butter
- 1 (16 ounce) package tofu, pressed and diced
- 4 cups cabbage, shredded
- 2 medium apples, grated
- 1 medium shallot, grated
- 6 tablespoons vegan mayonnaise
- 1 tablespoon apple cider vinegar
- Salt and black pepper
- 4 6-inch hoagie rolls, toasted

Directions and Total Time: approx. 30 minutes

In a saucepan, combine broth with butter and hot sauce and bring to a boil. Add tofu and reduce the heat to a simmer. Cook for 10 minutes then remove from heat and let sit for 10 minutes to marinate. Toss cabbage and rest of the ingredients in a salad bowl. Prepare and set up a grill on medium heat. Drain the tofu and grill for 5 minutes per side. Lay out the toasted hoagie rolls and add grilled tofu to each hoagie. Add the cabbage mixture evenly between them then close it. Serve.

Per Serving: Calories 111, Fat 11g, Carbs 5g, Protein 1g

989. Vegan Carrots and Broccoli

Ingredients for 6 servings

- 4 cups broccoli florets
- 2 carrots, peeled and sliced
- 1/4 cup water
- 1/2 lemon juice
- 1 teaspoon garlic, minced
- 1 tablespoon olive oil
- 1/4 cup vegetable stock
- 1/4 teaspoon Italian seasoning
- Salt

Directions and Total Time: approx. 15 minutes

Add oil into the inner pot of instant pot and set the pot on sauté mode. Add garlic and sauté for 30 seconds. Add the sliced carrots and broccoli florets and cook for 2 minutes. Add remaining ingredients and stir everything well. Seal large-sized pot with lid and cook on high for 3 minutes. Once done, release pressure using quick release. Remove lid. Stir well and serve.

Per Serving: Calories 51, Fat 2.6g, Carbs 6.3g, Protein 2g

990. Vegetables Tempura

Ingredients for 4 servings

- 4 cups of sliced zucchini
- 4 asparagus
- 4 carrots
- 1 egg
- 2 cups of frying oil
- 1 cup of flour
- 1 ½ cup of iced sparkling water
- Salt and pepper to taste

Directions and Total Time: approx. 15 minutes

Wash and cut all the vegetables in sticks. In a bowl whisk together the flour with iced water until smooth. Heat a pan with the oil, dip the vegetables in the egg and then in the flour mixture, and then deep fry it for 5 minutes. Pat dry on kitchen paper then serve with salt and pepper.

Per Serving: Calories 334, Fat 15g, Carbs 19g, Protein 6g

Ingredients for 4 servings

- 1 can chickpeas
- 3 tablespoons flour
- 4 cloves minced garlic
- 2 minced shallots
- 2 tablespoons sesame seeds
- 4 tablespoons olive oil
- ⅓ cup fresh parsley
- 1 teaspoon salt, pepper, cumin, cardamom, and coriander

Directions and Total Time: approx. 2 hours and 15 minutes

In a blender, combine the chickpeas, garlic, shallots, sesame seeds, parsley, salt, pepper, cumin, cardamom, and coriander. Pulse until a crumbly dough forms. Add flour and pulse until the dough is smooth. Refrigerate the mixture for up to 2 hours. Form the falafel into 2-inch balls. In a medium-heat skillet, add olive oil and fry the falafel on all sides for about 5 minutes.

Per Serving: Calories 545, Fat 22.4g, Carbs 69.2g, Protein 21.3g

992. Vegetarian Mac and Cheese

Ingredients for 10 servings

- 2 cups frozen mixed vegetables
- 16 ounces elbow macaroni pasta
- 1 teaspoon garlic powder
- 1 cup cheddar, shredded
- 1 cup milk

Directions and Total Time: approx. 30 minutes

Pour the prepared 4 cups of water into the Instant Pot. Add the pasta, garlic powder and a little bit of salt and pepper. Mix well. Seal the large-sized pot with a lid and set it to manual. Cook at high pressure for 4 minutes. Release the pressure quickly. Stir in the vegetables, cheddar and milk. Cover the pot. Press sauté. Simmer until the vegetables have softened.

Per Serving: Calories 456, Fat 4.9g, Carbs 77.5g, Protein 22.1g

993. Vegetarian Tartare

Ingredients for 4 servings

- 1 beef tomato
- Basil to taste
- 1 tablespoon olive oil
- 1 small zucchini
- 1 cup of radishes
- 1 carrot
- 1 cucumber
- 1 tablespoon soy sauce
- Salt and pepper to taste

Directions and Total Time: approx. 20 minutes

Cut all the vegetables into little cubes as a tartare. Mix them all together in a bowl with salt, pepper, olive oil, chopped basil, and soy sauce. Cut this mixture in a tartare shape with the help of a rounded cut in 4 servings. Place the dish in the fridge and serve cold with some basil.

Per Serving: Calories 160, Fat 10g, Carbs 15g, Protein 5g

Ingredients for 3 servings

- 2 garlic cloves, minced
- 2 yellow onions, chopped
- 4 scallions, chopped
- 2 carrots, grated
- 2 teaspoons of cumin, ground
- ½ teaspoon of turmeric powder
- Salt and black pepper, to the taste
- ¼ teaspoon of coriander, ground
- 2 tablespoons of parsley, chopped
- ¼ teaspoon of lemon juice
- ½ cup of almond flour
- 2 beets, peeled and grated
- 2 eggs, whisked
- ¼ cup of tapioca flour
- 3 tablespoons of olive oil

Directions and Total Time: approx. 20 minutes

In a bowl, combine the garlic with the onions, scallions, and the rest of the ingredients except the oil, stir well and shape medium fritters out of this mix. Heat up a large-sized pan with the oil over medium-high heat, add the fritters, cook for 5 minutes on each of the side, arrange on a platter, and serve.

Per Serving: Calories 209, Fat 11.2g, Carbs 4.4g, Protein 4.8g

995. Veggie, Tofu Skewers

Ingredients for 4 servings

- 3 cups of firm tofu cut thick pieces
- 1 red pepper
- 2 zucchini
- 1 cup of breadcrumbs
- 3 cups of olive oil for frying
- 5 lemon slices
- Salt and pepper to taste
- Fresh thyme to taste
- Basil to taste
- Chives to taste
- Rosemary to taste

Directions and Total Time: approx. 25 minutes

Prepare the herbs mixture. Mix all the herbs and grind them together. Cut all the vegetables into cubes and start filling the skewers alternating tofu and vegetables. Roll the filled skewers on the breadcrumbs and fry them in hot oil. Serve with a sprinkle of herbs, salt and pepper, and lemon slices.

Per Serving: Calories 487, Fat 20g, Carbs 10g, Protein 22g

996. White Gazpacho

Ingredients for 4 servings

- 4 cups of iced water
- 5 cups of water
- 2 cups of peeled almonds
- 1 cup of old bread
- 2 garlic cloves
- ½ cup of olive oil
- 3 tablespoons apple vinegar
- Salt and pepper to taste

Directions and Total Time: approx. 2 hours and 15 minutes

Pour the old bread in the water for 5 minutes then drain it and squeeze it. Toast the almond in a pan for a couple of minutes. Blend together the almonds, the bread, and 1 cup of iced water for 1 minute. Keep blending and then add the rest of the water, the garlic, oil, salt, pepper, and vinegar. Place in the fridge for 2 hours. Serve the gazpacho in 4 bowls with toasted almonds.

Per Serving: Calories 394, Fat 20g, Carbs 20g, Protein 10g

Ingredients for 2 servings

- 4 cups sliced zucchini
- ½ cup halved cherry tomatoes
- 1 teaspoon minced garlic
- 1 tablespoon olive oil
- ½ cup parmesan cheese
- ¼ cup breadcrumbs
- 4 tablespoons fresh basil
- 1 teaspoon salt and pepper

Directions and Total Time: approx. 55 minutes

In a medium-heat saucepan, add the olive oil and cook the zucchini, salt, and pepper for 10 minutes. Add the garlic and cook until fragrant. In a baking dish, add the zucchini, tomatoes, and basil. Top with breadcrumbs and parmesan cheese. Bake the dish for 30 minutes in a 350°F oven.

Per Serving: Calories 185, Fat 9.7g, Carbs 20.4g, Protein 7.3g

998. Zucchini Casserole

Ingredients for 4 servings

- 1 medium red onion, sliced
- 1 green bell pepper, thin strips
- 4 medium zucchinis, sliced
- 1 15-ounce can dice tomatoes, with the juice
- 1 teaspoon of sea salt
- ½ teaspoon black pepper
- ½ teaspoon basil
- 1 tablespoon extra-virgin olive oil
- ¼ cup grated parmesan cheese

Directions and Total Time: approx. 4 hours and 30 minutes

Combine the onion slices, bell pepper strips, zucchini slices, and tomatoes in the slow cooker. Sprinkle with salt, pepper, and basil. Cover and cook on low within 3 hours. Drizzle the olive oil over the casserole and sprinkle with the Parmesan. Cover and cook on low within for 1½ hours more. Serve hot.

Per Serving: Calories 219, Fat 16g, Carbs 3g, Protein 10g

999. Zucchini Ribbons with Ricotta

Ingredients for 4 servings

- 3 tablespoons of olive oil
- 1 garlic clove, minced
- 1 teaspoon of lemon zest
- 1 tablespoon of lemon juice
- 4 zucchinis, cut into ribbons
- Salt and black pepper to taste
- 2 tablespoons of chopped fresh parsley
- ½ ricotta cheese, crumbled

Directions and Total Time: approx. 10 minutes

Whisk 2 tablespoons oil, garlic, salt, pepper, and lemon zest, and lemon juice in a bowl. Warm the remaining olive oil in a large-sized skillet over medium heat. Season the zucchini ribbons with salt and pepper and add them to the skillet; cook for 3-4 minutes per side. Transfer to a large-sized serving bowl and drizzle with the dressing, sprinkle with parsley and cheese and serve.

Per Serving: Calories 134, Fat 2g, Carbs 4g, Protein 2g

1000. Zucchini with Egg

Ingredients for 2 servings

- 1 1/2 tablespoons olive oil
- 2 large zucchinis, cut into large chunks
- Salt and ground black pepper to taste
- 2 large eggs
- 1 teaspoon water, or as desired

Directions and Total Time: approx. 15 minutes

Cook the oil in a frying pan over medium heat; sauté zucchini until soft, about 10 minutes. Season the zucchini well. Lash the eggs using a fork in a bowl. Pour in water and beat until everything is well mixed. Pour the eggs over the zucchini; boil and stir until scrambled eggs and no more flowing, about 5 minutes. Season well the zucchini and eggs.

Per Serving: Calories 213, Fat 7g, Carbs 2g, Protein 2g

1001. Apple Mash

Ingredients for 4 servings

- 1 cup of water
- 2 apples, peeled, cored and sliced
- A pinch of sea salt
- 1 butternut squash, peeled and dig medium chunks
- 2 tablespoons of syrup
- 1 yellow onion, chopped
- ½ teaspoon of pie spice

Directions and Total Time: approx. 25 minutes

Put the water in your instant pot, add the steamer basket inside, add squash pieces, onion and apple slices inside, cover and cook on High for 8 minutes. Transfer squash, onion and apple to a bowl, mash employing a potato masher, add a pinch of salt, syrup and pie spices, stir well, divide among plates and function an entremots. Enjoy!

Per Serving: Calories 142, Fat 2g, Carbs 5g, Protein 6g

1002. Asian Bok Choy

Ingredients for 4 servings

- 2 tablespoons of butter, melted
- 2 cloves of garlic, minced
- 1 (1/2-inch) slice of fresh ginger root, grated
- 1 ½ pounds of Bok choy, trimmed
- 1 cup of vegetable stock
- Celery salt and black pepper to taste
- 1 teaspoon of Five-spice powder
- 2 tablespoons of soy

Directions and Total Time: approx. 10 minutes

Press the "Sauté" button to heat up the moment Pot. Now, warm the butter and sauté the garlic until tender and fragrant. Now, add grated ginger and cook for an extra 40 seconds. Add Bok choy, stock, salt, black pepper, and Five-spice powder. Secure the lid. Choose "Manual" mode and High pressure; cook for six minutes. Once cooking is complete, use a fast pressure release; carefully remove the lid. Drizzle soy over your Bok choy and serve immediately. Bon appétit!

Per Serving: Calories 83, Fat 6.1g, Carbs 5.7g, Protein 3.2g

1003. Baked Potatoes

Ingredients for 4 servings

- 2.2 pounds of Golden potatoes, peeled and diced
- 2 sprigs of rosemary
- 1 clove of garlic
- 7 teaspoons of extra virgin olive oil
- Salt to taste

Directions and Total Time: approx. 1 hour and 15 minutes

Preheat the oven to 400°F. Place diced potatoes in a bowl. Season with extra virgin olive oil, and salt, and toss to combine. Spread the potatoes on an oiled baking sheet. Add the sprigs of rosemary, and a whole clove of garlic, without peeling it. Bake for about 35 minutes, until crisp, and golden brown, stirring once halfway through cooking. Serve, and enjoy

Per Serving: Calories 264, Fat 10.4g, Carbs 37g, Protein 5.5g

1004. Baked Tomato

Ingredients for 4 servings

- Whole grain bread
- Salt and pepper to taste
- 1 tablespoon of finely chopped basil
- 2 cloves of garlic. Finely chopped
- Extra virgin oil
- 2 large tomatoes

Directions and Total Time: approx. 32 minutes

Preheat your oven to 400°F. Use the olive oil to brush the bottom of a baking dish. Set aside. Slice the tomatoes into a thickness of ½ inch. Lay the tomato pieces into the baking dish that you had prepared earlier. Sprinkle some basil and garlic on top of the tomatoes, season with pepper and salt to taste. Then drizzle the slices of tomatoes with olive oil and then place the baking dish into the oven. Bake for about 20-25 minutes. Remove from the oven, give it a few seconds to cool down, and then serve and enjoy.

Per Serving: Calories 342, Fat 10g, Carbs 45g, Protein 16g

1005. Balsamic Beets

Ingredients for 6 servings

- 3 medium beets, sliced
- 1/3 cup of balsamic vinegar
- 1 teaspoon of rosemary, chopped
- 1 garlic clove, minced
- ½ teaspoon of Italian seasoning
- A drizzle of olive oil

Directions and Total Time: approx. 40 minutes

In a bowl, mix rosemary with vinegar, garlic, Italian seasoning, and the beets, toss and leave aside for 10 minutes. Place beets and the marinade on aluminum foil pieces, add a drizzle of oil, seal edges, place on a preheated large-sized grill pan over medium heat, and cook for 25 minutes. Unwrap beets, peel, cube them, divide between plates and serve as a side dish.

Per Serving: Calories 100, Fat 2g, Carbs 2g, Protein 4g

1006. Basil Artichokes

Ingredients for 4 servings

- 1 red onion, chopped
- 2 garlic cloves, minced
- Salt and black pepper to the taste
- ½ cup of veggie stock
- 10 ounces of canned artichoke hearts, drained
- 1 tablespoon of olive oil
- 1 teaspoon of lemon juice
- 2 tablespoons of basil, chopped

Directions and Total Time: approx. 22 minutes

In a hot large-sized pan, heat the oil, then add the onion and garlic, stirring continuously for 2 minutes. Toss in the artichokes and the other ingredients, simmer for another 10 minutes, then divide among plates and serve as a side dish.

Per Serving: Calories 105, Fat 7.6g, Carbs 6.8g, Protein 2.5g

Ingredients for 2 servings

- 3 large eggs
- 1 tablespoon of good quality unsalted butter
- Freshly ground black pepper
- Salt to taste
- 1/4 teaspoon of thyme leaves

Directions and Total Time: approx. 16 minutes

Fill a medium pan most of the way with water and heat until boiling. When water is bubbling, tenderly put eggs in water and flip using a large spoon. While your eggs are cooking, place one tsp of margarine in a microwave-safe bowl and microwave until dissolved, for around 20 seconds. In the meantime, take the pan and cautiously spill out the excessive water carefully. Cautiously remove shell from every egg, wash to remove any shell parts, and add in the softened margarine. Add the thyme leaves as well as the salt and pepper for flavor.

Per Serving: Calories 160, Fat 12g, Carbs 1g, Protein 14g

1008. Braised Garlic Threat

Ingredients for 3 servings

- 1 tablespoon of extra-virgin vegetable oil
- 2 garlic cloves, minced
- 2 large-sized Belgian endive, halved lengthwise
- 1/2 cup of apple vinegar
- 1/2 cup of broth, preferably homemade
- Salt and black pepper, to taste
- 1 teaspoon of cayenne pepper

Directions and Total Time: approx. 6 minutes

Press the "Sauté" button to heat up the moment Pot; heat the oil. Once hot, cook the garlic for 30 seconds or until aromatic and browned. Add Belgian endive, vinegar, broth, salt, black pepper, and cayenne pepper. Secure the lid. Choose "Manual" mode and Low pressure; cook for two minutes or until tender when pierced with the tip of a knife. Once cooking is complete, use a fast pressure release; carefully remove the lid. Bon appétit!

Per Serving: Calories 91, Fat 6.4g, Carbs 3.6g, Protein 1.8g

1009. Bread Sauce

Ingredients for 12 servings

- 1 yellow onion, peeled and chopped
- 2 garlic cloves, peeled and crushed
- 6 cloves
- 26 ounces of milk
- 6 bread slices, torn
- 2 bay leaves
- Salt, to taste
- 2 tablespoons of butter
- Heavy cream

Directions and Total Time: approx. 20 minutes

Set the moment Pot on Manual mode, add the milk and warm it up. Add the garlic, cloves, onion, bay leaves, and salt, stir well, and cook for 3 minutes. Add the bread, stir, cover, and cook on the Manual setting for 4 minutes. Release the pressure, uncover the moment Pot, transfer the sauce to a blender, add the butter and cream, discard the bay leaves, and blend well. Return the sauce to the moment Pot set it on Manual mode and simmer sauce for 3 minutes.

Per Serving: Calories 113, Fat 5g, Carbs 11g, Protein 3g

Ingredients for 4 servings

- 1-pound of broccoli florets
- 2 garlic cloves, minced
- 1 tablespoon of olive oil
- ¼ cup of roasted peppers, chopped
- 2 tablespoons of balsamic vinegar
- Salt and black pepper to the taste
- 1 tablespoon of cilantro, chopped

Directions and Total Time: approx. 10 minutes

In a medium-high-heat pan, heat the oil, then add the garlic and peppers and sauté for 2 minutes. Toss in the broccoli and the other ingredients, simmer for another 8 minutes over medium heat, divide into plates, and serve as a side dish.

Per Serving: Calories 193, Fat 5.6g, Carbs 8.6g, Protein 4.5g

1011. Broccoli Rabe and Burrata

Ingredients for 6 servings

- 1 bunch of broccoli rabe
- 1 to 2 tablespoons of olive oil
- 2 garlic cloves, sliced
- ¼ teaspoon of red-pepper flakes
- 4 ounces of burrata mozzarella
- ½ tablespoon of fresh lemon juice
- 2 tablespoons of crushed, toasted pistachios
- Flaky sea salt, to serve

Directions and Total Time: approx. 19 minutes

Boil the broccoli in salted water for approximately about 3 minutes then drain. Sauté the garlic with 2 tbsp of oil in a skillet for 30 seconds. Add in the broccoli rabe and red pepper flakes and cook for 5 minutes. Transfer the rabe onto a plate and garnish with the rest of the ingredients. Serve.

Per Serving: Calories 357, Fat 28g, Carbs 7.4g, Protein 21.4g

1012. Broccoli Sauce

Ingredients for 4 servings

- 6 cups of water
- 3 cups of broccoli florets
- 2 garlic cloves, minced
- Salt and ground black pepper, to taste
- ⅓ cup of coconut milk
- 1 tablespoon of wine vinegar
- 1 tablespoon of nutritional yeast
- 1 tablespoon of vegetable oil

Directions and Total Time: approx. 16 minutes

Put the water into the moment Pot. Add the broccoli, salt, pepper, and garlic, stir, cover, and cook on the Manual setting for six minutes. Release the pressure, uncover the moment Pot, strain the broccoli and garlic, and transfer to a kitchen appliance. Add the coconut milk, vinegar, yeast, olive oil, salt, and pepper and blend well. Serve over pasta.

Per Serving: Calories 128, Fat 10g, Carbs 6g, Protein 5.4g

1013. Brussels Sprouts and Pistachios

Ingredients for 4 servings

- 1 pound of Brussels sprouts, lengthwise
- 4 shallots, peeled and quartered
- ½ cup of roasted pistachios, chopped
- ½ lemon, zested and juiced
- ¼ teaspoon of fine sea salt
- ¼ teaspoon of black pepper
- 1 tablespoon of olive oil

Directions and Total Time: approx. 16 minutes

Preheat the oven to a heat of 400F. Line a baking sheet with foil. In a bowl, toss the shallots and Brussels sprouts in olive oil. Make sure the sprouts are well coated. Season with the salt and pepper before spreading them onto the baking sheet. Bake for 15 minutes. Your vegetables should be lightly caramelized as well as tender. Take the sheet out of the preheated oven and toss the sprouts with the lemon zest, lemon juice, and pistachios. Serve and enjoy!

Per Serving: Calories 126, Fat 7g, Carbs 14g, Protein 6g

1014. Cabbage with Bacon

Ingredients for 4 servings

- 2 teaspoons of vegetable oil
- 4 slices of bacon, chopped
- 1 head of green cabbage, cored and dig wedges
- 1 cups of vegetable stock
- Sea salt, to taste
- 1/2 teaspoon of whole black peppercorns
- 1 teaspoon of cayenne pepper
- 1 herb

Directions and Total Time: approx. 10 minutes

Press the "Sauté" button to heat up the moment Pot. Then, heat vegetable oil and cook the bacon until it's nice and delicately browned. Then, add the rest of the remaining ingredients; gently stir to mix. Secure the lid. Choose "Manual" mode and High pressure; cook for 3 minutes. Once cooking is complete, use a fast pressure release; carefully remove the lid. Serve warm and enjoy!

Per Serving: Calories 166, Fat 13g, Carbs 5.8g, Protein 6.8g

1015. Caprese Style Portobello Mushrooms

Ingredients for 2 servings

- 2 large caps of Portobello mushroom, gills removed
- 4 tomatoes, halved
- Salt, and black pepper, to taste
- ¼ cup of fresh basil
- 4 tablespoons of olive oil
- ¼ cup of shredded Mozzarella cheese

Directions and Total Time: approx. 20 minutes

Preheat the oven to a heat of 400°F, and line a baking sheet with aluminum foil. In a bowl, add tomatoes, and season with salt, black pepper, basil, and oil, and mix well. Brush the mushrooms with oil, and spread the cheese evenly over the bottom of each mushroom cap. Top with the prepared tomato mixture. Arrange the portobello stuffed mushrooms on the prepared baking sheet, and bake in the oven for 15 minutes. Serve immediately.

Per Serving: Calories 315, Fat 29g, Carbs 14.2g, Protein 4.7g

1016. Carrot Sauce

Ingredients for 6 servings

- 4 tablespoons of butter
- 2 cups of juice
- Ground cinnamon
- Salt and ground black pepper, to taste
- Cayenne pepper
- 1 teaspoon of dried chervil
- 1 teaspoon of dried chives
- 1 teaspoon of dried tarragon

Directions and Total Time: approx. 25 minutes

Put the juice into the moment Pot, set the moment Pot on Manual mode, and convey to a boil. Add the butter, salt, pepper, cayenne and cinnamon, stir, cover and cook on the Manual setting for five minutes. Release the pressure, uncover the moment Pot, add the chervil, chives, and tarragon, stir, and serve.

Per Serving: Calories 149, Fat 7g, Carbs 19g, Protein 2g

1017. Cauliflower Fried Rice with Bacon

Ingredients for 4 servings

- 4 slices of bacon
- 1 small onion
- 1 head of cauliflower
- 1 cup of frozen mixed vegetables
- 1 teaspoon of Bragg's Liquid Amino

Directions and Total Time: approx. 15 minutes

In a wok or enormous sauté container over medium flame, cook bacon. Add the onions and pan-fried food until translucent. Set heat to high. Add the shredded cauliflower and pan-fried food for 1 moment. Add water and mixed vegetables, mix well, spread the dish and let the cauliflower blend steam for an additional 3 minutes or about just until tender. Add Bragg's Liquid Amino. Taste and add salt for extra flavoring as wanted.

Per Serving: Calories 492, Fat 22g, Carbs 28g, Protein 38g

1018. Cauliflower Mash

Ingredients for 4 servings

- 1/2 pound of cauliflower, dig florets
- 1/2 pound of kohlrabi, peeled and diced
- 1 cup of water
- 3/4 cup of soured cream
- 1 clove of garlic, minced
- Sea salt, to taste
- 1/3 teaspoon of ground black pepper
- 1/2 teaspoon of cayenne pepper

Directions and Total Time: approx. 15 minutes

Add 1 cup of water and a steamer basket to rock bottom of your Instant Pot. Then, arrange cauliflower and kohlrabi within the steamer basket. Secure the lid. Choose "Manual" mode and Low pressure; cook for 3 minutes. Once cooking is complete, use a fast pressure release; carefully remove the lid. Now, puree the cauliflower and kohlrabi with a potato masher. Add the remaining ingredients and stir well. Bon appétit!

Per Serving: Calories 89, Fat 6.5g, Carbs 3.6g, Protein 2.6g

1019. Cauliflower Steaks with Arugula

Ingredients for 4 servings

- 1 head cauliflower
- ½ teaspoon of garlic powder
- 4 cups o arugula
- 1 ½ tablespoon of extra-virgin olive oil
- 1 ½ tablespoon of honey mustard
- 1 teaspoon of freshly squeezed lemon juice

Directions and Total Time: approx. 25 minutes

Preheat the oven to a heat of 425°F, and line a baking sheet with aluminum foil. Cut the prepared head of the cauliflower in half lengthwise. Cut 1½-inch-thick steaks from each half. Spray both sides of each steak with cooking spray, and season both sides with garlic powder. Place the prepared cauliflower steaks on a lined baking sheet, and roast in the oven for 20 minutes, turning halfway through cooking. In a small-sized bowl, combine the olive oil, honey mustard, and lemon juice, and whisk with a fork. Top each cauliflower steak with a quarter of the arugula, and dressing, and serve.

Per Serving: Calories 115, Fat 6g, Carbs 14g, Protein 5g

1020. Chanterelles with Cheese

Ingredients for 4 servings

- 1 tablespoon of vegetable oil
- 2 cloves of garlic, minced
- 1 (1-inch) ginger root, grated
- 1/2 teaspoon of dried dill
- 1 teaspoon of dried basil
- 1/2 teaspoon of dried thyme
- 16 ounces of Chanterelle mushrooms, brushed clean and sliced
- 1/2 cup of water
- 1/2 cup of tomato purée
- 2 tablespoons of dry wine
- 1/3 teaspoon of freshly ground black pepper
- Kosher salt, to taste
- 1 cup of cheddar

Directions and Total Time: approx. 10 minutes

Press the "Sauté" button to heat up the moment Pot. Then, heat the olive oil; sauté the garlic and grated ginger for 1 minute or until aromatic. Add dried dill, basil, thyme, Chanterelles, water, tomato purée, dry wine, black pepper, and salt. Secure the lid. Choose "Manual" mode and Low pressure; cook for five minutes. Once cooking is complete, use a fast pressure release; carefully remove the lid. Top with shredded cheese and serve immediately. Bon appétit!

Per Serving: Calories 218, Fat 15.1g, Carbs 5.5g, Protein 9.9g

1021. Cheesy Olive Bread

Ingredients for 8 servings

- ½ cup of softened butter
- ¼ cup of mayo
- 1 teaspoon of garlic powder
- 1 teaspoon of onion powder
- 2 cups of shredded mozzarella cheese
- ½ cup of chopped black olives
- 1 loaf of French Bread, halved longways

Directions and Total Time: approx. 15 minutes

Preheat oven to a temperature of 350° Fahrenheit. Stir butter and mayo together in a bowl until it is smooth and creamy. Add onion powder, garlic powder, olives, and cheese and stir. Spread the mixture over French bread. Place bread on a large-sized baking sheet and bake for 10-12 minutes. Increase the heat to broil and cook it just until the cheese has melted and the bread is golden brown. Cool and chill. Preheat before eating.

Per Serving: Calories 307, Fat 17.7g, Carbs 30.1g, Protein 8g

1022. Chicken Kale Wraps

Ingredients for 4 servings

- 1 tablespoon of mayonnaise
- 1 teaspoon of Dijon mustard
- 3 medium kale leaves
- 3 ounces of cooked chicken breast, sliced
- 6 thin red onion slices
- 1 firm apple, cut into 9 slices

Directions and Total Time: approx. 10 minutes

Mix the mustard with mayonnaise in a small bowl. Spread the kale leaves onto the serving platter. Top the leaves with an even layer of mayo mixture. Place 1 ounces of chicken, 2 onion slices and 3 slices of apple on top of each leave. Roll the leaves to wrap the veggies. Cut each roll in half and serve.

Per Serving: Calories 216, Fat 4.4g, Carbs 38.9g, Protein 9.5g

1023. Chickpea and Beet

Ingredients for 4 servings

- 3 tablespoons of capers, drained and chopped
- Juice of 1 lemon
- Zest of 1 lemon, grated
- 1 red onion, chopped
- 3 tablespoons of olive oil
- 14 ounces of canned chickpeas, drained
- 8 ounces of beets, peeled and cubed
- 1 tablespoon of parsley, chopped
- Salt, and pepper to the taste

Directions and Total Time: approx. 35 minutes

Heat a skillet with the oil over medium heat. Add the onion, lemon zest, lemon juice, and capers, and sauté for 5 minutes. Add the rest of the prepared ingredients, stir, and cook over medium-low heat for 20 minutes. Divide the mixture among plates, and serve.

Per Serving: Calories 199, Fat 4.5g, Carbs 6.5g, Protein 3.3g

1024. Citrus, Fennel and Avocado Bowl

Ingredients for 6 servings

- 3 tablespoons of olive oil
- Juice of 1 lemon
- 1 tablespoon of fresh mint, chopped
- 2 tablespoons of fresh parsley, chopped
- 1 teaspoon of kosher salt
- ½ teaspoon of black pepper
- 6 cups of arugula
- 2 oranges, peeled and chopped
- 2 blood oranges, peeled and chopped
- 1 ruby-red grapefruit, peeled and chopped
- 1 bulb of fennel, quartered and sliced
- 2 avocados, halved, pitted and sliced

Directions and Total Time: approx. 10 minutes

In a medium-sized bowl, mix black pepper, salt, parsley, mint, lemon juice and oil. Add the arugula into this mixture, toss well then spread it onto a platter. Top with the remaining ingredients and serve.

Per Serving: Calories 244, Fat 20.4g, Carbs 16.8g, Protein 2.9g

1025. Corn on Cobs

Ingredients for 2 servings
- 2 fresh corns on cobs
- 2 teaspoons of butter
- 1 teaspoon of salt
- 1 teaspoon of paprika
- 1/4 teaspoon of olive oil

Directions and Total Time: approx. 20 minutes

Preheat the air fryer to 400 F. Rub the corn on cobs with salt and paprika. Then sprinkle the corn on cobs with olive oil. Place the corn on cobs in the air fryer basket. Cook the corn on cobs for 10 minutes. Transfer the corn on cobs to the serving plates when the time is over and gently rub the butter. Serve the meal immediately. Enjoy!

Per Serving: Calories 122, Fat 5.5g, Carbs 17.6g, Protein 3.2g

1026. Cream of Sweet Potato

Ingredients for 4 servings
- 4 tablespoons of olive oil
- 1 garlic clove, minced
- 4 medium sweet potatoes
- 1 red onion, sliced
- 3 ounces of baby spinach
- Zest, and juice of 1 lemon
- A small bunch of dill, chopped
- 1, and ½ tablespoons of Greek yogurt
- 2 tablespoons of tahini paste
- Salt, and black pepper to the taste

Directions and Total Time: approx. 1 hour and 10 minutes

Preheat the oven to a heat of 350°F, and line a baking sheet with baking paper. Place the medium sweet potatoes on the baking sheet, and bake for 1 hour. Peel the medium sweet potatoes then cut them into wedges, and place them in a bowl. Add the garlic, oil, and the rest of the ingredients, and mix well. Divide the mixture among the plates, and serve.

Per Serving: Calories 214, Fat 3.4g, Carbs 6.5g, Protein 3.1g

1027. Crispy Herb Cauliflower Florets

Ingredients for 2 servings
- 1 egg, beaten
- 2 tablespoons of parmesan cheese, grated
- 2 cups of cauliflower florets, boiled
- ¼ cup of almond flour
- 1 tablespoon of olive oil
- Salt to taste
- ½ tablespoon of mixed herbs
- ½ teaspoon of chili powder
- ½ teaspoon of garlic powder
- ½ cup of breadcrumbs

Directions and Total Time: approx. 30 minutes

Combine garlic powder, breadcrumbs, chili powder, mixed herbs, salt, and cheese in a bowl. Stir the olive oil into the breadcrumb mixture well. Place flour in a bowl and place the egg in another bowl. Dip the cauliflower florets into the beaten egg, then in flour, and coat with breadcrumbs. Preheat your air fryer to 350°Fahrenheit. Place the coated cauliflower florets inside the air fryer basket and cook for 20-minutes.

Per Serving: Calories 253, Fat 11.3g, Carbs 9.5g, Protein 8.5g

1028. Crispy Rosemary-Garlic Potato Slices

Ingredients for 4 servings
- 1 tablespoon of rosemary needles
- 2 garlic cloves, sliced
- 3 tablespoons of olive oil
- 4 large potatoes, thinly sliced

Directions and Total Time: approx. 25 minutes

Preheat the grill to medium. Simmer the potatoes salted water for 3 minutes, drain well, place in a shallow baking tray, and gently toss with the tablespoons of olive oil, garlic, rosemary, and seasoning. In a single layer, spread into the grill; cook for 10-15 minutes or until golden and crisp.

Per Serving: Calories 245, Fat 9g, Carbs 39g, Protein 5g

1029. Crispy Spiced Cauliflower with Feta Cheese

Ingredients for 4 servings
- ¾ pound of cauliflower, chopped
- ½ tablespoon of ground toasted cumin seeds
- 1 garlic clove, grated
- 2 tablespoons of crumbled feta cheese
- 1 ½ tablespoon of freshly squeezed lemon juice
- 1 tablespoon of chopped fresh flat-leaf parsley
- Chili flakes
- Sweet smoked paprika
- Sea salt
- Canola oil

Directions and Total Time: approx. 15 minutes

In a large-sized skillet, heat the canola oil over medium-high heat. Add the chopped cauliflower, and sauté for about 2 minutes or until browned, and crispy. Season with salt, and you need to reduce heat to medium. Add the cumin, lemon juice, grated garlic, and a pinch of chili, and stir well. Transfer the chopped cauliflower to a serving platter, then top with the feta, parsley, and a pinch of paprika, and serve.

Per Serving: Calories 300, Fat 19.3g, Carbs 30.6g, Protein 13g

1030. Crispy Sweet Potato Fries

Ingredients for 4 servings
- 1 1/2 pounds of sweet potatoes
- Sea salt
- Garlic powder
- Onion powder

Directions and Total Time: approx. 25 minutes

In a cast-iron skillet over medium-high to high heat, add 1/2 to 1 inch of oil. When the oil is hot, and you can begin to see little air pockets forming, add the sweet potato fries to the container. Fry until they are brilliant darker, and marginally firm, around 10 minutes. Remove from oil and move to a paper towel to absorb excess oil. Add sea salt, garlic powder, and onion powder in a little bowl. Sprinkle flavoring over top of the sweet potato fries.

Per Serving: Calories 102, Fat 8g, Carbs 23.7g, Protein 4g

1031. Dandelion Greens

Ingredients for 6 servings

- 4 pounds of dandelion greens, stalks cut and discarded, and greens washed
- ½ cup of water
- ¼ cup of extra-virgin olive oil
- ¼ cup of lemon juice
- ½ teaspoon of salt
- ½ teaspoon of ground black pepper

Directions and Total Time: approx. 11 minutes

Add dandelion greens and water to the Instant Pot. Close lid, set steam release to Sealing, press the Manual button, and set time to 1 minute. When the timer beeps, quick-release the pressure until the float valve drops. Open lid and drain well. Combine the cup of extra-virgin olive oil, lemon juice, salt, and pepper in a small bowl. Pour over greens and toss to coat.

Per Serving: Calories 39, Fat 12g, Carbs 7g, Protein 1g

1032. Eggplant Ratatouille

Ingredients for 2 servings

- 1 eggplant
- 1 sweet yellow pepper
- 3 cherry tomatoes
- 1/3 white onion, chopped
- 1/2 teaspoon of garlic clove, sliced
- 1 teaspoon of olive oil
- 1/2 teaspoon of ground black pepper
- 1/2 teaspoon of Italian seasoning

Directions and Total Time: approx. 30 minutes

Preheat the air fryer to 360 F. Peel the eggplants and chop them. Put the chopped eggplants in the air fryer basket. Place the cherry tomatoes in the air fryer basket. Then add chopped onion, sliced garlic clove, olive oil, ground black pepper, and Italian seasoning. Chop the sweet yellow pepper roughly and add it to the air fryer basket. Shake the vegetables gently and cook for 15 minutes. Stir the meal after 8 minutes of cooking. Transfer the cooked ratatouille to the serving plates. Enjoy!

Per Serving: Calories 149, Fat 3.7g, Carbs 28.9g, Protein 5.1g

1033. Eggplant Rolls

Ingredients for 6 servings

- 1 eggplant, ½ inch sliced lengthwise
- 1/3 cup of cream cheese
- ½ cup of tomatoes, chopped
- 1 clove of garlic, minced
- 2 tablespoons of dill, chopped

Directions and Total Time: approx. 8 minutes

Slice your eggplant before brushing it down with olive oil. Sprinkle eggplant slices with salt and pepper. Grill the eggplants for three minutes per side. Get out a bowl and mix cream cheese, garlic, dill and tomatoes in a different bowl. Allow your eggplant slices to cool and then spread the mixture over each one. Roll them and pin them with a toothpick to serve.

Per Serving: Calories 91, Fat 7g, Carbs 2.1g, Protein 6.3g

1034. Fish and Tomato Sauce

Ingredients for 4 servings

- 4 cod fillets, boneless
- 2 garlic cloves, minced
- 2 cups of cherry tomatoes, halved
- 1 cup of chicken stock
- A pinch of salt and black pepper
- ¼ cup of basil, chopped

Directions and Total Time: approx. 40 minutes

Place the garlic, salt, tomatoes and pepper in a skillet and simmer over medium heat for 5 minutes, stirring occasionally. Add the fish and the rest of the ingredients, bring to a boil, cover the pan and cook for 25 minutes. Divide the mix on plates and serve.

Per Serving: Calories 180, Fat 1.9g, Carbs 5.3g, Protein 33.8g

1035. Flatbread Wraps

Ingredients for 4 servings

- 1 package of seven-grain pilaf
- 1 cup of English cucumber, chopped
- 1 cup of seeded tomato, chopped
- ¼ cup of feta cheese, crumbled
- 2 tablespoons of lemon juice
- 1 tablespoon of olive oil
- ¼ teaspoon of black pepper
- 1 cup of hummus
- 3 whole-grain white flatbread wraps

Directions and Total Time: approx. 25 minutes

Cook the seven-grain pilaf as per the instructions on the package. Meanwhile, mix the tomato and cucumber with oil, lemon juice, pepper, and cheese in a bowl. Drain and add the pilaf to the vegetables. Spread an even layer of hummus on one side of each flatbread. Spoon the pilaf mixture onto each slice of bread. Wrap the flatbreads and cut each sandwich in half. Serve and enjoy.

Per Serving: Calories 299, Fat 12.4g, Carbs 40.4g, Protein 15g

1036. Fried Green Beans

Ingredients for 2 servings

- ½ pound of green beans, trimmed
- 1 egg
- 2 tablespoons of olive oil
- 1¼ tablespoons of almond flour
- 2 tablespoons of parmesan cheese
- ½ teaspoon of garlic powder sea salt or plain salt
- freshly ground black pepper to taste

Directions and Total Time: approx. 25 minutes

Start by beating the egg and olive oil in a bowl. Then, mix the remaining Ingredients in a separate bowl and set aside. Now, dip the green beans in the egg mixture and then coat with the dry mix. Finally, grease a baking pan, then transfer the beans to the pan and bake at 250 degrees F for about approximate 12-15 minutes or until crisp. Serve warm.

Per Serving: Calories 334, Fat 23g, Carbs 10.9g, Protein 18g

1037. Garlicky and Buttery Fennel

Ingredients for 6 servings

- 1/2 stick of butter
- 2 garlic cloves, sliced
- 1/2 teaspoon of sea salt
- 1 ½ pounds of fennel bulbs, dig wedges
- 1/4 teaspoon of black pepper, or more to taste
- 1/2 teaspoon of cayenne pepper
- 1/4 teaspoon of dried dill
- 1/3 cup of dry wine
- 2/3 cup of chicken broth

Directions and Total Time: approx. 6 minutes

Press the "Sauté" button to heat up your Instant Pot; now, melt the butter. Cook garlic for 30 seconds, stirring periodically. Add the remaining ingredients. Secure the lid. Choose "Manual" mode and Low pressure; cook for 3 minutes. Once cooking is complete, use a fast pressure release; carefully remove the lid. Bon appétit!

Per Serving: Calories 111, Fat 5.7g, Carbs 2.1g, Protein 2.7g

1038. Greek-Style Potatoes

Ingredients for 4 servings

- ⅓ cup of olive oil
- 2 garlic cloves, chopped
- 1 ½ cups of water
- Salt and black pepper, to taste
- ¼ cup of lemon juice
- 1 teaspoon of rosemary
- 1 teaspoon of thyme
- 2 chicken bouillon cubes
- 6 potatoes, chopped

Directions and Total Time: approx. 1 hour and 40 minutes

Place the potatoes in a baking tray. Mix all the rest of the prepared ingredients in a large bowl and pour over the potatoes. Bake in a prepared preheated oven at a temperature of 350°F for 90 minutes. Serve and enjoy.

Per Serving: Calories 418, Fat 18.5g, Carbs 58.6g, Protein 7g

1039. Green Beans Entremots

Ingredients for 6 servings

- 5 cups of water
- 1 tablespoon of vegetable oil
- 2 tablespoons of thyme, chopped
- 1 cup of yellow onion, chopped
- 5 garlic cloves, minced
- 3 tablespoons of balsamic vinegar
- ½ cup of ingredient
- ½ cup of syrup
- 2 tablespoons of coconut aminos
- 2 tablespoons of red chili paste
- 2 tablespoons of mustard
- 1 and ½ cups of green beans
- A pinch of salt and black pepper

Directions and Total Time: approx. 24 minutes

Set your instant pot on sauté mode, add the oil, heat it up, add onion, stir and sauté for 3 minutes. Add garlic, thyme, vinegar and ingredient, stir and cook for 1 minute more. Add green beans, water, syrup, mustard, chili paste, salt, pepper and aminos, stir, cover and cook on High for 10 minutes Divide among plates and function an entremots. Enjoy!

Per Serving: Calories 160, Fat 2g, Carbs 7g, Protein 8g

1040. Green Spaghetti Sauce

Ingredients for 12 servings

- 2 pounds of green tomatoes, cored and chopped
- 1 white onion, peeled and chopped
- ¼ cup of currants
- 1 Anaheim chili pepper, chopped
- 4 red chili peppers, chopped
- 2 tablespoons of ginger, grated
- ¾ cup of sugar
- ¾ cup of white vinegar

Directions and Total Time: approx. 15 minutes

Within the Instant Pot, mix green tomatoes with onion, currants, Anaheim pepper, chili pepper, ginger, sugar, and vinegar, stir, cover and cook on the Manual setting for 10 minutes. Release the pressure for five minutes, uncover the moment Pot, transfer sauce to jars, and serve.

Per Serving: Calories 50, Fat 2g, Carbs 10g, Protein 1.5g

1041. Grilled Cheese on Garlic Bread

Ingredients for 4 servings

- 4 tablespoons of softened unsalted butter
- 1 tablespoon of fresh parsley, chopped
- 2 tablespoons of corino Romano cheese, grated
- 1 garlic clove, minced
- white bread slices
- 4 provolone cheese slice
- 1/2 cup of mozzarella cheese, shredded

Directions and Total Time: approx. 50 minutes

In a bowl, place the ground beef, the dressing mix, the egg, crushed crackers and onion. Combine well together before then forming them into hamburger patties. It would help if you were making the burgers as you allow the barbecue to heat up to a high temperature. Once the burgers are ready and the barbecue has reached the desired, you now place them on it. It is good to coat the grill with some oil to prevent the burgers from sticking to it. Then, you should actually cook each side of the burger for 5 minutes, and when do you serve them in a sesame topped bun.

Per Serving: Calories 258, Fat 14.1g, Carbs 23.3g, Protein 8.7g

1042. Grilled Garlic with Seasoning

Ingredients for 5 servings

- Dry seasonings of choice
- 1 jumbo fresh garlic head
- Extra-virgin olive oil to Scotch mist

Directions and Total Time: approx. 10 minutes

Trim off the topmost leaf tips of every clove to expose a teensy quantity of the clove while holding the full head of garlic. Keep the remaining leaves unbroken around the garlic head's body. Place the trimmed garlic head, trimmed side up, in an airtight microwave-safe bowl. Drizzle a tiny quantity of olive oil around the sides and top of the head. Season with salt and pepper to taste. Place garlic cloves on the center rack of the grill and roast at 400F for 20–30 minutes, or until soft and golden brown. Remove the garlic cloves from the grill, spread them over crusty toast, or add them to veggies, omelets, or pasta.

Per Serving: Calories 8, Fat 1g, Carbs 1g, Protein 1g

1043. Guacamole Quinoa Bowl

Ingredients for 6 servings

- 1 cup of quinoa, rinsed
- 2 avocados, halved and pitted
- ½ small white onion, diced
- ½ cup of fresh cilantro, chopped
- 2 tablespoons of lime juice
- ½ teaspoon of kosher salt
- 1 can of black beans
- 1 cup of cherry tomatoes, quartered
- Olive oil, for drizzling

Directions and Total Time: approx. 20 minutes

Boil the cup of quinoa as per the package's instructions and drain well. Mash the avocado in a medium-sized bowl then add the tablespoons of lime juice, salt, cilantro and onion. Fold in the tomatoes, quinoa and beans. Drizzle olive oil on top and serve.

Per Serving: Calories 359, Fat 15.3g, Carbs 45.9g, Protein 12.6g

1044. Guava Sauce

Ingredients for 6 servings

- 1 can of guava shells and syrup
- 2 onions, peeled and chopped
- ¼ cup of oil
- Juice from 2 lemons
- 2 garlic cloves, peeled and chopped
- 1-inch ginger piece, peeled and minced
- ½ teaspoon of nutmeg
- 2 Serrano chilies, chopped

Directions and Total Time: approx. 30 minutes

Put guava shells and syrup into the blender, pulse well and put aside. Set the moment Pot on Sauté mode, add the oil and warmth it up. Add the chopped onion and the prepared minced garlic, stir and cook for 4 minutes. Add the guava mix, ginger, juice, chilies, and nutmeg, stir, cover, and cook on High for quarter-hour. Release the pressure, uncover the moment Pot, and serve sauce with fish.

Per Serving: Calories 85, Fat 2.3g, Carbs 22g, Protein 3g

1045. Halloumi Cheese with Butter-Fried Eggplant

Ingredients for 2 servings

- 1 eggplant
- 3 ounces of butter
- 10 ounces of halloumi cheese
- 10 black olives
- Salt and pepper

Directions and Total Time: approx. 15 minutes

Cut the eggplant down the middle, longwise, and cut into pieces which are a big portion and an inch thick. Heat up a healthful dab of butter in an enormous pan. Add the cheese on one side of the dish and eggplant on the other. Season eggplant with salt and pepper Fry over medium-high heat for 5-7minutes. Flip the cheese after three minutes, with the aim that it's darker on the 2 sides. Mix the eggplant now. Present with olives.

Per Serving: Calories 110, Fat 9g, Carbs 10g, Protein 7g

1046. Healthy Mushrooms and Green Beans

Ingredients for 4 servings

- 1 pound of fresh green beans, trimmed
- 2 cups of water
- 6 ounces of bacon, chopped
- 1 small yellow onion, chopped
- 1 clove, minced
- 8 ounces of mushrooms, sliced
- A pinch of salt and black pepper
- A splash of balsamic vinegar

Directions and Total Time: approx. 16 minutes

Put the beans in your instant pot, add water to hide them, cover the pot, cook at High for 3 minutes, drain and leave them aside. Set your instant pot on Sauté mode, add bacon, brown it for 1 minute and blend with onion and garlic. Stir, cook 2 more minutes, add mushrooms, stir and cook until they're done. Return green beans to instant pot, add salt, pepper and a splash of vinegar, toss, divide among plates and function an entremots. Enjoy!

Per Serving: Calories 123, Fat 2g, Carbs 4g, Protein 3g

1047. Italian Garlic Mushrooms

Ingredients for 8 servings

- 1 teaspoon of ground black pepper
- 4 ounces of cheddar cheese, grated
- 2 tablespoons of garlic, minced
- 1 tablespoon of Italian seasoning
- 1 tablespoon of green chives
- 1-pound of mushroom, sliced
- ¼ teaspoon of salt
- 1 teaspoon of olive oil

Directions and Total Time: approx. 35 minutes

Sprinkle the mushrooms with salt. Combine the minced garlic with the ground black pepper and olive oil in a skillet and sauté for 1 minute. Add the sliced mushrooms and cook the mixture for 15 minutes, stirring constantly. Avoid browning the ingredients. Sprinkle with Italian seasoning and chives. Add the grated cheese and mix carefully until the cheese melts. Transfer to serving plates and serve hot.

Per Serving: Calories 84, Fat 6g, Carbs 3.1g, Protein 5.5g

1048. Lemon Faro Bowl

Ingredients for 6 servings

- 1 carrot
- 2 cups of vegetable broth, low sodium
- 1 cup of onion, pearled faro
- 2 avocados, peeled, pitted & sliced
- 1 lemon, small

Directions and Total Time: approx. 26 minutes

Preheat saucepan over medium-high heat. Add in a tablespoon of oil, and then throw in your onion once the oil is hot. Cook for about five minutes, frequently stirring to keep it from burning. Add in your carrot and 2 garlic cloves. Allow it to simmer for another minute while stirring constantly. Add in your broth and faro. Let it boil and adjust your heat to high to help. Once it boils, lower it to medium-low and cover your saucepan. Let it simmer for twenty minutes. The faro should be al dente and plump. Pour the faro into a bowl and add in your avocado and zest. Drizzle with your remaining oil and add in your lemon wedges.

Per Serving: Calories 279, Fat 12g, Carbs 19.3g, Protein 14g

1049. Lemon-Pignoli Zucchini

Ingredients for 6 servings

- 3 cups of orecchiette pasta
- 2 small zucchinis, sliced
- 1-pint cherry tomatoes, cut in half
- Grated zest and juice of 2 lemons
- ¼ cup of olive oil
- Salt and black pepper, to taste
- 1 ½ cups of crumbled feta cheese
- ½ cup of fresh basil leaves, chopped
- ½ cup of pine nuts

Directions and Total Time: approx. 10 minutes

Cook the pasta as instructions on the package. When it is cooked, drain and rinse under cold water then set it aside. Mix the tomatoes with zucchini, lemon peel, salt, pepper and lemon juice in a bowl. Stir in the pasta and toss well. Add the basil and feta cheese. Top with pine nuts and serve immediately.

Per Serving: Calories 370, Fat 24.8g, Carbs 28.7g, Protein 11g

1050. Lemony Carrots

Ingredients for 3 servings

- 3 tablespoons of olive oil
- 2 pounds of baby carrots, trimmed
- Salt and black pepper, to the taste
- ½ teaspoon of lemon zest, grated
- 1 tablespoon of lemon juice
- 1/3 cup of Greek yogurt
- 1 garlic clove, minced
- 1 teaspoon of cumin, ground
- 1 tablespoon of dill, chopped

Directions and Total Time: approx. 15 minutes

In a roasting pan, combine the carrots with the oil, salt, pepper, and the rest of the ingredients, except the dill, toss and bake at 400°F for 20 minutes. Reduce the temperature to 375°F and cook for 20 minutes more. Divide the mix between plates, sprinkle the dill on top, and serve.

Per Serving: Calories 192, Fat 5.4g, Carbs 7.3g, Protein 5.6g

1051. Margherita Slices

Ingredients for 4 servings

- 1 tomato, cut into 8 slices
- 1 clove of garlic, halved
- 1 tablespoon of olive oil
- ¼ teaspoon of oregano
- 1 cup of mozzarella, fresh & sliced
- ¼ cup of basil leaves, fresh, tron & lightly packed
- sea salt & black pepper to taste
- 2 hoagie rolls, 6 inches each

Directions and Total Time: approx. 20 minutes

Start by heating your oven broiler to high. Your rack should be four inches under the heating element. Lay the sliced bread on a rimmed baking pan. Broil for a minute. Your bread should be toasted lightly. Brush each one down with oil and rub your garlic over each half. Place the bread back on your baking sheet. Distribute the tomato slices on each one, and then sprinkle with oregano and cheese. Bake for one to two minutes, but check it after a minute. Your cheese should be melted. Top with basil and pepper before serving.

Per Serving: Calories 297, Fat 11g, Carbs 38g, Protein 12g

1052. Mashed Sweet Potatoes

Ingredients for 12 servings

- 3 pounds of sweet potatoes, cubed
- 1 cup of coconut milk, hot
- 6 garlic cloves, minced
- 28 ounces of veggie stock
- 1 herb
- ¼ cup of ghee, melted
- A pinch of salt and black pepper

Directions and Total Time: approx. 26 minutes

Put potatoes in your instant pot, add stock, garlic and herb, stir, cover and cook on High for 16 minutes. Drain potatoes, discard herb, transfer them to a bowl, mash employing a potato masher, mix with coconut milk and ghee and whisk rather well. Season with a pinch of salt and also pepper, stir well, divide among plates and function a entremots. Enjoy!

Per Serving: Calories 135, Fat 4g, Carbs 6g, Protein 4g

1053. Mediterranean Chicken Bites

Ingredients for 4 servings

- 20 ounces of canned pineapple slices
- A drizzle of olive oil
- 3 cups of chicken thighs
- A tablespoon of smoked paprika

Directions and Total Time: approx. 20 minutes

Situate pan over medium-high heat, add pineapple slices, cook them for a few minutes on each side, transfer to a cutting board, cool them down, and cut into medium cubes. Heat another pan with a drizzle of oil over medium-high heat, rub chicken pieces with paprika, add them to the large-sized pan and cook for 5 minutes on each side. Arrange chicken cubes on a platter, add a pineapple piece on each, and stick a toothpick in each. Serve.

Per Serving: Calories 120, Fat 3g, Carbs 14g, Protein 2g

1054. Mediterranean Sauteed Kale

Ingredients for 6 servings

- 12 cups of kale, chopped
- 2 tablespoons of lemon juice
- 1 tablespoon of olive oil
- 1 tablespoon of garlic, minced
- 1 teaspoon of soy sauce
- Salt and black pepper, to taste

Directions and Total Time: approx. 20 minutes

Add a steamer insert into a saucepan. Fill up the saucepan with water up until the bottom of the steamer insert. Cover and bring the water to a boil over medium-high heat. Add the kale to the steamer insert and steam for 7–8 minutes. Add the lemon juice, olive oil, garlic, salt, soy sauce, and black pepper to a large bowl. Mix well. Add the steamed kale, toss well, and serve.

Per Serving: Calories 91, Fat 4g, Carbs 14g, Protein 5g

1055. Mediterranean Slices

Ingredients for 4 servings

- 13-ounce of pack ready-rolled puff pastry
- 4 tablespoons of green pesto
- ¾ cup of frozen roasted peppers, sliced
- ¾ cup of frozen artichokes
- ½ cup of mozzarella cheese, grated

Directions and Total Time: approx. 30 minutes

Preheat the oven to a heat of 400°F and lightly grease a baking sheet. Unfold the puff pastry and cut it into four rectangles. Cut an edge of 0.4 inches inside each rectangle with a sharp knife and transfer the rectangles to the baking sheet. Layer all the rectangles with the pesto, followed by the peppers and artichokes. Put the large-sized baking sheet in the oven and bake for 15 minutes. Top with mozzarella cheese and bake for another 7 minutes.

Per Serving: Calories 606, Fat 42.6g, Carbs 46.2g, Protein 9.5g

1056. Mint Tabbouleh

Ingredients for 6 servings

- ¼ cup of fine bulgur
- 1/3 cup of water, boiling
- 3 tablespoons of lemon juice
- ¼ teaspoon of honey
- 1 1/3 cups of pistachios, finely chopped
- 1 cup of curly parsley, finely chopped
- 1 small cucumber, finely chopped
- 1 medium tomato, finely chopped
- 4 green onions, finely chopped
- 1/3 cup of mint, finely chopped
- 3 tablespoons of olive oil

Directions and Total Time: approx. 25 minutes

Take a large bowl and add bulgur and 1/3 cup of boiling water. Allow it to stand for approximately about 5 minutes. Stir in the teaspoon of honey and lemon juice and allow it to stand for 5 minutes more. Fluff up the bulgur with a small fork and stir in the rest of the ingredients. Season with salt and pepper. Enjoy!

Per Serving: Calories 150, Fat 13.5g, Carbs 9.2g, Protein 3.8g

1057. Minty Zucchini with Marinated Feta

Ingredients for 2 servings

- ¼ pound block of feta cheese, diced
- 1 bunch of mint leaves, chopped
- Black pepper, to taste
- 3 (1-inch) strips orange peel
- Crushed red-pepper flakes, to taste
- Olive oil, as needed
- 2 medium zucchinis, diced
- 1 teaspoon of salt
- ½ cup of roasted pistachios, shelled
- ¼ cup of dried currants

Directions and Total Time: approx. 10 minutes

Place the cheese cubes in a mason jar and top them with a pinch of red pepper flakes, black pepper, mint and orange peel then fill the jar with oil. Cover and marinate for 2 weeks at room temperature. Mix the zucchini with the rest of the ingredients in a suitable bowl. Top with cheese cubes and 1 tablespoon of marinating oil. Serve.

Per Serving: Calories 229, Fat 15.6g, Carbs 17.7g, Protein 9.9g

1058. Mushroom Shallot Sauce

Ingredients for 6 servings

- 2 tablespoons of extra virgin olive oil
- 1 pound of cleaned and sliced varied mushrooms
- 2 garlic cloves, peeled and minced
- 2 finely chopped shallots
- 1/3 cup of dry white wine
- 1 tablespoon of mustard (Dijon)
- 2 teaspoons of fresh thyme snipped

Directions and Total Time: approx. 20 minutes

In a large-sized nonstick skillet, heat the olive oil over medium heat. In a skillet, combine the mushrooms, garlic, and shallots and simmer, turning periodically, for about 5 minutes, or until soft. Reduce the heat to a low temperature and stir in the wine, mustard, and thyme. Cook for another 2–3 minutes, or until thoroughly mixed and heated. Serve with chicken or fish as the main course.

Per Serving: Calories 79, Fat 3g, Carbs 7g, Protein 2g

1059. Mustard Sauce

Ingredients for 4 servings

- 6 ounces mushrooms, chopped
- 3 tablespoon vegetable oil
- Ounces dry sherry
- 1 thyme sprig
- 1 clove, peeled and minced
- Ounces beef broth
- 1 tablespoon of balsamic vinegar
- 1 tablespoon of mustard
- 2 tablespoon of crème fraiche
- 2 tablespoons of fresh parsley, diced

Directions and Total Time: approx. 17 minutes

Set the moment Pot on Sauté mode, add the oil and warm it up. Add the garlic, thyme, and mushrooms, stir, and cook for five minutes. Add the sherry, vinegar, and stock, stir, cover, and cook on the Manual setting for 3 minutes. Release the pressure, uncover the moment Pot, discard the thyme, add the crème fraiche, mustard, and parsley, stir, set the moment Pot on Manual mode, and cook the sauce for 3 minutes, and serve.

Per Serving: Calories 67, Fat 0.4g, Carbs 4g, Protein 1g

1060. Olives and Carrots Sauté

Ingredients for 4 servings

- 1 tablespoon of green olives, pitted and sliced
- 3 tablespoons of olive oil
- 2 teaspoons of capers, drained and chopped
- ½ teaspoon of lemon zest, grated
- 1 and ½ teaspoons of balsamic vinegar
- ¼ teaspoon of rosemary, dried
- ¼ cup of veggie stock
- Salt and black pepper to the taste
- 2 pounds of carrots, sliced
- 2 spring onions, chopped
- 1 tablespoon of parsley, chopped

Directions and Total Time: approx. 30 minutes

In a large-sized pan, heat the oil and sauté the carrots for 5 minutes. Stir in the green olives, capers, and the other ingredients (except the parsley and chives), and simmer for 15 minutes over medium heat. Add the chives and parsley, toss, divide the mix between plates and serve as a side dish.

Per Serving: Calories 244, Fat 11g, Carbs 5.6g, Protein 6.3g

1061. Orange Ginger Sauce

Ingredients for 4 servings

- 3 oranges, freshly squeezed
- ¼ cup of mayonnaise (light)
- ¼ teaspoon of honey
- 2 tablespoons of fresh horseradish
- ¼ teaspoon of ground ginger
- 1 tablespoon of extra-virgin olive oil
- To taste, season with salt and freshly ground pepper
- A good sprinkling of all-purpose flour

Directions and Total Time: approx. 20 minutes

In a small saucepan, combine ginger, mayonnaise, orange juice, honey, olive oil, horseradish and salt & pepper. On low heat, whisk to combine. Whisk in the flour once the sauce has started to simmer. Cook, frequently whisking, for 1–2 minutes, or until sauce is smooth.

Per Serving: Calories 60, Fat 1g, Carbs 14g, Protein 2.6g

1062. Orange Sauce

Ingredients for 6 servings

- ¼ cup of wine vinegar
- 1 teaspoon of ginger paste
- 2 tablespoons of ingredient
- 3 tablespoons of sugar
- 1 cup of fruit juice
- 1 teaspoon of garlic, diced
- 2 tablespoons of agave nectar
- 1 teaspoon of vegetable oil
- 1 teaspoon of condiment
- 2 tablespoons of soy
- ¼ cup of vegetable stock
- 2 tablespoons of cornstarch

Directions and Total Time: approx. 17 minutes

Set the moment Pot on Sauté mode, add the oil and warmth it up. Add the diced garlic and ginger paste, stir, and cook for two minutes. Add the ingredient, sugar, fruit juice, vinegar, agave nectar, soy sauce, and condiment, stir, cover, and cook on the Manual setting for 3 minutes. Release the pressure, uncover the moment Pot, add the stock and cornstarch, stir, cover again, and cook on the Manual setting for 4 minutes. Release the pressure again, and serve your sauce.

Per Serving: Calories 80, Fat 7g, Carbs 5g, Protein 13g

1063. Paprika and Chives Potatoes

Ingredients for 2 servings

- 4 potatoes
- 1 tablespoon of olive oil
- 1 celery stalk, chopped
- 2 tomatoes, chopped
- 1 teaspoon of sweet paprika
- 2 tablespoons of chives, chopped

Directions and Total Time: approx. 68 minutes

Situate potatoes on a baking sheet lined with parchment paper bake at 350 degrees F for 1 hour. Cool the potatoes down, peel, and cut them into larger cubes. Preheat the pan with the oil over medium heat, add the celery and the tomatoes and sauté for 2 minutes. Add the potatoes and the rest of the ingredients, toss, cook everything for 6 minutes, divide the mix between plates and serve.

Per Serving: Calories 233, Fat 8.7g, Carbs 12.4g, Protein 6.4g

1064. Parsnip Fries

Ingredients for 2 servings

- 2 tablespoons of olive oil
- A pinch of sea salt
- 1 large bunch of parsnips

Directions and Total Time: approx. 22 minutes

Dissolve 2 tablespoons butter in a large pot set on moderate heat. Mix in the thyme and halibut and cook. Wash and peel the parsnips, then cut them into strips. Place the parsnips in a bowl with olive oil and sea salt and coat well. Preheat your air fryer to 360°Fahrenheit. Place the parsnip and oil mixture into the air fryer basket. Cook for 12-minutes. Serve with sour cream or ketchup.

Per Serving: Calories 262, Fat 11.3g, Carbs 10.4g, Protein 7.2g

1065. Pesto Broccoli Quinoa

Ingredients for 4 servings

- 2 and ½ cups of quinoa
- 4 and ½ cups of veggie stock
- A pinch of salt and black pepper
- 2 tablespoons of basil pesto
- 2 cups of mozzarella cheese, shredded
- 1-pound of broccoli florets
- 1/3 cup of parmesan, grated
- 2 green onions, chopped

Directions and Total Time: approx. 40 minutes

In a baking pan, combine the quinoa with the stock and the rest of the ingredients except the parmesan and the mozzarella and toss. Sprinkle the cheese on top and bake everything at 400 degrees F and bake for 30 minutes. Divide between large-sized plates and serve as a side dish.

Per Serving: Calories 181, Fat 3.4g, Carbs 8.6g, Protein 7.6g

1066. Plum Sauce

Ingredients for 20 servings

- 3 pounds of plums, pitted and chopped
- 2 onions, peeled and chopped
- 2 apples, cored and chopped
- 4 tablespoons of ground ginger
- 4 tablespoons of ground cinnamon
- 4 tablespoons of allspice
- 1 ½ tablespoons of salt
- 1 pint of vinegar
- ¾ pound of sugar

Directions and Total Time: approx. 25 minutes

Put the plums, apples, and onions into the moment Pot. Add the ginger, cinnamon, allspice, salt, and most the vinegar, stir, cover, and cook on the Manual setting for 10 minutes. Release the pressure, uncover the moment Pot, set it on Manual mode, add the remainder of the vinegar and therefore the sugar, stir, and cook until sugar dissolves. Keep sauce refrigerated until able to use.

Per Serving: Calories 100, Fat 10g, Carbs 23g, Protein 26g

Ingredients for 5 servings

- ½ cup freshly ground cayenne pepper
- 2 tablespoons caraway seeds, finely ground
- A quarter cup of cumin
- 1 tsp coriander (coriander seed)
- 2 teaspoons of salt
- 5 garlic cloves, peeled and smashed
- 1 teaspoon of water
- ½ cup extra-virgin olive oil

Directions and Total Time: approx. 20 minutes

In a mortar, combine all spices. Add the smashed garlic and salt to the spice combination and mash them together to make a paste. In a jar, combine the pasta, water, and 1/4 cup olive oil; stir thoroughly. Cover closely with the remaining olive oil and keep refrigerated. It will last for months.

Serving: Calories 5.7, Fat 0.3g, Carbs 1g, Protein 0.2g

1068. Rich Beets Entremets

Ingredients for 6 servings

- 6 beets, peeled and dig wedges
- A pinch of sea salt
- Black pepper to the taste
- 2 tablespoons of juice
- 2 tablespoons of vegetable oil
- 2 tablespoons of agave nectar
- 1 tablespoon of vinegar
- ½ teaspoon of lemon peel, grated
- 2 rosemary sprigs

Directions and Total Time: approx. 22 minutes

Put the beets in your slow cooker. Add a pinch of salt, black pepper, juice, oil, agave nectar, rosemary and vinegar. Stir everything, cover and cook on Low for 8 hours. Add lemon peel, stir, divide among plates and serve. Enjoy!

Per Serving: Calories 120, Fat 1g, Carbs 6g, Protein 6g

1069. Roasted Carrots

Ingredients for 4 servings

- 1 ½ pounds of carrots, peel and cut into slices
- ½ cup of Feta cheese, crumbled
- 2 tablespoons of dill, chopped
- 1 garlic clove, minced
- 2 tablespoons of olive oil
- 1 teaspoon of water
- 2 tablespoons of honey
- Pepper
- Salt

Directions and Total Time: approx. 30 minutes

Preheat the oven to 425° F. Arrange carrots onto the baking sheet. Mix together honey, water, oil, garlic, dill, pepper and salt and pour over carrots. Roast in preheated oven for 20-25 minutes. Stir halfway through. Top with Feta cheese and serve.

Per Serving: Calories 216, Fat 11.1g, Carbs 27.3g, Protein 4.4g

1070. Roasted Ranch Burger

Ingredients for 2 servings

- 2 pounds of lean ground beef
- Pack of ranch dressing mix
- 1 egg (lightly beaten)
- 6 ounces of crushed crackers
- 1 chopped onion

Directions and Total Time: approx. 50 minutes

In a bowl, put the minced beef, the egg, the dressing mix, crushed crackers & onion. Mix well together and then make patties for hamburger. It would be best to make the burgers as you allow the barbecue to heat up to a high temperature. When the burgers are done and the barbeque has also done as per required, then place them on. Coat the grill with oil to avoid the burgers from jutting to it. Then, cook each side of the burger for five minutes, till it's done. Enjoy it with sesame topped bun.

Per Serving: Calories 483, Fat 31g, Carbs 345g, Protein 21g

1071. Roasted Red Pepper Dip

Ingredients for 6 servings

- 4 large red bell peppers, seeded and quartered
- 1 large onion, chopped
- 2 tablespoons of extra-virgin olive oil
- 1 teaspoon of red wine vinegar
- 11/2 teaspoons of salt
- 1/4 teaspoon of black pepper
- 2 garlic cloves, peeled

Directions and Total Time: approx. 1 hour and 45 minutes

Heat the oven and line a rimmed baking sheet with aluminum foil. Merge the peppers and onion with olive oil, vinegar, salt, and pepper in a large bowl. Spread out the peppers and onion in a single layer on the prepared baking sheet. Roast for 30 minutes, then add the garlic cloves and roast for another 15 minutes, until the peppers blacken on the edges. Detach from the oven and set aside to cool. Fridge before serving.

Per Serving: Calories 85, Fat 5g, Carbs 9g, Protein 1g

1072. Roasted Tomatoes with Garlic and Thyme

Ingredients for 6 servings

- 2 teaspoons of fresh thyme leaves
- 2 pounds of small tomatoes, halved
- 1/2 teaspoon of chili pepper flakes
- Salt & black pepper, to taste
- 1 teaspoon of Sumac
- 2-3 minced garlic cloves
- Olive oil
- Crumbled feta cheese, as needed

Directions and Total Time: approx. 40 minutes

Let the oven preheat to 450 F. In a bowl, add tomatoes and spices with olive oil. Toss well. On a baking sheet, spread the tomatoes in one even layer. Roast for 30-35 minutes, till tomatoes are soft. Serve with feta cheese, thyme on top.

Per Serving: Calories 71, Fat 3g, Carbs 2g, Protein 6g

1073. Roasted Vegetables

Ingredients for 4 servings
- 1 zucchini, chopped
- ½ teaspoon of dried oregano
- ½ teaspoon of garlic powder
- 1 teaspoon of basil
- ½ teaspoon of parsley
- 2 tablespoons of olive oil
- 2 small onions, sliced
- 10 grape tomatoes
- 3 bell peppers, sliced
- ½ teaspoon of salt

Directions and Total Time: approx. 25 minutes

Preheat the oven to 425° F. In a bowl, add all ingredients and toss until well coated. Transfer vegetables onto the baking sheet and roast in preheated oven for 15 minutes. Stir halfway through. Allow to cool completely and serve.

Per Serving: Calories 168, Fat 8g, Carbs 24g, Protein 4.7g

1074. Salty Lemon Artichokes

Ingredients for 2 servings
- 1 lemon
- 2 artichokes
- 1 teaspoon of kosher salt
- 1 garlic head
- 2 teaspoons of olive oil

Directions and Total Time: approx. 60 minutes

Cut off the edges of the artichokes. Cut the lemon into the halves. Peel the garlic head and chop the garlic cloves roughly. Then place the chopped garlic in the artichokes. Sprinkle the artichokes with olive oil and kosher salt. Then squeeze the lemon juice into the artichokes. Wrap the artichokes in the foil. Preheat the air fryer to 330 F. Place the wrapped artichokes in the air fryer and cook for 45 minutes. When the artichokes are cooked – discard the foil and serve. Enjoy!

Per Serving: Calories 133, Fat 5g, Carbs 21.7g, Protein 6g

1075. Sausage with Greens

Ingredients for 4 servings
- 2 teaspoons of vegetable oil
- 2 pork sausages, casing removed sliced
- 2 garlic cloves, minced
- 1 medium-sized leek, chopped
- 1 pound of greens
- 1 cup of turkey bone stock
- Sea salt, to taste
- 1/4 teaspoon of black pepper, or more to taste
- 1 herb
- 1 tablespoon black sesame seeds

Directions and Total Time: approx. 10 minutes

Press the "Sauté" button to heat up the moment Pot. Then, heat the sesame oil; cook the sausage until nice and delicately browned; put aside. Add the garlic and leeks; still cook in pan drippings for a moment or two. Add the greens, stock, salt, black pepper, and herb. Secure the lid. Choose "Manual" mode and Low pressure; cook for 3 minutes. Once cooking is complete, use a fast pressure release; carefully remove the lid. Serve garnished with sesame seeds and enjoy!

Per Serving: Calories 149, Fat 7.2g, Carbs 6.1g, Protein 14.2g

1076. Sauteed Garlic Spinach

Ingredients for 4 servings
- ¼ cup of extra-virgin olive oil
- 1 large onion, thinly sliced
- 3 cloves of garlic, minced
- 6 (1-pound) bags of baby spinach, washed
- ½ teaspoon of salt
- 1 lemon, cut into wedges

Directions and Total Time: approx. 15 minutes

Cook the olive oil, onion, and garlic in a large skillet for 2 minutes over medium heat. Add one bag of spinach and ½ tsp. of salt. Cover the skillet and let the spinach wilt for 30 seconds. Repeat (omitting the salt), adding 1 bag of spinach at a time. Remove the cover once all of the spinach has been added and simmer for 3 minutes, allowing some moisture to escape. Serve with a squeeze of lemon over the top.

Per Serving: Calories 301, Fat 14g, Carbs 29g, Protein 17g

1077. Smoked Salmon, Avocado, and Cucumber Bites

Ingredients for 2 servings
- 1/2 cucumber, medium size
- 3 ounces of Smoked salmon
- 1/2 avocado, peeled, and remove the pit
- 1/2 tablespoon of Lime juice
- Salt and ground black pepper for garnish
- Chopped fresh chives for serving

Directions and Total Time: approx. 15 minutes

Cut the cucumber into 1/4th inch of thickness. Place them on a plate. In a bowl, add lime juice and avocado, mash with a fork until smooth. On each cucumber slice, spread the avocado mixture. On top, place a piece of smoked salmon. Add another slice of cucumber on top. Sprinkle salt and freshly ground black pepper on top. Serve right away with fresh chives.

Per Serving: Calories 243, Fat 15.4g, Carbs 29.4g, Protein 13.8g

1078. Sour Cream and Chive Egg Clouds

Ingredients for 4 servings
- 8 large pastured eggs
- 1/4 cup of sharp white cheddar cheese
- 1/4 cup of sour cream
- 1 teaspoon of garlic powder
- 2 chives and 2 teaspoons of salted butter

Directions and Total Time: approx. 6 minutes

Preheat stove to 450°. Line an oven tray with parchment paper. Separate the eggs, emptying the whites into an enormous blending bowl, and the yolks into singular ramekins. Utilizing an electric blender, whip the egg whites until they are fleecy and solid pinnacles have begun to frame. Utilizing an elastic spatula, delicately overlap in cheddar, cream, garlic powder, and half of the chives. Spoon blend into 8 separate hills on the parchment paper. Make a hole in the focal point of each cloud. Heat for 6 minutes or until the mists are golden on top and the yolks are set. Put a modest quantity of margarine over every yolk. Top with chives. Serve and Enjoy.

Per Serving: Calories 117, Fat 10g, Carbs 21g, Protein 6g

1079. Sour Onion Sauce

Ingredients for 2 servings

- 1 large onion; sliced
- 1-2 tablespoon of apple vinegar
- 1 cup of water or chicken broth
- 1 tablespoon of vegetable oil
- 2 teaspoons of almond flour
- 1 teaspoon of cayenne pepper
- 1 teaspoon of stevia powder
- 1/4 teaspoon of salt

Directions and Total Time: approx. 15 minutes

Connect the moment pot and press the *Sauté* button. Heat up the vegetable oil and add onions. Sprinkle with salt and stevia and cook for 2-3 minutes, or until translucent. Now add almond flour and provides it a good stir. Still cook for another minute then add cayenne pepper. Pour in water or chicken broth and sprinkle with apple vinegar. Bring it to a boil and press the *Cancel* button. Chill for a while and store until use

Per Serving: Calories 108, Fat 8.4g, Carbs 6g, Protein 1.4g

1080. Spanish Green Beans

Ingredients for 4 servings

- ¼ cup of extra-virgin olive oil
- 1 large onion, chopped
- 4 cloves of garlic, finely chopped
- 1-pound of green beans
- 1½ teaspoon of salt, divided
- 1 (15-ounces) can of diced tomatoes
- ½ teaspoon of freshly ground black pepper

Directions and Total Time: approx. 30 minutes

Position large pot over medium heat, cook olive oil, onion, and garlic. Cut the green beans into 2-inch pieces. Stir in the green beans and 1 teaspoon of salt in the saucepan, toss well, and simmer for 3 minutes. Add the diced tomatoes, the remaining ½ tsp. of salt, and black pepper to the pot. Continue to cook for just another 12 minutes, stirring occasionally. Serve.

Per Serving: Calories 200, Fat 13g, Carbs 24g, Protein 13.8g

1081. Spicy Garlic Pesto Sauce

Ingredients for 4 servings

- ¼ cup of extra-virgin olive oil
- ¼ teaspoon of crumbled red hot pepper flakes
- 4 garlic cloves, diced
- To taste, season with salt and freshly ground pepper
- Parmesan cheese, grated

Directions and Total Time: approx. 20 minutes

Warm olive oil in a medium-sized pan over medium heat. Sauté the garlic until it becomes translucent. Add the hot pepper flakes, then cook for 3–5 minutes on low heat. Serve with pasta of your choice. If preferred, top with grated Parmesan cheese.

Per Serving: Calories 234, Fat 23g, Carbs 1.9g, Protein 3g

1082. Spicy Pepper Beef Broth

Ingredients for 6 servings

- 2 pounds of beef bones
- 3 chili peppers; whole
- 4 garlic cloves; whole
- 1/4 cup of celery stalk; chopped.
- 1/4 cup of celery leaves; chopped
- 1/4 cup of onions; chopped.
- 3 tablespoon of wine vinegar
- 1/2 teaspoon of red pepper flakes
- 2 teaspoon of chili pepper
- 1 teaspoon of salt

Directions and Total Time: approx. 40 minutes

Place the bones within the pot and pour in enough water to hide. Add vegetables and drizzle with wine vinegar. Season with salt, chili pepper, and pepper flakes. Stir well and seal the lid. Set the actual steam release handle to the *Sealing* position and press the *Manual* button. Set the timer for 35 minutes on high. When done; release the pressure naturally and open the lid. Stir well again and strain the liquid. Chill for a short time and refrigerate.

Per Serving: Calories 17, Fat 0.4g, Carbs 0.8g, Protein 2g

1083. Spicy Zucchini

Ingredients for 4 servings

- 4 zucchinis, cut into ½-inch pieces
- 1 cup of water
- ½ teaspoon of Italian seasoning
- ½ teaspoon of red pepper flakes
- 1 teaspoon of garlic, minced
- 1 tablespoon of olive oil
- ½ can of crushed tomatoes
- Salt, to taste

Directions and Total Time: approx. 15 minutes

Add the water and zucchini to an Instant Pot. Seal the pot with the lid and cook on High for 2 minutes. Once done, release the pressure using quick release. Remove the lid. Drain the zucchini well and clean the Instant Pot. Add the tablespoon of oil to the Instant pot and set it to Sauté mode. Add the garlic and sauté for 30 seconds. Add the remaining ingredients and stir well. Cook for 2–3 minutes. Serve and enjoy.

Per Serving: Calories 69, Fat 4.1g, Carbs 7.9g, Protein 2.7g

1084. Spicy Zucchini Slices

Ingredients for 2 servings

- 1 teaspoon of cornstarch
- 1 zucchini
- 1/2 teaspoon of chili flakes
- 1 tablespoon of flour
- 1 egg
- 1/4 teaspoon of salt

Directions and Total Time: approx. 16 minutes

Slice the zucchini and sprinkle with chili flakes and salt. Crack the egg into the bowl and whisk it. Dip the zucchini slices in the whisked egg. Combine cornstarch with flour. Stir it. Coat the zucchini slices with the cornstarch mixture. Preheat the air fryer to 400 F. In the air fryer tray, place the zucchini slices. Cook the zucchini slices for 4 minutes. After this, flip the slices to another side and cook for 2 minutes more. Serve the zucchini slices hot. Enjoy!

Per Serving: Calories 67, Fat 2.4g, Carbs 7.7g, Protein 4.4g

1085. Spinach with Cheese

Ingredients for 4 servings

- 2 tablespoons of butter, melted
- 1/2 cup of scallions, chopped
- 2 cloves of garlic, smashed
- 1 ½ pounds of fresh spinach
- 1 cup of vegetable broth, preferably homemade
- 1 cup of cheese, cubed
- salt and ground black pepper, to taste
- 1/2 teaspoon of dried dill

Directions and Total Time: approx. 10 minutes

Press the "Sauté" button to heat up the moment Pot. Then, melt the butter; cook the scallions and garlic until tender and aromatic. Add the rest of the remaining ingredients and stir to mix well. Secure the lid. Choose "Manual" mode and High pressure; cook for two minutes. Once cooking is complete, use a fast pressure release; carefully remove the lid. Ladle into individual bowls and serve warm. Bon appétit!

Per Serving: Calories 283, Fat 23.9g, Carbs 6.4g, Protein 10.7g

1086. Squash Puree

Ingredients for 4 servings

- ½ cup of water
- 2 tablespoons of ghee
- 2 acorn squash, halved
- A pinch of salt and black pepper
- ¼ teaspoon of bicarbonate of soda
- ½ teaspoon of nutmeg, grated
- 2 tablespoons of syrup

Directions and Total Time: approx. 30 minutes

Put the water in your instant pot, add the steamer basket, add squash halves inside, season with a pinch of salt, pepper and bicarbonate of soda, rub a bit, cover and cook them on High for 20 minutes. Transfer squash to a plate, calm down, scrape flesh, transfer to a bowl and blend with ghee, syrup and nutmeg. Mash employing a potato masher, whisk well, divide among plates and function an entremots. Enjoy!

Per Serving: Calories 143, Fat 2g, Carbs 7g, Protein 2g

1087. Sriracha Sauce

Ingredients for 6 servings

- 4 ounces of red chilies, seeded and chopped
- 3 tablespoons of sugar
- 3 ounces of arbol chilies, dried
- 12 garlic cloves, peeled and minced
- 5 ounces of distilled vinegar
- 5 ounces of water

Directions and Total Time: approx. 27 minutes

Within the Instant Pot, mix the water with the sugar and stir. Add all the chilies and garlic, stir, cover and cook on the Manual setting for 7 minutes. Release the pressure, uncover the moment Pot, blend sauce using an immersion blender, add the vinegar, stir, set the moment Pot on Manual mode, and cook the sauce for 10 minutes. Serve when needed.

Per Serving: Calories 90, Fat 0.4g, Carbs 19g, Protein 2.4g

1088. Stewed Okra

Ingredients for 4 servings

- 4 cloves of garlic, finely chopped
- 1 pound of fresh or frozen okra, cleaned
- 1 (15 ounces) can of plain tomato sauce
- 2 cups of water
- ¼ cup of olive oil
- 1 onion, sliced
- ½ cup of fresh cilantro, finely chopped

Directions and Total Time: approx. 35 minutes

In a large-sized pot on medium heat, add the olive oil, onion, garlic, and salt. Cook until the onion is softened and the garlic is fragrant. Stir in the okra and cook for 3 minutes. Add the tomato sauce, water, cilantro, and black pepper; stir, cover, and let cook for 15 minutes, stirring occasionally. Serve warm.

Per Serving: Calories 201, Fat 12.9g, Carbs 18g, Protein 4g

1089. Sugary Carrot Strips

Ingredients for 2 servings

- 2 carrots
- 1 teaspoon of brown sugar
- 1 teaspoon of olive oil
- 1 tablespoon of soy sauce
- 1 teaspoon of honey
- 1/2 teaspoon of ground black pepper

Directions and Total Time: approx. 20 minutes

Peel and chop the carrot into strips. Then put the carrot strips in the bowl. Sprinkle the carrot strips with olive oil, soy sauce, honey, and ground black pepper. Shake the mixture gently. Preheat the air fryer to 360 F. Cook the carrot for 10 minutes. After this, shake the carrot strips well. Enjoy!

Per Serving: Calories 67, Fat 2.4g, Carbs 11.3g, Protein 1.1g

1090. Sweet Potato Marinara

Ingredients for 6 servings

- 1 cup of dry red wine
- 1 15-ounces can of sweet potato purée
- 3/4 cup of coconut cream
- ¼ cup of fresh basil leaves, chopped
- ¼ cup of fresh parsley leaves, chopped
- ¼ cup of parmesan cheese, grated

Directions and Total Time: approx. 20 minutes

Warm up the sweet potato in a saucepan on medium heat. Stir in the parsley, and basil an let it cook for approximately about 2 minutes. Add the cream and wine into the thick mixture. After boiling the sauce, cook it for approximately about 8 minutes on a simmer. Stir in the Parmesan and mix well. Serve.

Per Serving: Calories 128, Fat 7.4g, Carbs 8.5g, Protein 1.5g

1091. Tahini Spinach

Ingredients for 4 servings

- 10 spinach, chopped
- ½ cup of water
- 1 tablespoon of tahini
- 2 cloves of garlic, minced
- ¼ teaspoon of cumin
- ¼ teaspoon of paprika
- ¼ teaspoon of cayenne pepper
- 1/3 cup of red wine vinegar
- Sea salt & black pepper to taste

Directions and Total Time: approx. 10 minutes

Add your spinach and water to the saucepan, and then boil it on high heat. Once boiling reduces to low, and cover, allow it to cook on simmer for five minutes. Add in your garlic, cumin, cayenne, red wine vinegar, paprika, and tahini. Season with salt and pepper after whisking well. Drain your spinach and top with tahini sauce to serve.

Per Serving: Calories 69, Fat 3g, Carbs 8g, Protein 5g

1092. Taramasalata Sauce

Ingredients for 16 servings

- ½ of red onion, chopped roughly
- ½ cup of water
- 4 white sandwich bread slices
- ¼ cup of olive oil
- 3 tablespoons of white tarama (fish roe)
- 2 tablespoons of fresh lemon juice
- Pinch of sugar
- 1 cup of sunflower oil

Directions and Total Time: approx. 10 minutes

In a blender, add onion and water and pulse until smooth. Through a strainer, strain the onion puree into a bowl. In a food processor, add the onion puree, bread slices, olive oil, tarama, lemon juice, and sugar and pulse until smooth. While the motor is actually running, gradually add the sunflower oil and pulse until well combined. The sauce is ready to use.

Per Serving: Calories 170, Fat 17.2g, Carbs 3.8g, Protein 1.1g

1093. Tomato Basil Sauce

Ingredients for 4 servings

- 1 tablespoon of extra virgin olive oil
- 4 fresh garlic cloves, minced
- 1 finely chopped shallot
- 1 tin of chopped tomatoes with chiles (14.5 ounces), properly drained
- To taste, season with salt and freshly ground pepper
- 4 basil sprigs, chopped

Directions and Total Time: approx. 20 minutes

Mix olive oil, garlic, and shallot in a pan over medium-high heat. Garlic and shallot should be tender and fragrant after sautéing. Reduce the heat to a low setting. Cook, uncovered until tomatoes, salt and pepper, and basil are heated through and liquid absorbed. Serve over fish or chicken as a thick sauce.

Per Serving: Calories 52, Fat 3g, Carbs 5g, Protein 2g

1094. Tomato Sauce

Ingredients for 4 servings

- 1 ½ tablespoons of olive oil
- 1 ½ teaspoons of butter
- 2 cups of plum tomatoes, seeded and chopped finely
- 3 garlic cloves, minced
- 1 ½ tablespoons of capers
- 1 tablespoon of Dijon mustard
- 1 ½ tablespoons of fresh parsley, chopped
- 1 ½ tablespoons of fresh chives, minced
- ¼ teaspoon of red pepper flakes, crushed
- Salt and ground black pepper, as required

Directions and Total Time: approx. 13 minutes

In a large-sized wok, heat the olive oil with butter over medium-high heat and cook the tomatoes for about 6 minutes, stirring frequently. Stir in the garlic, capers, and mustard and bring to a boil. Adjust the heat to low and simmer for about 2 minutes or until slightly thickened, stirring occasionally. Remove from the heat temperature and stir in the remaining ingredients. Set aside to cool before serving.

Per Serving: Calories 82, Fat 7.1g, Carbs 3.3g, Protein 1.3g

1095. Turkish Beet Greens

Ingredients for 2 servings

- 2 cups of beet greens
- 7 dried Turkish figs, stemmed and quartered
- ½ cup of white grape juice
- 2 cups of fresh spinach
- 1 clove of garlic, minced
- 2 teaspoons of olive oil
- Salt, to taste
- ½-ounce parmesan cheese, grated (optional)

Directions and Total Time: approx. 20 minutes

Cook the beet greens, white grape juice, and figs over medium heat in a pan for about seven minutes before adding the olive oil, spinach, and garlic. Turn the heat down to low and cook for another three minutes before adding some salt. Add the parmesan cheese on top before serving.

Per Serving: Calories 328, Fat 7g, Carbs 49.4g, Protein 6.7g

1096. Tzatziki Sauce

Ingredients for 8 servings

- 2 ½ cups of yogurt
- 1 large cucumber, peeled and shredded.
- 1 garlic clove, minced
- 1 tablespoon of fresh mint, chopped
- 1 ½ tablespoon of white wine vinegar
- 2 tablespoons of olive oil
- ½ teaspoon of salt

Directions and Total Time: approx. 10 minutes

With a paper towel, line a strainer and add the yogurt on top. Place the strainer in a bowl and leave it for 2 hours. Place the peeled and shredded cucumber in a colander and sprinkle with salt. Let it sit for 10 minutes then transfer it into a bowl. Blend the yogurt with the rest of the ingredients in a blender. In a large-sized bowl, mix the yogurt with the cucumber. Serve.

Per Serving: Calories 157, Fat 5.6g, Carbs 13.5g, Protein 9.9g

Ingredients for 2 servings

- 14 ounces of oven-roasted vegetables
- 1 can of chopped tomatoes
- 1 can of kidney beans
- Salt and black pepper, to taste

Directions and Total Time: approx. 32 minutes

Preheat the oven to a heat temperature of 390°F and lightly grease a casserole dish. Arrange the oven-roasted vegetables in the casserole dish and place them in the oven. Bake for about 15 minutes and then stir in the kidney beans, tomatoes, salt, and black pepper. Bake for 15 more minutes. Remove from the oven and serve.

Per Serving: Calories 366, Fat 15g, Carbs 43.8g, Protein 14.4g

1098. White Lasagna Stuffed Peppers

Ingredients for 4 servings

- 2 large sweet peppers
- 1 teaspoon of garlic salt
- 12 ounces of ground turkey
- 3/4 cup of ricotta cheese
- 1 cup of mozzarella

Directions and Total Time: approx. 1 hour and 5 minutes

Preheat stove to 400. Put the cut peppers in a heating dish. Sprinkle with 1/4 teaspoon of garlic salt. Gap the ground turkey between the peppers. Sprinkle with another 1/4 teaspoon of garlic salt. Cook for 30 minutes. Partition the ricotta cheese between the peppers. Sprinkle with 1/2 teaspoon of garlic salt. Sprinkle the mozzarella on top. Put the cherry tomatoes in the middle of the peppers, if utilizing. Cook for an extra 30 minutes until the meat is cooked, and the cheese is golden.

Per Serving: Calories 297, Fat 18g, Carbs 8g, Protein 25g

1099. White Wine Sauce

Ingredients for 6 servings

- Cooking spray with olive oil
- 1/3 cup of white onion, finely chopped
- ½ cup of fat-free, low-sodium chicken broth
- A can ¼ cup dry white wine
- 2 tablespoons of white wine vinegar, aged
- 2 tablespoons of melted trans fat–free canola/olive oil spread
- 2 teaspoons of fresh chives, coarsely chopped

Directions and Total Time: approx. 20 minutes

Spray a large-sized skillet with cooking oil and heat over medium-high heat. Add the onion and cook for about 2 minutes. Bring to a boil with the chicken broth, wine, and vinegar. Cook for another 5 minutes, or until the liquid has been reduced to ¼ cups. Remove from the actual fire and stir in the melted canola/olive oil spread and chives before serving with chicken, pasta, or white fish.

Per Serving: Calories 59, Fat 5.7g, Carbs 1.6g, Protein 0.6g

Ingredients for 4 servings

- 6 tablespoons of olive oil
- 1 onion, peeled and chopped
- 2 garlic cloves, peeled and crushed
- 1 medium zucchini, sliced
- 1 medium summer squash, sliced
- Salt and black pepper, to taste
- 7 ounces of ripe tomatoes, chopped
- 4 ounces of mozzarella, torn
- ¼ cup of parsley leaves, chopped
- ¼ cup of basil leaves, torn

Directions and Total Time: approx. 27 minutes

Sauté the garlic and onion with oil in a large skillet for 10 minutes. Stir in the summer squash, zucchini, black pepper and salt then sauté for 2 minutes. Add the tomatoes and cook for approximately about 5 minutes. Garnish with basil, parsley and mozzarella. Serve.

Per Serving: Calories 477, Fat 27.1g, Carbs 16.1g, Protein 44.5g

1101. Almond Bites

Ingredients for 5 servings

- 1 cup of almond flour
- ¼ cup of almond milk
- 1 egg, whisked
- 2 tablespoons of almond butter
- 1 tablespoon of coconut flakes
- ½ teaspoon of baking powder
- ½ teaspoon of apple cider vinegar
- ½ teaspoon of vanilla extract

Directions and Total Time: approx. 24 minutes

Mix the whisked egg, almond milk, apple cider vinegar, baking powder, vanilla extract, and butter. Add the almond flour and coconut flakes, then knead the dough. If the dough is sticky, add more almond flour. Make medium-sized balls from the dough and place them on the rack of an air fryer. Press them gently with the use of the palm of your hand. Lower the air fryer lid and cook the dessert for 12 minutes at 360°F. Check if cooked; cook for 2 minutes more for a crunchier crust.

Per Serving: Calories 118, Fat 10.6g, Carbs 3.6g, Protein 4.1g

1102. Almond Cherry Crumble Cake

Ingredients for 4 servings

- 1/4 cup of almonds, slivered
- 1/2 stick of butter, at room temperature
- 1 teaspoon of ground cinnamon
- A pinch of grated nutmeg
- 1 cup of rolled oats
- 1/3 teaspoon of ground cardamom
- 1 teaspoon of pure vanilla extract
- 1/3 cup of honey
- 2 tablespoons of all-purpose flour
- A pinch of salt
- 1-pound of sweet cherries, pitted
- 1/3 cup of water

Directions and Total Time: approx. 15 minutes

Arrange the pound of cherries on the bottom of the Instant Pot. Sprinkle cinnamon, cardamom, and vanilla over the top. Add the water and honey. In a separate large-sized mixing bowl, thoroughly combine the butter, oats, and flour. Spread topping mixture evenly over cherry mixture. Secure the lid. Choose the "Manual" mode and High pressure; cook for 10 minutes. Once cooking is complete, use a natural pressure release; carefully remove the lid. Serve at room temperature. Bon appétit!

Per Serving: Calories 335, Fat 13.4g, Carbs 60.5g, Protein 5.9g

1103. Almond Orange Pandoro

Ingredients for 12 servings

- 2 large oranges, zested
- 2 ½ cups of mascarpone
- ½ cup of almonds, whole
- 2 ½ cups of coconut cream
- ½ pandoro, diced
- 2 tablespoons of sherry

Directions and Total Time: approx. 10 minutes

Whisk cream with mascarpone, icing sugar, ¾ zest and half sherry in a bowl. Dice the pandoro into equal sized horizontal slices. Place the bottom slice in a plate and top with the remaining sherry. Spoon the mascarpone mixture over the slice. Top with almonds and place another pandoro slice over. Continue adding layers of pandoro slices and cream mixture. Dish out to serve.

Per Serving: Calories 346, Fat 10.4g, Carbs 8.5g, Protein 7.7g

1104. Amaretto Ice Cream

Ingredients for 6 servings

- 5 cups of milk
- 1 cup of sugar
- 1 cup of fresh cream
- ¾ of amarettos
- ½ milk chocolate
- 3 tablespoons of powdered milk
- 1 teaspoon of Maizena

Directions and Total Time: approx. 55 minutes

Melt the chocolate and set it aside. Pour in a bowl the milk, the cream, milk powder, and Maizena and melt in the microwave until 85°. Mix and let it cool down. Add the milk chocolate, the amaretto, and the sugar and blend for 1 minute. Cover with foil and the you can place it in the fridge for 6 to 15 hours. Blend again the mixture and set it again in the freezer. Serve.

Per Serving: Calories 445, Fat 18g, Carbs 22g, Protein 10g

1105. Apple and Brown Rice Pudding

Ingredients for 6 servings

- 2 cups of almond milk
- 1 cup of long-grain brown rice
- ½ cup of golden raisins
- 1 Granny Smith apple, chopped
- ¼ cup of honey
- 1 teaspoon of vanilla extract
- ½ teaspoon of ground cinnamon

Directions and Total Time: approx. 30 minutes

Place all ingredients in the Instant Pot®. Stir to combine. Close lid, set steam release to Sealing, press the Manual button, and set time to 20 minutes. When the timer beeps, let pressure release naturally for 15 minutes, then quick-release the remaining pressure. Press the Cancel button and open lid. Serve warm or at room temperature.

Per Serving: Calories 218, Fat 2g, Carbs 51g, Protein 3g

1106. Apple Bread

Ingredients for 6 servings

- 3 cups of apples
- 1 cup of sugar
- 1 tablespoon of vanilla
- 2 eggs
- 1 tablespoon of apple pie spice
- 2 cups of white flour
- 1 tablespoon of baking powder
- 1 stick of butter
- 1 cup of water

Directions and Total Time: approx. 45 minutes

Mix in egg with 1 butter stick, sugar, and apple pie spice and turn using mixer. Put apples and turn properly. Mix baking powder with flour in another bowl and turn. Blend the 2 mixtures, turn and move it to spring form pan. Get spring form pan into air fryer and cook at 320F for 40 minutes. Slice. Serve.

Per Serving: Calories 401, Fat 9g, Carbs 29g, Protein 12g

1107. Avocado and Dark Chocolate Mousse

Ingredients for 4 servings

- 2 tablespoons of olive oil
- 8 ounces of dark chocolate, chopped
- ¼ cup of milk
- 2 ripe avocados, deseeded
- ¼ cup of honey
- 1 cup of strawberries

Directions and Total Time: approx. 10 minutes + freezing time

Cook the chocolate, olive oil, and milk in a saucepan over medium heat for 3 minutes or until the chocolate melt, stirring constantly. Put the avocado in a food processor, then drizzle with honey and melted chocolate. Pulse to combine until smooth. Pour the mixed, prepared mixture into a serving bowl, then sprinkle with strawberries. Chill for 30 minutes and serve.

Per Serving: Calories 654, Fat 47g, Carbs 56g, Protein 7.2g

1108. Avocado Mousse

Ingredients for 7 servings

- 2 avocados, peeled, cored, and mashed
- 3 tablespoons of erythritol
- ⅓ cup of heavy cream
- 1 teaspoon of almond butter
- 1 teaspoon of vanilla extract
- 1 teaspoon of cocoa powder

Directions and Total Time: approx. 20 minutes

Mix up the avocado with erythritol until smooth. Place the butter in a saucepan and allow it to melt. Add the mashed avocado mixture and cocoa powder, then stir well. Sauté the mixture for 3 minutes. Meanwhile, whisk the heavy cream at high speed for 2 minutes. Transfer the cooked avocado mash to the bowl and chill in ice water. Add the whisked heavy cream and vanilla extract when the avocado mash reaches room temperature. Stir gently. Transfer the mousse into small cups and chill for 4 hours in the fridge.

Per Serving: Calories 50, Fat 4.7g, Carbs 6g, Protein 1g

1109. Avocado Sorbet

Ingredients for 4 servings

- ¼ cup of sugar
- 1 cup of water
- 1 teaspoon of grated lime zest
- 1 tablespoon of honey
- 2 ripe avocados, pitted and skin removed
- 2 tablespoons of lime juice

Directions and Total Time: approx. 15 minutes

Combine together the prepared sugar and water in a small pan over medium flame. Continue until the sugar dissolves completely and then remove from the flame. Place the avocados in the food processor. Add the sugar and water mix along with the honey, lime zest, and lime juice into the food processor. Process until you reach a smooth consistency. Place the mix into a baking pan and cover with foil. Place the mix into the freezer until completely frozen. Upon serving, process the food in the food processor until you reach a smooth consistency.

Per Serving: Calories 390.3, Fat 6g, Carbs 19g, Protein 10g

1110. Banana Bread

Ingredients for 6 servings

- 3/4 cup of sugar
- 1/3 cup of butter
- 1 tablespoon of vanilla extract
- 1 egg
- 2 bananas
- 1 tablespoon of baking powder
- 1 and 1/2 cups of flour
- 1/2 tablespoon of baking soda
- 1/3 cup of milk
- 1 and 1/2 tablespoon of cream of tartar
- Cooking spray

Directions and Total Time: approx. 45 minutes

Mix in milk with cream of tartar, vanilla, egg, sugar, bananas and butter in a bowl and turn whole. Mix in flour with baking soda and baking powder. Blend the 2 mixtures, turn properly, move into oiled pan with cooking spray, put into air fryer and cook at 320F for 40 minutes. Remove bread, allow to cool, slice. Serve.

Per Serving: Calories 540, Fat 16g, Carbs 28g, Protein 18g

1111. Banana Chocolate Squares

Ingredients for 24 servings

- 2/3 cup of white sugar
- ¾ cup of cashew butter
- 2/3 cup of brown sugar
- 1 egg, beaten
- 1 teaspoon of vanilla extract
- 1 cup if banana puree
- 1 ¾ cups of flour
- 2 teaspoons of baking powder
- ½ teaspoon of salt
- 1 cup of semi-sweet chocolate chips
- ½ cup of almonds, chopped

Directions and Total Time: approx. 40 minutes

Preheat the oven to 350°F. In a medium-sized bowl, add the sugars and butter and beat until lightly colored. Add the egg, banana puree, and vanilla, then stir well Mix the baking powder, flour, almonds, and salt in another bowl. Add this mixture to the butter mixture. Stir in the chocolate chips. Prepare a baking pan and place the mixture in it. Bake for 20 minutes. Let it cool for 5 minutes before slicing into equal-size squares.

Per Serving: Calories 174, Fat 8.2g, Carbs 25.2g, Protein 1.7g

1112. Banana Cinnamon Cupcakes

Ingredients for 4 servings

- 4 tablespoons of avocado oil
- 4 eggs
- 1/2 cup of orange juice
- 2 teaspoons of cinnamon powder
- 1 teaspoon of vanilla extract
- 2 bananas, peeled and chopped
- 3/4 cup of almond flour
- 1/2 teaspoon of baking powder
- Cooking spray

Directions and Total Time: approx. 30 minutes

In a bowl, combine the oil with the eggs, orange juice and the other ingredients except the cooking spray, whisk well, and pour in a cupcake pan greased with the cooking spray. Introduce in oven for 20 minutes, at 350 degrees F. Cool the cupcakes down and serve.

Per Serving: Calories 142, Fat 5.8g, Carbs 5.7g, Protein 1.6g

Ingredients for 4 servings

- 2 kiwi, peeled and sliced
- 1 egg
- 2 ¼ cups of milk
- ½ cup of honey
- 1 teaspoon of vanilla extract
- 3 tablespoons of cornstarch

Directions and Total Time: approx. 20 minutes + chilling time

In a bowl, beat the egg with honey. Stir in 2 cups of milk and vanilla. Pour into a medium-sized pot over medium heat and bring to a boil. Combine cornstarch and remaining milk in a bowl. Pour slowly into the pot and boil for 1 minute until thickened, stirring often. Divide between 4 cups and transfer to the fridge. Top with kiwi and serve.

Per Serving: Calories 262, Fat 4.1g, Carbs 52g, Protein 6.5g

1114. Berry Sorbet

Ingredients for 4 servings

- 1 teaspoon of lemon juice
- ¼ cup of honey
- 1 cup of fresh strawberries
- 1 cup of fresh raspberries
- 1 cup of fresh blueberries

Directions and Total Time: approx. 10 minutes + freezing time

Bring the cup of water to a boil in a pot over high heat. Stir in honey until dissolved. Remove from the heat and mix in berries and lemon juice; let cool. Once cooled, add the mixture to a food processor and pulse until smooth. Transfer to a shallow glass and freeze for 1 hour. Stir with a fork and freeze for 30 more minutes. Repeat a couple of times. Serve in dessert dishes.

Per Serving: Calories 115, Fat 1g, Carbs 29g, Protein 1g

1115. Blackberries Tiramisu

Ingredients for 4 servings

- 4 cups of mascarpone cheese
- 1 cup of water
- 3 egg yolks
- 1 ½ cup of sugar
- 4 cups of blackberries
- 8 ladyfingers
- 3 tablespoons of sugar
- 1 lemon juice

Directions and Total Time: approx. 35 minutes

Wash the cups of blackberries and add them to a bowl with lemon juice and sugar. In a saucepan add the water, the sugar and cook at medium heat. In a large-sized bowl add the egg yolks and the sugar and whisk slowly adding the syrup. Continue whisking and slowly add the mascarpone. Blend the blackberries and set the compote aside. Start building the tiramisù bowl, layering the compote first, then the ladyfinger and the mascarpone mixture. Layer until the bowl is full.

Per Serving: Calories 140, Fat 10g, Carbs 61g, Protein 9g

1116. Blood Orange Soft Cake

Ingredients for 8 servings

- 2 blood orange, juiced + the zest
- 2 tablespoons butter, softened and cubed
- 1/2 cup of cornmeal
- 1 cup of all-purpose flour
- 2 teaspoons of baking powder
- 4 tablespoons of granulated sugar
- ½ teaspoon of salt
- 3 eggs
- 1/2 cup of plain yogurt
- Ice sugar to garnish

Directions and Total Time: approx. 60 minutes

Preheat the oven at 380 F. Take a large mixing bowl: add flour, baking powder and sugar. Then add the butter, and whisk with an electric mixer until creamy. While whisking add the eggs one by one, the orange zest and keep mixing until all ingredients are well combined. Once ready, pour the mixture in a cake pan previously covered with parchment paper. Bake the cake for about 35 minutes then sprinkle the ice sugar on top before serving.

Per Serving: Calories 360, Fat 17.4g, Carbs 45.9g, Protein 5.8g

1117. Blueberry and Oats Crisp

Ingredients for 8 servings

- 1 cup of rolled oats
- ½ cup of whole wheat flour
- ¼ cup of extra-virgin olive oil
- ¼ teaspoon of salt
- 1 teaspoon of cinnamon
- ⅓ cup of honey
- Cooking oil
- 4 cups of blueberries (thawed if frozen)

Directions and Total Time: approx. 15 minutes

Combine the rolled oats, flour, olive oil, salt, cinnamon, and honey in a large bowl. Spray a barrel pan with cooking oil all over the bottom and sides of the pan. Spread the blueberries on the bottom of the barrel pan. Top with the oat mixture. Place the pan in the air fryer. Cook at 350°F (177°C) for 15 minutes. Cool before serving.

Per Serving: Calories 304, Fat 18.9g, Carbs 23.8g, Protein 10g

1118. Blueberry Muffins

Ingredients for 4 servings

- 1 cup of whole wheat flour
- 1 teaspoon of baking powder
- ¼ cup of blueberries
- 1 teaspoon of vanilla extract
- 1 tablespoon of butter softened
- ¾ cup of sour cream
- 1 tablespoon of Erythritol
- Cooking spray

Directions and Total Time: approx. 4 minutes

In the mixing bowl, combine wheat flour and baking powder. Then add sour cream, vanilla extract, butter, and Erythritol. Stir the mixture well until smooth. You should get a thick batter. Add more sour cream if needed. After this, add blueberries and carefully stir the batter. Spray the muffin molds with the cooking spray. Fill ½ part of every muffin mold with batter. Preheat the oven to 365F. Place the muffins in the prepared oven and cook them for 25 minutes. The cooked muffins will have a golden color surface.

Per Serving: Calories 241, Fat 12.4g, Carbs 24.9g, Protein 1.9g

1119. Blueberry Scones

Ingredients for 10 servings

- 1 cup of white flour
- 1 cup of blueberries
- 2 eggs
- 1/2 cup of heavy cream
- 1/2 cup of butter
- 5 tablespoons of sugar
- 2 tablespoons of vanilla extract
- 2 tablespoons of baking powder

Directions and Total Time: approx. 20 minutes

In a medium-sized mixing bowl, combine the flour, baking powder, salt, and blueberries. Turn to combine. Mix heavy cream with vanilla extract, sugar, butter and eggs and turn properly. Blend the 2 mixtures, squeeze till dough is ready, obtain 10 triangles from mix, put on baking sheet into air fryer and cook them at 320F for 10 minutes. Serve cold.

Per Serving: Calories 525, Fat 21g, Carbs 37g, Protein 14g

1120. Bread Dough and Amaretto Dessert

Ingredients for 12 servings

- 1 pound of bread dough
- 1 cup of sugar
- 1/2 cup of butter
- 1 cup of heavy cream
- 12 ounces of chocolate chips
- 2 tablespoons of amaretto liqueur

Directions and Total Time: approx. 23 minutes

Cut dough into 20 slices and cut each piece in halves. Garnish dough pieces with spray sugar, butter, put into air fryer's basket and cook them at 350F for 5 minutes. Cook for 3 minutes still. Move to a platter. Dissolve the heavy cream in pan over medium heat, attach chocolate chips and turn until they melt. Set in liqueur, turn and move to a bowl. Serve bread dippers with the sauce.

Per Serving: Calories 179, Fat 18g, Carbs 17g, Protein 12g

1121. Brown Butter Financiers

Ingredients for 4 servings

- 1 cup of almond flour
- 3/4 cup and 2 tablespoons of sugar
- 5 tablespoons of flour
- 1 pinch of salt
- 4 large egg whites
- ½ teaspoon of vanilla extract
- 2 ½ ounces of brown butter

Directions and Total Time: approx. 27 minutes

Preheat your oven at a heat of 375°F. Grease a 24-cup mini muffin tray with butter. In a large-sized bowl, mix the almond flour with the salt, flour, sugar, egg whites, browned butter and vanilla in a medium bowl. Divide this mixture into muffin cups, press them down and bake them for approximately about 12 minutes. Allow them to cool and serve.

Per Serving: Calories 237, Fat 3.5g, Carbs 46.8g, Protein 6.1g

1122. Butter Walnut and Raisin Cookies

Ingredients for 8 servings

- ½ teaspoon of pure almond extract
- ½ teaspoon of pure vanilla extract
- 2 tablespoons of rum
- ½ cup of almond flour
- 1 stick of butter, room temperature
- 1/3 cup of cornflour
- 2 tablespoons of Truvia
- ¼ cup of raisins
- 1/3 cup of walnuts, ground

Directions and Total Time: approx. 25 minutes

In a small bowl, place rum and raisins and allow to sit for 15-minutes. Beat the butter with Truvia, vanilla, and almond extract until light and fluffy in a mixing dish. Then, throw in both types of flour and ground almonds. Fold in the soaked raisins. Continue mixing until it forms a dough. Refrigerate for approximately 20 minutes after covering. Meanwhile, preheat the air-fryer to 330°Fahrenheit. Roll the dough into small cookies, place them in an air-fryer cake pan; gently press each cookie with a spoon. Bake cookies for 15-minutes.

Per Serving: Calories 406, Fat 11.3g, Carbs 62.3g, Protein 5.7g

1123. Butterscotch Lava Cakes

Ingredients for 6 servings

- 7 tablespoons of all-purpose flour
- A pinch of coarse salt
- 6 ounces of butterscotch morsels
- 3/4 cup of powdered sugar
- 1/2 teaspoon of vanilla extract
- 3 eggs, whisked
- 1 stick of butter

Directions and Total Time: approx. 20 minutes

Add 1 ½ cups of water and a metal rack to the Instant Pot. Line a standard-size muffin tin with muffin papers. In a microwave-safe bowl, microwave butter and butterscotch morsels for about 40 seconds. Stir in the powdered sugar. Add the remaining ingredients. Fill the muffin pan halfway with batter. Secure the lid. Choose the "Manual" and cook at High pressure for 10 minutes. Once cooking is complete, use a quick release; carefully remove the lid. To remove, let it cool for 5 to 6 minutes. Run a small knife around the sides of each cake and serve. Enjoy!

Per Serving: Calories 393, Fat 21.1g, Carbs 45.6g, Protein 5.6g

1124. Caramel Cream

Ingredients for 8 servings

- 1 1/2 cup of sugar
- 4 cups of cold milk
- 8 eggs
- 2 teaspoons of vanilla powder

Directions and Total Time: approx. 1 hour and 18 minutes

In a nonstick pan, melt 1/4 of the sugar over low heat. When the sugar has turned into caramel, pour it into 8 cup-sized ovenproof pots covering only the bottoms. Whisk the 8 eggs with the remaining sugar and vanilla extract, then gradually add the milk. Stir the mixture well before dividing it between the two pots. Place the 8 pots in a larger, deep baking dish. Pour 3-4 cups of water into the dish. Place the baking dish in a preheated to 280 F oven for about an hour and bake but do not let the water boil, as the boiling will overcook the cream and make holes in it: if necessary, add cold water to the baking dish. Carefully take the pots out of the baking dish after removing them from the oven. Place a shallow serving plate on top, then invert each pot so that the cream unmolds. The caramel will form a topping and sauce.

Per Serving: Calories 213, Fat 16g, Carbs 25.4g, Protein 8g

1125. Caramel Popcorn

Ingredients for 20 servings
- 2 cups of brown sugar
- 1/2 cup of corn syrup
- 1/2 teaspoon of baking powder
- 1 teaspoon of vanilla extract
- 5 cups of popcorn

Directions and Total Time: approx. 1 hour and 30 minutes

Preheat the oven to a heat of 95° C (250° F). Put the popcorn in a large bowl. Melt the prepared 1 cup of butter in a medium-sized pan over medium heat. Stir in brown sugar, 1 tsp. of salt and corn syrup. Bring to a boil, constantly stirring — Cook without stirring for 4 minutes. Remove from heat and stir in soda and vanilla. Pour in a thin layer on the popcorn and stir well. Place in two large shallow baking tins and bake in the preheated oven, stirring every 15 minutes for an hour. Remove from the prepared oven and cool completely before slicing.

Per Serving: Calories 253, Fat 14g, Carbs 32.8g, Protein 8.4g

1126. Cherry Clafoutis

Ingredients for 6 servings
- 1 ¼ pounds of sweet cherries
- 3 large eggs
- ½ cup of all-purpose flour
- 1 teaspoon of vanilla extract
- lespoons of sugar
- 1 ⅓ cup of whole milk
- Softened butter, for the
- 1/8 teaspoon of almond extract
- 1 teaspoon of instant coffee
- 9 ounces of chocolate chips
- 1/2 cup of whole milk
- 1/3 cup of sugar

baking dish

Directions and Total Time: approx. 60 minutes

Preheat your oven at 375°F. Grease a 2 quarts of baking dish with butter. Spread the pitted cherries onto the baking dish. Blend the eggs with the flour, vanilla and the rest of the ingredients in a blender until smooth. Pour this mixed mixture into the baking dish and bake for 45 minutes. Serve.

Per Serving: Calories 352, Fat 15g, Carbs 51g, Protein 34g

1127. Chia Seed and Chocolate Pudding

Ingredients for 4 servings
- 2 cups of heavy cream
- ¼ cup of cocoa powder
- 1 teaspoon o vanilla extract
- ½ ground cinnamon
- ½ cup of chia seeds
- 2 tablespoons of chocolate shavings

Directions and Total Time: approx. 10 minutes + chilling time

Warm the cups of heavy cream in a saucepan over medium heat to just below a simmer. Remove from the heat and the allow it to cool slightly. In a large bowl, combine the warmed heavy cream, cocoa powder, vanilla extract, cinnamon, and salt and blend using an actual immersion blender until the cocoa is well incorporated. Put in the chia seeds and let sit for 15 minutes. Divide the mixture evenly between small glass bowls and refrigerate for at least 2 hours or until set. Serve chilled.

Per Serving: Calories 561, Fat 53g, Carbs 19g, Protein 8g

1128. Chocolate and Pecan Thins

Ingredients for 4 servings
- 4 ounces of dark chocolate
- 0.5 ounce of pecans, chopped
- 0.25 teaspoon of vanilla extract
- 1 teaspoon of licorice powder
- Baking tray lined with parchment paper

Directions and Total Time: approx. 15 minutes

Warm up a pan on a low heat and melt the chocolate, or place in the microwave as an alternative. Add the licorice and the vanilla extract and combine well. Take a baking tray and grease it, lining it with parchment paper. Pour the mixture onto the tray and add the pecans over the top. Allow to cool or place in the refrigerator if you want it faster! The mixture should set to a completely hard consistency - snap to break up, to around 15 pieces and enjoy!

Per Serving: Calories 60, Fat 5g, Carbs 3g, Protein 1g

1129. Chocolate Coffee Pots de Creme

Ingredients for 6 servings
- A pinch of pink salt
- 4 egg yolks
- 2 cups of double cream

Directions and Total Time: approx. 25 minutes

Place a metal trivet and 1 cup of water in your Instant Pot. In a saucepan, bring the cream and milk to a simmer. Then, thoroughly combine the egg yolks, sugar, instant coffee, and salt. Slowly and gradually whisk in the hot cream mixture. Whisk in the chocolate chips and blend again. Pour the mixture into mason jars. Lower the jars onto the trivet. Secure the lid. Choose the "Manual" mode and cook for 6 minutes at High pressure. Once cooking is complete, use a natural pressure release for 10 minutes; carefully remove the lid. Serve well chilled and enjoy!

Per Serving: Calories 351, Fat 19.3g, Carbs 39.3g, Protein 5.5g

1130.Chocolate Gelato

Ingredients for 4 servings
- 1 cup of heavy whipping cream
- 1/3 cup of powdered sugar
- 1 ½ tablespoons of unsweetened cocoa powder
- 2 large egg yolks
- ½ teaspoon of vanilla extract

Directions and Total Time: approx. 20 minutes

In a pan, add the heavy whipping cream and sugar over medium-high heat and bring to a boil, stirring frequently. Adjust the heat to low and simmer for about 1 minute. Stir in the cocoa powder and cook for about 2 minutes, stirring continuously. Remove from the heat temperature and you and set aside to cool for about 5 minutes. Meanwhile, in a bowl, add the egg yolks and vanilla extract and beat well. Slowly add the cream mixture into the egg yolks mixture, beating continuously until slightly frothy. Freeze for about 4-6 hours, stirring after every 1 hour.

Per Serving: Calories 176, Fat 13.7g, Carbs 12.3g, Protein 2.4g

1131. Chocolate Lava Cake

Ingredients for 4 servings

- 2 ounces of butter
- 0.25 teaspoon of vanilla extract
- 3 eggs
- 1 tablespoon of butter
- 2 ounces of dark chocolate
- 4 greased ramekin glasses

Directions and Total Time: approx. 15 minutes

Preheat the oven to 200°C. Take four ramekin dishes and grease with butter. Cut the dark chocolate up into very small pieces and add to a saucepan with the butter, allowing to melt. Add the vanilla to the chocolate once melted, and stir well. Take the pan off the heat and set to one side to cool down. Crack the three eggs into a large-sized bowl and beat for around 3 minutes. Pour the chocolate mixture into the eggs and mix together well. Pour into the prepared ramekins and cook in the oven. Turn the oven down to 175°C when you place the ramekins inside, and cook for 6 minutes. Serve whilst still hot

Per Serving: Calories 180, Fat 16g, Carbs 4g, Protein 4g

1132. Chocolate Mousse

Ingredients for 4 servings

- ¾ cup of milk
- 3.5 ounces of dark chocolate, grated
- 2 cups of Greek yogurt
- 1 tablespoon of honey
- ½ teaspoon of vanilla extract

Directions and Total Time: approx. 5 minutes with 2 hours chilling time

Put the milk and chocolate into a saucepan and gently heat until the chocolate has melted. Wait to boil, then add the honey and vanilla extract and stir well. Pour the chocolate mixture over the Greek yogurt in a bowl. Thoroughly combine all the ingredients before transferring to individual bowls or glasses. Refrigerate for at least 2 hours. The chocolate mousse can be stored in the refrigerator for up to 2 days.

Per Serving: Calories 328, Fat 18.2g, Carbs 25.4g, Protein 15.8g

1133. Chocolate Salami

Ingredients for 10 servings

- 1 ½ cup of butter
- 2 ½ dark chocolate
- 1 cup of pistachios
- ½ cup of icing sugar
- 1 ½ cup of biscuits
- 2 tablespoons of Grand Marnier

Directions and Total Time: approx. 35 minutes

Chop and melt the chocolate at bain-marie, let it cool down. In another bowl whisk the butter with the icing sugar, add the Grand Marnier and keep whipping. Add to the whipped butter the chocolate mixture, the biscuits, pistachios, and mix. Transfer the prepared mixture to the center of a parchment paper sheet and roll it, close it like a candy and keep it in the fridge for 2 hours. Unfold the salami and roll it in the icing sugar. Slice it and serve.

Per Serving: Calories 90, Fat 10g, Carbs 44.73g, Protein 6.5g

1134. Cinnamon Chickpeas Cookies

Ingredients for 12 servings

- 1 cup of canned chickpeas
- 2 cups of almond flour
- 1 teaspoon of cinnamon powder
- 1 teaspoon of baking powder
- 1 cup of avocado oil
- 1/2 cup of stevia
- 1 egg, whisked
- 2 teaspoons of almond extract
- 1 cup of raisins
- 1 cup of coconut, unsweetened and shredded

Directions and Total Time: approx. 30 minutes

In a bowl, combine the chickpeas with the flour, cinnamon and the other ingredients, and whisk well until you obtain a dough. Scoop tablespoons of dough on a baking sheet lined with parchment paper, introduce in oven for 20 minutes at 350 degrees. Let it cool and serve.

Per Serving: Calories 200, Fat 4.5g, Carbs 9.5g, Protein 2.4g

1135. Cinnamon Palmier

Ingredients for 30 servings

- 1/3 cup of granulated sugar
- 2 teaspoons of cinnamon
- 1/2 pound of puff pastry
- 1 egg, beaten (optional)

Directions and Total Time: approx. 20 minutes

Stir together the sugar and cinnamon. Spread the pastry dough into a large rectangle. Spread the cinnamon sugar in an even layer over the dough. From the long ends of the rectangle, loosely roll each side inward until they meet in the middle. If needed, brush it with the egg to hold it together. Slice the pastry roll crosswise into 1/4-inch pieces and arrange them on a lined with parchment paper baking sheet. Bake cookies in a preheated to 400 F oven for 12-15 minutes, until they puff and turn golden brown. Serve warm or at room temperature.

Per Serving: Calories 114, Fat 3g, Carbs 8g, Protein 6g

1136. Cinnamon Pear and Oat Crisp with Pecans

Ingredients for 4 servings

- 2 tablespoons of butter, melted
- 4 fresh pears, mashed
- ½ lemon, juiced and zested
- ¼ cup of maple syrup
- 1 cup of gluten-free rolled oats
- ½ cup of chopped pecans
- ½ teaspoon of ground cinnamon
- ¼ teaspoon of salt

Directions and Total Time: approx. 30 minutes

Preheat oven to a heat of 350 F. Combine the pears, lemon juice and zest, and maple syrup in a bowl. Stir to mix well, then spread the mixture on a greased baking dish. Combine the remaining ingredients in a small bowl. Stir to mix well. Pour the mixture over the pear mixture. Bake for 20 minutes or until the oats are golden brown.

Per Serving: Calories 496, Fat 33g, Carbs 50.8g, Protein 5g

1137. Cinnamon Stuffed Peaches

Ingredients for 4 servings

- 4 peaches, pitted, halved
- 2 tablespoons of ricotta cheese
- 2 tablespoons of liquid honey
- ¾ cup of water
- ½ teaspoon of vanilla extract
- ¾ teaspoon of ground cinnamon
- 1 tablespoon of almonds, sliced
- ¾ teaspoon of saffron

Directions and Total Time: approx. 25 minutes

Pour water in the saucepan and bring to boil. Add vanilla extract, saffron, ground cinnamon, and liquid honey. Cook the liquid until the honey is melted. Then remove it from the heat. Put the halved peaches in the hot honey liquid. Meanwhile, make the filling: mix up together ricotta cheese, vanilla extract, and sliced almonds. Remove the peaches from the honey liquid and arrange them on the plate. Fill 4 peach halves with ricotta filling and cover them with remaining peach halves. Sprinkle the cooked dessert with liquid honey mixture gently.

Per Serving: Calories 213, Fat 1.4g, Carbs 23.9g, Protein 1.9g

1138. Cocoa Brownies

Ingredients for 8 servings

- 30 ounces of canned lentils, rinsed and drained
- 1 tablespoon of honey
- 1 banana, peeled and chopped
- ½ teaspoon of baking soda
- 4 tablespoons of almond butter
- 2 tablespoons of cocoa powder
- Cooking spray

Directions and Total Time: approx. 30 minutes

Preheat the oven to 375°F. In a food processor, combine the lentils with the honey and the other ingredients except for the cooking spray and pulse well. Pour the mixture into a medium-sized pan greased with the cooking spray, making sure to spread the mixture out evenly. Bake in the preheated oven for approximately about 20 minutes. Cut the brownies and serve cold.

Per Serving: Calories 200, Fat 4.5g, Carbs 8.7g, Protein 4.3g

1139. Cocoa Bundt Cake

Ingredients for 10 servings

- 2 ½ cup of flour
- 1 sachet of baking powder
- 1 ½ cup of sugar
- ½ cup of oil
- A pinch of salt
- 2 ½ cup of water
- 2 tablespoons of cocoa powder

Directions and Total Time: approx. 55 minutes

In a bowl add the flour, the baking powder, salt, water, oil, and sugar and whisk all together. Divide the batter into 2 different portions and add the cocoa to one part. Pour the batter into the mold starting from the cocoa batter then add the white batter. Swirl with a stick the batter and bake for 25 minutes.

Per Serving: Calories 150, Fat 10g, Carbs 39g, Protein 6g

1140. Cocoa Cake

Ingredients for 6 servings

- 1 ounces of butter
- 3 eggs
- 3 ounces of sugar
- 1 tablespoon of cocoa powder
- 3 ounces of flour
- 1/2 tablespoon of lemon juice

Directions and Total Time: approx. 22 minutes

Merge in 1 tablespoon butter with cocoa powder in a bowl and beat. Merge in the rest of the butter with eggs, flour, sugar and lemon juice in another bowl, blend properly and move half into a cake pan. Set half of the cocoa blend, spread, add the rest of the butter layer and crest with remaining cocoa. Set into air fryer and cook at 360 F for 17 minutes. Allow to cool before slicing.

Per Serving: Calories 221, Fat 5g, Carbs 12g, Protein 7g

1141. Coconut Cake Balls

Ingredients for 8 servings

- 1 package of cake mix
- 4 cups of coconut milk
- 1 cup of cream cheese
- 1 cup shredded coconut
- 2 cups of dark chocolate
- 2 tablespoons of butter
- 2 tablespoons of oil

Directions and Total Time: approx. 1 hour and 30 minutes

Mix the cake mix with the milk and the oil. Pour in a baking sheet for 25 minutes and let it cool down. In a large-sized bowl whip the cream cheese. Add the rest of the milk and beat again. Stir in the cup of shredded coconut, dark chocolate, and butter. Crumble the cake inside the cream cheese mixture. Scoop some balls and freeze them for 30 minutes. Roll in the grated coconut and refrigerate for another hour.

Per Serving: Calories 81, Fat 5g, Carbs 10g, Protein 1g

1142. Coconut Rice Pudding

Ingredients for 4 servings

- ½ cup of rice
- ¼ cup of shredded coconut
- 3 tablespoons of Swerve
- 1 ½ cups of water
- 14 ounces of coconut milk
- Pinch of salt

Directions and Total Time: approx. 13 minutes

Spray the inside of an Instant Pot with cooking spray. Add all the ingredients to its inner pot and stir well. Seal the pot with the lid and cook on High for 3 minutes. Once done, allow to release the pressure naturally for 10 minutes. Then release the rest of the remaining pressure using quick release. Remove the lid. Serve and enjoy.

Per Serving: Calories 302, Fat 23.5g, Carbs 33.3g, Protein 3.8g

1143. Coffee Granita

Ingredients for 8 servings

- 4 cups of hot brewed extra strong coffee
- 2 teaspoons of ground cinnamon
- ½ cup of Erythritol
- 1 ¼ cups of heavy cream, divided

Directions and Total Time: approx. 10 minutes

In a large bowl, add coffee, cinnamon, and erythritol and stir until sugar is completely dissolved. Add ¼ cup of cream and beat until well combined. Refrigerate for about 30 minutes. Remove from refrigerator and transfer the mixture into a shallow baking dish. Freeze for about 3 hours, scraping after every 30 minutes with the help of a fork. With a foil paper, cover tightly and freeze before serving. While serving, in a bowl, add the remaining cream and beat until soft peaks form. Place the granita in serving glasses. Place cream over each glass evenly and serve.

Per Serving: Calories 67, Fat 7g, Carbs 1g, Protein 0.5g

1144. Cranberry Applesauce

Ingredients for 8 servings

- 1 cup of whole cranberries
- 4 medium tart apples, peeled, cored, and grated
- 4 medium sweet apples, peeled, cored, and grated
- 1 ½ tablespoon of grated orange zest
- ¼ cup of orange juice
- ¼ cup of dark brown sugar
- ¼ cup of granulated sugar
- 1 tablespoon of unsalted butter
- 2 teaspoons of ground cinnamon
- ½ teaspoon of ground cloves
- ¼ teaspoon of ground black pepper
- ⅛ teaspoon of salt
- 1 tablespoon of lemon juice

Directions and Total Time: approx. 30 minutes

Incorporate all ingredients in the Instant Pot®. Seal then, set the Manual button, and time to 5 minutes. When the timer actually beeps, let the pressure release naturally, about 25 minutes. Open the lid. Lightly mash the fruit with a fork. Stir well. Serve warm or cold.

Per Serving: Calories 136, Fat 4g, Carbs 3g, Protein 9g

1145. Cranberry Pound Cake

Ingredients for 8 servings

- 1 cup of almond flour
- 1/3 teaspoon of baking soda
- 1/3 teaspoon of baking powder
- 1 tablespoon of Truvia for baking
- ½ teaspoon of ground cloves
- ½ cup of cranberries, fresh or thawed
- 2 eggs plus 1 egg yolk, beaten
- ½ teaspoon of vanilla paste
- 1 stick of butter
- ½ teaspoon of cardamom
- 1/3 teaspoon of ground cinnamon
- 1 tablespoon of browned butter

Directions and Total Time: approx. 30 minutes

Preheat your air-fryer to 355°Fahrenheit. Whisk the flour, baking soda, baking powder, Truvia, crushed cloves, cinnamon, and cardamom in a mixing basin. In another bowl, add a stick of butter and vanilla paste, mix the eggs, and whisk until light and fluffy. Add the flour/sweetener mixture to the butter/egg mixture and fold in cranberries and browned butter. Add the mixture into greased cake pan. Bake in preheated air-fryer for 20-minutes.

Per Serving: Calories 346, Fat 21.6g, Carbs 34.5g, Protein 4.7g

1146. Fig and Honey Buckwheat Pudding

Ingredients for 4 servings

- 1/2 teaspoon of ground cinnamon
- 1/2 cup of dried figs, chopped
- 1/3 cup of honey
- 1 teaspoon of pure vanilla extract
- 3 ½ cups of milk
- 1/2 teaspoon of pure almond extract
- 1 ½ cups of buckwheat

Directions and Total Time: approx. 20 minutes

In your Instant Pot, combine all of the ingredients listed above. Secure the lid. Choose the "Multigrain" mode and cook for 10 minutes under high pressure. Once cooking is complete, use a natural pressure release; carefully remove the lid. Serve topped with fresh fruits, nuts, or whipped topping. Bon appétit!

Per Serving: Calories 320, Fat 7.5g, Carbs 57.7g, Protein 9.5g

1147. Fig Cookies

Ingredients for 24 servings

- 1 cup of flour
- 1 egg
- 1/2 cup of sugar
- 1/2 cup of figs, chopped
- 1/2 cup of butter
- 1/4 cup of water
- 1/2 teaspoon of vanilla extract
- 1 teaspoon of baking powder
- A pinch of salt

Directions and Total Time: approx. 25 minutes

Cook figs with water, stirring, for 4-5 minutes, or until thickened. Set aside to cool. Scourge butter with sugar until light and fluffy. Beat in the egg and vanilla. In separate bowl, incorporate together flour, baking powder and salt. Blend this into the egg mixture. Stir in the cooled figs. Drop teaspoonful of dough on a greased baking tray. Bake in a preheated to 375 degrees F oven until lightly browned. Remove cookies and cool on wire racks.

Per Serving: Calories 111, Fat 9g, Carbs 5g, Protein 3g

1148. Frosty Strawberry Dessert

Ingredients for 16 servings

- 1 cup of flour, white sugar, whipped cream
- 1/2 cup of chopped walnuts, butter
- 2 cups of sliced strawberries
- 2 tablespoons of lemon juice
- 1/4 cup of brown sugar

Directions and Total Time: approx. 26 minutes

Preheat oven to 175°C (350 degrees Fahrenheit). Mix flour, brown sugar, nuts, and melted butter. Bake for just approximately 20 minutes or until crispy on a baking sheet. Remove the pan from the oven and cool completely. Beat the egg whites to snow. Keep beating until you get firm spikes while slowly adding sugar. Mix the strawberries in the lemon juice and stir in the egg whites until the mixture turns slightly pink. Stir in the whipped cream until it is absorbed. Crumble the walnut mixture and spread 2/3 evenly over the bottom of a 9-inch by 13-inch dish. Place the strawberry mixture on the crumbs and sprinkle the rest of the crumbs. Place in the freezer for two hours. To make cutting easier, take them out of the freezer a few minutes before serving.

Per Serving: Calories 184, Fat 9.2g, Carbs 29.4g, Protein 2.2g

Ingredients for 4 servings

- 2 cups of plain yogurt
- 2 tablespoons of honey
- 1 teaspoon of vanilla extract
- A pinch of salt
- 2 mangoes, cut into chunks

Directions and Total Time: approx. 15 minutes + straining time

Place an actual fine sieve lined with cheesecloth over a bowl and spoon the yogurt into the sieve. Allow the liquid to drain off for 12-24 hours. Transfer the strained yogurt to a bowl and mix in the honey, vanilla, and salt. Set it aside. Heat your grill to medium-high. Thread the fruit onto skewers and grill for 2 minutes on each side until the fruit is softened and has grill marks on each side. Serve with labneh.

Per Serving: Calories 292, Fat 6g, Carbs 60g, Protein 5g

1150. Fruit Tart

Ingredients for 10 servings

- 3 cups of whole wheat flour
- 1 cup of oil
- 1 cup of sugar
- 1 egg
- 1 egg yolk
- 1 teaspoon of baking powder
- 1 teaspoon of vanilla extract
- A pinch of salt
- 2 ½ cup of marmalade without sugar

Directions and Total Time: approx. 45 minutes

In a bowl add the sugar, flour, baking powder, vanilla extract, and salt and create a well. Break the 1 egg in the center of the well and mix and add the oil slowly. Mix a bit and create a solid dough, then roll it out between two sheets of parchment paper. Place the dough in a butter and flour baking pan and pour inside it the marmalade. Bake at 170° for 30 minutes.

Per Serving: Calories 350, Fat 15g, Carbs 42g, Protein 7.2g

1151. Glazed Pears with Hazelnuts

Ingredients for 4 servings

- 4 pears, peeled, cored, and quartered lengthwise
- 1 cup of apple juice
- 1 tablespoon of grated fresh ginger
- ½ cup of pure maple syrup
- ¼ cup of chopped hazelnuts

Directions and Total Time: approx. 30 minutes

Put the pears in a pot, then pour in the apple juice. Bring to a boil over medium-high heat, and then reduce the heat to medium-low. Stir constantly. Cook covered for just about 15 minutes or until pears are tender. Meanwhile, combine the ginger and maple syrup in a saucepan. Bring to a boil over medium-high heat. Stir frequently. Turn off the heat, transfer the syrup to a small bowl, and sit until ready to use. Transfer the pears to a large serving bowl with a slotted spoon, then top the pears with syrup. Spread the hazelnuts over the pears and serve immediately.

Per Serving: Calories 287, Fat 3.1g, Carbs 34.4g, Protein 2.2g

Ingredients for 4 servings

- 8 slices of pineapple
- ½ cup of macadamia nuts, chopped
- ½ cup of chocolate cream and hazelnut spread
- ¼ cup of double cream
- ½ cup of mascarpone Italian cheese
- 1 teaspoon of whipped cream
- 4 cherries

Directions and Total Time: approx. 17 minutes

Preheat the skillet at medium temperature for 3 minutes. Add the macadamia nuts and store them for 3 minutes, stir constantly. Preheat the Round Grill at medium-high temperature for 3 minutes. Add the pineapple slices and roast each side for 2 minutes. In a bowl, add the chocolate cream, double cream and mascarpone cheese; stir until a uniform mixture is achieved. Spread four slices of pineapple with the mixture and cover with the remaining slices to form the sandwiches. Garnish with the cream, cherries and nuts.

Per Serving: Calories 344, Fat 9.3g, Carbs 46g, Protein 18g

1153. Hazelnut and Olive Oil Bread

Ingredients for 9 servings

- 1 1/4 cups of hazelnut meal
- 3/4 cup of flour
- 1/4 cup of brown sugar
- 1/4 cup of powdered sugar + quarter cup of for glaze
- 1 teaspoon of kosher salt
- 1 zested lemon juiced
- 1 teaspoon of vanilla
- 1/2 cup of olive oil extra-virgin

Directions and Total Time: approx. 10 minutes

Heat your oven to 375°F. Mix everything except 1/4 cup of sugar in a bowl. Press dough into a dish of 8x8-inch. Bake for around 5 minutes. Cut shortbread into squares and allow them to cool. Whisk rest of sugar and 1 tbsp of lemon juice in a bowl and drizzle over cookies.

Per Serving: Calories 276, Fat 21.2g, Carbs 20.1g, Protein 3.6g

1154. Ice Cream Sandwich Dessert

Ingredients for 12 servings

- 22 ice cream sandwiches
- Frozen whipped topping in 16 oz. container
- 1 jar (12 ounces) Caramel ice cream
- 1 ½ cups of salted peanuts

Directions and Total Time: approx. 20 minutes

Cut a sandwich with ice in two. Place a whole sandwich and a half sandwich on a short side of a 9 x 13-inch baking dish. Repeat this until the bottom is covered, alternate the full sandwich, and the half sandwich. Spread half of the whipped topping. Pour the caramel over it. Sprinkle with half the peanuts. Do layers with the rest of the ice cream sandwiches, whipped cream, and peanuts. Cover and freeze for 2 months. Remove from the freezer after approximately 20 minutes before serving. Cut into squares.

Per Serving: Calories 559, Fat 28.8g, Carbs 31g, Protein 10g

1155. Jasmine Rice Pudding with Cranberries

Ingredients for 4 servings

- 1 cup of apple juice
- 1 heaping tablespoon of honey
- 1/3 cup of granulated sugar
- 1 ½ cups of jasmine rice
- 1 cup of water
- 1/4 teaspoon of ground cinnamon
- 1/4 teaspoon of ground cloves
- 1/3 teaspoon of ground cardamom
- 1 teaspoon of vanilla extract
- 3 eggs, well-beaten
- 1/2 cup of cranberries

Directions and Total Time: approx. 20 minutes

Thoroughly combine the apple juice, honey, sugar, jasmine rice, water, and spices in the inner pot of your Instant Pot. Secure the lid. Choose the "Manual" mode and cook for 4 minutes at high pressure. Once cooking is complete, use a natural pressure release for 5 minutes; carefully remove the lid. Press the "Sauté" button and fold in the eggs. Cook on "Less" mode until heated through. Ladle into individual bowls and top with dried cranberries. Enjoy!

Per Serving: Calories 402, Fat 3.6g, Carbs 81.1g, Protein 8.9g

1156. Lemon Curd

Ingredients for 2 servings

- 4 tablespoons of butter
- 1 cup of sugar
- 2/3 cup of lemon juice
- 3 eggs
- 2 teaspoons of lemon zest
- 1 ½ cups of water

Directions and Total Time: approx. 20 minutes

Whip together the butter and sugar until well combined. Add 2 whole eggs and just the yolk of the other egg into the batter. Squeeze in the lemon juice. Pour the mixture into the two jars and close them securely. Place the steaming rack in the Instant Pot and pour 12 cups of water into the bottom. Place the jars on the rack and cook for 10 minutes at HIGH PRESSURE. Allow for a 10-minute natural release before rapidly releasing the remaining pressure. Replace the lids on the jars and stir in the zest.

Per Serving: Calories 45, Fat 1g, Carbs 8g, Protein 1g

1157. Lemon Easy Sorbet

Ingredients for 6 servings

- 2 ½ cups of caster sugar
- The peel of 1 lemon
- 2 cups of lemon juice
- 2 tablespoons of vodka
- 2 cups of water

Directions and Total Time: approx. 20 minutes

In a saucepan mix the water, the sugar, and the lemon peel and bring to a boil. Stir for approximately 5 minutes and then turn off the heat and let it cool. Take off the lemon peel and add the vodka and lemon juice. Set the mixture in a box then put it in the refrigerator for 5 hours. Every 1-hour mix the sorbet and incorporate the ice crystals. After 5 hours and 5 mixings, the sorbet should be ready. Keep it in the fridge and serve iced with some lemon zest or a little bit of iced vodka.

Per Serving: Calories 150, Fat 1g, Carbs 40g, Protein 2g

1158. Lemon Sorbet

Ingredients for 4 servings

- 2 tablespoons of fresh lemon zest, grated
- ½ cup of pure maple syrup
- 2 cups of water
- 1 ½ cups of fresh lemon juice

Directions and Total Time: approx. 10 minutes

Freeze the ice cream maker tub for about 24 hours before making this sorbet. Add all the ingredients except the lemon juice in a pan and simmer them over medium heat for approximately about 1 minute or until the sugar dissolves, stirring continuously. Remove the pan from the heat and stir in the lemon juice. Transfer the prepared mixture into an airtight container and refrigerate for about 2 hours. Now, transfer the mixture into an ice cream maker and process it according to the manufacturer's directions. Return the ice cream to the airtight container and freeze it for about 2 hours.

Per Serving: Calories 127, Fat 0.8g, Carbs 29g, Protein 0.8g

1159. Licorice and Chocolate Ice Cream

Ingredients for 4 servings

- 1 ½ cup of dark chocolate
- 6 cups of almond milk
- 1 cup of sliced diced banana
- ½ cup of honey
- 1 tablespoon of dark cocoa
- 1 teaspoon of pure licorice
- ½ teaspoon of xanthan

Directions and Total Time: approx. 25 minutes

Boil 50 ml of almond milk and dissolve the licorice in it. Melt the chocolate and let it cool down a little bit. Blend the rest of the milk, the dissolved licorice, the banana, cacao, and honey. Add the melted chocolate and blend again. Add the xanthan gum and keep blending for 1 minute. Pour the mixture into a freezing pan and freeze for 4 to 6 hours. Serve.

Per Serving: Calories 342, Fat 10g, Carbs 35g, Protein 19g

1160. Light Pine Nuts Cookies

Ingredients for 12 servings

- 1 ½ cup of flour
- 3 tablespoons of sugar
- 3 tablespoons of dark cocoa
- ¾ cup of chopped dark chocolate
- 3 tablespoons of pine nuts
- 1 teaspoon of baking powder
- A pinch of salt
- Oil to taste
- Water

Directions and Total Time: approx. 25 minutes

Chop the chocolate in pieces, place it into a bowl then add all the other dry ingredients and mix. Slowly add the oil, and water, and mix creating a dough. Place a parchment paper sheet on a baking sheet and place the cookies onto it. Bake at 170° for 15 minutes.

Per Serving: Calories 150, Fat 10g, Carbs 20g, Protein 9g

1161. Mango Mug Cake

Ingredients for 2 servings

- 1 medium-sized mango, peeled and diced
- 2 eggs
- 1 teaspoon of vanilla
- 1/4 teaspoon of grated nutmeg
- 1 tablespoon of cocoa powder
- 2 tablespoons of honey
- 1/2 cup of coconut flour

Directions and Total Time: approx. 15 minutes

Combine the coconut flour, eggs, honey, vanilla, nutmeg and cocoa powder in two lightly greased mugs. Then, add 1 cup of water and a metal trivet to the Instant Pot. Lower the uncovered mugs onto the trivet. Secure the lid. Choose the "Manual" mode and High pressure; cook for 10 minutes. Once cooking is complete, use a quick pressure release; carefully remove the lid. Top with diced mango and serve chilled. Enjoy!

Per Serving: Calories 268, Fat 10.5g, Carbs 34.8g, Protein 10.6g

1162. Maple Baked Pears

Ingredients for 4 servings

- 4 Anjou pears, halved and cored
- ¼ teaspoon of ground cinnamon
- ½ cup of pure maple syrup
- 1 teaspoon of pure vanilla extract

Directions and Total Time: approx. 35 minutes

Preheat your oven to 375 °F. Line a baking sheet with parchment paper. Carefully, cut a small sliver off the underside of each pear half. Arrange the pear halves onto the prepared baking sheet, cut side upwards, and sprinkle with cinnamon. In a small bowl, add the maple syrup and vanilla extract and beat well. Reserve about 2 tablespoons of the maple syrup mixture. Place the remaining maple syrup mixture over the pears and bake for 25 minutes or until lightly browned. Remove from the preheated oven and immediately drizzle with the reserved maple syrup mixture. Serve warm.

Per Serving: Calories 227, Fat 0.4g, Carbs 58.5g, Protein 0.8g

1163. Mascarpone and Fig Crostini

Ingredients for 8 servings

- 1 long French baguette
- 4 tablespoons of (½ stick) salted butter, melted
- 1 (8-ounce) tub of mascarpone cheese
- 1 (12-ounce) jar of fig jam or preserves

Directions and Total Time: approx. 20 minutes

Preheat the oven to 350°F. Slice the bread into ¼-inch-thick slices. Lay out the sliced bread on a single baking sheet and brush each slice with the melted butter. Put the single baking sheet in the oven and toast the bread for 5 to 7 minutes, just until golden brown. Let the bread cool slightly. Spread it about a tea spoon or so of the mascarpone cheese on each piece of bread. Top with a teaspoon or of your choice of the jam. Serve immediately.

Per Serving: Calories 445, Fat 24g, Carbs 48g, Protein 3g

1164. Mini Orange Tarts

Ingredients for 2 servings

- 1 cup of coconut flour
- 1/2 cup of almond flour
- A pinch of grated nutmeg
- A pinch of sea salt
- 1/4 teaspoon of ground cloves
- 1/4 teaspoon of ground anise
- 1 cup of brown sugar
- 6 eggs
- 2 cups of heavy cream
- 2 oranges, peeled and sliced

Directions and Total Time: approx. 45 minutes

Begin by preparing and preheating your oven to 350 degrees F. Thoroughly combine the flour with spices. Stir in the sugar, eggs, and heavy cream. Mix again to combine well. Divide the batter into six lightly greased ramekins. Top with the oranges and bake in the preheated oven for about 40 minutes until the clafoutis is just set. Bon appétit!

Per Serving: Calories 398, Fat 28.5g, Carbs 24.9g, Protein 11.9g

1165. Mint Strawberry Treat

Ingredients for 6 servings

- Cooking spray
- ¼ cup of stevia
- 1 ½ cups of almond flour
- 1 teaspoon of baking powder
- 1 cup of almond milk
- 1 egg, whisked
- 2 cups of strawberries, sliced
- 1 tablespoon of mint, chopped
- 1 teaspoon of lime zest, grated
- ½ cup of whipping cream

Directions and Total Time: approx. 55 minutes

Preheat the oven to 350°F. Whisk the egg and almond milk in a bowl. Add the flour, baking powder, stevia, and grated zest. Mix well. Add the whipping cream and stir for 10 more minutes. Add the mint and strawberries, and lightly mix with a spoon. Grease 6 ramekins with the cooking spray and evenly distribute the strawberry mixture between them. Bake for 30 minutes. Let them cool, then serve.

Per Serving: Calories 274, Fat 9.1g, Carbs 41g, Protein 4.5g

1166. Mint-Watermelon Gelato

Ingredients for 4 servings

- ¼ cup of honey
- 4 cups of watermelon cubes
- ¼ cup of lemon juice
- 12 mint leaves to serve

Directions and Total Time: approx. 10 minutes + freezing time

In a food processor, blend the watermelon, honey, and lemon juice to form a purée with chunks. Transfer to a freezer-proof medium container and place in the freezer for 1 hour.

Remove the container from and scrape with a fork. Return the to the freezer and repeat the process every half hour until the sorbet is completely frozen, for around 4 hours. Share into bowls, garnish with mint leaves, and serve.

Per Serving: Calories 149, Fat 0.4g, Carbs 38g, Protein 1.8g

1167. Moroccan Stuffed Dates

Ingredients for 30 servings

- 1 pound of dates
- 1 cup of blanched almonds
- 1/4 cup of sugar
- 1 1/2 tablespoon of orange flower water
- 1 tablespoon of butter, melted
- 1/4 teaspoon of cinnamon

Directions and Total Time: approx. 15 minutes

Incorporate the almonds, sugar and cinnamon in a food processor. Stir in the butter and orange flower water and process until a smooth paste is formed. Roll small pieces of almond paste the same length as a date.

Take one date, make a vertical cut and discard the pit. Insert a piece of the almond paste and press the sides of the date firmly around. Repeat with all the remaining dates and almond paste.

Per Serving: Calories 102, Fat 7g, Carbs 5g, Protein 2g

1168. Mousse Treat

Ingredients for 8 servings

- 8 ounces of chopped baking semisweet chocolate
- 4 egg yolks
- 2 ½ cups of whipping cream
- ¼ cup of sugar

Directions and Total Time: approx. 25 minutes

Blend egg yolks in a blender with slow addition of sugar. Heat whipping cream at medium flame, pour half of the hot whipping cream into the egg mixture and mix well. Pour the egg mixture back to hot whipping cream in a saucepan at low flame and cook for the next five minutes. Add and mix chocolate and cook until chocolate melts. Refrigerate for two hours till it gets chilled. Using a beater, beat cream, and mix in a chocolate mixture. Put one spoon of mixture in each serving dish.

Per Serving: Calories 430, Fat 33g, Carbs 27g, Protein 5g

1169. Olive Oil Brownies

Ingredients for 9 servings

- ¼ cup of olive oil
- ¼ cup of Greek yogurt
- ¾ cup of sugar
- 1 teaspoon of vanilla extract
- 2 eggs
- ½ cup of flour
- ⅓ cup of cocoa powder
- ¼ teaspoon of baking powder
- ¼ teaspoon of salt
- ⅓ cup of walnuts, chopped

Directions and Total Time: approx. 32 minutes

Preheat the oven to a heat of 350°F and line a baking pan with parchment paper. Blend the olive oil and sugar in a blender. Add the vanilla extract and mix well. Add the beaten eggs, walnuts, and yogurt and mix well. Blend the flour, cocoa powder, salt, and baking powder in another bowl and add them to the olive oil mixture. Decant the mixture into the baking pan. Bake for 25 minutes. Let it cool and cut in squares.

Per Serving: Calories 150, Fat 8.4g, Carbs 56.5g, Protein 54.1g

1170. Pain Perdu with Oranges

Ingredients for 6 servings

- 12 slices of bread
- 3 cups of milk
- 1 cup of fresh cream
- 4 eggs
- 1 ½ cup of sugar
- 2 oranges
- 1 vanilla stem
- 2 tablespoons of butter

Directions and Total Time: approx. 40 minutes

In a bowl add the eggs, the seeds of the vanilla bean, sugar, milk, and cream, and whisk. Peel the oranges, cutting the peel off and slicing them. Brown the butter in a pan and add the bread dipped in the egg mixture. Fry the slices on both sides, add the oranges, the rest of the sugar, and serve.

Per Serving: Calories 650, Fat 16g, Carbs 35g, Protein 19g

1171. Peach Pudding

Ingredients for 6 servings

- 3 cups of chopped peaches
- ½ cup of almond flour
- ½ cup of rolled oats
- ½ cup of brown sugar
- ½ cup of olive oil
- 2 teaspoons of cinnamon powder
- 2 tablespoons of cornstarch
- 1 lemon zest

Directions and Total Time: approx. 50 minutes

In a large-sized bowl mix the peaches with the cinnamon, the lemon zest, and the cornstarch and place them in a baking pan. In a bowl mix the flour, the oats and the oil, and the sugar and create some crumbs. Place the crumbs on top of the peaches and bake them for 35 to 40 minutes.

Per Serving: Calories 235, Fat 2g, Carbs 57g, Protein 3.5g

1172. Peaches Cake

Ingredients for 10 servings

- 1 peach
- 1 ½ cup of sugar
- 3 eggs
- 2 teaspoons of baking powder
- 2 ½ cups of peach yogurt
- 3 ¾ cups of all-purpose flour
- ½ cup of oil

Directions and Total Time: approx. 60 minutes

In a large-sized bowl whisk together the eggs and the sugar. When fluffy, add the yogurt. Add the oil then slowly add the flour and the baking powder. Mix with a spatula, chop the peach in little peaches and add them to the mixture. Grease a pan and pour the batter in it and cook at slow heat for 40 minutes or just until the bottom of the cake is cooked. Turn the cake and keep cooking for 10 minutes. Take the cake off the pan and let it cool down. Serve with a sprinkle of icing sugar.

Per Serving: Calories 350, Fat 10g, Carbs 61g, Protein 9g

1173. Plums Delight

Ingredients for 8 servings

- 3 eggs
- 1/3 teaspoon of pure hazelnut extract
- 2 tablespoons of Truvia for baking
- 1/3 cup of almond flour
- A pinch of salt
- 1 ½ cups of plums, pitted and halved
- 1/3 cup of heavy cream

Directions and Total Time: approx. 28 minutes

Firstly, butter 2 mini pie pans. Lay the plum halves on the bottoms of pans. In a saucepan, over medium heat, warm the milk and heavy cream until well heated. Remove the pan from heat. Using a wire whisk, incorporate the flour. In a small-sized bowl, whisk the eggs, along with Truvia and salt, until creamy. Whisk in the creamy milk mixture. Pour the mixture over the plums. Bake at 335°Fahrenheit for about 18-minutes.

Per Serving: Calories 175, Fat 6.1g, Carbs 25.7g, Protein 4.9g

1174. Poached Apples with Greek Yogurt and Granola

Ingredients for 4 servings

- 4 medium-sized apples, peeled
- 1/2 cup of brown sugar
- 1 vanilla bean
- 1 cinnamon stick
- 1/2 cup of cranberry juice
- 1 cup of water
- 1/2 cup of 2% Greek yogurt
- 1/2 cup of granola

Directions and Total Time: approx. 20 minutes

Add the apples, brown sugar, water, cranberry juice, vanilla bean, and cinnamon stick to the inner pot of your Instant Pot. Secure the lid. Choose the "Manual" mode and cook for 5 minutes at High pressure. Once cooking is complete, use a natural pressure release for 5 minutes; carefully remove the lid. Reserve poached apples. Press the "Sauté" button and let the sauce simmer on "Less" mode until it has thickened. Place the apples in serving bowls. Add the syrup and top each apple with granola and Greek yogurt. Enjoy!

Per Serving: Calories 247, Fat 3.1g, Carbs 52.6g, Protein 3.5g

1175. Portuguese Orange Mug Cake

Ingredients for 2 servings

- 2 tablespoons of butter, melted
- 6 tablespoons of flour
- 2 tablespoons of sugar
- ½ teaspoon of baking powder
- ¼ teaspoon of salt
- 1 teaspoon of orange zest
- 1 egg
- 2 tablespoons of orange juice
- 2 tablespoons of milk
- ½ teaspoon of orange extract
- ½ teaspoon of vanilla extract
- Orange slices for garnish

Directions and Total Time: approx. 12 minutes

In a bowl, beat the egg, butter, orange juice, milk, orange extract, and vanilla extract. In another bowl, combine the flour, sugar, baking powder, salt, and orange zest. Pour the listed dry ingredients into the wet ingredients and stir to combine. Spoon the mixture into 2 mugs and microwave one at a time for 1-2 minutes. Garnish with orange slices.

Per Serving: Calories 302, Fat 17g, Carbs 33g, Protein 6g

1176. Raspberry Tart

Ingredients for 6 servings

- 3 tablespoons of butter softened
- 1 cup of wheat flour, whole wheat
- 1 teaspoon of baking powder
- 1 egg, beaten
- 4 tablespoons of pistachio paste
- 2 tablespoons of raspberry jam

Directions and Total Time: approx. 25 minutes

Knead the dough: combine softened butter, flour, baking powder, and egg. You should get the non-sticky and very soft dough. Press the dough into the springform pan to make a pie shell. Bake it for 10 minutes at 365°F. After this, spread the pie crust with raspberry jam and then with pistachio paste. Bake the tart at 365°F for another 10 minutes. Cool the cooked tart and cut on the servings.

Per Serving: Calories 311, Fat 11.4g, Carbs 14.9g, Protein 1.9g

1177. Rhubarb Strawberry Crunch

Ingredients for 18 servings

- 1 cup of white sugar
- 3 tablespoons of all-purpose flour
- 3 cups of fresh strawberries, sliced
- 3 cups of rhubarb, cut into cubes
- 1 ½ cups of flour
- 1 cup of packed brown sugar
- 1 cup of butter
- 1 cup of oatmeal

Directions and Total Time: approx. 30 minutes

Preheat the oven to 190 ° C. Incorporate white sugar, 3 tablespoons flour, strawberries and rhubarb in a large bowl. Place the mixture in a 9 x 13-inch baking dish. Mix 1 ½ cups of flour, brown sugar, butter, and oats until a crumbly texture is obtained. You may want to use a blender for this. Crumble the mixture of rhubarb and strawberry. Bake for 45 minutes.

Per Serving: Calories 253, Fat 10.8g, Carbs 32g, Protein 2.3g

1178. Rice Pudding

Ingredients for 8 servings

- 4 cups of milk
- 1 orange zest
- 2 orange juice
- 1 cinnamon stick
- 1 ½ cup of rice
- 1 ½ sugar
- 10 plums
- 3 cups of raisins
- 2 cups red wine

Directions and Total Time: approx. 2 hours and 10 minutes

In a saucepan add milk, orange zest, and cinnamon stick and bring to a simmer. Add the rice and the sugar slowly until reduced, stirring for 1 hour. Remove from heat. Take off the zest and the cinnamon stick. Let the rice cool down and pour into a bowl. In a pot add the fruit, wine, sugar, the orange juice and bring to a boil. Cook for 15 minutes until thick. Serve the rice in bowls with fruit and juice on top.

Per Serving: Calories 430, Fat 16g, Carbs 35g, Protein 19g

1179. Rice Pudding with Dried Figs

Ingredients for 2 servings

- 3 cups of milk
- 1 cup of water
- 2 tablespoons of sugar
- 1/3 cup of white rice, rinsed
- 1 tablespoon of honey
- 4 dried figs, chopped
- 1/2 teaspoon of cinnamon
- 1/2 teaspoon of rose water

Directions and Total Time: approx. 45 minutes

In a deep saucepan, bring the milk, water and sugar to a boil until the sugar has dissolved. Stir in the rice, honey, figs, raisins, cinnamon, and turn the heat to a simmer; let it simmer for about 40 minutes, stirring periodically to prevent your pudding from sticking. Afterwards, stir in the rose water. Divide the pudding between individual bowls and serve. Bon appétit!

Per Serving: Calories 228, Fat 6.1g, Carbs 35.1g, Protein 7.1g

1180. Ricotta Brulee

Ingredients for 4 servings

- Fresh raspberries
- 1 cup of whole milk Ricotta cheese
- 1 tablespoon of granulated sugar
- ½ teaspoon of lemon zest, finely grated
- 1 tablespoon of honey

Directions and Total Time: approx. 21 minutes

Take a large bowl, stir in the lemon zest, ricotta, and honey. Combine the ingredients well. Place 4 ramekins and divide the batter among them. Add the sugar on top if you don't have a kitchen torch. Add all of the ramekins to a baking sheet and place them on the oven rack. Keep the rack on the highest level and turn on the broiler. Once the Ricotta is golden-brown and starts to bubble, turn off the oven. Top with the raspberries once it has cooled down. Serve it cold.

Per Serving: Calories 254, Fat 14.7g, Carbs 8g, Protein 12.8g

1181. Rose Crème Caramel

Ingredients for 2 servings

- 2 eggs
- 1 cup of low fat cream
- 1 cup of milk
- 2 tablespoons of sugar
- 1 tablespoon of rose syrup
- Caramel syrup
- 2 tablespoons of sugar
- 2 tablespoons of water

Directions and Total Time: approx. 35 minutes

Mix the tablespoons of water and sugar in a saucepan and cook until it caramelizes, stirring occasionally. Divide the caramel into 4 ramekins. Preheat your oven at 350°F. In a bowl, beat the eggs with rose syrup, sugar, cream and milk. Divide this mixture into the ramekins then bake for 25 minutes. Allow the crème caramel to cool then refrigerate for 6 hours. Run a knife around the dessert and flip onto a serving plate. Serve.

Per Serving: Calories 358, Fat 20.8g, Carbs 31.9g, Protein 13.1g

1182. Small Pumpkin Pastry Cream

Ingredients for 8 servings

- 1 can of 16 ounces of prepared pumpkin
- 1 14-ounces of can sweeten condensed milk
- 3 beaten eggs
- 1 teaspoon of finely chopped polished ginger (optional)
- 1 teaspoon of ground cinnamon
- ¼ teaspoon of ground cloves
- 1 cup of water

Directions and Total Time: approx. 15 minutes

Mix the pumpkin, milk, eggs, cinnamon, ginger, and cloves. Pour into individual cups for custard. Cover each cup firmly with the foil. Pour the water into the pot. Position the cups on the rack of the pot. Close and secure the lid. Place the pressure regulator on the vent tube and cook for 10 minutes once the pressure regulator begins to rock slowly. Cool the pot quickly. Let the cream cool well in the refrigerator. If desired, serve with whipped cream.

Per Serving: Calories 207, Fat 36.4g, Carbs 39.4g, Protein 3.8g

1183. Spanish Crumble Cakes

Ingredients for 2 servings

- 2 cups of flour
- 1 cup of butter, softened
- 1 cup of sugar
- 1 egg
- 1 teaspoon of lemon zest
- 1 teaspoon of orange zest
- 1 tablespoon of orange juice
- 1/2 cup of almonds, blanched and finely ground

Directions and Total Time: approx. 35 minutes

Beat butter with sugar, lemon, and orange zest until light. Combine in the flour using a wooden spoon. Add ground almonds, stir, then knead with your hands until dough clings together. Divide it into three parts. Seal and chill for at least half an hour. On a well-floured surface, roll out each piece of dough until it is 1/4 inch thick. Cut into different shapes. Arrange cookies on an ungreased baking sheet. Beat together egg and orange juice and brush this over the cookies. Bake in a preheated to 350 degrees F oven for 7-8 minutes, or until edges are lightly golden. Set aside and keep in an airtight container.

Per Serving: Calories 113, Fat 8g, Carbs 5g, Protein 4g

1184. Spanish Nougat

Ingredients for 24 servings

- 1 1/2 cup of honey
- 3 egg whites
- 1 ¾ cup of almonds, toasted and chopped

Directions and Total Time: approx. 32 minutes

Bring the cup of honey to a boil in a saucepan over medium heat, then cool. Beat the egg whites to a thick glossy meringue and fold them into the honey. Bring the mixture back to medium-high heat and let it simmers, constantly stirring, for 15 minutes. When the color and consistency change to a dark caramel, remove from heat, add the almonds and mix through. Pour the heated mixture into a 9x13 inch pan lined with foil. Cover with another piece of foil and even out. Let cool completely. Place a wooden board weighted down with some heavy cans on it. Leave like this for 3-4 days, so it hardens and dries out. Slice into 1-inch squares.

Per Serving: Calories 189, Fat 12g, Carbs 29.1g, Protein 5.8g

1185. Spiced Hot Chocolate

Ingredients for 4 servings

- ¼ teaspoon of cayenne pepper powder
- 4 squares of chocolate
- 4 cups of milk
- 2 teaspoons of sugar
- ½ teaspoon of ground cinnamon
- ½ teaspoon of salt

Directions and Total Time: approx. 15 minutes

Place milk and sugar in a pot over low heat and warm until it begins to simmer. Combine chocolate, cinnamon, salt, and cayenne pepper powder in a bowl. Slowly pour in enough hot milk to cover. Return the pot to the heat and lower the temperature. Stir until the chocolate has melted, then add the remaining milk and combine. Spoon into 4 cups and serve hot.

Per Serving: Calories 342, Fat 23g, Carbs 22g, Protein 12g

1186. Spicy Fruit Salad

Ingredients for 1 serving

- 1 cup of mixed fruit: apricots, peaches, yellow plums, and mango
- 2 tablespoons of brown sugar
- 1 teaspoon of ginger
- 1 teaspoon of nutmeg
- 1 teaspoon of cinnamon
- 1 lemon zest
- ½ cup of water
- A pinch of black pepper
- Basil leaves to taste

Directions and Total Time: approx. 10 minutes

Bring to a boil the water and sugar with the spices in a pot. Simmer until the mixture has become thick and of the consistency of a syrup. Mix in a little bowl the chopped fruit and toss it with the syrup. Sprinkle with lemon zest, black pepper, and some basil leaves.

Per Serving: Calories 122, Fat 0.6g, Carbs 30.6g, Protein 1.4g

1187. Strawberry Angel Food Dessert

Ingredients for 18 servings

- 1 angel cake (10 inches)
- 2 packages of softened cream cheese
- 1 cup of white sugar
- 1 container of frozen fluff, thawed
- 1 liter of fresh strawberries, sliced
- 1 jar of strawberry icing

Directions and Total Time: approx. 15 minutes

Crumble the cake in a 9 x 13-inch dish. Beat the cream cheese and sugar in a medium bowl until the mixture is light and fluffy. Stir in the whipped topping. Crush the cake with your hands, and spread the cream cheese mixture over the cake. Combine the strawberries and the frosting in a bowl until the strawberries are well covered. Spread over the layer of cream cheese. Cool until ready to serve.

Per Serving: Calories 261, Fat 11g, Carbs 10g, Protein 3.2g

1188. Strawberry-Pomegranate Molasses Sauce

Ingredients for 6 servings

- 3 tablespoons of olive oil
- ¼ cup of honey
- 2 pints of strawberries, hulled and halved
- 1 to 2 tablespoons of pomegranate molasses
- 2 tablespoons of chopped fresh mint
- Greek yogurt, for serving

Directions and Total Time: approx. 15 minutes

In a small-sized saucepan, heat the olive oil over medium heat. Add the strawberries; cook until their juices are released. Stir in the honey and cook for 1 to 2 minutes. Stir in the molasses and mint. Serve warm over Greek yogurt.

Per Serving: Calories 189, Fat 7g, Carbs 24g, Protein 4g

1189. Stuffed Peaches

Ingredients for 6 servings

- 6 peaches, pits and flesh removed
- Salt
- ¼ cup of coconut flour
- ¼ cup of maple syrup
- 2 tablespoons of coconut butter
- ½ teaspoon of ground cinnamon
- 1 teaspoon of almond extract
- 1 cup of water

Directions and Total Time: approx. 14 minutes

In a large-sized bowl, mix the flour with the salt, syrup, butter, cinnamon, and half of the almond extract and stir well. Fill the peaches with this mix, place them in the steamer basket of the Instant Pot, add the water and the rest of the almond extract to the Instant Pot, cover and cook on the Steam setting for approximately 4 minutes. Release the pressure naturally, divide the stuffed peaches on serving plates, and serve warm.

Per Serving: Calories 160, Fat 6.7g, Carbs 12g, Protein 4g

1190. Sugar-Coated Pecans

Ingredients for 12 servings

- 1 egg white
- 1 tablespoon of water
- 1-pound of pecan halves
- 1 cup of white sugar
- 1/2 teaspoon of ground cinnamon

Directions and Total Time: approx. 1 hour and 15 minutes

Preheat the oven to a heat of 120 ° C (250 ° F). Grease a baking tray. In a bowl, whisk the egg whites and water until frothy. Combine the sugar, ¾ teaspoon of salt, and cinnamon in another bowl. Stir the pecans into the egg whites until they are completely covered. Remove the nuts from the shells and toss them in the sugar until well coated. Place the nuts on the baking sheet that has been prepared. Bake for 1 hour at 250 ° F (120 ° C). Stir every 15 minutes.

Per Serving: Calories 328, Fat 27.2g, Carbs 38.4g, Protein 3.8g

1191. Vanilla Apple Pie

Ingredients for 8 servings

- 3 apples, sliced
- ½ teaspoon of ground cinnamon
- 1 teaspoon of vanilla extract
- 1 tablespoon of Erythritol
- 7 ounces of yeast roll dough
- 1 egg, beaten

Directions and Total Time: approx. 65 minutes

Separate the dough into two pieces by rolling it out and cutting it in half. Line the springform pan with baking paper. Place the first dough part in the springform pan. Then arrange the apples over the dough and sprinkle it with Erythritol, vanilla extract, and ground cinnamon. Then cover the apples with the remaining dough and secure the edges of the pie with the help of the fork. Make the small cuts on the surface of the pie. Brush the pie with beaten egg and bake it for 50 minutes at 375F. Cool the cooked pie well, and then remove it from the springform pan. Cut it on the servings.

Per Serving: Calories 140, Fat 3.4g, Carbs 23.9g, Protein 2.9g

1192. Vanilla Bread Pudding with Apricots

Ingredients for 6 servings

- 2 tablespoons of coconut oil
- 1 1/3 cups of heavy cream
- 4 eggs, whisked
- 1/2 cup of dried apricots, soaked and chopped
- 1 teaspoon of cinnamon, ground
- 1/2 teaspoon of star anise, ground
- A pinch of grated nutmeg
- A pinch of salt
- 1/2 cup of granulated sugar
- 2 tablespoons of molasses
- 2 cups of milk
- 4 cups of Italian bread, cubed
- 1 teaspoon of vanilla paste

Directions and Total Time: approx. 20 minutes

Add 1 ½ cups of water and a metal rack to the Instant Pot. Grease a baking dish with a nonstick cooking spray. Throw the bread cubes into the prepared baking dish. In a mixing bowl, thoroughly combine the remaining ingredients. Pour the mixture over the bread cubes. Cover with a piece of foil, making a foil sling. Secure the lid. Choose the "Porridge" mode and High pressure; cook for 15 minutes. Once cooking is complete, use a quick pressure release; carefully remove the lid. Enjoy!

Per Serving: Calories 410, Fat 24.3g, Carbs 37.4g, Protein 11.5g

1193. Vanilla Cake

Ingredients for 10 servings

- 3 cups of almond flour
- 3 teaspoons of baking powder
- 1 cup of olive oil
- 1 and ½ cup of almond milk
- 1 and 2/3 cup of stevia
- 2 cups of water
- 1 tablespoon of lime juice
- 2 teaspoons of vanilla extract
- Cooking spray

Directions and Total Time: approx. 35 minutes

Mix the almond flour with the baking powder, the oil, the rest of the ingredients except the cooking spray in a bowl, and whisk well. Pour the batter into a prepared cake pan and bake for 25 minutes at 370°F. Leave the cooked cake to cool down, cut, and serve!

Per Serving: Calories 200, Fat 7.6g, Carbs 5.5g, Protein 4.5g

1194. Vanilla Cheesecake Squares

Ingredients for 6 servings

- ½ cup butter, melted
- 1 (12-ounces) box of butter cake mix
- 3 large eggs
- 1 cup of maple syrup
- 1/8 teaspoon of cinnamon
- 1 cup of cream cheese
- 1 teaspoon of vanilla extract

Directions and Total Time: approx. 55 minutes + chilling time

Preheat oven to 350 F. In a medium-sized bowl, blend the cake mix, butter, cinnamon, and 1 egg. Then, pour the prepared mixture onto a baking pan that has been buttered. Mix together maple syrup, cream cheese, the remaining 2 eggs, and vanilla in a separate bowl and pour this gently over the first layer. Bake for 45-50 minutes. Remove and allow to cool. Cut into squares.

Per Serving: Calories 160, Fat 8g, Carbs 20g, Protein 2g

1195. Vanilla-Poached Apricots

Ingredients for 6 servings

- 1 ¼ cups of water
- ¼ cup of marsala wine
- ¼ cup of sugar
- 1 teaspoon of vanilla bean paste
- 8 medium apricots, sliced in half and pitted

Directions and Total Time: approx. 30 minutes

Place all items in the Instant Pot and combine well. Seal tight, click the Manual Instant Pot. Stir to combine. Close the lid, set the steam release to Sealing, press the Manual button and set the timer to 1 minute. When the alarm beeps, quick-release the pressure until the float valve drops. Set the Cancel and open the lid. Let stand for 10 minutes. Carefully remove apricots from poaching liquid with a slotted spoon. Serve warm or at room temperature.

Per Serving: Calories 62, Fat 1g, Carbs 5g, Protein 2g

1196. Wine Figs

Ingredients for 2 servings

- 1/2 cup of pine nuts
- 1 cup of red wine
- 1 pound of figs
- Sugar, as needed

Directions and Total Time: approx. 8 minutes

Slowly pour the wine and sugar into the Instant Pot. Arrange the trivet inside it; place the figs over it. Close the lid and lock. Ensure that you have sealed the valve to avoid leakage. Press MANUAL mode and set timer to 3 minutes. After the timer reads zero, press CANCEL and quick-release pressure. Carefully remove the lid. Divide figs into bowls, and drizzle wine from the pot over them. Top with pine nuts and enjoy.

Per Serving: Calories 95, Fat 3g, Carbs 5g, Protein 2g

Ingredients for 4 servings

- 4 ½ cup of Greek yogurt
- 1 ½ cup of blackberries
- 1 ½ cup of blueberries
- 2 tablespoons of sugar
- ½ cup of water
- 1 lime
- Water

Directions and Total Time: approx. 25 minutes

In a saucepan add the fruit, water, and sugar and let it cook for 10 minutes. In another bowl add the lime zest to the yogurt then start layering the ingredients in 4 glasses. Start by adding one layer of yogurt and 1 layer of fruit compote and go on. Place in the fridge before serving.

Per Serving: Calories 85, Fat 1g, Carbs 21g, Protein 6.2g

1198. Yogurt Ice Cream

Ingredients for 3 servings

- ⅓ ounces of whole milk
- 2 ounces of powdered milk
- 10 ½ ounces of yogurt
- ¼ ounces of cream
- 2 ounces of honey
- 4 ounces of brown sugar
- 1 vanilla pod

Directions and Total Time: approx. 20 minutes

Mix the cream, sugar, milk, whole milk, honey and vanilla in a bowl. Pour this mixture into a pan and heat to 185°F then remove from the heat. Stir in the yogurt and allow the mixture to cool. Cover and refrigerate overnight. Transfer the mixture into an ice-cream maker and churn as per the machine's instructions. Transfer the ice-cream into a container and freeze for 4 hours. Serve.

Per Serving: Calories 345, Fat 1.8g, Carbs 69.5g, Protein 12.5g

1199. Yogurt Moose with Sour Cherry Sauce

Ingredients for 6 servings

- 1 1/2 cups of Greek yogurt
- 1 teaspoon of vanilla extract
- 4 tablespoons of honey
- 1 1/2 cups of whipped heavy cream
- 2 cups of sour cherries
- 1/4 cup of white sugar
- 1 cinnamon stick

Directions and Total Time: approx. 20 minutes

Combine the yogurt with vanilla and honey in a bowl. Fold in the heavy whipped cream then spoon the mousse into serving glasses and refrigerate. For the sauce, combine the cherries, sugar, and cinnamon in a saucepan. Allow it to rest for just approximately 10 minutes then cook on low heat for 10 minutes. Cool the sauce down and then spoon it over the mousse. Serve it right away.

Per Serving: Calories 245, Fat 12.1g, Carbs 5.8g, Protein 29.7g

1200. Yogurt with Berries Compote

Ingredients for 2 servings

- 5 cups of fresh berries
- 3 tablespoons of brown sugar
- 1 lemon
- A pinch of cinnamon and ginger
- 2 tablespoons of 0% fat Greek yogurt

Directions and Total Time: approx. 15 minutes

In a saucepan add the berries and the sugar and let it simmer for 5 minutes. Turn the heat to medium and keep simmering it for 10 minutes, add the juice of the lemon, its zest, the cinnamon, and ginger. Mash the fruit with a spoon or a masher and let it cook for 5 minutes more. Turn off the heat temperature of the oven and let it cool. Serve a little bowl of compote with 2 tbsp. of Greek yogurt.

Per Serving: Calories 222, Fat 1.4g, Carbs 55.5g, Protein 3g

	Breakfast	Lunch	Dinner	Total Calories
DAY 1	Breakfast Quinoa Calories: 287	Seafood Paella Calories: 507	Chicken Rice Noodle Soup Calories: 306	1100
DAY 2	Tuna Breakfast Quiche Calories: 151	Chicken and Artichokes Calories: 552	Orecchiette Pasta Calories: 321	1024
DAY 3	Vegetable and Hummus Bowl Calories: 392	Spinach Pesto Chicken Breasts Calories: 493	Pasta and Chickpeas Calories: 250	1135
DAY 4	Orzo and Veggie Bowls Calories: 411	Oregano Grilled Chicken Calories: 479	Chicken Curry Rice Calories: 232	1122
DAY 5	Potato Hash Calories: 535	Creamy Swordfish Calories: 340	Oyster Stew Calories: 264	1144
DAY 6	Almond Grits with Honey Calories: 131	Parmesan Pork Chops Calories: 574	Cheesy Beet Soup Calories: 309	1014
DAY 7	Cheese Egg Quiche Calories: 182	Garlic Pork Rinds Calories: 621	Creamy Chicken Salad Calories: 200	1003
DAY 8	Artichoke Frittata Calories: 199	Marinated Grill Chicken Calories: 530	Egg Salad Calories: 341	1070
DAY 9	Chili and Cheese Frittata Calories: 381	Turkey and Cilantro Broccoli Calories: 438	Garbanzo Bean Salad Calories: 268	1087
DAY 10	Quinoa and Eggs Pan Calories: 304	Chicken in Wine Sauce Calories: 462	Peaches Caprese Calories: 250	1016
DAY 11	Ham Muffins Calories: 343	Turkey Curry Calories: 400	White Bean Soup Calories: 264	1007
DAY 12	Artichoke and Spinach Frittata Calories: 190	Meat Pie with Yogurt Calories: 503	Mushroom Risotto Calories: 363	1056
DAY 13	Kale Egg Cupcakes Calories: 213	Dill Beef Brisket Calories: 556	Cauliflower Curry Calories: 243	1012
DAY 14	Avocado Toast Calories: 348	Mahi-Mahi and Mushrooms Calories: 444	Shrimp Scampi Calories: 231	1023
DAY 15	Eggs on Greens Calories: 158	Baked Dijon Salmon Calories: 552	Orzo-Veggie Pilaf Calories: 476	1186
DAY 16	Zucchini and Quinoa Pan Calories: 310	Lamb Chops Calories: 465	Lemony Salmon Calories: 232	1007
DAY 17	Seeds and Lentil Oats Calories: 204	Citrus Clams Calories: 514	Asparagus Pasta Calories: 307	1025
DAY 18	Brown Rice Salad with Cheese Calories: 480	Grilled Swordfish Calories: 398	Chorizo White Bean Stew Calories: 386	1104
DAY 19	Egg Breakfast Bowl Calories: 325	Buttered Pork Chops Calories: 450	Chard and Couscous Calories: 300	1075
DAY 20	Raspberry Oats Calories: 289	Balsamic-Honey Glazed Salmon Calories: 454	Lemon Spaghetti Calories: 398	1141
DAY 21	Garlic Bell Pepper Omelet Calories: 272	Walnut Turkey and Peaches Calories: 500	Cheesy Tilapia Calories: 235	1007
DAY 22	Orange French Toast Calories: 394	Garlic Meatballs Calories: 468	Baked Trout with Dill Calories: 194	1056
DAY 23	Jalapeno Cheddar Waffles Calories: 338	Buttery Fish and Polenta Calories: 450	Broccoli Pesto Spaghetti Calories: 284	1072
DAY 24	Spinach and Egg Scramble Calories: 296	Rosemary Meatballs Calories: 477	Lamb and Potatoes Stew Calories: 411	1184
DAY 25	Egg Scramble with Veggies Calories: 338	Moist Shredded Beef Calories: 456	Veggie Salad Calories: 327	1121
DAY 26	Quinoa and Apple Porridge Calories: 225	Mediterranean Tuna Capellini Calories: 410	Rice with Pork Chops Calories: 375	1010
DAY 27	Nectarine Bruschetta Calories: 347	Cod Fettuccine Calories: 431	Brown Rice Pilaf with Raisins Calories: 320	1098
DAY 28	Stuffed Pita Breads Calories: 382	Smoky Pork and Cabbage Calories: 484	Melon Salad Calories: 218	1084
DAY 29	Mushroom Egg Casserole Calories: 152	Chicken Pesto Pasta Calories: 521	Saffron Risotto Calories: 392	1065
DAY 30	Tempeh Bacon Calories: 394	Thyme Ginger Garlic Beef Calories: 452	Spicy Mushroom Soup Calories: 244	1090

CONCLUSION

The Mediterranean Diet Cookbook is a step-by-step guide that will help you lose weight, boost your energy, and increase your overall well-being. As America looks ever more like the Mediterranean region, people are realizing that the Mediterranean Diet is by far the healthiest eating plan in the world.

The Mediterranean Diet focuses heavily on fresh fruits and vegetables, whole grains (and not just wheat), and olive oil. The traditional Italian Diet also emphasizes a healthy intake of fish, seafood, poultry, legumes, nuts and seeds, and olive oil. It is by no doubt one of the most effective diets for losing weight. It is a healthy way to diet and reduces body fat. This Cookbook teaches you how to eat healthily and lose weight while still having delicious meals to satisfy your family.

In this Cookbook, you will find the complete guide to eating healthy and losing weight by following the Mediterranean Diet. You will learn how to cook healthy dinners that will keep you full until your next meal. This diet plan helps you eat lean proteins, fruits, vegetables, and whole grains without having to leave the comfort of your own home.

Earlier this year, you might have noticed that the Mediterranean Diet became a whole lot more popular. Everyone from your favorite celebrities to your local restaurant is cutting back on their consumption of red meat and eggs. This is because the Mediterranean Diet is known to be very healthy, and many people are beginning to adopt it as well.

The Mediterranean Diet is actually quite different from the Standard American Diet (SAD), but both can be very beneficial to your health. We should take a look at the major differences between the two diets.

The Mediterranean Diet emphasizes vegetables, fruits, nuts, and beans over meat and dairy products. This diet actually reduces the number of calories you consume along with processed foods due to its emphasis on whole grains, vegetables, fruits, and nuts.

The Mediterranean Diet encourages eating fish that are high in omega-3 fatty acids, which helps lower your cholesterol levels and protects against heart disease.

The Mediterranean Diet also encourages drinking wine with most meals. Studies show that wine lowers bad cholesterol while increasing good cholesterol in your body; thus making it actually a great addition to a healthy lifestyle like the Mediterranean Diet.

Lastly, the Mediterranean Diet also encourages you to eat more fiber, since it helps reduce symptoms of constipation and diabetes by keeping your blood sugar levels stable and helping you feel full longer after meals. This is why it's recommended that you include more fruits and vegetables in your diet when trying to lose weight since they are packed with fiber that helps slow down digestion and keeps you feeling full longer after meals, as well as reducing cravings for snacks or sugary foods.